The Dynamic Spread of Buddhist Print Culture
Volume 1

The Dynamic Spread of Buddhist Print Culture

Mapping Buddhist Book Roads in China and Its Neighbors

Volume 1

By

Shih-shan Susan Huang

BRILL

LEIDEN | BOSTON

Originally published in hardback in 2024 as Volume 7 in the series CROS.

Cover illustration: Detail. Frontispiece to the *Lotus Sutra*, juan 1. Illustrated by Wang Yi. Southern Song. Woodblock print. Concertina. © National Palace Museum

This publication was sponsored by the Chiang Ching-kuo Foundation for International Scholarly Exchange.

The Library of Congress has cataloged the earlier hardback edition as follows:

Library of Congress Cataloging-in-Publication Data
Names: Huang, Shih-shan Susan, author.
Title: The dynamic spread of Buddhist print culture : mapping Buddhist book roads in China and its neighbors / by Shih-shan Susan Huang.
Description: Leiden ; Boston : Brill, 2024 | Series: Crossroads—history of interactions across the silk routes, 2589-885X ; volume 7 | Includes bibliographical references and index.
Identifiers: LCCN 2024039229 (print) | LCCN 2024039230 (ebook) | ISBN 9789004680814 (hardback) | ISBN 9789004700017 (ebook)
Subjects: LCSH: Printing—Social aspects—China. | Buddhist prints—China. | Buddhist literature—China. | Book industries and trade—China—History. | Buddhism—Economic aspects—China. | Buddhist civilization. | China—Commerce—History.
Classification: LCC Z186.C5 H775 2024 (print) | LCC Z186.C5 (ebook) | DDC 306.6/9430951—dc23/eng/20240912
LC record available at https://lccn.loc.gov/2024039229
LC ebook record available at https://lccn.loc.gov/2024039230

Typeface for the Latin, Greek, and Cyrillic scripts: "Brill". See and download: brill.com/brill-typeface.

ISBN 978-90-04-74581-0 (paperback, vol. 1, 2025)
ISBN 978-90-04-74587-2 (paperback, vol. 2, 2025)
ISBN 978-90-04-74602-2 (paperback, set, 2025)
ISBN 978-90-04-68081-4 (hardback)
ISBN 978-90-04-70001-7 (e-book)
DOI 10.1163/9789004700017

Copyright 2024 by Shih-shan Susan Huang. Published by Koninklijke Brill BV, Leiden, The Netherlands.
Koninklijke Brill BV incorporates the imprints Brill, Brill Nijhoff, Brill Schöningh, Brill Fink, Brill mentis, Brill Wageningen Academic, Vandenhoeck & Ruprecht, Böhlau and V&R unipress.
Koninklijke Brill BV reserves the right to protect this publication against unauthorized use. Requests for re-use and/or translations must be addressed to Koninklijke Brill BV via brill.com or copyright.com.

This book is printed on acid-free paper and produced in a sustainable manner.

For David

∵

Contents

Volume 1

PART 2
Buddhist Printing in North and Northwest China

Volume 2

PART 3
The Mongol Era

Acknowledgements

I was introduced to Buddhist print culture quite unexpectedly. As an art history master's student at National Taiwan University, I took Professor Shih Shou-chieh's Yuan painting seminar. While much of the course focused on landscape painting, a session on Buddhist and Daoist themes (which I liked most) included printed and hand-painted frontispieces from a special exhibition of the *Lotus Sutra* that was then being held at the National Palace Museum. A "frontispiece," as I learned, is an image decorating the opening of a book and a very common artistic feature in Buddhist books. These prints' minute details immediately made a strong impression on me. The black ink lines and busy narrative scenes, many of which contain complex architectural, figural, and landscape motifs, mimic the pictorial quality of paintings. Over the course of my career, as I became more aware and interested in Chinese religions and broader visual and material culture, I was ever more intrigued by Buddhist print culture. It was this curiosity, as it grew and developed, that led me to write this book.

I have worked on this book for a full decade. My gratitude to all the many people who have helped me in so many ways over this long journey would be impossible to fully express.

First and foremost, I would like to thank an exceptional team of individuals, who, in myriad ways, took care of the many "nuts and bolts" aspects of this book and contributed to its realization. I much appreciate the constructive feedback of the anonymous reviewers; their critical suggestions helped me produce a stronger book. I am grateful to the very good people at my publisher, Brill, who were willing to publish such a thick manuscript with hundreds of illustrations, maps, diagrams, and tables. I was very fortunate to have Patricia Radder as my editor and blessed by her depth of experience, efficiency and patience. I thank her for always responding to my inquiries, big and small, and for securing a grant from the Chiang Ching-kuo Foundation to help defray costs and keep the book affordable. I appreciate the endorsement of the series editor, Angela Schottenhammer, who, upon my initial inquiry, expressed great interest in including my book in her exciting series *Crossroads—History of Interactions across the Silk Routes*. I am immensely thankful for Livia Kohn's great editorial help, she, herself a renowned Daoist scholar and experienced editor/publisher. Livia thoroughly edited the manuscript multiple times at different stages and also helped to prepare the index.

At Rice University, I am grateful to have had a number of very smart and able undergraduate students who worked as research assistants for this project.

Their impressive multi-disciplinary backgrounds, sophisticated research skills, and impeccable work ethic were great assets that I was fortunate to be able to call upon. Rita Zhaorui Xiong (Architecture, class of 2022) designed all the complex and beautiful maps and diagrams. We spent endless hours discussing how to transform a wealth of historical data into clear and readable visual images; she even consulted a Japanese color manual to help with color-design. Cuiyuanxiu Chen (Computer Science and Art, class of 2024), Lauren Weisizhe Ma (Architecture, class of 2024), and Jingyi (Eponine) Zhou (Philosophy and Art History, class of 2021) meticulously checked through all the footnotes and the bibliography. Thanks to their great attention to detail, we were able to catch many inconsistencies and errors.

Over the years I received generous support from multiple organizations which gave me leave time from teaching, provided financial support for field trips, and contributed toward subvention for this project. They include the Chiang Ching-kuo Foundation for International Scholarly Exchange (CCKF), the American Council of Learned Societies (ACLS), and the Asian Cultural Council (ACC) travel fellowship. I am equally grateful to the Huntington Library, Art Museum, and Botanical Gardens in San Marino, California. They agreed to serve as the host institute for my ACLS residential fellowship in 2017–18. I also remain very grateful to Rice University for the continued support I've received from across our campus. This has included a Research and Promotion Fellowship for Associate Professors from the School of Humanities, a Scholarly and Creative Works Subvention Fund award from the Office of Research, a teaching release fellowship and a Spatial Humanities fellowship from the Humanities Research Center, and generous support on multiple occasions from the Department of Art History, the Department of Transnational Asian Studies, and the Chao Center for Asian Studies.

I benefited greatly from the questions and feedback I received from students, colleagues and other attendees at the lectures and conference presentations I have given on materials related to this book. I thank all the hosts and audiences at these institutions: in China, Fudan University and Shaanxi Normal University; in the UK, University of Cambridge; in Europe, the European Institute for Chinese Studies (EURICS), and the University of Leiden; in Israel, Hebrew University of Jerusalem; in Japan, Rissho Kosai-kai International and University of Tokyo; in Taiwan, Academia Sinica, and National Palace Museum, Southern Branch; in the USA, Pomona College, Princeton University, University of California, Berkeley, University of Chicago, University of Oregon, University of Pennsylvania, University of Washington, University of Wisconsin-Madison, and Yale University.

I owe special thanks to Sören Edgren, Thomas Ebrey, Patricia Buckley Ebrey, Yong Cho, Anne Saliceti-Collins, Paul Copp, and Richard J. Smith for reading parts of the manuscript at various stages and giving me valuable input. My very close colleague at Rice, Nanxiu Qian, who passed away in 2022, was a tremendous help with translations of some arcane Chinese sources. I will miss her generosity and knowledge dearly. I would like to acknowledge my friend, Yung-Yi Julie Chou, who inspired me to bring humanities scholarship to life through mapping. After chatting about my "book roads" project, she came up with some mapping drafts which eventually became maps 0.1 and 10.4 in this book.

I have received so much help from so many members of the Rice community. They include colleagues and staff in both the Department of Art History and the Department of Transnational Asian Studies. I'd like to thank my esteemed colleagues Diane Wolfthal, Eric Huntington, Lisa Balabanlilar, Sonia Ryang, Linda Neagley, Graham Bader, Leo Costello and our wonderful staff members Kelley Vernon, Chelsey Denny, Hae Hun Matos. In addition, the librarians at the Fondren library, Anna L. Shparberg, Heidi and Scott Vieira, Angela Brown, Jane Zhao, all have my sincere gratitude. I'd also like to thank several of my undergraduate and graduate students including Tian Chen, Beatrice Chan, Dan Shan, and Ruoxin Wang.

I would also like to thank numerous friends and colleagues from all around the world for their continued encouragement and help. They include Stanley Abe, Alain Arrault, Christopher Atwood, Qianshen Bai, Alice Bianchi, Franck Billé, Michal Biran, Phillip Bloom, Elizabeth (Lulu) Brotherton, Mengge Cao, Mengyuan Chai, Fong-fong Chen, Huaiyu Chen, Hui-hung Chen, Yi-Rong Chen, Yunru Chen, Hsiao-wen Cheng, Lucille Chia, Shih-hua Chiu, Insoo Cho, Wonhee Cho, Eric Tzu-Yin Chung, Vincent Durand-Dastès, Julie Nelson Davis, Karl Debreczeny, Hilde De Weerdt, Fei Deng, Xiaolin Duan, Ling-guang Fang, Patrice Fava, Devin Fitzgerald, Sherry Fowler, Imre Galambos, Noga Ganany, Chiara Gasparini, Zhaoguang Ge, Anne Gerritsen, Jacques Giès, Vincent Goossaert, Valerie Hansen, Yan-chiuan He, Bryce Heatherly, Martin Heijdra, Satomi Hiyama-Karino, Ka-yi Ho, Jeehee Hong, Ming-liang Hsieh, Shu-wei Hsieh, Tsung-hui Hsieh, Che-ying Hsu, Ya-hwei Hsu, Lan-yin Huang, Li-Yun Huang, Graham Hutt, Seinosuke Ide, Shinobu Iguro, Tomoyasu Iiyama, Masaaki Itakura, Weiwei Jia, Ni Jiang, Takahiko Kameyama, Ming-yi Kao, Yury Khokhlov, Hiromi Kinoshita, Kōichi Kitsudō, Steve Kossak, Lingling Kuo, Nikita Kuzmin, John Lagerwey, Rongdao Lai, Seunghye Lee, Sonya Lee, June Li, Xingming Li, Yuhang Li, Yutong Li, Yunyun Liang, Fan Lin, Fu-shih Lin, Huan Shen Lin, Hui Sheng Lin, Li-chiang Lin, Sheng-chih Lin, Wei-cheng Lin, Kate Lingley, Stephen

Little, Heping Liu, Jui-Ch'i Liu, Shiyee Liu, Shu-fen Liu, Wei-Ting Liu, Yisi Liu, Darui Long, Hui-chen Lu, Hui-wen Lu, Ling-en Lu, Yu-ping Luk, Meng-ching Ma, Pierre Marsone, Michael Meng, Natsuimi Morihashi, Masaki Mukai, Julia Murray, Mika Natif, Isao Nishitani, Fei Pan, Maddalena Poli, Amelia Ying Qin, Hosung Shim, Pénélope Riboud, Lilla Russell-Smith, Norifumi Sakai, Bryan Sauvadet, Dominick Scarangello, Joseph Scheier-Dolberg, Angela Sheng, Sha Wutian, Yue Shu, Rui Shi, Ching-fei Shih, Chun-Tsui Tracy Shih, Adam Smith, Nancy Steinhardt, Lucien Sun, Jin Tao, Stephen F. Teiser, John Teramoto, Maromitsu Tsukamoto, Wen-e Tung, Daniel Tuzzeo, Maggie Wan, Cheng-hua Wang, Ching-ling Wang, Lanzhen Wang, Michelle C. Wang, Xin Wen, Andrew West, Jiang Wu, Wu Hung, Yi-ting Wu, Clarissa von Spee, Jisheng Xie, Xiong Wenbin, Márton Vér, Venerable Shi Zhiru, Lei Xue, Jie Yang, Kaikai Xu, Chia-ling Yang, Li Wei Yang, Zhiguo Yang, Yi-chun Yeh, Lidu Yi, Mimi Yiengpruksawan, Yu-chi Yu, Yusen Yu, Xinhua Yuan, Shubin Zhang, Judith Zeitlin, Minhao Zhai, Jianyu Zhang, Yunshuang Zhang, Yuzheng Zhang, Xiuying Zhou, Peter Zieme.

I dedicate this book to David Brody in honor of our 20 years together. I thank him for all the love, laughter, delicious food, travel, art, and music we've shared and for the wisdom he has brought to my life.

S.H.
January 2024

Illustrations

Figures

Diagrams

Maps

Tables

Chronology

China	Northern and Mongol Regimes	Japan/Korea
Shang dynasty, ca. 1600–1050 BCE		
Zhou dynasty, ca. 1050–256 BCE		
Qin dynasty, 222–207 BCE		
Han dynasty, 207 BCE–220 CE		
Western Han dynasty, 207 BCE–8 CE		
Wang Mang's Xin dynasty, 8–25		
Eastern Han dynasty, 25–220		
Three Kingdoms, 220–265		
(Western) Jin dynasty, 265–316		
(Eastern) Jin dynasty, 317–420		
Northern and Southern Dynasties, 420–589		
Sui dynasty, 581–618		
Tang dynasty, 618–907		
Taizong (r. 626–649)		
Empress Wu Zetian (r. 690–705)		
Xuanzong (r. 712–756)		(J) Heian, 794–1185
Wuzong (r. 840–846)		
Five Dynasties and Ten Kingdoms,	Khitan Liao, 907–1125	
907–960	Taizu (r. 916–926)	(K) Koryŏ, 935–1392
Song dynasty, 960–1127	Taizong (r. 927–947)	
Northern Song, 960–1127	Shenzong (r. 982–1031)	
Taizong (r. 976–997)	Xingzong (r. 1031–1055)	
Zhenzong (r. 997–1022)	Daozong (r. 1055–1101)	
Renzong (r. 1022–1063)		
Huizong (r. 1100–1126)	Tangut Xi Xia, 1038–1227	
Southern Song, 1127–1276	Huizong (r. 1068–1086)	
Lizong (r. 1224–1264)	Renzong (r. 1139–1193)	
		(J) Kamakura,
	Jurchen Jin, 1115–1234	1185–1333
	Zhangzong (r. 1189–1208)	

(*cont.*)

China	Northern and Mongol Regimes	Japan/Korea
Yuan dynasty, 1260–1368	Pre-Yuan Mongol Empire,	
Shizu (Kublai; r. 1260–1294)	1206–1260	
Chengzong (Temür, r. 1294–1307)	The Ilkhanate, 1260–1502	
Renzong (Ayurbarwada, r. 1311–1320)	The Golden Horde,	
Yingzong (Shidibala, r. 1320–1323)	ca. 1260–1502	
Wenzong (Tuq Temür, *r. 1328–1332*)	The Chaghadaids and the	
Shundi (Toghan Temür, r. 1333–1370)	Ögödeids, 1260–1370	(J) Muromachi,
Ming dynasty, 1368–1644		1333–1568
Taizu (r. 1368–1398)		
Yongle (r. 1402–1424)		(K) Chosŏn, 1392–1910
Xuanzong (r. 1425–1435)		
Yingzong (r. 1436–1465)		
Jiajing (r. 1521–1567)		(J) Edo, 1600–1868
Qing dynasty, 1644–1912		

Introduction

This book explores the dynamic spread of Buddhist print culture in China and its neighbors, as seen in map 0.1. Ample printed specimens—many of which bear illustrations—were discovered in remote archaeological sites, retrieved inside statues (both in China and elsewhere), or published in large compilations.[1] What makes these printed images and texts so remarkable is their common ties to Buddhism. Their sheer quantity is daunting and puzzling, but it also presents an unprecedented opportunity for new levels of understanding. What are the implications of Buddhist printed materials that spread vastly across China and its neighbors over centuries? Where and how were these materials produced? Where and how did they spread? Who created, distributed, sponsored, and used them?

Responding to these initial questions, this book examines major Buddhist printed images and texts produced over six centuries, from 850 to 1450. These works are not merely examined as static cultural relics but holistically as objects "on the move," transmitted along networks. Such networks appear in "Buddhist Book Roads," manifest in transnational and multicultural contexts, connect to other cultural products. By applying interdisciplinary approaches that matter in art history, the history of print and book culture, religious studies, and digital humanities, this study intends to shed new light on the "life" of Buddhist print culture from visual, textual, social, and religious perspectives. Doing so, it takes into account both the initial phase of manufacturing and the subsequent stages of circulation and reception.

FIGURE 0.0 ← Detail of fig. 0.5a. *Diamond Sutra* (Or.8210/P.2). 868. Tang. Woodblock print. The British Library

1 To name a few, for archaeological finds in Khara Khoto, Inner Mongolia, see ECHSCWX. For Buddhist printed texts discovered inside Chinese and Japanese Buddhist statues, see Rosenfield 1968–1969; Goepper 1983; Wood 1986; Shanxi sheng wenwuju 1991; Shen 2001; Huang 2011a. For the 106 volumes of the Chinese Buddhist illustrated woodblock printing, see ZGFJBHQJ; ZGFJBHQJBB.

© SHIH-SHAN SUSAN HUANG, 2024 | DOI:10.1163/9789004700017_002

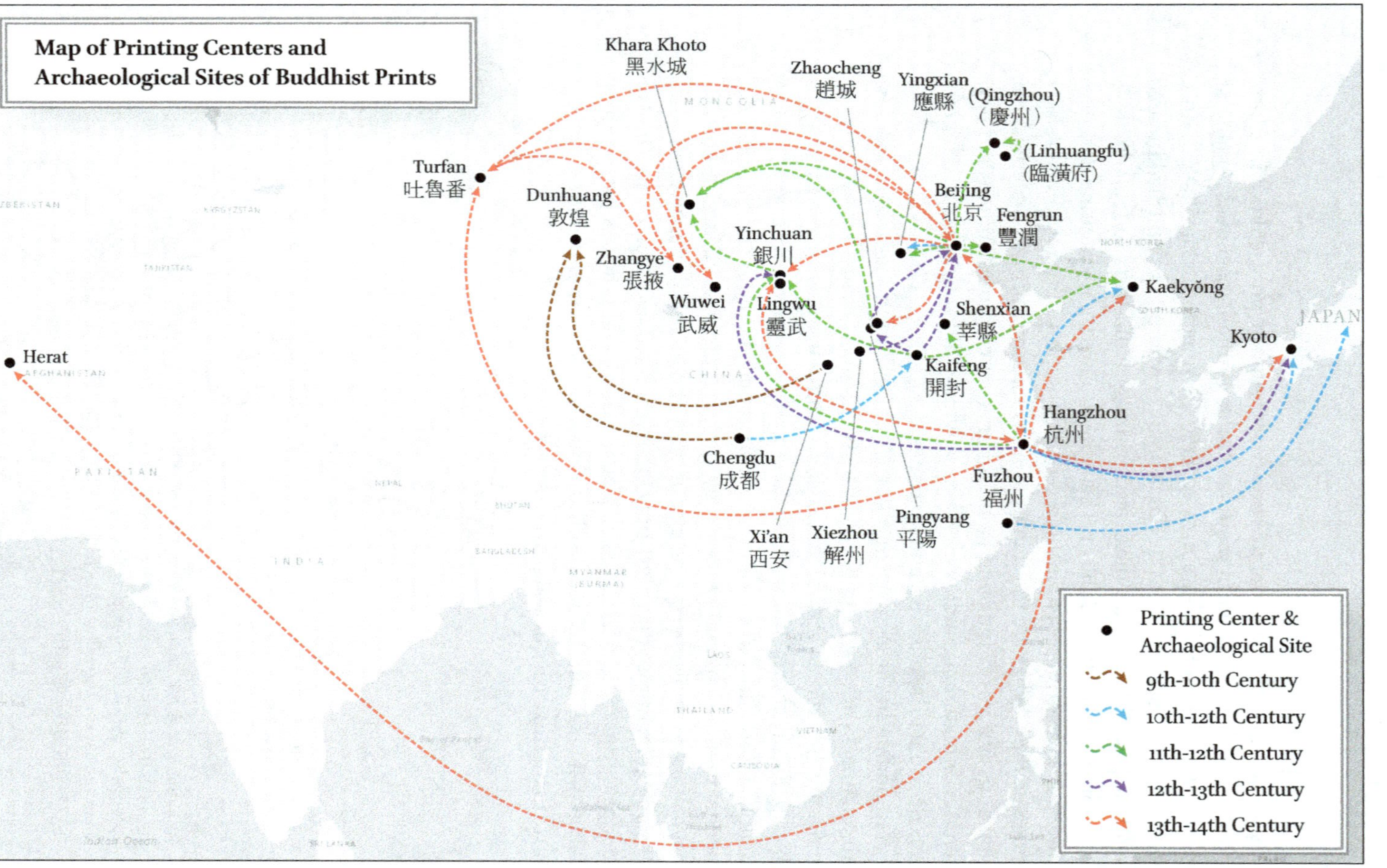

MAP 0.1 Map of printing centers and archaeological sites of Buddhist prints. By Rita Xiong

1 Primary Sources

Two groups of raw materials discovered at the turn of the twentieth century—one in Inner Mongolia (figs. 0.1–0.2) and the other in Eastern Central Asia (fig. 0.3)—show the entangled nature of the primary sources and the complex issues this book explores.

The first group contains two frontispieces proceeding two different sets of the *Lotus Sutra* (figs. 0.1–0.2), one of the most popular Buddhist scriptures widely circulated in the Sinosphere. They are among thousands of printed documents retrieved by the Russian expedition Pyotry Kuzmich Kozlov led in 1908–1909. It focused on Khara Khoto (Black Water) (map 0.1), an ancient city in Inner Mongolia that yielded fruitful cultural relics associated with the Xi Xia 西夏 kingdom (map 0.2), established by the Tanguts in what is today northwest China.[2] One frontispiece (fig. 0.1), produced by two documented Chinese block cutters commissioned by the Tangut emperor, is an early example of Buddhist printing sponsored by the Xi Xia royal house.[3]

The other frontispiece (fig. 0.2), as indicated by the publisher's colophon right of the illustration, was made by the Yan Family (Hangzhou Yanjia 杭州晏家) printshop in Hangzhou (map 0.1), located in south China, over 2700 km away from Khara Khoto. Most likely, a document like this was transmitted to Xi Xia through interstate trade routes, border markets, or even illegal channels.[4] The Yan Family printshop is one of the earliest documented commercial publishers active in Northern Song Hangzhou. One of its products (fig. 0.4), dated 1069 and deposited in a pagoda in Shenxian, Shandong (map 0.1),[5] a Northern Song Buddhist ruin located about 933 km north of Hangzhou, is similar to the Xi Xia frontispiece (fig. 0.1), but shows more sophisticated details. Considered together, these two prints suggest that illustrated scriptures produced in eleventh-century south China made their way to the northwest and subsequently inspired Xi Xia Buddhist print culture, which prospered in the twelfth century.

---

2 Thousands of printed and written documents, and paintings, retrieved by Kozlov and currently housed at the Institute of Oriental Studies and the State Hermitage Museum, Saint Petersburg, have been published in ECHSCWX; EGABCHY; Piotrovsky 1993.

3 For the colophon, see ECHSCWX 1: 270. The set contains six extant frontispieces; see ECHSCWX 1: 1, 17, 32, 241, 257, 310; Huang 2014d, 144. Shi Jinbo identifies them as Chinese; see Shi 1988, 148.

4 For more about the book smuggling, see De Weerdt 2006.

5 Cui 1982; Su 1999, 143–45; Huang 2011a, 146–54; Huang 2014b, 406–407, 413–14, 417; Huang 2014d, 144–45, 172.

FIGURE 0.1 Frontispiece to the *Lotus Sutra*, juan 3 (TK 3). 1146. Xi Xia. Woodblock print. Institute of Oriental Manuscripts, St. Petersburg

FIGURE 0.2 Frontispiece to the "Guanyin" Chapter of the *Lotus Sutra* (TK 167). Northern Song. Woodblock print. Institute of Oriental Manuscripts, St. Petersburg

FIGURE 0.4 Frontispiece to the *Lotus Sutra*, juan 3. 1069. Northern Song. Woodblock print. Discovered in the Buddhist pagoda, Shenxian, Shandong

The second group (fig. 0.3), virtually combined with the help of computer technology, consists of fragments retrieved further west, in the Turfan basin (map 0.1). They were discovered among the ruins of the medieval Uighur kingdom of Qocho (Gaochang 高昌) and first taken to Europe together with a "large quantity of woodcuts and block prints" by Albert von Le Coq, who led multiple Prussian expeditions to Turfan in 1902–1907.[6]

In 1922–1923, the sinologist Thomas Carter went to Berlin to inspect select specimens from the crates. He subsequently published an exclusive "witness report" in a paper entitled "The Printing of the Uigur Turks." This later became part of a classic book on Chinese print culture, published under the title *The Invention of Printing in China and its Spread Westward*.[7] Here Carter contrasts the messy and destructive condition of these printed specimens with the "neatly piled rolls" sealed in the Dunhuang 敦煌 "library cave," attributing the fragmented nature to a possible Buddhist persecution.[8] Yet, he was

6 The printed specimens brought to Berlin by Le Coq may originally have been numerous, retrieved from various sites in the Turfan basin, such as Gaochang (Turfan itself), Sangim, Toyoq, and Murtuq. Carter identifies Murtuk as the site where "a large proportion of the best block prints were found," and names Toqun, located "at the western edge of the Turfan oasis," as the "most western point at which" woodblock-printed specimens were discovered. See Carter 1955, xxi, xiv, 142–44.

7 The revised edition published in 1955 is cited most widely; see Carter 1955, 140–49.

8 Carter cites signs of destruction in a particular monastery, where "the floor was covered knee deep with" "waste paper," amid which lay the dead bodies of Buddhist monks killed "while the systematic destruction of their library was going on" (Carter 1955, 142–43). For select

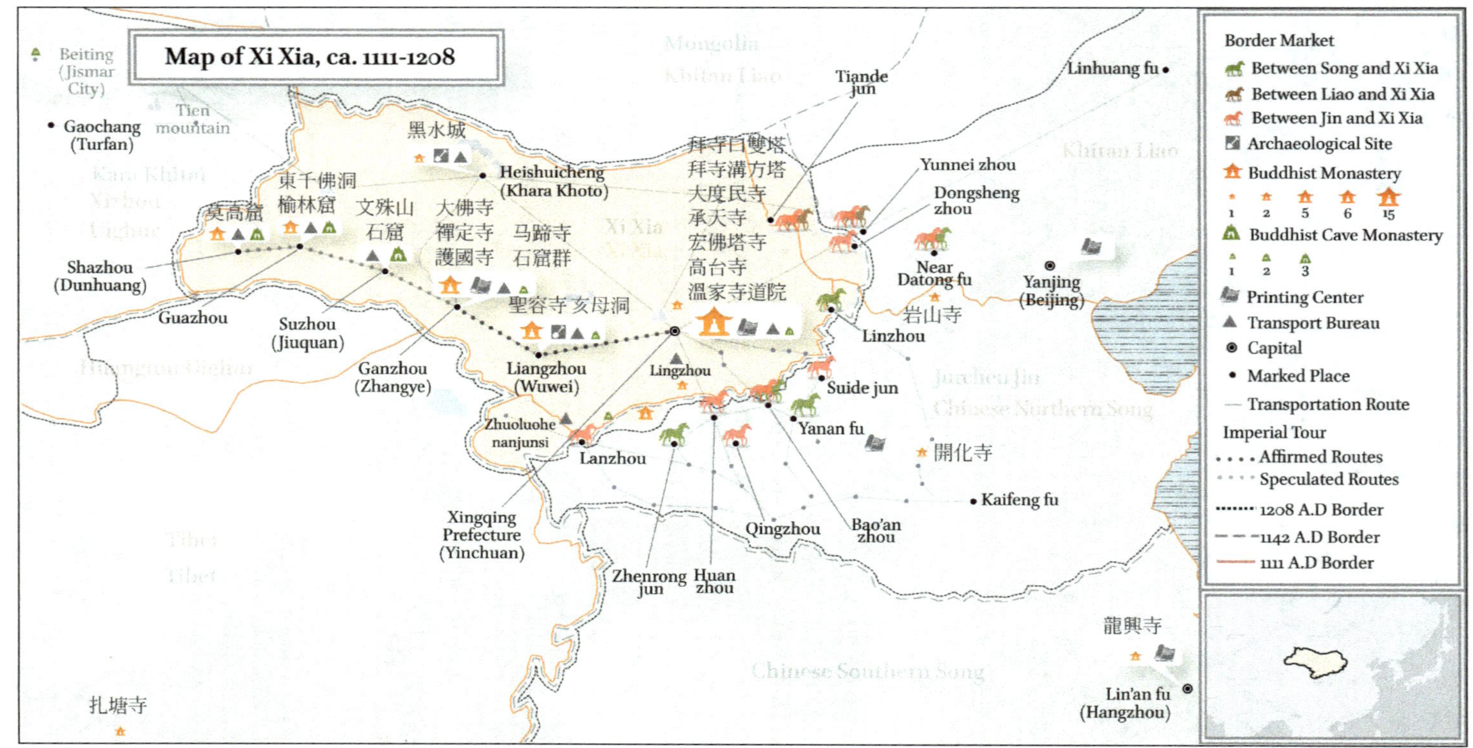

MAP 0.2 Xi Xia and its neighbors. By Rita Xiong

FIGURES 0.3A–B Two fragments of a Buddhist frontispiece. Yuan. Woodblock print. Museum für Asiatische Kunst, Berlin. a. MIK III 4633b1. b. MIK III 4633a

wrong to claim that these finds represent so-called "Uighur printing" produced in Central Asia.[9] After a century of studies, moreover, scholars deciphering fragments containing old Uighur writings have concluded that most printed fragments discovered in Turfan were in fact not made locally but in major printing centers such as Beijing and Hangzhou under the Mongol Yuan dynasty in China, going back to the thirteenth and fourteenth centuries (map 0.1).[10]

A case in point is a rare "family portrait" of an elite Uighur family (figs. 0.3a–b). The men and women in the woodcut are dressed in Mongolian clothing fashion, reflecting the family's adaptation of Mongol customs. Although their clan originated in the Uighur homeland in eastern Central Asia, many members worked for the Mongol court in Yuan China in the thirteenth and fourteenth centuries. Most prominent among them was Mengsusu 蒙速速 (Mungsuz; 1206–1267), the leading man in the bottom row. Serving Qubilai Khan (Hubilie 忽必烈, r. 1271–1294), he was a high-ranking minister who helped the Mongol to fight the Southern Song. Many of his sons, also represented here, held high governmental positions in the Yuan capital Dadu 大都, modern Beijing.[11] These fragments were likely parts of a Buddhist frontispiece, produced in Yuan China and subsequently transported to the Uighur homeland in Turfan via Uighur and Mongol networks.

The two groups of sources discussed so far share certain key features. First, they were retrieved in northwest China, where a relatively cold and dry climate helped to preserve the fragile printed specimens. This, however, does not mean that no Buddhist prints circulated in south China.[12] Second, they were imprints discovered far removed from their original places of production. This suggests that they may have been transported over long distances. Third, they show Inner Asian peoples, such as the Tanguts and Uighurs, as major actors in the dynamic spread of Buddhist print culture.

Previous scholars working on Chinese print culture have focused mostly on historically transmitted Confucian classics, popular textbooks, study and

---

studies of the nature of the Dunhuang "library cave," see Rong 2013, 124, 130, 341, 380; Van Schaik and Galambos 2012, 18–28; Galambos 2020, 253.

9 Carter published a frontispiece, which he wrongly attributes to the Song period (Carter 1955, 89 recto). I re-identify this frontispiece as a product of Yuan Dadu, associated with a relative of the Uighur chief *Köncök*; see "The *Iduq qut* Frontispiece" in ch. 7 below (fig. 7.11a).

10 See, for example, Zieme and Kudara 1985; Zieme 1996; Zieme 2007.

11 Franke 1978; Kitamura 1987; Ebert 1990; Dang 2000; Nishiwaki 2009, 165.

12 A rare exception is the Northern Song tomb of a lay woman in Jiangsu, which yields many exquisite illustrated texts, both printed and hand copied. See Zhu 1984; Suzhou bowuguan et al. 1982; ZGBHQJ 1: 36 (fig. 47); Jiangyin bowuguan 2009, 190–97. For two major monographs on commercial publishing in Fujian, see Chia 2002a; Brokaw 2007a.

household guides, elite notebooks, local gazetteers, maps, medical and technical handbooks, illustrated fictions, painting manuals, and more.[13] They have largely neglected Buddhist printing as have historians, bibliographers, and scholars of literature.[14] Their main concern has been on issues of elite print culture, the cultural and social history of books and printing, including the origin and evolution of printing, the tension between manuscript and print culture, commercial publishing, networks of block cutters, printers, and publishers, knowledge and technological transfer, editions, East-West connection, and the relationship between texts and images.[15] Based on their work, a "publishing boom" theory, which may or may not be applicable to Buddhist materials, has been widely accepted, attributing greater dissemination of knowledge to larger print runs.[16]

Within the corpus of Buddhist printed materials, images embedded in texts deserve more attention. Scholars working on Buddhist texts tend to be most concerned with the textual tradition, where key issues are canon formation, bibliographical documentation, and editorial comparison.[17] On the side of art history, researchers who work on printed images tend to be drawn largely to Ming-Qing illustrated books and other commercial prints. Their fruitful scholarship addresses the image-text relationship in secular novels, plays, and Confucian books; the significance of professional painting manuals in disseminating knowledge of famous paintings across East Asia; and the commercialization, materiality, and European reception of single-sheet colored prints

13 For a study of the 11th-to-17th century local gazetteers, see Dennis 2015 (for the mapping of block cutters' business zones in Jiangxi, Beijing/Handan, and Jiangnan, see map 4.1–4.3).

14 Lucille Chia studies extensively the donors' colophons in Song-to-Ming Buddhist sources, including the Qisha Canon, the Jiaxing Canon, and other Ming-Qing popular Buddhist imprints; see Chia 2015a–b.

15 For the state of the field, see Brokaw 2005a–b; Brokaw 2007b. For select studies, see Carter 1955; Tsien 1985; Edgren 1984; Edgren 1989; Cherniack 1994; Hegel 1998; Chia 2002a; Chia 2003; Brokaw and Chow 2005; Zhang and Han 2006; Brokaw 2007a; Zhang and Han 2009; McDermott 2006; Chow 2007; Chia and De Weerdt 2011. For more about the images and texts, see Chia 2002b; Murray 2005; Brokaw 2007b, 278–79. For more on Song scholars' critical views toward printing, especially on Confucian subjects, see Kieschnick 2002, 182; Drège 1991, 101–3; for a counter argument, citing evidence of Song scholars' enthusiasm in print culture, see Huang 2014b, 391–92.

16 This is the general assumption made by scholars examining the history of the book; see the summary in Brokaw 2007b, 266–74. For more speculation of Chinese print runs, see Tsien 2002, 166–67.

17 See Wu and Chia 2015; Li and He 2003; Li 2002b.

made in Suzhou.[18] Some studies of Buddhist printed images, often centered on a specific work, tackle issues concerning iconography, images and texts, painting and printing, regional styles, as well as donors and block cutters.[19] Given the growing datasets and transnational trends of scholarship, it is now possible to expand the research agenda to a broader scope and context.

Buddhist woodcuts, that is, mass-produced printed images on paper, or impressions taken from them constitute a large corpus of visual data in traditional Chinese art, closely connected with images made in other media. They are also among the earliest examples of what is now called *banhua* 版畫, "woodblock print pictures," a term first introduced from the Japanese.[20] Buddhist woodcuts exhibit rich visual knowledge and ideas borrowed, edited, and repurposed from various existing cultural sources and media. Unlike Buddhist art in other media, such as wall paintings and stone carvings crowding temples and grottoes, printed images mass-produced on paper and embedded in books are portable objects circulated by people over long distances. Compared to a Buddhist text written in a specific language that defined and limited its readership, a printed image presented no language barrier. It could transcend cultural and linguistic boundaries and exert a great impact beyond its original religious context. Buddhist printed illustrations transmitted internationally thus opened the door for foreign artists to the rich visual repertoire of Chinese images.

2 Formative Years: 850–1450

The core of the book treats the six centuries from 850 to 1450, the formative period of Buddhist print culture with many references to later times.[21]

18 For a comprehensive history of the illustrated print culture, see Zhou 1998; Kobayashi 2017 (84% of the book deals with Ming-Qing secular woodcuts). For major publications of plates, see OFZGBCT; ZGBHQJ; ZGBHSTL; ZGGDBHCK; Takimoto 1988; Takimoto 2009; Zhou 2008; Zheng 2012. For more about the Ming-Qing print culture, see Clunas 1997a, 181–85; Clunas 1997b, 134–48; Clunas 2013, 134–37; Clunas 2017, 74–75, 124–26; Edgren 2011; Kobayashi 2017, 114–713; Kobayashi 2018; Lin 2012; Lin 2015; Lin L. 2019; Lin L. 2023; Ma 2002; Ma 2010a–b; Murray 2005; Park J. 2012; Park 2018, esp. 147–73; Wang C. H. 2014; Wang C. 2016; Wang 2020, 119–53, 159–63, 211–30, 235–75; Wang C. 2022; Wang 2024; Lai 2018; Hsu W. 2021; Farrer and McLoughlin 2022.

19 See Miya 1983a–b; Drège 1999; Huang 2011a–b; Huang 2014b; Zhang J. 2014; Sun B. 2016; Kobayashi 2017, 3–52; Zhang J. 2021. For select visual studies of Daoist woodcuts, see Chia 2011; Huang 2012; Wan 2010; Wan 2016a–b; Wan 2017b.

20 Huang 2017c, 2.

21 For a study that questions the conventional dynastic approach in historical inquiries, see Wu 2022b.

Not only relevant to Buddhist printing, this time period is also relevant in the periodization of Chinese print culture and Buddhist exchanges. Lucille Chia and Hilde De Weerdt, for example, call the period from 900 to 1400 the "first golden age of woodblock printing."[22] Adding to this, Joseph McDermott and Peter Burke identify 1450–1850 as the "first four centuries" of the "Age of European Expansion" and as a period of "considerable expansion of printing in East Asia."[23] Tansen Sen characterizes the seventh-to-fifteenth centuries as the key period when multiple Buddhist centers emerged across Asia.[24] In world history, Jerry Bentley identifies 500 to 1500 as the age of "hemispheric integration," because cross-cultural interaction during this period "brought about an impressive degree of integration in the eastern hemisphere."[25] He further divides it into two sub-periods, distinguishing the "post-classical age" of 500–1000 from the "age of transregional nomadic empires," 1000–1500.[26] More recently, Valerie Hansen sees the year 1000 as the beginning of globalization.[27]

Buddhism and printing have been closely related since the beginning of woodblock technology. It is now widely accepted that woodblock printing was invented in China in the seventh century and that the earliest imprints were mostly Buddhist.[28] The year 850 marks the approximate time when Buddhist printed books reached maturity. The famous *Diamond Sutra* scroll dated 868 (figs. 0.5a–b), originally discovered in the Dunhuang "library cave" in Gansu (map 0.1), northwest China, and now in the British Library, is considered the

22 Chia and De Weerdt 2011, 1. Inoue Susuma identifies the late Ming period in the sixteenth century as the golden age of book culture, although the data he draws on do not really include Buddhist materials; see Inoue 2002. For a book review, see Brokaw 2005b, esp. 149; Brokaw 2007b, 260.

23 McDermott and Burke 2015, 5.

24 Sen 2014, xvi–xix.

25 Bentley 1998, esp. 238.

26 Bentley 1996, esp. 756.

27 Hansen 2020.

28 Timothy Barrett argues that Empress Wu 武 (r. 690–705) "discovered printing" by sponsoring millions of Buddhist *dharani* texts (Barrett 2008, esp. 89–90). The eight-century miniature scrolls of Buddhist printed *dharani* charms found in Korea and Japan are indeed the earliest extant specimens of printed texts (Hickman 1975; Tsien 1985, 149–51; Yiengpruksawan 1987; Kornicki 1998, 114–17; Kornicki 2012). For more on the origin of woodblock printing, see Barrett 1997; Chia and De Weerdt 2011, 1–3. Some studies shed light on early Daoist and Confucian use of printing technology. For the Daoist use of ritual seals as a kind of "proto-printing," see Strickmann 1993; Huang 2017a, 78–80; DZ 1270, 32: 578. For printed sacred images recorded in a seventh-century Daoist monastic manual, see Barrett 1997, 540; Kohn 2004, 98; DZ 1125; Schipper and Verellen 2004, 451–52. For morality books printed in the eleventh century with Laozi as alleged author, see Bell 1992. For the printing of the Confucian classics in tenth-century Sichuan, see Zhang and Han 2006, 1: 21; McDermott 2006, 9–10.

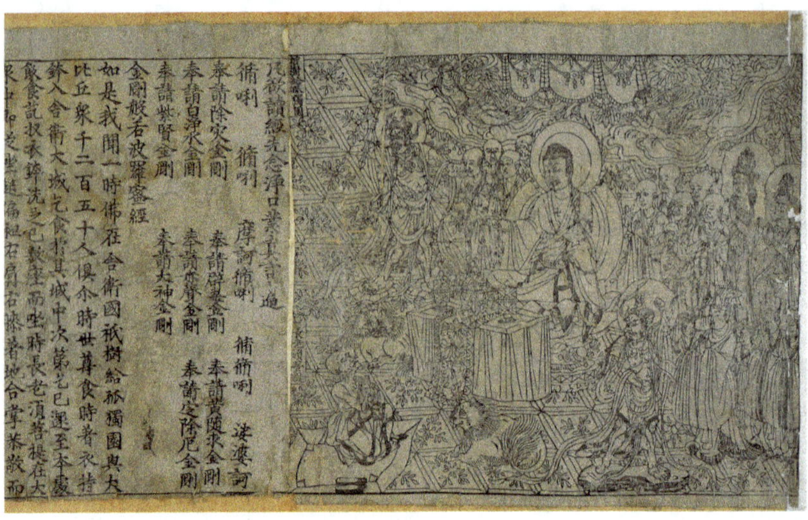

a

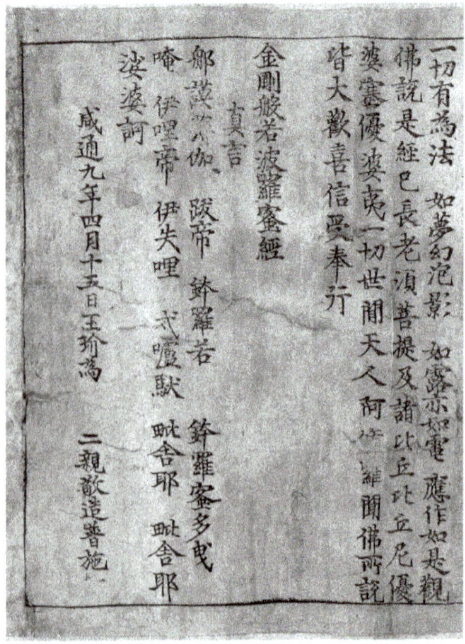

b

FIGURES 0.5A–B
Details. *Diamond Sutra* (Or.8210/P.2). 868. Tang. Woodblock print. The British Library

world's earliest printed book.[29] It is decorated with a frontispiece (fig. 0.5a)—an illustration preceding the text and placed to the right of the written part. It represents the Buddha in a palatial setting, turning his face toward the lower left to preach to a kneeling monk. This leftward facing composition

29 The book has recently been repaired; see Wood and Barnard 2010.

departs from the frontally-positioned buddha-preaching scene depicted in earlier mural conventions and may cater to the right-to-left reading habit of a Buddhist scroll-book or traditional handscroll painting.[30] Later this became the standard template for Buddhist frontispiece art.

A donor's dedicatory colophon (fig. 0.5b), printed at the end of the scroll, identifies a layman named Wang Jie 王玠 as the sponsor of the printing on behalf of his deceased parents. Without specifying the print run, he claims to distribute the book widely, which suggests that he printed multiple copies. Given the book's sophisticated quality, Susan Whitfield speculates that it may have been produced in Chengdu, Sichuan (map 0.1). This was a thriving printing center at the time, located over 2000 km southeast of Dunhuang.[31] This hypothesis is indirectly supported by numerous other tenth-century hand-copied *Diamond Sutra* manuscripts based on the printed edition made in Sichuan as well as miscellaneous Chengdu printed artifacts, all found in Dunhuang.[32]

The period from the tenth to the fourteenth centuries constitutes constitutes the golden age of Buddhist print culture.[33] Multiple printing centers developed (map 0.1): Hangzhou 杭州 in the south, Pingyang 平陽 and Beijing 北京 in the north, and Yinchuan 銀川 in the northwest. In Song China, illustrated Buddhist texts were produced by both government and commercial organizations. Transmitted beyond the Song, they then inspired printers in other countries, such as Korea and Japan, to produce their own versions. Buddhist print culture also thrived under the regimes of non-Han peoples, including the Khitan Liao (see ch. 4), the Jurchen Jin 金 and the Tangut Xi Xia as well as the Mongol Yuan 元, whose royal families was among the most significant supporters.

The period covered in this book ends around 1450, when coincidentally the first book was printed in Europe using movable type—the famous Bible by Johannes Gutenberg (ca. 1400–1468). A well-known landmark in world history, this has often mistakenly been described as the beginning of printing worldwide. More important for our purposes, Buddhist print culture was firmly established by then. A case in point is a Buddhist book widely popular

30 Huang 2011b, 141; Huang 2014b, 390. See also Wang M. 2022, 224.

31 Whitfield 2018, 237–38.

32 Both literary and visual sources account for the thriving print and book culture in ninth-century Chengdu; its diverse products range from the privately printed calendars, to Buddhist sutras, to other publications on the yin-yang, divination, astronomy, and geomancy. See JWDS, 589; Tsien 1985, 151–52; Zhang and Han 2006, 1: 21–22; Chia and De Weerdt 2011, 2–3n3; Huang 2018b, 38–39*n*12.

33 For case studies of the visual culture of the Middle Period, see Ebrey and Huang 2017.

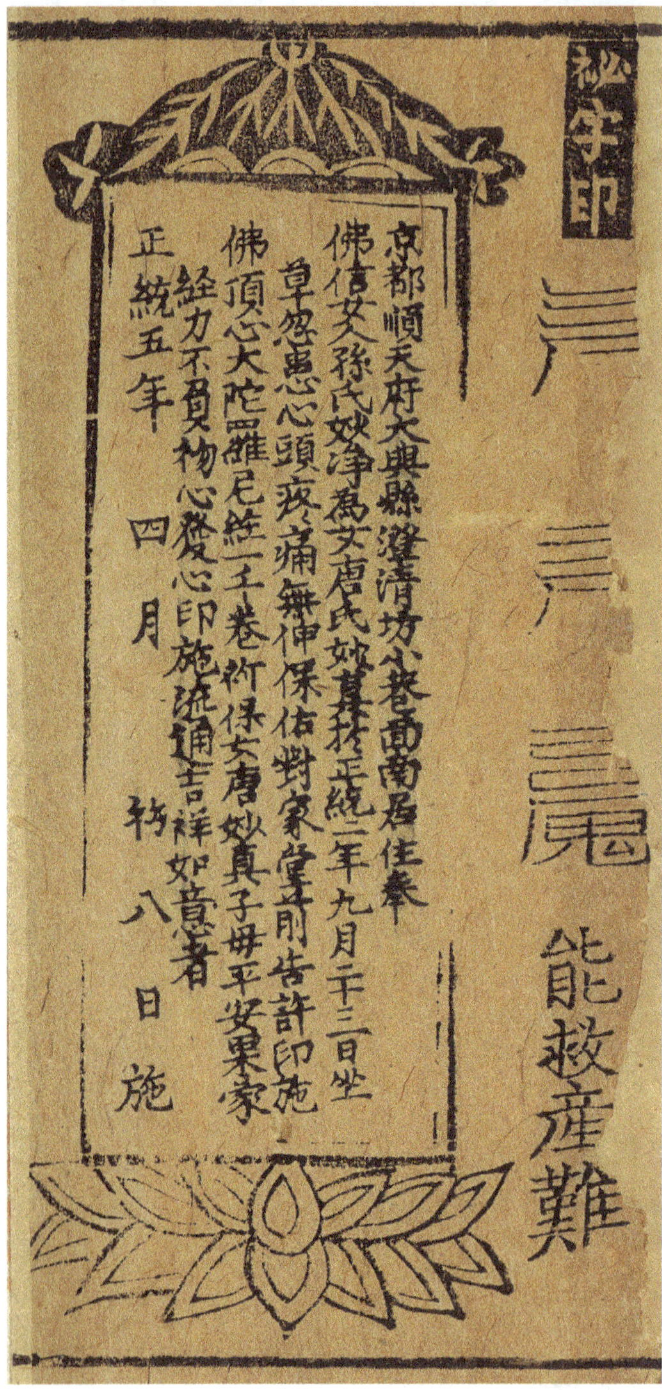

FIGURE 0.6
Detail. *Dharani Sutra*. 1440. Ming. Woodblock print. Indianapolis Museum of Art at Newfields

in fifteenth-century Beijing, which was originally an indigenous Chinese text (figs. 0.6, 12.13a, 12.14, 12.16a–d). Integrating long-standing devotion to the compassionate bodhisattva Guanyin 觀音 (Avalokiteśvara), talismanic culture, and common popular beliefs, this book gained currency especially because of its acclaimed healing power. Multiple printed specimens dated to the mid-fifteenth century suggest that they share standardized designs, with customized colophons added at the end. Women and their families, concerned with possible childbirth complications, were its main donors.

A prime example from the Indianapolis Museum of Art at Newfields bears a dedicatory colophon that identifies a woman named Sun Miaojing 孫妙淨 from Beijing's Chengqing 澄清 Ward (map 11.1) as the donor (figs. 0.6, 12.16a–d; Table 12.1, no. 13). She funded one thousand copies in 1440 to fulfill a promise she made three years earlier. Her daughter Tang Miaozhen 唐妙真 suffered from severe chest pain while in labor. Woman Sun prayed to Guanyin and vowed that, should her daughter be free from pain and deliver her baby smoothly, she would distribute one thousand copies of the *dharani* text to thank the deity. Donors like her, who sponsored Buddhist printing as a token of gratitude responding to blessings, must have provided convincing testimonials that caused more people to turn to Buddhism for help and support wider runs of printing. Buddhist print culture continued to thrive after 1450, but the basic paradigms and repertoire were set.

3 Printing for Merit

Buddhist printing was greatly stimulated by the concept of merit accumulation. Individuals could earn merits for a variety of good deeds related to books,[34] notably financial donation, production, copying, and the general veneration of Buddhist texts. Merits could also be transferred from one person to another: to a deceased parent (fig.0.5b), a sick daughter (fig. 0.6), a ruler, or any sentient being.[35] An extreme case is exemplified by a tenth-century farmer who commissioned a manuscript containing handmade copies of both the *Diamond Sutra* and the *Scripture of the Ten Kings of Hell*, later found at

34 Kieschnick 2002, 164–85. For a study of Buddhist printing for merit, drawing donors' colophons attached to Buddhist printed texts as primary sources, see Chia 2015a.

35 Kieschnick 2002, 170–71; Teiser 2017, 322.

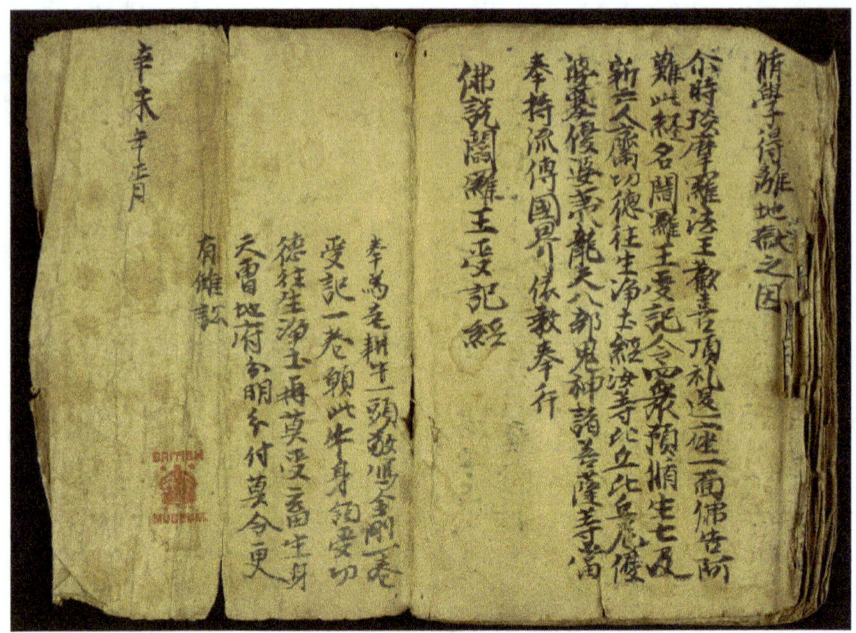
脩學得離地獄之因
爾時琰摩羅法王歡喜頂禮退坐一面佛告阿
難此經名閻羅王受記令四衆預脩生七及
新亡人廣功德往生淨土經汝等比丘比丘尼優
婆塞優婆夷天龍八部鬼神諸菩薩等當
奉持流傳國界依教奉行
佛說閻羅王受記經
奉為老耕牛一頭敬寫金剛一卷
受記一卷願此牛身領受功
德往生淨土再莫受畜生身
天曹地府分明分付莫令更
有讎訟
辛未年正月
BRITISH MUSEUM

FIGURE 0.7 Detail. *Diamond Sutra* and the *Scripture of the Ten Kings of Hell* (Or.8210/S.5544). 911. Ink on paper. Dunhuang manuscript. The British Library

Dunhuang (fig. 0.7). He, with great compassion, decided to transfer merits to his aged plow ox (*lao gengniu* 老耕牛).[36]

Mahayana Buddhism, which exerted a profound influence on East Asian societies, promoted a "cult of books," urging adepts to worship and venerate them.[37] The *Lotus Sutra*, one of its most popular scriptures, encourages adepts to accumulate merit by reading and preaching it, and also by copying and keeping the scripture.[38] The widespread notion of "more books, more merit" is vividly reflected in later popular liturgical paintings, which depict the courts of the Kings of Hell (figs. 0.8, 5.29).[39] Here books are used as a material means to measure karmic merit. Escorted by a goddess who holds a flying banner, a family consisting of a man, two adult women, and a child all well-dressed

36 For an inspiring study, see Teiser 1994, 136. See also Kieschnick 2002, 172.

37 Kieschnick 2002, 164–65; Wu 2015, 46–47; Yü 2020, 1.

38 Kieschnick 2002, 165. For more on the *Lotus Sutra*, see Stevenson 2007; Teiser and Stone eds. 2009; Campany 2018; Lopez and Stone 2019.

39 Cf. a similar Ming hanging scroll at Harvard Art Museums; "1979.406: One of the Ten Kings of Hell," Accessed October 30, 2023. https://harvardartmuseums.org/collections/object/201976.

For more about the *Ten Kings of Hell* texts and images, see Teiser 1994; Ledderose 2000, 163–85.

FIGURE 0.8 Detail of fig. 5.29. *King of Hell*. 17th century. Ming. Ink and color on paper. Hanging scroll. Musée des Arts Asiatiques-Guimet

in contrast to other sinners depicted in the same painting stand in front of a "scale of karma" waiting to be judged.[40] Because they sponsored books that outweigh the negative impacts of their past actions, they are spared the punishments of hell. The presence of lay women as patrons of Buddhist books

40 The scale of karma is a recurring motif in pictures of the *Ten Kings of Hell*. Cf. similar motifs depicted in the tenth-century Dunhuang manuscripts (Teiser 1994, 174, 187).

echoes many cases of elite and non-elite women's patronage of Buddhist books as discussed below.

Interpreting the proliferation of Buddhist print culture as a product of merit-making challenges the common "publishing boom" theory that equates larger print runs with a widening readership. Numerous Buddhist printed texts deposited in Buddhist pagodas and statues—including also those found in other East Asian countries—provide evidence to the contrary.[41] Originally concealed inside devotional statues or pagodas and not meant for ordinary reading, they are, as Hsueh-man Shen notes, "text-relics."[42]

Also, while printing provides a more efficient way to mass-produce Buddhist texts, it never entirely replaced hand-written copies, partly because of the "sacred value" or merit accrued by manually copying a sutra—sometimes even with one's own blood (fig. 11.1) as "a devotional act."[43] This also explains why, even in this age, when copies of Buddhist texts were routinely mass-produced, there were still some patrons in East Asia, especially those tied to aristocratic or elite classes, who preferred hiring scribes and illustrators to produce limited editions of hand-written manuscripts with hand-painted illustrations. Some of these manuscripts (figs. 3.33a, 3.42a, 3.59) may even have been copied from printed works (figs. 3.31, 3.35, 3.39).

The reception of different printed copies of the Buddhist canon,[44] often composed of thousands of texts, also deserves re-evaluation. In the Song-to-Ming periods, multiple editions were compiled, mass-produced, and distributed widely; some even made their way to other parts of Asia. While most versions were sponsored by the ruling classes, some were funded by the general public. The motivation for producing new editions of the canon, even though older ones were still available, may have been related to the inclusion of newly-translated or collated texts promoted by individuals who had compiled or sponsored them. The new editions may also have celebrated specific donors and local communities. Not all copies were "read" in the traditional sense. Rather, they were stored in temple libraries as devotional objects or used for what Jiang Wu calls "symbolic" reading.[45]

41 Even though researchers call attention to comparable deposit practices associated with the later Hunan Daoist statues, no books were found in the surveyed cases. For more studies, see Fava 2013; Robson 2014; Robson 2016; Arrault 2020, 123–61.

42 Shen 2019, 33.

43 Kieschnick 2002, 184.

44 For recent studies of the Buddhist canon, see Wu and Chia 2015; Long and Chen 2019.

45 Wu 2015, esp. 60. For a theoretical study of the devotional uses of sacred texts, Buddhist and Daoist alike, see Campany 1991.

4 The Network Approach

Mapping Buddhist imprints in space enables us to see them as potential "things in motion," traveling through both integrated networks and extensive Book Roads. A preliminary mapping (map 0.1), based on extant imprints of images and texts, connects major printing centers with sites where some extant specimens were discovered. Each dotted line linking two locations denotes the potential linkage of two places; arrow markings suggest the direction of movement of certain Buddhist imprints from production to final destination. For the sake of visual clarity and aesthetics, all links between points of connection are drawn in a wavy fashion rather than straight lines that would demarcate the most direct path (or edge) between two places.

Lines are further colored in purple, blue, green, yellow, and red to refer to different historical periods. While there were fewer identifiable routes of connection in the ninth and tenth centuries (marked in purple and blue), the web in the thirteenth and fourteenth centuries (marked in red) shows an exponential expansion, reaching all the way into Central and West Asia. Across various periods, Hangzhou and Beijing stand out as the busiest hubs of transmission: they embody the most intense convergences of outbound, inbound, and long-distance movements. In the Mongol era, both cities produced Buddhist imprints that reached Turfan, the Uighur homeland in eastern Central Asia. Because Central Tibet was a special district controlled by the Yuan, imprints made in Beijing at that time also made their way there. Then again, a potential route connects Hangzhou with Herat in today's Afghanistan. This is inferred from a visual comparison elaborated in detail below (figs. 0.19, 0.21; see ch. 3). In East Asia, Buddhist imprints produced in Hangzhou make up the bulk of those transmitted to Japan and Korea by sea.

To date, researchers in multiple fields have applied various network approaches to examine artistic, cultural, social, and religious connectivity, exchange, and interaction in Asia and beyond.[46] A network is a proposed web

---

46 For the state of the field of network analysis, see a bibliography, see the Historical Network Research (HNR), "HNR Bibliography," The Historical Network Research Community, Accessed December 24, 2023. https://historicalnetworkresearch.org/hnr-bibliography-categories/#Art%20History.

Social structure, culture, and human agency form three major modes of network analysis; see Emirbayer and Goodwin 1994. For religious networks, see Guillot et al. 1998; Collar 2013; Sen 2014; Meinert 2016; *BuddhistRoad* Team 2018; Bryson 2018; Kim 2019. For maritime networks in Asia, see Schottenhammer 2005; Schottenhammer 2008; Schottenhammer 2010; Schottenhammer 2015; Schottenhammer 2023. Xin Wen re-interprets the Silk Road as "the King's Road," seeing it as a "traveler-centered" network and as "a diplomatic route, rather than a commercial one." He highlights the role played by the "Kings of Eastern

consisting of various points of connections: hubs, major centers, minor nodes, and routes.[47] It is productive to go beyond a singular network framework, and visualize the entire system as made up of numerous intertwined and overlapping networks. Scholars studying the spread of Buddhism throughout Asia have shown that Buddhist networks were embedded in other types, including long-distance trade and various social and political networks.[48] These eventually came to include connections provided by Buddhist monasteries and quite possibly involved the repurposing of older connections.[49] Suffice it to say, a network is rarely "exclusive to one group of people" nor is it "a single type of commodity" or "a specific religious tradition."[50] Based on this, this study will apply the overlapping and multi-layered network model to the study of Buddhist print culture.

Texts and images, two different but interrelated types of primary sources, may shed light on different networks. An example appears in Megan Bryson's study of the religious network of the medieval kingdom of Nanshao and Dali that ruled southwest China (modern Yunnan). It was arguably a part of the "southern or southwest Silk Road" and "a transit hub linking China, Southeast Asia, India, and Tibet."[51] Texts and images pertinent to the Yunnan "regional form" of the so-called Acuoye Guanyin bodhisattva reveal two kinds of "mutually constitutive" networks. Whereas the texts suggest a "documented network" with Tang-Song China, the images point to a "represented network" more closely tied to India.[52] Pertinent to this, this book treats abundant images transmitted in Buddhist print culture as primary sources and argues that visual

---

Eurasia" who created and maintained the network and by the numerous diplomatic envoys who were the main travelers. See Wen 2023. For applications of social network analysis and digital humanities in archaeology, history, and art history, see Knappett 2013; De Weerdt 2016; Rice 2017; Hsu 2018. For interdisciplinary studies of the Silk Road, taking into account both material artifacts and manuscripts, see Wang and Overbey eds. 2023.

47 While hubs and nodes are used in this study in a loose way, some scholars have a stricter differentiation of the terms. To see how hubs, major centers, and minor nodes are defined in archaeological studies, see Ray Rivers, Carl Knappett and Tim Evans in Knappett 2013, 125–50; Meinert 2016, 9; Bryson 2018, 82–83.

48 Neelis 2011, esp. 311–19; Neelis 2014, 3, 5; Sen 2017, 111–94 (for a provocative map marking the "Afroeurasian interlocking circuits," see 123); Sen 2018, 3–4; Sen 2023, 839–45; Li Y. 2023. Not all Buddhist networks overlap with economic hubs; see Bryson 2018, 83.

49 Frasch 1998, 70–71.

50 Sen 2017, 112.

51 Bryson 2018, 106.

52 Bryson 2018, 82. More and more visual studies of the Dali Buddhist art highlight the diverse artistic and religious elements. For the long Buddhist handscroll attributed to Zhang Shengwen, see Lee Y. 2023; for fragments of printed frontispieces, see Chen J. 2023.

materials allow us to see additional dimensions of cultural transfers than what we can see by relying solely on textual data.

Metaphors involving roads, seas, and waterways are effective to help researchers re-conceptualize a trans-regional or intra-Asia framework. Taking the cue of the oft-cited Silk Road,[53] Carmen Meinert and others promote the counterpart of the border-crossing "Buddhist Road," applying it to trace the spread of Buddhist ideas, materials, and other trends across pre-modern eastern Central Asia.[54] The Buddhist Road goes beyond state-based boundaries, highlighting interconnectivities, circulations, and the dynamics between the local and the global. An inspiring graph published by Meinert's team shows the transmission processes in a series of "feedback loops" or circular movements that originate from a node, travel to other nodes, and then bounce back to the original point with added feedback.[55]

Equally powerful is the notion of Book Roads (*shuji zhilu* 書籍之路), a road-based concept famously coined by the sinologist Wang Yong in his ground-breaking studies of book-based cultural exchanges between China and Japan. Wang originally saw the eastbound Book Roads as a counterpart of the westbound, material-based Silk Road.[56] More recent studies, however, see these two models not as mutually exclusive but as complementary. Book Roads can be extended beyond the Sino-Japanese context as well.[57] Qin Hualin, for example, asserts that those in the Song and Yuan included not only eastern routes to Japan and Korea, but also northern ones into the Liao-Jin territories and northwestern ones into Xi Xia. The northwest-bound Book Roads, Qin adds, connected book production centers in Jiangnan with Dunhuang, Turfan, and Khara Khoto.[58]

Going beyond roads, there is the metaphor of the "Mediterranean Sea," first raised in a Western context by the French scholar Fernand Braudel to refer to a fluid, interlocking, and connected system. Scholars have transferred this

---

53 For the inter-regional connections along the Silk Road, see Hansen 2015; Wong and Heldt 2014; Wang and Overbey eds. 2023. For a study of the "metal road," tracing the early transmission of the bronze and iron technologies by the Xiongnu steppe people in Eastern Eurasia, see Yang et al. 2017; Yang et al. 2020.

54 For select publications, see *BuddhistRoad* Team 2018; Meinert 2016; Heirman et al. eds. 2018; Meinert and Sørensen eds. 2020; Kasai and Sørensen eds. 2022. For more, see Ruhr-Universität Bochum, "BuddhistRoad project homepage," Accessed December 24, 2023. https://buddhistroad.ceres.rub.de/en/publications/.

55 *BuddhistRoad* Team 2018, 218. For a related concept of "relational religion," see Meinert 2016, 7*n*9.

56 Wang Yong 2003a–b; Wang Y. 2009.

57 See Mizuguchi Motoki 水口幹記 in Wang Y. ed. 2013, 30–43.

58 Qin 2016, esp. 34–35.

to varying Asian contexts to assess maritime networks.[59] Initiated by Denys Lombard, they reframe the Indian Ocean and beyond, including seas of south-eastern China, as the "Southeast Asian Mediterranean."[60] Tilman Frasch, furthermore, identifies the Bay of Bengal as the "Buddhist Mediterranean," because it linked the Indian Buddhist site Bodhgaya with Burma and Sri Lanka in a triangle.[61] Reconceptualizing the Mediterranean metaphor in an East Asian context, Angela Schottenhammer coined the term "East Asian Mediterranean" in her study of maritime history connecting China, Japan, and Korea.[62] Sujung Kim adopted this in her transnational study of a Silla deity, whose cult spread from Korea to Japan and China.[63] Building upon these studies, this book encourages us to consider Buddhist Book Roads.

Pertinent to the larger-network mode of thinking, Joseph McDermott and Cynthia Brokaw acknowledge two Western theoretical models of the "communications circuit," originally proposed to track the circulation of printed books in eighteenth-century Europe.[64] While one visualizes a people-based cycle, tying author, publisher, bookseller, and reader in a full circle,[65] the other focuses more on "the life of the book," linking publishing, manufacture, distribution, reception, and survival.[66] Assessing both models in the context of Chinese Buddhist books, it is often hard to trace their communication circuit, since information on block cutters and publishers is sparse, and we know hardly anything about illustrators or sutra copyists, whose transcribed works provided the basis for the cutters. Still, as we shall see, alternative approaches, such as mapping various Buddhist networks that involve associated temples and donors, and the visual analysis of the images embedded in printed texts, can yield fruitful results in tracing the social and artistic life of a Buddhist book.

As part of the boom in "big data" and digital humanities,[67] the newly developed geographic information system (GIS) is the digital technology most

59 For the original use of "Mediterranean" as a metaphor, see Braudel 1972–1973.

60 Guillot et al. 1998.

61 Frasch 1998.

62 Schottenhammer 2005; Schottenhammer 2008.

63 Kim 2019.

64 Brokaw 2005b, 139; McDermott 2006, 115; Darnton 1982; Adams and Barker 1993.

65 For the diagram of the communications circuit, see Darnton 1982, 68.

66 For a diagram of the revised "cycle of the book," see Adams and Barker 1993, 14.

67 For the state of the field, see Bol 2020a. To date, the most popular method adopted by scholars of Chinese studies is the social network analysis (SNA), a highly computational, data-driven, and quantitative method that investigates the ties between people on the basis of biographical sources. For select model studies in history, art history, and Buddhism, see De Weerdt 2016; Hsu 2018; Bingenheimer 2020. Two databases are worth noting. The China Biographical Database Project (CBDB), compiled by Peter Bol and his team at

pertinent to our study. According to Peter Bol, GIS "allows the user to overlay different kinds of data that have spatial attributes, and thus to see correlations that would remain opaque if one relied solely on statistical analysis."[68] Among the different software programs, ArcGIS "is the most sophisticated and powerful."[69] Under Bol's leadership, the China Historical GIS (CHGIS) provides downloadable datasets, with which users can "create new data layers."[70] Turning to Chinese Buddhist studies, new waves of studies apply GIS and spatial humanities to map complex pilgrimage routes and networks of religious sites.[71] In sum, these various network approaches all provide useful models for the current study.

4.1 *Mapping Buddhist Book Roads*

Mapping the geographical distribution of Buddhist Book Roads and networks appears to be an efficient way to better visualize the interconnectivity of the networks pertinent to Buddhist print culture. While it is relatively easy to locate specific places, it is challenging to connect them due to the lack of direct information regarding the routes of transfer. For this book, I have created customized maps, both in macro and micro scales, that highlight the relationship between the centers of Buddhist print culture and other nodes of multi-layered infrastructures, ranging from trade routes and border markets to more complicated postal relay systems.

For example, the northwest-China network spanning Xi Xia and Yuan China from the eleventh to the fourteenth centuries developed first under the Xi Xia (see ch. 6). A specially designed map (map 0.2) shows that Xi Xia printing hubs, notably the capital Xingqing 興慶 (modern Yinchuan 銀川) and Ganzhou 甘州 (modern Zhangye 張掖), overlap with political centers, transportation bureaus, and Buddhist temples and grottoes. They are all located along the most traveled "Buddhist Road" that ran from the capital west to Dunhuang. In addition, the Xi Xia kingdom was surrounded by diverse Buddhist cultures flourishing in all directions: Khitan Liao, Jurchen Jin, and Song Chinese in the

Harvard University, contained biographical information about approximately 515,488 individuals as of December 2021; see Harvard University, China Biographical Database Project (CBDB), Accessed December 24, 2023). https://projects.iq.harvard.edu/cbdb.

The Historical Social Network of Chinese Buddhism dataset, compiled by Marcus Bingenheimer and his team, gathers 17,500 persons and their connections; see Marcus Bingenheimer, "Historical Social Network of Chinese Buddhism," Chinese Buddhism SNA. Accessed December 24, 2023. https://github.com/mbingenheimer/ChineseBuddhism_SNA.

68 Bol 2020b, 513.

69 Bol 2020b, 513.

70 Bol 2020b, 514–19.

71 See case studies contributed by various researchers in Wu ed. 2022.

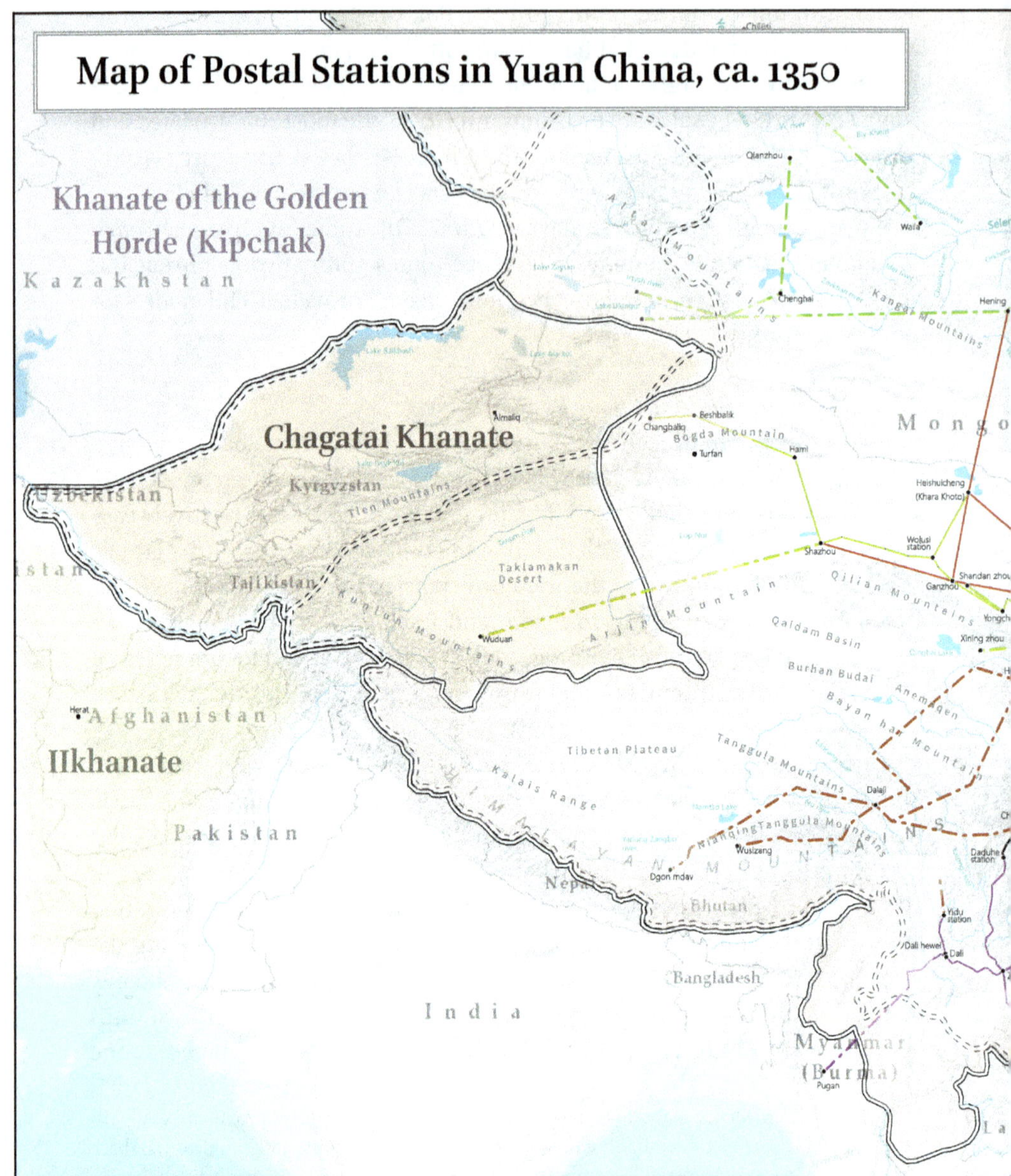

MAP 0.3 The Mongol Yuan Postal Relay System, ca. 1350. By Rita Xiong

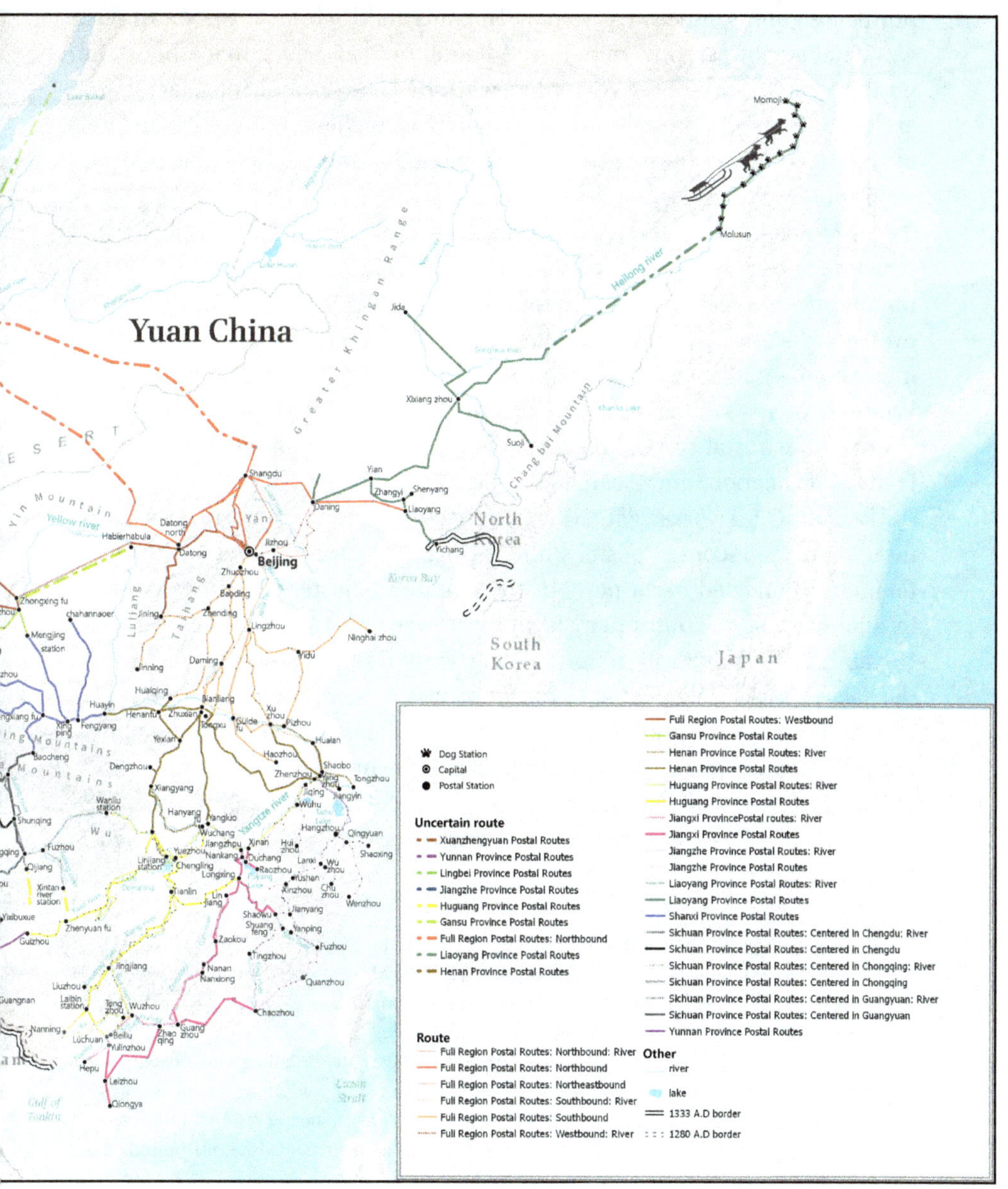
Yuan China
Greater Khingan Range
Heilong river
Chang bai Mountain
Momoji
Molusun
Jida
Xixiang zhou
Suoji
Yian
Zhangyi
Shenyang
Liaoyang
Yichang
North Korea
South Korea
Japan
Shangdu
Daning
Yan
Datong
Habierhabula
Beijing
Jizhou
Zhuozhou
Baoding
Zhending
Lingzhou
Ninghai zhou
Yidu
Daming
Jinning
Huaiqing
Bianliang
Xu zhou
Pizhou
Huaian
Henanfu
Zhuxian
Guide fu
Haozhou
Shaobo
Zhenzhou
Tongzhou
Jiangyin
Yexian
Dengzhou
Xiangyang
Hanyang
Wuhu
Hangzhou
Qingyuan
Shaoxing
Wuchang
Yangtze river
Jiangzhou
Nankang
Duchang
Raozhou
Longxing
Tianlin
Zhongxing fu
Chahannaoer
Jining
Mengjing station
Huayin
Fengyang
Baocheng
Shunqing
Fuzhou
Qijiang
Xintan river station
Zhenyuan fu
Guizhou
Jingjiang
Liuzhou
Laibin station
Wuzhou
Nanning
Luchuan
Beiliu
Yulinzhou
Zhao qing
Guang zhou
Hepu
Leizhou
Qiongya
Nanan
Nanxiong
Chaozhou
Quanzhou
Tingzhou
Zaokou
Shaowu
Yanping
Jianyang
Wenzhou
Dog Station
Capital
Postal Station
Uncertain route
Xuanzhengyuan Postal Routes
Yunnan Province Postal Routes
Lingbei Province Postal Routes
Jiangzhe Province Postal Routes
Huguang Province Postal Routes
Gansu Province Postal Routes
Full Region Postal Routes: Northbound
Liaoyang Province Postal Routes
Henan Province Postal Routes
Route
Full Region Postal Routes: Northbound: River
Full Region Postal Routes: Northbound
Full Region Postal Routes: Northeastbound
Full Region Postal Routes: Southbound: River
Full Region Postal Routes: Southbound
Full Region Postal Routes: Westbound: River
Full Region Postal Routes: Westbound
Gansu Province Postal Routes
Henan Province Postal Routes: River
Henan Province Postal Routes
Huguang Province Postal Routes: River
Huguang Province Postal Routes
Jiangxi ProvincePostal routes: River
Jiangxi Province Postal Routes
Jiangzhe Province Postal Routes: River
Jiangzhe Province Postal Routes
Liaoyang Province Postal Routes: River
Liaoyang Province Postal Routes
Shanxi Province Postal Routes
Sichuan Province Postal Routes: Centered in Chengdu: River
Sichuan Province Postal Routes: Centered in Chengdu
Sichuan Province Postal Routes: Centered in Chongqing: River
Sichuan Province Postal Routes: Centered in Chongqing
Sichuan Province Postal Routes: Centered in Guangyuan: River
Sichuan Province Postal Routes: Centered in Guangyuan
Yunnan Province Postal Routes
Other
river
lake
1333 A.D border
1280 A.D border

north, east, and southeast; as well as Tibetans and Uighurs in the southwest, west, and northwest. Government-run border markets, clustering around the northeast, east, and southeast borders with the Liao, Jin, and Song, facilitated exchange. Consequently, related ideas, materials, and people flowed in and out of the Xi Xia kingdom to generate a dynamic Buddhist network beyond the state's borders.

The Mongol Yuan postal relay system, a massive courier and transport infrastructure built in the thirteenth and fourteenth centuries, provides a yet larger framework that may have facilitated the transfer of Buddhist printed books over long distance. According to Marco Polo, there was a station every 25 to 30 miles; if on an urgent mission, one could travel up to 200 to 300 miles a day.[72] While historians such as Dang Baohai have done substantial work reconstructing the Yuan postal system, no researcher to date has attempted to turn the textual information into a searchable map.[73]

Using ArcGIS, I worked with Rita Xiong to create an online map that retrieves more than 940 recorded postal stations (map 0.3). Dadu, the hub of the system, was connected to all parts of the empire in clusters of routes marked in different colors. Routes marked in green went westward and reached the Uighur homeland in Eastern Central Asia. From Dadu to Central Tibet, where the Sakya sect, closely related to the Yuan, was located (see ch. 7), one could take routes marked in red, light green, blue, and dark brown. An interactive, multi-layered version of the map, available online in open access,[74] provides a mapping exercise that demonstrates how the circulation of Buddhist printing, that is, the Buddhist network in the northwest first cultivated under Xi Xia rule (map 0.2), could have overlapped with this larger Yuan postal system.

---

72 Morgan 2007, 91–92; Dang 2006, 5–6. For the responsibility of the persons in charge of a station, see Dang 2006, 34–36. For more studies of the Mongol postal and communication system, see Dang 2001, 2003a, 2004b, 2005, 2006; Fu 2011, 102–16; Tian 1994; Morgan 2007, 90–94; Allsen 2009, 144–46; Kim 2023, 432–37.

73 Exceptionally, Hosung Shim creates three sectional maps detailing the postal roads between Qaraqorum and Mt. Tianshan, along Uighuristan, and along Tarim Basin; see Shim 2014, 423 (map 4), 426–27 (maps 5–6). For a study of the postal system in the Islamic world, see Silverstein 2007 (for four maps detailing the routes of different periods and regions, see 14, 95–96, 171). For the map of "Mongol *jam* highways," see Kim 2023, 435.

74 Shih-shan Susan Huang and Rita Xiong, "Multi-layered Mapping: the Postal Relay System and Circulation of Buddhist Printing under Mongol Rule," ArcGIS, Accessed December 24, 2023. https://www.arcgis.com/home/webmap/viewer.html?webmap=eb0c810a6f304144a8045bfca5d95df7&extent=80.0359,21.1824,142.8338,50.7195.

This ArcGIS map is created by integrating various historical sources, scholarly publications, GIS website information, and other digital tools. The primary sources are *Jingshi dadian: zhanchi* 經世大典·站赤, *Yuan Shi*, and many others which are collected and analyzed in Dang 2006.

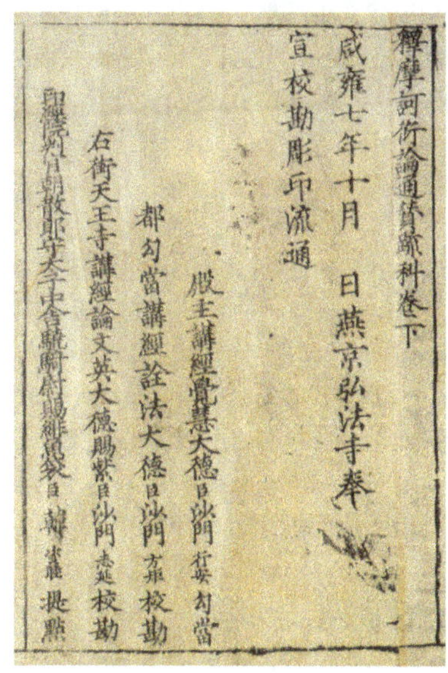

釋摩訶衍論通贊疏科卷下
咸雍七年十月　日燕京弘法寺奉
宣校勘彫印流通
殿主講經覺慧大德臣沙門 行安 勾當
都勾當講經詮法大德臣沙門 方矩 校勘
右街天王寺講經論文英大德賜紫臣沙門 志延 校勘
印經院判官朝散郎守太子中舍驍騎尉賜緋魚袋臣 韓 資睦 提點

FIGURE 0.9
Detail. *Shimoke yanlun tong zan shu ke*, juan 2. 1071. Liao. Discovered in the Wooden Pagoda, Fogong Monastery, Yingxian, Shanxi

Another key feature is temples that play a major role in Buddhist networks. Large-scale temples located on "a network of highways," such as those thriving in Beijing from the Liao to the Ming, exert a lasting legacy beyond dynastic changes.[75] They were major sites of Buddhist book production and textual collections widely connected to other temples beyond the city.

The Hongfasi 弘法寺 (Monastery of the Vast Dharma) (fig. 0.9; map 4.2), for example, had close links with the Khitan Liao ruling house in the eleventh century. It was in charge of collating, printing, and distributing Buddhist imprints, later deposited into the Buddhist statue of the wooden pagoda of the Fogongsi 佛宮寺 (Monastery of the Buddha's Palace; hereafter called the Fogong Pagoda) in Yingxian 應縣, Shanxi (fig. 4.6)—a complex timber structure completed in 1056 under the patronage of the Liao Empress Renyi 仁懿 (?–1076).[76] In subsequent years, the Hongfa Monastery remained the most important temple to preserve and print Buddhist texts, including various editions of the Buddhist canon produced under the Jurchen and Mongols (see pt. 3).

The other temple with a lasting network is the Qingshousi 慶壽寺 (Monastery of Auspicious Longevity), located along the south wall of the Yuan capital Dadu (map 7.1). With the generous support of the court and members of the elite—including a Korean king—it accumulated a rich collection of Buddhist

75 Neelis 2011, 5–6. Cf. Zürcher 1999, 11. For a study of Daoist temple networks in Ming China, see Wang R. 2022.

76 Steinhardt 1997; Zhang C. et al. 2001.

books. It also grew into an international Buddhist hub, where Tibetans, Tanguts, Uighurs, and Koreans clustered together (see ch. 7). In the fifteenth century, after the Ming capital was relocated to Beijing, it housed a governmental bureau in charge of various Buddhist printing projects (see ch. 11). Possibly still in possession of earlier Yuan blocks or books, this produced new editions of texts drawing on older resources.

Temples in more provincial areas are harder to trace. One exception is the Tianningsi 天寧寺 (Monastery of Heavenly Peace) in Anyi 安邑, Xiezhou 解州 (modern Yuncheng 運城) in southern Shanxi, active in the twelfth century under Jurchen rule. It served as the headquarters of the Jin Canon block-cutting, a project funded mostly by local villagers that took over thirty years. Based on donors' colophons retrieved from extant imprints, map 0.4 outlines a local network of the Jin Canon. The Tianning Monastery is its hub, connecting to a community reaching as far as 200 miles in today's Shanxi and Shaanxi provinces (see ch. 5). Humble villagers who had no money contributed raw materials such as tree branches, animals, and fabric. The project later caught the attention of the Jurchen court, who in turn sponsored the transportation of the blocks to the Hongfasi in Beijing. There, temples and individuals nationwide could pay to request copies of selected texts: the Jin Canon thus became a major model for later versions of the Buddhist canon compiled afterwards (see ch. 7).

Erik Zürcher and Jason Neelis, to account for the spread of Buddhism, have identified long-distance transmission as an alternative model to the vision of "point-to-point diffusion."[77] They characterize long-distance transmission as the "irregular travel by foreign monks, unusual hybrid images" and "long and difficult routes of communication."[78] This resonates with Michal Biran and others' re-examination of nomads as agents of cultural change, attributing the "cross-cultural encounters" and "the movement of ideas, texts, and artifacts" over long distance to the "actual physical movement and mobilization of individuals and groups."[79] These models are useful to assess the role of the elite Uighurs—such as those illustrated in the Turfan fragments (fig. 0.3)—in their contributions to the dynamic transfer of Buddhist print culture. The vast Mongol postal relay system made the long-distance Buddhist Book Roads possible, connecting various printing centers in Yuan China with the Uighur center in Turfan.

---

77 Neelis 2011; Zürcher 1999.

78 Neelis 2011, 4–7 (esp. 6), 311–19; Zürcher 1999, esp. 15.

79 Biran 2014, 5; Biran 2018.

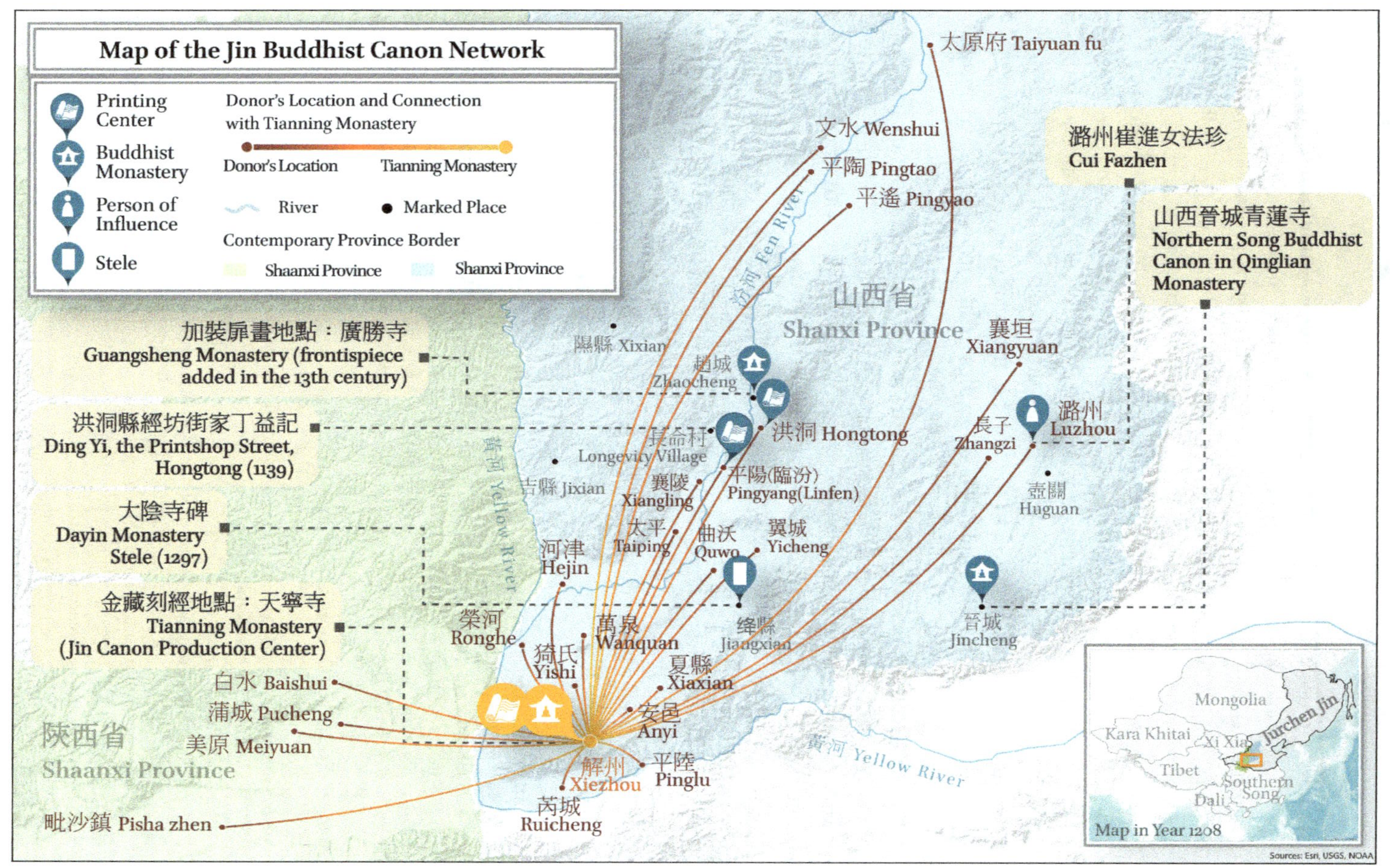

MAP 0.4 Map of the Jin Canon Network. By Rita Xiong

5 Visual Dimensions

From the outset, Buddhists used woodblock printing to reproduce not only texts but also images, since they believed any form of image-making was highly meritorious (see ch. 3). After returning from India in 645, the pilgrim-monk Xuanzang 玄奘 (602–664) supposedly printed an image of the bodhisattva Samantabadhra (Puxian 普賢) on paper, reproducing it in enormous quantities that were loaded on animals to be distributed to the masses.[80] Reflective of this is a coarse Dunhuang print, likely dated to the tenth century (fig. 0.10).[81] The upper register represents Puxian riding on an elephant in the center, accompanied by two figures on both sides; they are shown on swirling clouds with a radiating background. In the lower register, a dedicatory prayer by the military officer Yang Dongqian 楊洞芊 expresses his desire for peace on the borders.[82]

A rare Northern Song block fragment in the New York Public Library (fig. 0.11, 2.26), arguably one of the earliest extant blocks from Julu 巨鹿, Hebei, in north China, offers a rare glimpse of the "original" material matrix with which images were imprinted.[83] The front shows sets of little buddhas (fig. 0.11), rendered next to two identical talismanic seals and the text; the back (fig. 2.26), possibly carved for a different purpose, shows a seated monk on a chair.[84] Religious woodblocks are rarely treated as collectible by traditional art collectors. Stored mainly for practical functions, they tend to wear out after repeated use and are often replaced with recut blocks.[85]

---

80 This oft-cited anecdote, likely derived from post-Tang sources, specifies that the image was imprinted on the so-called huifeng zhi 回鋒紙; see YXZJ 5: 7a; SF 119 xia: 16a; Tsien 1985, 148–49; Zhang and Han 2006, 1: 11. For an in-depth study of Xuanzang and Empress Wu as major agents of Buddhist artistic and cultural transmission, see Wong 2018, 23–94.

81 For more discussion of this image, see Matsumoto 2019, 1: 443, 445; 2: 251 (pl. 144c).

82 The artifact, discovered in the Dunhuang library cave, has no other extant comparable duplicate.

83 The block is about 43.5 cm wide. See Edgren 1984, 58–59; Tsien 1985, fig. 1053a; Tsien 2002, 153–54, 158 (figs. 1–3).

84 Below the monkish image are two additional engraved markings, one showing a seal, and the other is a seal-to-be.

85 For the Korean blocks collected in the Haeyinsa 海印寺 (Monastery of the Ocean Seal), South Korea, originally from the first and second editions of the Korean Buddhist Canon, dated to the eleventh and fourteenth centuries respectively, see Kungnip Chungang Pangmulgwan 2018, 110, 112. For Japanese illustrated woodblocks dated to the fourteenth century and later, see Uchida 2011, 14–15, 132–48. For an extant Ming Daoist block (in British Library) bearing a frontispiece design comparable to that preserved in the Ming Daoist Canon, see Delacour 2010, 167.

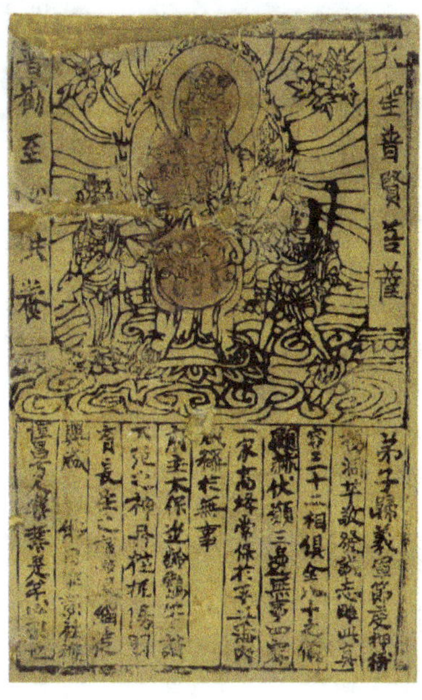

FIGURE 0.10
Samantabhadra. Tenth century. Guiyijun period. Woodblock print. The British Museum

FIGURE 0.11 The front of a block retrieved from Julu, Hebei. Northern Song. Woodblock fragment. Spencer Collection, The New York Public Library

5.1 *Modular Designs*

In order to mass-produce illustrated prints efficiently, Buddhist woodcut makers adopted the fundamental strategy to make compartmentalized designs, which entailed the use of existing pictorial motifs retrieved from different kinds of media. During the process of image transfer, some modifications occurred, including changes in the details of individual motifs and the combination or regrouping of individual motifs into larger clusters. They in turn formed larger, standardized templates or compositions that could be applied by other workers to make multiple similar designs. Because they are highly schematic and look as if they were created from modules, they are also called modular designs.[86]

The notion of standardization and modularization in mass-produced manufacture goes back to ancient Chinese crafts, notably the First Emperor's "magical army" of thousands of terra-cotta warriors. The seemingly unique figurines, as outlined in Lothar Ledderose's seminal book, *Ten Thousand Things: Module and Mass Production in Chinese Art*, are in fact the result of a highly standardized procedure, made possible by the activation of a vast workforce in assembly-line fashion.[87] Each figurine consists of seven standardized units in clay molds, including "a plinth, the feet, the legs below the garment, the torso, the arms, the hands, and the head."[88] The workers created a limited repertoire of these standardized units, including, at least, eight types of heads, eight types of torso, two types of hands, and more.[89] They then recombined the basic components to make thousands of figurines. In a similar vein, Ledderose examines other module-based mass-produced arts, including porcelain, timber buildings, Buddhist paintings, words printed with moveable type, and so on. Although he does not discuss the woodblock prints, we can assume that they are manufactured in a similar manner.

Zhang Xiumin notes that the print-culture marketplace in Middle-Period China was wide open.[90] There were few constraints on the reproduction of previously printed materials—unless, of course, such materials were official publications of the state. According to William Alford, throughout the imperial era, Chinese governments saw no need to develop "comprehensive, centrally promulgated, formal legal protections" of the sort we now associate with concepts such as "intellectual property" and "copyright."[91] A wide range of people including artists, politicians, and other thinkers constantly sought new ideas in past conventions with the effect that no one could be said to own the past. Song-dynasty publishers copied or recreated popular editions of books printed by other publishers.[92] Similarly, designers of Buddhist woodcuts copied or

86 See my earlier studies of the modular designs in the Song and Xi Xia Buddhist printed frontispieces in Huang 2011b; Huang 2014b; Huang 2014d; Huang 2017b; Huang S. 2021a.

87 Ledderose 2000, esp. 51–74.

88 Ledderose 2000, 70.

89 Ledderose 2000, 72.

90 Zhang and Han 2006, 143; Huang 2011a, 152–53.

91 For a full discussion, see Alford 1995, esp. ch. 2. This author would like to thank Richard Smith for his help with the source.

92 For more about the possible block sharing among publishers, see Chia 2002a, 165.

borrowed readymade printed materials already illustrated in other works. This free borrowing led to the heavy use of standardized templates and modular designs in Buddhist print culture.[93]

5.1.1 Memes and Memeplexes

On a more conceptual level, modular designs can be further compared to memes or meme complexes called "memeplexes," borrowing the theory of memes first proposed by the British evolutionary biologist Richard Dawkins.[94]

In his book *The Selfish Gene*, he creates an analogy between genetic and cultural evolution and coins the word "meme" on par with "gene," indicating a unit of cultural transformation or imitation. He says,

> We need a name for the new replicator, a noun that conveys the idea of a unit of cultural transmission, or a unit of *imitation*. 'Mimeme' comes from a suitable Greek root, but I want a monosyllable that sounds a bit like 'gene'. I hope my classicist friends will forgive me if I abbreviate mimeme to *meme*. If it is any consolation, it could alternatively be thought of as being related to 'memory', or to the French word *même*. It should be pronounced to rhyme with 'cream'.[95]

Just as some genes replicate more successfully than others, Dawkins adds, certain memes appear to be more successful "in the meme-pool than others." Furthermore, like the replications of genes that go through mutations, the transmission of memes is "subject to continuous mutation and also to blending."[96] Thanks to the nature of human creativity, a constant process of imitating, varying, and recombining old memes, new ones are created. Areas of cultural mutation evolving through non-genetic means include musical composition, clothing fashion, religion, art, and architecture.[97] Perhaps the most widely received usage of meme is by internet users.[98] A popular internet meme can spread vastly from person to person or one social network to another. Internet memes go "viral" when they are "shared," "tweeted," and "retweeted" multiple

93 Huang 2011a, 153; Zhang and Han 2006, 143.
94 Dawkins 1976.
95 Dawkins 1976, 192.
96 Dawkins 1976, 194–95.
97 Dawkins 1976, 190, 192.
98 Note that in Dawkins' original discussion of memes he cited internet as well, although the notion of meme as received by web users nowadays is a more recent development. See "Wikipedia: Internet Meme," Wikimedia Foundation, last modified December 23, 2023, 15:10 (UTC). https://en.wikipedia.org/wiki/Internet_meme.

times; they are posted on various websites or sent to individual email accounts through group email lists.

Competitive memes often get passed on as a cluster, known as the "memeplex," an abbreviated term based on Dawkins's notion of the "co-adapted meme complex."[99] According to Susan Blackmore, these "memeplexes" are sets of "co-memes" that are "mutually-assisting" or "mutually suitable;" they travel together to increase the survival rate of being copied or passed on.[100] Religions and the internet are examples of powerful memeplexes.[101]

Dawkins's theoretical paradigm is insightful especially because it helps to broaden the dichotomous image-and-text classification of knowledge, pushing us to treat modular designs in an even broader cultural context, seeing them as parts of the multi-faceted manifestations of cultural trends and ideas, which got spread and shared across media in varying historical contexts.

5.2 *Transmedia and Transnational Spread*

Artists and artisans turned modular designs into a multitude of images in various media. A good example is the modular design representing the popular Buddhist iconography known as *Amitabha Welcoming*, evident in Xi Xia images discovered in Khara Khoto, Inner Mongolia (figs. 0.12–0.14, 6.15).[102]

A brightly colored painting (fig. 0.12), this depicts Amitabha Buddha and two bodhisattvas descending on clouds to welcome a deceased person. It shares a modular design of the same trio in two printed frontispieces (fig. 0.13).[103] Another comparable work is a little-studied fragmented drawing (fig. 0.14) that preserves a partial view of the two bodhisattvas: one leans in profile while the other is shown with his face positioned frontally. Quite like the painting, this may have been used as a preparatory drawing for a more finished work.[104] It is also possible that the woodcut designers used a similar modular design to cut the block (see ch. 6). This modular design must have been popular in Xi Xia, as it transformed into recurring miniature decorative patterns filling the

99 Dawkins 1976, 197–98; Blackmore 1999, 19.

100 Blackmore 1999, 19. Cf. Dawkins 1976, 197–98.

101 Blackmore 1999, 187–218.

102 For studies of the *Amitabha Welcoming* portable paintings discovered in Khara Khoto, see Lee 1996; Saliceti-Collins 2007, 78–89; Wang M. 2022. For more comparisons of the Sino-Japanese productions, see Ide 2001, 56–57; Wang M. 2022, 217–42 (for related ritual texts in Chinese, Tangut, and Sanskrit discovered in Khara Khoto, see 228–29).

103 For the other image, see Wang M. 2022, 227 (fig. 6.14). Michelle Wang notes that the major difference between the two printed frontispieces lies in whether or not a reborn baby is depicted; see Wang M. 2022, 226–27, 230.

104 For more study, see EGABCHY 1: 221.

FIGURE 0.12 *Greeting the Soul to the Pure Land of Amitabha* (x. 2411). Xi Xia. Ink and color on linen. Hanging scroll. The State Hermitage Museum, St. Petersburg

FIGURE 0.14 *Greeting the Soul to the Pure Land of Amitabha* (x. 2533). Xi Xia. Ink on paper. Drawing. The State Hermitage Museum, St. Petersburg

halo of Amitabha, depicted in the other painting showcasing the Western Pure Land.[105]

The strongest memes of all modular designs transmitted in Buddhist print culture are connected to the *Lotus Sutra*. They include its most popular "Universal Gateway" chapter, which expounds the miracles of Avalokiteśvara and is often printed and circulated independently. The legacy of these memes was international and went far beyond Buddhism itself (see ch. 3).

A now-lost Chinese print version of the "Universal Gateway" chapter supposedly inspired an anonymous Japanese illustrator to produce a painted version

105 For a plate, see Piotrovsky 1993, 191.

FIGURE 0.13 *Amitabha Welcoming* (TK 244). Xi Xia. Woodblock print. Institute of Oriental Manuscripts, St. Petersburg

in a handscroll, dated 1257 (figs. 0.15a–b).[106] The donor's inscription, originally accompanying the Chinese printed version, was faithfully transcribed by the Japanese calligrapher (fig. 0.15b). It notes that layman Qian Zhonghu 錢仲虎 from Yunjian 雲間 (today's Shanghai) in the Southern Song ordered the artisan to cut blocks based on a book he purchased and in due course widely distributed the printed copies.[107]

Earlier researchers have stressed the prominent *yamato-e* Japanese style in the painted version, but equally notable is how faithful select scenes follow the

106 The Japanese calligrapher who transcribed the text is identified as Sugawara-no-Mitsushige; see Ford 1987, 26.

107 The Metropolitan Museum of Art website claims that the Chinese printed version was "based on an earlier painted handscroll," although the inscription only refers to the model as a "sutra" (*jing* 經) and does not specify if it was printed or painted, let alone if it is a "painted handscroll."

For a complete painting, see the Metropolitan Museum of Art, "'Universal Gateway', Chapter 25 of the Lotus Sutra," Asian Art, Accessed December 24, 2023. https://www.metmuseum.org/art/collection/search/44849.

a

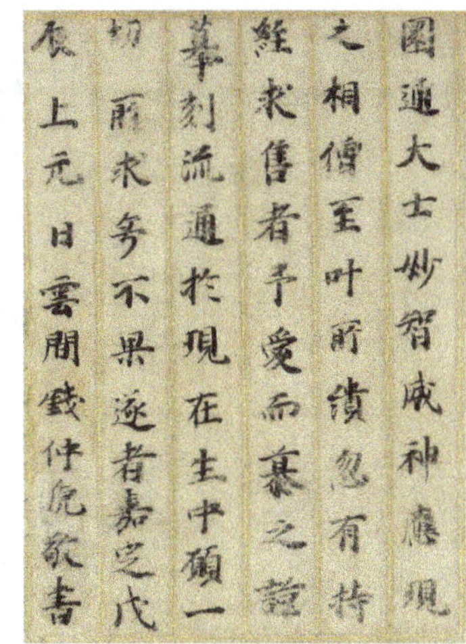

b

FIGURES 0.15A–B Details. "Universal Gateway" chapter of the *Lotus Sutra*. 1257. Kamakura period, Japan. Ink, color, and gold on paper. Handscroll. The Metropolitan Museum of Art

modular designs of their Chinese prototype. The scene depicting the manifestation of Avalokiteśvara in the form of monks and nuns in a cave-like setting (fig. 0.15a), for example, resembles a Chinese printed version dated to the late Yuan or early Ming (fig. 0.16).[108] The versions both carry a shared meme transmitted from the now-lost Southern Song printed version Qian once distributed.

This meme can be further connected to a still earlier theme in Buddhist print culture, staging a Buddhist monk meditating or conversing with his disciples in a cave-like structure (fig. 0.17). This is reflected in a Koryŏ Korean woodcut based on a Chinese work originally linked to the Northern Song imperial patronage (see ch. 2).[109] Going beyond Buddhist woodcuts, this meme also appears in a thirteenth-century fan painting, showing two men conversing in a cave (fig. 0.18), as well as fourteenth-century Daoist woodcuts (fig. 2.53).

---

108 Compositionally, this scene is similar to the other scene from the same set; see ZGFJBHQJ 4: 175; Machida Shiritsu Kokusai Hanga Bijutsukan 1988, 102 (pl. 16). According to Kazuma Kawase, select Chinese block cutters joined Japanese cutters to create blocks for what are known as the Buddhist Gozanban 五山版 editions, sponsored by major Zen temples in Kamakura and Muromachi Japan. The publications include Japanese reprint editions based on Chinese originals. For the Japanese illustrated printed copies based on Chinese Buddhist illustrated texts, see Kawase 1970, 212–17 (for further documentation of Chinese cutters in Japan, see 142–60); Li Pingfan in Machida Shiritsu Kokusai Hanga Bijutsukan 1988, 13.

109 Huang 2014b, 397 (fig. 6).

FIGURE 0.16 Detail, "Universal Gateway" chapter of the *Lotus Sutra*. Yuan. Woodblock print

FIGURE 0.17 Detail, *Secret Treasures*. Koryŏ period, Korea. Woodblock print. Nanzenji collection

FIGURE 0.18 *Conversation in a Cave*. 13th century. Southern Song. Ink on silk. Fan. The Metropolitan Museum of Art

FIGURE 0.19 Detail. Frontispiece to the *Lotus Sutra*, juan 5. Southern Song. Woodblock print. National Palace Museum

While some memes of Buddhist print culture derived from earlier pictorial conventions in non-Buddhist or non-printed sources, others were new inventions with widespread impact. Once transferred to "a new environment" or "unfamiliar cultural contexts," they came to tell an altered story.[110]

110 This is based on Lieselottes E. Saurma-Jeltsch's discussion of the agency of things and the flow of cultural transformations; see Saurma-Jeltsch 2010, 17.

FIGURE 0.20 *Tiling*. From *Danwon pungsokdo cheop*. By Kim Hongdo. 1780. Chosŏn period, Korea. Ink and color on paper. Album leaf. National Museum of Korea

A case in point is the strong meme of a building scene, newly standardized in Southern Song-to-Yuan Hangzhou frontispieces of the *Lotus Sutra* (figs. 0.19, 3.39, 3.57), quite different from earlier Buddhist mural conventions.[111]

111 Comparable but not identical mural prototypes in Dunhuang include the *Sutra on the Different Virtues and Fields of Merit*, depicted in the sixth-century Mogao Cave 296 and 302, the *Sutra of the Jewel Rain*, depicted in the early Tang Mogao Cave 321, and the *Sutra of Maitreya's Rebirth Below*, depicted in the eighth-century Yulin Cave 25. For plates, see

FIGURE 0.21 *The Building of the Castle of Khvarnaq*, Khamsa of Nizami (Or. 6810, F. 154V). 1494–1495. Timurid Empire. Ink, opaque watercolor and gold on paper. The British Library

FIGURE 0.22 *The Building of the Castle of Khawarnaq* (MS. 1654). By Sahifa Banu. Early 17th century, Mughal Empire. Opaque watercolor on paper. Golestan Palace Library, Tehran

It represents builders on the ground and also on the roof of the structure, working in pairs: a worker standing on the ground throws a brick to a worker crouching on the rooftop; another ground worker delivers a bulk of materials tied to a rope to a worker leaning on the roof.

The meme later moved into the international sphere (figs. 3.42a–3.43a), where it is vividly present in a Korean genre painting (fig. 0.19). It also appears in two related Islamic paintings: one was created in fifteenth-century Herat in the Timurid Empire (fig. 0.21); the other, quite possibly a copy of the former, goes back to the seventeenth century and was created by a court artist at the Mughal court in South Asia (fig. 0.22).[112] While no documentation can

DHSKQJ 6: 80 (fig. 60); 9: 87–88, 90–91; 21: 54, 103; Ma 2018, 34; Huang 2017c, 23*n*112, 67 (fig. 43). I thank Stephen F. Teiser for his valuable feedback.

112 Huang 2017c, 26–30.

reconstruct the exact itineraries of the meme's international transmission, one might hypothesize that these foreign artists were exposed to similar printed illustrations of the *Lotus Sutra* that had become available in their workplaces via transregional trade routes and entangled networks. All this demonstrates how image memes could transcend cultural, religious, and linguistic boundaries and travel even farther than texts.

6 About This Book

This book contains twelve chapters, grouped thematically and chronologically into four parts.

Part 1, "Connecting Print Culture with Other Media," tackles the question of how print culture intersected with other media, drawing mostly from early visual materials. Its three chapters show that Buddhist print culture shared much with other reproductive techniques and that visual trends traveled across media. Artists and artisans alike sometimes took the existing designs out of context, then modified, assimilated, and repurposed them.

Chapter 1, "Reproducing Images across Media," provides a broad survey of China's long history of reproducing texts and images in diverse media. It begins with Daoist seals and Buddhist stamps, moves on to the molded religious and daily objects including Buddhist clay tablets and molds for ceramics and pastry, textiles with printed designs, the embossed decorative paper, and ends with the rubbings of texts and images.

Chapter 2, "From Painting to Woodblock Printing and Back Again," elaborates the dynamic interconnectivity of print and painting. While some Buddhist woodcuts borrow elements from paintings, including both formats and motifs, others demonstrate how the unique characteristics of woodcuts, especially their angular and linear qualities, inspire the images made in other media.

Chapter 3, "Book Art of the *Lotus Sutra*," centers on the proliferation of highly artistic frontispieces printed in Song Hangzhou. Some of these books must have been transmitted cross-regionally and internationally along Buddhist networks and Book Roads, as they inspired other woodcut artisans and painters in Xi Xia, Korea, Japan, and, quite unexpectedly, Islamic painters in West and South Asia.

Part 2, "Buddhist Printing in North and Northwest China," maps multifaceted developments and cross-regional connections from the eleventh to the thirteenth centuries. The three chapters treat the understudied print culture associated with China's neighbors: Khitan Liao, Jurchen Jin, and Tangut Xi

Xia. Most materials investigated come from pagodas and other ruins in Inner Mongolia, Shanxi, Hebei, Ningxia, and Gansu.

Drawing on eleventh-century deposited texts as discovered in Liao pagodas in north China, chapter 4, "Mapping Buddhist Printing under Khitan Liao Rule," identifies two versions of the government-sponsored Buddhist canon and other texts as products printed in Yanjing, the Southern Capital. Here imperially-sponsored temples and elite monastics, block cutters, and printshops formed a vibrant network.

Chapter 5, "Southern Shanxi as the New Printing Center under Jurchen Jin Rule," focuses on a printing region that grew under Jurchen rule in the twelfth century. Family-owned printshops clustered in Pingyang produced a wide range of works, including reprint editions of Northern Song illustrated books, popular prints, and vernacular Buddhist texts sponsored by lay followers, who used them to pray for longevity and miracles. Southern Shanxi was also the birthplace of the influential Jin Canon. While the original blocks cut there contain only texts, four kinds of frontispiece designs attached to extant copies were added later by individual owners, sometime between the late twelfth and early fourteenth centuries.

Shifting to northwest China, chapter 6, "Tangut Royal Patronage and Xi Xia Buddhist Printing," examines syncretic Xi Xia Buddhist print culture from several perspectives: royal patronage, interstate connections, and the multi-ethnic and multi-lingual Buddhist community. Numerous illustrated printed texts in Chinese and Tangut reveal unprecedented, massive Buddhist printing activity in the late twelfth century, notably sponsored by Emperor Renzong and his wife, Empress Luo. Using a visual approach, the study identifies four groups of modular designs, used systematically by anonymous woodcut makers who worked in a workshop fashion to meet the Tangut ruling patrons' ambitious endeavors.

The four chapters of Part 3, "The Mongol Era," center on the Mongol empire. Along with the flow of people over long distances, imperial infrastructure networks and Buddhist Book Roads expanded further in the thirteenth and fourteenth centuries. Powerful non-Han people, especially members of the Mongol ruling class, Tangut and Tibetan monks, and elite Uighurs, were most active as sponsors, users, and transmitters of Buddhist print culture.

Chapter 7 explores the Yuan capital Dadu, an international metropolis and the hub of the empire's postal relay system. It focuses on Tibetan books sponsored by Mongol emperors and empresses that were dispatched to Tibet, on texts and images associated with the Uighurs that were transmitted to Turfan, as well as on two fourteenth-century imperially-sponsored versions of the

Buddhist canon, adorned with two kinds of frontispieces, one in Himalayan style and the other in northern Chinese mode.

Moving to south China, chapter 8, "Adorning the Buddhist Canon Printed in Yuan Hangzhou," examines the frontispiece templates adorning the Puning and Qisha Canons produced in Yuan Hangzhou. Although the majority of documented cutters, illustrators, and publishers were Chinese, the frontispieces depart from standard Song conventions and display a Sino-Himalayan style. This hybrid style reflects a further blending of Xi Xia prototypes, new waves of Himalayan Buddhist art, and Chinese elements.

Transitioning from the visual to the social and religious dimensions, chapter 9, "Tibetan and Tangut Monks," traces four influential foreign monks associated with the print culture in Yuan Hangzhou. These include the Tibetan master Danba and the three Tangut monks Yang Lianzhenjia, Guan Zhuba, and Li Huiyue. While the first three held close ties to the central political power, Li Huiyue was little documented: a Tangut monk in diaspora, he exhausted his personal savings to sponsor Buddhist sutra copying.

Chapter 10, "Elite Uighurs," evaluates the inter-regional network of leading Uighurs of strong Buddhist background who migrated to Mongol-Yuan China from their homeland in eastern Central Asia. Among pertinent printed fragments unearthed in Turfan, some depict Mengsusu and his family members, who had close ties to the Mongol court in Beijing. Others represent the narrative details of a *Lotus Sutra* frontispiece in Hangzhou style. The rubbing taken from a broken stele in Quanzhou sheds light on the vast temple network associated with the great Uighur donor Yiheimishi. Nearly 100 temples nationwide owned copies of the Buddhist canon; some were located in the northwest, where the Uighurs and Tanguts lived.

Going beyond the canonical, Part 4, "Printing Buddhism on the Ground," moves on to vernacular print culture. Supported by the general populace, fully illustrated popular Buddhist texts were appealing to them because they promised efficacy in granting protection and healing. In the fifteenth century, the most vibrant center of such productions was the Ming capital Beijing. Recurring motifs dealing with hell, animal killing, demons, sickness, and childbirth display a popular flavor not seen in the pictures accompanying earlier canons.

Chapter 11, "Illustrating Efficacy in *Diamond Sutra* Woodcuts," investigates hybrid productions that combine the classical *Diamond Sutra* with miracle stories about its wondrous powers. A standardized illustrated repertoire showcases female demons subjugated by guardians, imaginary journeys to the underworld court and back, and the sprouting of magical fungi in response to devotional sutra copying. The intended audience may have well been

Buddhists from Ming Beijing's transnational community, who encouraged a hybrid pantheon that mixed Buddhist and Daoist elements.

Chapter 12, "The Most Popular Book," features the indigenous *Dharani Sutra*. The text is a cultural melting pot, synthesizing miscellaneous beliefs while turning a Buddhist scripture into magical medicine. Two standard versions, one coarse and one more refined, widely circulated in Ming Beijing. Accompanied by lively narrative pictures and containing Daoist-inspired talismanic writs that promise to save women from childbirth complications, it was often printed on demand. Women and their families, preoccupied with potential dangers during childbirth or ardently desiring a baby boy, were the main supporters.

PART 1

Connecting Print Culture with Other Media

CHAPTER 1

Reproducing Images across Media

Woodblock printing was invented and applied to reproduce texts and images in the seventh to eighth centuries. By that time, several other techniques of reproduction were already in use, notably seals, molds, and rubbings. Each included a matrix for reproduction, be it in wood, clay, stone, or some other material. The end result was a copy created by the matrix, which could be reproduced on paper, textiles, or terracotta tiles, or even turned into three-dimensional ceramic objects. As woodblock printing developed, it also inspired these modes of image reproduction. Rather than placing them in a linear chronological order or treating some as part of the "pre-history of printing," I present them as co-existing throughout the Tang-through-Yuan period, relating to and enriching one another.[1] This interconnected world where the reproduction of images traversed the boundaries of various media sets the preliminary interface of Buddhist printing investigated in the chapters below.

I begin with seals and stamps, long regarded as the technical precursor of woodblock printing. I focus largely on those created and consumed in Daoist and Buddhist ritual, highlighting the mechanism concerning their designs, meanings, and functions. Artisans used clay molds to mass-produce religious and everyday objects, ranging from Buddhist votive tablets and architectural decors to ordinary ceramics, toys, and even pastry. Select preparatory clay molds survive alongside their products. Switching to fabrics, textiles with printed designs further suggest that their producers also used carved blocks similar to those applied in paper printing to reproduce designs. Around the eleventh century, artistic stationary mostly used by elite writers was embossed with intricate designs, some of which match paintings and images found in ceramics, books, textiles, and stone reliefs.

From a global perspective, the most unusual mode of reproduction was rubbings or "inked squeezes," that is, a way to transfer engraved writings or

FIGURE 1.0 ← One of the two stamps on the reverse side of a Dunhuang manuscript Pelliot chinois 4514 (10) 3. 10th century. Ink on paper. Bibliothèque nationale de France

1 Tsuen-hsuin Tsien cites seals, metal casting, stone engraving, rubbings and textiles with stencil-based designs as major "techniques for making reproductions" that "paved the way for the use of woodblock printing." See Tsien 1985, 133. Cf. Carter 1955, 11–14; Carter 1957, 22–32.

© SHIH-SHAN SUSAN HUANG, 2024 | DOI:10.1163/9789004700017_003

images from a stone surface to paper.[2] Some steles laid out carved images and texts in a book-like form, suggesting that they were created for reproduction purposes. While mainstream rubbings are all about calligraphy, there is also a rare illustrated rubbing album of Buddhist themes, which allows us to examine the cross fertilization of different techniques such as rubbings, painting, and woodblock printing.

1 Seals and Stamps

The Chinese joined other ancient civilizations in the Near East, Egypt, and Greece in creating seals and sealing practices, primarily for authentication and securing property. Some seals were deemed amuletic, wielding additional healing and protective powers, and as such used in religious or shamanic contexts.[3] In some cultures, especially in China, the impression of a seal was also called "seal" and was respected as equally authentic. As Verity Platt convincingly notes, impressing a seal—unlike other forms produced by printing, casting and molding—"is the only form of reproduction which was not carried out by specialist craftsmen within workshops but was frequently enacted by anybody who owned it." This "self-replicatory power" creates an automatic tension between the "original" and "copies," making seals a unique medium in the realm of visual and material culture.[4]

Seals were cut in relief (*yangke* 陽刻) or intaglio (*yinke* 陰刻) on hard-surface materials such as jade, ivory, and wood. In Chinese, "seal" as both noun and verb is *yin* 印. The term can also mean "print" or "printing" and refers primarily to woodblock printing as first applied in the seventh to eighth centuries.[5] The linguistic interchangeability of seal stamping and block printing indicates their close connection.[6] Unlike the picture-based seals from the Near East and Mediterranean, mainstream Chinese seals used in connoisseurship and authentication were heavily loaded with writings and scripts and only a few early examples bear pictorial images.[7] Of particular relevance to Buddhist

2 Tsien 1985, 140–45. Past scholarship of Chinese rubbings focuses more those reproducing writings/inscriptions and not images; see Carter 1957, 29–32.

3 Collon 1997; Huang 2017a, 70*n*2.

4 Platt 2006, 234, 238–39.

5 Carter 1957, 22–23; Tsien 1985, 136; Barrett 2001; Barrett 2008.

6 Huang 2017a, 71.

7 For selected ancient Chinese seals that bear images (birds, a horse-chariot, a tiger, a building), see Luo 1987; 2010, 52–55; Tseng 1993, 100; Collon 1997, 219.

printing, however, are seals and stamps used in ritual.[8] Their visual designs, different from mainstream non-religious seals, are often charged with religious meaning and they have more complex functions.

1.1 *Shamanistic and Daoist Seals for Exorcism and Healing*

The shamanistic use of seals can be traced back to the Han dynasty (202 BC–220 CE). Going beyond authentication and security, certain seals were used for exorcism and healing.[9] Selected inscriptions retrieved from seals and clay impressions for sealing (*fengni* 封泥) bear the names of the Monarch of Heaven (Tiandi 天帝) and the Yellow God (Huangshen 黃神); they were found in several archaeological sites such as Lelang 樂浪 commandery in today's Korea.[10] The best documented are seals bearing the four characters *huangshen yuezhang* 黃神越章 (fig. 1.1a), possibly translated as "The Yellow God's Conquering Statute," hereafter called Yuezhang Seals.[11] One double-sided seal shown here has the four characters on one side. Their script style matches that of Han official seals, while the other side (fig. 1.1b) contains twenty semi-graphic writs, each placed evenly within a square unit of a five-by-four grid.[12] The four-unit vertical column of four characters on the right of the impression reads "Demon [Killing] Seal" ([*sha*] *gui zhi yin* [殺]鬼之印).

Growing from these Yuezhang seals, Daoist seals associated with healing rituals in the Tang-through-Yuan dynasties bear more complicated graphic designs. Michel Strickmann studied one seal with complex graphic designs (fig. 1.2; hereafter called the Strickmann seal) illustrated in a Tang Daoist text.[13] It shows a scoop-shaped "doublet of the Northern Dipper and numerous renditions of the archaic logograph for the sun [*ri* 日]."[14] Beyond that, other legible

8 For more on Daoist seals, see Strickmann 1993; 2002; Wang 2000; Wang Y. 2001; Li and Lu 2002; Huang 2017a; Huang 2018a. For more on Buddhist ritual seals, see Copp 2011; Copp 2019.

9 Bumbacher 2012.

10 Liu D. 2022. A paper spell originally inserted inside a hole near the entrance of an ancient tomb in Turfan bears an unusual figural drawing with the caption which identifies the figure as the Yellow God. See Ma 2004, 64 (fig. 1); 18 (fig. 10). For more seal specimens bearing the characters "Tiandi" or "Huangshen," see Huang 2017a, 74–75 (figs. 1a–b, 2a–b); Liu Z. 2007, 138–40; Zhang and Bai 2006, 1:256. For more on clay impressions, see FNKL; Sun 2002a–b.

11 Wang 2000, 13, 20–21; Wang Y. 2001, 435–36, 440–41; Liu Z. 2007, 146–57; Luo 1987, 86–87; Verellen 2019, 282–84. I am grateful for Paul Copp's valuable input on this topic.

12 Luo 1987, 9–73.

13 Strickmann 1993, 10–20; 2002, 124–32; Verellen 2019, 281–82. Various Daoist seals illustrated in Southern Song-to-Yuan liturgical sources show two different graphic templates closely comparable to the seal; see Huang 2017a, 82 (figs. 7a–d).

14 Strickmann 1993, 19; 2002, 131 (fig. 1a–b).

a

b

FIGURES 1.1A–B The double-sided Yue Seal
a. The front side
b. The back side

FIGURE 1.2 A seal for healing. *Zhengyi fawen xiuzhen zhiyao*

words appear on the upper part, which invoke a constellation known as the Three Terraces (Santai 三台) and exorcistic actions such as "strike dead" (*sha* 煞) and "subjugate" (*fa* 伐). The overall graphic and script elements embedded in the seal match the Daoist master's visualization of stars and the classical analogy of healing to demon-killing during seal-healing performances.[15] The accompanying text provides step-by-step instructions, combining the stamping of the seal with visualizations, spells, and the use of additional ritual objects, such as a bowl of water, a sword, a bell, and a lithophone.[16] The healing performance comes to a climax as the Daoist master activates the seal's power by stamping an ailing body part while chanting a set formula.[17]

Using the Yuezhang Seal,	吾今以黃神越章之印，
I stamp on the patient's heart: it comes out of his heart!	印心從心出
I stamp the abdomen: it comes out of the abdomen!	印腹從腹出
I stamp the liver: it comes out of the liver!	印肝從肝出
I stamp the lungs: it comes out of the lungs!	印肺從肺出
I stamp the kidneys: it comes out of the kidneys!	印腎從腎出
I stamp the spleen: it comes out of the spleen!	印脾從脾出
I stamp the head: it comes out of the head!	印頭從頭出

15 Cf. a talisman evoking the Three Terraces, reproduced in Li and Li eds. 2022, 3: 220.

16 Huang 2017a, 78–79.

17 My translation is modified after Strickmann (2002, 129); I translate the verb *yin* as "stamp" and not as "seal."

FIGURE 1.3
Spells incised on the back of the Yellow God seal. *Daofa huiyuan*

I stamp the back: it comes out of the back!	印背從背出
I stamp the chest: it comes out of the chest!	印胸從胸出
I stamp the waist: it comes out of the waist!	印腰從腰出
I stamp the hands: it comes out of the hands!	印手從手出
I stamp the feet: it comes out of the feet!	印足從足出
Swiftly, swiftly, in accordance with the statutes and ordinances!	速出！速出！急急如律令

The testimonial of a Sichuan priest's use of the Yuezhang seal to cure a sick layman, recorded in multiple Tang and Song sources, connects the exorcistic action of stamping performed by the priest to an unexpected "end result"—the stamped impression visible on the back of a disease-causing bat that flew out of the patient's mouth.[18]

The Strickmann seal in turn inspired various Yuezhang seals associated with healing produced in the Southern Song and Yuan periods. They divide into two kinds—the "Yellow God" and the "Yuezhang Seal"—which usually form a pair, each bearing two incised surfaces, front and back.[19] While the designs on the front are similar to those of the Strickmann seal (fig. 1.2), selected back templates contain spells of more than a hundred legible characters in small regular script (fig. 1.3). They summon the Northern Dipper and other stars to

18 YJQQ 118, 4: 2650; Wang Y. 2001, 442; Huang 2017a, 85; Copp 2019, 32.

19 These paired seals are recorded in Southern Song-Yuan liturgical manuals; for visual examples, see Huang 2017a, 81–83.

subjugate evil spirits and heal ailments.[20] To date, these seal templates represent the most extreme cases of writings on a seal's surface. The Daoist obsession with writings on seals calls to mind a ten-centimeter Yuezhang seal with 120 incised characters mentioned by the early medieval Daoist writer Ge Hong 葛洪 (284–363).[21]

1.1.1 Materials and Designs of Daoist Seals

Although early shamanistic or Daoist seals were mostly made of hard materials such as stone, jade, bronze, and other metals, seals recorded in the Dunhuang manuscripts (dated before or around the tenth century) and the fifteenth-century imperially-sponsored Daoist Canon (*Daozang* 道藏) were mostly made of wood.[22] This preference for wood as a carving material is in line with the blossoming of woodblock printing in the Tang and Song, further connecting seal carving and woodblocks.

Meticulous guidelines of Daoist seal materials specify the priority of specific woods. Because peach trees, associated with a Daoist heaven called the Mountain of Jade Capital (Yujing shan 玉京山), are believed to have magical powers for expelling demons, peach wood is often ranked top for seal carving.[23] Jujube, maple, locust, pear, and sandalwood are also recommended, as they are dense in consistency and have smooth grain which facilitates carving.[24] This matches the woods commonly chosen for printing blocks in the Song and Yuan periods.

The most popular pigment used in Daoist seal imprints is cinnabar, still commonly used in traditional Chinese stamp pads. In Daoism cinnabar is associated closely with immortality.[25] It was sometimes mixed with bezoar (*niuhuang* 牛黃), "a mass retrieved from a cow's gastrointestinal system" and "highly regarded in Chinese medicine" for its "anti-toxic quality."[26]

While Daoist seals typically bear some sort of writing, most are illegible. Over 260 seal templates illustrated in the Daoist Canon show seal designs of

20 DZ 1185, 28: 241–42; Huang 2017a, 83–84.

21 Huang 2017a, 77.

22 For more on the Daoist Canon, see Huang 2012, 18–19.

23 DZ 1220, 29: 151. See also Huang 2017a, 87.

24 DZ 1220, 29: 151, 30: 103, 108, 120, 317; DZ 587, 10: 779; DZ 1412, 34: 401, 415; DZ 582, 10: 755; DZ 219, 3: 809; DZ 857, 18: 596. For the enigmatic "lightning-struck wood" (*leipi mu* 雷劈木) and "wood petrified by a dragon" (*longjing mu* 龍驚木), which have auspicious associations, see Huang 2017a, 87–88.

25 Because cinnabar contains mercury sulfide, which was believed to be able to be transformed into silver and gold, it has long been valued in Daoist alchemy; see Huang 2017a, 92.

26 Huang 2017a, 92.

FIGURE 1.4
Daoist ritual seal in seal script style. *Taishang zhuguo jiumin zongzhen biyao*

FIGURE 1.5
Seal of the Jade Emperor in heavenly script. *Sanjiao lingying jing*

FIGURE 1.6
Seal of the Thunderclap Bureau. *Daofa huiyuan*

four types, ranging between the two poles of the Daoist "imagetext" seesaw—all writing or pure graphic.[27] The four types attest to the interlocking relationship of text and image unique to Daoist visual culture.

The first type is entirely in seal script. Although such seals reflect the close relationship of Daoism to mainstream culture, they make up less than 8 percent of the seals surveyed, the smallest group of examples.[28] Exemplars typically evoke the judicial authorities in charge of major celestial bureaus crucial to Daoist rituals, such as the Seal of the Office of the Northern Ultimate for Expelling Perversities (*Beiji quxie yuan yin* 北極驅邪院印) (fig. 1.4).

The second type includes seals in heavenly scripts (*tianshu* 天書) (figs. 1.5, 1.6). They comprise the largest group, occupying over 40 percent of samples.[29] Daoist writs showcased in these seals depart from traditional writings with their own idioms—containing some word-like elements hard to decipher—and mix images with texts. The illegible Seal of the Jade Emperor (*Yudi yin*

27 For more discussions of the concept of "imagetext" in Daoist visual culture, see Huang 2012, 11, 14, 21, 34, 136, 139, 149, 154, 158, 165, 185, 242, 344.

28 Twenty seals of this category are reproduced in Wang 2000, 58–75; Wang Y. 2001, 472–93. For more discussion, see Huang 2017a, 48–51.

29 Huang 2018a, 52–66.

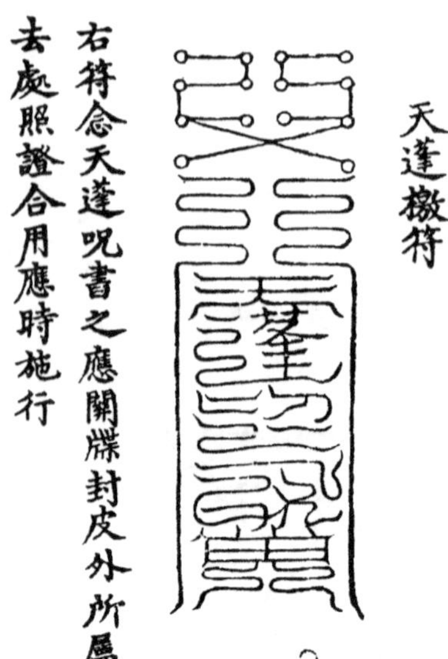

FIGURE 1.7
Talisman of Tianpeng. *Daofa huiyuan*

玉帝印) (fig. 1.5), used for summoning a celestial dragon in visualization to facilitate the adept's cosmic journey, is dominated by intertwined curvy lines just like clouds or cosmic *qi* in motion. The Seal of the Thunderclap Bureau (*Leiting dusi zhi yin* 雷霆都司之印) (fig. 1.6), on the other hand, used in Song-Yuan rituals to summon various thunder divinities, interspaces writing with ornamental dots and graphs. The word *lei* 雷, "thunder," on top of the right column of the seal template shows an incised ax-shaped pattern filled with three dots in the lower compartment.[30] This design is almost identical with an archaeological seal found in Heilongjiang 黑龍江 and dated to the twelfth century, when northeast China was under Jurchen Jin rule.[31]

The third type, which occupies over 30 percent of samples, involves talisman-inspired seals. The Strickmann seal discussed earlier is a good example (fig. 1.2).[32] Taking visual cues from talismans (fig. 1.7),[33] a seal designer would modify the typical elongated talismanic composition into a smaller, often square structure, truncating or simplifying it during transfer. Switching from writing with brush on paper to carving a seal on wood and other hard surfaces compromised the nuances of the thickening and thinning of calligraphic brushstrokes.

30 For more seals associated with thunder, see Li and Li eds. 2022, 3: 222, 325–26.

31 See the seal discovered in 1991, and measures 5.8 × 5.8 cm, reproduced in Huang 2018a, 65 (fig. 15d). Cf. a modern counterpart used by contemporary Daoists in Taiwan, reproduced in Huang 2018a, 66 (fig. 16c).

32 For more visual examples and discussions, see Huang 2018a, 66–71.

33 For more about Daoist uses of talismans, see Verellen 2019, 272–80.

FIGURE 1.8
Graphic Taiji Seal. *Daofa huiyuan*

FIGURE 1.9
Rubbing of a tile. Han. Discovered in the Han city ruins, Xi'an

The fourth type (fig. 1.8), which makes up about 15 percent, consists of purely graphic seals.[34] These swing to the other extreme: some show some graphic designs with reference to animated cosmic *qi* while others embody miniature diagrammatical renditions of Daoist ritual space and numerology charts. The Seal of the Great Ultimate (Taiji 太極) illustrated in a fourteenth-century Daoist compilation is a circular seal with fluid curvilinear patterns, which recall the design of palatial tiles retrieved in Han ruins in Xi'an (fig. 1.9).[35] Going beyond ancient ornamental conventions, however, here the overall design is more talismanic: the curvy graph occupying the upper half of the composition, for example, is created by an unbroken stroke traveling back and forth in left-right direction, just like writing a talisman.[36]

1.1.2 Buddhist Talismanic Seals

The few talismanic seals hand-drawn in eight-to-tenth century Dunhuang manuscripts (figs. 1.10–1.11) and other canonical sources cast light on their Buddhist counterparts used in healing and other ritual contexts.[37] However, no

34 Huang 2018a, 72–77.
35 Cf. the other similar Han tile, also discovered in Xi'an; see Zhao 1998, 345.
36 Huang 2018a, 72.
37 Copp 2011; Copp 2019; Lin 2021.

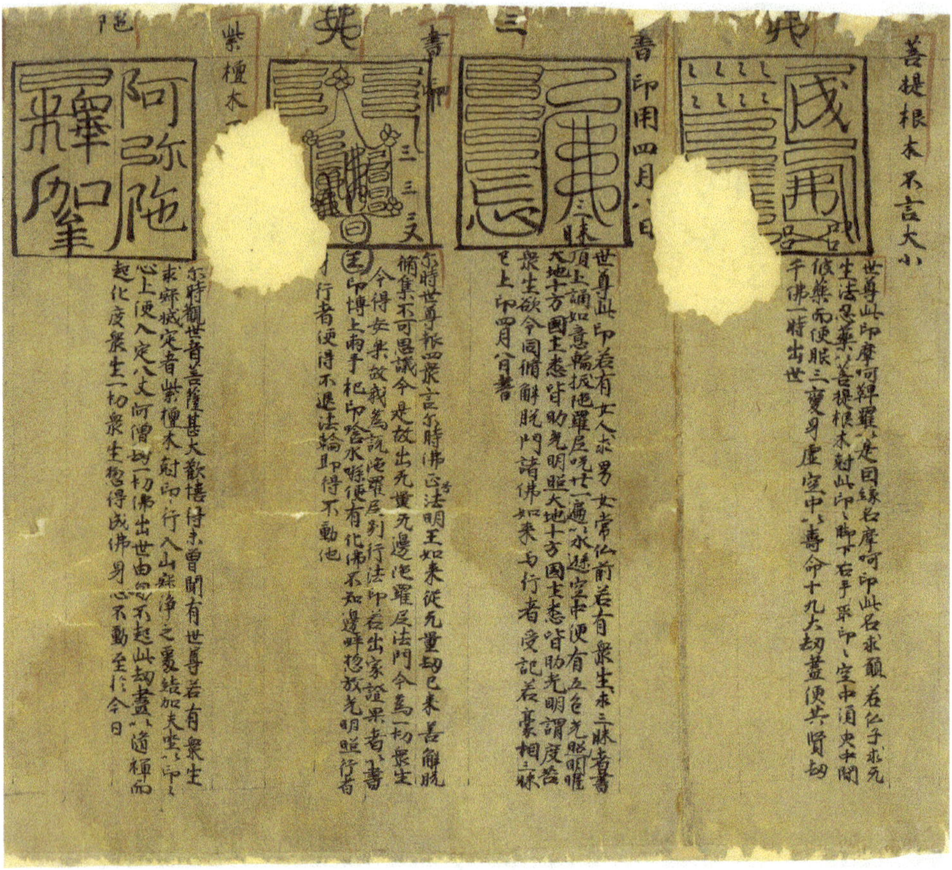

FIGURE 1.10 Detail of a Dunhuang manuscript (Pelliot chinois 3874). 10th century. Ink on paper. Handscroll. Bibliothèque nationale de France

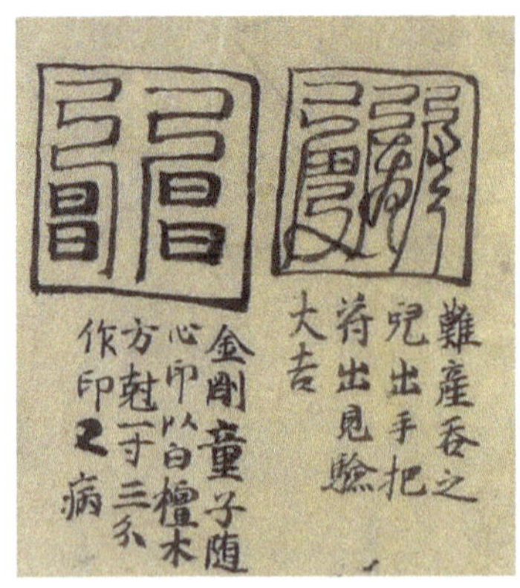

FIGURE 1.11 Detail of a Dunhuang manuscript (Pelliot chinois 2153). 10th century. Ink on paper. Handscroll. Bibliothèque nationale de France

physical seal or impression on paper corresponding to any of the seal samples illustrated in the Dunhuang texts has survived.

In terms of materiality, most Buddhist seals were supposed to be carved in sandalwood, peach, and jujube, just like their Daoist counterparts. However, some were also made from the uniquely Buddhist "wood of the root of the bodhi tree" (*puti gen mu* 菩提根木), taking the cue from the Buddha's biography that associates the bodhi tree with the site where he attained enlightenment.[38]

Regarding design, Buddhist seals show recurring switchback layers of undulations and sun-evoking logographs.[39] These features may well echo the basic graphic vocabulary of Daoist seals circulating in Dunhuang at that time, such as the True Seal in Dragon Seal Script (*Longzhuan zhenyin* 龍篆真印) illustrated in a Dunhuang manuscript dated to the mid-ninth to the eleventh century.[40]

Different from the Daoist prototype, however, are additional script-based logographs that evoke Buddhist divinities. Good examples in Dunhuang manuscripts on Tantric rituals associated with the bodhisattva Avalokiteśvara are seals bearing legible logographs that read, "becoming Buddha" (*chengfo* 成佛), "Amitabha Buddha" (Amituo 阿彌陀), and "Shakyamuni" (Shijiamou 釋伽牟) (fig. 1.10).[41] Inscriptions accompanying seal illustrations outline various goals such as extending life, facilitating meditation, conceiving children, safeguarding childbirth, and healing diseases.[42] Two therapeutic seals were transcribed twice in two comparable manuscripts (fig. 1.11).[43] The seal composed of three lines of vertical graphs, shown on the right of the cited detail, is considered efficacious in helping women with childbirth complications (*nanchan* 難產).[44] Although there is no specific information regarding what material was used, is it likely that a woman is advised to imbibe (*tun* 吞) the seal impressed on edible bamboo fiber (*zhumo* 竹膜) or ingest the paper with the impressed seal

38 For "the wood of the root of the Bodhi Tree," see two Dunhuang manuscripts (P. 2153 and P. 3874). See Copp 2011, 211.

39 For more visual examples illustrated in Dunhuang manuscripts, see Copp 2011, 215–24; 2019, 36; Huang 2017a, 90. For more examples from the canonical sources, see T.21.1420; T.21.1265; Strickmann 1993, 55–64; 2002, 170–78; Xiao 1993, 192–94. Buddhist talismans applied similar graphic designs; see Robson 2008.

40 See the seal illustrated in the Dunhuang manuscript (P. 3811), reproduced in Huang 2017a, 86 (fig. 9).

41 For more, see Copp 2011.

42 For seals whose graphic designs evoke Guanyin, see P. 2153, P. 2602, and P. 3835v, reproduced in Copp 2011, 216; Copp 2019, 36.

43 For the other Dunhuang manuscript recording the same seals in a slightly different order, see S. 2498. See also Huang 2017a, 90 (fig. 10c).

44 For more on the Dunhuang seals and talismanic writs associated with childbirth, see Lin 2017, 249–52.

FIGURE 1.12
A Buddhist wooden stamp (Pelliot Koutcha 512). Possibly 8th century. Discovered in Kucha, Xinjiang. Bibliothèque nationale de France

dissolved in liquid.[45] The other seal, on the left of the cropped detail, evokes the healing power of the Tantric deity Vajrakumara (Jingang tongzi 金剛童子).[46] Stamping the seal carved from white sandalwood on the patient is said to be efficacious in treating the sick.

1.2 *Buddhist Iconic Stamps*

Mainstream Buddhist stamping practices are apparent in Buddhist iconic stamps—a term used to refer to Buddhist seals bearing iconic designs, differentiating them from Daoist-inspired talismanic seals. Most visual examples survive as stamped markings on paper scrolls originally discovered in the Dunhuang library cave and dated to the ninth and tenth centuries.[47] The average size of the stamped impression is about six centimeters. This corresponds to some extant stamps from the eighth century, such as the wooden relief stamp discovered in Kucha (fig. 1.12), located west of Turfan in present-day

45 My speculation is based on the Daoist practice. See, for example, the use of bamboo fiber in the instruction of the Red Emperor's Talisman of Nurturing the Qi (*Chidi yangqi fu* 赤帝養氣符) in DZ 219, 3: 1038.

46 Cf. a seal with the identical design and accompanied inscription recorded in S. 2498, reproduced in Huang 2017a, 90 (fig. 10c).

47 The longest Dunhuang stamped scroll (P. 3938) measures about eight meters long and bears 2030 identical impressions. See Cohen and Monnet 1992, 43; Shen 2019, 81. Another Dunhuang scroll, now in the British Museum (1919,0101,0.260* Recto), also bears excessive numbers of stamped icons. It measures 555 centimeters long and bears 476 impressions of the stamped Dizang.

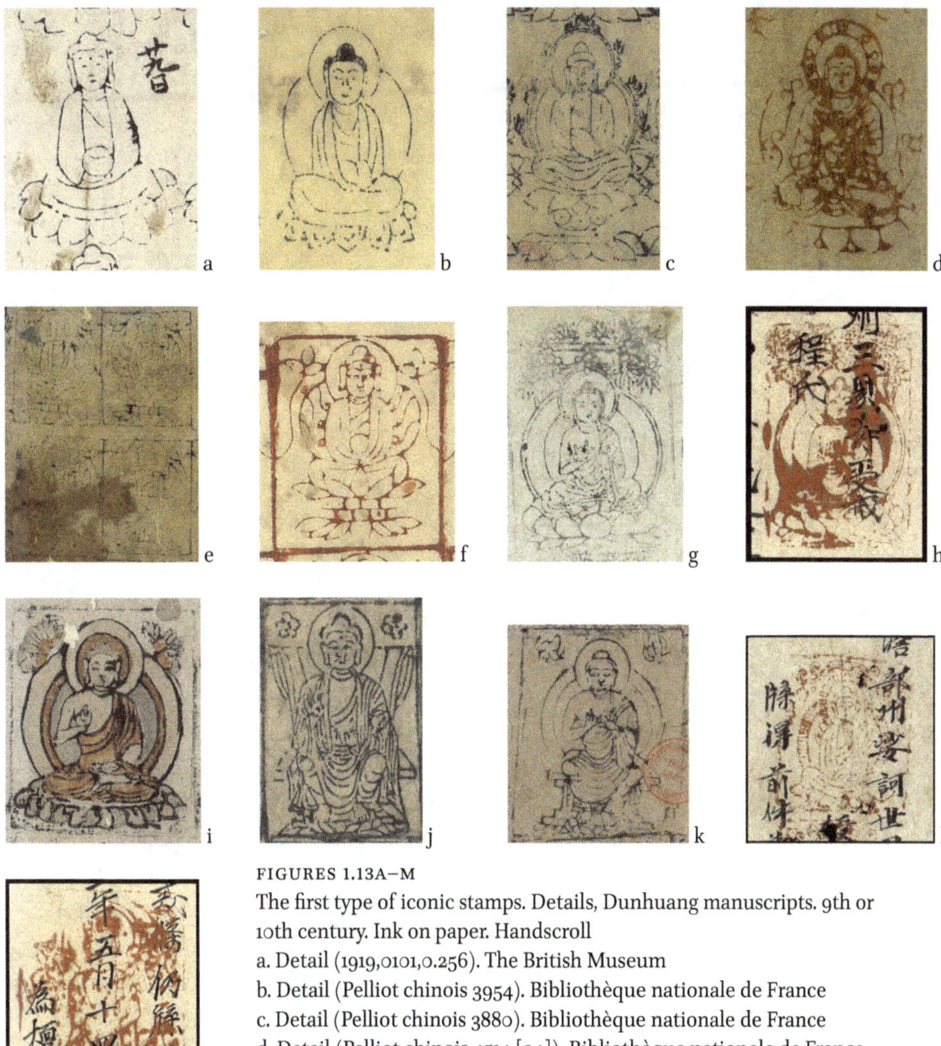

FIGURES 1.13A–M
The first type of iconic stamps. Details, Dunhuang manuscripts. 9th or 10th century. Ink on paper. Handscroll
a. Detail (1919,0101,0.256). The British Museum
b. Detail (Pelliot chinois 3954). Bibliothèque nationale de France
c. Detail (Pelliot chinois 3880). Bibliothèque nationale de France
d. Detail (Pelliot chinois 4514 [24]). Bibliothèque nationale de France
e. Detail (Pelliot chinois 4514 [19]). Bibliothèque nationale de France
f. Detail (Pelliot chinois 3528). Bibliothèque nationale de France
g. Detail (1919,0101,0.260 Recto). The British Museum
h. Detail of an ordination certificate (Or.8210/S.330). 982. The British Library
i. Detail (1919,0101,0.254). The British Museum
j. Detail (Pelliot chinois 4514 [17] B). Bibliothèque nationale de France
k. Detail (Pelliot chinois 4514 [23]). Bibliothèque nationale de France
l. Detail of an ordination certificate (Or.8210/S.532). 964. The British Library
m. Detail of a Dunhuang manuscript (Or.8210/S.330). 985. The British Library

n

o

p

q

r

FIGURES 1.13N–R
The second type of iconic stamps. Details, Dunhuang manuscripts. 9th or 10th century. Ink on paper. Handscroll
n. Detail (1919,0101,0.258). The British Museum
o. Detail (Pelliot chinois 3880). Bibliothèque nationale de France
p. Detail (1919,0101,0.252). The British Museum
q. Detail (1919,0101,0.257). The British Museum
r. Detail (1919,0101,0.260.+). The British Museum

Xinjiang.[48] To carve a relief stamp, the artisan left the surface of the contours of the imagery uncarved while scooping out the rest—a method comparable to most woodblock printing.

1.2.1 Types of Dunhuang Stamps

Extant Dunhuang manuscripts now housed in Paris, London, and China shed light on a rich repertoire of iconic stamped impressions on paper scrolls, presumably produced by local Buddhists in tenth-century northwest China. Twenty-four iconic impressed designs (figs. 1.13a–w) sum up the stamp repertoire circulating in the Dunhuang community. Designs divide into four types. The first type features a buddha, the second type a bodhisattva, the third a pagoda, and the fourth bears multiple figures or more complex designs.[49]

While most stamps were impressed in black ink, select samples, especially those retrieved from temple certificates, were produced in red (figs. 1.13d, 1.13f, 1.13h, 1.13l–m, 1.13q).[50] One unique stamp of a seated buddha (fig. 1.13i) shows

---

48 For a stamp discovered in Turfan and now in Berlin, see Carter 1955, unnumbered page between 40 and 41.

For a recent study of selected samples, linking the practice of reproduction to the Buddhist notion of authenticity, see Shen 2019, 80–86.

49 For some reproductions, see Cohen and Monnet 1992, 42–44, 46–47; Von Spee 2010, 61; Shen 2019, 80–82, 84; Matsumoto 2019, 2: 237–39.

50 Figs. 1.13e and 1.13f are impressions of the same stamp design in black and red respectively. There are multiple items of stamped buddhas in red comparable to P. 3528. See, for example, P. 5526 reproduced in Cohen and Monnet 1992, 42 (no. 23).

s

t

FIGURES 1.13S–T
The third type of iconic stamps. Details, Dunhuang manuscripts. 9th or 10th century. Ink on paper. Handscroll
s. Detail (Pelliot chinois 4514 [18]). Bibliothèque nationale de France
t. Detail (Pelliot chinois 3954). Bibliothèque nationale de France

FIGURE 1.14
Detail of a stupa with a seated buddha. Tang. Mural. West wall of the central pillar, Mogao Cave 431

multiple colors applied by hand after it was stamped in ink.[51] These specimens suggest that most wooden stamps used in Dunhuang were carved in relief fashion, just like the one retrieved in Kucha (fig. 1.12). Only one stamp showing eighteen miniature buddhas in a grid was cut in intaglio (fig. 1.13v).

The first type features a buddha (figs. 1.13a–m). Designs range from a plain seated buddha without any background or frame to a seated or standing buddha against botanical decors or floral curtains, either with or without a marked frame. Only one stamp, retrieved from an ordination certificate dated 982, represents a standing buddha (fig. 1.13m).

51 Agnew et al. 2016, 242–43.

FIGURE 1.13U
Detail of a Dunhuang manuscript (Pelliot chinois 4514 [19]). Ink on paper. Handscroll. Bibliothèque nationale de France

The second type features a single bodhisattva (figs. 1.13n–r). In addition to frontal designs (figs. 1.13n–o), two stamps feature figures with their face turned to one side and torsos in S shape (figs. 1.13p–q). One particular icon accompanied by a long lotus stem may represent Guanyin (fig. 1.13p). A unique monkish icon with a bold head can be identified as the bodhisattva Kṣitigarbha (Dizang 地藏) (fig. 1.13r); it is one of the 476 identical stamped images filling a 555-centimeter scroll.[52]

The third type appears only in two out of almost two dozen stamped templates (figs. 1.13s–t). It features a stupa with a buddha seated inside.[53] One design (fig. 1.13s) shows a gated stupa covered by a dome decorated with leafy motifs at the border. It resembles similar stupa designs depicted in Dunhuang murals from the seventh to tenth centuries, such as that from the Mogao 莫高 Cave 431 (fig. 1.14).[54]

The fourth type contains miscellaneous stamps with designs more complicated than the other three (figs. 1.13u–w). While they are all of different

52 Whitfield 1983, fig. 157. For the Japanese counterparts featuring the same deity (Jizō) dated to 1185–1392, see Nara Kokuritsu Hakubutsukan 1999, 43–47, 49–50.

53 For the stupa design in P. 3954, see Drège et al. 1986, 30; Cohen and Monnet 1992, 46 (no. 28); Shen 2019, 84 (fig. 3.8). Cf. a fragment scroll bearing more than twenty-three stamped images of the same stupa design, now in the National Library of China, see ZGFJBHQJBB, 1: 9–10.

54 DHSKQJ 21: 96 (fig. 81). For more on the types of stupas depicted in Dunhuang murals, see DHSKQJ 21: 207–14. For a stupa in a ninth-century Tibetan temple compound, illustrated in a Dunhuang manuscript, see Pelliot tibétain 993; Wu 2022a, 35, 290n.39. Cf. Japanese specimens of stupa-shaped stamps, dated to the Muromachi period; see Nara Kokuritsu Hakubutsukan 1999, 55 (nos. 61–62). The shape of a pagoda also plays an essential role in the practice of sutra copying. In the tenth century the *Heart Sutra* was transcribed in diagrammatic form mimicking a pagoda; see P.2168; S. 4289. For more about the word-pagodas in East Asian Buddhist art, see O'Neal 2018 (for the Chinese examples, see 122–30, figs. 3.1a–3.1b, 3.2); Chung 2022, 86–93.

FIGURE 1.15 Detail of Amitabha's Pure Land. 8th century. Tang. Mural. South wall of the main chamber, Yulin Cave 25

FIGURE 1.13V
Detail of a Dunhuang manuscript (Or.8210/S.330). 982. Ink on paper. Handscroll. The British Library

FIGURE 1.13W
A compound stamp (1919,0101,0.251.1). Tang. Ink on paper. The British Museum

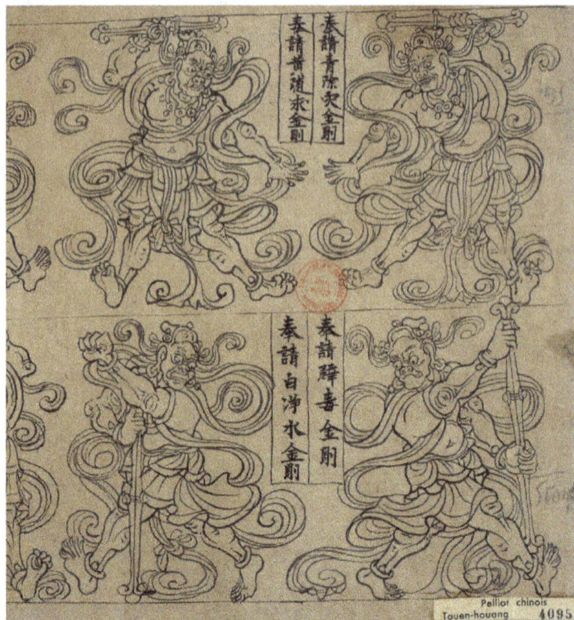

FIGURE 1.16 Drawing fragment of four guardians (Pelliot chinois 4095). Tang. Ink on paper. Bibliothèque nationale de France

compositions, both the first (fig. 1.13u) and second (fig. 1.0) contain a Buddhist triad; the third (fig. 1.13v) and fourth (figs. 1.13w) show multiple vignettes placed in a grid. The first example (fig. 1.13u), which survives in large quantities, depicts a triad with a seated buddha in the center flanked by standing bodhisattvas on either side. It may also reflect the legacy of earlier clay tablets from the seventh century (fig. 1.29).

The second example (fig. 1.0) is a mid-tenth century stamp representing paradise. It takes the triad design as the core, then adds complex architectural settings to the surrounding, resulting in a design that is almost twice the size of the average Dunhuang stamp.[55] It is in fact a miniature edition of the wall-size paradise paintings crowding the Dunhuang grottoes in the Tang period.[56] The

55 For dating, see Sha 2007, 90.

56 Each stamp is about 3.93 inches (or 10 cm) wide, and 5.11 inches (or 13 cm) high. Three extant fragments are in the Bibliothèque nationale de France. Each fragment of paper bears two stamped images, laid out vertically. These three items are: 1) Pelliot chinois 4514 (10), Pelliot chinois 4514 (10) 1; 2) Pelliot chinois 4514 (10), Pelliot chinois 4514 (10) 2; 3) Pelliot chinois 4514 (10), Pelliot chinois 4514 (10) 3. For a stamp impressed at the back of a Dunhuang document, see the back of Pelliot chinois 3024.

FIGURE 1.17 Detail of repetitive stamped spells in red. Xi Xia. Stamps on paper. Handscroll. Discovered in Baisigou Square Pagoda, Ningxia

FIGURE 1.18 Detail of stamped images of a Buddhist triad. Possibly 13th century. Ink on paper. Discovered at Bezeklik cave site, Turfan

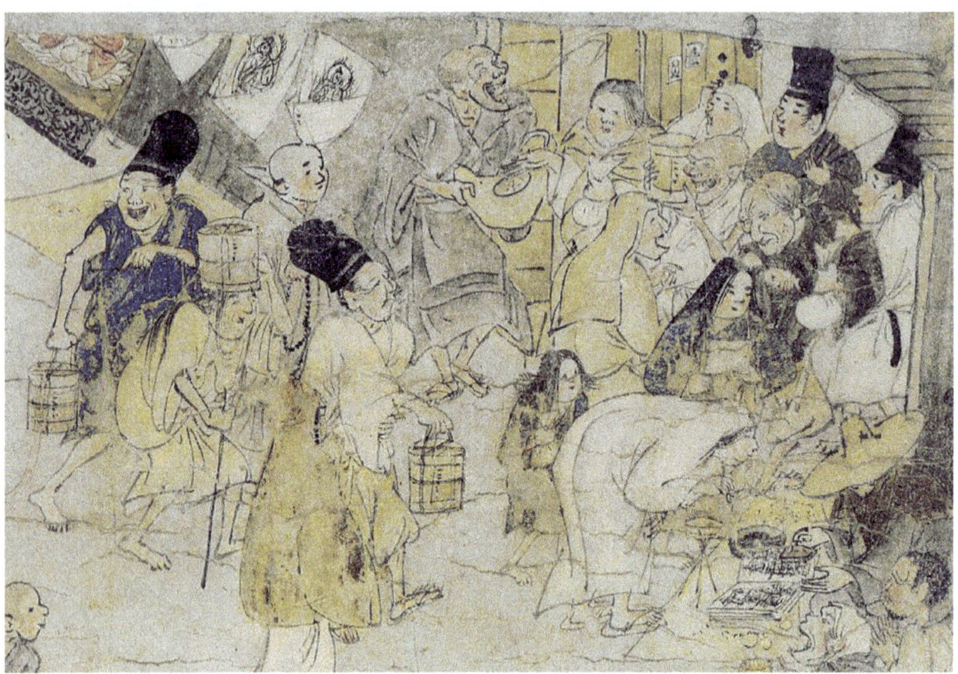

FIGURE 1.19 Detail. *Hungry Ghosts*. 12th century, Heian period, Japan. Ink and color on paper. Handscroll. Kyoto National Museum

stamp shows the triad of figures in the center, the lotus pond of rebirth in the foreground, and palatial architecture in the back. It also includes two symmetrically arranged towers and multi-storied buildings on both sides as well as musical instruments flying in the sky, altogether showing a striking similarity with the eighth-century mural on the south wall of Yulin Cave 25 (fig. 1.15).[57] While past scholarship has linked the stamp's representation to the *Amitabha Sutra*,[58] it is likely that the stamp's designer worked from the Pure Land stereotype standardized in Dunhuang murals.[59]

Moving on to "compound stamps," the third (fig. 1.13v) and fourth (fig. 1.13w) examples are both divided into a grid. The third example retrieved from the red stamped impressions on a temple ordination document is in a three-by-six grid. It places eighteen identical seated buddhas in box-like structures. The

57 DHSKQJ 21: 186 (fig. 172). Yulin Cave 25 has long been considered a cave constructed during the Tibetan occupation period. For more studies, see Xie and Huang 2007; Sha 2016.

58 Sha 2007, 86–91.

59 For a portable ninth-century Dunhuang painting in the British Museum (1919,0101,0.36) using the similar paradisal template to represent the assembly of the Medicine Buddha, with two additional Esoteric Buddhist iconographies added to the upper corners of the picture plane, see Sørensen 2015, 256–58 (fig. 7).

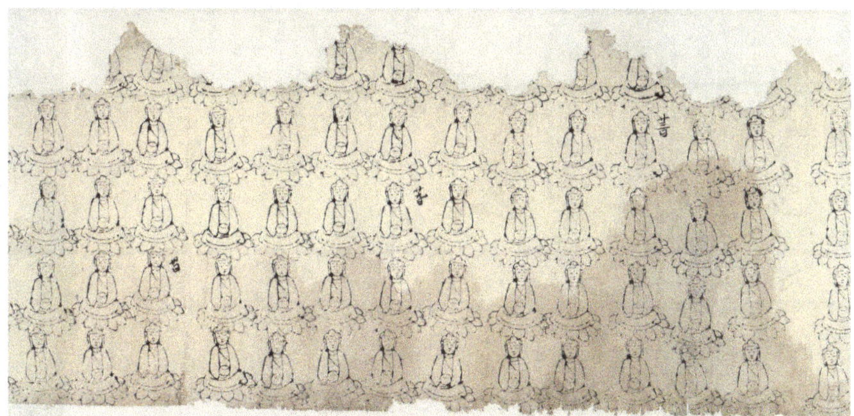

FIGURE 1.20 Detail of stamped images of Medicine Buddha (1919,0101,0.256). Tang. Print. Handscroll. The British Museum

FIGURES 1.21A–B Two sides of a wooden stamp (MG 23965). Tang. Musée des Arts Asiatiques-Guimet. a. Front side. b. Back side

fourth example features the four guardians known as vajrapāṇis (*Jingang* 金剛) in a two-by-two grid: the two on the upper and lower right vignettes form the mirror images of those on the upper and lower left. By impressing the stamp twice, lining the impressions next to each other, as reflected in the extant specimen preserved in the National Library of France,[60] the overall layout comes to resemble the hand-painted eight vajrapāṇis (fig. 1.16), illustrated in some Dunhuang manuscripts expounding the *Diamond Sutra* (see ch. 11).

Buddhist iconic stamps prospered beyond tenth-century Dunhuang, and comparable later examples were found in northwest China, Central Asia, and Japan. A Xi Xia paper fragment discovered in the Baisigou 拜寺溝 Square Pagoda in Ningxia preserves an array of repetitive stamped spells in red (fig. 1.17). The

60 For a visual example, see the stamped sample in Pelliot chinois 4514 (11).

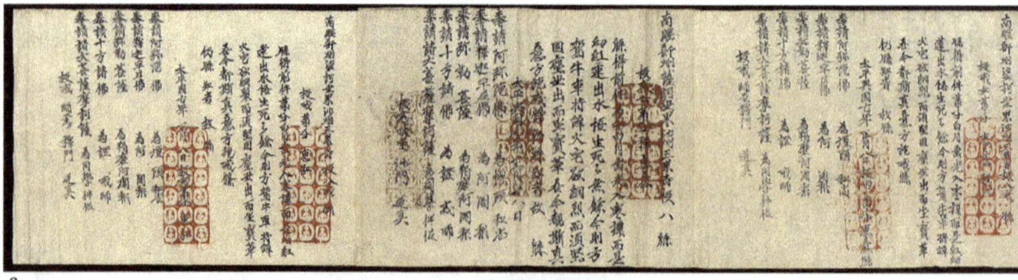

a

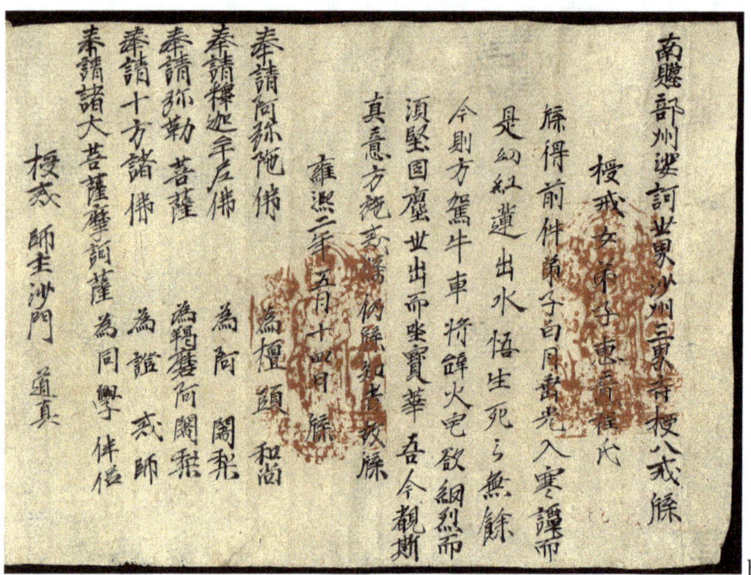

b

FIGURES 1.22A–B Details of a Dunhuang manuscript (Or.8210/S.330). 10th century. Ink on paper. Handscroll. The British Library
a. A composite document with six joined ordination certificates
b. Detail of a certificate dated 982

square "spell stamp" shows a seated buddha at the center, surrounded by Sanskrit charms.[61] Another paper fragment found in Turfan bears stamped images of a Buddhist triad (fig. 1.18), probably associated with the thirteenth-century Uighur Buddhist community.[62] The variety of Buddhist stamps made in Japan from the twelfth century onwards exceeds existing prototypes, adding unique Japanese designs such as the northern celestial king Vaiśravaṇa (Bishamon

61 Cf. the stamps discovered in Khara Khoto, reproduced in Despande 2008, 391 (no. 273). For other fragments impressed with identical stamp designs from the collection in St. Petersburg and mislabeled as Dunhuang materials, see ECDHWX 15: 255–57.

62 The Turfan stamp depicts a central seated buddha holding a canopy; he is surrounded by a bodhisattva and a monkish figure; see Tulufan bowuguan 1992, 106, 125.

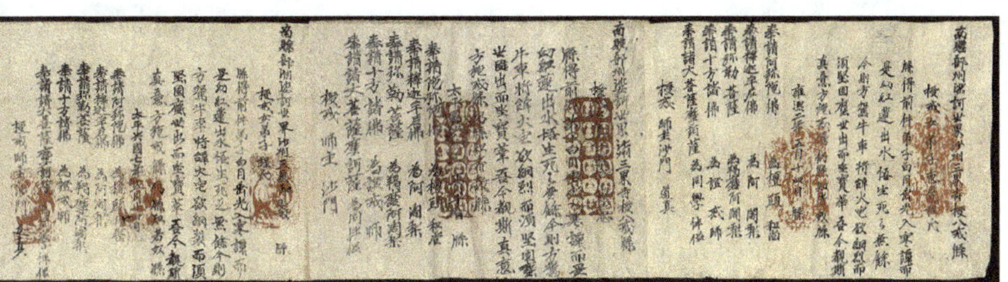

毘沙門), the wisdom king Vidyārājas (Myōō 明王), and the bag-carrying protector Mahākāla (Daikokuten 大黒天).[63] A lively scene retrieved from a twelfth-century Japanese handscroll painting of hungry ghosts depicts a person pressing a pagoda stamp in a booklet (fig. 1.19), two per page.[64]

1.2.2 Functions

Iconic stamps were used in various ways to reflect their different functions. Previous scholars have paid special attention to devotional, meritorious, and ritual practices evident in repetitive stamps that fill long paper scrolls, noting that in some occasions a devotee would recite prayers while stamping.[65] In an oft-cited scroll that is over five meters long, exceptional notes of dates were written in ink every twenty-one impressions of the Medicine Buddha (fig. 1.20), such as "the twenty-third day," "the twenty-ninth day," and "the thirtieth day."[66] These may well correspond to the Six Fasting Days, during which lay Buddhists performed the Ritual of the Eight Restrictions (Baguan zhai 八關齋).[67] That said, this is the only stamped scroll from Dunhuang that marks dates besides selected stamps. We know little about who stamped such extensive impressions on the Dunhuang scrolls; nor do we know if the persons stamping the impressions actually owned the stamps.

Interpreting the practice of ritual stamping on paper, scholars have linked them to practices performed during sand-buddha stamping assemblies

63 Ishida 1961 (for the Vaiśravaṇa stamped images dated 1162, see 87; for the stamped images of Myōō and the Great Dark Heaven, see 85, 89); Sasaki 2017, 286.

64 For more study of this scene, see Uchida 2011, 1, 7, 61. Numerous extant stamped images were preserved in miniature paper slips deposited in Buddhist statues as tokens of devotional offerings; see Uchida 2011, 2–60; Sasaki 2017, 166–67, 261–93.

65 Hou 1993, 293–94; Tai 2005; Dai 2016, 92; Shen 2019, 80.

66 The manuscript measures 108 centimeters long; see Von Spee 2010, 61; Agnew et al. 2016, 34 (fig. 16). Cf. the twelfth-century Japanese stamped paper specimens featuring the "one thousand buddhas" in Sasaki 2017, 261–93.

67 Tai 2005; Dai 2016, 92; Shen 2019, 80. For the Fast of Eight Restrictions, see *Baguan zhai jing* 八關齋經 in T.1.89: 913.

(*yinshafo hui* 印沙佛會) as documented in Dunhuang manuscripts.[68] Buddhists would gather on New Year's day or at the beginning of spring to seek the Buddha's blessing. They came together on sandy beaches near a body of water to "stamp the true presence of the ten thousand buddhas" (*yin wanfo zhi zhenrong* 印萬佛之真容) on the sand or reproduce molded stupas.[69] While images stamped on sand are ephemeral, some molded clay buddhas supposedly were relocated and mounted on the walls of selected cave temples in the Mogao grottoes.[70] The large Dunhuang wooden stamp with a seated buddha carved on one side (fig. 1.21a) and a handle on the reverse (fig. 1.21b) most likely is a sand-stamping tool used in such a ritual. The intaglio carving, different from the norm of relief stamps used to reproduce most of the impressions preserved in Dunhuang paper scrolls, would have created a vivid relief in the sand.[71] While the buddha images stamped on sand may appear more ephemeral than those stamped on paper, Wei-cheng Lin argues that it is the very nature of sand as a material, composed of infinite grains, that so powerfully embodies the notion of the "ten thousand buddhas."[72]

Additional Dunhuang iconic stamps go back to local temples where they served to authenticate ordination paperwork, functioning in a different context from long scrolls with repetitive stamped impressions. Over forty Dunhuang documents preserve stamped ordination certificates issued to lay Buddhists by local temples such as the Sanjiesi 三界寺 (Monastery of the Three Worlds) (figs. 1.22a–b, 1.23) and the Lingtusi 靈圖寺 (Monastery of Numinous Charts) (fig. 1.24), dating from 964 to 987. They were relatively smaller temples among the dozens of recorded local institutions in Dunhuang.[73] As Rong Xinjiang points out, the Sanjie Monastery "located in front of the Mogao caves," was the very temple that once owned the manuscripts and artifacts later discovered in the Dunhuang library cave.[74] Many extant documents associated with this

68 Hou 1984; Tan 1989; Wang S. and Wang Y. 2005.

69 See the Dunhuang manuscript (Pelliot chinois 3276V3), discussed in Wang S. and Wang Y. 2005, 55; Lin W. 2023, 68.

70 Tan cited Mogao Caves 212, 220, 285, and 492 as extant examples; see Tan 1989, 22–23; Wang S. and Wang Y. 2005, 53.

71 The artifact is 13 × 10.2 × 1 cm. According to Michelle McCoy, no "ink stains or reside" can be detected; see Agnew et al. 2016, 243–44.

72 Lin W. 2023, 68–69.

73 For more documented temples in Dunhuang, see Rong 2013, 119; Galambos 2020, 96; Wu 2022a, 34; Li 1988. Cf. the local Daoist temple Lingtuguan 靈圖觀 (Abbey of Numinous Charts; built 666), which owned copies of Daoist scriptures and issued Daoist ordination certificates; see Hao 2020, 91; Liu Y. 2006, 67; Wu 2022a, 37–38.

74 Rong Xinjiang proposed that the Dunhuang "library cave" was a "storeroom for the old and damaged sutras Daozhen collected in order to replenish the monastery's incomplete library," hence the materials in the library cave "were originally the library holdings and

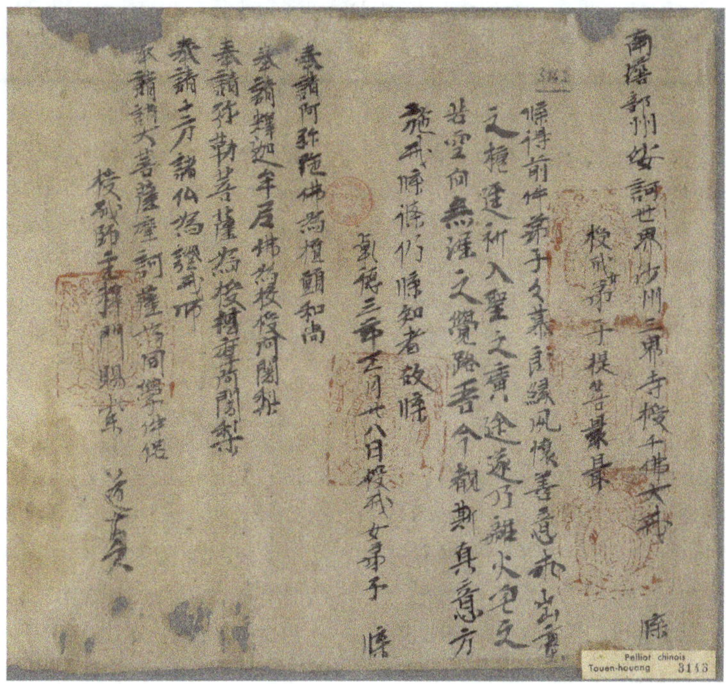

FIGURE 1.23 Detail of an ordination certificate. Dunhuang manuscript (Pelliot chinois 3143). 965. Ink on paper. Handscroll. Bibliothèque nationale de France

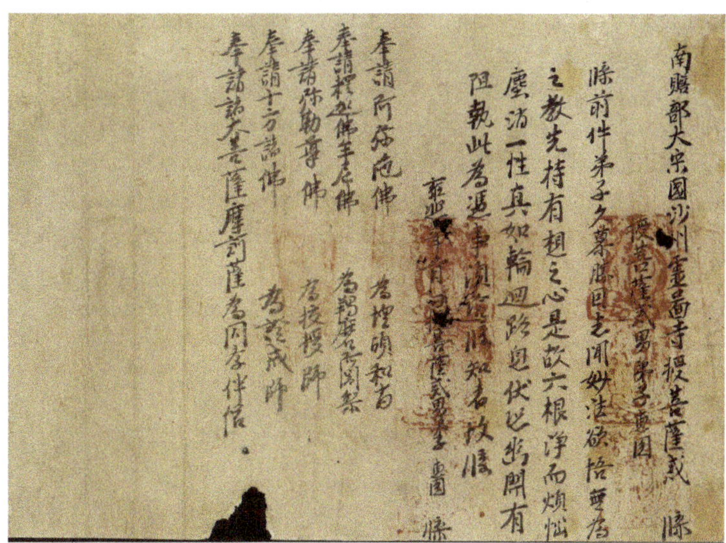

FIGURE 1.24 Detail of an ordination certificate. Dunhuang manuscript (Or.8210/S.4482). 984–987. Ink on paper. Handscroll. The British Library

temple bear the name of the resident monk Daozhen 道真 (ca. 915–987), who signed most of the ordination paperwork examined below. Daozhen is called Precept Master (*shoujie shi* 受戒師) and given various other titles in 964; he rose to the rank of District Sangha Recorder (*du senlu* 都僧錄) around 987. According to Stephen F. Teiser and others, he was deeply involved in repairing texts and documents stored at the Sanjie Monastery throughout his career.[75]

The certificates served as written testimony of their bearer's Buddhist standing as a follower of the religion's moral code or precepts (*jie* 戒). While the precepts came in different sets and levels—five, eight, ten, and more—they fundamentally required followers to refrain from killing, lying, stealing, and other forms of misconduct.[76] Surviving documents most likely are duplicates kept as temple records.[77]

Most certificates begin with naming the issuing temple and the specific ordination sanctioned, followed by the name of the ordinand (figs. 1.22b, 1.23, 1.24).[78] Next comes the main content, written in standard prose. It confirms that the ordaining master "has witnessed the sincere intention" (*du si zhenyi* 覩斯真意) of the supplicant and that the latter has taken the precepts and will cease to suffer in this life, a state that is compared to "a burning house" (*huozhai* 火宅) in reference to the famous parable of the *Lotus Sutra* (fig. 3.34d). Next comes the date of the ordination, followed by a series of evocations that summon a host of buddhas and bodhisattvas "to study [Buddhist teachings] together and accompany [the ordinand]" (*tongxue banlü* 同學伴侶). At the very end is the signature of the ordaining master; those issued at Sanjie Monastery were signed by Daozhen.[79] The entire affair concludes with a formal seal, usually a single temple stamp applied between two and seven times, usually superimposed on the names of the temple, the ordination master, and the supplicant.

Temple stamps come in at least four kinds. The first and most common bears a seated buddha (fig. 1.13l), as evident in two certificates issued by the Sanjie Monastery, dated to 965: one for the female disciple Putizuizui's 菩提最最 who took the Great Precepts of the Ten Thousand Buddhas (*qianfo dajie*

property of the Sanjie Monastery." See Rong 2013, 124, 130, 341, 380. Sam van Schaik and Imre Galambos expanded Rong's explanation by considering the cave as the "waste repository" or "book cemetery" of "sacred relics." See Van Schaik and Galambos 2012, 18–28; Galambos 2020, 253.

75 For a detailed study of Daozhen, see Teiser 1994, 138–51. See also Van Schaik and Galambos 2012, 23; Sørensen 2020, 8–9, 14.

76 For more studies, see Wang S. 1997; Dai 2016; ZGFJBHQJ 1: 98–123.

77 Wang S. 1997, 38.

78 In addressing the location of the Sanjie Monastery, a Buddhist cosmological location—the Southern Continent (Nanzhan bu 南瞻部) in the human world, is added to the name of the county—"Shaozhou" 沙州.

79 Wang S. 1997, 39.

FIGURE 1.25
Detail of a stamp impressed on the back of a Dunhuang manuscript (Pelliot chinois 3024). Ink on paper. Handscroll. Bibliothèque nationale de France

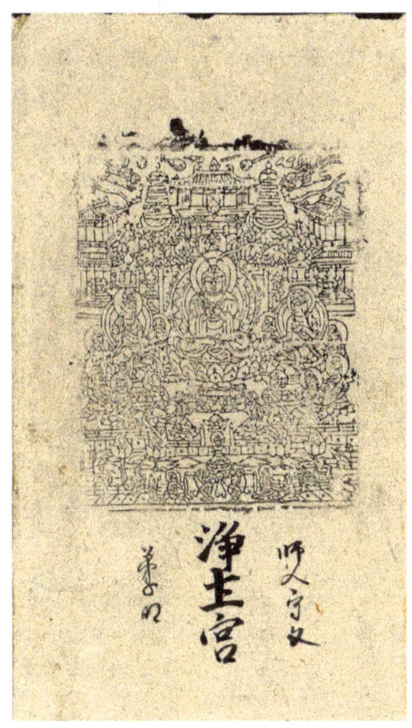

FIGURE 1.26
Detail. The reverse side of a Dunhuang manuscript (Or.8210/S.4644). 10th century. Ink on paper. Handscroll. The British Library

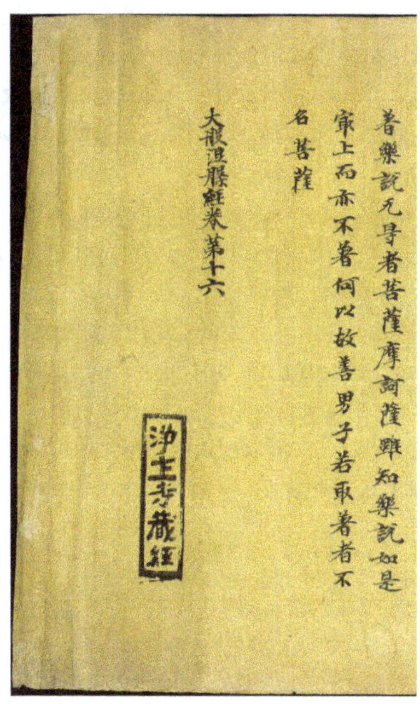

FIGURE 1.27
Detail of the *Da niepan jing*, juan 16. Dunhuang manuscript (Or.8210/S.5296). Tang. Ink on paper. Handscroll. The British Library

千佛大戒) (fig. 1.23); the other for the male disciple Li Han'er's 李憨兒 when he obtained the Five Precepts.[80] Intriguingly, the same stamp also appears in a later certificate issued by the Lingtu Monastery, dated 984–987 (fig. 1.24). Here it appears on the certificate for the male disciple Huiyuan 惠圜 who received the bodhisattva precepts, the most advanced codes recorded in Dunhuang ordination paperwork. Huiyuan's certificate is incomplete: it misses the ordaining monk's signature.

A 250-centimeter-long composite manuscript (fig. 1.22a) containing six certificates issued by the Sanjie Monastery, dated 982–985, showcases the other three kinds of iconic temple stamps (figs. 1.13m, 1.13h, 1.13v). Five of the certificates were issued to Woman Cheng 程, Buddhist name Huiyi 惠意. The first, dated 985, concerns her taking the Eight Precepts and bears an unusual stamp of a standing buddha (figs. 1.13m, 1.22b). Her three other certificates, second, fourth, and fifth in the document, are all associated with the same Eight Precepts she took repeatedly in 982 and 984 (fig. 1.22a). They are stamped with a compound seal showing multiple small buddhas in a grid (fig. 1.13v). The last certificate, dated 982 and placed second in the document, was stamped three times with a delicate stamp bearing a seated buddha (fig. 1.13h).

It is likely that the four kinds of iconic stamps retrieved from this paperwork were monastic stamps owned by local temples. Also pertinent in this context is the oversized "Pure Land Stamp" bearing the complex paradise design discussed earlier (fig. 1.0). Different from the four stamps on the front of documents, this appeared on the back of several Buddhist sutra copies (figs. 1.25–1.26) and may have served as a sign to mark it as monastic property. An example is the long composite scroll that transcribes extracts from the *Avatamsaka Sutra* (*Huayan jing* 華嚴經) and other sutras. The stamp here was impressed twice on the back of the scroll (fig. 1.25). In another example, a hand-written text was added below, identifying the paradise as the Pure Land Palace (Jingtu gong 淨土宮) and juxtaposing it with the names of a Buddhist master and his disciple (fig. 1.26).[81] It is tempting to identify this palace with the Jingtusi 淨土寺 (Pure Land Monastery), a temple in Dunhuang with a sizable collection of Buddhist manuscripts.[82] Discovered in the Dunhuang library cave, they still bear an ownership seal of the temple. Different from pictorial

80 At least seven other ordination certificates issued by the Sanjie Monastery and dated 964–966 and 983 were issued to Li Han'er; see Sørensen 2020, 14. Two of the seven documents do not have a precise date; see Wang S. 1997, 37–38. For the other Sanjie Monastery certificate (Dx 2889) associated with the Ten Thousand Buddhas Precept and issued by Monk Daozhen, see Hao 2020, 33 (fig. 2.28).

81 Sha 2007, 86; cf. two repetitive stamped samples in P.4514 (10), reproduced in 87.

82 The temple also functioned as a place for education; see Galambos 2020, 96–97. For more documentations of the Jintusi in Dunhuang manuscripts, see Rong 2013, 99, 307, 487.

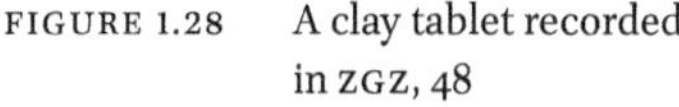

FIGURE 1.28 A clay tablet recorded in ZGZ, 48

FIGURE 1.29 The clay tablet of a Buddha triad. 7th century. Tang. Nara National Museum

stamps, this is purely textual and reads, "Sutra collected by the Pure Land Monastery" (Jingtusi cangjing 淨土寺藏經) (fig. 1.27).[83]

To sum up, the many impressed stamps preserved in Dunhuang manuscripts shed light on the diverse uses of stamps in the Buddhist community in the ninth and tenth centuries. Although both Daoists and Buddhists used seals, the repetitive application of iconic stamps as a material means of accumulating merit is a uniquely Buddhist practice. Contrary to mainstream Daoist seal designs, which often mix illegible magical writs with apparently abstract graphs evoking the sun, thunder, clouds, and stars, most Buddhist stamps are iconic, figural, and representational. Some of these designs are comparable to the Buddhist clay tablets we will examine below.

2 Molded Religious and Daily Objects

Clay or wooden molds were widely used in Tang-Song times to make objects for religious or everyday purposes. They include clay tablets, molded pagoda and tomb decors as well as molds for making toys, ceramics, and pastry.

83 Cf. a seal sample reproduced in Sha 2004, 122. Other Dunhuang manuscripts bearing the same temple seal impression include P. 2004 (a Daoist text; see Hao 2020, 19 [fig. 2.10]), P. 2039, P. 2100, P. 2175, P. 2188, P. 2219, P. 2263, P. 2284, P. 2290, P. 2298, P. 2320, P. 1832, and S. 5296.

FIGURES 1.30A–B Samples of two sides of a pagoda clay tablet. 7th century. Tang. National Museum of China
a. Front
b. Recto

FIGURES 1.31A–B Details of a clay tablet. Xi Xia. Discovered in Khara Khoto. a. Front. b. Recto

2.1 *Buddhist Clay Tablets*

Hundreds of Buddhist tablets with an average height of ten centimeters were mass-produced in seventh-century Chang'an 長安 using clay molds. Often referred to as "merit-accumulating clay" (*shanye ni* 善業泥) or terracotta buddhas (*taofo* 陶佛), they are believed to have been sponsored to accumulate religious merit.[84] Linking the practice to India, it is commonly assumed that

84 For select studies, see Li L. 2013; Wong 2018, 29–37; Hida 2018, 49–84; Shen 2019, 106–36. For Huang Jun's 黃濬 (ca. 1890–1937) collection of rubbings detailing the different types

FIGURE 1.32 A votive tablet of a multi-armed, multi-headed Guanyin. Xi Xia. Clay. Excavated in Khara Khoto

FIGURE 1.33 A mold of a multi-armed, multi-headed god. Northern Song. Clay. Discovered in Qingzhou, Shandong

the Chinese pilgrim-monks Xuanzang and Yijing 義淨 (635–713) played major roles in their transmission in addition to bringing back Buddhist sutras and teachings.[85] Comparative extant clay tablets, stupas, and seals produced in medieval India, Tibet, Burma, and Japan attest to shared yet diverse practices across Buddhist Asia.[86]

---

of visual designs and inscriptions, see ZGZ. Cf. a mid-fifteenth-century European votive clay mold in circular shape depicting the relief image of Saint Eustachius; see Parshall et al. 2005, 61 (pl. 1e).

85 Tan 1989, 22–23; Li L. 2011; Wong 2018, 37; Shen 2019, 111–12. While clay tablets could be used individually as votive objects in a domestic setting, their most crucial role, according to Hida Romi, was to furnish the surface of a pagoda, creating an overall effect of infinite buddhas, which in turn would have facilitated the devotees' visualization practice. See Hida 2018, 83–84.

86 For a 11th-to-12th-century stupa-shaped clay "sacchaya" discovered in eastern India and now in the British Museum, see Liao Yang in Xiong and Li 2016, 16 (fig. 6). For more on the Tibetan "tsha tsha," see Xiong and Li 2016. The practice of clay tablets also recalls the textual discourse of the so-called "sand stamp" (*yinsha* 印沙), "released buddha" (*tuofo* 脫佛), and "released stupa" (*tuota* 脫塔) recorded in Dunhuang manuscripts; see Tan 1989. For studies of Xuanzang and his legacy in visual cultures, see Nara Kenritsu Bijutsukan 1999; Liu S. 2012; Liu 2017; Liu Y. 2018; Wong 2002; Wong 2018, 21–94.

FIGURE 1.34
Detail of a molded brick.
ca. 990. Northern Song. Po Pagoda, Kaifeng, Henan

Most Tang clay tablets feature iconic designs, such as a buddha or bodhisattva (fig. 1.28),[87] or again a triad (fig. 1.29), echoing the repertoire of Buddhist iconic stamps (figs. 1.13p, 1.13u). One exceptional design represents an elaborate multi-storied pagoda with two buddhas seated inside (fig. 1.30a).[88] The inscription on the reverse of the design—citing from a different specimen (fig. 1.30b)—identifies the donor as Monk Falü 法律, who was from the Zhixiangsi 至相寺 (Monastery of Utmost Phenomena) located in Mt. Zhongnan 終南 outside Chang'an.[89] In 650, he commissioned 84,000 copies of such miniature jeweled pagodas (*duobao ta* 多寶塔), a term deriving from the *Lotus Sutra*.

Post-Tang Buddhist clay tablets found in sites associated with the Xi Xia and Northern Song suggest that the tradition continued into the twelfth century, complete with an expansive iconographic repertoire. Beyond Tang figures and different from them, as evident in Xi Xia clay tablets discovered in Khara Khoto, multi-armed, multi-headed divinities appear, celebrated in Esoteric and Himalayan Buddhism (figs. 1.31a–1.33). One specimen features the guardian deity Yamantaka on the front and Tibetan and Sanskrit charms on the back (figs. 1.31a–b).[90] Another tablet (fig. 1.32) shows a multi-armed, multi-headed

87 This reproduced image from Huang Jun's catalogue of clay tablets compares closely to the extant clay tablet in National Museum of China, published in Li L. 2013, 222 (fig. 25).

88 Li L. 2013, 215–16; Wong 2018, 29–31 (fig. 1.3); Shen 2019, 117–18 (fig. 4.7).

89 Note that my translation of the term "biqiu Falü" 比丘法律 is different from the translation by Hsueh-man Shen, who translated the term as "monks and Vinaya masters"; see Shen 2019, 117. For the location of Zhixiansi, see Hida 2018, 83.

90 Chen and Tang 2010, 200 (fig. 3.23–2); Zhang and Cai eds. 2020, 25. For a comparable clay tablet featuring a similar icon, discovered in the other Xi Xia ruins in Haimudong 亥母洞, Wuwei, Gansu, see Chen and Tang 2010, 200 (fig. 3.23–1).

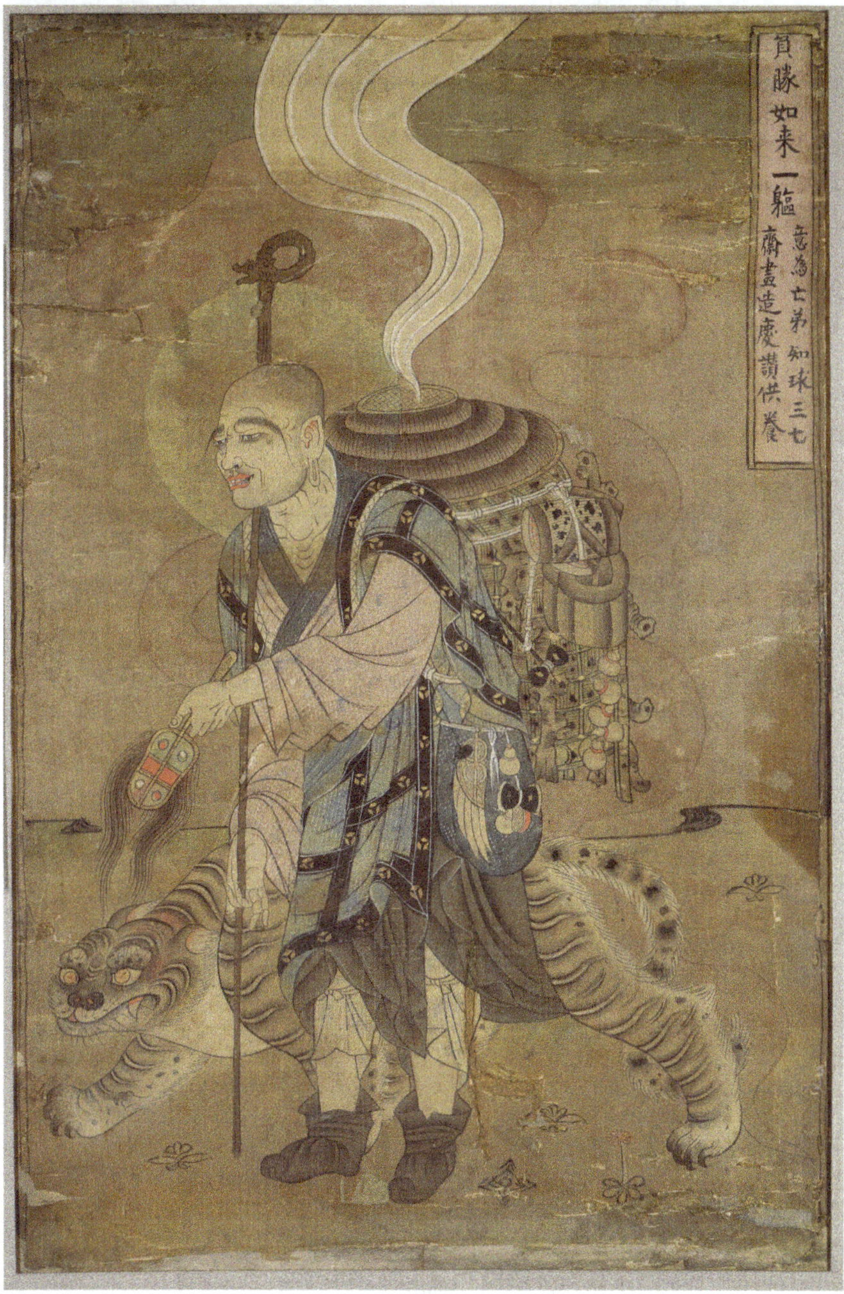

FIGURE 1.35 *Itinerant Pilgrim Monk Accompanied by a Tiger*. ca. 900. Tang. Ink and color on silk. Hanging scroll. Musée des Arts Asiatiques-Guimet

Guanyin in relief, with other smaller deities above and below.[91] A similar Northern Song tablet (fig. 1.33), found in Qingzhou 青州, Shandong, shows a multi-armed, multi-headed deity in relief and its corresponding clay mold in intaglio.[92]

2.2 *Molded Decors for Buddhist Pagodas*

Clay molds were also the source for tiles and decorative surfaces that furnished religious buildings and tombs, as well as for toys and ceramic utensils. Many extant brick tiles originally from the Po ta 繁塔 (Po Pagoda) in Kaifeng 開封, dated to 990 represent a molded design of a pilgrim-monk (fig. 1.34), who carries a longish pack of scrolls and is accompanied by a tiger.[93] Attached to the upper part of his pack is an umbrella-like canopy. Suspended from its rim is a censer that produces smoke to repel insects. Molded bricks with similar designs, dated to 1068, also appear in a pagoda at the Da Pumensi 大普門寺 (Great Monastery of the Universal Gateway) in Xiangshan 香山, Henan—about 132 km southwest of Kaifeng.[94] Their pictorial convention can be linked to more than a dozen ninth-to-tenth-century portable paintings and drawings originally discovered in Dunhuang (fig. 1.35).[95] The latter reflect a common visual stereotype of a traveling monk accompanied by a tiger, carrying a pack, and

91 Chen and Tang 2010, 199 (fig. 3.22); Zhang and Cai eds. 2020, 21. For more about Xi Xia clay tablets, see Chen and Tang 2010, 197–201; Niu 2013, 145–71; Lei et al. 1995, 175 (pl. 24); Zhang and Cai eds. 2020, 8–41.

92 For its corresponding mold, see Wei 2010, 103.

93 For more visual examples of the tiles adorning the Po Pagoda, see Kaifengshi bowuguan ed. 2019, 212–15 (for the template of a pilgrim monk, see 213). The Po Pagoda was related to the imperially sponsored the Tianqingsi 天清寺 (Monastery of Heavenly Clarity); see Sun X. 2012, 103. Cf. other samples of similar molded bricks reproduced in Yu 1997, 3:232 (fig. 241). Prior to the Northern Song, the exterior surfaces of the seventh-century pagoda of the Xiudingsi 修定寺 (Monastery of the Cultivation of Samadhi) in Anyang, Henan are filled with 3775 molded relief tiles with "seventy-two different designs"; see Shen 2019, 113, 115 (fig. 4.6); Jia 2020, 284 (fig. 4–2–22); Li J. 2023. Selected tiles originally from the pagoda are now in the San Francisco Asian Art Museum, the Philadelphia Museum of Art, and the Royal Ontario Museum.

94 For the visual example, see Sun X. 2012, 104 (fig. 2). The Northern Song stone pagoda dated 960 in Lingyinsi 靈隱寺 (Monastery of Numinous Seclusion), Hangzhou also bears a comparable figural design; see Sun X. 2012, 106 (fig. 5). The east (Zhenguo 鎮國) and west (Renshou 仁壽) pagodas of the Kaiyuansi 開元寺 (Monastery of Opening the Prime) in Quanzhou, dated to around the thirteenth century, are both decorated with stone relief carvings that represent monks in different figural designs. The monkish motif of the west pagoda bears a cartouche that reads, "Tang Sanzang" 唐三藏, referring to the Tang pilgrim-monk Xuanzang. For plates and more discussion, see Yu 2010, 32 (figs. 8–9).

95 Wong 2002.

FIGURE 1.36
A molded child with a backpack. Song. Terra cotta. Discovered in Qingzhou, Shandong

FIGURE 1.37
A clay mold of a child holding a lotus leaf. Xi Xia. Discovered in Linqiangsai, Ningxia

FIGURE 1.38
A molded child carrying a backpack. Terracotta. Discovered in Zhengzhou, Henan

a

b

FIGURES 1.39A–B Decorative bricks. Jin. Terracotta. Discovered in tombs in Houma, Shanxi
a. Tomb (65H4M104)
b. Tomb of Dong Ming

holding a walking staff in one hand and a flywhisk in the other.[96] A standard cartouche identifies the figure as Baosheng rulai 寶勝如來, possibly a title

96 Chen Yuquan 2009, 324 (fig. 4–21); Wong 2002, fig. 10. Dorothy Wong mentioned additional mural examples in Dunhuang Mogao Cave 45, 363, 306, and 308; see Wong 2002,

honoring Xuanzang.[97] Citing the temple murals known as "the traveling monk" (*xingseng* 行僧), recorded in the ninth-century *Records of Famous Paintings of All Dynasties* (*Lidai minghua ji* 歷代名畫記), recent scholarship suggests that these specimens may in fact reflect the Xuanzang-inspired pictorial convention as it spread from Chang'an.[98]

2.3 *Toys versus Tombs*

Most likely artisans had the liberty of recycling or repurposing molded designs. Many clay artifacts and molds document just how religious and secular elements intersected at the time (figs. 1.36–1.38).[99] Song specimens were made in the early twelfth century.[100] Others, excavated in south China, acknowledge such Jiangsu artisans as Bao Chengzu 包成祖 and Sun Rong 孫榮.[101]

Many specimens highlight children (figs. 1.36–1.38) and may have served as toys.[102] One discovered in Qingzhou (fig. 1.36) mimics the stereotype of a pilgrim-monk as seen in the brick from the Po Pagoda (fig. 1.34) while replacing the key figure with a child. Still, even this shows the towering pack and canopy, from which miscellaneous things are suspended.[103] Other recurring designs have a child holding a large lotus leaf (fig. 1.37) and a young herb-picker dressed in a leaf skirt carrying a pack (fig. 1.38).[104] These designs further overlap with funerary decors common at the time. Interior bricks found in Jin tombs

---

64–65. For more about tigers and monks in medieval Chinese Buddhism, see Chen H. 2023, 63–99.

97 Akiyama 1966; Chen Yuquan 2009, 109–10, notes 232–36; Wong 2002; Wong 2018; Wang H. 2016.

98 Sun X. 2012, 104. For the mural of a traveling monk in Changshousi 長壽寺 (Monastery of Extended Longevity) painted by Wu Daozi 吳道子, see LDMHJ, 135.

99 Wei 2010; Li Jinxing 1998.

100 Wei 2010, 19–20.

101 The clay molds discovered in Pingjiang bear such trademarks that read "Bao Chengzu from Pingjiang" (Pingjiang Bao Chengzu 平江包成祖) "Bao Chengzu from the Wu county" (Wujun Bao Chengzu 吳郡包成祖), and "Sun Rong of Pingjiang" (Pingjiang Sun Rong 平江孫榮); see Wei 2010, 18.

102 Wei Yaojin further cited the baby boy-praying custom associated with the Double Seven (Qixi 七夕) festival, on which day those who prayed to have baby boys venerated a type of clay child dolls known as *mohele* 磨喝樂 or *mohouluo* 磨睺羅. See Wei 2010, 9–17; DJMHL, 54. In Southern Song Hangzhou, *mohouluo* clay dolls were sold in the Zhong'an 眾安 Bridge area where bookshops selling Buddhist printed books clustered; see Wei 2010, 10; SSGJ, 302.

103 For its corresponding mold, see Wei 2010, 223. For more comparable specimens, see Li Jinxing 1998, 186, 188, 206.

104 For its corresponding mold, see Wei 2010, 159. Cf. Xi Xia molded designs discovered in Ningxia; see Li Jinxing 1998, 184–88 (figs. 71–73). Cf. the Liao brick relief carving at the base of the North Pagoda in Chaoyang, Inner Mongolia; see Liaoning sheng wenwu kaogu yanjiusuo et al. eds. 2007, color plate 95.4.

FIGURE 1.40
A plate mold with the carved garden scene at the base. Jin. Terra cotta. Discovered in Jingjing, Hebei

FIGURE 1.41
A modern wooden mold depicting the celestial palace in the moon

in Houma 侯馬, Shanxi, for example, depict similar low reliefs of a child holding a lotus leaf (fig. 1.39a) and an herb-picker wearing a shawl and a skirt made of leaves (fig. 1.39b).[105] Unlike the young herb-picker in the other specimen (fig. 1.38), the one here looks older: he has a mustache, holds an axe, and is accompanied by a goat.

2.4 *Molds for Ceramics and Pastry*

Typically, disposable molds for utensils and food containers have not survived since they were used regularly to meet everyday demands. After the eleventh century, they came to play a key role in ceramic manufacture, replacing earlier, labor-intensive manual work in shaping and carving decorations. A mushroom-shaped clay mold and a finished Yaozhou stoneware bowl at the Metropolitan Museum show just how, by using a clay mold for a bowl with its outer surface fully carved with floral patterns, Song potters could create a molded stoneware bowl with its interior surface impressed with decorations.[106]

Going beyond ornamental designs, more and more molds feature pictorial compositions. For example, the Jin mold of a shallow plate, discovered in a kiln site in Jingjing 井陘, Hebei bears an intricately carved garden scene at the base of the plate mold (fig. 1.40).[107] The garden features water fowl swimming in a lotus pond in the foreground, and has a garden rock and banana trees inside a balustrade in the background. Later transferred, the garden scene also appears on the interior of a finished ceramic plate. As I show below, similar memes were also adopted by Buddhist woodcut designers in the Song and Xi Xia (figs. 6.67c, 6.68a–b, 6.68d, 6.68f, 6.69a). Alternatively, bowl-shaped molds with interior decorations were used to produce ceramic bowls with external ornaments.[108]

While it is hard to find an extant mold for medieval pastry, some modern Taiwanese wooden molds for traditional moon cakes (fig. 1.41) show what they may have looked like.[109] The example here has a handle; the concentric round shape carved in the center matches the pattern impressed on the surface of a

105 For the bricks representing a child holding a lotus stem, see Shanxi sheng kaogu yanjiusuo 1999, 220–21. For an immortal-like man dressed in a skirt made of leaves, see 218. For more studies on the modular designs of decorative bricks in Song-Jin brick tombs, see Deng 2015, 71–73; 2017, 42–44; 2019, 71–76.

106 Leidy 2015, 13 (fig. 6).

107 Cf. similar clay molds with floral or pictorial designs, discovered in the same site and dated 1189 and 1206 respectively; see Hebei bowuyuan 2014, 158–59, 224–25.

108 For a bowl-shaped Yaozhou ware mold with carved patterns on the interior, see Shaanxi sheng kaogu yanjiu suo 1998, color plate 16.1.

109 For more Taiwanese wooden pastry molds, see Jian 1999. For rare specimens of medieval pastries discovered in the tombs at Astana, including "a jam tart, and in a variety

FIGURE 1.42 Textile fragment with printed designs. Tang. Silk. Discovered in Astana, Xinjiang. Xinjiang Museum

moon cake, complete with a central design representing a rabbit in the process of making the elixir in the moon palace.

of shapes including buns, straws and twists," see Whitfield and Sims-Williams 2004, 325 (cat. 287).

a

b

c

FIGURES 1.43A–C Details. *Assembly of Buddha Shakyamuni*. Liao. Dyed tabby weave silk. Discovered in the Fogong Pagoda, Yingxian, Shanxi
a–b. Details of Specimen Yi
c. Detail of Specimen Jia

3 Textiles with Printed Designs

Chinese artisans have used carved blocks to print decorative designs on textiles since ancient times.[110] While printed designs in early textiles were merely ornamental, more complex pictorial representations were introduced during the Tang-and-Liao period.[111]

A Tang silk fragment discovered in Astana, Xinjiang is among the earliest extant specimens with printed pictorial designs (fig. 1.42). Colored in dark yellow, it shows two repetitive scenes of an animated design: an archer on a running horse turns around to shoot a lion. Additional animal motifs have a hound jumping through a grassy mound in the foreground as he chases a rabbit, while three birds soar into the sky ahead of the rider. The overall design was printed onto the fabric from a block about thirty centimeters wide.

Discovered in the eleventh-century Liao Fogong Pagoda in Shanxi, three rare pieces of clamp-resist, dyed tabby weave silk indicate a technological breakthrough at the time (figs. 1.43a–c).[112] The fabric is printed in red, blue, and yellow, with details of figures' faces added manually. It is likely that the three colors were applied in separate steps, probably beginning with red, followed by blue and yellow. Applying the ancient *jiaxie* 夾纈 technique, the fabric is printed using two identically-sized blocks, each carved with a mirror image of the other. To make the print, the fabric is placed on the inked blocks, which are then folded like a book to create the symmetrical image.[113] The design shows a seated, front-facing buddha flanked by twelve figures (fig. 1.43a). All three examples are differentiated by hand-painted additions to the underlying print. The hand-painted details serve not only to customize each print but also to add greater individuality in the flanking figures (figs. 1.43b–c). These additions

110 For example, the diamond-shaped patterns of Han-dynasty Mawangdui silk may have been created by using a block bearing four-diamond-shaped patterns cut in relief. Each diamond-shaped pattern is about 0.4 cm high and 0.22 cm wide. The extant fragment shows about 20 of them. Thomas Carter discussed printed designs of textiles in western history, citing the sixth-century specimens discovered in Egypt as the earliest extant specimens; he also mentioned tenth-century Dunhuang textiles as the Chinese counterpart; see Carter 1955, 194–95; Carter 1957, 166–71 (esp. 168–69).

111 For early and medieval specimens of textiles, see Machida Shiritsu Kokusai Hanga Bijutsukan 1988, 66–71 (for Qing-dynasty wooden molds, see 72). For the European use of printed designs on textiles in the Middle Ages, see the oft-cited Sion textile dated around the second half of the fourteenth century, an early European counterpart whose printed narratives depict the legend of Oedipus. See Parshall et al. 2005, 64–65 (no. 2).

112 Kuhn et al. 2012, 304–305.

113 The characters indicating "Hail Shakyamuni Buddha" (*Nanwu shijia mouni fo* 南無牟尼佛) are printed in reverse on the right half, further supporting this hypothesis.

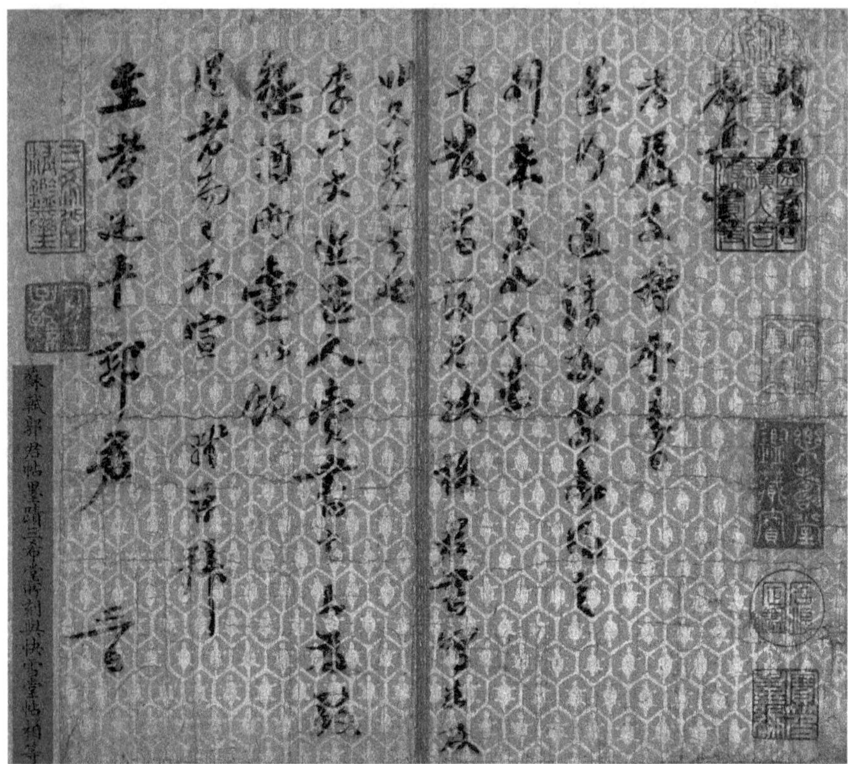

FIGURE 1.44 Detail. Digital photography of *Letter to Filial Gentleman Guo Tingping* by Su Shi. 1075. Northern Song. Ink on decorative paper. Album leaf. National Palace Museum

range from the exaggerated eyebrows of one of the figures (fig. 1.43b) to the addition of new facial features positioned to turn a head in an opposite direction (fig. 1.43b) from what occurred in the original print (fig. 1.43c).

4 Embossed Decorative Paper

By the tenth century, advanced technologies in textile making and woodblock printing stimulated the creation of decorative papers. Also using clay molds, they were mostly used by the elite as refined stationary.[114]

114 He Yanquan published his scholarly findings in an exhibition catalogue, including impressive reproductions of more than a dozen kinds of precious Song decorative letter paper, using special photography technologies; see He ed. 2017. Cf. Song decorative letter paper

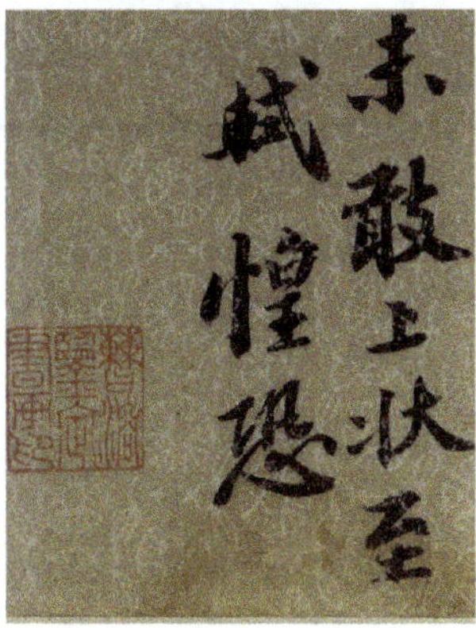
未敢上狀至
軾惶恐

FIGURE 1.45
Detail. Digital photograph of *Letter "Pingshi"* by Su Shi. Northern Song. Ink on decorative paper. Album leaf. National Palace Museum

FIGURE 1.46 Detail of decorative paper attached to the *Medicine Buddha* print. Liao. Discovered in the Fogong Pagoda, Yingxian, Shanxi

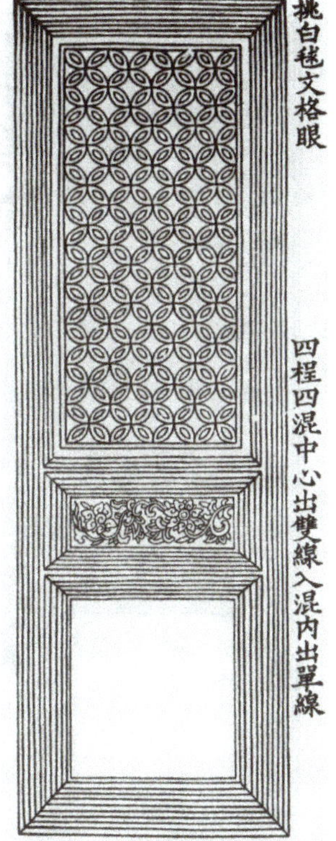

FIGURE 1.47
Detail of the ornamental designs of a door. YZFS, 32: 5a

FIGURE 1.48 Detail. Frontispiece to the *Lotus Sutra*, juan 1. Illustrated by Wang Yi. Southern Song. Woodblock print. National Palace Museum

Makers of letter paper—called *qian* 箋—copied patterns on textiles. The "fish-eggs paper" (*yuzi qian* 魚子箋) and "gauze-patterned paper" (*luoqian* 羅箋) made in Sichuan, for instance, were created "with starch on a piece of closely-woven cloth from which a hidden design like fish eggs resulted."[115] Besides gauze (*luo* 羅), twill damask (*ling* 綾) and patterned tabby weave silk fabric (*qi* 綺) were used in Song-Yuan papermaking.[116] The intricate designs of textiles further enriched the decorative repertoire of Song embossed paper.[117]

By the tenth and eleventh centuries, papermakers applied woodblock printing to create "pressed floral paper" (*yahua qian* 砑花箋).[118] The process involved first carving ornamental or pictorial designs on a woodblock, then pressing either the front or back of the paper onto it with the help of a wooden hammer, a piece of polished jade, shell, or agate with a smooth surface. The medieval printer Yao Yi 姚顗 (866–940) was lauded for creating the "lustrous letter papers in small pamphlets" (*yaguang xiaoben* 砑光小本), perhaps because his decorated designs were coated with a layer of lustrous glue (*jiao* 膠).[119] Yao used fragrant gharuwood (*chenxiang* 沉香) for his blocks and created intricate designs of "landscape, trees, branches of flowers and fruits, lions and phoenixes, insets, fishes, the God of Longevity, the Eight Immortals," and even archaic seal script characters traceable to those cast on ancient bronze bells and vessels.[120] Compared to traditional woodblock printing, whose impressions were printed on paper in ink, woodblocks for decorative letter paper did not use ink. Rather, they were often left empty or furnished with subtle ingredients such as glue mixed with lustrous mica powder or subdued pigments in white, yellow, and brown. This resulted in decorated paper with delicately embossed, translucent designs similar to watermarks today.[121] He Yanquan links the subtle taste to the

---

bearing Japanese Heian poems, reproduced in Tōkyō Kokuritsu Hakubutsukan et al. 2023, 68–71; Nezu Bijutsukan 2023, 114–29.

115 Tsien 1985, 94; see also He 2017, 14–16.

116 He 2017, 15.

117 For example, letter paper in subdued circular floral patterns used by the Northern Song scholar Zhang Fangping 張方平 (1007–1091) recalls the similar floral patterns in the Northern Song silk brocade used in issuing the governmental document; see He 2017, 21 (fig. 4); He ed. 2017, 51 (no. 2).

118 For more about the decorative paper in Asia, see Tsien 1985, 85–96, esp. 94; Yu 2021; Tōkyō Kokuritsu Hakubutsukan et al. 2023, esp. 52–53, 67–73, 76–87; Nezu Bijutsukan 2023, 111–36.

119 QYL 4: 8a. See also Tsien 1985, 94; He 2017, 13.

120 QYL 4: 8a.

121 The tools for pressing the paper to create embossed designs were referred to as "lustrous shell" (*beiguang* 貝光) in the Ming dynasty; see He 2017, 20–21. Tsuen-hsuin Tsien regarded such translucent designs "forerunners of the watermark." See Tsien 1985, 94.

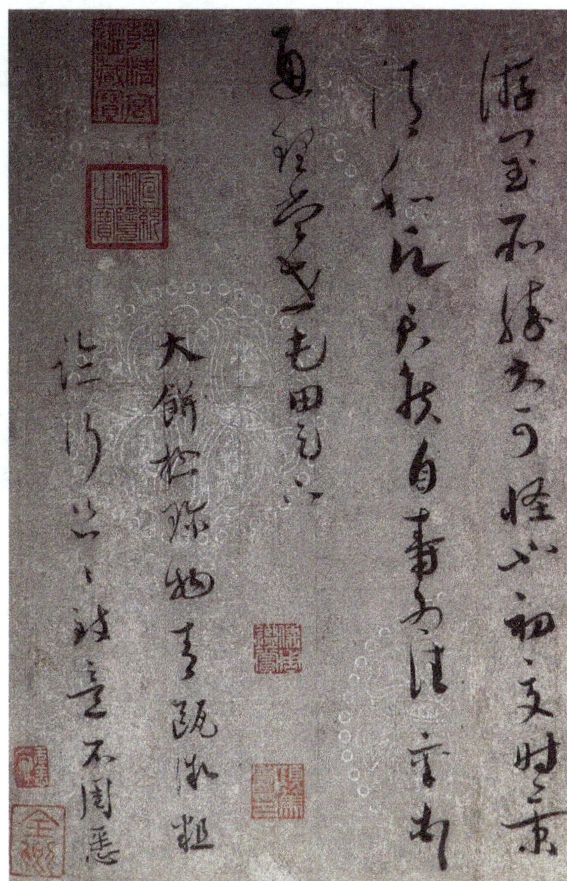

FIGURE 1.49
Detail. Digital photograph of the *Letter to Feng Jing of the State Farms Bureau* (*"Siyong"*) by Cai Xiang. 1051. Northern Song. Ink on decorative paper. Album leaf. National Palace Museum

incised or embossed designs in Song ceramics, reproduced by applying recyclable clay molds with carved designs.[122]

In practical application, when someone wrote on such a paper, the decorated part coated with lustrous substances would often resist the ink, leaving a semi-transparent quality of the brushstrokes. An excellent example is Su Shi's *Letter to Filial Gentleman Guo Tingping*, dated around 1075 and now at the National Palace Museum (fig. 1.44). Su wrote it on a piece of exquisite paper decorated with subtle geometric patterns, each unit showing a turtle in bird's-eye-view inside a hexagonal shape. While viewers may not discern the pale, silver gray graphic patterns at first glance,[123] digital photography after special image processing brings to light the astonishing lustrous grandeur

122 The Song decorative paper's subtle designs are especially comparable to the understated decorative aesthetics of the Ding ware 定窯 porcelains; see He 2017, 19.

123 For a plate, see He 2017, 65.

FIGURE 1.50 Detail. A Child's Coat with Ducks in Pearl Medallions. 700s. Iran or Central Asia, Sogdiana. Silk. The Cleveland Museum of Art

FIGURE 1.51 Yue ware plate with the incised design of paired butterflies. Liao. Stoneware. Discovered in the tomb of the Princess of the Chen kingdom and her husband, Inner Mongolia

of the design. The decorated surface in mica appears partially ink-resistant, making the calligraphic strokes superimposed on the decorative surface semi-translucent.[124]

4.1 *Ornamental Designs*

Echoing the variety made by Yao Yi, extant letter papers attest to a wide design repertoire that divides into two categories, ornamental (figs. 1.44, 1.45, 1.49) and pictorial (figs. 1.52).[125] While most extant specimens from the Northern Song are rendered in subtle and subdued tones, those from the Southern Song show designs in more discernible ways.[126] They reflect visual connections with designs in other media, including textiles, architecture, print, ceramics, jade, paintings, and so on.

Mainstream ornamental designs feature roundels, curvy botanical patterns, and other geometric structures. They often match weaving designs applied to silks and the ornamental patterns on carved doors and windows—a good example being the floral roundels of the letter paper used by Su Shi (fig. 1.45).

124 Cf. the original view of the work, reproduced in He 2017, 64–65. For more examples and discussions, see He 2017, 16.

125 This is based on the findings by He 2017, 19.

126 He 2017, 25.

They call to mind the decorative paper attached to a single-sheet print produced in the north during the eleventh-century under the Khitan Liao (figs. 1.46, 2.3). They also compare to the openwork architectural decors of a door panel, illustrated in the government-sponsored architectural handbook *Building Standards* (*Yingzao fashi* 營造法式), compiled by the architect-official Li Jie 李誡 (1035–1110), and published in 1103 (fig. 1.47).[127] Similar roundel designs are re-applied in the Southern Song frontispiece to the *Lotus Sutra* (fig. 1.48) printed in Hangzhou (see ch. 3 below).

Ornamental designs in Northern Song embossed decorative paper absorbed existing conventions from multiple media. The paper used by the calligrapher Cai Xiang 蔡襄 (1012–1067) to write a letter in 1051, for instance, is embossed with sparsely arranged roundels framed by pearl-like dots (fig. 1.49).[128] Digital photography with enhanced contrast reveals that each roundel contains a pair of butterflies. This elegant design combines multiple existing ornamental idioms. The pearl roundel convention can be traced to an earlier ornamental idiom, widely transmitted along the Silk Road in multiple media, including textiles (fig. 1.50),[129] paintings, ceramics, metal ware, and so on.[130] The paired butterflies were popular in the tenth and eleventh centuries, seen for example in the Yue ware plate discovered in the Liao tomb of Princess Chen and her husband in Inner Mongolia (fig. 1.51).[131]

---

127 Guo 1999; Steinhardt ed. 2002, 150–61; Xu 2017; Cheng 2010. Cf. a screen (unearthed from a Yuan tomb in Shanxi) bearing the similar designs; see Shoudu bowuguan 2016, 184.

128 This was the farewell letter to Feng Jing 馮京 (1021–1094), written by Cai Xiang when he was about to leave Hangzhou. For more details, see the catalogue entry of no. 4 in He 2017, 221.

129 According to the Cleveland Museum of Art, this child's coat with ducks in pearl medallions can be dated around the early eighth century. Its inner lining "is a twill damask with a floral pattern made in China. The combination of Sogdian and Chinese silks in one garment with Tibetan ownership history is evidence of the vital exchange and cultural interaction among the peoples living along the trade routes of the Silk Road." See The Cleveland Museum of Art, "Child's Coat with Ducks in Pearl Medallions," Collections, Accessed December 24, 2023. https://www.clevelandart.org/art/1996.2.1.

130 For more studies of the chained-pearl-roundels as decorative modes in multicultures, see Meister 1970; Bo 1990; Xu and Zhao 1991; Zhao 1995, 1997; Wu 1984, 1999; Sheng 1999; Compareti 2004; Whitfield 2018, 207–10; Xie and Zhu 2018. According to Jiang Boqin, the roundels depicted in Dunhuang cave temples feature hunters, winged horses, and birds; see Jiang 1994, 79–80.

131 For the excavation report, see Neimenggu wenwu 1987. Cf. the Liao jade pendant and the white ceramic plate, both found in the Liao pagoda in Zhaoyang 朝陽, Liaoning 遼寧. For plates, see Liaoning sheng wenwu et al. 2007, pl. 53.1; Beijing Liao Jin chengyuan bowuguan 2012, 55; Shoudu bowuguan 2018, 282.

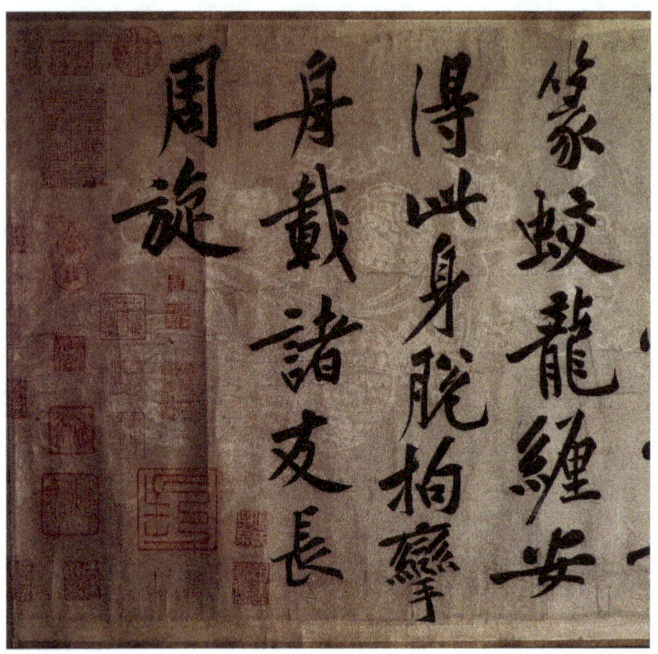

FIGURE 1.52 Detail. Digital photograph of the *Poem on the Hall of Pines and Wind* by Huang Tingjian. Northern Song. Ink on decorative paper. Handscroll. National Palace Museum

FIGURE 1.53 Detail. *Three Melons*. Song. Ink and colors on paper. Hanging scroll. National Palace Museum

FIGURE 1.54 Detail of a decorative paper. Edo period, Japan

4.2 *Pictorial Designs*

Song decorated letter paper embossed with picture-like designs is most exquisite. Extant specimens suggest that pictorial themes related to Song paintings, especially in the categories "flowers and birds" (*huaniao* 花鳥), "grass and insects" (*caochong* 草蟲), and "fruits and vegetables" (*shuguo* 蔬果). These constitute the largest group of paintings documented in Emperor Huizong's 徽宗 (r. 1100–1126) catalog. Their predecessors may have derived from simpler designs in earlier ceramics or metal wares.

Huang Tingjian's 黃庭堅 (1045–1105) *Poem on the Hall of Pines and Wind* (*Songfeng ge* 松風閣) (fig. 1.52), although well-known as a calligraphic masterpiece, is rarely examined from the perspective of its intricate paper.[132] It is among the finest Chinese papers decorated in gauze weaving patterns, visible only with special digital image processing.[133] Researchers have connected its

132 For more studies, see Wang C. 2005; He 2017, 16. The *Poem on the Hall of Pines and Wind* is now mounted with a frontispiece on gold-sprinkled paper, with hand-painted pictorial designs of two birds perching on floral branches; see He 2017, 167–68. A very similar sheet of paper was cut into pieces to make the Persian book of *Makhzan al-asrar* (*The Treasury of Secrets*), dated 1478, now in New York Public Library; see Yu 2021, 97–101, esp. figs. 3–4.

133 He 2017, 14–15, 23, 184. Huang himself once created pressed designs of reeds to his paper by using a woodblock. In 1104, when he was in exile in the remote Yizhou 宜州, Guangxi 廣西, he made decorated paper by himself with a block bearing the designs of reeds and geese (*luyan qianban* 蘆雁箋板) he received from his friend Danghuan 黨渙 and a

FIGURE 1.55 Ding Ware bowl with embossed designs. 12th–13th centuries. Song-Jin. Ceramic. National Palace Museum

FIGURE 1.56 Detail of a melon on the vine. Southern Song. Stone carving. Tomb of An Bing, Huaying, Sichuan

FIGURE 1.57 A plate with fruit designs. Southern Song. Gilt silver. Excavated in Taining, Fujian

melons-and-vines design to later paintings of similar themes. They include the anonymous painting representing three melons and vines (fig. 1.53), probably from the late thirteenth century, often linked with the so-called Biling 毘陵 school of professional paintings associated with the region of Changzhou 常州, Jiangsu,[134] and a melon painting by Qian Xuan 錢選 (1239–1299).[135] In spite of the overall similarity, the design on the decorative paper appears more graphic and two-dimensional than the melon painting, for the embossed melons and leaves show little overlap in contrast to their painted counterparts, which are juxtaposed in overlapping positions, suggesting hidden pictorial space.

The design of melons and vines on embossed paper enjoyed a long-lasting history and was even transmitted to Japan, where papermakers produced their own version.[136] An example is the hand copy of poetry extracted from thirty-six Heian poets printed in yellow mica on paper patched in various colors—a clear transformation of the subtle Song taste (fig. 1.54).[137]

Beyond painting, melons and vines appear also in tomb decors and ceramic and metal wares, symbolizing the prosperity of people's offspring.[138] This is most evident in a Ding 定 Ware dish dated to the Jin-Yuan period, pairing melons and vines with babies (fig. 1.55) and a stone relief (fig. 1.56) in the tomb of the Southern Song official An Bing 安丙 (1148–1221), found in Huaying 華鎣, Sichuan.[139] Other artifacts discovered in Fujian and Jiangsu (fig. 1.57) show that melon vines integrated with other auspicious fruit motifs, such as lychees and pomegranates as decoration on silver fruit-plates.[140] Such shared designs in porcelain, stone, and silverware go beyond what Jessica Rawson outlined in her earlier study, where she identified silverware as the stylistic and technological forerunner of porcelain all through the seventh to the fifteenth centuries.[141]

---

jade or crystal hammer as his paper-pressing tool. One may even speculate that Huang's choice of the letter paper reflects his personal liking of melon, as he once composed a poem inspired by tasting the melon in summer; see the poem entitled "Notes after Tasting the Melon" (*Shigua you gan* 食瓜有感) in SGSJZ, *waiji bu*, 4: 3–2; Yang 2010, 3: 108.

134 Most extant Biling paintings are in Japanese collections. For more studies of the Biling school paintings, see Shimada 1948; Miyazaki 1996.

135 Wang C. 2005, 9–15.

136 For a nineteenth-century Chinese multi-colored letter paper with melon decorations (East Asian library, University of Chicago), see Tsien 1985, 92 (fig. 1077).

137 Ishida 1961, 63.

138 Wang C. 2005, 11.

139 Yang 2010, 3: 107 (fig. 1–27). For more molded pictorial designs of the Song-Jin Ding Ware dishes and bowls, see Guoli gugong bowuyuan 2014, 194, 196, 200, 203, 206–209, 222–27, 237–39.

140 Yang 2010, 3: 108. For more about the objects excavated from the tomb of An Bing, see Sichuan sheng wenwu et al. 2008. Cf. a similar silver plate discovered in Jiangsu; for a drawing of the plate bearing the fruit decors, see Xiao and Wang 1986, 73 (fig. 4).

141 Rawson 1986.

5 Rubbings

Rubbings, traced by textual sources back to the Tang, had a direct impact on "the making of books by inked impressions from wood."[142] Filled with black ink in the background and today called "black tigers,"[143] they are a prime form of Chinese art. In fact, China was one of the earliest civilizations to take advantage of rubbings as a key means to transmit aesthetic beauty combined with knowledge and information.[144] Since most rubbings—typically calligraphic rather than pictorial—were reproduced from outdoor steles or stone carvings, whose surfaces tend to deteriorate or are damaged over time, they vary in the degree of visibility.[145] Still, they closely match woodblock prints in technique, but with some differences in execution.

5.1 *Early Calligraphic Rubbings*

In the mid-seventh century, the government established official positions for rubbing specialists (*tashu shou* 搨書手) in charge of issuing "authorized rubbings of inscriptions in stone."[146] Literary sources describe them as *daben* 打本, that is, "patted copies," and the technique as *da* 打 or *moda* 模打, literally "patting."[147] The process involves laying a piece of paper on an engraved surface, then pressing it tightly so that engraved indentations show through. Next, one uses a cloth-pad loaded with sand or heavy powder and dipped in ink to pat through the paper surface until all the "background" of the engraved content turns black. This singles out the engraved content: because it is below the surface of the inked paper, it remains free from ink and stands out in white.

Early rubbings are treasured for their value of preserving the calligraphy of famous masters. They are, however, "second-hand" reproductions, since they

142 Carter 1955, 19.

143 For an introduction to Chinese rubbings, see Starr 2008.

144 The making of rubbings in the West is a relatively recent phenomenon traceable to the nineteenth century. For the rubbings of tombstones in New England, see Gillon 1981.

145 For a theoretical study of the materiality and historicity of Chinese rubbings, see Wu 2003. For more about the making processes and materiality of steles and rubbings, see Luo 2023, 137–49, 244–77.

146 XTS, zhi 47: 1210; zhi 49: 1294. See also Carter 1955, 20, 23 (endnote 6). For a new study of the Tang scribes, see Zhou 2020.

147 For Tang-Song documentations of the term "moda," see T50.2053: 269b; MZML 6: 18; YLMC 6: 106. For the term "daben," see the imperial order dated 725 regarding the issuing of the rubbing of the stele newly erected in Mt. Hua; see XTS, 27: 12a; THY 27: 520. Also, see the reference of the "daben" of the *Stone Classics in Three Scripts* (*Santi shijing* 三體石經) in four pieces of paper, recorded in Dou Ji's 竇臮 commentary (dated 775) on *Xu shufu* 述書賦 in QTW 447: 4561–2.

a

b

FIGURES 1.58A–B Details. The *Diamond Sutra* (Pelliot chinois 4503). 824. Tang. Rubbing. Handscroll. Bibliothèque nationale de France

are impressions taken from engraved copies and not carved by the calligrapher himself. The Dunhuang library cave yielded three specimens, all attributed to famous masters of the Tang.[148] The rubbings of the *Diamond Sutra* (figs. 1.58a–b), now mounted as a handscroll, bear the date of 824 and preserve the signature of the calligrapher Liu Gongquan 柳公權 (778–865) as well as the names of the engravers Qiang Yan 強演 and Shao Jianhe 邵建和.[149] They reflect Tang imperial connections, Liu Gongquan being "the most productive court calligrapher of Buddhist texts" in the ninth century; the two engravers served as Officials of Engraved Jade Books (Yuce guan 玉冊官) under the Imperial Secretariat (Zhongshu sheng 中書省).[150] Truncated Chinese characters marking the incomplete sequence of the text, such as the fifth (fig. 1.58b), seventh, ninth, and twelfth, found in various sections of the rubbings, may refer to their original numbered text-bearing slabs.[151]

The Northern Song court applied rubbing techniques to the production of "engraved model-letters compendia" (*fatie* 法帖).[152] The process involved engraving individual characters "cropped" or selected from a wide range of famous calligraphic works onto a hard surface, such as wood blocks or stone slabs, making rubbings from them, then cutting and remounting the latter into book form. The now-lost imperial compendium of the *Model Letters in the Chunhua Archives* (*Chunhua ge tie* 淳化閣帖), published at the court of Emperor Taizong 太宗 (r. 976–997) in 992 and named after his Chunhua 淳化 reign (990–995), represents the earliest example of this sort. The compendium supposedly was "engraved in wooden plates in ten volumes."[153] Later manuals were largely engraved on stone surfaces, such as the *Daguan Manual of Model*

---

148 Cf. the *Hot Spring Inscription* (*Wenquan ming* 溫泉銘) accredited to Emperor Taizong 太宗 (r. 626–649), whose inscription bears the date of 653 (Pelliot chinois 4508). For more studies, see Chen 1958; Carter 1955, 20, 23 (endnote 5); Pelliot 1953, 21–24. The other rubbings discovered in Dunhuang, the *Inscription for the Reliquary Stupa in Honor of the Yi Master from the Huadu Monastery* (*Huadusi guseng Yi chanshi shelita ming* 化度寺故僧邕禪師舍利塔銘), mounted as a booklet, were taken from a seventh-century stele (engraved in 631) transferring the writings of the calligrapher Ouyang Xun 歐陽詢 (557–641). These rubbings are now divided between the The Bibliothèque nationale de France (P. 4510) and the British Library (Or.8210 S.5791).

149 Tsui 2014, 242; Cheng 2008, 84–86. Some scholars treat this rubbing as a ninth-century object, others are more dubious about its Tang date. For more studies, see Starr 2008, 15; Onoe and Shimonaka, 1954–1968, 171; Monnet 2004, 49–50; Luo 2023, 245.

150 Cheng 2008, 79–80, 86; Tsui 2014, 242–43.

151 I thank Shi Rui of Beijing University for his insight.

152 McNair 1994 (esp. 209), 1995.

153 The manual assembles more than 400 characters retrieved from some one hundred calligraphers. For more studies of the Song model letters, see McNair 1994, 209–25 (for Wang Zhu, see 210); 1995, 106–109. Most extant rubbings "were actually taken from re-engravings done in the Ming and Qing dynasties." See McNair 1994, 210 (footnote 4).

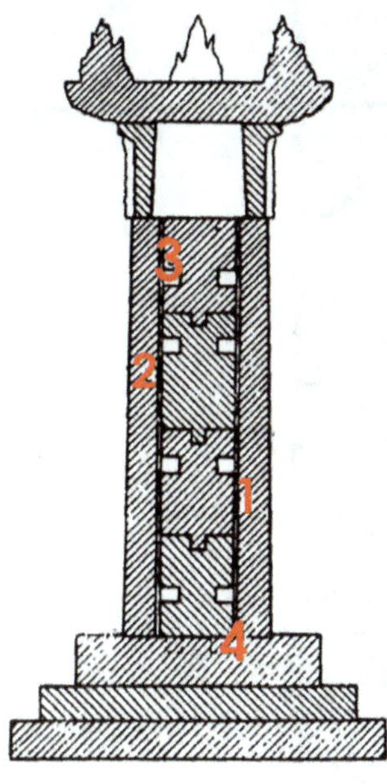

DIAGRAM 1.1
Diagram indicating the locations of the deposited artifacts found inside the stele of the *Classic of Filial Piety on the Stone Platform*
1. Location of the rubbing of the *Preface to the Buddhist Canon* by Huairen
2. Location of the single-sheet print of *Dongfang Shuo Stealing the Peaches*
3. Location of the fragmented documents in Jurchen script
4. Location of the Jin coins that bear "Zhenglong yuanbao." Reconfigured after Liu and Zhu 1979, 1 (detail of fig. 1)

Letters (*Daguan tie* 大觀帖) compiled during the Daguan 大觀 reign (1107–1110) under Emperor Huizong in 1109. Woodblocks are still used in the same fashion today.

Even though both rubbing making and printing may use wood as primary material for engraving and paper for impression, the former process is more complex and time-consuming, and also involves certain differences in execution.[154] Table 1.1 illustrates the similarities and differences between rubbing (*ta* 拓) and printing (*yin*). Unlike printing blocks, where content is engraved in a mirror image and often in relief, the matrix for rubbings shows the text straight and executes content in intaglio style, that is, incised below the surface of the hard material (*yinke*). In rubbings, moreover, the paper or impression-to-be is placed on top of the engraved surface, with its front facing up; in woodblock printing, it is placed with its front facing down and touching the engraved surface.[155] Ink, moreover, is applied to different places: in rubbings, it is directly patted onto the front of the paper, while in woodblocks it is applied to the surface of the carved block.

154 Tsien 1985, 143; Carter 1955, 19.

155 In the case of a rubbing, "the direction of the text on the paper is the same as that on the stone from which it is taken." See Carter 1955, 19.

FIGURE 1.59
Preface to the Buddhist Canon. Jin. Rubbing. Discovered inside the Stele Compound bearing the *Classic of Filial Piety* by Tang Emperor Xuanzong engraved in 745. Stele Forest, Xi'an

TABLE 1.1 Comparison of rubbing and printing

	Rubbing (*ta*)	Printing (*yin*)
Matrix	Stone or wood	Wood
End product material	Paper	Paper
Characters engraved	Regular	Mirror image (or reverse)
Carving style	Carve the content (*yinke*)	Carve out the part that is not the content (*yangke*) [not always]
Placement of the front side of the paper in relation to the engraved surface	Face up	Face down
Where the ink is applied	The front side of the paper	The surface of the cut block

The Stele Forest (Beilin 碑林) in Xi'an is a fruitful site for the study of steles and rubbings,[156] especially a four-sided stele compound known as the *Classic of Filial Piety on the Stone Platform* (*Pingtai xiaojing* 石台孝經). It includes four limestone slabs on four sides connected by a central pillar; each slab is 125 cm wide and 590 cm high.[157] During repairs in 1973, specialists discovered historical artifacts inside the object (diagram 1.1).[158] Among them is a rubbing of the *Preface to the Buddhist Canon* (*Shengjiao xu* 聖教序), written in Wang Xizhi's calligraphy and assembled by the Tang monk Huairen 懷仁 (fig. 1.59); it is based on a separate Tang stele, now also in the Forest. Dated by scholars to the Jin or Song period, it was folded and deposited in the mid-section behind

156 The Stele Forest as a site assembling steles can be traced to the Northern Song period under the reign of Emperor Huizong. By the end of Northern Song, there were more than forty stone carvings and steles of Tang and Song periods assembled in the Stele Forest. For the history of the Stele Forest, see Lu 1998, esp. 94.

157 For more detailed measurements of the stele compound, see Liu and Zhu 1979, 1. Cf. the measurements reported in Lu 1998, 46. The placement of the stele compound in the pavilion along the axis of the Stele Forest may be traced to the thirteenth century. This is based on the stele (*Dayuanguo Jingzhao fu chongxiu Xuanshengmiao ji* 大元國京兆府重修宣聖廟記; this was carved on the opposite side of the Song stele referred to as *Xingqing chi xieyan shi* 興慶池楔宴詩) dated 1273, also in the Stele Forest; see Lu 1998, 131. Prior to its relocation to the central axis of the Stele Forest, the stele compound may have been displayed in a Confucian Temple (Wenmiao) nearby; see Lu 1998, 103–104.

158 For a report, see Liu and Zhu 1979.

a b

FIGURES 1.60A–B Rubbings of a Buddho-Daoist Stele. Northern Song. National Museum of Asian Art
a. Stele with Buddhist and Daoist texts inscribed by Yuan Zhengji. 968
b. Stele with Daoist Triad and Daoist Scriptures transcribed by Pang Renxian. 980

the north-facing stele (marked as 1 in diagram 1.1). Although the rubbing is a one-piece artifact, it is made of multiple pieces of paper pieced together.[159]

159 According to Qi Gong, it is more likely a Jin rather than a Song rubbing; see Zhang 1979, 78–79; Qi 1999. Cf. Luo 2023, 155–57. The engraved texts on the stele include not only the preface, written by the Tang emperor Taizong, but also a follow-up essay by Xuanzang thanking the emperor, as well as the *Heart Sutra*. Multiple Northern Song versions of the rubbings of Huairen's Preface are all cut and remounted into manuals. Compared to these Northern Song extant rubbings, the stele-size rubbing discovered inside the stele compound indicates minor damage of selected characters, suggesting that it was made after the Northern Song. That it still preserves the complete text suggests that the rubbing was made prior to the time when the upper part of the stele was broken.

5.2 *Book-Form Steles for Rubbing-Making*

Also in the Stele Forest is a double-sided Buddho-Daoist stele engraved in 968 on one side (Fig. 1.60a; Table 1.2) and in 980 on the other (Fig. 1.60b; Table 1.3).[160] It assembles multiple Buddhist and Daoist texts, with a layout that departs from the conventional stele format, where the engraved text runs vertically from top to bottom. Here the texts are laid out in multiple registers, each resembling the layout of a book, so that lines contain eleven to fourteen characters. Its overall format recalls the textual layout of the *Diamond Sutra* rubbing scroll (fig. 1.58b).[161] Three out of five texts bear frontispiece-like illustrations preceding the texts; their illustrators were also noted in the stone inscriptions (Tables 1.2–1.3).

The earliest extant stone carving with multi-register layout is the imperially-sponsored *Stone Classic of the Kaicheng Reign* (*Kaicheng shijing* 開成石經), completed in 837. Relocated to the Stele Forest by the time the Buddho-Daoist stele was created, it refers to a large corpus of classical texts engraved in elegant regular script on 114 double-sided stele-sized stone slabs.[162] Each slab divides into eight registers from top to bottom, and each line contains ten characters—most likely matching the size of an open book page. Having texts engraved facilitates mass production by rubbings, made with sheets of hand-made paper placed on the stone surface register by register; they could then be cut and remounted into book format. This connection between steles and printed books echoes Rong Xinjiang's study, where he calls attention to selected Dunhuang manuscripts that transcribe the contents of Tang steles.[163]

Compared to the ninth-century *Stone Classic of the Kaicheng Reign*, the book-inspired design of the tenth-century double-sided Buddho-Daoist Stele is even more pronounced. One example is the side engraved in 968 (fig. 1.61a). It divides evenly into five registers, each demarcated by border lines on the top and bottom, quite like those in a printed book. Their height is about 25 cm and their width less than 64 cm—the same as a sheet of paper before folding for a typical string-bound book.[164]

First at the top is the Buddhist *Mārīcī Sutra Preached by the Buddha* (*Foshuuo Molizhitian jing* 佛說摩利支天經), complete with a picture engraved to the right of the first register. The placement of the illustration recalls the format of

160 For the rubbing, see Beijing tushuguan jinshizu 1989, 37: 19. For a recent study, see Li S. 2012 (cf. his table in 254).

161 Each line of the text of the *Diamond Sutra* rubbing scroll contains eleven characters.

162 XABLQJ 107: 14–15.

163 Rong 2017. For the Dunhuang "composite" manuscript (P. 3720), certain sections of the scroll were copied after the inscriptions of the steles; see Galambos 2016b, 366, 369.

164 For the illustration, see ZGMSQJ, *Huihua pian* 13: 69 (fig. 60). For a sample of the border lines marked as "I" and "H" in the standard format of a Chinese printed book in Edgren 2007, 98.

TABLE 1.2 The front side of a Buddho-Daoist Stele engraved in 968

	Foshuo *Molizhitian jing* 佛說摩利支天經	***Huangdi yinfu jing*** 黃帝陰符經
Date of Engraving	The tenth month of 968	The eleventh month of 968
Calligrapher	Yuan Zhengji 袁正己	Yuan Zhengji 袁正己
Illustrator	Li Fenggui 李奉珪	Zhai Shousu 翟守素
Carver	An Renzuo 安仁祚	An Renzuo 安仁祚
Donors	Xu Zhishun 徐知舜 (primary sponsor) Liu Zhina (stone donor) 劉知訥 Fan Youyong 樊有永 and Fan Yousui 樊有遂	Wang Nengchu 王能處 (primary sponsor) Liu Zhina 劉知訥 (stone donor) Fan Youyong 樊有永 and Fan Yousui 樊有遂
Stele Location	Guozi jian 國子監	

TABLE 1.3 The back side of a Buddho-Daoist Stele engraved in 980

	Taishang laojun chang qingjing jing 太上老君常清靜經	*Taishang shengxuan huming jing* 太上昇玄消災護命經	*Taishang tianzun shuo shengtian dedao jing* 太上天尊說生天得道經
Date of Engraving	The second month of 980	The 15th day of the third month of 980	The 21st day of the third month of 980
Calligrapher	Pang Renxian 龐仁顯	Pang Renxian 龐仁顯	(none)
Illustrator	Bai Tingcan 白廷璨	(none)	(none)
Carver	An Wencan 安文璨	An Wencan 安文璨	(none)
Donors	Daoist Huang Xuanzhi 黃玄之 Daoist Liu Shousu 劉守素 Nine members of the Buxu Society Other thirty-eight donors	Liu She 劉陟 Fan Youyong 樊有永	(none)
Stele Location	Xuansheng miao 宣聖廟		

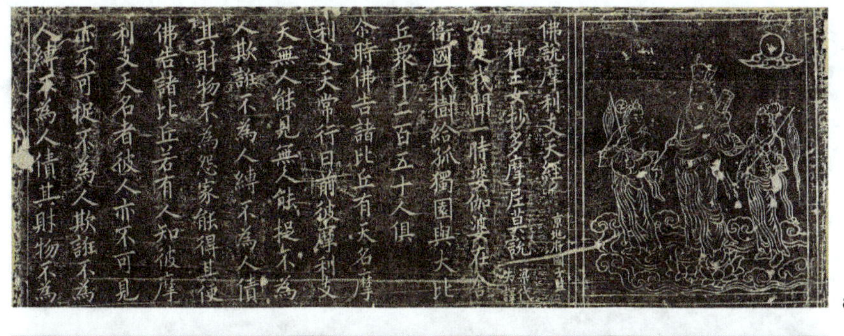

a

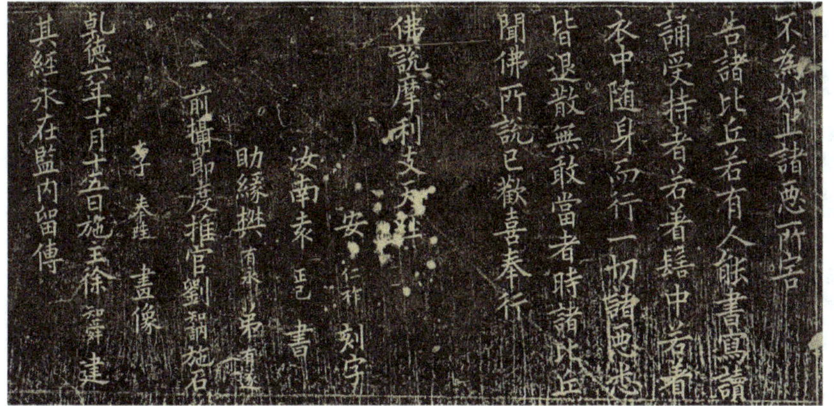

b

FIGURES 1.61A–B Details of 1.60a. Stele with Buddhist and Daoist texts inscribed by Yuan Zhengji. 968. Rubbing. National Museum of Asian Art

a frontispiece in textual printing. It depicts the fan-holding goddess Mārīcī and her two attendants processing in the clouds under a bird-bearing sun shown in the upper right corner.[165] The text reads from right to left, continues into the second register, and ends in the third, with eleven characters per line. The colophon (fig. 1.61b) at the end names the calligrapher Yuan Zhengji 袁正己, the frontispiece illustrator Li Fenggui 李奉珪, the carver An Renzuo 安仁祚, a Sogdian descendent whose other family members were also stone carvers,[166]

165 Cf. the Dunhuang illustration reproduced in Li S. 2012, 242 (fig. 5). Lee Yu-min sorts the visual and textual sources concerning the representations of Mārīcī from Tang-Song China as well as from the Xi Xia and Dali kingdoms; see Lee 2014, 7–29. While Lee tends to see the Mārīcī in the Song rubbing more of a continuity of the Dunhuang iconography (see Lee 2014, 15, 21), Li Song highlights the difference between the Dunhuang Mārīcī paintings and the Mārīcī engraving on Buddho-Daoist stele (Li S. 2012, 239–44).

166 Ai Xun's M.A. thesis documents three generations of the An family, all stone carvers active in the Wuwei and Xi'an areas. An Wenzuo belonged to the second generation, and An

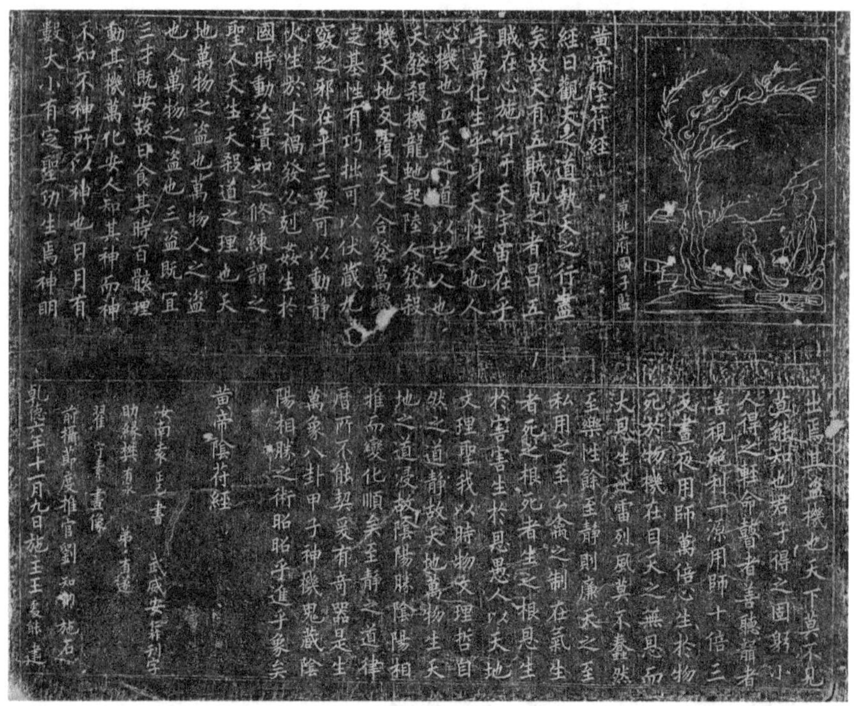

FIGURE 1.62 Detail of fig. 1.60a. Stele with Buddhist and Daoist texts inscribed by Yuan Zhengji. 968. Rubbing. National Museum of Asian Art

and donors led by Xu Zhishun 徐知舜 (Table 1.2).[167] Inscriptions both in the title and at the end of the colophon identify the National University (*Guozi jian* 國子監) in Jingzhao Prefecture (*Jingzhao fu* 京兆府; modern Xi'an), as its place of installation.

Following the *Mārīcī Sutra* is the *Yellow Emperor's Scripture of Hidden Contracts* (*Huangdi yinfu jing* 黃帝陰符經), also written by Yuan Zhengji and carved by An Renzuo; it runs from the fourth to the fifth registers (fig. 1.62).[168] This short Daoist text expounds the concept of cosmic forces and principles as well as "their seen or unseen influences in the human world."[169] It was later

Wencan 安文璨, who carved the back side of the same stele in 980, belonged to the third generation. See Ai 2020, esp. 13. I am grateful for Xin Wen's valuable insight and generous sharing of this M.A. thesis.

167 Cf. Li S. 2012, 254.

168 For the illustration, see ZGMSQJ, *Huihua pian* 13: 68 (fig. 59). The engraved text comes in the longer (*Huangdi yinfu jing*, DZ 31, 1: 821) and the shorter versions. For more studies, see Reiter 1984; Xiao 1996b; Louis 2012, 331.

169 See Florian C. Reiter's introduction to this text in Schipper and Verellen 2004, 320–21.

important in the Complete Perfection (Quanzhen 全真) school.[170] Aside from its Daoist nature, the text is often classified as military, possibly because it deals with martial arts of strengthening troops and fighting to victory.[171] As a result, the text appealed to rulers and political leaders.[172] This may explain why the opening of the engraved text includes a notation that states "National University of Jingzhao Prefecture" (Jingzhao fu Guozijian 京兆府國子監), indicating that it was displayed at the school.[173]

Like the *Mārīcī Sutra*, which has an illustration proceeding the text, the *Yellow Emperor's Scripture* bears a frontispiece-like illustration, this time by Zhai Shousu 翟守素 (fig. 1.61a). It depicts two figures seated under a tree against the background of distant mountains. The figures' positioning suggests a master-disciple relationship, as one is an older man seated on a rock and holding a staff, the other a scholar in a long robe with loose sleeves who is kneeling and bowing before the first. A zither, a stage prop often associated with scholarly self-cultivation, rests on the ground. As explained by many Ming-Qing writers, the scenario may reflect the story of the Yellow Emperor asking the immortal Guangchengzi 廣成子 about Dao in the mountains.[174]

The engraved illustration is among the earliest examples of the so-called *Picture of Asking about Dao* (*Wendao tu* 問道圖), a meme that depicts a scholarly disciple conversing with an elderly master. The meme was transmitted in both Daoism and Buddhism, as evident in the Southern Song painting by Ma Gongxian's 馬公顯 depiction of the scholar official Li Ao 李翱 conversing with

170 For the various Song-Jin-Yuan commentaries, see Schipper and Verellen 2004, 691–700.

171 Schipper and Verellen 2004, 320.

172 The Khitan Liao King of Dongdan 東丹王 (also known as Li Zanhua 李贊華 or Yelü Bei 耶律倍, 899–937), for example, owned a copy of the *Scripture of the Hidden Contrast* in his collection of books on Daoism and medicine. See Huang 2014a, 1011–12; Louis 2012, 331. For a study of Li Zanhua's biography, see Louis 2012. It is also likely that as a military leader he found the content dealing with the martial arts of strengthening the troops and fighting victoriously particularly appealing; see Huang 2014a, 2012.

173 In a similar vein, the other stele dated 966, which was also erected in the National University in Song Xi'an, bears the engraved text by the famous artist Guo Zhongshu 郭忠恕 (?–977) in seal script, clerical script, and ancient small script. Li Song mentioned a model letter manual based on the *Yinfu jing* transcribed by Ouyang Xiu 歐陽修 (dated 637); see Li S. 2012, 245.

174 Some Ming and Qing writers identified the image as the Yellow Emperor consulting the Dao with the Daoist Guangchengzi; see SMJH 5: 10685; SY 4: 124–25. 181; Gao et al. 1999, 26: 2633–42. Li Song offers a different reading of the iconography, supporting the Qing writer Bi Yuan 畢沅 (1781) to identify the illustration as the story of the "Encounter between Li Quan and the Old Mother of Mt. Li" (*Li Quan yu Lishan laomu* 李荃遇驪山老母), see Li S. 2012, 237–38, 244–49. Li cites two visual features as his main evidence for this argument. First, he identifies the Li-Guo style old tree with knots and angular twigs as the representation of fire or flame; second, he sees the old man seated on the rock as an old woman.

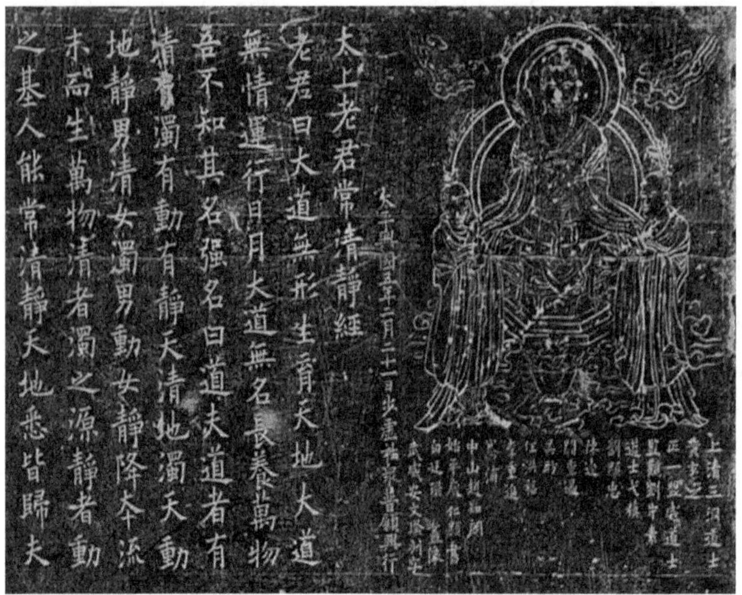

FIGURE 1.63 Detail of fig. 1.60b. Daoist *Scripture of Constant Clarity and Stillness, as Spoken by the Most High Lord Lao*. 980. Northern Song. Rubbing. National Museum of Asian Art

the Chan master Yaoshan 藥山, a theme associated with this Buddhist school,[175] and the Yuan mural decorating the tomb of the Daoist Feng Daozhen 馮道真 in Datong 大同, Shanxi.[176]

The book-inspired format continues on the back of the stele engraved in 980 (fig. 1.63). It lists three Daoist texts that share a frontispiece-like illustration in the beginning, designed by the otherwise unknown painter Bai Tingcan 白廷璨 (Table 1.3).[177] The iconic triad features the Most High Lord Lao (*Taishang laojun* 太上老君) seated frontally in the center and two attendants flanking his sides.[178] This iconic presence of Lord Lao in the frontispiece is particularly fitting for the first text to the left of the illustration: the *Scripture of Constant Clarity and Stillness of the Most High Lord Lao* (*Taishang laojun chang qingjing jing* 太上老君常清靜經), a highly popular Daoist text.[179] The

175 The painting is now in the Nanzenji collection, Kyoto, Japan. For a plate, see Fong 1992, 268 (fig. 112).

176 Huang 2014a, 157, 200 (fig. 38).

177 Huang 2014a, 1021–22.

178 For more stylistic analysis of the triad, see Li S. 2012, 249–51.

179 The text blends the worldview of the *Daode jing* with the practice of Daoist observation of the self, others, and the mind to obtain the Dao. Cf. DZ 620; for an English translation

layout spreads across four registers, each line containing thirteen or fourteen characters. Matching the front of the stele, the text follows a book-like format, although calligrapher, carver, and donors are different (Table 1.3). The inscriptions below the illustration indicate that the carving was supported by a Daoist group known as Pacing the Void Society (*Buxu she* 步虛社), led by two priests (*daoshi* 道士).[180] The stele was initially carved to serve as a model for mass production rubbings as made clear in the inscription: "Members of the Pacing the Void Society wish to distribute [the carved material] to the public" (*buxu shezhong puyuan xing xing* 步虛社眾普願興行).[181]

In sum, the Buddho-Daoist stele provides important material evidence of book-form steles or stone carvings coming in vogue during the Tang and Song periods. Steles, in other words, were the matrix for the reproduction of rubbings, which, after further cutting and remounting often were transformed into a book.

5.3 *Illustrated Rubbings Mounted in Albums*

Engraved images were similarly reproduced through rubbings. Zhang Yanyuan 張彥遠 (815–ca. 875), in his *Records of Famous Paintings of All Dynasties*, notes that people in the past enjoyed "making rubbings from paintings" (*tahua* 拓畫).[182] In the Song, there were also "compiled manuals of pictorial rubbings" (*huatie* 畫帖).[183] For example, Zeng Hongfu 曾宏父, a Southern Song scholar official from Luling 廬陵, Jiangxi 江西, compiled a two-volume manual of pictorial rubbings in 1237–1252. This was part of his great endeavor to put together over forty volumes of calligraphic rubbings, known as the *Rubbing Manual of the Phoenix Villa* (*Fengshu tie* 鳳墅帖).[184] Exclusively featuring Song

---

of this scripture, see Kohn 1993a, 25–29. On the imperial level, Patricia Ebrey points out that Emperor Huizong once bestowed a copy of the scripture transcribed by himself on his beloved Daoist priest Liu Hunkang 劉混康 (1036–1108) as a farewell gift upon Liu's return to Mt. Mao 茅山 after his first stay in the capital in 1102. Founders of Complete Perfection identified it as one of the major reference texts required for adepts' daily practice. For more studies of this scripture, and its reception in Liao-Song-Yuan China, see Huang 2014a, 1021–22.

180 They were Huang Xuanzhi 黃玄之, the Priest of the Highest Clarity Three Cavern (Shangqing sandong daoshi 三清三洞道士), and Liu Shousu, with the rank of Covenant of Orthodox Unity (Zhengyi mengwei daoshi 正一盟威道士).

181 For more documentation of the members of the Daoist community recorded in this stele, see Li S. 2012, 249–50, 254–55.

182 LDMHJ 2: 127a.

183 SKPX, 2: 7–8. Cf. Aimi 1955, 65.

184 For a new study of the *Rubbing Manual of the Phoenix Villa*, see Shih 2023, 75–110. An incomplete of twelve volumes of the *Fengshu tie* in the Shanghai Library collection

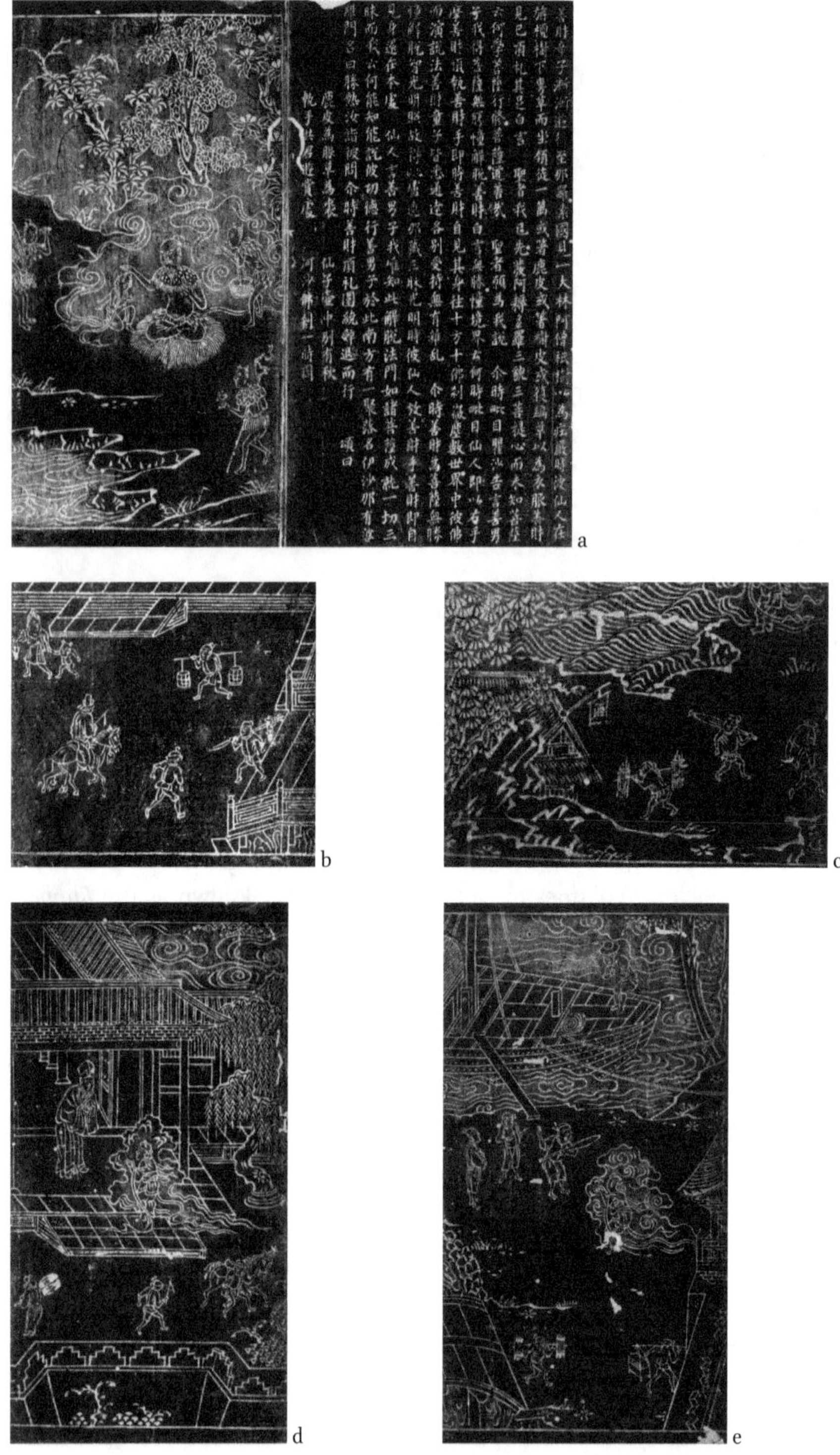

FIGURES 1.64A–E Details. *Illustrated Sutra of Sudhana's Pilgrimage as Described in the Avatamsaka Sutra*. Song. Rubbings. Album

men of letters, the original stone engravings were installed in the Phoenix Mountain Academy (*Fengshan shuyuan* 鳳山書院) in Jizhou 吉州, Jiangxi.[185] The now-lost pictorial rubbings feature *Ink Play of the Xuanhe Reign* (*Xuanhe moxi* 宣和墨戲), *Painting of the Rain-praying Ritual in the Wind* (*Fengyu tu* 風雩圖) by Wu Daozi 吳道子, and the twelve-section *Pictures of the Nine Songs* (*Jiuge tu* 九歌圖) by Li Boshi 李伯時 [Li Gonglin 李公麟].[186]

A rare Song specimen of illustrated rubbings mounted in album form is the *Illustrated Sutra of Sudhana's Pilgrimage as Described in the Avatamsaka Sutra* (*Huayan ru fajie pin Shancai canwen bianxiang jing* 華嚴入法界品善財參問變相經) (figs. 1.64a–g), inspired by widely circulating literature pertinent to this sacred text.[187] Since its appearance in a Chinese auction in 2014, it has gained wider attention, receiving enthusiastic endorsements by experts from various fields. They have recognized it as an authentic Northern Song work, likely dated from the late eleventh to the early twelfth centuries. The extant illustrations represent the first portion of the original program. It contains an incomplete collection of twenty-eight illustrations, part of the original fifty-four, plus accompanying texts featuring narrative depictions of Sudhana's visits to fifty-three sages.[188]

The rubbings were probably reproduced from an engraved stone model, whose pictorial designs were copied from an original set of illustrations, painted by a Chan monk associated with the Yanqingsi 延慶寺 (Monastery of Extended Felicitations) in Jiangxi and well connected to the scholarly circle of the time. He is called Master Zhong (*Zhong shangren* 忠上人, *Zhong shi* 忠師), the Old Man from Yanqing (Yanqing lao 延慶老), or Zhong from Yanqing (Yanqing Zhong 延慶忠) in several Northern Song colophons, written by well-known scholar officials such as Zhang Shangying 張商英 (1043–1122), Huang Tingjian, and Su Che 蘇轍 (1039–1112). This suggests that these Song

preserves such calligraphic samples by Huang Tingjian, Yue Fei 岳飛, Fan Chengda, and so on. For the plates, see Qi and Wang 2002.

185 SKPX, 2: 7–8.

186 Aimi 1955, 65.

187 For classic studies, see Aimi 1954; Aimi 1955; Fontein 1967, esp. 40–52. For more about the paintings of the Child Sudhana's visits to sages, see Chen Junji 2012a–b.

188 The album's circulation in Japan may be traced back to the Southern Song period around the 1250s. This is indirectly supported by documentation in Japan, which indicates that Monk Shinkai 心海 copied part of the text from the original set of the rubbings in 1251, and acknowledged that the original set, which belonged to the monk Kanryōbō 觀良房 of the Chisoku-in 知足庵 temple, was brought back from China by Monk Shōgambō 聖願房; see Aimi 1954, 3, 6; Fontein 1967, 40; Shao and Li 2015, 45–46, 52.

FIGURE 1.65
Rubbing of a tomb engraving copied after a painting by Li Gonglin (dated 1090). Yuan. The tomb of Zheng Ze, Luoyang, Henan

FIGURE 1.66 Detail. *Up the River during Qingming Days*. Northern Song. Ink and color on silk. Handscroll. The Palace Museum, Beijing

scholars saw Master Zhong's original paintings in the late eleventh century and regarded him as a revered member of their circle.[189]

189 These colophons, now lost in their original form, were recorded in a text copied by a thirteenth-century Japanese monk. They were retrieved from *Wu xiang zhishi song* 五相知識頌, which was thought to be included in the original work. For a full transcription of the colophons and eulogies, see Shao and Li 2015, 45; for English translations, see Fontein 1967, 42–44. For more on Master Zhong, see Aimi 1954, 4–5; Aimi 1955, 60–62. For a study of Master Zhong, see Zhang X. 2019.

Su Che compared Master Zhong's style to that of the scholar-painter Li Gonglin 李公麟 (1049–1106), whose now-lost multiple paintings based on the *Avatamsaka Sutra* were once in Emperor Huizong's imperial collection.[190] One can surmise the stylistic connection between the two by comparing Master Zhong's rubbings (figs. 1.64b) with an unusual Yuan tomb engraving (fig. 1.65), copied after Li's hanging scroll painting. The tomb engraving surprisingly preserves Li's signature dated 1090 and a poem originally inscribed by Su Shi.[191]

The "Y-shaped" trees in Master Zhong's rubbing (fig. 1.64d) also recall a similar rendition in Li's attributed painting, the *Classic of Filial Piety* (fig. 2.56), executed in plain linear drawing (*baimiao* 白描) style. Furthermore, the minute architectural, naval, and figural (figs. 1.64b–e) motifs in Master Zhong's rubbings are similar to designs in the Northern Song painting widely referred to as *Up the River during Qingming Days* (*Qingming shanghe tu* 清明上河圖; fig. 1.66), although those in the rubbings tend to be rather angular, simpler, and more schematic.[192] Master Zhong's artistic legacy may have also been transmitted in Chan Buddhist circles of the Southern Song. His compositional scheme of a wine shop with a flying banner (fig. 1.64c), depicted behind the protruding rocks along the river shore, compares closely to the splash-ink landscape handscroll painting, *Returning Sails off Distant Shore* (*Yuanpu guifan* 遠浦歸帆) attributed to the Chan monk-painter Muxi 牧谿 who was active in the thirteenth century.[193] The backing paper of the album bears a temple stamp that reads, "Great Canon of the Dongchan Monastery" (*Dongchan dazang* 東禪大藏), indicating that the paper may have been recycled from the Northern Song Chongning 崇寧 Canon, printed in the Dongchansi 東禪寺 (Eastern Meditation Monastery) in Fujian.[194]

In many ways the rubbing album stands at the crossroad of painting, rubbings, and printing. Its being transferred originally from a painting by Master Zhong points to a direct connection between rubbing and painting. The nuanced inking technique skillfully applied to various details throughout the album supports this further. The episode illustrating Sudhana's visit to an immortal (fig. 1.64a), "seated on straw at the foot of sandalwood tree and clad

190 Shao and Li 2015, 45; Fontein 1967, 44; Aimi 1955, 61.

191 This is from the tomb of Zheng Ze 鄭擇, whose ancestor Zheng Juzhong 鄭居中 (1059–1123) was Li Gonglin's younger colleague in Kaifeng; see Chen and Zhao 1991, 99; Hsu Y. 2021, 130, 161 (fig. 9).

192 For a study of the furniture motifs, see Shao and Li 2014.

193 The painting is in the Kyoto National Museum collection. For a plate, see Nezu Bijutsukan 2004, no. 64.

194 The character "dong" 東 is missing from the damaged stamp; see Aimi 1954, 7. Jan Fontein even speculated that the album may be printed in the same temple; see Fontein 1967, 46.

FIGURE 1.64F Detail. *Illustrated Sutra of Sudhana's Pilgrimage as Described in the Avatamsaka Sutra*. Song. Rubbings. Album

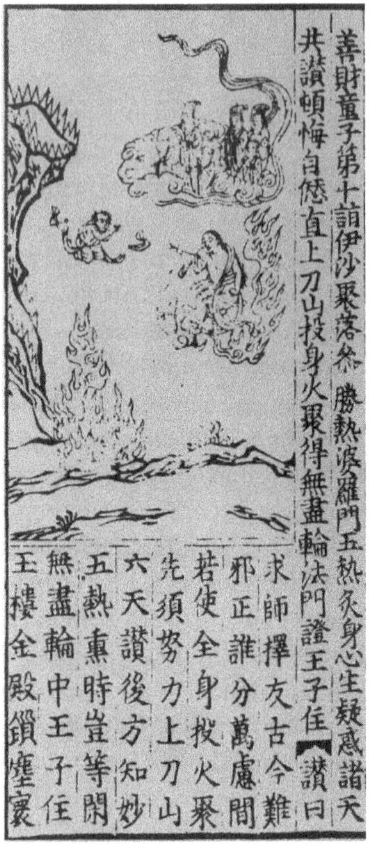

FIGURE 1.67 Detail. *Illustrated Eulogies by Mañjuśrī*. Southern Song. Woodblock print. Concertina. Otani University Library

in the bark of trees," offers a good example.[195] The ink applied in the waterscape in the foreground, as well as the clouds surrounding the sage and the tree in the background, is lighter than that found elsewhere. Similarly, in the twenty-third visit to Captain Vaira (fig. 1.64e), lighter ink appears in the seascape with the boat and in the clouds or vapors surrounding Sudhana. The visual effect of the variation of ink tones in the rubbings mimics the ink wash quality of a painting.[196]

195 Quoted from Jan Fontein's summary of the episode; see Fontein 1967, 8 (for the image, see fig. 11).

196 For example, see the cloud and water in Fontein 1967, figs. 9, 12–13, 15b, 16.

FIGURE 1.64G
Detail. *Illustrated Sutra of Sudhana's Pilgrimage as Described in the Avatamsaka Sutra*. Song. Rubbings. Album

It is likely that Master Zhong's rubbing album inspired later woodblock illustrations. Previous scholars have noted that many of its illustrations closely match those in the printed scroll *Illustrated Eulogies by Mañjuśrī* (*Wenshu zhinan tuzan* 文殊指南圖讚) (fig. 1.67), produced in Hangzhou during the Southern Song.[197] This is most evident when comparing the two versions' depictions of the tenth visit to the sage (figs. 1.64f, 1.67), an ascetic who advised Sudhana to jump from "the Sword Mountain immersed in flames on all sides."[198] In both versions, the Sword Mountain is depicted as a towering cliff with pointed blades on one side. The positioning of the figures differs, though. In the rubbing, the sage and Sudhana converse in the foreground; in the woodblock, both are in the air, indicating that they are jumping off the mountain.

As Jan Fontein suggests, the Northern Song album may form a stylistic and iconographic source (fig. 1.64g) for another later wooden column with exquisite

197 Fontein 1967; Chen Y. 2023.
198 For a summary of this episode, see Fontein 1967, 8.

FIGURE 1.68 Detail. Four columns from a Chinese temple. Wood. Collection of the Honolulu Museum of Art

FIGURE 1.69 *The Thousand-Armed Guanyin* (EO1232). 10th century. Woodblock print. Musée des Arts Asiatiques-Guimet

FIGURE 1.70
Detail. The "Universal Gateway" chapter of the *Lotus Sutra*. Yuan

narrative carvings of the Sudhana story, now in the Honolulu Academy of Arts (fig. 1.68).[199] The representations of Sudhana's (second) visit to Meghaśrī in both cases form the closest match. In both versions, the child encounters a monk in front of a pillar-shaped mountain, modeled after Mt. Kunlun 崑崙山 with its vertical pillar soaring from the water and supporting a wider platform on top.[200] A pair of circular symbols representing the sun and the moon appear on both sides of the mountain.

The dark aesthetic of the "black tiger" rubbings, especially the darkened background of the reproduced images, may have inspired some woodcut artisans to transfer the rubbing effect to print. A rare Dunhuang single-sheet print (fig. 1.69), reflecting the darkened background of a rubbing, features an Esoteric ritual icon—the Thousand-Armed Guanyin—his retinue surrounding him and vajras framing the print in darkened background.[201] A commercial

199 The image discussed is from one of the four undated columns that are believed to originally support "a canopy in a Buddhist temple." See Fontein 1967, 65–77 (for the detail shown here, see pl. 21a).

200 Huang 2014c, 162–63, 203–204.

201 Copp 2014, 125–26, 271 (note 151).

printshop active in fourteenth-century Hangzhou further effectively borrowed the effect to create a dramatic scene in the fully illustrated "Universal Gateway" chapter of the *Lotus Sutra* (fig. 1.70).[202] Here, the blackening effect is particularly powerful as it highlights the destroying power of the demons attacking the devotee on a boat amidst the turmoil seascape.

•••

The various reproductive strategies evident in seals, clay-molded objects, textiles, decorative letter paper, and rubbings reveal both the overlapping and distinctive features of these media. While Daoists and Buddhists made ample use of seals, their approaches differed. Daoists used seals largely in exorcism and healing rituals, applying them on a patient's body to release malignant or demonic entities. Responding to the seals' ritual functions, their aniconic designs feature a mixture of magical writs and graphs, evoking the sun, thunder, and stars.

This differs from the mainstream Buddhist iconic stamps, which feature buddhas, bodhisattvas, and guardians. The stamped specimens preserved in Dunhuang manuscripts suggest at least two ways Buddhists used them. First, devotees impressed the same stamp repetitively on a piece of paper to accumulate merit. Second, temples or monks used iconic stamps to authenticate ordination certificates that documented the formal taking of precepts.

Like stamped impressions on paper, iconic clay tablets carved in relief constitute another type of reproductive artifact stimulated by Buddhist devotion. While some designs of merit-accumulating clay tablets associated with the Tang capital Chang'an are comparable to Dunhuang iconic stamps, those produced under the Xi Xia represent multi-armed Himalayan Buddhist deities not seen in earlier stamps or tablets. In a world where multiple reproductive means were available to artisans, the opportunities to borrow and transfer memes in and out of different contexts were infinite. This explains why molded toys showcasing children are similar to painting-inspired pilgrim-monk tiles decorating Buddhist pagodas or to bricks of herb-picking immortals decorating tombs. The close sharing of embossed letter papers, paintings, ceramics, and metal ware, and the similarity between illustrated rubbings and woodblock-printed illustrations, highlight the fluid transfer of images across media, although with each change in material artists confronted technical challenges posed by their unique quality and limitations.

---

202 This illustrated book was published by the Yang Family publisher; for the location, see "C" in map. 3.1 in ch. 3 below.

CHAPTER 2

From Painting to Woodblock Printing and Back Again

Among images in various media, paintings stand out as the most direct visual resources for Buddhist printed images from the tenth to thirteenth centuries.[1] As Buddhist visual print culture developed, the traffic of artistic borrowing, sharing, and transformation went both ways, from painting to printing, and back. This chapter explores the dynamic interconnectivity of woodblock images and paintings, with special attention to painting-inspired printed illustrations created in the Buddhist context. It begins with textual sources detailing the relationship between painting and printed imagery, then moves on to types of printed images closely related to paintings: single-sheet prints and landscape woodcuts. The final section considers the "woodcut effect" in prints and painting, reflecting both the visual novelty and the limitation of the media and technology transfer.

1 Textual Documentations

Eleventh-century textual sources provide a glimpse of how paintings were transferred into printed images. At the Northern Song court, artists created various sets of didactic illustrations celebrating moral paradigms and virtues of past emperors, first in paintings, later in print, so that the materials could be widely shared among officials and imperial household members.[2] They were particularly used as visual aids in the education of the child-emperor Renzong 仁宗 (r. 1022–1063), who ascended the throne at the age of 12. In 1049, the leading court painters Gao Keming 高克明 and others first drafted the ten-scroll *Pictures of the Precious Instructions of the Three Reigns* (*Sanchao xunjie tu*

FIGURE 2.0 ← Detail of fig. 2.29d. Landscape Illustration from the *Secret Treasures*. Northern Song. Woodblock print. Handscroll. Harvard Art Museums

1 Shih 2014, 32.

2 At least three sets of illustrations were mentioned: *Contemplating Texts and Viewing the Past* (*Guanwen langu* 觀文覽古), *Treasured Lessons of the Three Reigns* (*Sanchao baoxun* 三朝寶訓), and *Imperial Processions* (*Lubu* 鹵簿); see HCL 1: 53.

© SHIH-SHAN SUSAN HUANG, 2024 | DOI:10.1163/9789004700017_004

三朝訓鑒圖) to commemorate a hundred virtuous events of the previous three rulers. The pictures were then transferred into woodblock versions: they were noted for the comprehensive layout of palace buildings, landscape settings, imperial carriages, and guards as well as the minute execution of human figures, often less than an inch tall.[3] Sometime before 1052, Renzong himself made a painting of the healing bodhisattva Nāgārjuna (Longshu 龍樹) to pray for his aunt who was going blind; in due course, he ordered court painters to transfer the painting to woodblock prints for wider distribution.[4]

The Northern Song court stored image-bearing blocks or molds (*mo* 模), so they could be used to make more copies as needed. Some showing Buddhist icons were held in the Institute for Dharma Transmission (Chuanfayuan 傳法院), supervised by the imperially sponsored Taiping xingguosi 太平興國寺 (Monastery of Great Peace and a Prosperous State) in Kaifeng.[5] During his visit in 1073, the Japanese monk Jōjin 成尋 (1011–1081) and his disciples stayed in its guest house. They requested printed copies of Buddhist icons to be sent to Japan, using the mold of the Five Hundred Arhats (*Wubai luohan moyin* 五百羅漢模印) and the Six Chan Patriarchs of the Bodhidharma Sect (*Damo liuzu mo* 達摩六祖模) stored in the repository.[6]

Beyond of the court, scholars, collectors, and elite monks actively transferred scenes from paintings onto woodblocks. As the scholar Chen Shidao 陳師道 (1053–1102) recalled, the elite Chan Master Datong 大通 (d. 1108),[7] a friend of many well-known scholars, once reproduced Li Gonglin's painting of the seated Guanyin in single-sheet prints and distributed them to Buddhist devotees.[8] Another member of the same elite circle, Mi Fu 米芾 (1015–1107), took note of a scholar-friend who decorated a new standing screen with a woodblock version of a handscroll painting by Gu Kaizhi 顧愷之 (ca. 344–405), called *Wise and Virtuous Women* (*Lienu tu* 列女圖), then available in a Tang copy.[9] Song paintings by monks and scholar artists, too, were transferred into

---

3 THJWZ 6: 492–93. Cf. SCSSLY 50: 659; THJWZ 3: 476. See also Murray 2007, 75–77; Huang 2011b, 140; 2014b, 395. Gao Keming was good at painting landscape, figures, horses, birds and flowers, and insects; see SCMHP 2: 453. He was skillful in painting miniature scenes (*xiaojing* 小景) in fan or screen format; see THJWZ 4: 482. Gao's family graveyard was recently discovered in Chengdu, Sichuan in 2018.

4 Huang 2011b, 140.

5 Tsukamoto 2016, 227; Chen Yuquan 2009, 143; SHY 200, *daoshi* 2: 6; Su 1999, 17.

6 Wang L. 2009, 14–15, 515, 528. In the sixth month of 1073, Jōjin's five disciples returned to Japan from the seaport Mingzhou 明州, today's Ningbo. See Wang L. 2009, 9–10.

7 For more on Master Datong, see XCLAZ 70: 10b–11a.

8 HSXSJ 17: 4b–5a. See also Su 1999, 76; Huang 2011b, 137–38.

9 HS, 978. The opening of the eleventh-century illustrated book *Newly Printed Biographies of Virtuous Women from Ancient Times* (*Xinkan gu lienü zhuan* 新刊古列女傳), reprinted

printed versions. During Guo Ruoxu's 郭若虛 life time (*c.*1074), for example, screens sold in Sichuan were decorated with print versions of landscape and architectural paintings originally created by the tenth-century monk-painter Chu'an 楚安.[10] Last but not least, Su Shi fondly compared refined decorative paper-printed water designs to waterscape paintings.[11]

2 Single-Sheet Prints

Among the earliest image-bearing printed products are single-sheet prints. They are impressions on single pieces of vertical paper, extant in specimens from the tenth to the twelfth centuries.[12] Additional mounting and coloring features make their overall designs look like mock paintings in hanging scroll format (figs. 2.1a, 2.2a, 2.3).

Certain Dunhuang single-sheet prints (figs. 2.1a, 2.2a), probably from the tenth century, are among the earliest woodblock prints mimicking paintings.[13] One rare specimen is now in the British Museum (fig. 2.1a). When first published by Aurel Stein in *Serindia* (fig. 2.4),[14] it was pasted side by side with another, almost identical print onto a piece of recycled paper that depicts an auspicious winged horse-dragon, a chain of coins associated with exorcism, and an official receiving celestial writs from the horse-dragon (fig. 2.5).[15] The

by the Qian'an 建安 publisher Yu Renzhong 余仁仲 (ca. 1127–1279), listed Liu Xiang 劉向 (77–6 BCE) as the compiler of the text and Gu Kaizhi as the illustrator, although the printed illustrations minimally reflect Gu's painting style. Cf. a Song-dynasty handscroll bearing a similar title of virtuous women and attributed to Gu Kaizhi, now in the Palace Museum. For more about the pictorial tradition associated with female moral models, see Wu 2019, 61–91.

10 THJWZ 2: 476. For the printing industry in the Tang-Song transition, see Wu and Chia eds. 2015, 152–53. Among the physical examples of screens examined in the latest scholarship of Chinese screens, none is decorated with printed designs; see Wu ed. 2021.

11 JJDPWJSL 60; Su 1999, 77; Huang 2014b, 391. Su Shi once owned twenty-four water paintings by his contemporary Sichuan painter Pu Yongsheng 蒲永昇; see THJWZ 4: 486.

12 In modern Taipei, Taiwan, a popular type of single-sheet prints for funeral uses depicts Amitabha Buddha leading the deceased souls in a boat to the Western Pure Land; see TWZJZLHB 1.34: 20–21.

13 Huang 2014b, 392; Shen 2019, 50.

14 Stein 1921, vol. 4. pl. CI.

15 For more on the drawing, see Whitfield 1983, pl. 60; Matsumoto 2019, 1: 451–52. Guolong Lai interprets the winged animal as the *baize* 白澤 spirit powerful in exorcism; see Lai 2014, color plate 1 (unnumbered page), 79–81. The practice of pasting multiple prints together onto the paper surface may be deemed as a devotional act of collecting. For a similar specimen, see Pelliot chinois 4514 (2) 28.

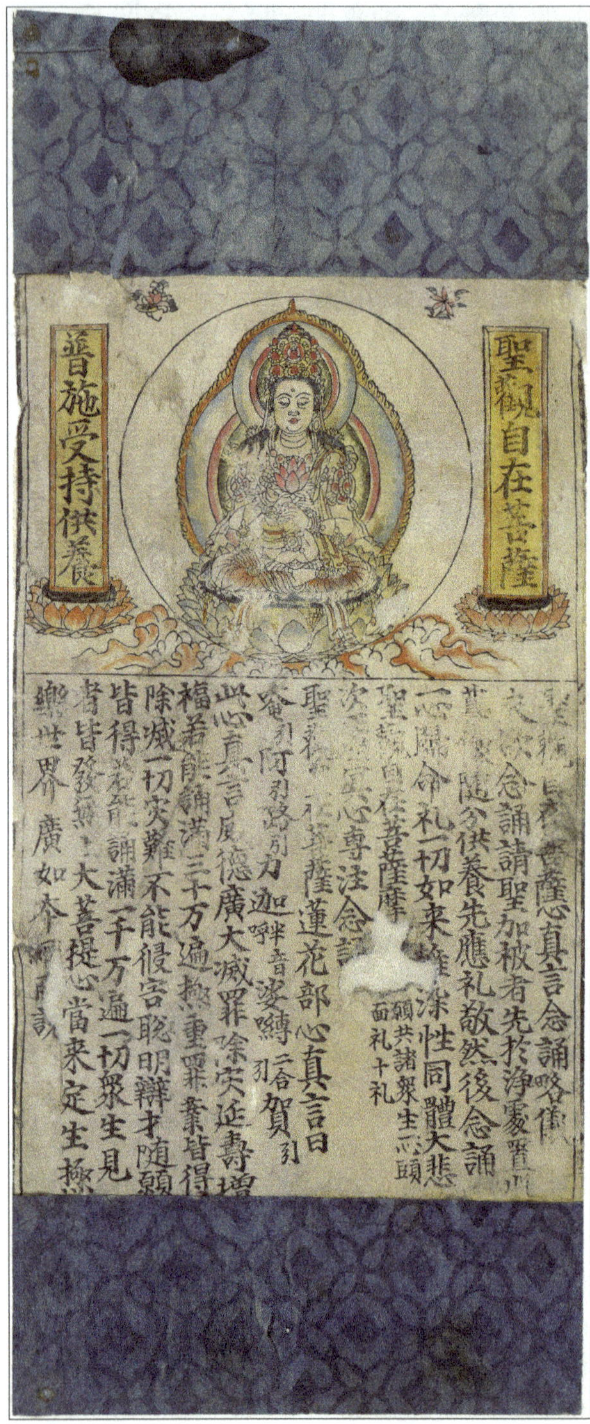

FIGURE 2.1A
Avalokiteśvara (1919,0101,0.234). 10th century. Hand-colored woodblock print. Single sheet. The British Museum

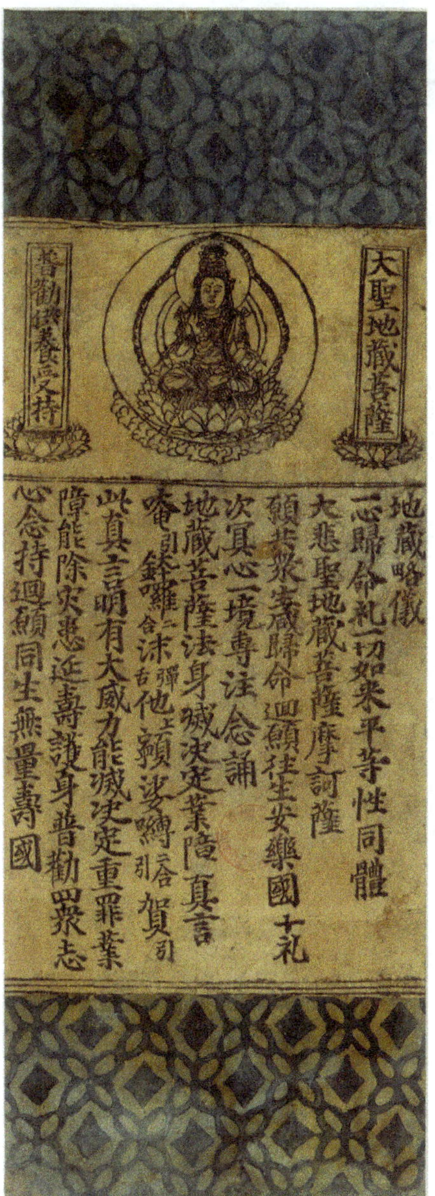

FIGURE 2.2A *Kṣitigarbha*. 10th century. Woodblock print with added mount and colors. Bibliothèque nationale de France

FIGURE 2.3 *Medicine Buddha* (*jia* version). 11th century. Liao. Woodblock print with added colors. Discovered in the Fogong Pagoda, Shanxi

FIGURE 2.4 Two single-sheet prints pasted side by side on a recycled piece of painting. Discovered in Dunhuang library cave

FIGURE 2.5
Yu Receiving the Writings of the Luo River (1919,0101,0.157). 9th century. Tang. Ink and colors on paper. The British Museum

cartouche in the upper right corner identifies the deity as the Sage Guanyin Bodhisattva (*Sheng Guanzizai pusa* 聖觀自在菩薩). Its counterpart on the left reads, "to distribute widely, keep, and venerate" (*pushi shouchi gongyang* 普施受持供養), suggesting that the printed image was circulated widely as a devotional image. Matsumoto Eiichi links its iconographic features to the textual account of the icon recorded in the Esoteric liturgical manual translated by Monk Bukong 不空 (705–774).[16] The printed text in the lower register of the sheet offers directions for the liturgical procedure to be used with the image. It states that a devotee should first place it in a purified location and pay homage before reciting the relevant spell (*zhenyan* 真言), also transcribed in the text. It further states that by reciting the spell 300,000 times one will expunge all karmic sins, be free from disasters, obtain intelligence, and have all wishes granted. It goes on to instruct the reader that after 10,000,000 recitations he will be reborn in a blissful land.

2.1 *Mounting Format*

The print originally pasted on the left top of the recycled image-bearing paper has additional mounting decorations (figs. 2.1a, 2.4). Two pieces of blue paper with printed designs, each measuring about 6 or 7 cm high, were pasted onto the top and bottom of the print, extending its overall length. A closer look at the juncture of the lower register and the added blue paper shows that the latter covers some of the printed words of the prayer (fig. 2.1b). This confirms that the blue paper was separate, pasted on the single-sheet print. Similar decorative paper was attached to the other single-sheet print from Dunhuang that features the image of the bodhisattva Kṣitigarbha (figs. 2.2a–b).[17] The floral patterns here recall printed designs of flowers and linked leaves in Tang tabby-weave silk fragments, found in the library cave (fig. 2.6),[18] where the Guanyin and Dizang prints were originally discovered.

Indeed, the two prints share many visual features and may well have been produced and mounted by the same workshop. In addition to their shared mounting style, the two icons (figs. 2.1c, 2.2c) are similar in facial features, crowns, arm bracelets, body contours, seated positions, lotus thrones, and even multi-layered halos and clouds. The shared visual details challenge the assumption that each individual icon possesses individual iconographic features. It suggests instead that they reflect the makers' shared stock motifs and designs. They may have sold at a higher price than those without additional

16 Matsumoto 2019, 1: 444; T.20.1031: 5a.

17 Monnet 2004, 82; Whitfield et al. 1990, 101.

18 Kuhn et al. 2012, 242–43 (fig. 5.48a).

FIGURE 2.1B Detail of fig. 2.1a

FIGURE 2.2B Detail of fig. 2.2a

FIGURE 2.6
Fragment of plain woven textile made of silk, tie-dyed in blue, orange, yellow and green with floral designs (MAS.878). Tang. The British Museum

decorative paper on the borders (fig. 2.4). The Guanyin print (fig. 2.1a), with all its extra coloring, might have cost even more than that of Dizang (fig. 2.2a).

So far, the prints showing Guanyin (fig. 2.1a) and Dizang (fig. 2.2a) are the only extant Dunhuang works mounted on decorative printed paper. Their style imitates that of a hanging scroll painting, whose top ("heavenly head," *tiantou*

FIGURE 2.1C Detail of fig. 2.1a

FIGURE 2.2C Detail of fig. 2.2a

天頭) and bottom ("earthly head," *ditou* 地頭) are often mounted with additional brocades as protective fabrics to facilitate suspension.[19] Textual records suggest that such prints may have hung in Buddhist ceremonial spaces. As recorded by the eleventh-century monk and writer Wenying 文瑩, a Chan Buddhist hall in Changsha 長沙, Hunan 湖南 displayed a single-sheet print of Guanyin bodhisattva mounted as a hanging scroll.[20]

More single-sheet prints imitating hanging scroll paintings were produced in north China in the eleventh and twelfth centuries. They include two identical prints of the Medicine Buddha (fig. 2.3) made under Khitan Liao rule and discovered inside a statue (diagram 4.1c) in the Fogong Pagoda in Yingxian, Shanxi (fig. 4.6).[21] When first discovered, one specimen was attached to a wooden roller at the bottom and had a string attached at the top, suggesting that it was designed as a hanging scroll. Both prints were adorned with decorative paper in interlinking circles and flowers on top (fig. 1.46).[22] Compared to the Dunhuang prototype (fig. 2.1a), the two Liao prints are taller in height, making their size more comparable to a hanging scroll painting. An oversized Medicine Buddha is seated in the center, with two monkish disciples and two groups of heavenly guardians placed symmetrically on both sides. Small seated buddhas, each accompanied by a cartouche, manifest in the sky.

Beyond religious specimens, there is the print called *Four Beauties* (fig. 2.7), dated to the twelfth or thirteenth centuries and produced by the commercial printshop of the Ji 姬 Family in Pingyang, southern Shanxi. Two pieces of dark gray paper are pasted onto the top and the bottom, mimicking mounting brocades of a hanging scroll painting. Within the print itself, both upper and lower parts are filled with ornamental designs. The upper band, wider than the lower, shows flowers and a pair of birds in flight. It also has additional motifs in truncated reverse-V shape at the center imitating "frightened swallows" (*jingyan* 驚燕), a standard mounting element in hanging scroll paintings that indicates brocade strings suspended from the top.[23] The cutter intentionally

---

19 For more on the history of mounting in Chinese paintings, see Gulik 1958; Xu 1981; Ebrey 2008, 114–16.

20 The print was said to be "hung" (*xuan* 懸) in the Buddhist hall; see YHQH 5: 54–55; Huang 2011b, 138, 157n; Huang 2014b, 392. For a similar documentation of hanging a printed image in a twelfth-century Japanese monastic context, see Sasaki 2017, 179.

21 Cf. the other specimen in Shanxi sheng wenwuju et al. 1991, 13 (color pl. 14).

22 Cf. the roundel patterns in the Northern Song decorative letter paper, and the graphic designs of the windows and door panels showcased in the manual *Yingzao fashi* discussed in ch. 1 above.

23 For comparable "M-shaped tassels hanging from the top" of a scroll, depicted in the painted tomb (dated 1309) in Xingxian 興縣, Shanxi, see Wang Yudong 2012, 29 (fig. 12); McCausland 2014, 131 (fig. 79), 133 (fig. 83); Wu 2017, 22 (fig. 33).

FIGURE 2.7
Four Beauties. Jin. Woodblock print. Single sheet. Discovered in Khara Khoto, Inner Mongolia. The State Hermitage Museum, St. Petersburg

used the relief carving method to ink the background of the frightened swallows, the paired phoenixes, and the floral designs.[24] The effect complements the attached dark gray paper and frames the overall design.

24 Kobayashi 2017, 76.

FIGURE 2.8
Detail of a carved brick. Northern Song. Guanlinmiao tomb, Luoyang, Henan

FIGURE 2.9 Detail of a mural. 1169. Jin. Painted tomb in Yuquan Village, Lingchuan, Shanxi

As the subject matter celebrates theatrical performances in Jin popular culture, a print like this may have been used in a performance context. This is suggested by a molded brick recovered from a mid-twelfth-century tomb that shows an actor unfolding an image-bearing hanging scroll at the opening of a play (fig. 2.8).[25] It may also have hung in a domestic space, as indicated by two birds-and-flowers meta-paintings on the east wall of a Jin tomb, recently discovered in southern Shanxi (fig. 2.9).[26] This location is over 160 miles from Pingyang, where the *Four Beauties* was printed.[27] In addition, there is the meta-painting of a scholar's portrait in the early twelfth-century work, *Scholar in his Studio* (fig. 2.10a).[28] This small piece hangs against a screen painting of reeds and waterfowls frolicking along the shore. All these mock hanging scrolls have dark mounted material on top and bottom and show two white strings on top.

25 Zhang F. 2014, 341–42; Dong 1959; Luoyangshi wenwu 2011; Deng 2017, 42–45; 2019, 71–73.

26 Cf. another Jin tomb (dated 1228) in central Shanxi, where its wall painting represents a mock calligraphic hanging scroll; see Hsu Y. 2021, 136, 163 (fig. 11).

27 Xie et al. 2010, 1: 112–13; Li J. et al. 2018. For more visual examples of hanging scroll paintings depicted on walls of Song-Yuan tombs, see Wu 2017, 21 (fig. 31); Deng 2019, 108 (fig. 2.23), 111 (fig. 2.28); Li Q. 2018.

28 For the painting's representation of the "space for a scholar" (*wenren kongjian* 文人空間), see the entry by Chen Yunru in Lin et al. 2006a, 217–20. For more discussions, see Lin P. 1996, 97fig5, 6; Huang 2011b, 151fig24, 162n94; Wu 2022d, 126–31.

FIGURE 2.10A *Scholar in his Studio.* 12th century. Northern Song. Ink and color on silk. Album leaf. National Palace Museum

2.2 *Coloring*

Another feature to increase the painting-inspired quality of single-sheet prints appears in hand-painted colors. This is different from multi-color printmaking popular from the seventeenth century onward.[29] A good example is the Guanyin print with extra mounting design (figs. 2.1a, 2.1c). While seven or more extant Dunhuang prints have identical designs, suggesting that they all came from the same block, only this one bears hand-painted colors.[30] They

29 For more studies, see Wang C. 2016; Farrer and McLoughlin 2022.

30 These specimens are dispersed in Paris, London, New Delhi, and Shanghai Library. For more examples, see Pelliot chionis 4514 (6)2, Pelliot chinois 4514 (6) 3, Pelliot chinois 3965.

were added carefully in various details to bring out the liveliness of the featured icon as well as enhance the print's overall decorative flavor. Guanyin's lips, jewelry crown, arm bracelets, necklace, and chest-area lotus, are all hand painted in bright red. Her hair is colored blue; her skirt is bright orange. The same orange hue fills parts of the clouds below her seat and appears in the two lotus bases of the framed cartouches on the sides. The different layers of her circular halo are colored in green, red, light blue, and orange to enhance its illuminating effect. Her lotus throne appears partly in light blue and partly in light green, highlighting the nuanced gradation of the flower petals. Given that coloring was complex, required a high level of skill, and applied many diverse and often hard-to-get pigments, it is reasonable to assume that colors were added by professional artisans. While not as colorful as the Guanyin print, the Liao Medicine Buddha prints described earlier were also hand painted partially in orange and light green, with orange dominant in selected icons' robes and halos (fig. 2.3).

Unlike this print (fig. 2.1a), another Guanyin representation from Dunhuang in single-sheet print shows her standing (fig. 2.11a) and has rather amateur levels of coloring. While the image is impressed from an elongated block with a visible frame,[31] the text below it is printed from a separate block. Dated 947, it identifies Lei Yanmei 雷延美 as the cutter and Cao Yuanzhong 曹元忠 as the donor. The latter served as imperial commissioner of the Guiyi army stationed at Dunhuang from 946 to 970. Several duplicates of the same image-and-text prints survive (fig. 2.11b), but only this one shows colors in red, white, and green on the icon.

Guanyin's face in the hand-painted version appears in almost opaque beige, concealing the detailed facial features of the original monochrome print (fig. 2.11b). This suggests that it was added by an amateur, possibly the print's owner. Similarly, a group of identical printed slips with Guanyin images, also from Dunhuang, show some amateur coloring (figs. 2.12a–c). Unlike the British Museum specimen, which is a plain single printed slip (fig. 2.12a), the two in the Bibliothèque nationale de France show colors manually added to parts of the slips. In one case (fig. 2.12b), Guanyin's halo appears in yellow; in another (fig. 2.12c), which has two identical slips pasted side by side, both the floral

31 Multiple copies survive. An extant collage in the British Museum (1919,0101,0.244) shows nine prints of the Guanyin blockprints arranged in a 3 × 3 grid; see Whitfield et al. 1990, pl. 84; Shen 2019, 86 (fig. 3.10). Beyond the U.K. and Paris collections, one specimen is at the Metropolitan Museum of Art (Gift of Paul Pelliot through the Morgan Library, 1924), and the other is at the Royal Ontario Museum (no. 927.24).

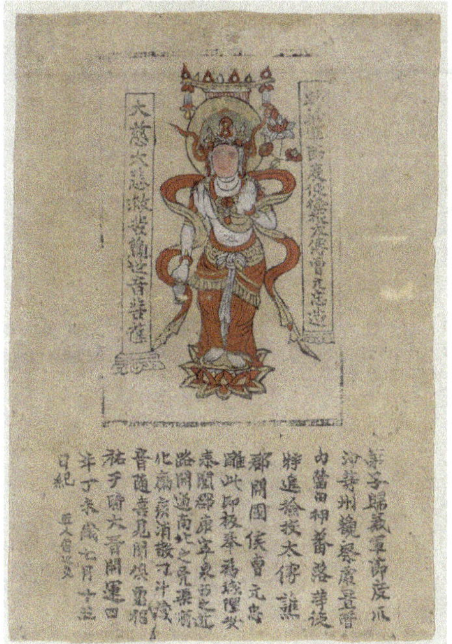

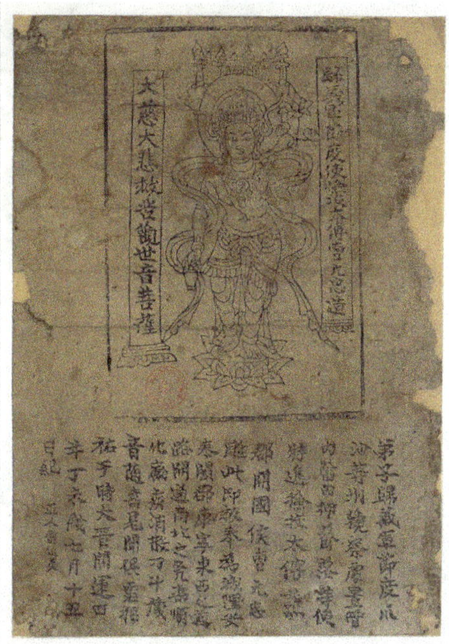

FIGURES 2.11A–B Two specimens of the "compound prints" with the standing Guanyin on top and the colophon below. Text Dated 947. Discovered in the Dunhuang library cave
a. The hand-colored version (EO 1218 D Recto). Musée des Arts Asiatiques-Guimet
b. The monochrome version (Pelliot chinois 4514 [6] 1). Bibliothèque nationale de France

border and the deity's willow branch are in this color. Slips like these may have been used in daily chanting of the deity's name.

An unusual example of multi-colored application is the enigmatic tri-colored single-sheet print (fig. 2.13), discovered inside the four-sided Tang stele mentioned earlier and housed in the Forest of Steles (diagram 1.1). It shows the legendary immortal Dongfang Shuo 東方朔 carrying a branch with the peaches of immortality he stole from the Queen Mother of the West. Printed mostly in gray, it shows the peach leaves in blue-green as well as his shoes, hat, and sleeve borders in black. The print was meant to mimic a painting, since it carries the signature "Painted by Wu Daozi" (Wu Daozi bi 吳道子筆), the famous Tang painter (ca. 680–759), in the upper left corner, followed by a seal stamped in red.[32] As suggested by Tsuen-hsuin Tsien, the print may "have been used

32 Cf. the oft-cited rubbing of a stone carving (associated with Mt. Heng 恆) depicting an animated demonic attendant, with a comparable signature that reads "painted by Wu Daozi." See ZGMSQJ, *Huihua bian* 19: 85 (fig. 73).

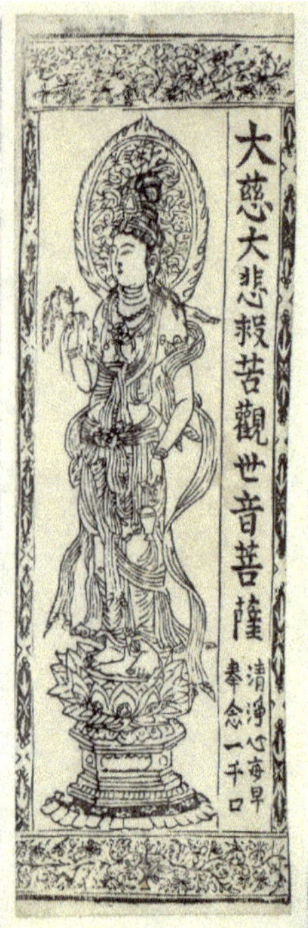

a

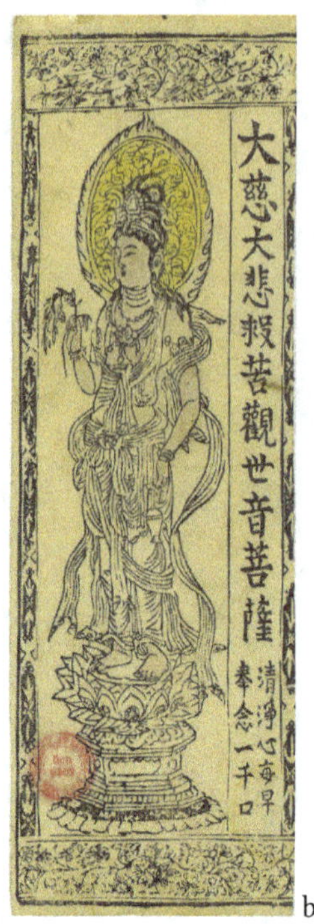

b

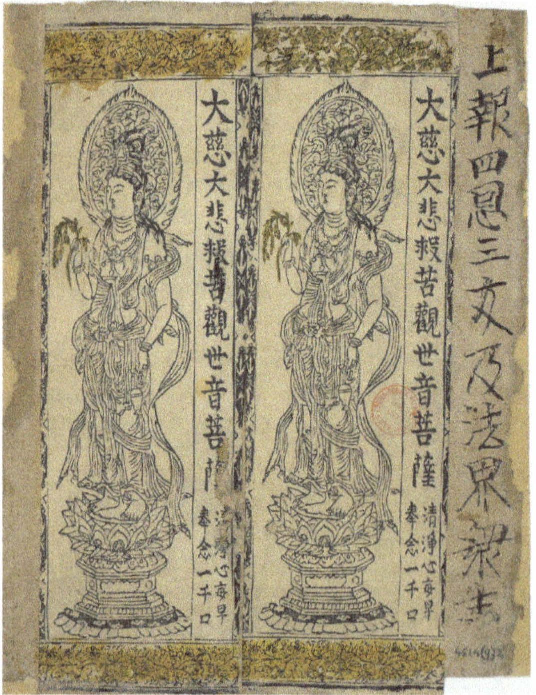

c

FIGURES 2.12A–C
Guanyin printed slips. 10th century. Late Tang or early Five Dynasties. Woodblock prints
a. Guanyin print (1919,0101,0.240). The British Museum
b. Guanyin print (Pelliot chinois 4514 [9] 12). Bibliothèque nationale de France
c. Guanyin prints (Pelliot 4514 [9] 13). Bibliothèque nationale de France

FIGURE 2.13
Dongfang Shuo Stealing the Peaches of Immortality. Jin. Single sheet print in grey, black, and blue-green. Stele Forest, Xi'an

FIGURE 2.14
Dongfang Shuo Stealing the Peach of Immortality. Silk tapestry. Yuan. The Palace Museum, Beijing

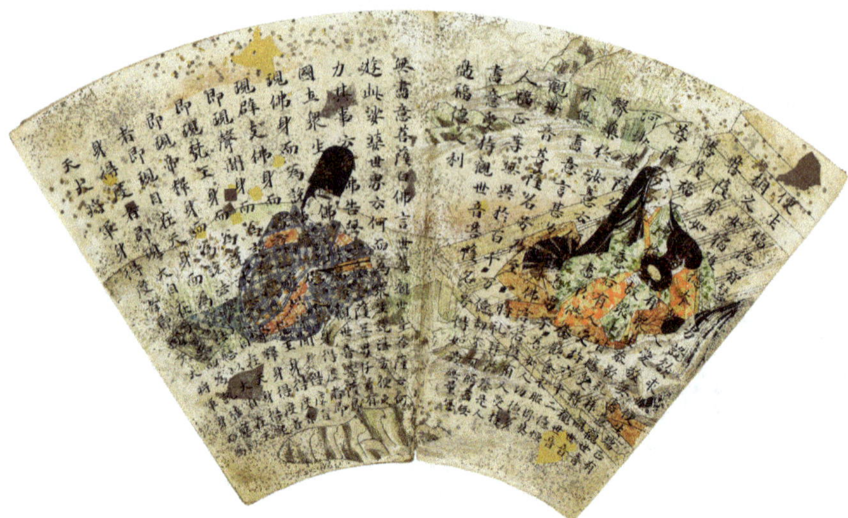

FIGURE 2.15 Detail. *Lotus Sutra*. 12th century. Heian period, Japan. Printed underdrawing, ink and color painted on golden flake paper. Tokyo National Museum

for house decoration or as one of the New Year pictures"; it may well be the product of "a commercial printer" in the printing center of Pinyang in southern Shanxi "under the Jurchen in the early twelfth century."[33] The dramatic image of Dongfang Shuo, moreover, which reflects "the humorous performance of a popular tale,"[34] was transmitted widely and in multiple media, including a Yuan-dynasty tapestry (fig. 2.14).

Prints in multiple colors—whether hand painted or printed—are rare between the Tang and Yuan dynasties;[35] most East Asian woodblock images before the sixteenth century were in monochrome ink. Beyond China, an exception appears in medieval Japan: the twelfth-century *Lotus Sutra* fan-shaped booklet associated with the Heian court.[36] Taking advantage of woodblock techniques, the designer first printed pale-colored underdrawings—grasses, rocks, ground, and figural contours—on paper decorated with golden flakes (fig. 2.15). A colorist then added bright colors and additional details manually

33 Tsien 1985, 280–82 (fig. 1188). For more on this area, see ch. 5 below.

34 Zhang F. 2014, 349.

35 For studies of color prints in China, 1600–1800, see Farrer and McLoughlin 2022.

36 Akiyama et al. 1972; Miya 1989, 93. For more sutra copies of the *Lotus Sutra* in medieval Japan, see Sudō 2015.

FIGURE 2.16
Saint Christopher. 1423. Southern Germany or German Switzerland. Hand-colored woodcut. John Rylands Library, Manchester, England

onto the printed design. In a final step, a skillful sutra copyist transcribed sections of the text in ink and golden pigment onto the painted surface.

Looking further afield, quite a few early woodcuts produced in fifteenth-century Europe bear hand-painted colors.[37] An early extant specimen is *Saint Christopher*, dated 1423 and first printed in monochrome ink with multiple colors added later (fig. 2.16).[38] The saint's multi-layered garments are differentiated in blue, yellow, and beige. Other motifs in the surrounding setting appear in soft tones: mountains and plants in green; buildings, tree trunks, a water mill, and a rabbit in yellow; and water partially in light blue. The only color that stands out is red, used selectively to highlight the cross within the halo of the baby Jesus, seated on the saint's shoulders. Other early prints of

37 Parshall et al. 2005.

38 Hults 1996, 24.

FIGURE 2.17 *Portrait of a Female Donor*. By Petrus Christus. ca. 1455. Netherlandish. Oil on panel. National Gallery of Art

this sort were mostly colored by hand, causing scholars to speculate that those without colors were never sold. The coloring trend also manifests in paintings of the time.[39] Similarly, the oil painting, *Portrait of a Female Donor*, by the Netherland-inspired painter Petrus Christus (ca. 1455), depicts a colored single-sheet print of Saint Elizabeth pasted on the wall (fig. 2.17); next to her a female devotee kneels in front of her prayer book.[40]

2.3 *The Maitreya Print Designed by a Court Painter*

The Chinese single-sheet prints discussed so far are all associated with north and northwest China. In contrast, the famous *Maitreya* print of the (fig. 2.18a), re-discovered in the 1950s inside a tenth-century Chinese Buddhist statue of Shakyamuni in the Seiryōji 清涼寺 (Monastery of Clarity and Purity) in Kyoto, Japan,[41] reveals the artistic quality of Buddhist prints circulating in the south. Still, even that is based on a painting designed by a court painter working for the Northern Song court in Kaifeng. The print contains writing that sheds light on its maker, donor, and date of production. A colophon dates it to 984 and stresses that its purpose was "to distribute it widely" (*pushi* 普施) (fig. 2.18b), a term mirroring the phrase found in the Dunhuang Guanyin prints (figs. 2.1a, 2.1c, 2.4). It suggests that the extant specimen was not the only copy printed in the tenth century.

The print has long been recognized as a masterpiece of Chinese woodcutting. It is closely linked to imperial fame since it was "painted by Gao Wenjin, attendant-in-waiting" (*daizhao Gao Wenjin hua* 待詔高文進畫) (ca. 950–after 1022) (fig. 2.18c), as outlined in the cartouche on the upper right (fig. 2.18c). Heping Liu connects this print to Gao Wenjin's now-lost painting of Maitreya, originally in display in Empress Dowager Liu's 劉 (969–1033, r. 1022–33) Buddhist chapel in the inner court.[42] The cartouche on the upper left reads,

39 In an interior scene of the *Annunciation* by the Master of Flémalle (Royal Museums of Fine Arts of Belgium), dated 1415 to 1425, a slightly worn single-sheet print is filled with multiple colors. It has similar iconography and was found attached to the mantel of the fireplace with "dabs of red wax." For a plate, see Areford 2010, 1.

40 For the plate, see Huang 2017c, 47 (fig. 11).

41 The Shakyamuni statue was made in Taizhou 台州, Zhejiang in southeastern coastal China and commissioned by the Japanese monk Chōnen 奝然 (938–1016), who traveled in Song China from 983 to 986. Carved out of a single log of wood, its spacious interior was capable of holding deposited objects. For more studies, see Henderson and Hurvitz 1956; Maruo et al. 1966; Nara Kokuritsu Hakubutsukan 1996, 126–28; Huang 2012, 76–77; Wang Z. 1994; Tsukamoto 2016; Nagaoka 2021.

42 Empress Liu's veneration of Maitreya reflects her political ambition modeled after Empress Wu in the Tang; see Liu 2003, 139–82. For more about Empress Dowager Liu, see Lee H. 2008.

a

FIGURES 2.18A–D *Maitreya*. Illustrated by Gao Wenjin. 984. Northern Song. Woodblock print. Single sheet. Seiryōji, Kyoto. a. The complete view. b–d. Details of 2.18a

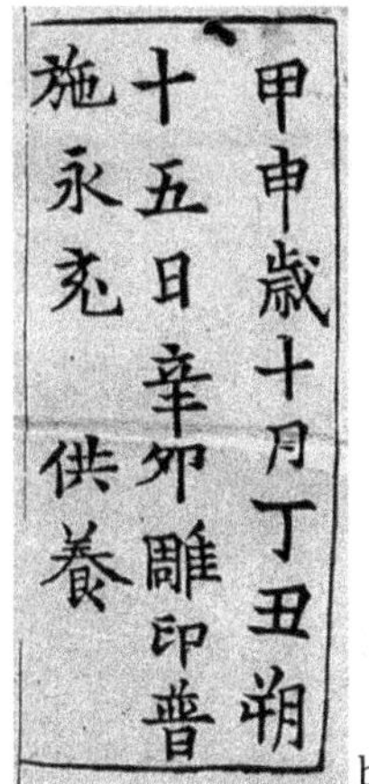

"carved by Monk Zhili from Yuezhou" (*Yuezhou seng Zhili diao* 越州僧知禮雕) (fig. 2.18d), prompting scholars to identify it as a product from Zhejiang. Going beyond the face value of the cartouche, however, it is more plausible to identify Monk Zhili not as the block cutter but as the supervisor of the printing.[43]

Stylistically, the *Maitreya* print connects southern print culture based in Zhejiang with Northern Song court painting based in Kaifeng. Before becoming part of the Northern Song in 978, Hangzhou was the capital of the Wu-Yue Kingdom (907–978), whose territory covered what is today Zhejiang plus parts of Jiangsu and Fujian.[44] The two female attendants standing in the foreground (fig. 2.18e)—especially their wheel-shaped hairdos, rounded faces in three-quarter view, and long and parallel drapery lines—recall the style of the now-lost Daoist handscroll by Wu Zongyuan 武宗元 (ca. 1004–1050) (fig. 2.19), formerly in the C. C. Wang Family collection.[45] The block cutter transferred Gao Wenjin's painting with great skill, carving out the surrounding parts of each line in order to capture the lively variation of thick and thin in the drapery lines. The main icon has long been identified as Maitreya, mainly due

43 Tsukamoto Maromitsu questions the identity of the monk Zhili from Yuezhou, seeing him as an undocumented monk-artisan relocated to Kaifeng from Zhejiang and different from the well-known monk Zhili from Siming recorded in Song Buddhist history; A revisionist argument he proposes, then, is to re-situate the production context of the Maitreya print in the Northern Song capital Kaifeng, highlighting the monumental (six-*chi*-tall) Tang Maitreya sculpture installed in the imperially-sponsored Xianggusi 相國寺 as its possible prototype. See Tsukamoto 2016, 199–200, 202–205, 227.

44 For the Buddhist print culture under the Wu–Yue rule, see Huang 2011a, 137–46.

45 Huang 2014b, 402–403; Huang 2017c, 4–5. For a complete reproduction of Wu Zongyuan's handscroll, see ZGHHQJ 3: 76–87 (pl. 65). For more studies, see Xu 1956; Barnhart 1983, 52–53; Huang 2012, 288–89. Cf. Li Song's different view of the painting in Li S. 2008.

FIGURE 2.18E Detail of 2.18a. *Maitreya*. Illustrated by Gao Wenjin. 984. Northern Song. Woodblock print. Single sheet. Seiryōji, Kyoto

FIGURE 2.19 Detail. *Immortals and Elders in Audience with the Prime*, by Wu Zongyuan. 11th century. Northern Song. Ink on paper. Handscroll

to the Tusita (*doushuai* 兜率) Heaven evoked in the eulogy by the Zhejiang Monk Zhongxiu 仲休 (active late tenth century),[46] which appear printed on the right of the icon. Researchers have also called attention to the feathered fan held in Maitreya's right hand as a new feature introduced to the iconography at that time. It later spread east to Japan and west to the Xi Xia Buddhist grottoes.[47] Nevertheless, similar conventions—such as hair spreading widely

46 For more biographical study of Monk Zhongxiu, see Tsukamoto 2016, 192, 197–99; Liu 2003, 171*n*124.

47 Izumi 2010, 189–216; Kitsudō 2019.

over shoulders, the icon placed in a seated posture, and the spacious arrangement and decorative details of the lotus throne—also appear in a slightly later Northern Song court painting featuring the Esoteric Buddhist Peacock King (fig. 2.20). The latter may well have been originally used in court rituals praying for rain.[48] The composite image of a Buddhist sacred object on top of a rock formation (fig. 2.18g) serves as a prototype for a variety of images made in the early twelfth century, such as *Scholar in his Studio* (fig. 2.10b), *Listening to the Qin* associated with Emperor Huizong (fig. 2.21),[49] and the stone reliquary (fig. 2.22) found in the Shaolinsi 少林寺,[50] Dengfeng 登封, Henan. However, in these three examples, the Buddhist sacred object is replaced with an image of flowers in a vase or a variation thereof. In all four examples, the aggregate grouping of object on rock formation is located in the center-foreground of each composition.

The tenth-century print culture of the south, particularly of the Wu-Yue kingdom, may also have served as a stylistic inspiration for the *Maitreya* print. This is evident from a twelfth-century Japanese copy of the now-lost single-sheet print called *Manifestations of Guanyin* (*Yingxian Guanyin* 應現觀音), commissioned in 974 by "Qian Shu, great general under heaven, king of Wu-Yue" (*tianxia dayuanshuai Wu Yue guowang Qian Shu* 天下大元帥吳越國王錢俶) (fig. 2.23).[51] The Japanese drawing was made as a copy of the Wu-Yue print of the *Manifestations of Guanyin*. Scholars surmise that the print may be part of a 20,000-copy printing of the so-called *Twenty-four Manifestations of Guanyin* (*Ershisi yingxian Guanyin xiang* 二十四應現觀音像), produced on plain silk. As his biography notes, the Wu-Yue Monk Yanshou 延壽, who worked for many royally-sponsored Buddhist printing projects, was in charge of this massive printing project and received 1000 *guan* 貫 in royal funds issued by Qian Shu.[52]

48 The Peacock King may be a Northern Song court painting made in the eleventh or early twelfth century. For more discussions, see Masuki 2008; Huang 2017c, 5*n*14; Huang 2002, 98–101.

49 For a complete view of the painting, see Palace Museum, "Tingqin tu 听琴图," Gugong minghuaji 故宫名画记, Accessed December 24, 2023. https://m-minghuaji.dpm.org.cn/paint/appreciate?id=na7xf64uvkwrsd5fj2z2ynzcek8iqtbb.

50 The reliquary is dated to the early twelfth century. For the carvings on all four sides of the reliquary, see ZGMSQJ, *Huihua bian* 19: 70–71 (fig. 61).

51 Takimoto 1988, fig. 6; Nara Kokuritsu Hakubutsukan 2009, 22, 275; Uchida 2001; Uchida 2011, 156–65, 172–74; Masuki 2012, Masuki 2014; Huang 2011a, 142–46; 2017c, 8–9; Sasaki 2017, 177–78.

52 This is based on the twelfth-century edition of the *Yongming Zhijue chanshi fangzhang shilu* 永明智覺禪師方丈實錄, compiled by Monk Yuanzhao 元照 (1048–1116), now in the National Library collection. See Masuki 2019, 37–38; Zhang 1978, 75, 76n9. For more

FIGURE 2.18F
Detail of 2.18a. *Maitreya*. Illustrated by Gao Wenjin. 984. Northern Song. Woodblock print. Single sheet. Seiryōji, Kyoto

FIGURE 2.20
Detail. *Peacock King*. Northern Song. Ink and color on silk. Hanging scroll. Ninnaji, Kyoto

FIGURE 2.18G Detail of 2.18a. *Maitreya.* Illustrated by Gao Wenjin. 984. Northern Song. Woodblock print. Single sheet. Seiryōji, Kyoto

FIGURE 2.10B Detail of 2.10a. *Scholar in his Studio.* 12th century. Northern Song. Ink and color on silk. Album leaf. National Palace Museum

FIGURE 2.21 Detail. *Listening to the Qin*, by Emperor Huizong. Early 12th century. Northern Song. Ink and color on silk. Hanging scroll. The Palace Museum, Beijing

FIGURE 2.22 Detail of the stone reliquary. Early 12th century. Northern Song. Stone linear engravings. Shaolin Temple, Dengfeng, Henan

FIGURE 2.23 *Manifestations of Guanyin*. 12th century. Kamakura period, Japan. Ink on paper. Drawing. Tokyo. The Gotoh Museum

According to Uchida Keiichi, many stylistic characteristics are comparable to the *Maitreya* print. They include rounded facial features, slightly downward gaze, drapery lines, clouds, and decorative motifs of vajras filling part of the borders.[53] It is therefore likely that the *Maitreya* print, although transferred from a painting by the court painter Gao Wenjin who worked in Kaifeng, was in fact cut and printed in Zhejiang.

The print-inspired drawing of the *Manifestations of Guanyin*, moreover, bears a seal of the Buddhist Kōzanji 高山寺 (Monastery of the High Mountain), a temple northwest of Kyoto, founded by the Monk Myōe 明恵 (1173–1232). This suggests that the drawing was once in this temple's collection, an active site in Sino-Japanese image transfer.[54] To preserve Buddhist iconographies transmitted from China, the temple administration assembled artisans to make copies—mainly in the form of drawings—of rubbings and prints transmitted from Song China.

Much information on early Chinese Buddhist illustrative prints relies on Japanese drawings copied later. The drawing *The Six Patriarchs* (fig. 2.24a), also with multiple Kōzanji seals, provides an additional example.[55] An inscription in the lower left corner makes it clear that it is a Japanese copy of a Northern Song print: "Block-cut and stored in the imperial inner court on the first day of the eleventh month of the first year of the Zhiyuan reign, by imperial order. Supervised by the official Chen Lu 陳陸 of the Inner Service of the Yellow Gate."[56] The original block was cut in 1054, just two years after Emperor Renzong had his painting of the healing bodhisattva transferred onto a print. Altogether the evidence reflects the court's active production of Buddhist prints under Renzong. The theme of the drawing—the Six Chan Patriarchs—further calls to mind a block Jōjin 成尋 (1011–1081) saw in the Xianshengsi 顯聖寺 (Monastery of Radiant Sagehood) in 1073. This is recorded in his travel diary, *Record of My Pilgrimage to Mounts Tiantai and Wutai* (*San Tendai Godaisan ki* 參天台五臺山記).[57] It is thus possible that the Kōzanji drawing is based on an impression

about other massive printing projects of pictures and texts Monk Yanshou supervised, see Zhang 1978, 75; Zhang and Han 2006, 36–37.

53 Nara Kokuritsu Hakubutsukan 2009, 23, 275; Uchida 2011, 156–65, 172–74; Huang 2011a, 144; 2017c, 8–9.

54 For a catalogue of the paintings, drawings, and other cultural artifacts in the Kōzanji collection, see Kyoto Kokuritsu Hakubutsukan 1981. For more about Myōe and the temple, see Myōe Shōnin to Kōzanji Henshū Iinkai hen ed. 1981.

55 Shih 1998, 158–59; Uchida 2011, 176–78; Sasaki 2017, 162–64; Huang 2017c, 6–7.

56 My transliteration is based on that published in Nara Kokuritsu Hakubutsukan 2009, 275; Uchida 2011, 177. Cf. a different transliteration of the official's name as Chen Xuan 陳絃 in Shih 1998, 159; Huang 2017c, 6.

57 Hirabayashi 1978, 201, 205; Wang L. 2009, 530. For more on Jōjin, see Borgen 2007.

of the mold of the Six Chan Patriarchs, transmitted to Japan by Jōjin's disciples. Positioned vertically, the drawing depicts the six leading masters in three rows, from the upper right all the way to the lower left. Each patriarch is depicted as an eminent monk surrounded by disciples and attendants.

Although it is "copy of a copy," the drawing shows selected details that connect directly to Tang–Song models. The first patriarch (fig. 2.24b), for instance, links the work to an earlier pictorial convention as preserved in the album *The Six Venerable Monks*, attributed to the eighth-century painter Lu Lengjia 盧棱伽 (fig. 2.25).[58] The version here is most likely a Southern Song court copy of a now-lost Tang painting, collected by the Mongol Princess Sengge Ragi (Dachang gongzhu 大長公主; ca. 1283–1331).[59] Furthermore, the fourth patriarch (fig. 2.24c), depicted as an old monk seated on a bamboo armchair with a tightly-woven bamboo mat on its back, matches a standard pictorial convention in Song Buddhist art. It calls to mind the carved image on the back (fig. 2.26) of the double-sided block retrieved from Julu, Hebei (fig. 0.11).[60] This location is not far from Kaifeng, where the Kōzanji drawing's original block was made.[61]

More motifs of this kind appear widely in Southern Song and Yuan China as well as in the neighboring states of Xi Xia and Dali 大理 (937–1253). They include the long *Handscroll of Buddhist Images* by Zhang Shengwen 張勝溫 of the Dali kingdom, dated to around 1180 (fig. 2.27).[62] While some scholars have identified the figures as the sixteen arhats, a stereotypical group in Buddhist iconography, Lee Yu-min sees them as a representation of sixteen patriarchs, unique to Buddhist history in Yunnan. She has also proposed that the handscroll may have functioned as a small pictorial sample used in transferring stock images to larger-scale temple murals in Dali.[63] Its modular design was also adopted also in later paintings depicting a Chan master conversing with

58 See Gugong bowuyuan 2008, 98.

59 The album bears the princess' well-documented collection seal that reads, "Library of the Imperial Elder Sister" (*Huangjie tushu* 皇姐圖書), placing it historically into a dynastic transaction. For more studies, see Shih 1998, 166; Huang 2017c, 7 (esp. footnote 23); Huang 2002, 392–95. For the Princess Sengge and the culture of appreciating and collecting art at the Mongol Yuan court, see Chen Y. 2016.

60 Edgren 1984, 58–59; Tsien 1985, fig. 1053c; Tsien 1993, 265–73; Huang 2017c, 7.

61 A rare painted tomb of the monk Zhirou 志柔, active under the Khitan Liao and excavated in Inner Mongolia, bears a surprisingly similar scene of a monk seated on a bamboo chair. For a color reproduction of the mural, see Jin 2008, pl. 1 (unnumbered page).

62 Lee Y. 2023; Huang 2017c, 7.

63 Lee 2010, 133–35. A rare Dali painted frontispiece was likely inspired by the Song Hangzhou printed prototype. See National Museum of Asian Art, "The Buddha Addressing Yamaraja at Kusinagara," Accessed December 24, 2023. https://asia.si.edu/explore-art-culture/collections/search/edanmdm:fsg_F1926.1/.

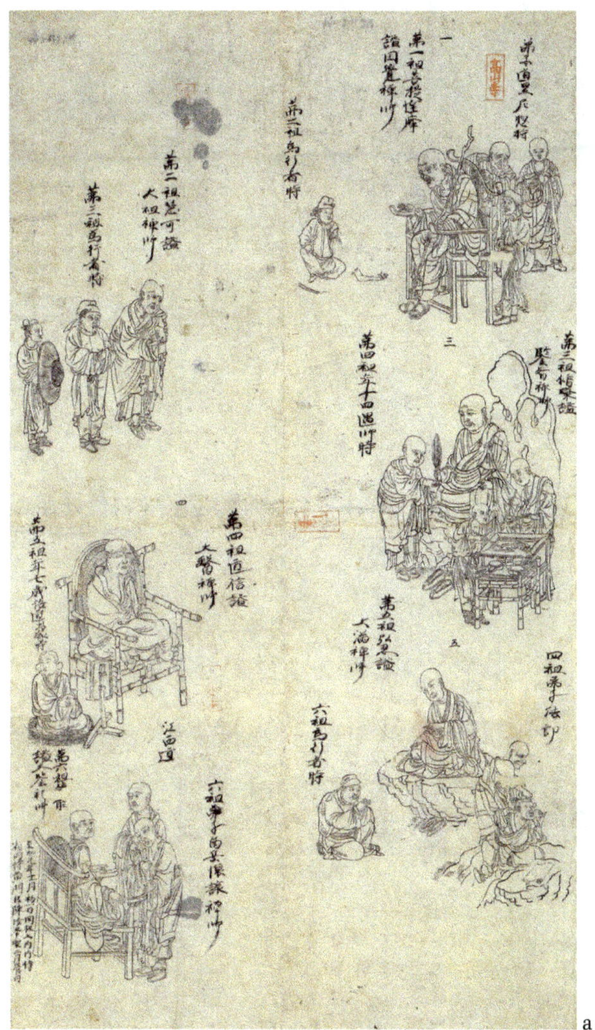
a

b

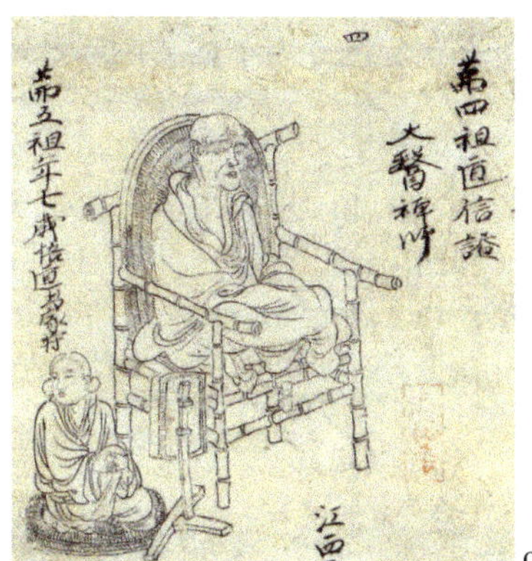
c

FIGURES 2.24A–C *The Six Patriarchs*. Kamakura period, Japan. Ink on paper. Drawing. Kōzanji, Kyoto
a. A complete view
b–c. Details

FIGURE 2.25 Detail. *The Six Arhats*. Attributed to Lu Lengjia. Southern Song. Ink and color on silk. Album leaf. The Palace Museum, Beijing

a scholar (fig. 2.28) and echoes a recurring meme, often associated with the story of the Tang-dynasty scholar-official Xiao Yi 蕭翼 tricking a monk, originally found in Wang Xizhi's *Preface to the Orchid Pavilion Gathering* (*Lanting ji xu* 蘭亭集序), a calligraphic piece coveted by the Tang emperor Taizong 太宗 (r. 626–649).[64]

64 Craig Clunas rightly notes that Emperor Taizong was the "patron of the Eighteen Scholars depicted on the scroll" (Clunas 2017, 46–47). For four versions of paintings depicting the story of Xiao Yi obtaining the Orchid Pavilion Preface calligraphic piece by trickery, see

FIGURE 2.26 Detail of the back of a block retrieved from Julu, Hebei. Northern Song. Woodblock fragment. Spencer Collection, The New York Public Library

FIGURE 2.27 Detail. *Handscroll of Buddhist Images*, by Zhang Shengwen. ca. 1180. Dali Kingdom. Ink, color, and gold on paper. Handscroll. National Palace Museum

FIGURE 2.28 Detail. *The Eighteen Scholars of the Tang*. 17th century. Ming or Qing. Ink and color on silk. Hanging scroll. Yale University Art Gallery

3 The *Secret Treasures* Woodcuts

The exquisite landscape illustrations accompanying the *Imperially Composed Explanation of the Secret Treasures* (*Yuzhi mizang quan* 御製秘藏詮; hereafter called the *Secret Treasures*) are among the most artistic early woodcuts in East Asia inspired by paintings (figs. 0.17, 2.29a–p, 2.30a–n, 2.31).[65] The original text, composed by the Northern Song emperor Taizong with annotations by elite monks, is a collection of poetry-based commentaries to the Buddhist canon.[66] Scholars have noted that the initial work was not included in the Kaibao 開寶 Canon, the first printed Buddhist collection cut and printed in tenth-century Sichuan, but was added later.[67] Its key illustrations appear in three versions of Chinese and Korean copies, most likely printed in the late eleventh to early twelfth centuries. Due to lack of documentation, the date when the illustrations were initially designed remains controversial.[68] Although they serve as illustrations to imperial commentaries, there seems to be no direct relation between them.[69] Unlike mainstream icon-based Buddhist art, the *Secret Treasures* woodcuts are devoid of any icons and only feature figures in landscape.

The Chinese version, now in the Harvard Art Museums (figs. 2.29a–d; hereafter called Harvard specimens), contains four illustrations in three handscrolls, pertinent to different sections of the thirteenth chapter. Scholars have long recognized the Harvard specimens as early twelfth-century Northern Song copies, printed from original tenth-century blocks. This is evidenced by a stamped colophon at the end of the third scroll (fig. 2.29e). It identifies the monk Jianluan 鑒巒, abbot of the Qingliansi 青蓮寺 (Monastery of the Green

---

the three handscrolls in Palace Museum in Beijing, the Liaoning Provincial Museum, and National Palace Museum in Taipei, as well as the album leaf attributed to Qiu Ying in Freer Gallery.

65 Loehr 1968; Chen Yuquan 2009; Egami and Kobayashi 1994; Huang 2017c; Takenami 2021.

66 Taizong's devotion to Buddhism is further documented in a posthumous stele in commemoration of him; the stele was erected in the Buddhist pilgrimage site Bodhgaya, India, in 1033 under the patronage of the Northern Song Empress Dowager Liu 劉 (969–1033). See Jinah Kim 2021, 9–10 (fig. 4).

67 The best evidence is in the record of the Japanese monk Jōjin, who listed a "thirty-juan *Secret Treasures*" as part of the "newly-printed sutras" he requested from and granted by the Xiansheng Monastery; see Chen Yuquan 2009, 163. The extant specimens at Harvard Art Museums do not bear any character from the *qianziwen* 千字文, which is used in numbering the Kaibao Canon; see Wu and Chia eds. 2015, 153–73 (esp. 160).

68 Li 2002b, 58–63.

69 Huang 2017c, 12.

Lotus) in southern Shanxi (map 0.3), as having raised the funds for the printing in 1108 (see ch. 5).[70]

The two Korean versions, probably from the eleventh century, contain more illustrations. Ninety-six woodcuts appear in the copy that is today held in the Nanzenji 南禪寺 (Southern Meditation Monastery), a temple in southeast Kyoto (figs. 2.30a–b; hereafter called Nanzenji specimens), while four woodcuts are in a version housed in the Sung Am Archives of Classical Literature (Songam Kosŏ Pangmulgwan 誠庵古書博物館) in Seoul (fig. 2.31).[71] The woodcuts seem to represent two different but closely related versions, recut under Koryŏ royal patronage from the tenth-century Chinese Kaibao Canon, possibly transmitted to Korea as a diplomatic gift.[72] Given the highly similar style and quality of all three versions, they can be said to reflect a common style of Chinese woodcuts in the period of the tenth-to-twelfth centuries.

Egami Yasuhi and Kobayashi Hiromitsu, who published fifty-one Nanzenji specimens from the first ten chapters,[73] note that the remaining forty-five illustrations from the other unpublished nine extant chapters (with the seventeenth chapter missing) are mere repetitions.[74] Four of the fifty-one illustrations (fig. 2.30b) share identical designs with the Harvard specimens, (figs. 2.29b), although they accompany different chapters.[75] Close comparisons

70 Li F. 2003, 185–86; Chen Yuquan 2009, 165–68; Loehr 1968; Barnhart 1969; Kim 2003; Su 1999, 79–83; Wu and Chia eds. 2015, 160–61; Sun B. 2016; Huang 2017c, 11–19; Takenami 2021, 115. Chen Yuquan argue that the Harvard specimens are printed from the blocks cut around 988–995; these blocks have not been integrated into the Kaibao Canon; see Chen Yuquan 2009, 16–22.

71 Egami and Kobayashi 1994; Kim 2003, 106–107; Kim 2011. Yi Sŏng-mi does not see these versions as faithful "recut" versions of the Chinese original. Rather, she argues that the Koryŏ versions do not merely reflect the Chinese prototype but also demonstrate the early Koryŏ landscape painting style; see Yi 1986; Chen Yuquan 2009, 29–30. Cf. Chen Yuquan 2009, 24–25, 29–31. For more about the use of the Kaibao Canon as a diplomatic gift, see Kurz 2001; Li F. 2003; Sloane 2010; Tong 1991.

72 For more historical records of the Sino-Korean artistic and Buddhist exchanges, including the "Buddhist canon gifted in the Yuanfu 元符 (1098–1100) reign," and the Korean painters coming to the Xiangguosi 相國寺 Monastery in Northern Song Kaifeng to make copies of the murals, see Zhang 2020, esp. 77, 78–80.

73 Egami and Kobayashi 1994.

74 For example, the first illustration of the first chapter is identical with the fifth illustration of the tenth chapter, as well as the fifth illustration of the twentieth chapter. For the correlative chart of all the illustrations in the Nanzenji collection, see Egami and Kobayashi 1994, 182.

75 This revised the earlier knowledge of the relation between the Harvard and the Nanzenji collections posited by Max Loehr and Yi Sŏng-mi. For the scholarship review, see Chen Y. 2009, 25–26. However, Chen's claim that there are only 50 specimens in the Nanzenji collection needs to be corrected (see 25). The four Chinese illustrations are accompanied

a

b

c

d

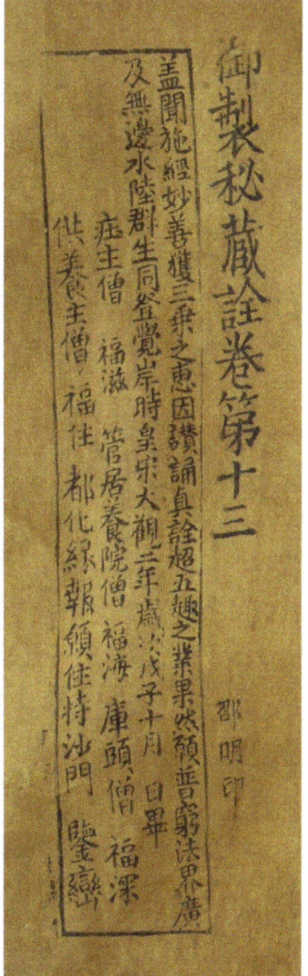

御製秘藏詮卷第十三
邵明印
蓋聞施經妙善獲三乘之惠因讚誦真詮超五趣之業果然願普窮法界廣
及無邊水陸群生同登覺岸時皇宋大觀二年歲次戊子十月 日畢
莊主僧 福滋 管居養院僧 福海 庫頭僧 福深
供養主僧 福住 都化緣報願住持沙門 鑒巒

e

FIGURES 2.29A–E
Details. Landscape illustrations of the *Secret Treasures*. 1108. Northern Song. Woodblock prints. Handscroll. Harvard Art Museums
a. Scroll 1, section 3: landscape illustration 1 (1962.11.1)
b. Scroll 2, section 2: landscape illustration 2 (1962.11.2)
c. Scroll 2, section 6: landscape illustration 3 (1962.11.1–3)
d. Scroll 3, section 3: landscape illustration 4 (1962.11.3)
e. Detail, colophon bearing the date of 1108. Scroll 3, section 6: Leaf 15 (1962.11.1–3)

FIGURES 2.30A–B Details. Landscape Illustrations of the *Secret Treasures*. Koryŏ period, Korea. Woodblock print. Nanzenji, Kyoto
a. Vol. 4, woodcut 2
b. Vol. 10, woodcut 4

FIGURE 2.31 Detail. Landscape Illustrations of the *Secret Treasures*. Woodblock print. Koryŏ period, Korea. Sung Am Archives of Classical Literature, Seoul

FIGURE 2.29F Detail of fig. 2.29b. Landscape illustrations of the *Secret Treasures*. Scroll 2, section 2: landscape illustration 2. Harvard Art Museums

FIGURE 2.30C Detail of fig. 2.30b. Landscape Illustrations of the *Secret Treasures*. Vol. 10, woodcut 4. Koryŏ period, Korea. Woodblock print. Nanzenji, Kyoto

of various details of the Harvard and Nanzenji specimens further show that the Chinese and Korean sets are based on differently cut blocks.[76] This is evident particularly from a detail that shows a partially hidden pavilion (figs. 2.29f, 2.30c). In the Nanzenji sample (fig. 2.30c), a pillar supporting the base of the

with different sections of the thirteenth chapter. In the Korean cases, the four identical compositions are inserted to accompany different sections of the 5th, 8th, 9th, 10th, 15th, 18th, 19th, 20th chapters respectively. For a chart, see Egami and Kobayashi 1994, 182. See also Huang 2017c, 12 (esp. footnote 49).

76 Cf. Chen Yuquan's visual comparisons of selected details of the four templates, which lead to his conclusion that the Nanzenji specimens were later and cruder than the Harvard specimens; see Chen Yuquan 2009, 25–28, 271–78 (figs. 1.31–1–65).

FIGURE 2.32 Fragment of a landscape drawing. Possibly Xi Xia. Ink on paper. Discovered in Khara Khoto

pavilion on the water is more slanted than its counterpart in the Harvard version (fig. 2.29f). The three groups of grasses on the slope in the Nanzenji sample, too, are more loosely constructed, different from the dense clusters in the Harvard specimens. Last but not least, the overhanging boulder in front of the roof of the pavilion in the Nanzenji version has an additional line next to the dots on the boulder not seen in the Harvard counterpart.

Based on the Nanzenji specimens, it is likely that Emperor Taizong's original compilation consisted of twenty chapters of texts, each with five landscape-based illustrations.[77] The woodcut designers recycled and reassembled selected stock motifs and compositional templates to create seemingly different images. To produce such a large collection of landscape woodcuts, it is reasonable to assume that the designer drafted the compositions on semi-transparent paper, transferred them onto blocks, and then had cutters execute the blocks accordingly. Such preparatory drawings may be similar to the so-called "landscape powder drawings" (*shanshui fentu* 山水粉圖), mentioned by various Tang poets such as Chen Zi'ang 陳子昂 (661–702) and Li Bo 李白 (701–762).[78] A rare archaeological specimen of a landscape drawing on paper, discovered in the Xi Xia ruins in Khara Khoto (fig. 2.32; hereafter called the Khara Khoto drawing), possibly dated to the twelfth century,[79] provides a sense of what such a

77 The texts composed by Emperor Taizong were completed in 983–988; see Chen Yuquan 2009, 11–13.

78 Sha 2007, 25–26. For more textual and visual discussion of landscape paintings in Buddhist context, see Li X. 2017.

79 Stein 1928, 3: plate LXI (K.K. II. 0313. b). Wen Fong dated the drawing to the late 12th-early 13th century; see Fong 1992, 105 (fig. 35). The composition of the Khara Khoto drawing

preparatory drawing may have looked like. Comparable to the recurring scenarios featured in the *Secret Treasures* woodcuts, the Khara Khoto drawing reveals clusters of mountains far and near, a boat in the waterscape, and minute travelers walking on a bridge or a path in the foreground.

3.1 *Landscape Style*

Stylistically, the *Secret Treasures* woodcuts display a landscape style that blends Tang and Song traditions.[80] The connection to Tang landscape art (fig. 2.33) is evident in the woodcut's depiction (fig. 2.30d) of a diagonal positioned cliff with a slanted platform on top and smaller units of rock formation underneath.[81] The compositional convention was to place a slope on one side of the foreground and a vertical cliff on the other side of the middle ground, sandwiching waterscape recessing to the depth in between (fig. 2.29g). This recalls an earlier counterpart in a monochrome wall painting, dated to 904 (fig. 2.34) and recently unearthed in a woman's tomb in Wangmucun 王母村, Hebei.[82] Selected details from the Harvard specimens, including the parallel texture brushstrokes (fig. 2.29h) and the towering mountains (fig. 2.29i), echo the tenth-century "period style" of landscape paintings and woodcuts discovered in tombs, both in the north and the south. Obviously similar are the wall painting from the tomb of Wang Chuzhi (dated 924) in Quyang (fig. 2.35),[83] Hebei, and the tenth-century hanging scroll discovered in a Liao tomb in Yemaotai 葉茂台, Liaoning (fig. 2.36).[84] The short and crossed linear markings on mountains (fig. 2.29j), furthermore, call to mind similar patterns in the printed frontispieces to the *Golden Light Sutra* (*Jin guangming jing* 金光明經), dated to 988 (figs. 2.37a–b). This was discovered in the tomb of a lay woman, the Fourth Daughter of the Sun Family (Sun Siniang 孫四娘; d. after 1054) in Jiangyin 江陰, Jiangsu.[85] In comparison to the classic repertoire of landscape

---

recalls a miniature screen painting depicted in the oft-cited *Double Screen* (*Chongping huiqi* 重屏會棋) attributed to Zhou Wenju 周文矩 (Palace Museum); for a plate, see Huang X. 2021, 142 (fig. 26).

80 Huang 2017c, 13; Kobayashi 2017, 33–52; Takenami 2021, 127–32.

81 See also DHSKQJ 18: 145 (fig. 121).

82 Hebeisheng wenwu yanjiu suo et al. 2019. The wall painting in the Wangmucun tomb is executed in monochrome ink; see Zheng 2021, 89–90.

83 Hebeisheng wenwu yanjiu suo et al. 1998 (color pl. 14); ZGCTBHQJ 1: 96.

84 Liaoning sheng bowuguan 2004, 39; Yang 1975; Li Q. 2004; Huang 2014c, 147–49 (for more scholarship review, see 148n146), 195 (fig. 31).

85 Suzhou bowuguan 2012, 16–23; Suzhou bowuguan et al. 1982; Zhu 1984; Zhang J. 2014; Huang 2017c, 49 (fig. 16); ZGBHQJ 1: 36 (fig. 47); Sudō 2021, 72–73.

FIGURE 2.30D Detail. Landscape Illustrations of the *Secret Treasures*. Vol. 3, woodcut 2. Koryŏ period, Korea. Woodblock print. Nanzenji, Kyoto

FIGURE 2.33 Detail of landscape. 8th century. Tang. Mural. North wall of the main chamber, Mogao 320, Dunhuang, Gansu

FIGURE 2.29G Detail of fig. 2.29a. Landscape illustrations of the *Secret Treasures*. 1108. Northern Song. Woodblock prints. Handscroll. Harvard Art Museums

FIGURE 2.34 Landscape. 904. Tang. Painted tomb no. 1 of Woman Cui, Wangmu village, Pingshan county, Hebei

FIGURE 2.29H Detail of fig. 2.29d. Landscape illustrations of the *Secret Treasures*. 1108. Northern Song. Woodblock prints. Handscroll. Harvard Art Museums

FIGURE 2.35 Detail of a landscape wall painting. 924. Five Dynasties. Mural. Tomb of Wang Chuzhi. Quyang, Hebei

paintings cited in Max Loehr's classic study,[86] including the northern landscape tradition associated with Jing Hao 荊浩 (active 850–911) and Guan Tong 關仝 (active 907–960), and the southern landscape style associated with Dong Yuan 董源 (active 930–960), these archaeological materials bear more reliable dates and therefore prove to be more useful in dating the woodcuts.

86 Loehr 1968, 34–54.

FIGURE 2.29I Detail of fig. 2.29b. Landscape illustrations of the *Secret Treasures*. 1108. Northern Song. Woodblock prints. Handscroll. Harvard Art Museums

FIGURE 2.36
Detail. *Playing Chess in the Deep Mountains*. 10th century. Liao. Ink and color on silk. Hanging scroll. Liaoning Provincial Museum

FIGURE 2.29J Detail of fig. 2.29a. Landscape illustrations of the *Secret Treasures*. 1108. Northern Song. Woodblock prints. Handscroll. Harvard Art Museums

a

FIGURES 2.37A–B
Details. Frontispiece to the *Golden Light Sutra*, juan 2. 988. Northern Song. Woodblock print. Excavated from the tomb of Sun Siniang (d. after 1054), Suzhou
a. Detail of 2.37b
b. A complete view

b

3.2 *Huts, Pavilions, and Fences*

Huts, pavilions, and fenced residences stand out as three major recurring architectural motifs dotting the mountainous landscape in the *Secret Treasures*. A monk's hut, a dwelling set against rustic mountains, is the most recurring motif (figs. 2.29k, 2.30e–j).[87] The dome-shaped hut is made of multi-layered dry stalks of plants, rendered in short vertical lines. Its U-shaped open entrance is sometimes decorated with drapes of raised curtains and there are intricate netted patterns and pieces of furniture in its interior. Human figures, such as a monk or a scholar-official, stand outside the hut and bow to a monk seated inside.

A good example appears in the Chinese version (fig. 2.29k). Set in a natural landscape in which mountains and water evoke a reclusive lifestyle, the hut appears in the upper left corner of the composition, securely "sandwiched" between a cliff on the right and a slope on the left. Inside the hut, a senior monk is seated on an armed chair, possibly resembling the now-lost Northern Song print *The Six Patriarchs*, copied in the Japanese drawing (fig. 2.24b). A layman accompanied by another monk bows to the seated master. Judging from his hat and robe, he may also be a scholar official. Comparative motifs retrieved from the Korean version in the Nanzenji collection (figs. 2.30e–j) show modifications of the hut motif, evident in the nuanced changes in the figural representations outside, the furnishing details inside, the furniture pieces, and the strategy of switching its orientation to create mirror images.

The hut in its various modes calls to mind the stereotypical Buddhist hut as defined by the Northern Song monk Daocheng 道誠 (active 1004–1024):

87 Cf. some of these examples reproduced in Huang 2014b, 400 (figs. 10–11); 2017c, 55 (fig. 25); Sun B. 2016, 424 (fig. 2).

FIGURE 2.29K
Detail of fig. 2.29a. Landscape illustrations of the *Secret Treasures*. 1108. Northern Song. Woodblock prints. Handscroll. Harvard Art Museums

> According to the *Buddhist Names*, a hut is a rounded shelter made of thatch ... the Indian monks and laymen lived in huts for self-cultivation.[88]
>
> 《釋名》曰：草為圓屋曰庵 ... 西天僧俗修行多居庵。

Daocheng's link of the Buddhist hut to the Indian meditative tradition can be further supported by visual evidence in ancient Indian art. According to Kazi Ashraf, the Brahmanic's forest dwelling in ancient Gandhara stone carvings is often represented as an ascetic's hut or "forest hut." Its visual feature highlights the "rounded leaf roof or of reed construction natural to a forest environment."[89] A stone relief dated sometime from the sixth to the fourth centuries BCE (fig. 2.38), for example, juxtaposes two dome-shaped huts side by side, with inhabitants and entrances facing the opposite side. The hut on the left, noted for repetitive short vertical lines, mimicking a hut made of reeds, especially is comparable to Chinese counterparts seen in the *Secret Treasures* woodcuts. However, while the ancient Indian motif undoubtedly resembles the medieval Chinese hut, it requires further evidence to establish a direct connection.

The hut motif in Chinese visual culture is often associated with eremitism, meditation, and self-cultivation.[90] In Buddhist pictorial art, huts appear in wall

88 T.54.2127: 263b. Cf. the translation in Pan 2007, 75.

89 Ashraf 2013, 11; for more visual examples, see 6 (fig. 1.4), 12 (fig. 1.11), 40 (fig. 1.8). This author is grateful for Eric Huntington's input.

90 Beyond Buddhist art, it was featured on the cover page of the fourteenth century *Newly Illustrative Fiction of the Three Kingdoms* published in Jianyang, Fujian; see Huang 2014b, 401 (fig. 13); Kobayashi 2017, 109–10 (figs. 1–2).

FIGURES 2.30E–J Details of the hut motifs. Landscape Illustrations of the *Secret Treasures*. Koryŏ period, Korea. Woodblock print. Nanzenji, Kyoto
e. Vol. 1, woodcut 6
f. Vol. 7, woodcut 2
g. Vol. 8, woodcut 2
h. Vol. 1, woodcut 5
i. Vol. 6, woodcut 4
j. Vol. 7, woodcut 1

FIGURE 2.38 Detail of two ascetic huts. 6th–4th century BCE. Gandhara. Stone relief

paintings and woodcuts associated with various texts, such as the *Diamond Sutra* (fig. 11.11c), the *Lotus Sutra* (fig. 3.37b), the *Maitreya Sutra* (figs. 6.2–6.6), and more.[91] The recluse's hut depicted on the north wall of the ninth-century monumental wall painting of the *Maitreya Sutra* in Yulin Cave 25 (fig. 2.39) is among the earliest Dunhuang examples.[92] Placed at the foot of the mountain, facing a meandering stream and a wooden bridge, the hut is a resting place for the practitioner who meditates in a cave nearby. Dome-shaped, it is delineated in short, vertical ink lines, drawn against the color wash in dark and light brown. Its overall design matches that of huts in the *Secret Treasures* woodcuts. Nearby a monk or hermit is meditating in a cave, whose geographic features recall the grotto landscape in the Nanzenji woodcuts (figs. 2.30a).

Mural images of huts in the mid-tenth century Mogao Cave 61, built by the Dunhuang governor Cao Yuanzhong and his wife, are further visual predecessors (fig. 2.40). More than thirty recluses' huts are dotted in the

91 For more visual examples, see Huang 2014b, 401 (figs. 12–13); 2017c, 56 (fig. 26); 2018b, 106 (fig. 18). For the hut motifs depicted in Xi Xia Buddhist mural, see Yulin Cave 3 reproduced in Zhang S. 2019, 24 (fig. 3).

92 This monkish figure is identified as the Buddha's principle disciple Jiaye 迦葉 (Mahākāśyapa or Kāśyapa); see Huang 2017c, 14. For more about the Yulin Cave 25, especially the Tibetan donor and the dating, see Xie and Huang 2007.

FIGURE 2.39
Detail. *Maitreya Sutra Tableaux*. 9th century. Tang. Mural. North wall of the main chamber. Yulin Cave 25, Guazhou, Gansu

FIGURE 2.40 Detail of the Panoramic View of Mt. Wutai. 10th century. Five Dynasties. Mural. West wall of the main chamber, Mogao Cave 61, Dunhuang, Gansu

thirteen-meter-long wall-size mural showing Mt. Wutai.[93] Often located at the foot of a mountain or hidden amid its middle level, dome-shaped huts provide man-made structures for devout lay Buddhists and monks to retreat from the world and meditate. Some bear cartouches with specific names, such as the Auspicious Hut (Jixiang an 吉祥菴) and the Pure Wind Hut (Qingfeng an 清風菴) on top of the Southern Terrace. Other examples include the Hut of Monk Zifu (Zifu heshang an 資福和尚菴), Fourth Master Zhao's Hut (Zhao Sishi zhi an 趙四師之菴), and Hut of Dharma Florescence (Fahua zhi an 法華之菴), each shown with its owner meditating inside.[94] Unlike the crowded atmosphere of the mural showing Mt. Wutai with its dense cluster of temples, traveling pilgrims, and auspicious omens, the landscape depicted in the *Secret Treasures* woodcuts evokes a more serene and solitary environment.

Around the same time, the formula of "one hut, one meditator" was applied more widely to re-invent the "thousand buddhas" (*qianfo* 千佛) pictorial genre, which aids meditation and visualization. Examples include the east and west (fig. 2.41) walls of Cave 19, the Western Thousand Buddhas Grottoes (Xi qianfo dong 西千佛洞), about 22 miles west of today's Dunhuang city, Gansu.[95] The hut motif, repeated in multiple rows, is drawn out in a simple, frontal, reverse U shape. Within each U-shaped hut is a seated monk; only one hut shows two seated monks.

Compared to the hut motifs depicted in Mogao Cave 61, the huts in the *Secret Treasures* woodcuts show more interior designs, including a chair, a desk, curtains, and decorative wall patterns (figs. 2.29k, 2.30e–j). The attention to material details is further elaborated in the Northern Song mural imagery of a deity's hut associated with the Jataka story concerning the daughter of a deer as recounted in the *Sutra of Repaying the Parents*. This is found in the Kaihuasi 開化寺 (Monastery of Opening Transformation) in Gaoping 高平, Shanxi, built around 1073 and painted by Guo Fa 郭發 and others in 1096 (fig. 2.42).[96] Positioned in three-quarter view, the dome-shaped hut has an open entrance framed by knotted straw along the arch-shaped border. The interior is filled with material abundance, including multi-layered shelves, a short table, and clothes hanging on a rack.

---

93 Heller 2008. For more plates, see Dunhuang yanjiu yuan 1993, fig. 78; DHSKQJ, 18: 180. For more studies of Mogao Cave 61, see Lee 2012; Lin W. 2013; Lin W. 2014.

94 Huang 2017c, 14; Zhang S. 2019, 22–24.

95 For a recent study that dates this cave to the Uighur occupation period, see Yin 2019, 306–307. See also DHSKQJ 2: 185.

96 For the story, see T.3.156: 138–41. Cf. the depiction of the same Jataka story in the Tang Mogao Caves 112 and 85 reproduced in DHSKQJ 9: 126 (fig. 110), 140 (fig. 121).

FIGURE 2.41 Detail. Meditative monks in U-shaped huts. 10th century. Five Dynasties. Mural. West wall of Cave 19, Western Thousand Buddha Grottoes, Dunhuang, Gansu

FIGURE 2.42
Detail of a hut. The Deer Lady Jataka. 1096–1097. Northern Song. Mural. North wall of Kaihua Monastery, Gaoping, Shanxi

l

m

FIGURES 2.29L–M Motifs of pavilions by the waterscape. Landscape illustrations of the *Secret Treasures*. 1108. Northern Song. Woodblock prints. Handscroll. Harvard Art Museums
l. Detail of fig. 2.29c. Scroll 2, section 6
m. Detail of fig. 2.29d. Scroll 3, section 3

The other recurring architectural design in the *Secret Treasures* woodcuts is a pavilion, originally rooted in Chinese artistic visions of eremitism. Three of the four Harvard specimens depict such a motif (figs. 2.29b–d). While none shows figures inside a pavilion, two examples depict a monk-style traveler crossing a river nearby (figs. 2.29l–m). Similar pavilions appear also in the Korean specimens both in the Nanzenji (fig. 2.30a) and Archives (fig. 2.31) versions. An eighth-century landscape mural (fig. 2.43), recently discovered in the tomb of Han Xiu 韓休 in Xi'an and dated to around 740, represents a Tang prototype.[97] Wen Fong has convincingly traced the pictorial convention of a pavilion by the water to the tenth-to-eleventh-century Jiangnan landscape of eremitism. Examples here include the much-debated *Riverbank*, attributed to Dong Yuan (figs. 2.44, 3.21b), and the *Lofty Scholar*, attributed to Wei Xian 衛賢 (active 961–975) (fig. 2.45). Both artists were active in the Southern Tang (937–975) kingdom in south China.[98]

Representing the ideal dwelling of a lofty recluse, both paintings have elaborate sections near the foreground that depict a scholar, his wife, and child gathering in a pavilion by the water. The common narrative mode, in Shih Shou-chien's words, expresses the pictorial intention (*huayi* 畫意) of "the lofty

97 For more studies of the wall paintings of this tomb, see Zheng Y. 2015; Zheng Y. 2021, 85, 86; Guo 2017; Qiang 2016, 111; Shih 2017a, 28; Wu 2022c, 128–33.

98 Fong 2014, 206–209, figs. 22–24.

FIGURE 2.43 Landscape mural. ca. 740. Tang. Mural. North wall of the tomb of Han Xiu, Xi'an. Xi'an Historical Museum

scholar in streams and mountains" (*Jiangshan gaoyin* 江山高隱).[99] Based on its style, *Riverbank* is more likely to date from the early half of the eleventh century, while *Lofty Scholar* is a pre-Song painting that was included in Emperor Huizong's collection by the early twelfth century. Its extant version presents an authentic "Xuanhe mounting style" (*Xuanhe zhuang* 宣和裝), sanctioned by Emperor Huizong's court.[100]

Fenced residential compounds dotting the *Secret Treasures* woodcuts form the third group of recurring motifs. Often showing a half-open gate (fig. 2.30k), fences consist of densely woven bamboo or wood. They are comparable to

99 Shih 2010, 95, fig. 27; 2017a, 34; Huang 2014b, 410.

100 For more on the Xuanhe mounting, see Xu 1981, 83; Ebrey 2008, 115 (fig. 4.5).

FIGURE 2.44
Detail. *Riverbank*, attributed to Dong Yuan (ca. 930s–960s). Possibly 11th century. Ink and color on silk. Hanging scroll. The Metropolitan Museum of Art

FIGURE 2.45
Detail. *Lofty Scholar*, by Wei Xian. 10th century. Five Dynasties. Ink and color on silk. Hanging scroll. The Palace Museum, Beijing

FIGURE 2.30K
Detail. Landscape Illustrations of the *Secret Treasures*. Vol. 5, woodcut 1. Koryŏ period, Korea. Woodblock print. Nanzenji, Kyoto

FIGURE 2.46
Detail. *Wintry Trees and Layered Banks*, attributed to Dong Yuan. 10th century. Five Dynasties. Ink and light colors on silk. Hanging scroll. Kurokawa Institute of Ancient Cultures, Hyogo

the fences depicted in *Wintry Trees and Layered Banks* (fig. 2.46), attributed to Dong Yuan.[101]

3.3 *Figures in Landscape*

The main protagonists in the *Secret Treasures* woodcuts are master monks, supporting roles being played by lay scholars and assistant monks. Master-and-disciple conversations often take place in a natural space enclosed by

101 Takenami Haruka also compares the similar fence motifs in *Secret Treasures* woodcuts and the *Wintry Trees and Layered Banks*; he treats the *Wintry Trees* as a Southern Song copy; see Takenami 2015, 217–96, esp. 254. For a complete view, see Nezu Bijutsukan 2023, 50.

n

o

FIGURE 2.29N–O Details of figures. Landscape illustrations of the *Secret Treasures*. 1108. Northern Song. Woodblock prints. Handscroll. Harvard Art Museums
n. Detail of fig. 2.29b. Scroll 2, section 2: landscape illustration 2
o. Detail of fig. 2.29c. Scroll 2, section 6

trees (fig. 2.29n) and isolated by water (fig. 2.29o). The intermingling of monks and scholarly figures, moreover, provides the visual prototype for an emerging genre of painting in the Northern Song that features scholarly gatherings in private garden settings, to which elite lay Buddhists were also invited. For example, in the Taipei version of *Mountain Villa* (fig. 2.47), attributed to Li Gonglin and executed in monochrome ink linear drawing style, two monks are seated among a group of scholars on a plateau against the waterfall.[102]

Complementing the seated monk surrounded by disciples are travelers moving through the landscape (figs. 2.30l–n). Whether monks or laymen, they either walk on foot or ride on a horse or donkey, sometimes alone, sometimes in the company of other travelers. While some figural motifs (fig. 2.30l) can be readily associated with stereotypical lay travelers dotting tenth-to-eleventh-century landscape paintings (fig. 2.48), a selective few derive from Tang-Song Buddhist art featuring a traveler with a pack on his back.[103]

102 For more on this painting and the social and cultural milieu of Li Gonglin, see Harrist 1998.

103 For more visual comparisons of travelers in *Secret Treasures* woodcuts and Tang-Song paintings, see Chen Yuquan 2009, 325–26.

FIGURE 2.47 Detail. *The Mountain Villa*, attributed to Li Gonglin. Possibly Northern Song. Ink on paper. Handscroll. National Palace Museum

There are two main motifs of travelers: one is a monk holding a walking stick and accompanied by a tiger (fig. 2.30m); the other features a layman with a fully loaded pack on his back and a flywhisk and staff in his hands (fig. 2.30n).[104] These figural motifs derive from the visual meme of a pilgrim monk carrying a pack and accompanied by a tiger (figs. 1.34–1.35). The designer of the *Secret Treasures* woodcuts as well as other Northern Song artisans working in various media may well have had access to this visual model transmitted in north China. A possible forerunner is the traveling monk walking on a busy urban street, depicted in *Up the River* (fig. 2.49a).[105] His walking stick peeks out from

104 See Chen Yuquan 2009, 109–10, 318 (fig. 4–1), 324 (fig. 4–21).

105 Sun 2012, 106–107.

FIGURE 2.30L
Detail. Landscape Illustrations of the *Secret Treasures*. Vol. 3, woodcut 1. Koryŏ period, Korea. Woodblock print. Nanzenji, Kyoto

FIGURE 2.48
Detail. *A Solitary Temple Amid Clearing Peaks*, by Li Cheng. Northern Song. Ink and light color on silk. Hanging scroll. The Nelson-Atkins Gallery, Kansas City, Missouri

m

FIGURES 2.30M–N Details. Landscape Illustrations of the *Secret Treasures*. Koryŏ period, Korea. Woodblock print. Nanzenji, Kyoto
m. Vol. 8, woodcut 2
n. Vol. 2, woodcut 5

his pack while his canopy overflows with all sorts of suspended objects. The international appeal of the pilgrim-monk meme is further reflected in other visual examples in Xi Xia, Japanese (fig. 2.50),[106] and Tibetan Buddhist art.

3.4 *Interpreting the Woodcuts*

Previous scholars have noted that the landscape woodcuts bear no direct relation to the commentaries they accompany. What, then, is their meaning?

In Tang-Song Buddhist pictorial art, landscape motifs have often been associated with sites of magical manifestation. Examples include two artifacts discovered in the Dunhuang library cave. The first, an exquisite piece of Tang embroidery (fig. 2.51), shows a standing Buddha enclosed in a rocky environment. It was originally commissioned by the Buddhist leader Yiming 義明 of the Chongjiaosi 崇教寺 (Monastery of Venerating the Teaching) in

106 In the fourteenth century Kamakura printed frontispiece shown here, the traveling monk wears a necklace decorated with skulls, standing amid the pantheon flanking the central Buddha. An ink colophon written at the end of this printed text is dated 1383. Cf. Mitsui 1986, 86 (fig. 104). For more multi-cultural visual examples representing the pilgrim monk, see Nara Kenritsu Bijutsukan 1999; Wong 2002.

FIGURE 2.49A
Detail. *Up the River during Qingming Days.* Northern Song. Ink and color on silk. Handscroll. The Palace Museum, Beijing

FIGURE 2.50 Fragment of vol. 157 of *Perfection of Wisdom Sutra*. 1383. Kamakura period, Japan. Woodblock print. Concertina. The Metropolitan Museum of Art

the late seventh to early eight centuries. Now known as the Liangzhou 涼州 icon, named after its first appearance in Liangzhou (today's Wuwei 武威, Gansu), it represents the miraculous icon (*ruixiang* 瑞像) that emerged "from the living rock of a mountain."[107] A second example is a painting (fig. 2.52) that depicts the Mañjuśrī bodhisattva and his entourage floating on clouds above panoramic mountains. Zhao Xiaoxing interprets this as the magical

107 See Zhao Feng and Michelle McCoy in Agnew et al. 2016, 204–206 (pl. 19); Ma 2008; Wu 2023, 206 (fig. 4.26).

manifestation of Mañjuśrī in his sacred abode, Mt. Wutai.[108] Related to the notion of landscape motif and sites of magical manifestation, Liu Shufen pays special attention to cave formations in Song arhat paintings. She identifies the caves depicted as the "arhat caves" (*luohan dong* 羅漢洞), linking them to arhat worship in medieval China, when devotees turned natural mountain caves into temples. She cites anecdotes that describe monks visiting the caves having magical visions of arhats drinking tea and lecturing there.[109] It is likely that the *Secret Treasures* woodcuts' representations of monks' activities in landscape echo all these various visual and religious trends.

Different from such icon-based images, the *Secret Treasures* woodcuts are aniconic. Featuring monks and laymen in nature, they depict mountains as sites of self-cultivation, meditation, and sermons.[110] Images of monks meditating in huts, grottoes, and rustic dwellings show them conversing with their disciples in the mountains. They celebrate a reclusive life-style in pursuit of Buddhist attainment through self-cultivation, just as travelers moving through the landscape evoke pilgrims' progress toward enlightenment and salvation.[111] They all suggest a Buddhist life-style as advocated by the Chan school, whose early eleventh-century codes advocate aniconic practice in a life of labor and humility. Chan Buddhists eschewed icons in public halls and required monks to treat each other as peers, all the while attending to mundane chores, such as gardening, cleaning, cooking, and other housekeeping tasks.[112] The *Secret Treasures* woodcuts reflect these concerns. With the exceptions of a miniature stupa that may bear a Buddha image, there are hardly any iconic representations in the woodcuts. Instead, quite a few scenes highlight tasks of labor, such as sweeping the floor, fetching water from the stream, preparing tea, and the like.[113]

---

108 Zhao X. 2017, 107.

109 Similar scenes are depicted in paintings of the *Five Hundred Arhats* composed by Southern Song Ningbo workshop painters; see Liu 2022, 816–37.

110 Chen Yuquan 2009, 100–35, 318, 323–25 (figs. 4–18, 4–19, 4–20, 4–21, 4–22, 4–1); Shih 2012, 78–79; Huang 2014b, 396–97; Huang 2017c, 13; Takenami 2021, 132–38. For earlier Buddhist examples showing an icon against a mountain background, see the Tang embroidery of the Fanhe icon (British Museum [Ch.00260]; see Wu 2022a, 193; Wu 2023, 205) and the Northern Song portable painting showing the manifestation of the Wenshu bodhisattva in Mt. Wutai (Musée Guimet [EO 3588]; see Zhao X. 2017, 107).

111 Huang 2017c, 11–15.

112 For the Chan Buddhist codes compiled by the Northern Song monk Daoyuan 道原 (ca. 1004), see T.51.2076: 251. For more studies of the Chan codes, see Lin W. 2003, 384–86; Chen Yuquan 2009, 114–16.

113 For a scene depicting a boy sweeping the floor near the fence, see Huang 2014b, 400 (fig. 11).

FIGURE 2.51 *Shakyamuni Preaching on the Vulture Peak*. Tang. Silk embroidery on hemp cloth. Hanging scroll. The British Museum

FIGURE 2.52 *Mañjuśrī on His Lion* (EO 3588). 9th century. Ink and color on silk. Hanging scroll. Musée des Arts Asiatiques-Guimet

FIGURE 2.53 *Refined Cultivation along the Pan River*. Illustration from the *Xuanfeng qinghui tu*. Reprint dated 1305. Yuan. Woodblock print. Tenri Central Library, Tenri University, Japan

Compared to landscape paintings showing a hermit's dwelling (figs. 2.44, 2.45), the *Secret Treasures* woodcuts express eremitism more religiously and relate landscape to cosmology. Multiple Nanzenji specimens depict grottoes in the mountains or facing a body of water (figs. 0.17, 2.30a).[114] Symbolizing reclusion, meditation, and enlightenment, images of caves in religious art evoke places of retreat (fig. 2.39). Daoists, furthermore, link grotto landscapes with the transformative concept of the grotto-heaven (*dongtian* 洞天),[115] a site embodying reclusion, self-cultivation, spiritual transcendence, immortality, and paradise. A good example is the Yuan-dynasty illustration entitled *Refined Cultivation along the Pan River* (*Panxi lianxing* 磻溪鍊行) (fig. 2.53), which depicts the ascetic practice of Qiu Chuji 丘處機 (1148–1227), leading Daoist master of the Complete Perfection school and founder of its Dragongate (Longmen 龍門) branch, active in north China.[116] Like the Buddhist monk

114 For visual examples, see Huang 2017c, 48 (fig. 13).

115 Verellen 1995; Huang 2012, 21–22, 105–106, 113–14, 116–20, 123, 134, 235, 345.

116 Huang 2014b, fig. 8. Cf. the other illustration in the same book, reproduced in Huang 2017c, 51 (fig. 19); Sun B. 2016, 438 (fig. 6); Kobayashi 2017, 91 (fig. 9). For more studies, see Katz 2001; 2003; Chia 2011, 193–201; Dang 2007, 442–51; Kobayashi 2017, 89–94.

seated in the *Secret Treasures* woodcuts, the Daoist master rests in a cave overlooking the mountains.

4 The Woodcut Effect

Being fundamentally different as an artistic medium, woodblock printing cannot match every characteristic of painting. It is impossible in a woodblock to match the nuanced ink or color gradation created by painting as, for example, in the nuanced materiality of wooden surfaces that shows tree rings in Song paintings, achieved by applying varied ink washes.[117] On the other hand, given that the engraving tool is sharp and the block surface hard, woodblocks excel at creating intricate images made of repeated lines. As a result, angular, parallel, and intertwined lines form their basic visual idioms. This applies clearly to images of huts (figs. 2.29k, 2.30e–j), pavilion rooftops (figs. 2.29l–m), fences (fig. 2.30k), as well as water waves and mountains (fig. 2.0).

The fascination with interwoven lines in woodblock printing can be further linked to the style of "ruler-lined painting" (*jiehua* 界畫), which reached its prime in the Northern Song. Extant paintings offer meticulous pictorial examples, ranging from buildings through interwoven tents (fig. 2.49b) to minute ropes and brooms (fig. 2.54).

Stone carvings, where images are made on hard surfaces just as in woodblock prints, demonstrate a similar linear quality. A good example is the *Stele Picture with Eulogy of Shangu Rowing Back* (*Shangu Fanzhao tu zanbei* 山谷返棹圖贊碑), originally engraved in Dangtu 當塗, Anhui 安徽 in 1256 (fig. 2.55) and copied from what looks like a hanging-scroll painting by Mou Zicai 牟子才 (1223 *jinshi*), produced while he served as official there.[118] The engraved boat carrying the Northern Song scholar-in-exile Huang Tingjian has a most intricate cover made of interwoven bamboo.

The angular and linear quality evident in woodblocks like those in the *Secret Treasures* in turn may have inspired paintings. This is most evident in monochrome, plain linear drawings associated with the scholar-painter Li Gonglin. As noted earlier, Li's now-lost Guanyin painting was transferred to single-sheet prints distributed by his friend, the monk Datong. In Li's *Pictures of the Classic of the Filial Piety* (fig. 2.56), the angular and schematic leaves mimic those in

117 Visual examples include the percussion depicted in the *Great Exorcism*, the wooden screen in Liu Songnian's 劉松年 *Arhat*, and the *Weaving Machine* by Chen Juzhong 陳居中; see Huang 2017c, 15–16.

118 QDYY, 175–76; Beijing tushuguan jinshizu 1989, 44: 123; Huang 2017c, 16. For a recent study, see Brotherton 2020.

FIGURE 2.49B Detail. *Up the River during Qingming Days*. Northern Song. Ink and color on silk. Handscroll. The Palace Museum, Beijing

FIGURE 2.54
Detail. *Great Exorcism*. Southern Song. Ink, color, and gold on silk. Hanging scroll. The Palace Museum, Beijing

FIGURE 2.55 *Stele Picture with Eulogy of Shangu Rowing Back*. 1256. Southern Song. Rubbing. National Library of China

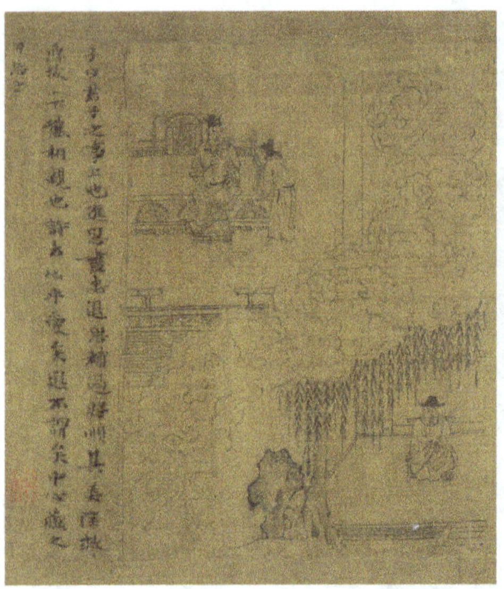

FIGURE 2.56 Detail. *The Classic of the Filial Piety*, by Li Gonglin. ca. 1085. Northern Song. Ink on silk. Handscroll. The Metropolitan Museum of Art

FIGURE 2.29P Detail of fig. 2.29d. Landscape illustrations of the *Secret Treasures*. Scroll 3, section 3: landscape illustration 4. 1108. Northern Song. Woodblock prints. Handscroll. Harvard Art Museums

the *Secret Treasures* woodcuts (figs. 2.0, 2.29p).[119] Similarly, in *Mountain Villa* attributed to Li (fig. 2.47), angular slices of rock formations flanking a group of monks and scholars, inspired by the *Secret Treasures*, recall the angular mountains in its woodcuts.[120] The painting repurposes the cave motif, replacing the solo monk with a group.[121] All these visual connections further support the hypothesis that Li, a scholar artist fully aware of the thriving print culture, may have created paintings in the angular woodcut effect.[122]

---

119 According to Richard Barnhart, this illustrates the first sentence of the seventeenth chapter of the *Classic of the Filial Piety*, highlighting the service of the ruler; see Barnhart et al. 1993, 147–49.

120 Huang 2017c, 18–19.

121 See Huang 2014b, 397–98 (figs. 6–7).

122 This echoes Robert Harrist's observation that Li Gonglin "had access to a living tradition of pictorial illustration in Buddhist ... woodblock prints" and that "woodblock prints provide an especially rich store of images that were an important part of visual culture during the time of Li Gonglin" (Harrist 1998, 98). For more about Li's use of past styles, see Barnhart 1976.

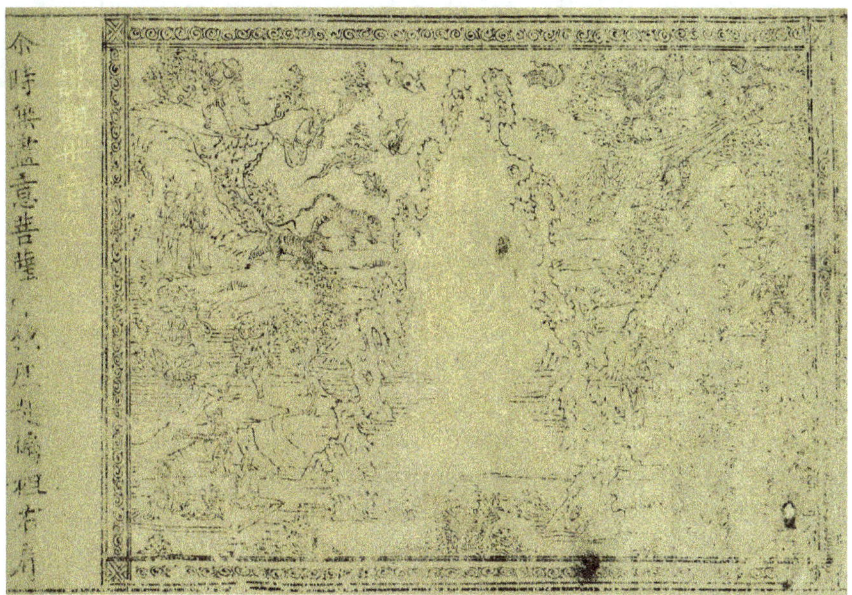

FIGURE 2.57 Frontispiece to the *Guanyin Sutra*. 1054. Northern Song. Ink and gold on paper. Manuscript. Excavated from the tomb of Sun Siniang (d. after 1054), Suzhou

Going beyond landscape paintings in plain linear style associated with Li Gonglin, some hand-painted Buddhist frontispieces closely compare to woodcut counterparts, providing further evidence of painting styles inspired by woodblock printing. The most unusual of them is a refined illumination mounted as a frontispiece to the hand-copied *Guanyin sutra* (fig. 2.57), discovered in the eleventh-century tomb of Lady Sun Siniang in Suzhou, Jiangsu.[123] Executed in ink and gold, it can be seen as an alternative linear painting or drawing. The central icon is the seated Guanyin bodhisattva, drawn in almost invisible golden pigment. Flanking him are figures in landscape done in minute monochrome linear drawing style. They spread out the picture plane in a symmetrical fashion, expounding selected episodes from the scripture celebrating Guanyin's efficacy. The maker of the frontispiece chose a unique brushstroke in executing short, pointed, angular lines that mimic the woodcut style. This is most evident in the agitated contour of the eroded rock formation flanking the central figure; it is also visible in the punctuated brushstrokes on the surface of the cliff in the upper left corner of the picture plane.

Although the frontispiece bears no specific date, another scroll, this one of the *Diamond Sutra*, executed in a similar style as the *Guanyin Sutra* and found

123 Suzhou bowuguan 2012, 42–43. For an archaeological report, see Suzhou bowuguan et al. 1982.

in the same tomb, contains a colophon dated to 1054. It identifies Lady Sun as the donor.[124] We can thus assume that the *Guanyin Sutra* was also sponsored by Lady Sun and compiled around 1054. Based on this, Sudō Hirotoshi speculates that it may have been a Suzhou product.[125] The composition of its frontispiece possibly borrows from the standardized template widely shared by printed frontispieces at that time. It resembles the composition of that of the printed *Lotus Sutra* (fig. 0.2) and bears the trademark of the commercial Yan Family printshop in eleventh-century Hangzhou. It was discovered in the Xi Xia ruins in Khara Khoto.[126] In both versions, the rocky mountain flanking the central Guanyin contains repetitive motifs that mimic the profile of a bird's head, echoing the bird-shaped Vulture Peak where the Buddha preached the sermon at the core of this scripture.[127] During the Song, Hangzhou was an international center of art and print culture. Many versions of the printed frontispieces and illustrations of the *Guanyin Sutra* published there have become models for other paintings produced elsewhere, including China's neighbors in East and West Asia.[128]

---

124 Suzhou bowuguan 2012, 36–39.

125 Sudō 2021, 74–75.

126 Huang 2014b, 414.

127 For more visual examples in Buddhist and Daoist art evoking the bird's head, see Huang 2012, 142–45; Wang Y. E. 2005, 192–200.

128 For the legacy of the Hangzhou Buddhist printing in Korean and Islamic paintings, see Huang 2011b, 151–54; 2017c, 26–27; for its connection to Japanese Buddhist illuminations, see Zhang 2020.

CHAPTER 3

Book Art of the *Lotus Sutra*

The growing artistic exchange between painting and printing led to the proliferation of fully illustrated Buddhist print books in the Song and Yuan periods. The illustrated *Lotus Sutra of the Wonderful Dharma* (*Miaofa lianhua jing* 妙法蓮華經, often abbreviated either *Lianhua jing* 蓮華經 or *Fahua jing* 法華經) appears in abundant versions, showing just how advanced print culture was at the time.[1] Mounted in concertina or accordion-scroll format, it was printed in Hangzhou and nearby Zhejiang, the historical center of artistic and book culture since the tenth century.[2] Printed images are often attached to the opening of chapters as frontispieces; they also appear as sequential illustrations embedded in the text.

The visual repertoire of the *Lotus Sutra* here (figs. 3.1a, 3.2a) differs from earlier conventions as preserved in mainstream Buddhist art forms such as sculptures (fig. 3.3), murals, manuscripts, and calligraphic steles (fig. 3.4).[3] It reflects visual memes book-makers edited, reassembled, and repurposed on the basis of broader sources. The Song collector Ye Mengde 葉夢得 (1077–1148) marveled at the superior quality of print books made in Hangzhou.[4] Modern scholars, examining the local print culture, have followed his lead and produced many studies on the complex relationship between different versions of the same texts. They have also documented the pervasive network of itinerant block cutters, printers, and publishers, and called attention to the artistic

FIGURE 3.0 Detail. Frontispiece to the *Lotus Sutra*, juan 1. Illustrated by Wang Yi. Southern Song. Woodblock print. Concertina. National Palace Museum
←

1 For the most-cited version translated by Kumārajīva in 406, see T. 9.262.

2 For Buddhism and print culture in tenth-century Hangzhou sponsored by the Wu–Yue rule, see Huang 2011a, 137–46; Welter 2022. Hangzhou as a historical printing center in Song-Yuan periods should include other neighboring places in Zhejiang, such as Huzhou 湖州, Shaoxing 紹興, and Pingjiang 平江, see Su 1999, 85–86, 90–91. For more on the cutters active in the Hangzhou neighborhood, see Su 1999, 93; Edgren 1989.

3 For Dunhuang murals, see DHSKQJ 7: 10–120. For select studies of the *Lotus Sutra* art, see Wang E. 2005; Huang 2011a–b; Zhang Y. 2009; Zhang 2013; Zhang and Zhang 2012; Zhang B. 2014; Zhang Y. 2016; Zhang J. 2017.

4 SLYY 8, 116.

© SHIH-SHAN SUSAN HUANG, 2024 | DOI:10.1163/9789004700017_005

a

b

FIGURES 3.1A–B
Frontispiece to the *Lotus Sutra*, juan 2. Illustrated by Wang Yi. Southern Song. Woodblock print. Concertina. National Palace Museum
a. The overall view
b. Detail of two monks

quality of some pictorial prints.[5] Building upon this, this discussion of *Lotus Sutra* book art focuses on recurring visual memes, showing their standardization and proliferation. The trendsetting impact of the text extends not only to Buddhist visual culture in Korea and Japan but also to paintings of non-Buddhist themes in Inner and West Asia.[6]

5 Fontein 1967; Edgren 1989; Su 1999, 84–91; Miya 1983a–b; Cui 1982; Zhang and Han 2006, 48–56.

6 The *Lotus Sutra* frontispieces produced in Japan and Korea produced before the sixteenth century were mostly painted and not printed; see Tanabe 1988, 63–97; Tanabe 2009; Nara Kokuritsu Hakubutsukan 1996, 211–15; Kungnip Chungang Pangmulgwan 2007.

a

b

c

d

FIGURES 3.2A–D
Frontispiece to the *Lotus Sutra*, juan 1. 1331–1349. Yuan. Woodblock print. Concertina. National Palace Museum

FIGURE 3.3
Buddha Shakyamuni and Prabhutaratna. 518. Northern Wei. Bronze and gold. Musée des Arts Asiatiques-Guimet

法蓮華經一千部金字三
十六部用鎮寶塔又寫一
千部散施受持靈應既多
具如本傳其載 勅內侍
吴懷寶賜金銅香爐高一

FIGURE 3.4
Detail. *Stele of the Jeweled Pagoda.* Calligraphy and text by Yan Zhenqing. 752. Tang. Rubbing

1 *Lotus Sutra* Experiences

The *Lotus Sutra* has been among the most widespread Buddhist scriptures in Inner and East Asia since medieval times.[7] After its debut in India in approximately the first century CE,[8] it was translated into Chinese at least six times between the third and seventh centuries. The most cited version, used in this study, was translated in 406 by the erudite monk Kumārajīva (Jiumoluoshi 鳩摩羅什, 344–413), a native of Kucha in Central Asia.[9] The text's teachings subsequently passed on to Korea and Japan as well as to other areas ruled by the Khitan, the Tangut, and the Uighur in north and northwest China as well as Central Asia.[10] This spread raised the *Lotus Sutra* to a level of importance equal to that of other great books representing major world religions. Donald Lopez describes it as the most "approachable" Buddhist text, citing its many story-based parables. In the mid-nineteenth century, he adds, it was the first Buddhist scripture "to be translated from Sanskrit into a European language" and "to appear in an American publication."[11]

Said to represent the Buddha's final (and thus highest and ultimate) teachings, the *Lotus Sutra* claims to be superior to all other Buddhist scriptures, just as the world peak Mt. Sumeru towers over all other mountains of the world.[12] It begins by establishing the setting: a cosmic and most dramatic assembly, hosted by Shakyamuni Buddha on the bird-shaped Vulture Peak (fig. 3.5).[13] There he delivers his ultimate message in story-based mode, so that all sentient beings can achieve buddhahood.[14] He begins by pointing out that visual approaches are the easiest way of teaching. This is known as "skillful means"

7 In the most recent publication, Chün-fang Yü highlighted the *Heart Sutra*, the *Diamond Sutra*, the *Lotus Sutra*, the *Vimalakirti Sutra*, and the *Nirvana Sutra* as the five major Buddhist texts of Chinese Buddhism; see Yü 2020, 29–64.

8 The *Lotus Sutra* was composed by different authors "between 100 BCE and 100 CE"; see Yü 2020, 32.

9 T.9.262. For a translation, see Hurvitz 2009. For a study of the social network of Kumārajīva in fourth-century China, see Bingenheimer 2020.

10 For the history of the *Lotus Sutra*, see Lopez 2016; Lopez and Stone 2019. The *Lotus Sutra* has been transcribed in Tangut script in gold on indigo paper, as well as printed in Chinese and Tangut with frontispieces; see Shi 1988, 160–61. The *Lotus Sutra* was translated into the Uighur version, preserved in fragments of written manuscripts found in Turfan and now in Berlin; see Peter Zieme's study in Yang trans. 2007, 36–38. For a study of the illustrated *Lotus Sutra* in Tangut script, printed in the Mongol era in the thirteenth century, see Arakawa 2018.

11 It was first translated into French in 1844; see Lopez 2016, 4.

12 T.9.262, 54a; Lopez and Stone 2019, 229.

13 Nara Kokuritsu Hakubutsukan 1996, 126.

14 Wang E. 2005, 194; Huang 2012, 145.

FIGURE 3.5
Lotus Sutra Tableaux. 984. Northern Song. Woodblock print. Single sheet. Seiryōji, Kyoto

or "expedient ways" of attaining the path of the buddhas (fig. 3.0). Making paintings (fig. 3.6a) or statues (fig. 3.6b) of Buddhist deities, even with humble means, is most meritorious. Visuals also have an encompassing appeal for children (fig. 3.6c), who may accumulate merit by drawing images of buddhas in the sand with "a blade of grass or a twig, a brush or a fingernail" or by playing with mud to build a miniature stupa.[15] Aside from granting merit through

15 T.9.262, 8c–9b; Lopez and Stone 2019, 61; Hurvitz 2009, 37.

a

b

c

FIGURES 3.6A–C Motifs of image-making from the *Lotus Sutra* frontispieces printed in Southern Song and Yuan Hangzhou. Woodblock print. National Palace Museum
a. Detail of fig. 3.37a. Frontispiece to the *Lotus Sutra*, juan 1, cut by Bian Ren and Qin Meng. Southern Song
b. Detail of 3.2a. Frontispiece to the *Lotus Sutra*, juan 1. Yuan
c. Detail. Frontispiece to the *Lotus Sutra*, juan 1, illustrated by Wang Yi, juan 1. Southern Song

image-making, the *Lotus Sutra* advocates the cult of the book by encouraging monks, nuns, and lay followers alike to recite and preach it (fig. 3.7). The sections entitled "The Expounder of the Dharma" and "Benefits Obtained by an Expounder of the Dharma" clearly praise the benefit of keeping, reading, and copying the text, reciting it from memory, and preaching its content to others.[16] All these are features that appear prominently in related miracle tales.

Compared to the *Diamond* and *Heart Sutras*, highly popular Buddhist scriptures also known well by their English titles, the *Lotus Sutra* is less arcane or philosophical in content, presenting more accessible descriptions of images, parables, and stories. Many of these have inspired fruitful visual and material representations. One example is the dramatic scene of the sudden appearance of the jeweled pagoda and Prabhutaratna, the buddha of the past, before Shakyamuni's assembly. It inspired the time-honored iconography of the "twin

16 These were referred to as the five practices of the dharma preacher, see Stevenson 2009, 136–37. See chs. 10 and 19 in T.9.262, 30–32, 47–50; Hurvitz 2009, 159–66, 242–54; Lopez and Stone 2019, 129–35, 201–205. The power of recitation and sutra copying is highlighted in many miracle tales of the *Lotus Sutra*; see Stevenson 2007, 320–35; Campany 2018, 35–36, 41–42. For the recurring metaphor of an incorruptible tongue as a result of reciting the *Lotus Sutra*, see Ho 2019a.

FIGURE 3.7
Detail of fig. 3.39. Frontispiece to the *Lotus Sutra*, juan 5. Illustrated by Wang Yi. Southern Song. Woodblock print. Concertina. National Palace Museum

buddhas," juxtaposing Shakyamuni and Prabhutaratna (fig. 3.3) as well as various forms of the jeweled pagoda (fig. 3.5).[17]

Many action-charged parables narrated by the Buddha, such as the three carts outside the burning house (fig. 3.1a), the prodigal (or poor) son (fig. 3.1a), and the illusionary city (figs. 3.38b, 3.41a), are popular narrative themes in pictorial arts, found both in early cave murals and Song-Yuan print books.[18] The chapter called "Universal Gateway" celebrates the savior bodhisattva Guanyin (fig. 0.2), a key figure in Mahayana Buddhism. Most likely added to the text after the first century, it is by far the most popular.[19] Guanyin promises to rescue all devotees who suffer from burning, drowning, demonic attacks, imprisonment, or robbery as long as they call on her name with deep faith (figs. 3.8, 12.23).[20] The

17 This is from chapter eleven; see T.9.262, 32b–34b; Hurvitz 2009, 167–76; Lopez and Stone 2019, 136–48; Teiser and Stone eds. 2009. For more studies of the related arts, see Zhang Y. 2009; Zhang B. 2014. For visual examples related to this topic, see Chung 2022, 56–95.

18 For the seven parables, see chapters three to five, seven to eight, fourteen, and sixteen in T.9.262, 10–20, 22–29, 37–40, 42–44; Hurvitz 2009, 47–110, 120–53, 191–205, 219–25; Lopez and Stone 2019, 74–104, 110–23, 166–69, 179–91. For visual representations of the parables, see Chung 2022, 95–113.

19 See the twenty-fifth chapter in T.51.2067, 56–58; Hurvitz 2009, 288–94; Lopez and Stone 2019, 237–42. For classic scholarship on Guanyin in Chinese Buddhism, see Yü 2001; Yü 2020, 82–92.

20 Cf. a Dunhuang hanging scroll dated 985 and at the Harvard Art Museums; the painting depicts six comparable narrative scenes pertinent to Guanyin's miracles flanking the multi-headed and multi-armed Guanyin at the center; see Harvard Art Museums,

bodhisattva also grants their wishes such as for a male child (figs. 12.27, 12.29).[21] Because of its popularity, the chapter has circulated widely in many different formats and, as early as the third century, was an independent text known as the *Guanyin Sutra* (fig. 3.19). It was copied in at least a hundred Dunhuang manuscripts, some of which bear hand-painted illustrations (fig. 12.27).[22] It also stimulated numerous derivatives of Chinese indigenous scriptures that circulated widely in the Song, Jin (fig. 5.26), Xi Xia (fig. 5.35), Yuan, and Ming (see ch. 12)—all accompanied by illustrations. A now-lost Southern Song print inspired an artist in Kamakura Japan to produce a painted version (fig. 0.15a), which closely resembles Yuan woodcuts (fig. 0.16).[23]

While some parables and stories of the *Lotus Sutra* hold a strong appeal for ordinary folk, others have more impact on the Buddhist clergy. For example, the parable of medicinal herbs, which compares the Buddha's encompassing benevolence to rain as it nurtures trees and grasses, was recited by monks to call down rain.[24] Perhaps the most extreme story that triggered monastics' self-immolation is the story of the Medicine King who burnt his arms "for the sake of the dharma" but was quickly restored.[25] Since the fourth century, numerous monks and nuns were so inspired by this story that they wrapped "themselves in waxed cloth" and "set themselves alight."[26] Other "cultic interests" in the Sui and Tang, as Daniel Stevenson points out, were inspired by the ascetic story of the bodhisattva Never Disparaging, who never criticized anyone and endured people throwing rocks on him.[27]

"1943.57.14: Eleven-Headed Guanyin," Paintings, Accessed December 24, 2023. https://harvardartmuseums.org/collections/object/204072.

21 Lopez and Stone 2019, 238; Huang 2018b, 70, 117 (fig. 37).

22 See the frontispiece to the *Guanyin Sutra* copied in a multiple-text Dunhuang booklet (P. 3932). Also, the Dunhuang manuscript (S.413) is a copy of the "Universal Gateway" chapter in scroll format; it bears two delicately drawn images: the Guanyin bodhisattva at the opening, and a seated buddha at the end.

23 Ford 1987, 26–27.

24 For more about the parable, see Lopez and Stone 2019, 97–104. For the story of Monk Huiyuan 慧遠 dated 645, see X.78.1539, 5a–b. Cf. a similar story recounted by Japanese Monk Jōjin, see Hirabayashi 1978, 226.

25 See chapter twenty-three in T.9.262, 53–54; Hurvitz 2009, 269–76; Lopez and Stone 2019, 223–36.

26 Lopez and Stone 2019, 225–26. For more studies, see Benn 2007, 2009; Stevenson 2007, 316–20; Yu 2012. For a summary of stories of self-immolation in Tang Buddhist sources, see Lin 2001. For a story of a monk reciting the chapter of the Bodhisattva Medicine King and visualized the pure land, see T.51.2067, 22c.

27 See the twentieth chapter in T.9.262, 50b–51c; Hurvitz 2009, 257–62. The Three Stages movement (Sanjie jiao 三階教) promoted by Monk Xinxing 信行 (540–94) was inspired by Bodhisattva Never Disparaging; see Stevenson 2009, 137, 148*n*6.

FIGURE 3.8 Guanyin's miracles (MG17665). 950–1000. Ink and color on silk. Hanging scroll. Musée des Arts Asiatiques-Guimet

1.1 *Japanese Pilgrimage Accounts*

Pilgrimage accounts by Japanese monks who visited Tang-Song China provide live reports of *Lotus Sutra* practices in various monastic settings. In 839–840, the monk Ennin 圓仁 (794–864), whose travel diary is the first extant "account of life in China by any foreign visitor,"[28] stayed in the Fahuayuan 法華院 (Cloister of Dharma Florescence), named after *Lotus Sutra* teachings.[29] Located on Chishan 赤山 (Red Mountain) in the Weihai 威海 peninsula of Shandong, it hosted lectures of the *Lotus Sutra* over two months. Both preaching monks and lay audience—40 to 250 in number—were mostly Korean from the Silla kingdom, located across the strait from Shandong. Three monks and one traveler also came from Japan.[30] As Edwin Reischauer notes, what Ennin encountered here was perhaps a Korean immigrant community "near the usual landfall for ships bound from Korea to China and the point from which they left the Chinese coast on the homeward voyage." The cloister had "twenty-nine Korean inmates"; "around it lived a large number of Korean laymen."[31]

Throughout his travels in China, especially to the capital Chang'an, the pilgrimage site Mt. Wutai in Shanxi, and the southern trading hub of Yangzhou 揚州, Ennin observed the widespread presence of the *Lotus Sutra*. He noted that there were numerous monastic lectures on the text, a temple mural depicting its recitation, and exquisite treasures of hand-written copies.[32] He also recorded a miracle associated with the text: thanks to a monk's recitation of the text, the building he stayed in was not damaged by a fire that burnt down the rest of the temple.[33] In letters petitioning the Tang court to allow his team to stay in China longer, Ennin repetitively stressed that he was "versed in lecturing on the *Lotus Sutra*" and that his fellow Japanese monks were also well versed in it. This reflects the fact that the *Lotus Sutra* was deemed essential for Buddhist priesthood at the time.[34]

---

28 See Valerie Hansen's "Foreword" in Reischauer 2020b, xii. For the classic translation of Ennin's travel diary in English, *The Record of a Pilgrimage to Tang in Search of the Law* (*Nittō guhō junrei gyōki* 入唐求法巡禮行記), see Reischauer 2020a.

29 Reischauer 2020b, 174. While the lecture series featured the *Lotus Sutra* in the winter, in the summer the lectures switched to the *Golden Light Sutra*; see Reischauer 2020a, 131; T.16.665.

30 Reischauer 2020a, 131, 160; Reischauer 2020b, 174, 185, 282–83. See also Bai et al. 1992, 190; Stevenson 2009, 143–44.

31 Reischauer 2020b, 282.

32 Reischauer 2020a, 67, 229, 234–35, 249, 265, 271–72, 298–99; Reischauer 2020b, 174, 184.

33 Reischauer 2020a, 67–68; Reischauer 2020b, 191–92.

34 Reischauer 2020a, 319, 328; Reischauer 2020b, 231.

Another Japanese visitor was the monk Jōjin who traveled to China in 1072–1073 (see ch. 2). He personally performed "esoteric rites of the *Lotus Sutra*" and formal rituals of repentance in the name of the bodhisattva Samantabhadra in the Guoqingsi 國清寺 (Monastery of State Clarity) on Mt. Tiantai 天臺山 (Heavenly Terrace Mountain). He also took note of *Lotus Sutra* chanting he observed in many other temples and documented various artifacts inspired by the text, including a printed ritual manual he received at the imperially-sponsored Xiansheng Monastery in Kaifeng. Other things he mentions are *Lotus Sutra*-inspired altars, ritual spaces, and temple halls, mostly in monasteries of the Tiantai school. As regards works of art and other material objects, he describes the "*Lotus Sutra* Mandala Painting," "a manuscript copy of the *Lotus Sutra* in the empress' palace," "a seven-chapter *Lotus Sutra* manuscript copied in golden pigment and deposited in a gilded gold sutra box," and "a stone stele of the *Lotus Sutra*."[35] Among Buddhist books he shipped back to Japan is also the *Record of Magical Responses of the Lotus Sutra* (*Fahua ganying zhuan* 法華感應傳),[36] compiled by the monk Zongxiao 宗曉 (1151–1214) from Ningbo in the Southern Song, possibly one of many collections of miracle tales circulating at the time.

Indeed, by the eleventh century, a Buddhist confession ritual known as "Samadhi of the Dharma Florescence" (Fahua sanmei 法華三昧) inspired by the *Lotus Sutra* was performed widely among Tiantai followers and especially promoted by the Song monk Zunshi 遵式 (964–1032) in the Tianzhusi 天竺寺 (India Monastery) in Hangzhou.[37] Its ritual space contains the *Lotus Sutra* as the sole object placed on the altar: there are no iconic images, relics, or other scriptures. Focused on the text, the ritual evokes the devotees' active visualization of the myriad gods mentioned in the sutra.

1.2 *Materiality in Miracle Tales*

Numerous miracle tales of the *Lotus Sutra* reveal repeated narrative patterns and cultural schemas that shed light on how audiences responded to and evaluated the authority, meaning, and power of a scripture, including from material and visual perspectives.[38] The eighth-century *Records of Advocating and Praising the Lotus Sutra* (*Hong zang fahua zhuan* 弘贊法華傳), compiled by

35 Hirabayashi 1978, 55, 116–17, 124, 187, 208, 277; Wang L. 2009, 303, 305–307, 326, 609, 629, 654, 674; Huang 2014b, 405; Huang 2020, 47.

36 Wang L. 2009, 246.

37 T.46.1941.

38 Stevenson 2007, 2009; Campany 2018. For more on the authority and power of the text, and the "narrative patterns" and "cultural schemas" in Buddhist miracle tales, see Campany 2018, 1, 50 (esp. his citations of Sherry B. Ortner and Gary L. Ebersole in

the monk Huixiang 惠詳 (ca. 639–after 706),[39] contains accounts that highlight the efficacy of visual and material culture as inspired by the *Lotus Sutra*.[40] The first category, devoted to images and icons (*tuxiang* 圖像), features a curious landscape-infused votive altar in monumental size, designed by the monk Huihao 惠豪 for a new temple in Nanjing in 423 that soon became a model for other altar designs. Measuring about 89.3 meters deep and 103.5 meters wide, it was decorated with a *Picture of the Vulture Peak* (*Lingjiu shan tu* 靈鷲山圖), which highlights animals, birds, and Buddhist deities amid transforming mountains and forests.[41] The mountain imagery could appear in painting, sculpture, or relief.

The text further describes multiple architectural constructions inspired by the *Lotus Sutra*, including temple halls (*tang* 堂) and lecture podiums (*tai* 台), all reflecting the "dharma florescence" (*fahua* 法華) and closely resonating with Jōjin's records. Jeweled pagodas proliferated.[42] Named directly after the jeweled pagoda mentioned in the sutra, they served as preservation sites for *Lotus Sutra* copies. As rubbings of the *Stele of the Jeweled Pagoda* (*Duobao ta bei* 多寶塔碑) by the famous calligrapher Yan Zhenqing 顏真卿 (709–785) (fig. 3.4) document, when the imperially-sponsored Jeweled Pagoda in Chang'an was consecrated in 752, one thousand copies of the *Lotus Sutra*, together with a

footnotes 108–109); for similar miracle tales compiled or translated in Japan and Korea, see 25 (footnote 2).

39 A story featuring a postmortem judgement at the underground bureau explicitly claimed that the benefit of reciting the *Lotus Sutra* is superior to that of reciting any other scriptures, as a monk reciting the *Lotus Sutra* was granted the rebirth in heaven, while the other monks reciting other Buddhist scriptures were dispatched to the animal realm. The sutras recited by those monks sent to the animal realm include the *Vimalakirti Sutra* (*Weimo jing* 維摩經), the *Nirvana Sutra* (*Niepan jing* 涅槃經), and the *Golden Light Sutra*; see the story of Monk Falang 法朗 in T.51.2067, 33.

40 In addition to images, accounts are grouped under the following categories, listed accordingly: translation (*fanyi* 翻譯), exegesis (*jiangjie* 講解), meditation and visualization (*xiuguan* 修觀), casting away the body (*yishen* 遺身), recitation of the sutra from memory (*songchi* 誦持), cyclic reading of the sutra (*zhuandu* 轉讀), and copying the sutra by hand (*shuxie* 書寫). See T.51.2067; Stevenson 2007, 312. For a study of the miracle tales recorded in this text, see Zhou Yutong 2009.

41 T.51.2067, 13b. The original measurements were given in *zhang* 丈 unit. Calculating one *zhang* in the fifth century as equivalent to approximately 235 cm, the altar may measure around 89.3 × 103.5 meters. Cf. the other landscape painting of the Vulture Peak entitled *Picture of the Vulture Peak* (Qishejue shan tu 耆闍崛山圖) recorded in the same text; see T.51.2067, 12b, 13b.

42 T.51.2067, 12–14. For a clay tablet of the Jeweled Pagoda dated 650, see fig. 1.30a in ch.1 this book.

special copy transcribed in blood and thirty-six written in gold pigment, were deposited in the pagoda to grant divine protection.[43]

Going beyond images and icons, Huixiang's work shows how the material appeal of the *Lotus Sutra* is evident in miracle tales, especially noting the magical power of the books. A good example is the story of the seventh-century nun Miaozhi 妙智, recorded under the category of hand-copying the sutra (*shuxie* 書寫).[44] She took care of her personal copy with ritualistic devotion and made regular offerings to the book "according to proper ritual procedure," insisting that anyone borrowing her copy had to wash hands, change robes, and undergo a period of fasting. A governor who did not follow these rules opened her copy, and immediately the scripture turned into a piece of blank yellow paper. When he fetched the nun to ask her about this, he was shocked to see that the very same copy was again full of text—and not only that, but the words were written in characters that floated gently in the air.[45] Deeply moved by the magical power of the sutra, he vowed to have one thousand copies made. Miaozhi then advised him on proper procedure, going into great detail on how to plant the right trees, water them with fragrant water, and collect their bark. From there, he had to hire the right craftsman to make paper and find a scribe who would fast and bathe before doing anything relating to the sutra.[46]

1.2.1 Sutra Copies in Gold and Silver

Sutra copies written in gold and silver pigments or in freshly pricked human blood mixed with ink were deemed most efficacious.[47] Copies in so-called gold-script (*jinzi* 金字) indicate texts written in gold mud (*nijin* 泥金), that is,

43 The stele was originally erected in the Qianfu Ward; it is currently in the Stele Forest in Xi'an. Other treasures deposited to the pagoda include a bronze incense burner, 3000 relics placed inside a stone container, and a stone portrait of the monk who initiated the pagoda project. In addition, another one thousand copies of the *Lotus Sutra* were commissioned for wide distribution. For the complete reproductions of the rubbings, see Kakui and Fujiwara eds. 1988. The other Tang pagoda in the Zishengsi 資聖寺 (Monastery of Endowed Sageliness) also had one thousand copies of the *Lotus Sutra* deposited; murals here were pained by such great painters as Wu Daozi, Han Gan 韓幹, Li Zhen 李真, and Bian Luan 邊鸞. See THJWZ, 488.

44 T.51.2067, 45a; translated by Stevenson 2007, 332–34.

45 T.51.2067, 45a; Stevenson 2007, 333.

46 Stevenson 2007, 334.

47 For blood writing in Buddhism, see Kieschnick 2000; Yu 2012, 43; Li 2020, 121–23. For an anecdote of a girl copying the *Lotus Sutra* with her own blood pricked from the tongue, and further stitching each character with her own hair, cited from the Qing sources, see Li 2020, 140. For a visual sample of a *Lotus Sutra* copied in blood, see Pakhoutova and Helman-Wazny 2012, fig. 35 (unnumbered page).

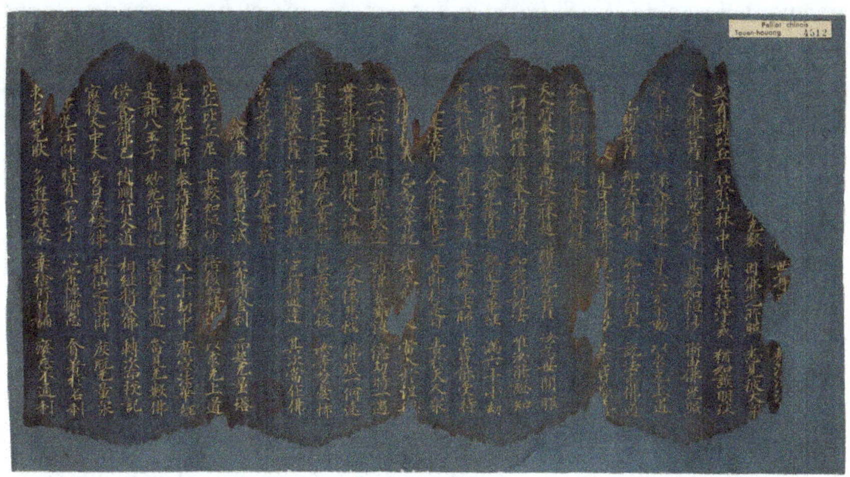

FIGURE 3.9 Fragment of the *Lotus Sutra*. Dunhuang Manuscript (Pelliot chinois 4512). Tang. Golden pigment on indigo-dyed paper. Bibliothèque nationale de France

using gold as ink created by mixing powdered gold with a binding material.[48] Such texts were considered especially efficacious in granting rebirth in the golden paradise, the Western Pure Land—west being associated with metal and thus gold.[49]

The tradition of copying Buddhist scriptures in gold may go back to the Tang. In 840, when the Japanese monk Ennin visited Mt. Wutai, he spotted a *Lotus Sutra* copied in gold. This may be similar to the Buddhist canon in gold and silver characters (*jinyin zi* 金銀字) he saw during the same trip; it was written on "dark blue paper" (*gan bizhi* 紺碧紙) and mounted "with rollers of white sandalwood, jade, and ivory."[50] A Dunhuang manuscript (fig. 3.9) preserving a

48 For a study of the East Asian Buddhist manuscripts "written with gold and/or silver ink on dark indigo dyed paper" with "drawn frontispiece illustrations in gold and/or silver ink," see Edgren 2019. See also Shen 2019, 57–59; Zhang 2023, 124–31.

49 Pakhoutova and Helman-Wazny 2012, fig. 14 (unnumbered page). For the notion of the gold-script *Lotus Sutra* that can grant one rebirth in the golden paradise, see the T.51.2067, 96b. For more records of the *Lotus Sutra* copies in golden pigment, see T.49.2035, 402c; T.51.2068, 96a; X.75.1513, 281b.

50 Bai et al. 1992, 282; Ten Grotenhuis 1999, 81; George 2009, 109; Shen 2019, 58. Ennin documented the engraved inscription on a revolving sutra cabinet, which mentions "gold writings on silver paper made in China" was collected in the Diamond Cave in Mt. Wutai; see Bai et al. 1992, 293. For more on the devotional use of Buddhist art in Ennin's diary, see Hansen 2014.

fragment of a gold *Lotus Sutra* on indigo paper may well be contemporaneous with those recorded by Ennin.[51]

Shifting to the south, King Qian Shu of the tenth-century Wu-Yue kingdom famously commissioned twenty sets of the gold-copied *Lotus Sutra* to donate to various temples throughout his state.[52] From the same period are also several other *Lotus Sutra* sets, now in Shanghai and Suzhou collections.[53] A gold-and-silver set, dated 973, bears a colophon that identifies Du Yu 杜遇 as the lay donor who commissioned ten copies.[54] Furthermore, a seven-scroll *Lotus Sutra* copy, originally deposited in the Northern Song Ruiguang ta 瑞光塔 (Auspicious Light Pagoda) in Jiangsu (figs. 3.10a–b) and now in Suzhou Museum, is arguably the earliest extant gold-copied sutra that also has frontispieces drawn in gold and silver;[55] it was probably written on dark blue paper, as the colophon describes, using the term *bizhi* 碧紙.[56] Although there is no information regarding how many copies were produced, hand-copied manuscripts like these were most likely commissioned in much smaller number, unlike later printed counterparts, which were often commissioned in hundreds or thousands of copies by a single donor.

Although print books were on the rise in the Southern Song period and increasingly replaced manuscripts, the practice of copying sutras in gold continued. Thus, the *Record of Magical Responses of the Lotus Sutra* notes the marvel of the seven-scroll *Lotus Sutra* copied by the monk Ying 瑩. He transcribed the text mostly in silver, except for certain characters referring to buddhas and bodhisattvas, for which he used gold. He further treasured his personal copies by mounting them with jade rods and storing them in a container made

51 Monnet 2004, 34–35; cf. the other Dunhuang gold-script *Lotus Sutra* on indigo paper reproduced in 33 (Pelliot chinois 4511). Also, cf. S. 5720 in Wood and Barnard 2010, 39; Edgren 2019, 113–14.

52 One of the copies Qian Shu commissioned was bestowed to the Guoqing Monastery in Mt. Tiantai, where the Japanese monk Jōjin once visited; see T.49.2035, 206c; X.78.1540, 42c.

53 Zhang 2023.

54 DEPGZGMT 3: 138–39 (no. 02998); Zhang 2023, 125–26, 140n58; Shanghai bowuguan ed. 2023, 46–53.

55 Suzhou bowuguan 2006, 159–63; Sudō 2018; Sudō 2015, 101–102; Sudō 2021, 69–71; Zhang 2023, 132.

56 For more study of indigo paper, see Liu R. 2012; Zhang 2023, 126. The Ming author Gao Lian 高濂 (1573–1620) referred to the indigo paper used for gold-script sutra copies as the "porcelain indigo paper" (*ciqing zhi* 磁青紙), highlighting its cloth-like enduring quality; see ZSBQ, "Yanwen Qingshang qian" 燕閒清賞箋, 598. For more about the Ming imperial copies of the *Lotus Sutra* transcribed on indigo paper, see Gao 2022, 18–20.

a

b

FIGURES 3.10A–B Frontispieces to the *Lotus Sutra*. Repaired in 931. Gold and silver on indigo-dyed paper. Scroll. Discovered in the Ruiguang Pagoda. Suzhou Museum
a. Detail of juan 1
b. Detail of juan 3

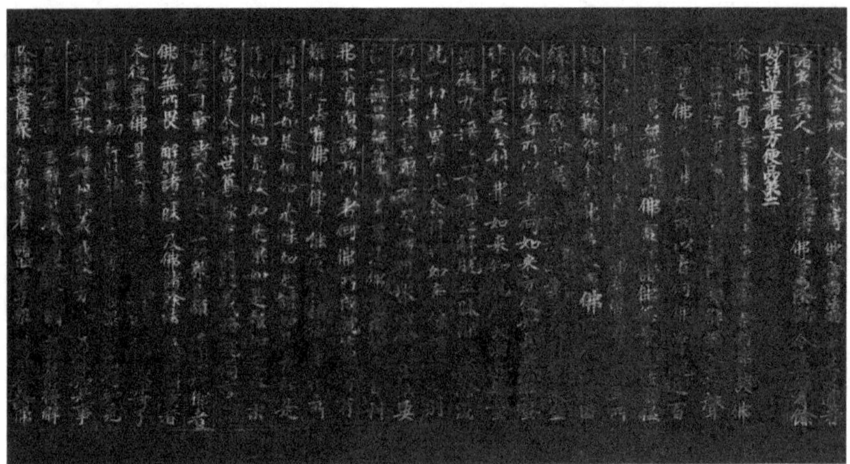

FIGURE 3.11 Detail. *Lotus Sutra*. 1033. Northern Song. Gold on indigo-dyed paper. Discovered in Hui'an Pagoda, Rui'an, Zhejiang

of carnelian. After Ying passed away, he left the sutra to his home temple: although it caught fire several times, the sutra copies remained intact.[57]

Ying's personal texts call to mind extant *Lotus Sutra* copies dated from 1033, for the most part written in silver with only selected words highlighted in gold, such as the title and honorific name of the Buddha, notably the terms *fo* 佛 and *rulai* 如來 (*tathagata*) (fig. 3.11).[58] The practice of copying sutras in gold was also common in Korea and Japan, so that, in 1003, the Japanese monk Jakushō 寂照 submitted a copy to the Song emperor Zhenzong 真宗 (r. 997–1022).[59] During the Mongol era, a hundred Korean monks were recruited from Koryŏ to Yuan Dadu in 1290 to copy the Buddhist canon (see ch. 7). They brought a gift of the *Lotus Sutra* copied in gold script.[60] Numerous extant specimens of Koryŏ copies of the *Lotus Sutra* lavishly decorated with frontispieces attest to

57 See the story of Ying from the Jiangdong Guangyan yuan 江東廣嚴院 in x.78.1540, 48b.

58 Cf. Shen 2019, 58 (fig. 2.11). The other example is the seven-scroll set dated 1044, donated by He Zizhi 何子芝 (from Guozhou 果州, Xichong 西充 county, Sichuan) and his family in honor of his deceased mother, Lady Yang. For more studies, see Wang Yanjing 2012; Zhang J. 2017; Zhang 2023.

59 T.49.2035, 402c. For studies of the sutra copies in Japan and Korea, see Sudō 2015; Sudō 2018; Sudō 2021, 83–86; Edgren 2019, 116–19.

60 HDJSY 8: 11; Chia 2015b, 198. For more about the Korean monks as sutra copyists or abbots in Yuan China and Koryŏ Korea, see Zhang 1999; Gui 2001; Tokushi 1939, 5–7; Kanda 1984, 432. For a reconstruction of Buddhist temples in the Koryŏ capital Kaesong in the twelfth century, see Zhang 2020.

FIGURE 3.12 Detail. Folio from the "Blue Qur'an." Late 9th to mid-10th centuries. Tunisia, North Africa. Gold and silver on indigo-dyed parchment. Codices. The Metropolitan Museum of Art

the international reputation of Korean sutra copies of that time (figs. 3.33a–b, 3.42a–b).[61]

The Buddhist preoccupation with sutra copies written in gold may reflect the common fascination with gold writings in Chinese religions. Many medieval Daoist texts instruct adepts to visualize the scriptures in their original cosmic state as written in golden characters (*jinzi* 金字) or as jade writs (*yuwen* 玉文), naturally formed in "the azure heavens" (*bikong* 碧空).[62] When ranking Daoist "perfect scriptures" (*zhenjing* 真經) in different materials, Tang monastic codes list gold and silver as the seventh and eighth most precious materials, below those engraved in gold or silver tablets yet above texts transcribed on bamboo tablets, walls, or leaves.[63]

61 Kungnip Chungang Pangmulgwan 2007. Zhang Jianyu re-identifies a hand-painted *Lotus Sutra* frontispiece in gold and silver at the MFA, Boston previously dated to the Yuan dynasty as a Koryŏ product; see Zhang J. 2021, 47 (fig. 5).

62 See, for example, see DZ 1, 1: 408a; YJQQ 23, 44, 105.

63 See ch. 6 "Copying Scriptures" of *Rules and Precepts for Worshiping the Dao* (*Fengdao kejie yingshi* 奉道科戒營始, DZ 1125) discussed in Kohn 2004, 103–104.

a

b

FIGURES 3.13A–B *Lotus Sutra* written in the shape of a pagoda. Attributed to Wen Zhengming. Ming. Gold pigment on indigo paper. Hanging scroll. National Palace Museum
a. Complete view
b. Detail

Similar practices are found in the Arabic and Persian worlds.[64] Since the ninth century or even earlier, extant specimens of the Blue Qur'an show that the sacred book was copied in gold and silver pigments on blue parchment (fig. 3.12) or paper, drawing "inspiration from Byzantine precedents." It "may have had a connotation of royalty," but also "of divine light shining through darkness."[65]

By Song times, *Lotus Sutra* copies in gold characters were also arranged in non-linear fashion, mimicking multi-storied pagodas. In this, they took their cue from the sutra's chapter on the Jeweled Pagoda while also building upon the earlier convention of copying the *Heart Sutra* in pagoda shape, as preserved in two extant Dunhuang manuscripts.[66] An anecdote of the Northern Song Emperor Huizong, compiled in a collection of miracle tales of the *Lotus Sutra* by the Ming-dynasty monk Yuanlu 圓錄, records that he awarded a pagoda-shaped *Lotus Sutra* copy to a Korean scholar from Koryŏ after the latter recited the entire scripture from memory.[67] According to Huizong's catalogue of imperial calligraphy, the monk Fahui 法暉 in 1112 presented the pagoda-shaped writings of ten Buddhist sutras as a birthday gift, including also the *Lotus Sutra*.[68] All the characters in these pagoda-shaped copies are executed minutely in regular script, each about half a sesame seed in size.[69] The overall visual effect may resemble a later gold-script *Lotus Sutra* pagoda on indigo paper, attributed to Wen Zhengming 文徵明 (1470–1559) (figs. 3.13a–b). Individual chapters were copied section by section along the tightly packed lines charted within the pagoda structure.[70] The overall layout and design reflect the Buddhist "imagetexts" popular at the time.[71]

64 George 2009; Yu 2021.

65 George 2009, 108. Beyond chrysography, Yusen Yu examines the metaphor and use of the gold-sprinked paper in Persian manuscripts; see Yu 2021, 107–10.

66 See Stein 4289 and Pelliot chinois 2168 dated to the ninth or tenth century. For more studies of the Buddhist writings in pagoda shape in China and Japan, see Yang B. 2014; O'Neal 2018; Kossak and Singer 1998, 19 (fig. 10).

67 X.78.1539, 11a. For more records of the *Lotus Sutra* copies in the form of a pagoda, see X.71.1414, 692a; X.71.1416, 426c; X.77.1524, 524a.

68 For the ten different sutras, see XHSP, 133. Monk Fahui was said to stay in a monastic site in Hangzhou in his late years; see "Guangjiao yuan" 廣教院 listed in XCLAZ 81, "Siguan" 寺觀 7, "Siyuan cheng wai" 寺院城外 5, 4109.

69 XHSP, 133.

70 The late Ming scholar Chen Jisheng 陳濟生 (1618–1664), for example, purchased a gold-script *Lotus Sutra* in the shape of a jeweled pagoda transcribed by Li Zhengqing 李正卿 of Xin'an 新安; see X.78.1541, 90b.

71 For more extant pagoda-shaped *Lotus Sutra* copies dated to the Yuan, Ming, and Qing periods, see Ge 1995, 10–15; Chung 2022, 86–93.

2 Frontispieces in Northern Song Hangzhou

Religious and ritual experiences associated with the *Lotus Sutra* in due course led to a great demand of copies, which in turn caused increased printing and more elaborate adornment of frontispieces. Pictorial designs typically match selected scriptural content. Departing from centralized and symmetrically composed large-scale murals or paintings of the sutra tableaux (*bianxiang* 變相), such as the ninth-century mural in Mogao Cave 159 at Dunhuang,[72] printed frontispieces in Hangzhou present a horizontal format, fitted to book size and full of innovative motifs and compositional schemes not seen earlier. They attest to a new kind of visuality, energized by Hangzhou print culture and reaching far beyond China and the Buddhist world.

The many printed frontispieces of the *Lotus Sutra* examined below show ample documentation concerning cutters but make little mention of illustrators. This may reflect the lack of specific illustrators making designs for woodcuts: cutters recycled existing designs or reassembled pictorial motifs to compose new images. Their standardization and modularization made it possible for non-illustrators like cutters to take charge of the image-making task.

In 1968, archaeologists working on a Northern Song pagoda in Shenxian 莘縣, Shandong (map 0.1), discovered multiple sets of the *Lotus Sutra* printed by the earliest documented commercial publishers active in Hangzhou in the eleventh century (table 3.1)—the printshops of the Qian (fig. 3.14a) and the Yan families (figs. 0.2, 0.4, 3.15a–b).[73] Extant specimens give the names of cutters such as Gou 垢, Nian 念, Wu Ling 吳鈴, and Ye Gui 葉桂, as well as of scribes Wang Suiliang 王遂良 (from Langxie 琅邪) and Zhang Yuexian 張月仙. Prior to publishing, the printed sutras were collated by monks holding administrative positions in Kaifeng and Hangzhou (Table 3.1; fig. 3.15b).[74] Selected few frontispieces dated to the 1060s and reproduced in scholarly publications reflect a local style as well as a copyright-free market, where publishers re-created popular editions of illustrated books printed by others.[75] A controversial *Lotus Sutra* silver frontispiece on indigo paper (fig. 3.16a), which scholars date variously from Song to Ming,[76] closely resembles the frontispiece created by the Yan Family dated 1069 (fig. 0.4). This reflects the common template in painted and printed frontispieces.

72 DHSKQJ 7: 94 (fig. 81). For more Dunhuang murals with centralized and symmetrical compositional schemes, see Mogao Caves 85, 61, 55 in DHSKQJ 7, 108–109, 112–13, 119.

73 For select plates, see Zhejiangsheng bowuguan ed. 2019, 210–17; Su 1999, 143–45.

74 Cui 1982, 41–42; Su 1999, 144.

75 Zhang 1989, 143; Huang 2011a, 152–53.

76 Chung 2022, 128–37 (esp. 129). For earlier publications supporting the Ming date, see Ge 1995, 46–47, 88–89; Huang 2011b, 143 (fig. 11A); Huang 2014b, 408–409.

TABLE 3.1 Northern Song *Lotus Sutra* Printed Copies Discovered in the Pagoda in Shenxian, Shandong

Publisher		Yan Family	Qian Family	Qian Family	Yan Family	Yan Family (?)
		1042	1060	1063	1068	1069
Chapter Number (Juan) with an Extant Frontispiece	1		x	x	x	x
	2		x	x	x	x
	3			x		x
	4		x		x	x
	5	x	x	x	x	x
	6	x	x	x	x	x
	7			x	x	
Cutters			垢刀（卷二） 垢刀（卷四）	念刀（卷三）		吳鈴刀（卷首） 葉桂刀（卷三）
Scribes			琅邪王遂良書（卷五）	琅邪王遂良書（卷五）	琅邪王遂良書（卷五）	張月仙（卷四） 琅邪王遂良書（卷五）
Collators			大宋嘉祐五年庚子正月杭州錢家重請講僧校勘兼于逐卷內重分為平聲為去聲字章并及添經音在后雕印施行	管內副僧正講經律賜紫崇因大師可中校勘	大宋熙寧元年。。。杭州晏家再請僧校勘又命工重開印造廣行天下願與受持人同契法華聖會	住持沙門審蘊校勘東京左街副僧錄前譯證義兼綴文講天臺教。。。制慈云大師賜紫清儒校勘東京右街僧錄。教門。。。宣教大師智林校勘 東京。。行僧錄譯經証義兼綴文知教習公事。廣辯大師賜紫善初勘
Other Documentations					杭州新開大字經懺	杭州新開大字經懺上柱國鄭國公夏？序言

FIGURE 3.14A Frontispiece to the *Lotus Sutra*, juan 4. Published by the Qian Family. 1060. Northern Song. Woodblock print. Discovered in the Buddhist pagoda, Shenxian, Shandong

a

大宋熙寧元年戊申歲杭州晏家
再請僧校勘又命工重開印造廣行天
下願與受持人同契　法華聖會
妙法蓮華經卷第一　爲平聲　爲去聲

b

FIGURES 3.15A–B
Details. *Lotus Sutra* published by the Yan Family. Northern Song. Discovered in the Buddhist pagoda, Shenxian, Shandong
a. Frontispiece, juan 4. 1068
b. Detail of the colophon, juan 1. 1060

FIGURE 3.16A Frontispiece to the *Lotus Sutra*, juan 3. Possibly Northern Song. Silver on indigo paper. © National Palace Museum

2.1 *Local Conventions*

The frontispieces in the version printed by the Qian (figs. 3.14a) and Yan (figs. 0.4, 3.15a) Families are highly similar in style. This is evident in their compositional schemes and decorative designs, which can in turn be traced back to local conventions.

In terms of composition, certain schemes take their cue from the tenth-century *Dharani Sutra* (fig. 3.17) made in Hangzhou.[77] This is most evident in the insertion of an architectural motif on the left edge of the picture plane (figs. 0.4, 3.14a), and in a pagoda placed near the center of the composition (fig. 3.14a); these motifs may refer to different narrative scenarios expounded in the *Lotus* and *Dharani Sutras*. In the latter, the building placed diagonally on the left edge of the frontispiece shows the house of a brahmin who stands in front with the Buddha beside him, witnessing the miracle of a ruined stupa-mount returning to radiance. The stupa behind the Buddha indicates "the treasure stupa in its original form."[78]

In the *Lotus Sutra*, both the 1060 frontispiece by the Qian Family (fig. 3.14a) and that of the Yan Family dated to 1069 (fig. 0.4) place architectural motifs in the left corners of the compositions. Along the left border of the 1060

77 Cf. the other extant version at the National Palace Museum; see Song ed. 2014, 32–33.

78 Wang Y. E. 2003, 492; Yu P. 1990, 126–28; Huang 2011a, 139–40.

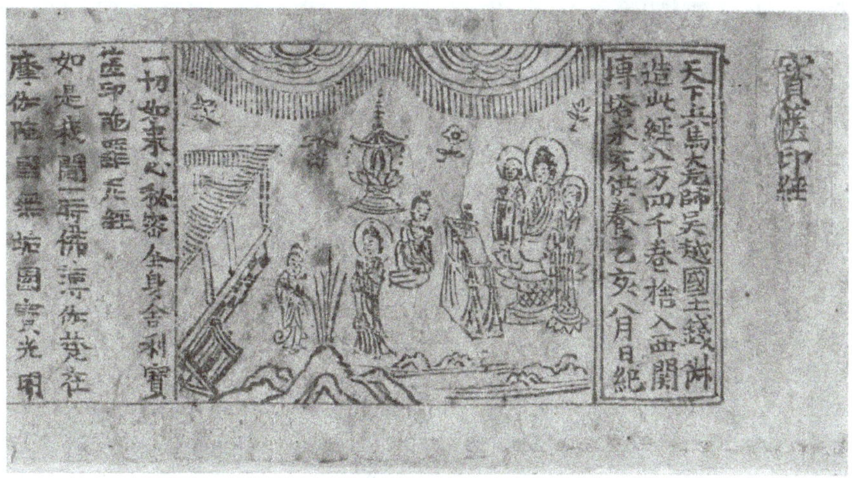

FIGURE 3.17 Frontispiece to the *Dharani Sutra*. 975. Woodblock print on paper. Handscroll. Harvard Art Museums

FIGURE 3.14B
Frontispiece to the *Lotus Sutra*, juan 4. Published by the Qian Family. 1060. Northern Song. Woodblock print. Discovered in the Buddhist pagoda, Shenxian, Shandong

FIGURE 3.18
Detail. Frontispiece to the *Lotus Sutra*, juan 3. Published by the Yan Family. 1069. Northern Song. Woodblock print. Discovered in the Buddhist pagoda, Shenxian, Shandong

frontispiece, the diagonally positioned house shows a man lying in bed with another standing beside him. They reflect the parable of a drunken man who was ignorant of the priceless jewel his friend had sewn into his coat.[79] In the 1069 frontispiece (fig. 0.4), the gated city in the upper left corner illustrates the parable of the illusionary city, while the fenced-in hut shows the parable of the medicinal herbs. The pagoda, moreover, placed in the middle of the 1060 frontispiece represents the sudden appearance of the buddha of the past in the jeweled pagoda.

As regards ornamental designs, the motif of fringed and tasseled curtains running along the upper border of the frontispieces and the leafy botanical branches sticking out of the Buddha's seat (figs. 0.4, 3.14a–b, 3.15a, 3.18) call to mind earlier local traditions.[80] The curtains recall tenth-century frontispieces produced in the Zhejiang area. Examples include the hand-painted *Lotus Sutra* frontispiece in gold and silver pigments on indigo paper, discovered in the Ruiguang Pagoda (figs. 3.10a–b),[81] and the mass-produced frontispieces of the *Dharani Sutra* scrolls, inserted into the bricks of the Leifeng Pagoda, built by King Qian Shu of the Wu-Yue kingdom (fig. 3.17).[82] Similar curtain décors also appear in the upper border of the frontispiece to the *Guanyin Sutra* (fig. 3.19), dated to around 1054 and originally commissioned by the local military official Ge You 葛誘. It was discovered in the tomb of the lay Buddhist woman Sun Siniang in Jiangsu—a tomb that yielded an impressive personal collection of illustrated Buddhist books (figs. 2.37b, 2.57, 11.5a).[83] The visual meme of the curtain decors tends to survive: in similar designs still visible in the twelfth-century Korean frontispiece as well as in the hand-painted frontispiece (fig. 3.16a).[84] Although not identical, the botanical branches behind the Buddha's seat (figs. 3.14b, 3.18) resemble the leafy plants

79 T.9.262, 29a; Hurvitz 2009, 151. The jewel symbolizes "the Buddhahood we are endowed with, although, like the drunken man, we are oblivious of the fact." See Yü 2020, 40.

80 For comparisons of these motifs, see Huang 2011b, 142; Huang 2014b, 406–409.

81 Cf. Chung 2022, 266 (fig. 1). The curtain motifs also appear in the early Northern Song *Lotus Sutra* manuscript copies (dated 973) donated by Du Yu; see Shanghai bowuguan ed. 2023, 51, 53.

82 The colophon of the frontispiece claims that Qian Shu made eighty-four thousand copies of this sutra and interred them in the brick pagoda at Xiguan as eternal offerings. For more about the various versions of the *Dharani Sutra* frontispieces commissioned by King Qian Shu dated 956, 965, 975 and the Korean copy dated 1007, see Edgren 1972; Huang 2011a, 137–42; Huang 2020, 46–47; Pak 2013, 79–81. For the latest study of the Leifeng Pagoda, see Welter 2022, esp. 73–107.

83 Jiangyin bowuguan 2009, 188–97; Suzhou bowuguan 2012, 16–27, 36–43.

84 For the Koryŏ gold frontispiece on indigo paper in Danzan jingja, Nara, reproduced in Pal and Meech 1988, 262–63; Huang 2011b, 143 (fig. 12).

FIGURE 3.19 Frontispiece to the *Guanyin Sutra*. ca. 1054. Northern Song. Woodblock print. Concertina. Discovered in the tomb of Sun Siniang (d. after 1054), Jiangyin, Suzhou

surrounding him in the gold and silver frontispiece of the *Lotus Sutra* discovered in the Ruiguang Pagoda (fig. 3.10b). Similar visual memes were also adopted in Xi Xia frontispieces, produced in northwest China in the late twelfth century (see ch. 6) (figs. 6.65a–c, 6.67a, 6.67b).

2.2 *A Memeplex Based on Landscape Painting*

The parable of the medicinal herbs was one of the most popular items depicted at the time, showing up in many printed versions of the *Lotus Sutra* produced in eleventh-to-twelfth century Liao (fig. 4.31a–b), Xi Xia (fig. 0.1), and Japan.[85] Beyond existing pictorial conventions for *Lotus Sutra* frontispieces specifically and Buddhist art in general, the designer of the Yan Family frontispiece (figs. 0.4, 3.20) borrowed various narrative motifs from landscape painting that were current in tenth-to-eleventh-century Jiangnan (figs. 3.21a–b). He then

85 Cf. other approaches depicting the parable of the medicinal herbs in the *Lotus Sutra* frontispieces produced in eleventh-century Liao in Huang 2011b, 146 (fig. 16; figs. 4.31a–b of this book), and in the twelfth century Japanese painted frontispiece painted in gold on indigo paper, at the Metropolitan Museum of Art; see The Metropolitan Museum of Art, "'Parable of the Medicinal Herbs,' Chapter 5 of the Lotus Sutra," Asian Art, Accessed December 24, 2023. https://www.metmuseum.org/art/collection/search/45624.

FIGURE 3.20 Detail of fig. 0.4. Frontispiece to the *Lotus Sutra*, juan 3. 1069. Northern Song. Woodblock print. Discovered in the Buddhist pagoda, Shenxian, Shandong

FIGURE 3.16B Detail. Frontispiece to the *Lotus Sutra*, juan 3. Possibly Northern Song. Silver on indigo paper. National Palace Museum

FIGURE 3.21A–B
Riverbank, attributed to Dong Yuan (ca. 930s–960s). Possibly 11th century. Ink and color on silk. Hanging scroll. The Metropolitan Museum of Art
a. Detail
b. Complete view

b

FIGURE 3.22 Detail. *Lotus Sutra Tableaux*. 8th century. Tang. Mural. North wall, Mogao Cave 23, Dunhuang, Gansu

repurposed them to represent the parable of the medicinal herbs (fig. 3.20), according to which the Buddha appeared in the world like "a great cloud universally covering all" and "raining down" on "all grasses and trees, shrubs and forests, and medicinal herbs," which all "flourished together."[86]

As depicted in the lower left corner (figs. 0.4, 3.20), the story is depicted as a man riding an ox and two farmers returning to a fenced hut on foot. Juxtaposing this with matching scenes found in a painted frontispiece introduced above (figs. 3.16a–b), some meticulous details emerge that are hard to recognize in the Northern Song print version. Through the fence, the viewer can see a hut with no walls, only a roof; inside, a kettle sits on a table near a bench. While the scene does not directly represent the cloud and the rain highlighted in the parable, it indirectly suggests rainy weather through the dress of the two farmers conversing outside the fence: they wear hats and raincoats made of rushes. A little further on, the man riding the ox comes around the corner; he, too, is covered with a raincoat made of rushes. The subtle depiction of the rain in the Hangzhou frontispiece is contrary to earlier Buddhist conventions as reflected in the eighth-century Dunhuang mural of the parable of the herbs (fig. 3.22).[87]

86 These phrases are quoted from the translation in Hurvitz 2009, 95–96, 98. For the original Chinese text, see T.9.262, 19b–20a.

87 DHSKQJ 7: 75 (fig. 65).

Here farmers and an ox are seen working in a field under large dark clouds, with falling rain depicted in both vertical lines and dots.

The return-home scene in both printed (figs. 0.4, 3.20) and painted (figs. 3.16a–b) frontispieces may be inspired by certain trends in landscape painting that circulated in tenth-to-eleventh-century Jiangnan. The prototype appears in the oft-cited painting *Riverbank* (figs. 2.44, 3.21a–b), attributed to the tenth-century Southern Tang painter Dong Yuan and most likely dating from the early eleventh century.[88] It shows a man riding a buffalo plus a barefoot farmer. Both dressed in raincoats made from rushes, they are proceeding toward the entrance of a fenced dwelling. Although comparable to the *Lotus Sutra* frontispieces, here the buffalo, the farmer, and the fenced residence are surrounded by servants, women, and children. Together, they constitute a visual repertoire representing the domestic life of a recluse-scholar set in a pavilion overlooking a body of water (fig. 2.44).[89] Taken out of context, however, the combination of a man riding an ox, farmers wearing raincoats, and a fenced hut (fig. 3.21a) form a visual memeplex, moving from the landscape of eremitism to the book art of the *Lotus Sutra*, which is then further transmitted from painting to printing.

2.3 *Expansion to the Xi Xia Kingdom*

A frontispiece to the "Guanyin" Chapter of the *Lotus Sutra* (fig. 0.2), discovered in the Xi Xia ruins in Khara Khoto, bears the trademark of the Yan Family publisher, suggesting that it was produced in Hangzhou.[90] The three-fold frontispiece depicts Guanyin seated in the center, flanked by a spectrum of narrative scenes that are rendered in a continuous landscape background to illustrate selected miracles. The arrangement does not necessarily follow the sequence of the text, but matches compositional schemes in earlier paintings.[91]

Viewed clockwise, the scenes correspond to various perilous situations resolved by chanting Guanyin's name. For instance, on the right are weather gods representing thunder, lightning, wind, and rain; they cause a thunderstorm which endangers umbrella-holding travelers while a snake and insect spread poisonous vapor over another group. On the left, a person is pushed off cliff while two tigers threaten a different group of travelers. The overall

88 Shih 2010, 89–118. Cf. Wen C. Fong in Hearn and Fong 1999, 3–57.

89 Shih 2010, 108–11.

90 Huang 2011a, 153–54 (fig. 4.9); 2011b, 147 (fig. 18); 2014b, 414. While most scholars take this as a Northern Song Hangzhou product, Sören Edgren proposed in a personal exchange that due to its lesser quality it may be a Xi Xia copy based on the original by the Yan Family.

91 For the miracles of Guanyin rescuing people in such perilous situations, see T.9.262, 56c–58b; Hurvitz 2009, 287–94.

FIGURE 3.23 Frontispieces to the *Lotus Sutra*. 1146. Xi Xia. Woodblock print. Institute of Oriental Manuscripts, St. Petersburg

compositional scheme closely matches eleventh-century frontispieces produced in the Jiangnan area, such as the hand-painted (fig. 2.57) and printed (fig. 3.19) frontispieces to the *Guanyin Sutra*. Both are marked as the personal property of the Buddhist laywoman Sun Siniang and date to around 1054. Further comparisons with the tenth-century Dunhuang hanging-scroll painting (fig. 3.8) of Guanyin's miracles suggest that some motifs showcased in the Yan Family frontispiece, such as the cliff-jumping and the snake and insect, were transmitted from still earlier visual memes beyond the local Jiangnan tradition.

More printed frontispieces of the *Lotus Sutra* made in Xi Xia and discovered in Khara Khoto attest further to the stylistic legacy of Song Hangzhou. A potent example appears in an incomplete set of six frontispieces (figs. 0.1, 3.23) that have a dedicatory colophon by the Xi Xia emperor Renzong 仁宗 (r. 1139–1193) in the first frontispiece and provide the date 1146 at the end of the seventh chapter.[92] The first (fig. 3.23) and third (fig. 0.1) largely match the Yan Family frontispieces dated 1068 (fig. 3.15a) and 1069 (fig. 0.4), respectively. This is especially clear in a group of motifs regarding merit-accumulating image-making, depicted in the lower left corners of the first frontispieces (figs. 3.15a, 3.23). Both show an artist painting a hanging scroll on the ground, a sculptor making a sculpture, one group of children drawing a pagoda in the sand, and another

92 The seven chapters are numbered TK 1–TK 4, TK 9–TK 11, although chapter two no longer contains a frontispiece. For the entire set, see ECHSCWX 1: 1–49, 225–70; for the dating, see 270. For more study, see Huang 2014b, 417 (fig. 28).

making a miniature stupa from mud.[93] Also, as discussed in the introduction, the return-home scene in the parable of the medicinal herbs is similar, depicted in both the Yan Family (fig. 0.4) and the Xi Xia (fig. 0.1) versions of the third frontispieces. The Xi Xia frontispieces omit some decorative and narrative details and in general, there is a sense of roughness in them, perhaps because they represent woodcuts made during an earlier development of Buddhist print culture in the early twelfth century. Soon after, more and more ambitious and innovative frontispieces appeared, sponsored by Xi Xia royalty: Buddhist print culture from Northern and Southern Song Hangzhou continued to serve as a major inspiration.

3 Publishers and Bookshops in Southern Song Hangzhou

The international reputation of Buddhist illustrated woodcuts in Hangzhou grew even stronger in the late twelfth century, when the Southern Song court moved its capital there. Bustling official and commercial printing enterprises at the time are particularly vivid in Sören Edgren's classic study. He documented 317 titles of books, directly or indirectly related to Hangzhou, and mapped out eighteen commercial bookshops, defined loosely as "printers, booksellers, and kiosks" (map 3.1).[94] The shops also included those selling the "paper horses" (*zhima* 紙馬), a general term for miscellaneous kinds of printed ephemera, ranging from single-sheet prints of gods and symbols to ritual paper money and effigies for burning.[95]

The main bookstore district appears on the historical *Capital Map* (*Jingcheng tu* 京城圖), preserved in the *Gazetteer of Lin'an during the Xianchun Reign* (*Xianchun Lin'an zhi* 咸淳臨安志), compiled during 1268–1273 (map 3.2).[96] It was marked by local landmarks, such as the Zhong'an 眾安 Bridge and the

93 For more discussion of the Southern Song-inspired raised terrace in the Xi Xia frontispiece (fig. 3.23), see Zhang J. 2021.

94 Edgren 1989, esp. 4 (the map of commercial printers and booksellers), 31–45.

95 See the accounts of the Qingming festival in DJMHL, 7: 43; XHLRFSL, 10. Wang Shucun cites various historical sources to discuss the "paper of the gods of the epidemics in five colors" and the "paper of five messengers of epidemics" to be pasted on walls or doors to get rid of disease; see Wang S. 2008, 20. Some Southern Song commercial bookstores that published books referred to themselves as "paper horse shops" (*zhimapu* 紙馬鋪) or "paper shops" (*zhipu* 紙鋪); see Su 1999, 87. For a store that sold printed maps known as Routes for Visiting the Capital (*Chaojing licheng tu* 朝京里程圖), see Zhang and Han 2006, 56.

96 XCLAZ. For more study of the maps preserved in the local gazetteer *Xianchun Lin'an zhi*, see Jiang 2015.

Commercial Publishers & Booksellers In Southern Song Hangzhou, 1127-1279

— Road ~ Canal ■ National/ Imperial Places

Zhong'an Bridge ▬ City Walls and Gates

● Publishers/bookshops/kiosks

A Guo Family Paper and Bookshop near the Qiantang Gate
錢塘門裡車橋南大街郭宅紙（經）鋪

B Lu Family Bookshop in front of National University
太學前陸家

C Yang Family Bookshop in the north of the Zhong'an Bridge
眾安橋北楊家

D Chen Family Bookshop
眾安橋南街東開經書鋪賈官人宅

E The Family of the Official Jia Bookshop to the south of the Zhong'an Bridge
棚北睦親坊陳宅書籍鋪

F Wang Nian (Sanlang) Family Bookshop
棚前南街經坊王念三郎家

G Wang Balang Family Bookshop
修文坊相對王八郎家經鋪

H Chen Family Bookshop
輓鼓橋南河西岸陳宅書籍鋪

I Chen Family Bookshop
洪橋子南河西岸陳宅書籍鋪

J Wang Erlang Family Shop
積善坊王二郎

K Zhong Family Shop at the east bank of the Mao'er Bridge
貓兒橋河東岸開牋紙馬鋪鍾家

L Zhang Family Bookshop in the Central
中瓦子張家

M Rong Liulang Family Bookshop in the Central Market
中瓦南街東經史書籍鋪榮六郎家

N Zhao Family Bookshop
清河坊北街西面東雙桂趙宅書籍鋪

O Yin Family Bookshop in front of the Imperial Ancestral Temple
太廟前尹家書籍鋪

P Bookshop at the Dayin Ward
大隱坊

Q Juyuan Ting Bookshop
橘園亭

R Shen Erlang Family Bookshop
大街棚前南鈔庫相對沈二郎經坊

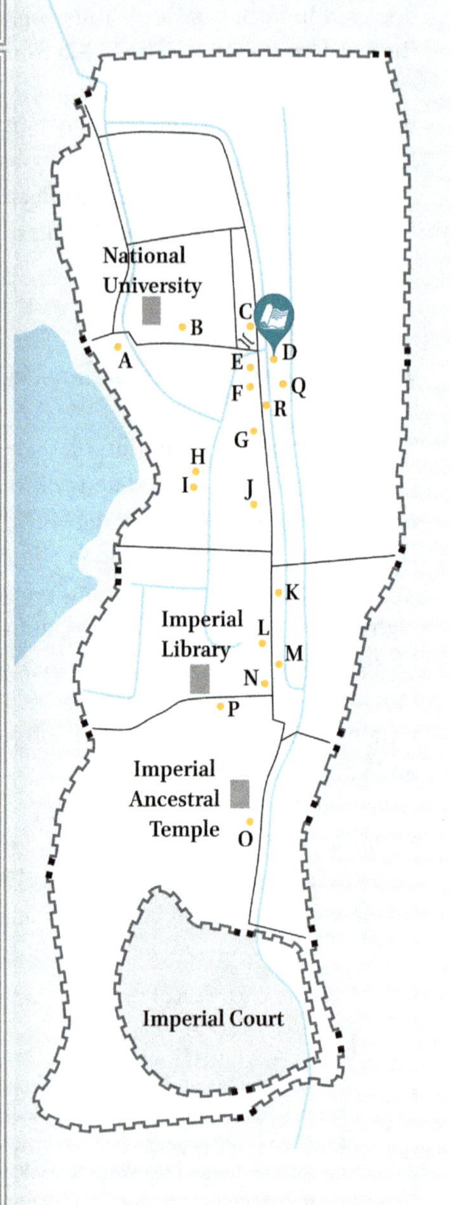

MAP 3.1 Publishers/bookshops in Southern Song Hangzhou. By Rita Xiong based on the map published in Edgren 1989, 4

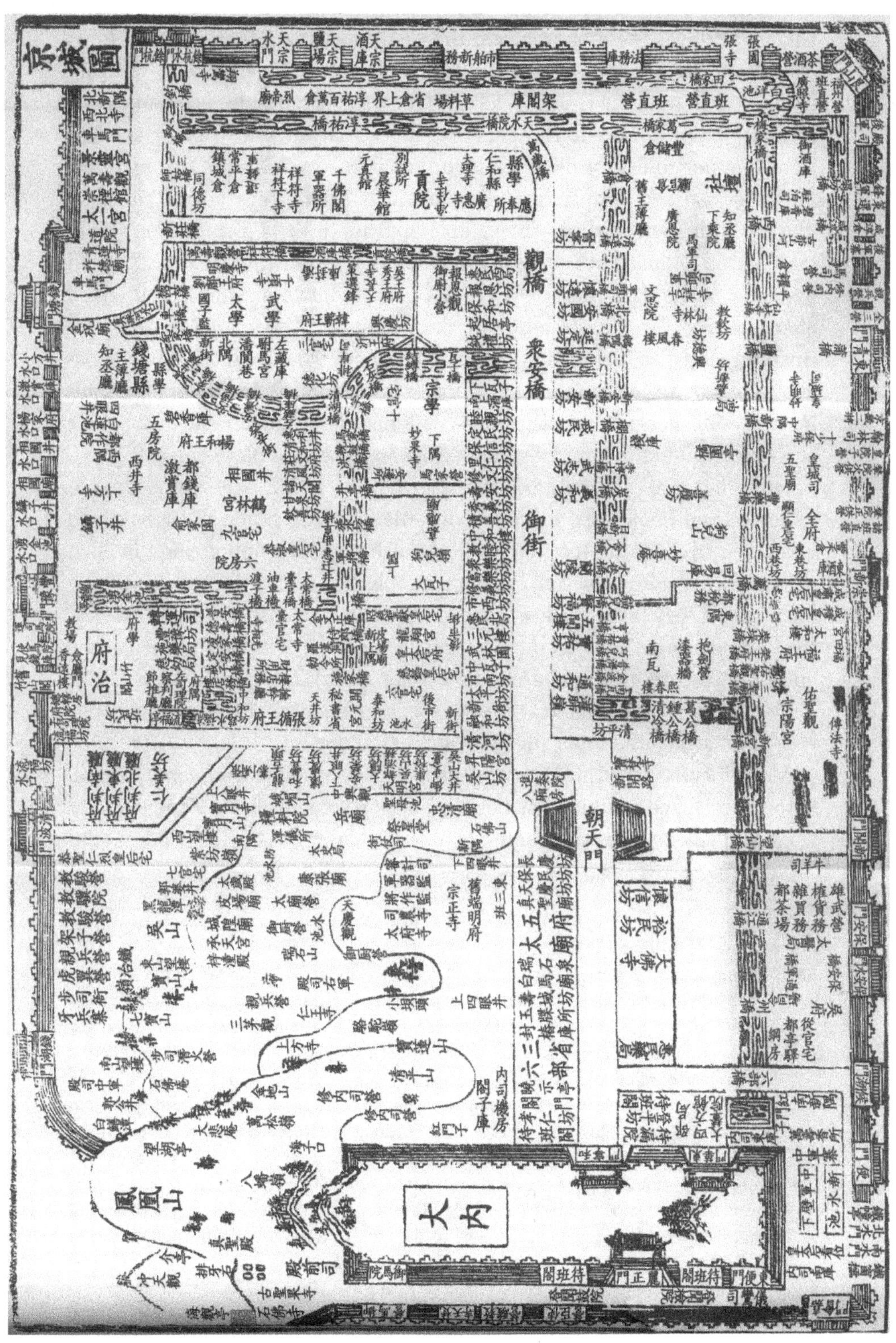

MAP 3.2 The Map of the Southern Song Capital. *Xianchun Lin'an zhi*

Guan 觀 Bridge. The area was near the Central Market (*Zhong wazi* 中瓦子) along Imperial Street (*Yujie* 御街) and not far from the Imperial Library (*Mishu sheng* 秘書省) and the Grand Academy (*Taixue* 太學). Besides bookstores, the area also housed numerous "divination stalls" that provided mantic services from "physiognomy, astrology, and word analysis" to "trigrams and pictures" (*guaying* 卦影).[97] Temple divination booklets often consisted of collected illustrated divination slips. An example appears in the *Divination Slips from the Tianzhu* [*Monastery*] (*Tianzhu lingqian* 天竺靈籤) (fig. 3.24), associated with the Shang Tianzhusi 上天竺寺 (Upper India Monastery), also called Shangzhusi 上竺寺, in the hilly suburb marked on the *Map of the West Lake* (map 3.3) and also included in the same Southern Song gazetteer. Such booklets were sold in local stationery shops or bookstores.[98] In addition to commercial publishers and lay consumers, Buddhist clergy and temples—typically clustered around the West Lake (fig. 3.25; map 3.3)—also played an active role in publishing and purchasing books.[99]

Some local bookshops moved from Kaifeng to Hangzhou after the north was taken over by the Jurchen kingdom of Jin, which soon created its own thriving print culture (see ch. 5). For example, the family bookshop of Rong Liulang's 榮六郎 (Sixth Fellow Rong) located "to the east of South Street at the Central Market" ("M" in map 3.1), as specified in a colophon printed at the end of an 1152 reprint of the medieval Daoist work *Book of the Master Who Embraces Simplicity* (*Baopuzi* 抱朴子), was previously near the Xiangguosi 相國寺 (Monastery of Supporting the State) in Kaifeng.[100]

Most documented Hangzhou publishers or bookshops were family-based. Some specialized in Buddhist books and clustered near the Zhong'an and Guan Bridges, such as the Family of Wang Nian 王念 ("F" in map 3.1) who

97 Liao 2001, 250, 270–73; Huang S. 2007, 285.

98 Huang S. 2007, 290; ZGFJBHQJ 2: 112–96. For more about the cutter Wang Yao who produced the Map of the West Lake, see Jiang 2015, 21. For more discussions of select places on the Map of the West Lake, see Duan 2023, 174–76 (fig. 1); Duan 2020, 16–17.

99 The section shown here features a temple colored in orange that contained a large Buddha torso; it may refer to Dafosi 大佛寺 (Great Buddha Temple) near the West Lake. See Jiang 2015, 235. Selected Buddhist temples were further known for their participation in the printing of Buddhist books. In the Northern Song, the Huayan Society of lay Buddhists organized by the abbot of the Longxingsi 龍興寺 (Monastery of Dragonlike Prosperity) contributed funds to print the *Avatamsaka Sutra* with a frontispiece. The *Guanyin Sutra* printed in 1116 by the Fachangyuan 法昌院 (Cloister of Dharma Flourishing) in Hangzhou was discovered in a pagoda in Lishui 麗水, Jiangsu. For more about temple publishing in Song Hangzhou, see Zhang and Han 2006, 49–50 (fig. 12), 52; Duan 2023, 176.

100 See Su 1999, 87, 150 (fig. 43); Edgren 1989, 32; Zhang and Han 2006, 55.

MAP 3.3 The Map of the West Lake by the cutter Wang Yao. *Xianchun Lin'an zhi*

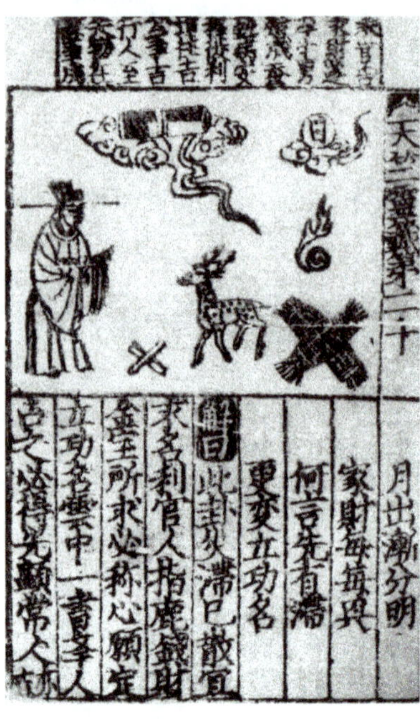

FIGURE 3.24
Detail. Lot 20 from *Tianzhu lingqian*. Southern Song. Woodblock print. National Library of China

FIGURE 3.25 Detail. *Scenic Attractions of West Lake*. 14th century. Late Yuan or early Ming. Ink and color on paper. Handscroll. National Museum of Asian Art

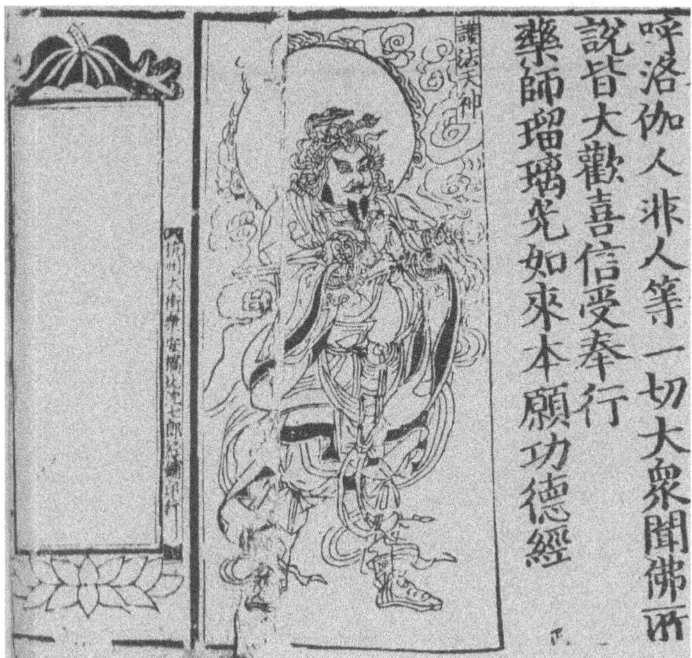

FIGURE 3.26 Detail of the publisher's colophon. *Scripture of the Medicine Buddha*. Yuan. Woodblock print

published an illustrated version of the *Diamond Sutra* (fig. 11.12b).[101] Wang Nian was also known as Third Fellow (Sanlang 三郎), maybe indicating that he was born as the third son. It is likely that other publishing businesses run by Wang family members were his relatives, including, for example, Wang Erlang 王二郎 (Second Fellow Wang) ("J" in map 3.1) and Wang Balang 王八郎 (Eighth Fellow Wang) ("G" on map 3.1). Some publishers probably continued their family-based business over several generations, lasting through the political changes of dynastic transition. The Shen Family bookshop run by Shen Erlang 沈二郎 (Second Fellow Shen), marked as "R" of map 3.1, was managed by the seventh and eighth sons of the family in the Yuan period. The seventh son, Shen Qilang 沈七郎 (Seventh Fellow Shen), published the illustrated *Scripture of the Medicine Buddha* (fig. 3.26). The eighth son, Shen Balang 沈八郎 (fig. 3.27a), similarly ran a shop in the Muqin 睦親 Ward (map 3.2) near

101 For the colophon, see Huang 2018b, 104 (fig. 15). Wang Erlang's shop published the *Lotus Sutra* as well; see Zhang and Han 2006, 55.

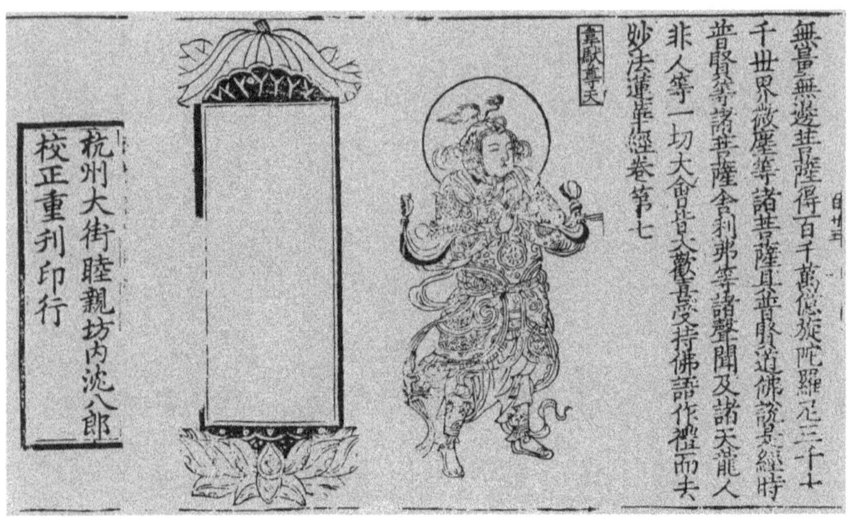

FIGURE 3.27A Detail of the publisher's colophon. Reprint of the *Lotus Sutra*. Yuan. Woodblock print

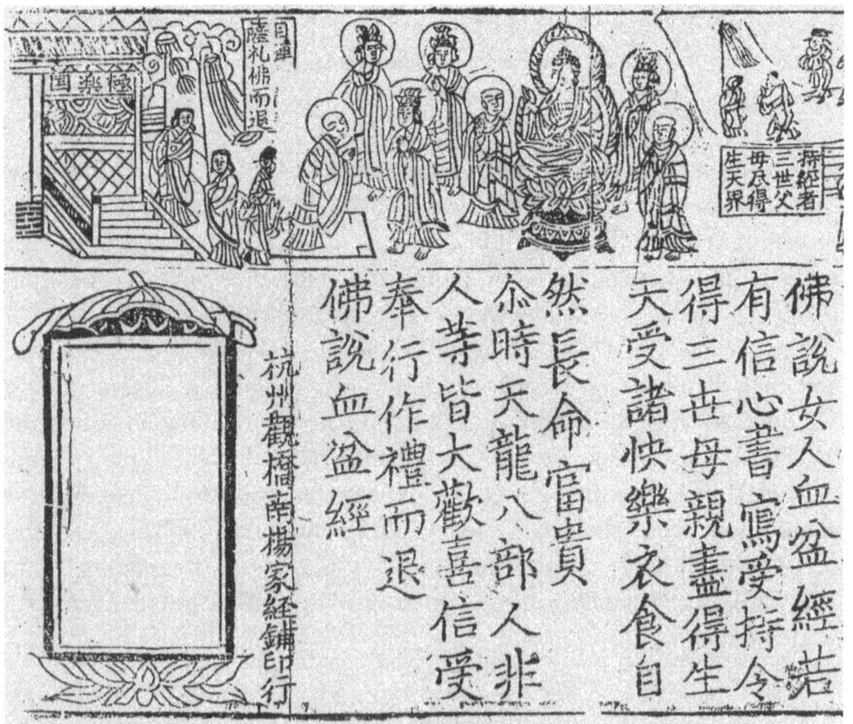

FIGURE 3.28 Detail. *Blood Pond Sutra* published by the Yang Family. Yuan

the Zhong'an Bridge in the Yuan dynasty. He was in charge of reprinting the *Lotus Sutra* (figs. 3.27a–b).[102]

Similarly, the Yang 楊 Family ("C" on map 3.1) who owned a publishing business from the Southern Song to Yuan dynasties, reached its prime time in the latter, when it participated in publishing the "Universal Gateway" chapter of the *Lotus Sutra* (fig. 1.70), the indigenous *Blood Pond Sutra Preached by the Buddha* (*Foshuo xuepen jing* 佛說血盆經) (fig. 3.28), and frontispieces adorning the Yuan Buddhist canon (figs. 8.10, 8.24a).[103] Transitioning to the Ming, the Yang Family was still in business in the late fourteenth century, evident in its reprint edition of the temple divination booklet associated with Hangzhou's Shang Tianzhu Monastery. Although related to the Southern Song edition (figs. 3.24, 12.30a–b), this edition shows a different page layout with much rougher illustrations.[104]

4 Three Southern Song Versions

At least three versions of *Lotus Sutra* frontispieces associated with Hangzhou are available in multiple copies or derivative designs. Extant specimens and copies made in Korea and Japan suggest that many were transported to neighboring countries after being printed in Hangzhou. There they inspired both printed and hand-written copies. Two of the three versions (3.29a, 3.34a) feature a single frontispiece design, while the third consists of a set of seven different frontispieces (figs. 3.1a, 3.36, 3.37a–b, 3.38a, 3.39, 3.40a, 3.41a). They adorn the opening of one chapter each in the seven-chapter version of the *Lotus Sutra*. In terms of publisher's information, the first version was printed by the bookshop of the Official Jia (Jia guanren 賈官人) (figs. 3.29a–c), and there is some information about the block cutters who worked on all three (figs. 3.29d, 3.34b, 3.37c). A rare signature of an otherwise undocumented painter preserved in an extant set of the third version sheds light on the frontispiece illustrator (fig. 3.40b).

4.1 *First Version: Bookshop Printed*

The first version published by the bookshop of the Official Jia survives in multiple printed specimens, all with the same basic designs but cut by different

102 See also Su 1999, 88. The renown Chen Family (Chen zhai 陳宅) Publisher was also located at the Muqin Ward.

103 Chia 2015a, 115–16.

104 Huang S. 2007, 244*n*4; ZGFJBHQJ 5: 18.

cutters.[105] The specimen cited here (fig. 3.29a) was first discovered in a Japanese wooden statue of the bodhisattva Jizō 地藏 (Kṣitigarbha), dated 1249 (fig. 3.30). Originally associated with the Buddhist monastery Jizōin 地藏院 (Cloister of the Bodhisattva Kṣitigarbha) in Kyoto, it is now in the Museum für Ostasiatische Kunst in Cologne, Germany (hereafter called the Cologne frontispiece).[106] The archival photograph provided by the Museum shows the thick Southern Song *Lotus Sutra* in accordion form, displayed to the right of the statue and juxtaposed with other objects removed from it (fig. 3.30).[107] They include over six thousand votive slips of an impressed buddha (*inbutsu* 印佛), each showing a stamped Amitabha.[108] Before these artifacts were removed from the statue, the slips were "used as stuffing" to fill its lower part and "keep the other offerings securely in place." The *Lotus Sutra* itself was at the very center of the objects, deep in the chest area, quite possibly because it was the sole precious Chinese book among the many items deposited.

The publisher's stamped colophon at the end of the Cologne frontispiece provides the street address for the bookshop: "South of the Zhong'an Bridge in Lin'an City [Hangzhou], the Sutra Bookshop of the Official Jia" (*Lin'an fu Zhong'an qiao nan Jia Guanren jingshupu* 臨安府衆安橋南賈官人經書鋪) (figs. 3.29b–c). While the address corresponds to "D" in map 3.1, an area where bookshops clustered, the shop itself was a well-documented commercial enterprise, specializing in Buddhist illustrated books. The publisher's most refined Buddhist publication is the fully illustrated book in folded-scroll format, the *Illustrated Eulogies by Mañjuśrī* (figs. 1.67, 6.67c, 6.69a–b).[109]

The Cologne frontispiece, showing a frontal and symmetrical composition, bears the signature of the cutter Ling Zhang 凌璋 in the lower left corner (fig. 3.29d). This is identical with its other extant copy, now in the National Library in Beijing.[110] The netted curtain motifs (fig. 3.29e) decorating the upper border are comparable to the Northern Song *Lotus Sutra* printed by the Qian and Yan Family bookshops (figs. 3.14a, 3.15a) and other tenth-century frontispiece designs (figs. 3.10a–b, 3.17). Selected figural motifs highlight non-Chinese features: on the left are two celestial musicians playing the flute and clappers

105 Huang 2020, 54–58.

106 The statue was associated with the famous sculptor Kōen 西信 (1207–after 1275); see Goepper 1983.

107 Covaci 2016, 123.

108 For more studies of the practice of the Buddhist stamps and prints in Japan, see Sasaki 2008; Sasaki 2017. For studies of the texts and artifacts deposited in religious statues in Asia, see Robson 2014, 2016; Bentor 1994; Robson et al. 2019; Arrault 2020.

109 Fontein 1967, 23–40; Huang 2017c, 22, 61–63 (figs. 36–38); Chen 2023.

110 For a plate, see Fontein 1967, 21–22 (fig. 7a).

(fig. 3.29f), labeled Gandharva (Qiantapo 乾闥婆); on the right are two heavenly guardians with pointed mustaches and exotic hats, labeled Kimnara (Jinna luowang 緊那羅王) (fig. 3.29g). These divinities all appeared in the *Lotus Sutra* as celestial beings attending the Buddha's assembly.[111]

An almost identical specimen in the collection of Unryū-in 雲龍院 (Cloud Dragon Cloister), a sub-temple of Sennyūji 泉涌寺 (Monastery of the Bubbling Spring) in Kyoto, was printed from a different block cut by Lü Bin 呂斌 active in the mid-twelfth century.[112] The publisher's stamped colophon at the end of the book is identical with that in the Cologne version. This suggests that the use of multiple blocks in reproducing the same frontispiece design entailed a large number of imprints serving the popular market. Documented cutters were itinerant artisans, mostly from Zhejiang and Jiangsu, including Ningbo.[113] By comparing the various versions with those that show both cutters' names and specific publication dates, it is possible to track printed productions even without specific dates to particular cutters. The information makes it clear that the first version of the *Lotus Sutra* in this format was published in the mid-twelfth century.

Extant Chinese and Korean copies sharing the same frontispiece design suggest its wide circulation and transnational legacy. A Yuan reprint with recut blocks survives in various specimens (fig. 3.31),[114] printed from different blocks that share a common frontispiece design. One was printed by the Shen Family (figs. 3.27a–b); the other preserves the older version's documentation of the names of two Southern Song cutters, Fang Zhi 方至 and Fang Zaiming 方再明, active in the first quarter of the thirteenth century.[115] Unlike the Southern Song prototype (figs. 3.29a, 3.29e), however, none of the Yuan reprint specimens bear any curtain designs in the upper border. Moreover, an elaborate poem entitled *Emperor Renzong's Imperial Eulogy to the Lotus Sutra* (*Renzong Huangdi yuzan lianjing* 仁宗皇帝御贊蓮經) (fig. 3.31), consisting of four lines of seven characters each, is added to the left of the original frontispiece in both specimens. The Northern Song emperor Renzong was among the most fervent imperial supporters of Buddhist printing.[116]

---

111 T.9.262, 2a.

112 For a plate, see Machida Shiritsu Kokusai Hanga Bijutsukan 1988, 29, 87 (fig. 10); Nara Kokuritsu Hakubutsukan 1996, 203 (pl. 198).

113 Su 1999, 86. For more on the documented cutters, see Wang Z. 1990.

114 ZGFJBHQJ 4: 135; Nara Kokuritsu Hakubutsukan 1996, 203 (pl. 199).

115 Nara Kokuritsu Hakubutsukan 1996, 281 (see cat. entry no. 199).

116 Renzong's *Eulogy of the Lotus Sutra* was added to the Northern Song illustrated *Lotus Sutra* manuscript (dated 1044) when the sutra was remounted in the Ming; for a transliteration of the eulogy, see Wang Yanjing 2012, 139–40. It also appears in the seven-volume

a

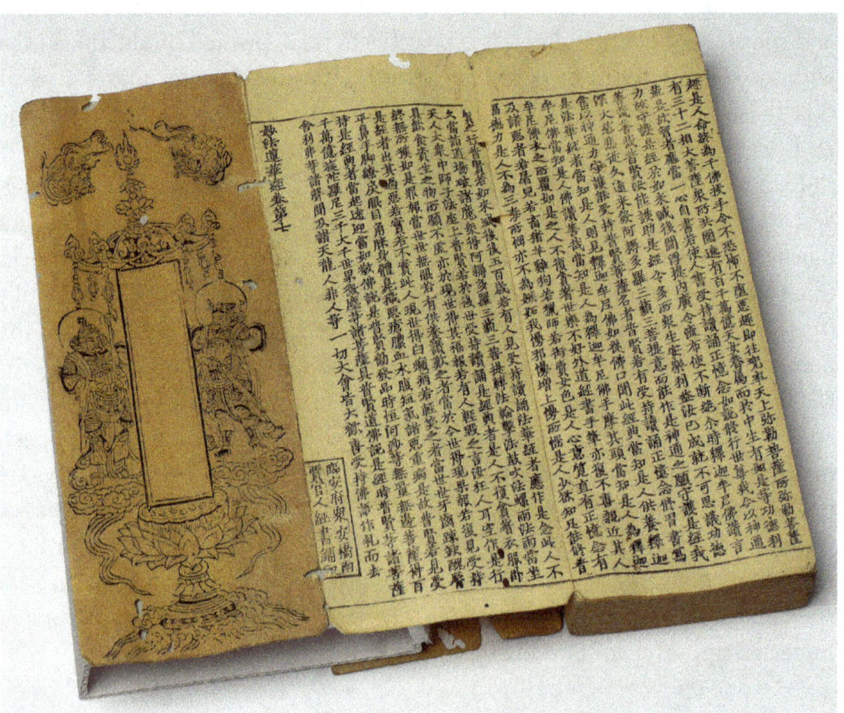

b

FIGURES 3.29A–G Details. The *Lotus Sutra* printed by the Family of the Official Jia. Southern Song. Woodblock print. Concertina. Museum für Ostasiatische Kunst
a. Frontispiece cut by Ling Zhang
b. Detail. The final section of the *Lotus Sutra*
c. Detail. The publisher's colophon
d. Detail. The signature of the cutter Ling Zhang
e. Detail of the netted curtain motif
f. Detail of celestial musicians (Gandharva)
g. Detail of heavenly guardians (Kimnara)

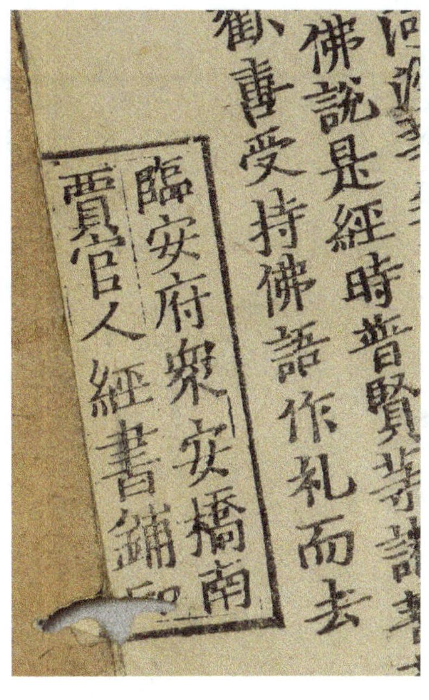

c

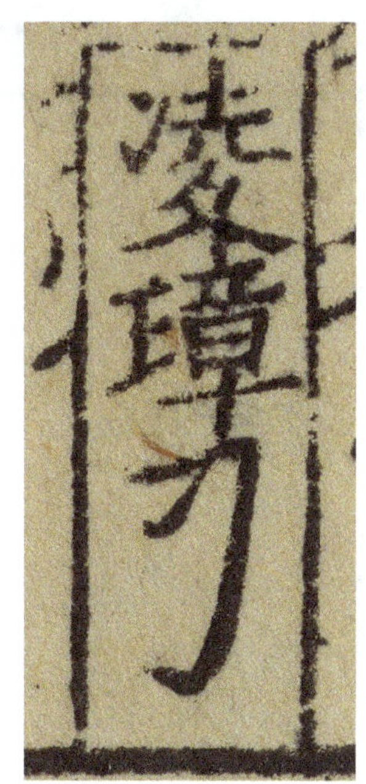

d

e

f

g

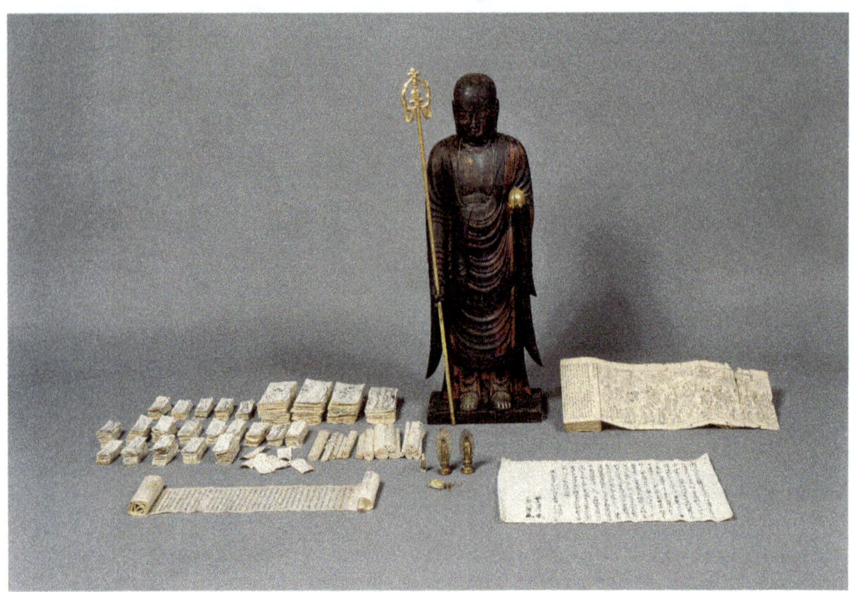

FIGURE 3.30 The statue of the Jizō bodhisattva and the artifacts originally deposited inside. 1249, Kamakura period, Japan. Museum für Ostasiatische Kunst

FIGURE 3.27B Detail. Frontispiece to the *Lotus Sutra*. Yuan. Woodblock print

The Korea copies, available in both printed and painted versions (figs. 3.32, 3.33a), closely follow Southern Song-to-Yuan designs, although without an imperial eulogy.[117] Whereas the overall composition matches the *Lotus Sutra*

version of the Yuan printed *Lotus Sutra* at the National Palace Museum; see Chung 2022, 23–24 (for the complete text of Renzong's eulogy as recorded in a Yuan source, see 23*n*1).

117 Kim 2017, 72, 356; Kungnip Chungang Pangmulgwan 2018, 108 (fig. 110); Nabeshima hokokai 2012, 26–27.

FIGURE 3.31 Frontispiece to the *Lotus Sutra*. Yuan. Woodblock print. Concertina. Daitōkyu Kinen Bunko

FIGURE 3.32 Frontispiece to the *Lotus Sutra*. 14th century. Koryŏ period, Korea. Woodblock print. Concertina. Horim Museum

convention associated with Southern Song-to-Yuan Hangzhou, a guardian motif now proceeds the frontispiece, appearing on the right. In this, the composition departs from standard Chinese conventions, which tend to show the guardian at the end of the scripture (figs. 3.26, 3.27a). He is called the "benevolent deity who protects the dharma" (*hufa shanshen* 護法善神), a phrase that resonates with the cartouche on a Liao frontispiece that also shows a guardian (fig. 4.27). The hand-painted version copied in gold and silver, in particular, is associated with Korean royalty and aristocracy: it bears a dedicatory colophon (fig. 3.33b) that pays tribute to an emperor or king.[118] The person in question may be the Koryŏ king Ch'ungsŏk 忠肅 (r. 1313–1330, 1332–1339), who not only grew up in the Yuan capital Dadu, but also was closely connected to the Mongol imperial family through his marriage to the grand-daughter of the Yuan emperor Qubilai Khan. Among the donors listed in the colophon was the leading monk Hyŏn Ch'ŏl 玄哲, also known as "Master Pillar"

118 Nabeshima hokokai 2012, 26–27.

a

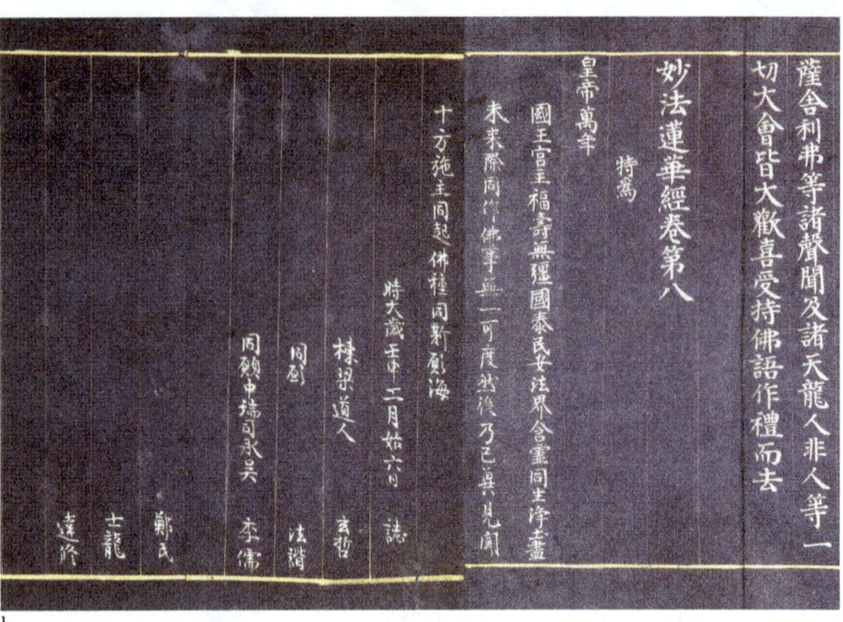

b

FIGURES 3.33A–B Details. *Lotus Sutra*. 1332. Koryŏ period, Korea. Gold and silver on indigo-dyed paper. Nabeshima Hokokai collection
a. Detail of the hand painted frontispiece
b. Dedicatory colopho

(Tongyangtoin 棟梁道人), whose style name appears here and also in the over-sized Avalokiteśvara painting by the Koryŏ court painter Sŏ Kupang 徐九方, dated 1323.[119]

4.2 *Second Version: in Small Characters*

The second version with a single frontispiece is attached to the first scroll of the eight-*juan Lotus Sutra* in small characters (*xizi* 細字), arguably the most popular frontispiece design that made its way to Japan (fig. 3.34a).[120] Based on the information of documented cutters including Chen Gao 陳高 (ca. 1260) from Siming 四明 (modern Ningbo) (fig. 3.34b), this version is dated around 1160.[121]

One extant copy, now at the U.S. Library of Congress (figs. 3.34a–d), was originally discovered inside the late thirteenth-century (around 1292) statue of the Infant Shōtoku Taishi 聖徳太子 (574–622) (fig. 3.35), now at the Harvard Art Museums.[122] Before being removed from the statue in 1936, the Library of Congress copy was deposited inside the statue together with many Japanese objects, all dating from 1160 to 1292 and ranging from miniature wooden statues to a hand-copied booklet of the *Lotus Sutra*. There was also a six-inch charm-slip, showing a stamped standing Amitabha above and a handwritten inscription below: "Each day one-hundred times [from among the prayers for the sake of] ten-thousand men."[123] The slip recalls similar items deposited in

119 For a plate see Sanekata and Shirahara eds., 2016, 63 (pl. 22); for the latest scholarship of the painting, including a conservation report, see 112–17, 146–50. For an introduction to the Koryŏ Buddhist painting, see Lippit 2008.

120 Huang 2020, 49–54. For the complete work, see Library of Congress, "Miao fa lian hua jing: qi juan Recto," Book/Printed Material, Accessed January 2, 2024. https://www.loc.gov/resource/lcnclscd.2014514056.1A000/?st=gallery.

121 Other cutters whose names appear throughout the printed text include Hong Xin 洪新, Hong Mao 洪茂, and Jiang Hui 蔣暉. These cutters cut the blocks of other non-Buddhist books published in Hangzhou from 1146 to 1164. For more information of these extant copies, see Nara-ken Kyōiku Iinkai 2001, pls. 26–27; Weidner ed. 1994, 305n2; Miya 1983a, 26–27; Li L. 2014, 63–87. It is possible that Chen Gao was related to the other Siming cutter Chen Zhong 陳忠 who cut the blocks of the *Avatamsaka Sutra*; see Zhang and Han 2006, 657.

122 John Rosenfield estimates about one hundred or more such Infant Shōtoku statues made in medieval Japan, with about forty dated to "the late thirteenth or early fourteenth centuries." See Rosenfield 1968–1969, 57. For more studies of the arts and images inspired by the cult of Shōtoku, see Carr 2012; for alternative sculptural forms representing Shōtoku as a Buddhist lecturer and a youth respectively, see 36, 39, 120.

123 Selected artifacts found inside the statue are at the Harvard Art Museums; see Harvard Art Museums, "Prince Shōtoku: The Secrets Within," May 25, 2019–August 11, 2019, University Teaching Gallery, Harvard Art Museums, Accessed December 24, 2023. https://www.harvardartmuseums.org/exhibitions/5756/prince-shotoku-the-secrets-within.

the Cologne statue. As a whole they reflect a common practice among East Asian Buddhists of filling holy statues with charms, sutras, and other sacred objects.[124]

Extant specimens of the second version include the one originally deposited in the Harvard statue, another one based on different blocks and now at the Harvard Art Museums, and others from temples in Japan.[125] A close comparison between the samples now held in the Library of Congress and the Harvard Art Museums shows that they were based on different blocks, although both were cut by the same cutter, namely Chen Gao. Rosenfield and others have identified thirty scenes with accompanying colophons in the frontispiece, linking their content to the *Lotus Sutra*.[126] A diagram reconfigured from the one published by Li Ling highlights the frontispiece's compositional layout of ten major episodes (diagram 3.1).[127] It shows that the arrangement of various episodes in a frontispiece does not follow any textual order but works according to a tripartite scheme, divided by two pagodas positioned in the third and the sixth folds of the eight-fold composition. The composition shows a prominent seven-storied pagoda on the right, encircled by eight seated buddhas and complete with a colophon that reads "variant buddha manifestations" (*fenshen zhufo* 分身諸佛). This illustrates the famous episode of visualizing the treasure pagoda.

Matching it is a smaller, five-storied pagoda on the left (fig. 3.34c). A figure to its right raises his right arm, which is on fire. This refers to the story of the "Medicine King burning his arm" (*Yaowang ranbi* 藥王燃臂), as stated in the accompanying cartouche. Quite different from the mainstream Buddhist frontispiece design, in which a buddha-preaching scene occupies a prominent size and placed at the right of a frontispiece, the buddha-preaching scene associated with the preface of the sutra here is of a rather small size and pushed to the upper corner.

Besides the compartmentalized compositional scheme, certain narratives pertinent to select parables also exhibit novelty. The scene labeled "three carts leave the dwelling" (*sanju chuzhai* 三車出宅) (fig. 3.34d), for example,

124 For an introduction to the Japanese tradition of depositing objects and books in Buddhist statues, see Brinker 2011; Wu 2011.

125 There are at least six extant copies in the world collections; note that the one Marsha Weidner listed as from the National Palace Museum may be a mistake; see Weidner 1994, 305*n*2. For a comparable specimen in a temple in Nara, see Nara Kokuritsu Hakubutsukan 2009, 79; for the one at Harvard Art Museums, see Shih-shan Susan Huang's entry in Von Spee et al. 2024, 143–45.

126 Rosenfield 1968–69, 63–69; Li L. 2014, 72–78.

127 Cf. the diagram published in Li L. 2014, 72 (fig. 13).

a

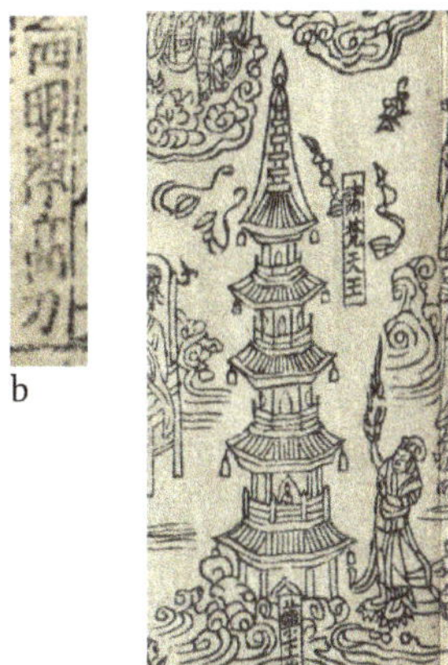

b

c

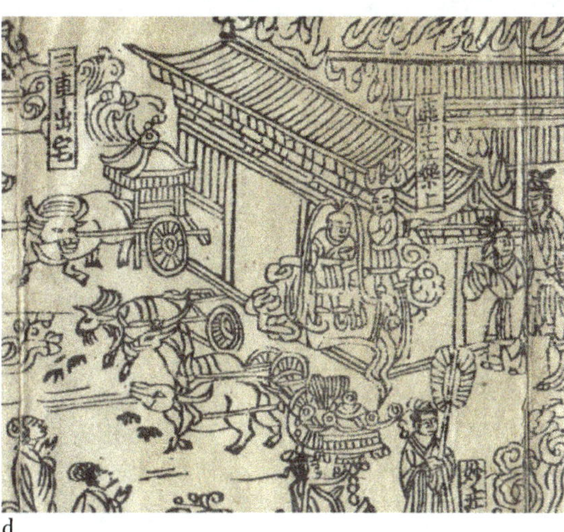

d

e

FIGURES 3.34A–E Frontispiece to the *Lotus Sutra*. ca. 1160. Southern Song. Woodblock print. Concertina. Library of Congress, Washington, D.C.
a. Complete view
b. Detail of the cutter's signature
c. Detail of the Medicine King burning his arm
d. Detail of the parable of the burning house
e. Detail of the parable of the medicinal herbs

FIGURE 3.35
Prince Shōtoku at Age Two. ca. 1292. Kamakura period, Japan. Japanese cypress; assembled woodblock construction with polychromy and rock-crystal inlaid eyes. Harvard Art Museums

represents arguably the most famous parable.[128] It depicts four animal-driven carts outside a burning house, inside of which two children are playing. A larger cart, covered with a rooftop and pulled by a water buffalo, is juxtaposed with three smaller carts, pulled by a goat, a deer, and an ox. The unusual juxtaposition of a larger cart with three lesser ones departs from the stereotyped template of the parable, which only shows three lesser carts (fig. 3.37b). The story uses the father as a metaphor of the Buddha, his deluded children are ordinary human beings, and the burning house is the world of suffering. In order to trick the children to leave the burning house, the father offers them their favorite carts drawn by a goat, a deer, and an ox. As soon as the children have left the house, the father gives them a still bigger cart pulled by a white water buffalo. Researchers interpret these carts as symbolic images of different levels of the Buddhist teaching. The three lesser carts indicate more "provisional" and "conventional" teachings, while the greater cart stands for the "one grand single cart-vehicle"—most likely Mahayana Buddhism, but possibly also the *Lotus Sutra* specifically, the text that sums up the "ultimate" truth.[129]

128 Rosenfield 1968–69, 66; Li L. 2014, 73–75 (fig. 15).
129 Rosenfield 1968–69, 66; Yü 2020, 35–36.

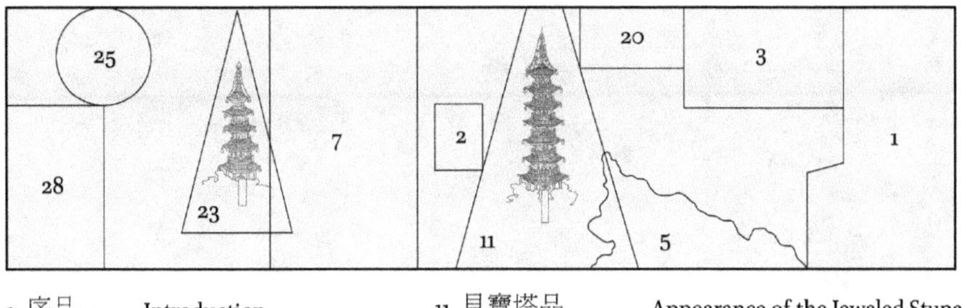

1. 序品	Introduction	11. 見寶塔品	Appearance of the Jeweled Stupa
2. 方便品	Skillful Means	20. 常不輕菩薩品	Bodhisattva Never Disparaging
3. 譬喩品	A Parable	23. 藥王菩薩品	Bodhisattva Medicine King
5. 藥草喩品	Parable of Medicinal Herbs	25. 普門品	Universal Gateway
7. 化城喩品	The Apparitional City	28. 勸發品	Encouragement of Bodhisattva Universally Worthy

DIAGRAM 3.1 Mapping major episodes of the *Lotus Sutra* as depicted in the Southern Song "second version." By Rita Xiong

Another novel rendition features the parable of the medicinal herbs, depicted in the lower right border of the picture plane and labeled "three grasses and two trees" (*sancao ermu* 三草二木) (fig. 3.34e).[130] Departing from the eighth-century Dunhuang mural (fig. 3.22), the Northern Song prototype featured in the Yan Family frontispiece (fig. 0.4, 3.20), the hand-painted frontispiece (fig. 3.16a–b), and the Xi Xia version (fig. 0.1), this scene is devoid of any figure or architectural motif, showing only shrubs and trees that grow on a slope by the water.[131] These different grasses and trees are linked to "different kinds of Buddhists," whom the Buddha, here comparable to invisible rain, nurtures without discrimination.

4.3 *Third Version: with Seven Frontispieces*

The third version comes in seven volumes, decorated with seven different frontispieces. Scholars refer to it as the "large character set" (*dazi ben* 大字本) in contrast to the second version whose text is in smaller characters.[132] Most artistic, it shows highly standardized compositional schemes and modular motifs, and, as extant specimens suggest, was produced in multiple sets in the broader Zhejiang area around the mid-twelfth century.[133] It also inspired some

130 It also differs from the depiction in the third version (3.38a) discussed below.

131 Rosenfield 1968–69, 66.

132 Huang 2011b, 155.

133 Miya 1983a; Huang 2011b, 147–52; Zhang J. 2021. For additional specimens not mentioned in this book, such as the set with the signature of the cutter Li Du 李度 at the National Library in Beijing, and the frontispiece cut by Xu Xi 徐禧 from Fengjing 風涇 (near Shaoxing, Zhejiang), see ZGFJBHQJ 2: 98–101, 108–109; Zhang J. 2021, 42–43.

FIGURE 3.36 Frontispiece to the *Lotus Sutra*, juan 5. Southern Song. Woodblock print. Concertina. Rikkyoku-an, Kyoto

Korean and Japanese painted and printed products from the fourteenth and fifteenth centuries. In addition, one motif regarding a construction scene is most enduring: it was adapted by foreign painters working on fifteenth-century Islamic illuminations (figs. 0.21–0.22) and in eighteenth-century Korean genre painting (fig. 0.20).

While the extant sets of this group do not bear identical frontispiece designs, they share standardized compositional schemes with minor differences. Among the most studied specimens is the twelfth-century set in the Rikkyoku-an 栗棘庵, a sub-temple of Tōfukuji 東福寺 (Eastern Monastery of Good Fortune) in Kyoto (fig. 3.36).[134] Chen Gao, who also cut the second version of the *Lotus Sutra* frontispiece (fig. 3.34b), was one of its cutters.[135] Two comparable sets in the National Palace Museum are from the same time period. One, highly comparable to the Ritsukyoku'an set, was cut by Bian Ren 邊仁 and Qin Meng 秦孟 (figs. 3.6a, 3.37a–c).[136] The other set, arguably the most refined, was illustrated by the little-known artist Wang Yi 王儀 (figs. 3.1a–b, 3.38a–3.40b;

134 For the plates of the complete set of seven frontispieces, see Machida Shiritsu Kokusai Hanga Bijutsukan 1988, 84–85. For a classic study, see Miya 1983a, 29–32, 78–79; for Chen Gao, see 104. See also Nara Kokuritsu Hakubutsukan 1996, 205; Nara Kokuritsu Hakubutsukan 2009, 80; ZGFJBHQJ 2: 92–93; Chung 2022, 110 (fig. 1).

135 Sudō 2015, 179.

136 Ge 1995, 24–25, 78–79; Chung 2022, 20–21, 98–99, 102–103, 106–107.

a

b

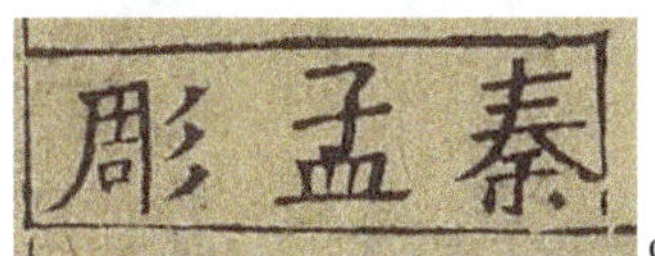

c

FIGURES 3.37A–C Frontispieces to the *Lotus Sutra* cut by Bian Ren and Qing Meng. Southern Song. Woodblock print. Concertina. National Palace Museum
a. Frontispiece to juan 1
b. Frontispiece to juan 2
c. "Cut by Qin Meng." Detail of 3.37b

a

b

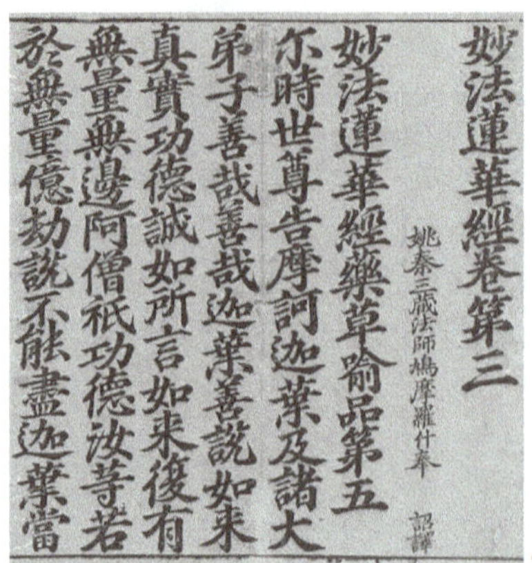

妙法蓮華經卷第三
姚秦三藏法師鳩摩羅什奉　詔譯
妙法蓮華經藥草喻品第五
尒時世尊告摩訶迦葉及諸大
弟子善哉善哉迦葉善說如来
真實功德誠如所言如来復有
無量無邊阿僧祇功德汝等若
於無量億劫說不能盡迦葉當

c

FIGURES 3.38A–C
Frontispiece to the *Lotus Sutra*, juan 3. Illustrated by Wang Yi. Southern Song. Woodblock print. Concertina. National Palace Museum
a. Complete view
b. Detail of fig. 3.38a
c. Detail of the text

FIGURE 3.39 Frontispiece to the *Lotus Sutra*, juan 5. Illustrated by Wang Yi. Southern Song. Woodblock print. Concertina. National Palace Museum

hereafter called the Wang Yi set),[137] though without any information on its cutters. The sutra (fig. 3.38c), copied from the original manuscript written by Su Shi (*Su xieben* 蘇寫本), was printed on Southern Song imitation paper, originally produced in the Northern Song in the Jinsusi 金粟寺 (Monastery of the Golden Chestnut) in Haiyan 海鹽, Zhejiang and accordingly known as Jingu paper.[138] A recurring motif depicting two monkish figures (fig. 3.1b), standing at the lower right corner of each frontispiece of the Wang Yi set, suggests that monks representing a certain temple may have been its donors.[139] A further set, dated 1261 and now in the National Library of China (figs. 3.41a–b),[140] was produced by a cutter with the surname Fan 范 from Jian'an 建安, Fujian 福建—likely an itinerant craftsman working in the Hangzhou region. Its main sponsor was Lu Daoyuan 陸道源 from Gui'an 歸安 county in Anji 安吉, Zhejiang. He left an impressive colophon (fig. 3.41b), mentioning over thirty villagers who donated various amounts to the project. Other copies of this version,

137 Ge 1995, 19–23; Chung 2022, 24–25 (pl. 6), 100–101 (pl. 45), 104–105 (pl. 48), 108–109 (pl. 51), 112–13 (pl. 54).

138 It is more common to see the Song printed sutras bearing the calligraphic styles of Tang calligraphers such as Ouyang Xun 歐陽詢 (557–641) (*Ou ti* 歐體) and Yan Zhengqing 顏真卿 (709–85) (*Yan ti* 顏體), and less common to have a printed sutra in the style of Su Shi. See Lin et al. 2006b, 238–43 (for the Southern Song imitation paper, see 240); Huang 2011a, 158. For more on the Jinsu paper, see Li 2002b, 48–52.

139 Huang 2020, 60–62.

140 ZGFJBHQJ 2: 202–203, 208–13.

a

b

FIGURES 3.40A–B
Frontispiece to the *Lotus Sutra*, juan 7. Illustrated by Wang Yi. Southern Song. Woodblock print. Concertina. National Palace Museum
a. Complete view
b. Detail of fig. 3.40a

moreover, were most likely transmitted to other parts of East Asia, where they inspired local productions in Korea (fig. 3.42a–b) and Japan (fig. 3.43a).[141]

141 The Mongol-Koryŏ intermarriage and tributary relation intensify the Sino-Korean exchanges. For more studies of Koryŏ royal members, officials, and Buddhist monks in Yuan China, see the temple gazetteer of the Huiyinsi 慧因寺 in Hangzhou, in ZGFSSZHK 20: 112–16; Chia 2015b, 198, 216–17*n*70–71. In the Yuan and Ming periods, there were more than fifty documented Chinese woodblock cutters who migrated to work in Japan; see Li Pingfan in Machida Shiritsu Kokusai Hanga Bijutsukan 1988, 13. For more about the Chinese cutters in Kamakura and Muromachi Japan, especially those associated

a

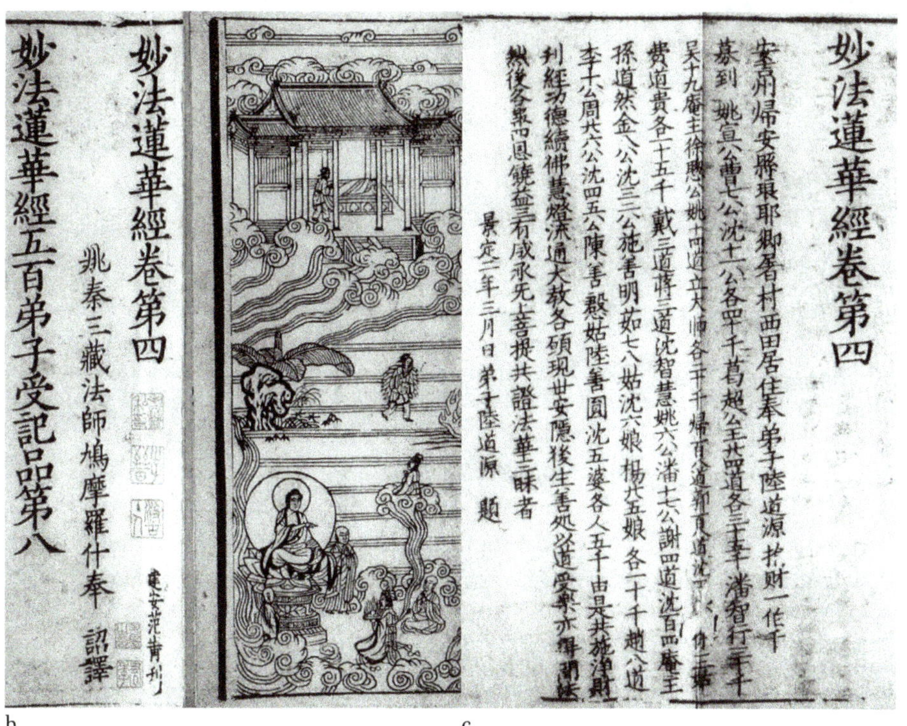

b c

FIGURES 3.41A–C Details. *Lotus Sutra*. 1261. Southern Song. Woodblock print. Concertina. National Library of China

a. Detail. Frontispiece to the *Lotus Sutra*, juan 3

b. Detail of the cutter's signature. *Lotus Sutra*, juan 4

c. Colophon. *Lotus Sutra*, juan 4

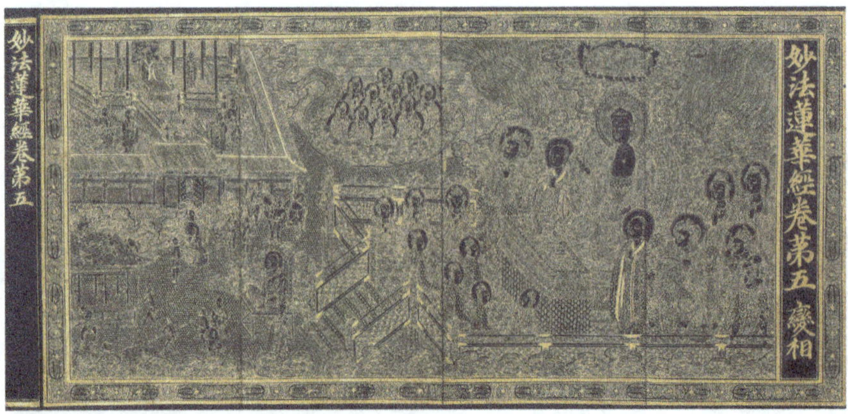

a

b

FIGURE 3.42A–B
Detail. Frontispiece to the *Lotus Sutra*, juan 5. 1340. Koryŏ period, Korea. Nabeshima Hōkokai Foundation, Saga, Japan

4.3.1 Principles of Composition

The frontispiece designs of the third version reflect highly standardized compositional schemes and modular motifs. The generic buddha-preaching scene on the right typically shows him on a raised terrace framed by balustrades;

---

with publishing the Gozanban literature, see Kawase 1970, 142–60. For a study of Gozan monks and Hangzhou in the twelfth and thirteenth centuries, see Duan 2023.

The printed *Lotus Sutra* in the Tōshōdai-ji 唐招提寺, Nara (fig. 3.43a) bearing an ink colophon dated 1412 is an eight-volume Japanese version in which the motifs originally used in the frontispieces of a seven-volume Southern Song Hangzhou version are reassembled in a series of eight frontispiece compositions. While the Tōshōdai-ji set has long been considered a Japanese copy of a Chinese original, it is not clear if any Chinese cutters had participated in creating the blocks.

FIGURE 3.43A Frontispiece to the *Lotus Sutra*. Before 1421. Kamakura period, Japan. Tōshōdai-ji, Nara

here it takes up a larger space, almost seventy percent of the composition.[142] In addition, the seven frontispieces deploy a variety of decorative patterns to furnish the balustrades, ranging from floral designs (fig. 1.48) through geometrics, honey-combs (fig. 3.44a), and phoenixes (fig. 3.44b) to meandering streams of water (fig. 3.44c). These patterns, widely cited by artisans working on the ruler-lined painting conventions, were standardized templates of doors (fig. 1.47), windows, balustrades (fig. 3.45), and ceilings in the government-issued architectural manual *Building Standard*.[143]

An overarching compositional principle shared by multiple frontispieces places a box-like architectural structure in the upper or lower left corner of the picture plane (figs. 3.1a, 3.37b, 3.38a, 3.39). In the second frontispiece (figs. 3.1a, 3.37b), this space shows the parable of the three carts, representing the burning house from a bird's eye view. In the third frontispiece the same space shows a frontally positioned walled city with an open gate (figs. 3.38a–b, 3.41a), matching the parable of the illusionary city.[144] Three travelers are arriving at the gate,

142 Zhang Jianyu characterizes this compositional scheme as the "buddha preaching on a raised terrace" (*gaotai shuofa* 高臺説法); see Zhang J. 2021.

143 Feng 2012, 124–25 (fig. 3.4); Huang 2011b, 150 (figs. 22A–C).

144 The architecture-based rendition of the illusionary city in Hangzhou woodcuts represents a new norm departing from the earlier landscape-based mural convention preserved in Tang Dunhuang grottos. Cf. the illusionary city depicted in the eighth century mural in Mogao Cave 103, which features travelers with an elephant and a donkey in a landscape setting with recessive mountain valleys; see DHSKQJ 7: 72 (fig. 61).

a b c

FIGURES 3.44A–C Details of the balustrades. Frontispieces to the *Lotus Sutra* illustrated by Wang Yi. Southern Song. Woodblock print. National Palace Museum
a. Detail of juan 4
b. Detail of juan 5
c. Detail of juan 7

FIGURE 3.45 Detail of a balustrade template. YZFS, juan 29

FIGURE 3.46
Fragment of the *Lotus Sutra* (no. 11503). Yuan (?). Woodblock print. Institute of Oriental Manuscripts, St. Petersburg

while two tigers linger nearby to signal the danger of their journey.[145] These stock motifs remained basically the same in the Yuan production (fig. 3.2a). Intriguingly, fragments of a printed frontispiece found in Turfan and now in St. Petersburg, Russia (figs. 3.46, 10.24), bear matching details of two tigers and three travelers in front of the walled city with an open gate. This suggests that these fragments, too, may have been part of the *Lotus Sutra* illustrations produced in Hangzhou and later transported to the Uighur community in the thirteenth century (see ch. 10).

4.3.2 Meta-Pictures

Standardization does not mean lesser artistic or creative quality. This is demonstrated in various minute meta-pictures depicted in extant specimens of the third version. A recurring scenario features a painter at work, illustrating the image-making merit advocated in the text. In the set cut by Bian Ren and Qin Meng (fig. 3.6a), a painter is seated on a stool outdoors, working on a vertical Buddha painting supported by a frame and held by two assistants who stand on each side.[146] The meme can be traced to a comparable scene in a mural in Dunhuang's Mogao Cave 72, dated to around the tenth century.[147] As part of a fantastic tableaux representing magical responses to an auspicious Buddha image, an intriguing sub-scene represents the action of making a pictorial copy of the auspicious image (fig. 3.47).[148] It shows a monk and a layman side by side, holding a vertical painting of a standing Buddha. A modern drawing copied after the mural reveals that the painting may refer to a painting-in-progress, for it is still tied to an outer frame with zigzag threads.[149]

This meme has been copied repeatedly in later Korean and Japanese hand-painted frontispieces dated to the fourteenth and fifteenth centuries.[150] Three Japanese *Lotus Sutra* frontispieces, likely produced by the same workshop

145 The dragon descending on the cloud is related to the other parable of medicinal herbs, depicted below. See Chung 2022, 103.

146 For a complete view of this frontispiece, see Ge 1995, 78 (fig. 8).

147 For more studies, see Wu 2022a, 214–25 (for the image, see 222); Wu 2022b, 111–13; Huo 1993. This author thanks Lucien Sun for his valuable feedback.

148 Wu 2022a, 222 (fig. 4.45); Wu 2023, 234 (fig. 4.45).

149 See Huo 1993, 40. The accompanying cartouche reads, "qing danqing qiaojiang miao shengrong zhenshen shi" 請丹青巧匠邈聖容真身時 (The moment when skilled craftsmen are invited to measure the true body in order to duplicate it). See Huo 1993, 44; Wu 2022a, 220; Wu 2023, 233; DHSKQJ 12: 159. Though not visible in the extant mural, Ma De observes that "there is a bare-chested painter mixing pigments in front of the frame." See Ma 2018, 36.

150 For Korean examples dated 1340, 1377, 1422, see Kungnip Chungang Pangmulgwan 2007, 97, 159, 249.

FIGURE 3.47 Details of two people holding a vertical painting tied to a frame. 10th century. Mural. South wall of Mogao Cave 72, Dunhuang, Gansu

a

b

c

d

FIGURES 3.48A–D Frontispiece to the *Lotus Sutra*. Kamakura period, Japan. Early 14th century. Spencer Collection, The New York Public Library
a. Complete View
b–d. Details

in the early fifteenth century, synthesize select templates and stock motifs from various designs of the third version, while also exhibiting apparently unique Japanese designs.[151] In the copy now in the New York Public Library (figs. 3.48a–b), a meme traceable to the third version design made in Hangzhou (fig. 3.6a) includes a painter seated on a stool working on a vertical painting and supported by an assistant who stands on the side.[152] Unique Japanese design elements not seen in the Hangzhou model include the vulture-shaped mountain in the upper right corner (fig. 3.48c),[153] which indicates the Vulture Peak where the Buddha preaches. In addition, as seen in the Japanese printed frontispiece (fig. 3.43b), the group of monks reciting the sutra in an outdoor

151 Sudō Hirotoshi re-identified three Japanese *Lotus Sutra* frontispieces in Cleveland Museum, New York Public Library, and Hazu 羽豆 Shrine as workshop products made in 1404 and 1408; see Sudō 2015, 185–207; Sudō 2018; Sudō 2021, 83–85. Cf. Zhang J. 2017; Zhang J. 2021, 45 (fig. 3); Covaci 2016, 126–27 (pl. 36).

152 Sudō 2015, 198–99.

153 The bird-mountain motif may derive from the earlier Japanese frontispiece art not exclusive to the *Lotus Sutra*; see the twelfth century examples, reproduced in Kungnip Chungang Pangmulgwan 2007, 283, 287; for more examples, see Sudō 2015, 84 (figs. 25–26), 86 (figs. 27–28), 237 (fig. 108).

FIGURE 3.43B Detail. Frontispiece to the *Lotus Sutra*. Kamakura period, Japan. Before 1421. Tōshōdai-ji, Nara

covered structure (fig. 3.48d), is also uniquely Japanese.[154] This type of architectural element is frequently featured in medieval Japanese paintings.[155]

In comparison, the scenario depicted in Wang Yi's set is more elaborate, presenting more informative details of material culture (fig. 3.0). The painter works in a sophisticated space, resembling an indoor studio. Seated on a screened couch, he holds a brush and adds touches to a hanging scroll depicting a seated buddha. The scroll-in-progress is mounted on a supporting frame, zigzag threads tying the upper part of the painting to the frame. The overall structure rests against a partially revealed painted screen, depicting plants and a garden rock. A side table next to the couch holds cups of pigments—probably the painter's utensils—and a miniature screen decorated with mock cursive-script calligraphy. This reflects a kind of desktop screen already depicted in the Northern Song *Up the River* scroll and the Jin-dynasty Yanshansi 巖山寺 (Monastery of the Cliff Mountain) mural; it may well reflect the dominant trend of material culture at the time.[156] The overall scenario, moreover, takes its visual cue from the pictorial convention featuring a scholar's space (fig. 2.10a).[157]

154 Sudō Hirotoshi noticed that the motif of monks reciting the sutra here is comparable to a handscroll painting depicting the Buddhist leader *Hōnen shonin* 法然上人; see Sudō 2015, 194–95.

155 For a prime example, see the 12th century illustrated handscrolls known as the *Shigisan engi emaki* 信貴山緣起絵巻, reproduced in Nara Kokuritsu Hakubutsukan 2016, esp. 36, 59, 102.

156 This type of desktop screen with calligraphic designs can be identified as the "yanping" 硯屏, and may be derived from the Northern Song literati circle of Su Shi and Huang Tingjian; see Wu Hung in Wu ed. 2021, 7. For more studies, see Zhang Z. 2021, 181–85 (for the Song and Jin visual examples, see figs. 34, 36); Huang X. 2021, 148–49.

157 Huang 2011b, 149.

FIGURE 3.49
Detail. *The Daoist Deity in Plain Drawing Style*, by Liang Kai. Southern Song. Ink on paper. Handscroll. Shanghai Museum

The motif of a painter in action is among the widely spread memes stimulated by *Lotus Sutra* frontispiece art of the Southern Song, not seen in Dunhuang murals. It was also adopted in the *Lotus Sutra* frontispiece printed in Yuan-dynasty Hangzhou (figs. 3.2a–b). Here the designer rearranged the painter's studio, placing artist, desk, and ink cake near a garden rock. The work in progress, showing an unfinished torso, is sewn to an outer frame by strings in a zigzag fashion that recalls the Wang Yi (fig. 3.0) and the Dunhuang (fig. 3.47) prototypes; it resembles the method still used by Himalayan painters making thangkas.[158]

Beyond the art of the *Lotus Sutra*, the meme of a painter at work is repurposed in a contemporaneous Daoist painting featuring the salvation of people by the deity Jiuku tianzun 救苦天尊 (Heavenly Worthy Who Saves from Suffering) (fig. 3.49). It was painted by Liang Kai 梁楷 (ca. 1140–1210), who was active in Hangzhou during the Southern Song.[159] Matching the *Lotus Sutra* prototype, the painter is dressed like a scholar-official with a formal cap and shown holding a pointed brush. The incomplete icon in his painting-to-be, laid slanted and held in a frame, appears to be a Daoist figure, complete with top knot.

Meta-pictures also appear in raised screened podiums, a Buddhist type of furniture designed for teaching and lecturing (figs. 3.7, 3.50). The screen attached to the seat is often decorated with painted bamboo or calligraphy in mock cursive script.[160] A pictorial predecessor appears in a late-eleventh-century mural

158 I appreciate Eric Huntington's insight on this topic.

159 For more plates, see Shanghai bowuguan 2019. For more studies of this painting, see Huang 2012, 6, 349*n*29; Huang 2022, 8*n*6.

160 According to Shi Rui, screens decorated with calligraphy by famous writers were already in vogue in the Sui-Tang times; see Shi 2017. For wall paintings from Song-Jin tombs in north China depicting calligraphic scrolls or screens, see Hsu Y. 2021, 160, 162–64.

FIGURE 3.50
Detail. Frontispieces to the *Lotus Sutra* illustrated by Wang Yi, juan 6. Southern Song. Woodblock print. Concertina. National Palace Museum

FIGURE 3.51 Detail of a couch decorated with a painted screen. ca. 1096. Northern Song. Mural. West wall of the Kaihua Monastery, Gaoping, Shanxi

at the Kaihua Monastery (fig. 3.51), Shanxi. It shows a nun lecturing on a couch, which is decorated with a painted screen of wintry trees and rocks.[161]

Moving from a painter's studio through a Buddhist teacher's study to a layman's bedroom depicted in the next scene (fig. 3.52), there is a screened bed in the upper left corner of the fourth frontispiece.[162] According to Zhang Zhihui, the division on the side of the bed is called a "pillow screen" (*zhenping* 枕屏). Screened beds grew popular at the Song time and are widely depicted in Song paintings.[163] The scene, representing the parable of a drunken man unaware that his friend has sewn a jewel in the seam of his robe, does not include many narrative details to convey its meaning. It simply depicts two people standing

161 For the explanation of the story, see Chen 2022, 100. Zhang Zhihui links this type of furniture to Chan Buddhism; see Zhang Z. 2021, 181. For more murals of the Kaihua Monastery, see ZGSGBHQJ 1: 140–83; Chen 2022.

162 For a complete view of the frontispiece, see Ge 1995, 21; Huang 2011b, 148 (fig. 20c). Cf. a plainer couch bed depicted in the same scene in other Southern Song printed versions and a Chinese-inspired Japanese hand painted version (dated 1163). See Ge 1995, 79 (fig. 8); Chung 2022, 107; Nara Kokuritsu Hakubutsukan 2009, 80 (pls. 74–75).

163 For textual documentations and visual examples, see Zhang Z. 2021, 177–80.

FIGURE 3.52 Detail. Frontispiece to the *Lotus Sutra* illustrated by Wang Yi, juan 4. Southern Song. Woodblock print. Concertina. National Palace Museum

beside a reclining man, his right arm supporting his head, in a bed with two panels showing ink-painted images of bamboo. Departing from an earlier Buddhist mural convention that shows the same parable in a group scene, with the drunkard seated languidly and two other men at a drinking table,[164] the Hangzhou frontispiece takes its cue from a non-Buddhist pictorial convention, such as the Southern Song court painting illustrating the classic reference to the *Odes of the State of Pin* (fig. 3.53), where a man lies in bed whiling away the summer.[165]

164 See, for example, the south wall of the main chamber of Mogao Cave 61 in DHSKQJ 7: 115 (fig. 105).

165 Fong 1992, 222–23 (pl. 30a); Wu 1996b, 160 (fig. 126); Huang 2011b, 150–51. For more motifs of the screened couches in Southern Song Hangzhou Buddhist woodcuts, see *Wenshu zhinan tuzan* in Fontein 1967, 23–27.

FIGURE 3.53 Detail. *Odes of the State of Bin*. 13th century. Southern Song. Ink on paper. Handscroll. The Metropolitan Museum of Art

4.3.3 The Construction Scene

Next, there is an architecture-based scene (figs. 0.19, 3.39), visible in the lower left corner of the fifth frontispiece. It depicts workers building a house, taking its cue from three-word *Lotus Sutra* phrases such as "erecting" (*li* 立) or "building" (zao 造) "monks' cells" (*sengfang* 僧坊).[166] The text describes this as a laborious way of accumulating merit and contrasts it with more expedient ways that would result in venerating the book:

> If, after the extinction of the tathagata [Buddha], there is anyone who accepts and keeps, reads and recites, preaches to others, writes down himself, or instructs others to write [the sutra], and thus honors the scriptural roll, he need not go further and erect stupa or monastery or build monks cells as offerings to the multitudinous monks.

> 如來滅後，若有受持、讀誦、為他人說，若自書、若教人書，供養經卷，不須復起塔寺，及造僧坊、供養眾僧。[167]

166 This phrase was mentioned three times in the scripture; see T.9.262, 45c.

167 T.9.262, 45c. My translation is largely based on that in Hurvitz 2009, 233. As Stephen F. Teiser pointed out, building monks' cells, stupas, or temples was considered one of seven

FIGURE 3.54
Detail. Frontispiece to the *Lotus Sutra*, juan 5. Yuan. Woodblock print. Concertina. National Palace Museum

The construction scene showing six builders is a novel meme, created by the illustrators of the third version (fig. 0.19). Its central feature has four figures in two teams. One team includes a worker on the right of the building who uses a rope to hoist a load of bricks to a fellow worker on the roof. The other team features a man on the ground who stands in a leaning position and is about to throw a brick to his partner crouching on the rooftop. The latter has both hands open, ready to catch. In addition, a fifth builder appears on the roof while a sixth one stands to the right of the building, shuffling a pile of mud on the ground.

This scene has been transmitted in highly consistent fashion within the East Asian tradition of *Lotus Sutra* frontispieces, including those printed or painted in Yuan Hangzhou (fig. 3.54),[168] Korea (fig. 3.42a–b),[169] and Japan (fig. 3.43a). Numerous Koryŏ Korean frontispieces show copies of this meme, although in

ways to make an offering in Buddhism; see Teiser 2022, 47. For Dunhuang murals, see the *Sutra on the Different Virtues and Fields of Merit*, depicted in the sixth-century Mogao Cave 296 and 302, reproduced in DHSKQJ 9: 87–88, 90–91; DHSKQJ 21: 54.

168 See Ge 1995, 30 (pl. 12); Chung 2022, 112–13.

169 Kungnip Chungang Pangmulgwan 2007, 107; Huang 2017c, 24–27.

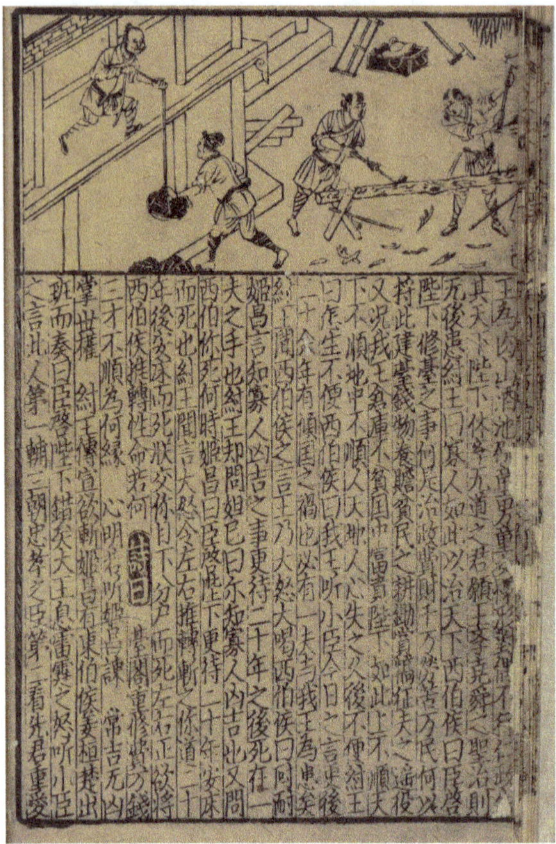
其天下陛下休學无道之君願王學堯舜之聖治則
无後患紂王曰寡人如此以治天下西伯侯曰臣啓
陛下修臺之事何足治政費財千万眾苦万民何以
將此建臺錢物養贍貧民之耕勸農桑減征夫之徭役
又況我王為庫不實國中富貴陛下如此上不順天
下不順地中不順人天地人心失之久後不便紂王
曰怎生不便西伯侯曰我王聽小臣今日之言忠後
二十余年有傾國之禍也必有一夫与我王為患矣
紂王聞西伯侯之言早王乃大怒大喝西伯侯曰匹耐
姬昌言知寡人凶吉之事更待二十年之後死在一
夫之手也紂王却問妲己曰你知寡人內吉也又問
西伯你死何時姬昌曰臣啓陛下更待二十年安床
而死也紂王聞言大怒令左右推轉斬之你道二十
年後果然而死狀交你自下分尸而死左右正欲將
西伯侯推轉性命若何 詩曰 臺閣重修費万錢
三才不順為何緣 心明不行聽姬昌諫 常吉无凶
掌世權 紂王傳宣欲斬姬昌有東伯侯姜桓楚出
班而奏曰臣啓陛下錯矣大王息雷霆之怒聽小臣
之言此人第一輔三朝忠孝之臣第二看先君重愛

FIGURE 3.55
Illustration of "Dukes of Eight States Repairing the Terraced Pavilion." *Xinkan quanxiang pinghua Wuwang fazhou*. Yuan. Woodblock print. Butterfly binding. National Archives of Japan

some cases the workers delivering the bricks are in front rather than to the right of the building.[170]

Moving beyond the *Lotus Sutra*,[171] the construction scene also appears in illustrations of the fourteenth-century novel *King Wu Attacking King Zhou* (*Wuwang fa Zhou* 武王伐紂) (fig. 3.55), printed by the Yu 虞 Family Publisher's Studio of Cultivating the Fundamental (Wuben tang 務本堂) in Jian'an 建安, northern Fujian.[172] Here the two teammates transporting bricks by rope

170 Huang 2011b, 152.

171 Huang 2011b, 151; 2017c, 23–30, 65–71 (figs. 40–47).

172 To view the illustrated book, see National Archives of Japan Digital Archive, "Xinkan quanxiang pinghua Wuwang fazhou" 新刊全相平話武王伐紂書 (9/45), Quanxiang pinghua 全相平話, Accessed January 7, 2024. <https://www.digital.archives.go.jp/img/2324050> For studies of the Jian'an printing, see Chia 2002a; Chia 2003. For more illustrative books published by the Yu Family publisher in 1321–33, see Takimoto 2009.

appear as workers renovating King Zhou's palatial pavilion. The illustration runs across two pages.

It is possible that the hand-painted Korean frontispieces of the *Lotus Sutra*, commissioned by aristocrats (fig. 3.42a–b), in turn triggered its appearance in later genre painting (fig. 0.20). The renowned Chosŏn painter Kim Hongdo 金弘道, also known as Danwon 檀園 (b. 1745), reconfigured it with a sense of humor in his oft-cited album celebrating ordinary people.[173]

Moving even further, and rather unexpectedly, the scene traveled far and wide, reaching the world of Islamic art in West and South Asia. Here it appears in two highly similar and closely related illustrations that depict workers building the Castle of Khvarnaq, painted in Timurid Herat in the fifteenth century (fig. 0.21) and in Mughal India in the early seventeenth (fig. 0.22).[174] According to Mika Natif, their similarity reveals artistic connections. The Timurid illustration, commissioned by a prince "at the court of Sultan Husayn in Herat," is from the *Khamsa* manuscript that transcribes poems by "the twelfth-century Persian poet Nizami." By the early seventeenth century, this text had been transmitted to "the royal Mughal library" of Emperor Jahangir (r. 1608–1627) and made available to the female artist Sahifa Banu, who painted the Mughal version.[175] Its visible modifications include making the castle "more three-dimensional" by applying European-inspired techniques, adding an image of a cross-legged ruler dressed in green to the left of the castle and altering the colors.[176]

At the center of the Timurid illustration (fig. 0.21), a worker dressed in red throws a brick to a fellow dressed in green who stands on wooden scaffolding. Near the red-clothed worker is another figure who delivers materials from a bowl by rope to a fourth who stands on top of the castle. The four workers making up a team can be seen as a modification of the construction meme of the *Lotus Sutra*. Even those shuffling dirt in the foreground recall the worker pushing around mud in the Chinese picture. They all, moreover, were closely copied in the Mughal painting.

While no direct source documents the Book Roads transporting the Hangzhou-based *Lotus Sutra* frontispieces to the Islamic world, scholars have long noted the complex interaction of Buddhism and Islam along the Silk

---

173 For a complete view of the 25 leaves in the alum, see "Wikipedia: *Danwon pungsokdo cheop*," Wikimedia Foundation, last modified October 12, 2023, 06:40 (UTC). https://en.wikipedia.org/wiki/Danwon_pungsokdo_cheop.

Burglind Jungmann mentioned that some of the leaves may be later additions; see Jungmann 2014, esp. 245–60 (figs. 111, 113, 116).

174 Natif 2018, 79–83 (figs. 24–25).

175 Natif 2018, 79.

176 Natif 2018, 77, 80–81.

FIGURE 3.56 Shakyamuni Offering Fruit to the Devil. *Jamiʿ al-Tawarikh* (MSS 727, folio 34a). 1314. Tabriz, Iran. Ink and watercolor on paper. Khalili Collections

Road, especially regarding the spread of "seemingly disappearing" Buddhism across thirteenth-century Iran under the Mongol Ilkhanate (1256–1335).[177] The Ilkhanate founder Hülegü (r. 1256–1265), a brother of Qubilai Khan, sponsored Buddhist temple construction in today's Khoy in northwest Iran. The descendants of artisans, builders, and Buddhists associated with this project later formed a Chinese immigrant community.[178] Furthermore, the Ilkhanid capital Tabriz, a hub along the Silk Road and a cosmopolitan city located at a major crossroad between East and West, is well known from the reports of the Venetian traveler Marco Polo (1254–1324), who passed through it on his return and described it as an international "market for merchandise from India and Baghdad, from Mosul and Hormuz, and from many other places."[179] While building the medical infrastructure in Tabriz, the erudite official, medical scholar, and historian Rashīd al-Dīn Hamadānī (1247–1318) assembled fifty eminent doctors, some of them from China. Chinese scholars well trained in medicine also participated in the compilation of a medical encyclopedia.[180]

In Tabriz, the government-funded manuscript workshop led by Rashīd al-Dīn produced the first world history called *Compendium of Chronicles*

177 For select studies, see Foltz 2010; Elverskog 2010; Prazniak 2013; Prazniak 2014; Prazniak 2019. For additional references to the studies of Chinese elements in Persian albums and the artistic exchanges between Ming China and the Timurid Empire, see Huang 2017a, 27–30 (footnotes 127–133); Yu 2018.

178 Prazniak 2014, 664; Chen 2019, 149.

179 Blair 2014, 321. Cf. Latham trans. 1958, 57–58; Canby 1993, 299; Prazniak 2013, 177–78. For more on Tabriz, see Prazniak 2013; Prazniak 2019; Blair 2014.

180 Prazniak 2014, 664; Chen 2019, 148; Berlekamp 2010; Huang 2012, 75.

(*Jamiʿ al-Tawarikh*).[181] It includes selected illustrations pertinent to the life of the Buddha, such as the scene preserved in the Arabian version dated 1314 (fig. 3.56).[182] In a landscape setting reminiscent of Chinese landscape painting, the Buddha Shakaymuni sits on the right, dressed in a turban like a Muslim prophet. He offers fruit to the demon Mara, seen standing on the left. A Buddhist monk from Kashmir was said to have been in Tabriz at that time, explaining the Buddhist story to Rashīd al-Dīn's team.[183] Some scholars even suggest that an unusual multi-headed icon depicted in the *Compendium of Chronicles* may have been inspired by Esoteric Buddhist iconography, imitating the multi-headed Avalokiteśvara.[184] A single-sheet print of filial sons (fig. 3.57), now in the Topkapi Palace and stylistically like a Yuan illustrated book printed in Fujian, may be an indirect source, opening further speculation about the transmission of Chinese woodcuts to West Asia through Mongol networks.[185] Indeed, these networks may have stimulated the transfer of Buddhist visual culture across vast continents (see pt. 3).

After Mongol rule, another significant art exchange between China and Persia occurred in the fifteenth century, featuring the Timurid court (r. 1370–1405) and the Ming rulers (1368–1644).[186] Shahrukh (r. 1405–1447) sent envoys to Ming China on overland routes in 1413 and 1419: they traveled through Dunhuang and Zhengding 正定 to reach Beijing. As David Roxburgh notes, they included the painter Ghiyath al-Din Naqqash, who may have been exposed to Buddhist paintings along the trip.[187] The Chinese official history *Veritable Records of the Ming* (*Ming shilu* 明實錄) recounts seventy-eight visits from Timurid envoys from 1387 to 1504. Exotic animals from West Asia, such as horses, lions, camels, and cheetahs constituted the main tributary inventory, although there was also

181 Blair 1995; Blair 2017. For a selection of the *Compendium of Chronicles* translated in English, see Rossabi 2011, 60–69, 104–14, 123–39, 170–71.

182 Khalili Collections, "Shakyamuni offering fruit to the devil (from the life of the Buddha) from The *Jamiʿ al-Tawarikh* of Rashid al-Din (MSS 727, folio 34a, Tabriz, Iran)," Accessed January 7, 2024. https://www.khalilicollections.org/collections/islamic-art/khalili-collection-islamic-art-the-jami-al-tawarikh-of-rashid-al-din-mss727-folio-34a/.

183 The Arabian text refers to the buddha as a prophet, and Mara as "Iblis or Shaitan (Satan)." For a full translation of the text pertinent to this illustration, see Canby 1993, 301–303. For more studies, see Blair 1995; Blair 2017; Prazniak 2013; Prazniak 2014; Prazniak 2019.

184 For a plate, see Roxburgh 2005, 199 (fig. 44).

185 For more on why this print was made in Yuan Fujian, see Huang 2017a, 29–30. For more about the arts of the filial stories in China and Korea, see Hsu Y. 2021, 123–28 (esp. 127*n*44).

186 Yu 2018, 58–64; Huang 2017a, 27; Zhang W. 2006 (for a detailed chart listing the dates, envoys, tributary objects from the Timurid court to Ming China from 1387 to 1504, see 266–74).

187 Roxburgh 2010; Huang 2017a, 27. Leo Jungeon Oh calls attention to the "Islamicized pseudo-Buddhist" iconography in Ilkhanid manuscripts (2015).

FIGURE 3.57 Depictions of the Filial Stories. Yuan. Hand-colored woodblock print. Single sheet. Topkapi Palace, Istanbul

gold and silver ware as well as jade stones and swords. The Ming court recompensed the envoys with various kinds of silk, clothing, ingots, paper money, and ceramics.[188] The Yongle 永樂 Emperor (r. 1402–1424) similarly sent multiple Chinese missions to the Timurid capital of Herat as well as to Samarkand. Morris Rossabi highlights a trip led by the famous Chinese diplomat and merchant Chen Cheng 陳誠 (1365–1458). Arriving in Herat in 1417, he presented the Timurid court with "a painting of a white horse that he had earlier offered as tribute to the Chinese emperor."[189] It is possible that some Chinese Buddhist books—including the Southern Song *Lotus Sutra* printed in Hangzhou—were also transferred as diplomatic gifts.

5 New Trends in the Yuan

Multiple copies of the seven-volume *Lotus Sutra* frontispieces, dated to the first half of the fourteenth century (figs. 3.2a–d, 3.54, 3.58) and now dispersed in various museum and library collections, attest to the legacy of the third version created in Yuan Hangzhou.[190] Dedicatory colophons, stamped at the end of several volumes in a set held by the National Palace Museum, indicate that at least four families from Jiaxing 嘉興 district near Hangzhou may have paid for the printing of individual volumes between 1331 and 1349.[191] Most prominent was the family of Yao Chen Daorong 姚陳道榮,[192] listed with his daughter and son in one colophon. Another names him along with two wives, sons, grand-daughter, and niece. Other sponsors include the Yang 楊, Gu 顧, and Xu 徐 families from the same community.[193]

188 Zhang 2006, 232–34, 266–74.

189 Rossabi 1976, 26. Cf. a cropped Ming painting depicting a white horse in a Persian album collected in Topkapi Palace Museum (H. 2154), reproduced in Watt et al. 2010, 23 (fig. 36); Yu 2018, 61. From 1413 to 1420, Chen Cheng made three trips to the Timurid court; see Zhang W. 2006, 83–84.

190 Miya 1983b; Huang 2020, 65–66. For the five sets at National Palace Museum, see Ge 1995, 28–31, 80–85, 107–109; Chung 2022, 24–25, 100–101, 104–105, 108–109, 112–13. For the set in the National Library, Beijing, see ZGFJBHQJ 4: 142–55.

191 For more information of the donors, see Ge 1995, 84–85, 107–109; Chung 2022, 23. The popular appeal of the *Lotus Sutra* in the Jiaxing region in the Yuan dynasty is further evident in two extant embroideries of the illustrated *Lotus Sutra*, sponsored by two lay Buddhist women—Li Delian 李德廉 and her niece Yao Huizhen 姚惠真—around 1366. For plates and study, see Huang and Yan 2000, 41; Zhang J. 2021, 46 (fig. 4).

192 For two colophons bearing his name and dated 1346, see Ge 1995, 84; Chung 2022, 23 (fig. 4).

193 For transliterations of the colophons, see Ge 1995, 107–109; for reproductions of select colophons, see 85.

FIGURE 3.58 Frontispiece to the *Lotus Sutra*, juan 7. Yuan. Woodblock print. Concertina. National Palace Museum

These donors are quite like lay figures depicted in the lower left corner of each frontispiece. Contrary to similar images in the Southern Song set illustrated by Wang Yi (figs. 3.0, 3.1b), which show two monks in the lower-left corner, here they clearly are families.[194] In select frontispieces (figs. 3.2c, 3.54, 3.58), the male donor holding an incense burner has a Mongolian hat; he stands with two women—perhaps his wives—and a boy, similarly capped.[195] The woman next to the man has a Buddhist text in her hands.

Comparing the compositional scheme of these Yuan frontispieces to their Southern Song prototypes, the main change appears in the increasing landscape elements in the background. No longer staged on a balustrade terrace, the Buddha and his entourage now are floating amid animated clouds, set against a landscape demarcated by trees and rocky terrain (fig. 3.3d). Judging from the extant specimens, one can surmise that, while the Yuan printed version did not spread as widely as its Southern Song predecessor, its landscape-infused frontispiece template reflected a new trend in frontispiece design. This template was partially copied in a contemporaneous hand-painted set (fig. 3.59), in gold on indigo paper, perhaps also produced in the Hangzhou area.[196]

194 For more images of multiple lay donors, see Ge 1995, 30–31, 80–83; Chung 2022, 23 (fig. 2), 105.

195 Cf. a similar hat worn by a young boy standing at a door, depicted in the Yuan painted tomb in Jinan, Shandong; see ZGCTBHQJ 4: 173.

196 Nara Kokuritsu Hakubutsukan 1996, 207, 282 (no. 203).

FIGURE 3.59 Frontispiece to the *Lotus Sutra*, juan 7. Yuan. Gold on indigo-dyed paper. Concertina. Tokugawa Art Museum

PART 2

Buddhist Printing in North and Northwest China

∴

化作大城鄉莊聚落舍宅
周匝有園林男女皆滿

CHAPTER 4

Mapping Buddhist Printing under Khitan Liao Rule

Buddhist printing developed in multiple centers in the tenth-to-twelfth centuries. While Hangzhou was the most thriving printing center of Buddhist books in Song-dynasty south China, other areas also prospered in the north and northwest, notably under the rule of the Khitan Liao 遼, Jurchen Jin 金, and Tangut Xi Xia 西夏 (see pt. 2).

This chapter focuses on Buddhist printing under Liao rule (907–1125). It draws on excavated materials in Buddhist pagodas to map the vast Buddhist network and Book Roads supported by the Khitan ruling class (map 4.1). At the center of this network is Yanjing 燕京 (modern Beijing), one of the Liao capitals, which emerged as a major Buddhist printing center in the eleventh century. Its temples and monastics were closely connected to the Liao ruling house and actively promoted Buddhist book production and distribution. Book Roads here extended north to Qingzhou 慶州 in Inner Mongolia, west to Yingzhou 應州 in Shanxi, and east to Fengrun 豐潤 in Hebei. Fragments of Liao Buddhist texts discovered in the Xi Xia ruins in Khara Khoto (ch. 6) and the Uighur homeland in Turfan (ch. 10) suggest that the Book Roads were further connected to the interstate network that reached out to northwest China and eastern Central Asia. The legacy of the Liao Buddhist print culture remained strong in north China under Jin (ch. 5) and Yuan (ch. 7) rules in the following centuries.

Archaeological finds of Buddhist print culture appear mainly in Inner Mongolia, Shanxi, and Hebei. A unique find involves specimens of mass-produced *dharani* texts, rolled up in pagoda-shaped reliquaries and deposited in an imperially sponsored pagoda in Inner Mongolia. Two versions of the Liao Canon (*Liao zang* 遼藏), discovered in Shanxi and Hebei, represent the most ambitious undertaking in this context. Although both the Khitan and the Jurchen created their own scripts, just like their Tangut counterpart who formed the Xi Xia kingdom, all extant Buddhist texts printed under Liao and Jin rule were in Chinese.[1] In this they differ from the Xi Xia, who not only translated

FIGURE 4.0 Detail of fig. 4.33a. *Lotus Sutra*, juan 4. 1025. Liao. Woodblock print. Discovered in the Fogong Pagoda, Yingxian, Shanxi
←

1 The Khitan script contains the large script, which is logographic, and the small script, which is syllabary.

© SHIH-SHAN SUSAN HUANG, 2024 | DOI:10.1163/9789004700017_006

MAP 4.1 A partial map of the Khitan Liao empire, with the Five Capitals, temples, and pagodas where Buddhist printed texts were excavated. By Rita Xiong

multiple Buddhist texts into Tangut, even from Chinese, but also printed them in their own language. While few printed sutras of the Liao bear illustrations, some frontispieces contain information on publishers and cutters in Yanjing and present exquisite designs different from those found in Hangzhou.

1 Khitan Liao Imperial Patronage

The Liao dynasty was founded by the Khitan people, whose homeland was in northeastern China (map 4.1).[2] At its greatest expansion, the empire extended from Manchuria to Mongolia, covering modern Liaoning, Heilongjiang, Jilin, Inner Mongolia, Mongolia, and parts of Russia.[3] To rule this huge empire, the Khitan adopted some aspects of the Chinese system while at the same time maintaining their own steppe customs. This resulted in the unique combination of a sedentary government and a traveling court that "moved around in tents and carts, following a pattern of seasonal movement to—and from—different locations."[4] Representing the "power of the north Asian tribal peoples," the name Khitan is "a synonym for China" in various Western languages, including "the Catai of Marco Polo."[5] In an introductory essay charting new approaches to their study, Valerie Hansen and François Louis assert that the Khitan Liao empire "formed a bridge" of an increasingly interconnected world,

2 The map is a partial map of the Khitan Liao Empire, focusing on the clusters of Buddhist temples and major archaeological sites relevant to the Buddhist printing. Selected Buddhist temples and major transportation routes marked on this map are based on the sectional maps published in Li Ruoshui's dissertation, citing Liao and Jin epigraphic sources and a wide range of local gazetteers; see Li R. 2015, 133, 136, 139, 143, 148, 272–309. For the Liao routes based on the Tang routes, see the maps of the Tang transportation routes in Yan 1986, 5: 1513, 1677, 1793. For a complete map of the Liao, see Shen et al. 2006, 371–73. Li Peng argued that the recently-discovered Fuju 福巨 ruins near Tongliao 通遼 city in Inner Mongolia was where the Khitan Liao originated; see Li P. 2017, 91. Cf. the Khitan homeland marked on a Liao map in Hansen and Louis 2013, 2.

3 Hansen and Louis 2013, 1; Di Cosmo 2006, 18.

4 Pursey 2019, 179. The seasonal traveling system was known as *nabo* 捺鉢; see Twitchett and Tietze 1994, 67, 79; LS 32: 373–75; Lu 2019, 6–8; Wittfogel and Feng 1949, 131–34; Zhuge 2016, 21–23; Shoudu bowuguan 2018, 104. For studies of the wall paintings of the four seasons decorating the East Mausoleum dedicated to the Emperor Shengzong and depicting the scenery of the imperial hunting, see Tamura et al. 1952–1953, 1: 40, 85.

5 Twitchett and Tietze 1994, 43; Di Cosmo 2006, 22. For more studies of the Khitan Liao and the world, see Hansen 2011, 2013, 2020.

linking "Western Europe, the Islamic world, and East Asia" hundreds of years "before the Mongols."[6]

Both textual and visual sources confirm that the Khitan ruling class first embraced Buddhist practices in their homeland of Inner Mongolia in the early tenth century. According to the official *Liao History* (*Liaoshi* 遼史), compiled in the fourteenth century, the Khitan ruler Yelü Abaoji 耶律阿保機 (872–926), later known as Emperor Taizu 太祖 (r. 916–926), built the Kaijiaosi 開教寺 (Monastery of Opening the Teaching) in his first walled-city in Longhua 龍化 prefecture in 902, before the dynasty was officially founded.[7] In 912, in order to house fifty monks captured near the Bohai 渤海 Sea, he built the Tianxiongsi 天雄寺 (Monastery of Heavenly Prowess) in the imperial city Linhuang 臨潢. Later known as the Supreme Capital (Shangjing 上京), it was the Khitan Liao's first imperial city "on a standard Chinese plan with walls."[8]

Recent archaeological finds in Balin zuoqi 巴林左旗 (Bairin Left Banner), Inner Mongolia, provide additional evidence. A stone sculpture of a seated monk (fig. 4.1), found near Abaoji's mausoleum (constructed around 927) outside of the Supreme Capital, may originally have been part of a ritual site used for imperial ancestral worship.[9] At the Xishanpo 西山坡 site in its southwest quarter (map 4.1), recent excavations have uncovered the foundations of one large and two small wooden pagodas,[10] part of a huge Buddhist compound, and unearthed fragments of terracotta sculptures with striking portrait-like facial features (fig. 4.2).[11]

After Abaoji passed away, his portrait was displayed in the temple for ancestral worship.[12] His successor, Emperor Taizong 太宗 (r. 927–947), enshrined a white-robed Guanyin he acquired in Youzhou 幽州 (near modern Beijing)

6 Hansen and Louis 2013, 9. For a comprehensive bibliography shedding light on the new approaches to the study of the Liao, see Hansen et al. 2013.

7 LS 1: 2; Wittfogel and Feng 1949, 298. The archaeological site in Fuju was linked to the early Liao's Longhua Prefecture; see Li P. 2016; Li P. 2017, 91.

8 Twitchett and Tietze 1994, 63. For more documentations of Buddhist temples in the Supreme Capital, see Chen and Zhu 2009, 685; Li R. 2015, 21–24, 132–33, 159.

9 There are also other fragments of a Buddhist sculpture and tiles bearing the character that reads "the buddha" (*fo* 佛); see Zhongguo shehui kexue yuan kaogu yanjiu suo Neimenggu di er gongzuodui et al. 2009, esp. 51.

10 Nancy Steinhardt associates the three pagodas with the so-called "architectural tripling" fashion prevailing in East Asia before the Khitan period; see Steinhardt 2022, 173–74.

11 I thank Michael Meng for his help. Cf. Shoudu bowuguan 2018, 30 (fig. 11). For more about the Liao Supreme Capital, see Dong 2019.

12 LS 1: 6; 37: 440–41; QDGZ 1: 6; T.49.2036: 652c. See also Wittfogel and Feng 1949, 298; Li R. 2015, 21–22. For more about the Khitan ruling class' use of imperial ancestral portraits in various media, including the paintings and statues in stone, metal, bronze, wood, see Zhang P. 2019, esp. 122–23.

FIGURE 4.1 Stone sculpture of a monk. 927. Liao. Discovered in the Khitan ancestral mausoleum. Balin Left Banner, Inner Mongolia

FIGURE 4.2 Terracotta sculptural fragments. Ruins of the Liao Supreme Capital in Xishanpo, Balin Left Banner, Inner Mongolia. Liao

in a temple on Mt. Muye 木葉,[13] a sacred mountain in the Khitan's ancestral homeland.[14] He had the bodhisattva worshiped as his "family deity" (*jiashen* 家神) along with other ancestral figures enshrined in nearby temples.[15] Later, some female imperial members were even named after Guanyin.[16]

While this Guanyin statue has not survived, numerous other versions are extant, either discovered at archaeological sites or continuously worshiped

13 Wittfogel and Feng 1949, 272; Li R. 2015, 128. For the most updated reconstruction of the location of Mt. Muye, see Li P. 2016, esp. figs. 1 and 5 on 2, 6. For imperial ancestral portraits enshrined there, see LS 37: 445; Zhang P. 2019, 122.

14 For an erudite speculation of the possible location of Mount Muye, see Marsone 2011a, 26–30 (for a map, see 29).

15 LS 32: 835; Wittfogel and Feng 1949, 309; Chen and Zhu 2009, 46. For the textual record of a statue of the white-robed Guanyin housed in the Tang-dynasty Minzhongsi in Beijing, see YYTZ 1: 24. For more on the goddess, see Yü 2001, 93–149, 234–62. For the worship activities on Mt. Muye, see Chen and Zhu 2009, 50–52.

16 For example, the Princess of Yan had the Buddhist childhood name "Daughter of Guanyin"; see LS 65: 1002; Zheng S. 1999, 532.

FIGURE 4.3
Details. White-robe Guanyin adorning a pagoda-shaped reliquary. Liao. Reliquary in wood; statue in amber. Discovered in the White Pagoda, Qingzhou, Inner Mongolia

in temples, revealing its iconography. For example, there is a rare miniature made from precious amber (fig. 4.3), originally serving as the top of a miniature pagoda-shaped reliquary and discovered in the imperially sponsored White Pagoda in Qingzhou (map 4.1), Inner Mongolia, constructed in the mid-eleventh century.[17] Decorated with a pearl on top of the forehead, the statue shows a goddess with a long piece of fiber draping from head to arms.[18] An alternative form appears in the colossal eleven-headed statue (fig. 4.4), enshrined in the multi-storied Guanyin Hall of the Dulesi 獨樂寺 (Monastery of Solitary Bliss) in Jizhou 薊州 (a suburb of modern Tianjin; map 4.1). Both the statue and the architecture were renovated around 984 to more closely reflect their Tang original by a local elite family named Han 韓, closely associated with the Khitan ruling house.[19]

17 Sun 2006, 77 (fig. 68); Balin youqi bowuguan 2017, 52–54.

18 Its overall style and iconography recall the tenth-century stone carved White-robed Guanyin guarding the entrance of the Yanxia Grotto in Hangzhou. Unlike the Liao Guanyin in amber holding a lotus in her hands, the stone Guanyin in the Yanxia Grotto is holding a chain of rosary; see Yü 2001, 182–83 (fig. 4.2).

19 For the stele dated 992 documenting the repair of the Guanyin Hall, see QLW 5: 103; Xu 2010, 146–47. The small buddhas atop the head of the Guanyin statue were remodeled in the Qing dynasty; see Yang 1988, 14. Liang Sicheng noted that a pagoda was built later on in a location where it meets the gaze of the Guanyin statue inside the hall; see

FIGURE 4.4 Detail of the Guanyin statue. ca. 984. Liao. Dule Monastery, Ji county, Tianjin

Khitan imperial family members were fervent supporters of Buddhism and its material culture.[20] Emperor Shenzong 聖宗 (r. 982–1031), named "Servant of Mañjuśrī" (Wenshu nu 文殊奴) since childhood, in the early eleventh century commissioned the printing of the first portion of the canon in Yanjing.[21] His successors, Xingzong 興宗 (r. 1031–1055) and Daozong 道宗 (r. 1055–1101), continued to support the printing of additional Buddhist texts (see below).[22] As a

Liang 2001, 1: 225; Zhang P. 2019, 12. According to Wei-cheng Lin, the "flights of stairs on the right side of the building" enable visitors to traverse "the interior space vertically." See Lin 2016, 113. For more about the statue, the temple, and the elite Han family, see Zhongguo wenwu yanjiu suo et al. 2007 (for a complete view of the statue, see 409–10, 437, 439); Chen 2007.

20 It has long been proposed that the Khitan Liao imperial families belonged to mainly two clans, the Khitan Yelű 耶律 and the Chinese Xiao 蕭 who had intermarried for generations. According to Pierre Marsone, however, the traditional assumption that most empresses marrying the Khitan rulers were from the Chinese Xiao clan is a false claim only recorded in Chinese sources; the so-called Xiao clan is most likely a collective term referring to various Khitan tribes. See Marsone 2011a, 37, 104–105. For Daoism under the Liao, see Huang 2014a, 1011–23. For more about the Khitan women, see Johnson 2011.

21 Wittfogel and Feng 1949, 294; Li and He 2003, 134–38; Yan et al. 1982, 13. Medieval Uighur and Khitan Buddhists often had names that commonly ended with the character "nu" 奴; see Kitsudō 2013, 232–33.

22 Li and He 2003, 139–40.

great supporter of the Huayan teachings, Daozong also composed the *Eulogies on the Avatamsaka Sutra* (*Huayan jing wu song* 華嚴經五頌) and showed a hand-written copy to his officials. He also had his elder son copy Buddhist texts;[23] the number of Buddhist monastics soared under his reign.[24]

Imperial women, too, were prominent Buddhist patrons. Thus, Empress Dowager Qin'ai 欽哀 (ca. 980–1057), foster mother of Emperor Xingzong, involved herself in the construction of the seven-storied White Pagoda in brick, located in Qingzhou near the imperial mausoleum dedicated to her husband.[25] It housed the reliquary with the miniature Guanyin in amber (fig. 4.3).[26] She also helped with the repair of Buddhist grottoes on Mt. Wuzhou 武州 in Datong. Later the Liao's Western Capital (map 4.1), it is best known for its cave temples and colossal Buddhist carvings sponsored by the Tuoba ruling class in the fifth century.[27] A huge terracotta eye bulb (fig. 4.5), likely a Liao product and originally filling the eye of a colossal buddha in Yungang 雲岡, may reflect her contribution to the repair project.[28]

---

23 In 1068, he composed the *Eulogy*; in 1072, he showed a hand-written copy of "five eulogies" to officials. In 1075, he ordered his elder son to copy Buddhist texts. See LS 22: 267, 23: 274; 23: 276; Wittfogel and Feng 1949, 305–306; Datong shi et al. 2008, 21.

24 In 1078, the government offered food to 360,000 monks all over the empire, marking a sharp increase compared to the number of 50,000 in 942. See LS 26: 314; Wittfogel and Feng 1949, 296.

25 De et al. 1994; Balin youqi bowuguan 2017; Lu 2019.

26 A stele deposited inside the pagoda names the imperial artisans and artists working on this project, including the little-known court painter Zhang Wenfu 張文甫 who "painted the entire pagoda." See Zhang P. 2019, 27. For a rubbing of the stele and the reconstruction of the imperial team working for the White Pagoda, see De et al. 1994, 23, 25. For a recent study of Zhang Wenfu, see Wei 2019.

27 This is based on the "Great Jin Stele of the Repair of the Great Cave Temples in Mt. Wuzhou in Western Capital" (*Dajin Xijing Wuzhoushan chongxiu dashiki si bei* 大金西京武州山重修大石窟寺碑文) published by Su Bai; see Su 1956, 79–80. For the ten temples in Wuzhoushan repaired or built under Liao rule, see Su 1956, 80–81 (footnote 26). For more material finds from the Liao Western Capital, see Beijing Liao Jin chengyuan bowuguan 2016; Shoudu bowuguan 2018, 91.

28 The eye, sold to Laurence Sickman by a local farmer during a visit to Yungang in 1932, was returned to China in the 1980s. See China News, "Yungang shifo taoyan liushi haiwai wushi nian jianzheng zhongmei wenwu qing" 云冈石佛陶眼流失海外 50 年见证中美文物情 (How the Buddha's Eye from the Yungang Grottoes, Lost Overseas 50 Years Ago, Documents the China-U.S. Love for Cultural Relics), April 4, 2014, 15:29, Accessed December 24, 2023. http://www.chinanews.com/cul/2014/04-05/6034101.shtml.

For the most updated study, see Li 2022. The eyeball returned by Sickman may originally come from the main buddha in Cave 18, or the side buddha in Cave 20; see Li 2022, fig. 4. For additional four extant samples of black glazed terracotta eyeballs in various sizes from Yungang grottoes, possibly added to the Northern Wei Yungang statues in the Liao-Jin periods, see Li 2022, fig. 1; for two other eyeballs of similar style, possibly taken from Yungang Cave 8, now in Kyoto National University, see fig. 2.

FIGURE 4.5
The cylinder pupil of a Buddha. Liao. Terracotta with black glaze on top. Yungang Grottoes Museum, Yungang

FIGURE 4.6 Fogong Pagoda, Yingxian, Shanxi. 1056. Liao

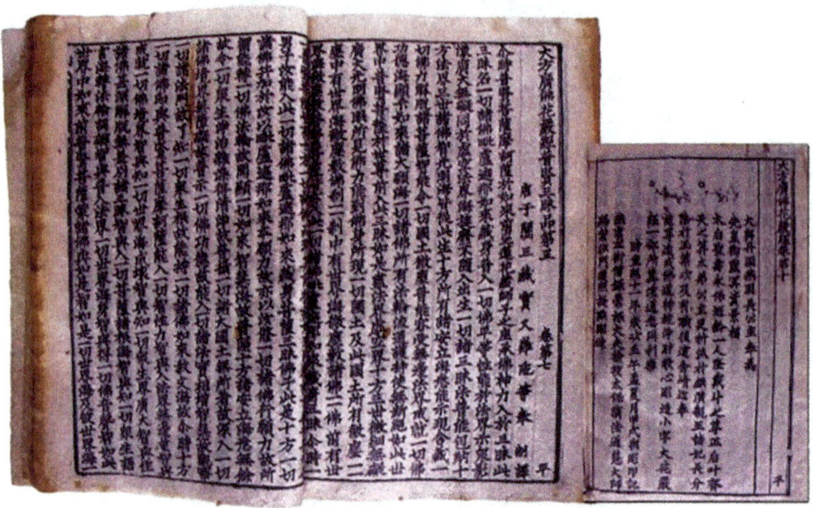

FIGURE 4.7 *Avatamsaka Sutra*. 1042. Liao. Woodblock print. Butterfly binding. Discovered in the Tiangong Pagoda, Fengrun, Hebei

Empress Renyi, Xingzong's wife, was another fervent supporter of Buddhism. With her support, the Fogong Pagoda was completed in 1056 in Yingxian (map 4.1; fig. 4.6). The tallest surviving wooden pagoda from this period, it overlooked the border of the Liao and Northern Song.[29] Abundant deposits discovered here include some single-sheet prints (fig. 2.3) and printed textiles

29 Du 2005; Chen 1980; Steinhardt 1997; Zhang et al. 2001. For Wei-cheng Lin's interpretation of the Fogong Pagoda as "a conceptual emanation of the Vairocana Buddha," see Lin 2016, 121–25.

(figs. 1.43a–c), as described earlier, as well as numerous Buddhist printed texts examined below.

Yet another active supporter of Buddhism was the Princess of Yan (Yanguo gongzhu 燕國公主) (970–1045), also known by her Buddhist childhood name "Daughter of Guanyin" (Guanyin nü 觀音女). She sponsored the printing of the *Avatamsaka Sutra* in Yanjing, discovered in the Pagoda of the Tiangongsi 天宮寺 (Monastery of the Heavenly Palace) in Fengrun, Hebei (fig. 4.7; map 4.1).[30] She also supported the erection of the Baoyansi 寶嚴寺 (Monastery of Treasured Awe) in Yizhou 懿州 (map 4.1), known for its elaborate sutra library and murals of stellar deities of the twenty-eight lodgings, painted by the little-known court painter Tian Chengzhi 田承制.[31] The Princess of Qin and Yue (Qin Yue gongzhu 秦越公主), active in the eleventh century, similarly donated her residence in the Tanyin Ward 棠陰坊 of Yanjing to the order: it was to become the new Haotiansi 昊天寺 (Monastery of Radiant Heaven) (map 4.2).[32]

By the mid-eleventh century, the Khitan Liao empire had five capitals: Supreme, Eastern, Southern, Central, and Western (map 4.1), each functioning "as the regional center of a circuit, a local administrative network."[33] The circuits of the Southern and Western Capitals absorbed the so-called Sixteen Prefectures of Yan and Yun (Yan Yun shiliu zhou 燕雲十六州) (maps 4.1, 4.3), previously occupied by the Later Jin kingdom and absorbed into the Liao realm in 938. The area marks the Liao border with the Northern Song and the Tangut Xi Xia, that is, "the Khitan control of all the strategic passes that defended northern China."[34] As illustrated in the thirteenth-century *Records of the Khitan Empire* (*Qidan guo zhi* 契丹国志), compiled by the Southern Song author Ye Longli 葉隆禮 (*jinshi* in 1247) (map 4.3), the Sixteen Prefectures constituted a "broad belt" to the south of the Great Wall, covering what is today

---

30 LS 65: 1002; Zheng S. 1999, 532–34; Fang 2015a, 22–23.

31 LDXBZ, 275–80; Zhang F. 2007, 64. For the location, see Wang and Pu 2016, 371.

32 Cf. the map of the Southern Capital in Shoudu bowuguan 2018, 83. The Princess's main motivation was to support the abbot Monk Zhizhi 智志, originally associated with the aristocratic clan; see the steles "Yanjing Dahaotian si chuan pusajie gu Miaoxing dashi yixing beiming" 燕京大昊天寺傳菩薩戒故妙行大師遺行碑銘 and "Miaoxing dashi xingzhuang bei" 妙行大師行狀碑 (dated 1108) in Xiang 1995, 509, 584–89. Also see QLW, 8: 199, 9: 249; LS 79: 1272; YYTZ 1: 23; Li R. 2015, 59–70, 63, 214; Li R. 2016, 294–96; Wittfogel and Feng 1949, 295; Xu 2010, 145–46.

33 Twitchett and Tietze 1994, 79. The Eastern Capital was established in 938, the Southern Capital was established in 938, the Central Capital was added in 1007, and finally, the Western Capital arose in 1044. See Twitchett and Tietze 1994, 79; Di Cosmo 2006, 18; Zhuge 2016, 13–27; Shoudu bowuguan 2018, 57, 82, 90, 92.

34 Twitchett and Tietze 1994, 70.

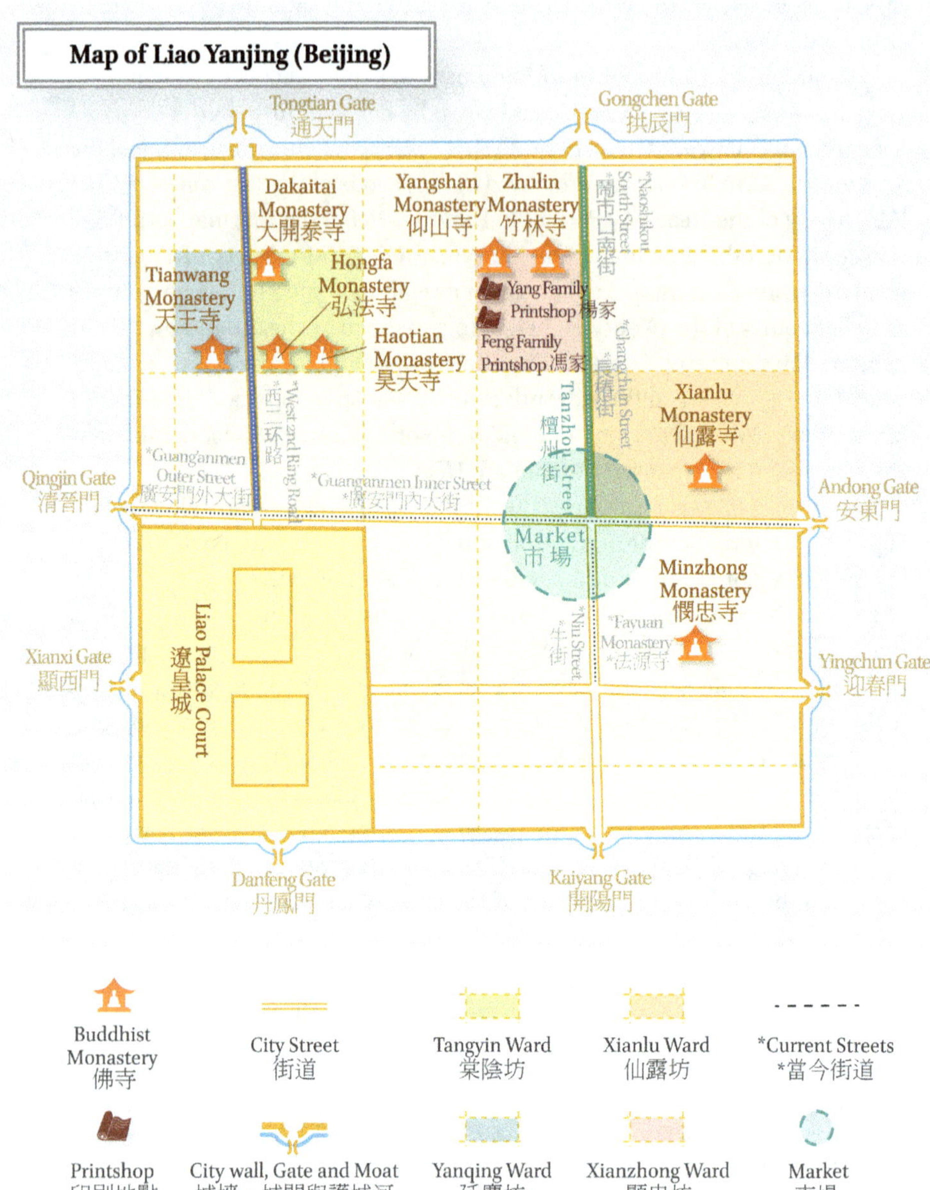

MAP 4.2 Map of Liao Yanjing with major Buddhist temples and printshops associated with Buddhist printing. By Rita Xiong

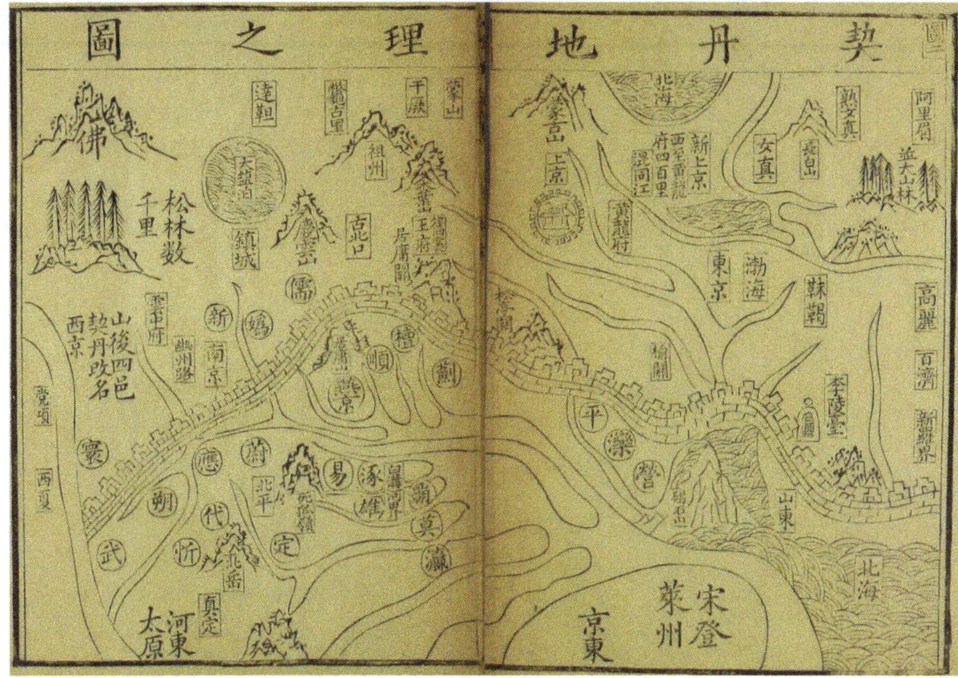

MAP 4.3 Map of the Complete Yan contributed to the Khitan by the Jin

Hebei and northern Shanxi.[35] They also include Yanjing at the center of the map, and Datong, marked as "Wu" 武. Both cities had accumulated a rich Buddhist material culture before Liao times and in due course further developed as prospering cultural centers.[36]

The five circuits were well connected through a courier and relay system known as *yidao* 驛道, which "was reserved for government use" and "envoys from foreign countries."[37] Lodgings, food, and horses were provided at stations run by local people. Scholars estimate that it may have taken about six days to deliver an imperial message "from the Korean border to the far western

35 The map is illustrated prior to the first *juan* of the book; see QDGZ.

36 Wittfogel and Feng 1949, 60. Regarding Tang or pre-Tang Buddhist temples in Beijing, the compiler of the *Yuan yi tong zhi* lamented that only Minzhongsi of the Tang survived after the Buddhist execution issued by the Tang Emperor Wuzong 武宗 (r. 840–846); see YYTZ 1: 25.

37 Wittfogel and Feng 1949, 161–62. For more Northern Song primary sources pertinent to the Liao transportation routes, see Chen and Zhu 2009, 747–48; Zhao Y. 2017, 15–18, 32–36, 87–88, 195–99.

FIGURE 4.8
Gilded tablet. Liao. Discovered in Chengde, Hebei. Hebei Museum

garrisons."[38] Such express service was only available for those who delivered "tributes of fresh things" and "memorials concerning litigations."[39] In addition, the Liao government issued a variety of travel passes to authorized travelers. One extant sample is an elongated gilded tablet, discovered in Chengde 承德, Hebei (fig. 4.8; map 4.1), possibly located along the transportation route between the Southern and Central Circuits.[40] It bears incised "small Khitan script" (Qidan xiaozi 契丹小字), which may read "Chi yi su" 敕宜速, meaning "Imperial order, better hurry!"[41]

Another feature was border markets between the Liao and its neighbors that facilitated cross-regional trade (map 4.1). For example, Xincheng 新城 and Xiongzhou 雄州 in modern Hebei were major hubs on the border between

38 Wittfogel and Feng 1949, 162.

39 Wittfogel and Feng 1949, 167.

40 For more examples, see ZGJYBLFLQQJ 2: 203. For the archaeological report, see Zheng 1974. Chengde was listed along the route connecting the Southern and Central Capitals, see Cheng 2015, 45–46.

41 Zheng 1974, 82–83. For a silver tablet with the same text, see ZGJYBLFLQQJ 2: 205 (fig. 370). For additional typologies of Liao travel passes in elongated, round, and fish shapes, see Chen and Zhu 2009, 148–53; Wittfogel and Feng 1949, 169.

the Liao and the Northern Song.[42] Dingzhou 定州 and Baozhou 保州 near the Bohai Sea were sites where the Liao traded with Korea and the Northern Song.[43] On the border between the Liao and the Xi Xia, Yunnei 雲内 and Tiande 天德 were significant market towns (map 0.2; see ch. 6).

In addition to such border markets, envoys from the Tangut Xi Xia, the Uighur kingdom, and Koryo Korea visited the Liao capitals, further enhancing exchange of Buddhist scriptures and other materials.[44] The Southern Capital Circuit, though tiny in comparison to the rest of the empire, housed the majority of Buddhist temples. Yanjing, the center of the Southern Capital Circuit, was the richest among the five and the most thriving printing center of Buddhist texts.[45] Numerous extant specimens of Buddhist printed texts and woodcuts deposited as treasures in pagodas were for the most part produced in Yanjing, indicating the width of the network and circulation.

2 Texts in Pagodas

Buddhist printed texts have survived mainly as deposited treasures in three pagodas (map 4.1; diagrams 4.1 a–c), White, Fogong, and Tiangong, built in 1049, 1056, and 1062, respectively.[46] Locations vary. In the White Pagoda, the texts appeared in the five-chambered cavity inside the stupa-shaped top (diagram 4.1a);[47] in the Fogong Pagoda, they were placed inside the tubular cache of the four-meter-high Buddhist statue on the fourth floor (diagram 4.1b);[48] and in the Tiangong Pagoda, they were found in the upper layer (diagram 4.1c).[49] The fact that so many Buddhist texts were deposited in pagodas around the mid-eleventh century reflects the overall preoccupation at the time with the

42 For a full list of border markets used by the Liao and the neighbors, see Chen and Zhu 2009, 607–15. For other border markets near the Liao-Xi Xia border, see Chen and Zhu, 2009, 611.

43 For more about the Liao-Northern Song diplomatic exchanges, especially regarding the material and visual culture, see Tsukamoto 2016, 452–59.

44 LS 22: 267; 23: 274; 26: 308; 14: 156; 24: 289; 37: 441; 115: 1527. In 1063, 1072, 1074, 1099, and 1107, the Liao government sent copies of the Liao Canon to Korea; in 1122, a Korean monk purchased three copies of the Liao Canon. See LS 23: 274; Chen and Zhu 2009, 402–403; Wittfogel and Feng 1949, 294. For more Liao-Korean Buddhist art connections, see Pak 2013. For Uighurs under the Liao, see Chen and Zhu 2009, 604; Kitsudō 2013, 227–29.

45 For more about the commerce in Yanjing, see Chen and Zhu 2009, 602–604.

46 For a summary of the deposited printed texts, see the chart in Bi 1996, 67–76.

47 Balin youqi bowuguan 1994, 2017; Sun 2006, 75 (fig. 62). Cf. Zhang P. 2019, 27 (fig. 1–19).

48 Shanxi sheng wenwuju et al. 1991; Zheng 1989; Zheng 1993; Shen H. 2006, 85–87.

49 Chen G. 1989; Zheng S. 1999; Tangshan shi Fengrun qu wenwu guanli suo 2010.

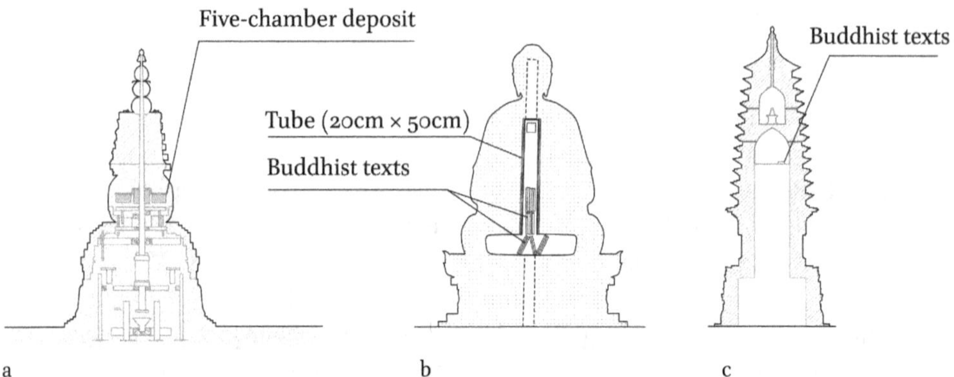

DIAGRAMS 4.1A–C Sectional drawings showing where the Liao printed texts were found as deposited treasures. By Rita Xiong. a. Sectional drawing of the top of the White Pagoda, Qingzhou, Inner Mongolia. b. Interior view of the seated Buddhist statue on the fourth floor of the Wooden Pagoda, Fogongsi, Yingxian, Shanxi. c. Drawing showing the Buddhist texts deposited in the upper register of the brick pagoda in conjunction with the Tiangongsi, Fengrun, Hebei

end of the world, referred to as the coming of the "end-time dharma" (*mofa* 末法). According to the Liao Buddhist calendar, 1052 was the year when the world would enter its final age, leading to a state when everything constituting the "Three Treasures of Buddhism" would vanish.[50] Quite likely, the Liao also inherited the practice of depositing reliquaries and scriptures in pagodas from the Tang.[51] Texts ranged from *dharani* spells to canonical scriptures, demonstrating the donors' collective efforts to prepare in the best way possible for the apocalyptic cleansing to come. Viewed as a whole, the materials reflect the "belief in the efficacy of Buddhist texts," which "not only functioned as shrines for the Buddha's relics but also gave physicality to the Buddha's presence."[52] Compared to those found in neighboring states, such as the Song and the Xi Xia, only few Liao Buddhist printed texts include images.

50 The Three Treasures refer to "the Buddha, the Dharama [law], and the monastic community" (Shen 2001, 267). For the shared temporal calculation of *mofa* under the Liao and in Japan; see Hansen 2020, 163–66; Yiengpruksawan 2018.

51 In his documentation of selected sites in Chang'an, the ninth-century author Duan Chengshi 段成式 (?–863) mentions 100,000 miniature clay and wooden pagodas buried in the Monastery of Zhao Jinggong 趙景公 in the Changle 常樂 Ward, and a thousand copies of the *Lotus Sutra* deposited in a pagoda of the Zishengsi 資聖寺 Monastery in the Chongren 崇仁 Ward; see TSJ 1: 181, 185.

52 Shen H. 2006, 84, 90; Shen 2019, 38–41.

2.1 *Dharani in Reliquaries*

The majority of printed texts in Liao pagodas feature *dharani* (*tuoluoni* 陀羅尼), magical spells believed efficacious for eliminating disasters.[53] The largest group was found in the White Pagoda in Inner Mongolia, rolled up in over a hundred miniature pagoda-shaped reliquaries (fig. 4.9).[54] In some cases, the silk wrapping bears the Chinese characters for "relic" (*sheli* 舍利) (fig. 4.10), equating the texts with the symbolic presence of the Buddha.[55] Unique among them are some cast on metal sheets, like printed scrolls and reliquaries most likely manufactured in the Supreme Capital and commissioned by the Liao royal house. Still, some printed texts indicate that they were based on a prototype first created in the Southern Capital Yanjing.

Among deposits found in the White Pagoda, about 108 reliquaries made of shared modules contain *dharani* printed on paper and cast on metal sheets. Neatly packed into each reliquary is the so-called "*dharani* on the Rod" (*zhangkan tuoluoni* 棖竿陀羅尼),[56] each set containing at least two paper scrolls with printed text (figs. 4.11–4.12) and a metal sheet with incised spells (fig. 4.13). The two paper scrolls, printed in Chinese, refer to a *dharani* scroll (fig. 4.11) and an instructive text that provides guidelines of how to "place" (*anzhi* 安置) the spells "inside buddha images" (*fo xingxiang zhong* 佛形像中) (fig. 4.12).[57] The instructive text was compiled by the monk Zhiguang 智光 of the Minzhongsi 憫忠寺 (Monastery of Sympathy and Loyalty) in Yanjing

53 For the Liao relic deposits in miniature-pagoda reliquaries, see Shen 2001; Shen et al. 2006, 242–51; Shen 2019, 37–41. For the *dharani* cult and materiality in medieval China, citing largely Tang and tenth century manuscripts and prints from Dunhuang, see Copp 2008; Copp 2014.

54 De et al. 1994, figs. 7–8; Shen 2001, 275 (fig. 8). For the latest publication of eighteen different miniature pagodas, see Balin youqi bowuguan 2017, 3–21, 23–54, 56–62.

55 De et al. 1994, 18. For a complete view of the pagoda-shaped reliquary illustrated here, see Balin youqi bowuguan 2017, 23–25. Cf. the other juxtaposition of a pagoda reliquary and the printed *dharani* scroll originally inserted inside, see Shen et al. 2006, 249. As Hsueh-man Shen pointed out, the cloth wrapping of a written *Lotus Sutra*, originally inserted in the other miniature pagoda-shaped reliquary excavated in the White Pagoda, further equates the wrapped sutra as "the embodiment of the whole body of the (Buddha's) relic" (quanshen sheli zai cijing zhong 全身舍利在此經中); see Shen 2001, 271; Balin youqi bowuguan 2017, 23–25 (for a complete view of the pagoda-shaped reliquary illustrated here), 97.

56 This term was stated in the stele dated 1049 and found in the same pagoda; see De et al. 1994, 21. Scholarly calculations of the total numbers of the miniature pagodas, ranging from 106 to 109, are not consistent. It is possible that the total number of the reliquaries was meant to correspond to the symbolic sacred number of 108 in Buddhism. Cf. De et al. 1994, 18, 20; Shen et al. 2006, 248; Shen 2019, 39. One printed *dharani* scroll was inserted inside the base of a bodhisattva statue; see De et al. 1994, 16 (fig. 37), 20.

57 De et al. 1994, 20, 23; Zhejiangsheng bowuguan 2014, 16.

FIGURE 4.9
Miniature pagoda-shaped reliquaries. Liao. Discovered in the White Pagoda, Qingzhou

FIGURE 4.10
Wrapped texts and the middle section of a miniature pagoda-shaped reliquary. Liao. Discovered in the White Pagoda, Qingzhou, Inner Mongolia

(map 4.2).[58] Colophons indicate that the copies, most likely printed in the Supreme Capital, were "reprint editions" distributed by the monk Zhiyuan 志淵 from the Fuxiansi 福先寺 (Monastery of Happiness First), also in the Supreme Capital. They were based on the "Yanjing edition" (*Yanben* 燕本) as transcribed by Pang Kesheng 龐可昇 and cut by Fan Zun 樊遵 (table 4.3), both active in the early eleventh century and named in other printed texts discovered in the Fogong Pagoda (tables 4.2, 4.3; see below).[59]

58 Cf. the map in Shoudu bowuguan 2018, 83. For more about Minzhongsi Monastery, see YYTZ, 1: 24–25; Xu 2010, 164–65.

59 Three extant specimens bear dates: 1007 for one and 1021 for the other two. On the identical copy with the date of 1021, see Balin youqi bowuguan 2017, 22. The information of the calligrapher and the cutter was retrieved from a specimen dated 1007; see De et al. 1994, 23. The calligrapher Pang Kesheng also transcribed the *Lotus Sutra* printed in 1025 in Yanjing and found in the Fogong Pagoda; see Shanxi sheng wenwuju et al. 1991, 33, 141. He also wrote the temple plaque of the Guangjisi 廣濟寺 (Monastery of Universal

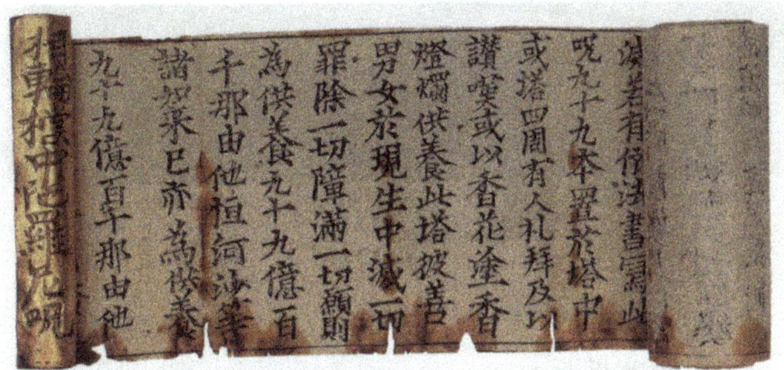

FIGURE 4.11
Detail of the "*Dharani* on the Rod." Early 11th century. Liao. Printed text on paper; gilded copper rod. Discovered in the White Pagoda, Qingzhou, Inner Mongolia

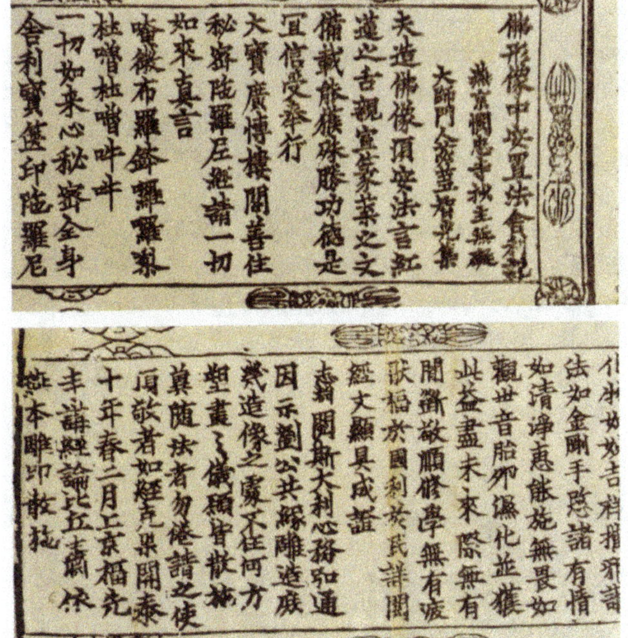

FIGURE 4.12
Details. Records of Placing the *Dharani* inside Buddha Imagery. 1021. Liao. Woodblock print. Scroll. Discovered in the White Pagoda, Qingzhou, Inner Mongolia

The "*dharani* on the Rod" appears in about 107 metal sheets of varied materials, including copper (fig. 4.13), silver, and gold (fig. 4.14). Most likely, these engraved sheets were manufactured by the same workshop associated with

Charity) in Hebei bestowed by the Liao court; see YYTZ 1: 36. The cutter Fan Zun also cut the *Chengzan dasheng gongde jing* 稱贊大乘功德經 printed in Sheshousi 聖壽寺 (Monastery of Sagely Longevity) in Yanjing and discovered in Fogong Pagoda. Fan may belong to the Fan family workshop whose other members were also Buddhist block cutters; see Yan 1983, 12. Fan Zun may be related to the other cutter Fan Chengzun, who cut the block of the *Lotus Sutra* found in the White Pagoda; see De et al. 1994, 23.

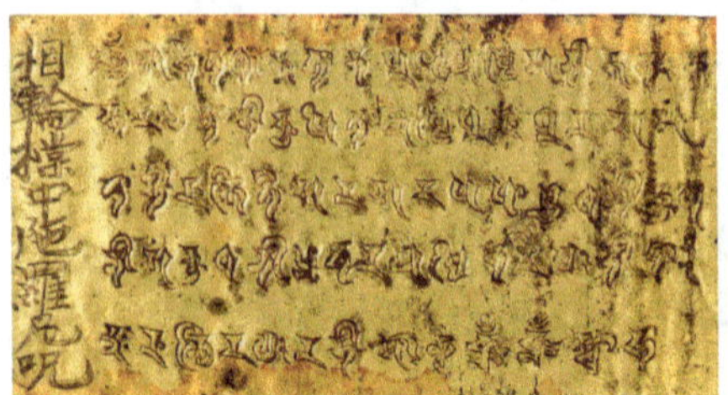

FIGURE 4.13 *Dharani* inside the Cavity of Chattra Parasols. Liao. Gilded copper sheet incised with dharani in Sanskrit. Museum of Balin Right Banner

FIGURE 4.14 Gold sheet with incised dharani. Liao. Discovered in the middle-chamber deposit, White Pagoda, Qingzhou. Museum of Balin Right Banner

the Liao court.[60] The apocalyptic anxiety at the time may well account for the choices of mixing more ephemeral printed paper scrolls with enduring metal sheets, the latter having a better chance of survival and thus transmission of the Buddhist teachings.[61] The shining quality of the gilded metal sheets, moreover, echoes the notion of "golden dharma relics" (*jin fa sheli* 金法舍利), as indicated by a stele inscription found in the same pagoda.[62] Each metal sheet lists a Chinese title on the left that reads "*dharani* inside the Cavity of Chattra Parasols" (*Xiangluntang zhong tuoluoni zhou* 相輪樘中陀羅尼咒) and displays incised Sanskrit spells extracted from a longer dharani scripture. Laid out horizontally and read from top to bottom, left to right, the spell starts with "Om" in the upper left corner and ends with "Ha" in the lower right.[63]

---

60 A now-lost example originally inserted in a reliquary in the North Pagoda, Zhaoyang, built around 1043, was said to be made by the artisan Zhang Congdao 張從道; the artisans in charge of incising the Sanskrit *dharani* were Hu Quanjin 扈全金 and Zhen Shouze 甄守則; see Liaoning sheng wenwu kaogu yanjiusuo et al. 2007, 69.

61 Shen et al. 2006, 244. Another enduring material Liao Buddhists turned to is limestone, evident in numerous Buddhist scriptures carved on thousands of stone slabs, preserved or buried in the Yunjusi 雲居寺 (Monastery of Dwelling in the Clouds) on Mt. Fang 房山 near modern Beijing. For a study of more than four thousand stone slabs of Buddhist scriptures sponsored by the Great Master Tongli in 1093–1095, see Ledderose 2004. For the local officials sponsoring the sutra carvings on Mt. Fang, see Xu 2010, 150. A group of carvers shared the family name Gong 宫; see Xu 2010, 185–86. For selected colophons, see Beijing tushuguan jinshi zu et al. 1987.

62 For more visual samples, see Balin youqi bowuguan 2017, 63, 67. For more about the stele, see De et al. 1994, 21; Shen 2019, 41.

63 The *dharani* was extracted from the *Rasmivimalavisuddhaprabha-dharani Sutra*; see Shen et al. 2006, 248. I would like to thank Tian Chen, Eric Huntington, and Xinyu Liang for their input.

Most exquisite among the pagoda-shaped reliquaries discovered in the White Pagoda (fig. 4.9) is the miniature gilded pagoda adorned with tassels and bells (fig. 4.15), found in the central room of the multichambered relic deposit.[64] Its overall design resembles a pagoda image printed in a *dharani* fragment in Chinese (fig. 4.16), also found in the White Pagoda. One of the select few image-bearing printed texts from the site, it lists its donor as the high-ranking monk Yungui 蘊珪, who served as the construction supervisor of the White Pagoda.[65]

The prevalent *dharani* culture in Khitan Liao is also reflected in other materials discovered beyond the White Pagoda. A printed booklet in butterfly binding (*hudiezhuang* 蝴蝶裝), found in the Tiangong Pagoda in Fengrun, Hebei (diagram 4.1c; map 4.1), shows assorted spells printed in both Sanskrit and Chinese (fig. 4.17).[66] Butterfly binding indicates a codex whose "large printed leaves were folded down the center and gathered into a pile."[67] Its prototype can be traced back to hand-copied codices in ninth-century Dunhuang, which may in turn be inspired by the manuscript format "transmitted by occidental religions, Nestorianism or Manichaeism."[68] Judging from its portable pocket size, this may originally have been used by a monk or lay follower for the chanting of daily prayers.[69]

In a funerary context, moreover, several extant "*dharani* coffins" were found in the Zhang family tombs in Xuanhua 宣化, Hebei (map 4.1). They show assorted spells from various sources. The example shown here is a coffin from the tomb of Zhang Kuangzheng 張匡正, who died in 1058 and was re-buried in the family graveyard in 1093 (fig. 4.18).[70] The *dharani* spells were transcribed in

---

64 For a metal scroll dated 1049 found inside the reliquary, see Shen et al. 2006, 250; Shen 2019, 38–39. Another *dharani* silver sheet found inside the same reliquary bears the name of a certain "Shanyou from the Supreme Capital" (Shangjing Shanyou 上京善友), most likely a craftsman based there; see De et al. 1994, 15, 19.

65 The *dharani* is entitled the *Great Light Six-character Dharani of the Sutra of the Magnificent Treasured King* (*Dasheng zhuangyan baowang jing liuzi daming tuoluoni* 大乘莊嚴寶王經六字大明陀羅尼). See De et al. 1994, 32; Wang et al. 2019, 77, 84–85; Li R. 2015, 26, 29–30, 202; Liu X. 2015, 276.

66 Fang 2015a, 18, 21–22 (for various sources of the assorted *dharani* charms, see 22); Zhongguo guojia tushuguan et al. 2012, 2: 56–57.

67 Tsien 1985, 229 (fig. 1157e), 231. Note that Chen Guoying made a mistake identifying this printed specimen as a "scroll"; see his listing of *Shengguang xiaozai jing* 聖光消災經 in Chen G. 1989, 81, 91.

68 Drège 2018, 28; Galambos 2020, 32.

69 Fang 2015a, 22.

70 For a transliteration of the *dharani* inscribed on the coffin, see Hebeisheng wenwu yanjiu suo 2001b, 1: 25–30; for the dating of the tomb, see the epitaph transliterated in 67–68. For the biography of Zhang Kuangzheng recorded in his tomb epitaph, see Xiang et al. 2010,

FIGURE 4.15
Miniature gilded pagoda. Liao. Gilded silver, silver, and pearls. Discovered in the middle-chamber deposit, White Pagoda, Qingzhou. Museum of Balin Right Banner

FIGURE 4.16 Fragment of the illustrated dharani donated by Monk Yungui of the Supreme Capital. Liao. Woodblock print. Discovered in the White Pagoda, Qingzhou, Inner Mongolia

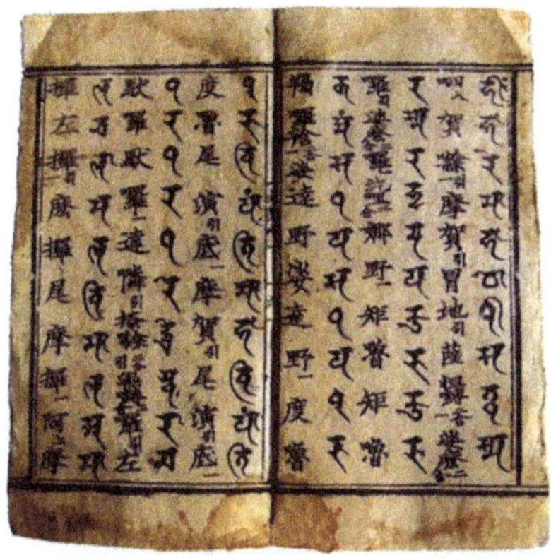

FIGURE 4.17
Detail of assorted *dharani* in Sanskrit and Chinese. Before 1062. Liao. Woodblock print. Butterfly binding. Discovered in the Tiangong Pagoda, Fengrun, Hebei

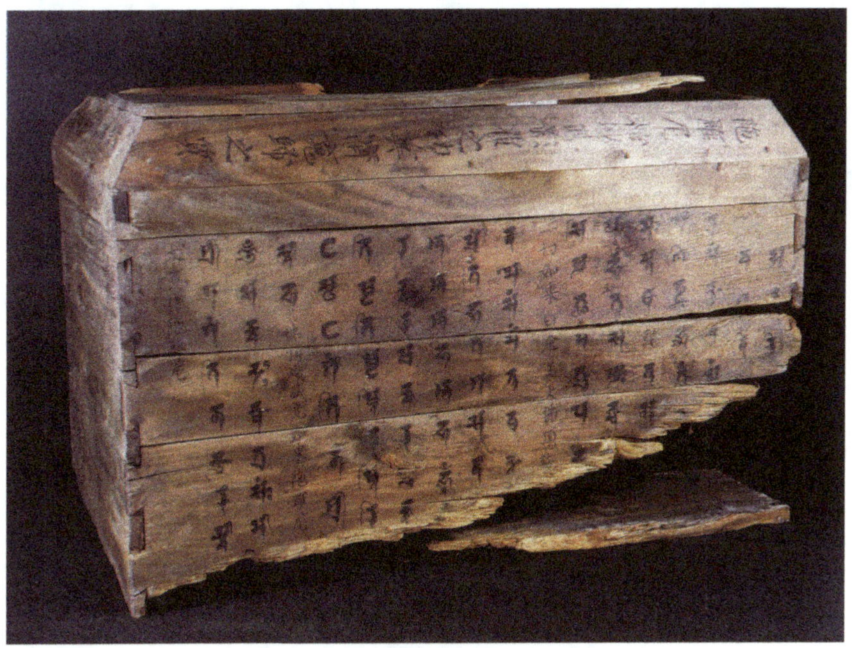

FIGURE 4.18 Wooden coffin with written dharani. ca. 1047. Liao. From the Tomb of Zhang Kuangzheng (M10), Xuanhua, Hebei

Siddham script, while the scriptures were in Chinese. The overall layout of the *dharani*, in vertical lines from right to left, follows the Chinese reading habit.[71] The text expresses the hope that the inscribed *dharani* spells help the deceased to avoid hell and be reborn in heaven.[72]

Going beyond the Khitan Liao, *dharani* spells were also common in south China and other parts of East Asia. Discovered in the Ruiguang Pagoda in Suzhou, Jiangsu, the *Dharani of the Chattra Parasols* dated 1017, printed on paper and transcribed in Chinese (fig. 4.19), reflects a similar practice in the Northern Song.[73] *Dharani* scrolls inserted into either architectural components or pagoda-shaped reliquaries were also widely present in medieval Korea and Japan.[74] As Peter Kornicki and T. H. Barrett note, there are two common features they share. One, the texts under evaluation "were not made for reading but rather were buried ... for future generations." Second, their common "use of precious metals" may reflect the notion that "more precious materials" are deemed "more efficacious."[75] Beyond Buddhism, the Khitan way of working with thin metal sheets and gold flakes also reflects a strong crafts tradition inherited from the Eurasian steppes.[76] This is evident in many exquisite funerary crowns made of thinly hammered gold and silver sheets (fig. 4.20).[77] Researchers further link the Liao practice of engraving Buddhist writings on

214–15. Cf. the *dharani* coffin of Zhang Wenzao transliterated in Hebeisheng wenwu yanjiu suo 2001b, 1: 82–88; for more discussion, see Shen 2005; Shen H. 2006, 87–89; Li Q. 2008, 75–84, 187–90, 199, 296–98.

71 I appreciate Yong Cho and Tian Chen for their help. For more study, see Shen 2005, 103–106, 107 (fig. 9), 110–11 (figs. 14–16), 139 (a chart of Buddhist texts where the *dharanis* were cited from).

72 Li Qingquan provocatively argued that both the shape and size of the *dharani* coffin compare closely to a Liao stone reliquary dated around the mid-eleventh century, providing further links between the funeral and Buddhist material cultures. Cf. the stone reliquary discovered in Liao pagoda on Mt. Fang, dated to around 1051, discussed in Li Q. 2008, 297–98.

73 It bears the colophon of a lay donor, named Zhu Congqing 朱從慶, who dedicated the copying of the *dharani* sutra to his deceased mother, Lady Zhou Liuniang 周六娘. The other similar *dharani* scroll dated 1071 was donated by a lay Buddhist Wu Song 吳聳 in honor of his deceased mother Lady Tang Qiniang 唐七娘. For both scrolls, see Suzhou bowuguan 2012, 30–35 (figs. 8–9).

74 Zhejiangsheng wenwu kaogu 2002; Qiu 1996; Zhejiangsheng bowuguan 2014, 14, 31; Shen 2001, 288 (figs. 37–38); 295–96; Shen 2019, 37–38 (fig. 1.13).

75 Kornicki and Barrett 2017, 119–20.

76 See, for example, the openwork golden plaque with disk pendants excavated in Liaoning and dated to the fourth century; James Watt traced it to the ornamental style of the Bactrian gold found in Tillya Tepe in Afghanistan dated to the first century; see Watt et al. 2004, 129.

77 For excavated examples, see Shoudu bowuguan ed. 2018, 204–205.

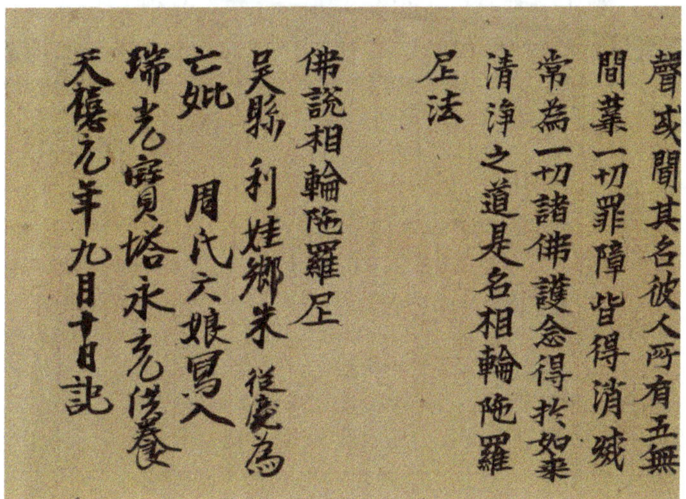
聲或聞其名彼人所有五無
間業一切罪障皆得消滅
常為一切諸佛護念得於如來
清淨之道是名相輪陁羅
尼法
佛說相輪陁羅尼
吳縣 利娃鄉朱 從慶為
亡妣 周氏大娘寫入
瑞光寶塔永充供養
天禧元年九月十日記

FIGURE 4.19 Detail of a hand-written colophon at the end of the printed *Dharani of the Chattra Parasols*. 1017. Northern Song. Woodblock print. Ink on paper. Handscroll. Discovered in the Ruiguang Pagoda, Jiangsu

FIGURE 4.20 Crown. Liao. Gilded and silver. Discovered in Xiaolamagou, Lingyuan, Liaoning. Liao

thin metal sheets to widely shared Buddhist practices in South, Southeast, and East Asia.[78] In spite of this, the sheer quantity of the Buddhist text-bearing metal sheets sealed in Liao pagodas is unprecedented and marks a unique facet in Liao material culture in response to apocalyptic fears.

2.2 *The Liao Canon*

To students of Buddhist books, the most exciting find of printed texts from the Liao pagoda deposits is the diverse specimens of the government-sponsored Liao Canon. Produced in the first half of the eleventh century, it has survived in two types of binding, matching the two major formats of book sat the time: scroll (or scroll and rod; *juanzhou zhuang* 卷軸裝) (figs. 4.21a–c) and butterfly (or booklet) (fig. 4.22).[79] Both are vividly depicted in the mural of the tomb of Zhang Kuangzheng (d. 1058, re-buried in 1093) in Xuanhua, Hebei (fig. 4.23).[80] Viewing these "scrolls and books" alongside with other "brush pens, ink and ink stones" depicted in other closely related painted tombs in the Xuanhua family graveyard, Hsueh-man Shen sees these images as mock material supplies for the tomb occupants "to duplicate scriptures in their tombs."[81]

Scroll binding often consisted of several sheets of paper pasted "end to end to form a continuous scroll" and fastened at the end to a rod.[82] The Liao Canon in this format was much like its Chinese counterpart—the Kaibao Canon—produced by the Northern Song court around 983, although the two versions differ in terms of textual layout.

Butterfly binding is a more efficient technique that developed in the ninth and tenth centuries. Also known as pasted-leaf (*nianye* 粘葉) or album-book (*shuce* 書冊) binding, here the book consists of printed pages "folded down the center and gathered into a pile."[83] It is often protected by a cover made of harder material—stiff paper or cloth—and pasted against the spine created by the folded page centers. When the volume was fully unfolded, it showed

---

78 For a broad assessment of this practice, see Kornicki and Barrett 2017 (for a list of examples in East Asia, see 119). Hsueh-man Shen suggests that the Liao practice may have been inspired by an eighth-century *Diamond Sutra* incised on gold sheets and originally deposited in a reliquary; see Shen 2019, 62–63 (see fig. 2.13).

79 Zhang and Han 2006, 152–56; 2009, 88–91; Tsien 1985, 228–31. For more studies of the Buddhist canons in the age of printing, see Long and Chen 2019.

80 Hebeisheng wenwu yanjiu suo 2001b, 1: 38, 2: color plate 16 (unnumbered page). For more about the Liao painted tombs in Xuanhua, see Hebeisheng wenwu yanjiu suo 2001a, 2001b; Shen 2005; Li Q. 2008; Wu 2010, 140–48, 160–62, 218, 220, 224–33.

81 Shen 2005, 134 (figs. 6–7).

82 Wu and Chia 2015, 32. See also Tsien 1985, 228–29.

83 Tsien 1985, 231; Li 2002b, 37–38; Zhang and Han 2006, 154–56; Wu and Chia 2015, 32.

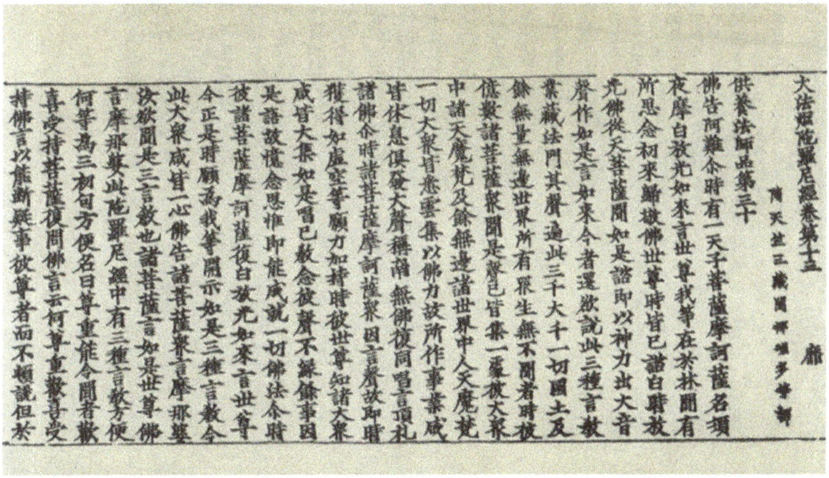

FIGURES 4.21A–C
Details. *Great Law Torch Dharani Sutra*, juan 13. Liao. Woodblock print. Discovered in the Fogong Pagoda, Yingxian, Shanxi

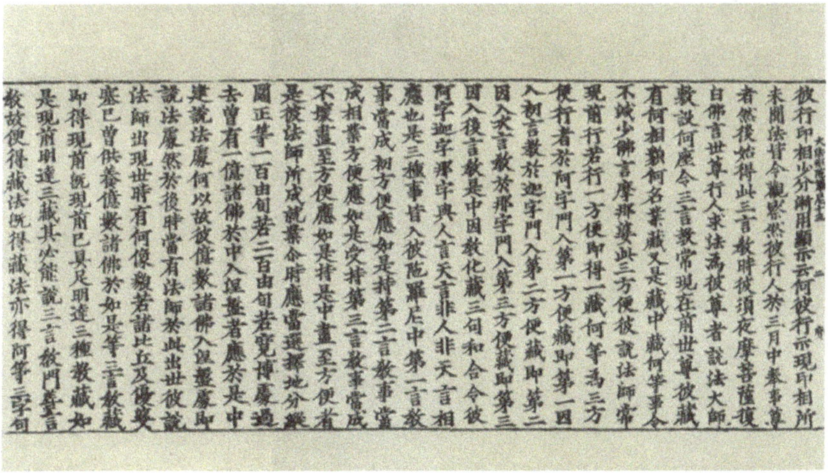

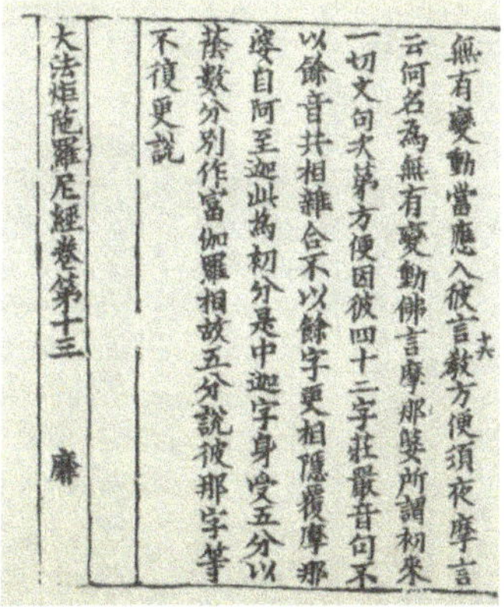

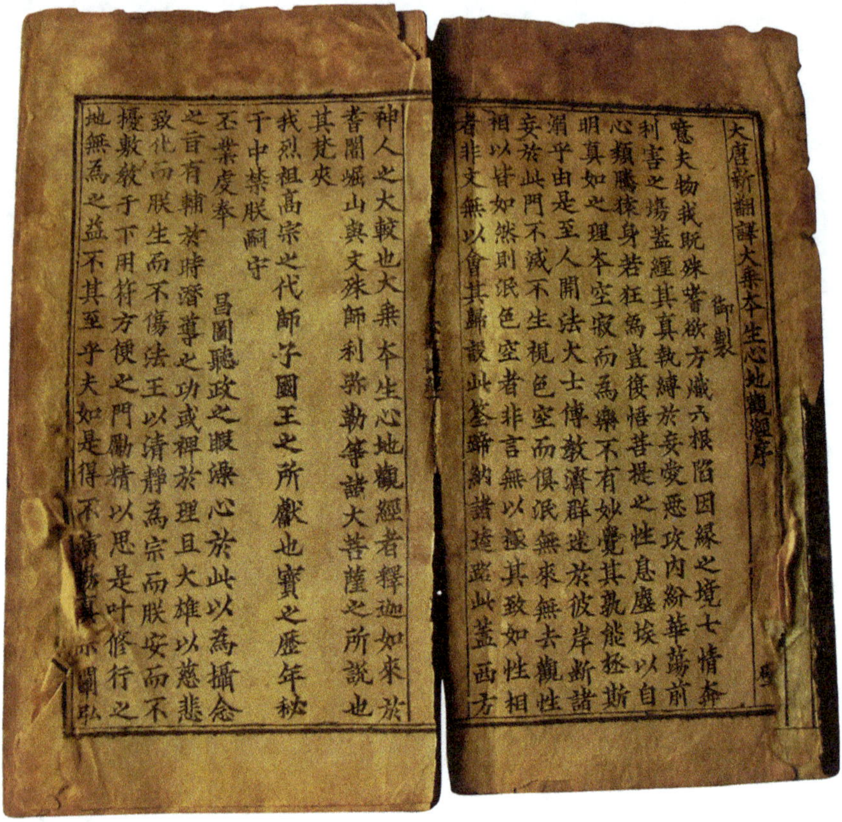

FIGURE 4.22 Detail. *Mahayana Origin of the Mind*. Liao Canon in small characters. 1070. Liao. Butterfly-binding. Discovered in the Tiangong Pagoda, Fengrun, Hebei

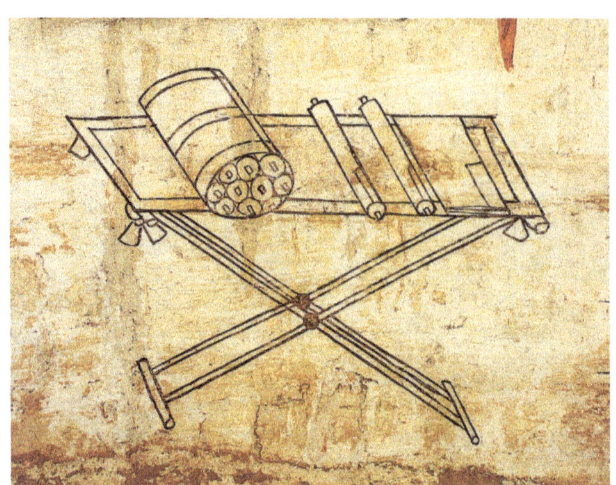

FIGURE 4.23 Detail of Buddhist texts in scroll and butterfly binding formats. 1093. Liao. Mural. West wall of the rear chamber of the tomb of Zhang Kuangzheng (Tomb M10), Xuanhua, Hebei

a continuous frame running across two pages, with block information listed along the spine's axis.

All the Liao Canon specimens discovered to date are in Chinese, with characters in scroll format larger than those in booklet or butterfly binding. Scholars accordingly call them the Liao Canon in large characters (*Liao dazi zang* 遼大字藏) (fig. 4.21a–c) and the Liao Canon in small characters (*Liao xiaozi zang* 遼小字藏) (fig. 4.22). Fang Guangchang identifies seven texts from the Fogong Pagoda as part of the Liao Canon in large characters (table 4.1) and one specimen from the Tiangong Pagoda deposits as belonging to the Liao Canon in small characters.[84] Most likely they were printed in Yanjing, as elite monks active there played a major role in compiling, collating, and supervising the process. The pagodas also yielded individually printed Buddhist texts in formats based on the Liao Canon; however, they bear additional colophons that list their donors in Yanjing.

2.2.1 In Scroll Format (Large Characters)

Within the scroll format, certain concrete criteria, as pointed out by Fang Guangchang, allow the identification of specific editions. They include mounting style, numbering system, framing design, frame measurements (*kuang* 框) of each block, and paper size.[85] When looking for common ground with other texts of the same edition, frame measurements are most crucial. If a text shares the same compositional layout as one from the canon but is printed on different sized paper, most likely it was printed later.[86]

As shown in table 4.1, seven texts from the Fogong Pagoda with closely comparable visual features can be identified as surviving specimens of the same edition of the Liao Canon.[87] It applies a unique numbering system that uses individual characters from the *Essay in a Thousand Words* (*Qianzi wen* 千字文) to mark cases (*han* 函) of texts in order.[88]

84 For selected pages of these printed texts, see Shanxi sheng wenwuju et al. 1991, 19–27, 39–79. Cf. different opinions proposed in Luo 1988, 1992; Zheng 1989; Zheng 1993; Li and He 2003, 127–60.

85 Fang 2004, 176–79.

86 Fang 2004, 184.

87 My chart consolidates the data presented in two charts in Fang 2004, 183–84. For the reproductions of these texts, see Shanxi sheng wenwuju et al. 1991, 19–27, 39–79.

88 This feature alone cannot determine whether or not a text is from the canon, as the *Thousand Words* numbering system can be applicable to either a text that is from the canon or a text reprinted after the one in the canon; see Fang 2004, 176. For a slightly different scholarly opinion, which identified twelve items as the Liao Canon, see Li 2002b, 90–91.

TABLE 4.1 Extant texts from the Liao Canon in large characters. Discovered in the Fogong Pagoda, Shanxi

No.*	Title	*Qianzi wen*	Lines/ block	Words/ line	Block numbering	Frame height (cm)	Frame length (cm)	Paper length (cm)	Frame style
1	大方廣佛華嚴經卷四七	垂	27	17	華嚴 47, 2, 垂 (right margin)	22	50–54.1	29.7	Single-line frame
7	大法炬陀羅尼經卷一三	靡	27	17	大法炬陀羅尼 13, 2, 靡 (right margin)	22	53–54	29.5	Single-line frame
8	大方便佛報恩經卷一	欲	27	17	報恩經 1, 15, 欲字號 (right margin)	22.3	53.8–55	28.4	Single-line frame
9	中阿含經卷三六	清	27	17	中阿含經 36, 2, 清 (right margin)	22.3	53.4–53.8	29.7	Single-line frame
10	阿毗達磨發智論卷一三	弟	27	17	發智論 13, 2, 弟 (right margin)	22.4	53.5–55.8	29.1	Single-line frame
11	佛說大乘聖無量壽決定光明王如來陀羅尼經	刻	27	17	大乘聖無量壽陀羅尼經 2, 刻 (right margin)	21.8	53.5	29.2	Single-line frame
12	一切佛菩薩名集經卷六	勿	28	17	佛菩薩名集 6, 20, 勿 (right margin)	24	55–55.2	28.9	Single-line frame

* This refers to the serial no. published in Shanxi sheng wenwuju et al. 1991.

For example, the thirteenth chapter of the *Great Law Torch Dharani Sutra* (*Dafaju tuoluoni jing* 大法炬陀羅尼經) in its opening shows a number based on the 181st character (*mi* 靡) of the *Thousand Words* (fig. 4.21a).[89] This means that the text was originally placed in the 181st case of the Liao Canon. Another unique marking in large collections of printed texts is the information added to each individual block, most importantly the "block number" (*banpian hao* 版片號).[90] Often marked on the margin of a block, this provides its sequential relation to other blocks of the same edition and thus facilitates block storage and ease of access.[91] Besides the block number, information also includes the abbreviated title of the text, the order of the specific block, and sometimes a number based on the *Thousand Words* (figs. 4.21b–c).[92] For example, the second block of the *Great Law Torch Dharani Sutra* (fig. 4.21b) provides block information in smaller characters on the right margin. It begins with the title (*Dafaju tuouloni* 大法炬陀羅尼) and the volume number (*juan* 13). Leaving a small space, it then says "second" (*er* 二), indicating that this is the second block of the text. After another space, it has the character *mi*, the marker from the *Thousand Words* assigned to the text's case.

Regarding the layout of lines and characters, all seven texts listed in table 4.1 have seventeen characters per line and for the most part twenty-seven lines per block. The size of each paper and the length and width of each block frame are also highly similar. The layout of the Liao Canon, especially in scroll format, and the textual organization in lines of seventeen characters match the version consulted and documented by the Korean monk Sugi 守其 (ca. 1236), who was in charge of the printing of the Korean Buddhist canon, starting in 1236.[93] Still, there are a few inconsistencies in the minute details. For example, three out of seven texts end with a title and a *Thousand Words* character within a lined column (figs. 4.21c), a format not seen in the other four.[94]

Traces of individual temple seals stamped on three deposited texts suggest that they did not belong to the same set but were assembled from two

89 Cf. T.21.1340.

90 The block information is not seen in Buddhist manuscripts; see Fang 2004, 178.

91 The first page often omits the block information, and the last page often simplifies the block information; see Fang 2004, 178.

92 The block numbering system is unique to a printed Buddhist canon not seen in a hand-copied canon; the earliest printed Buddhist canon bearing the block numbering system is the Northern Song Kaibao Canon. See Fang 2004, 174, 177–78.

93 Fang 2015a, 12–13; Grayson 2002, 97.

94 Shanxi sheng wenwuju et al. 1991, 47, 52, 74. Cf. the other four texts whose titles are not listed within a specifically lined column; see Shanxi sheng wenwuju et al. 1991, 27, 63, 77, 79.

FIGURES 4.24A–B
Temple stamps at the back of Buddhist printed texts. Liao. Discovered in the Fogong Pagoda, Yingxian, Shanxi
a. "Baoyan." Back of the *Avatamsaka Sutra*, juan 47
b. "Shenbo yunquan yuan cang jing ji." Back of the *Great Law Torch Dharani Sutra*, juan 13

different temple collections.[95] Thus, a seal reading "Baoyan" 寶嚴 (fig. 4.24a) stamped on the reverse side of the *Avatamsaka Sutra* may be related to a certain Baoyansi.[96] Another temple seal reads, "Record of Scriptural Collecting, Cloister of the Sacred Slopes and Cloudy Springs" (*Shenpo yunquan yuan cangjing ji* 神坡雲泉院藏經記) (fig. 4.24b). This was stamped on the reverse side of both the *Great Law Torch Dharani Sutra* and the *Middle Length Āgama Sutras* (*Zhong ahan jing* 中阿含經).[97] A larger implication is that the Baoyansi and the otherwise unknown Shenpo yunquan yuan 神坡雲泉院 (Cloister of Sacred Slopes and Cloudy Springs), which both contributed their book collections to the deposit in the Fogong Pagoda, may be connected to the Fogong Monastery.

The three texts with temple stamps are among the select few Liao printed scriptures adorned with frontispieces.[98] It is likely that these images were produced separately from the texts and attached later by individual temples.[99] The two frontispieces associated with the Shenpo yunquan Cloister show the same

95 Fang 2004, 185.

96 Researchers suggested that it may be the Baoyansi Monastery in Zhuozhou 涿州 to the north of today's Beijing (Map. 4.1 of this book), whose monk left a written colophon in red at the end of the *Avatamsaka Sutra* commentaries also deposited in the Fogong Pagoda; see the introductory essay in Shanxi sheng wenwuju et al. 1991, 40. The other possible association is the Baoyansi Monastery in Yizhou built by the Khitan Princess of the Yan.

97 Cf. the same seal stamped on the reverse side of the *Zhong ahan jing*, reproduced in Shanxi sheng wenwuju et al. 1991, 63. Among the Fogong Pagoda finds, eight printed specimens bear stamped seals in red; see Yan et al. 1982, 18. For the Liao specimen of the *Zhong a han jing* transmitted to the Uighur homeland and discovered in Turfan, see Kitsudō 2013, 229–233 (esp. figs. 1–5).

98 ZGFJBHQJ 3: 1–10.

99 Fang 2004, 185.

a

b

FIGURES 4.25A–B Identical frontispiece designs. Liao. Woodblock print. Discovered in the Fogong Pagoda, Yingxian, Shanxi
a. Frontispiece to *Great Law Torch Dharani Sutra*, juan 13
b. Frontispiece to the *Middle Length Āgama Sutras*, juan 36

design cut from the same block (figs. 4.25a–b).[100] They represent a crowned icon seated in the center and surrounded by a pantheon of bodhisattvas and guardians, plus a kneeling figure in the foreground with his back to the viewer. Similar modular designs of a kneeling figure were popular also in printed frontispieces produced under the royal patronage of the Tangut Xi Xia (figs. 5.15a, 5.17, 6.55–6.58), produced in twelfth-century northwest China.[101]

The *Avatamsaka Sutra* with the seal of the Baoyan Monastery is decorated with a simpler frontispiece (fig. 4.26), originally depicting a standing guardian. In the upper left corner is an incomplete cartouche, which reads, "Protects the Law" (*hufa* 護法). The simple design of a heavenly guardian reflects the popularity of the imagery of the heavenly king in Liao Buddhist art, evident also in two other printed frontispieces discovered in the Tiangong (fig. 4.27) and Fogong (fig. 4.28) Pagodas as well as in the gilded silver reliquary discovered in the North Pagoda (fig. 4.29). The solo standing guardian depicted in the Tiangong Pagoda frontispiece (fig. 4.27), also bears an elongated cartouche in the upper left corner of the narrow frontispiece. It reads "benevolent deity who protects the law," a term that also accompanies the standardized guardian motif which appears in the opening of a Koryŏ frontispiece design (fig. 3.32). A seated heavenly king in the Fogong frontispiece (fig. 4.28) and the North Pagoda reliquary (fig. 4.29), moreover, serve as prototypes of the mid-thirteenth century frontispiece design featured in the reprint of the Jin Canon (*Jin zang* 金藏) (fig. 5.18a), using funds contributed by a layman named Zhang who lived in Beijing under Mongol rule.

Most likely major temples across the Khitan empire housed copies of the government-sponsored Liao Canon.[102] According to an epigraphic record dated 1068, monks of the Qingshui yuan 清水院 (Cloister of Pure Water), on Mt. Yangtai 陽臺 in a northwestern suburb of Yanjing, once constructed "inner and outer repositories" (*nei wai zang* 內外藏) in order to store 579 cases (*zhi* 帙) of the Liao Canon.[103] The term "inner repositories" may refer to wall cabinets

100 Drège 1999, 46; Huang 2014b, 421; Huang 2014d, 150, 175 (figs. 22–23).

101 Huang 2014d, 153–56, 177 (figs. 30, 32).

102 For literary sources of bookcases built inside Liao temples to store copies of the Liao Canon, see Zhang and Han 2006, 166–68.

103 It survives today under the name Dajuesi 大覺寺 (Monastery of Great Awakening) near Beijing. For a punctuated transliteration of the record, see Xiang 1995, 332–33. Deng Conggui 鄧從貴 was the major donor who contributed land and funds for the Pure Water Hall. Also see Wittfogel and Feng 1949, 295 (Table 11); Zhang and Han 2006, 167–68.

FIGURE 4.26
Frontispiece to the *Avatamsaka Sutra*, juan 47. Liao. Woodblock print. Discovered in the in the Fogong Pagoda, Yingxian, Shanxi

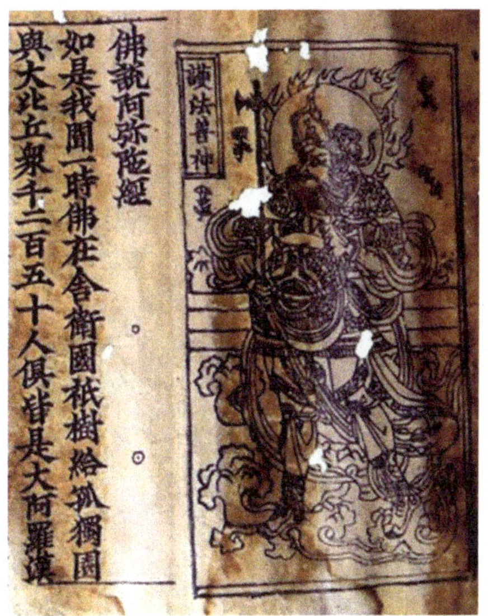

FIGURE 4.27 Detail. Frontispiece to the *Amitabha Sutra*. Liao. Woodblock print. Scroll. Discovered in the Tiangong Pagoda, Fengrun, Hebei

FIGURE 4.28 Frontispiece to the *Lotus Sutra*, juan 1. Butterfly binding format. Discovered in the Fogong Pagoda, Yingxian, Shanxi. Liao. Woodblock print

FIGURE 4.29 Reliquary in the shape of a miniature coffin. Liao. Gilded silver. Discovered in the North Pagoda, Zhaoyang, Liaoning

built along the interior walls of a temple hall, while "outer" ones may indicate free-standing and/or revolving cabinets.[104] The eleventh-century *Building Standards*, compiled and printed by the Northern Song government, provides sample designs.[105] A rare extant specimen of an inner repository appears in custom-made wooden wall cabinets found in the Shang Huayansi 上華嚴寺 (Upper Avatamsaka Monastery), constructed in the Western Capital in 1038 (map 4.1; fig. 4.30). Arguably the oldest surviving Buddhist repositories, they may once have held all 579 portfolios of the scroll-format Liao Canon in large characters.[106]

104 Li R. 2015, 215–16.

105 YZFS, 32: 19–22.

106 This is based on a Jin stele dated 1162; see Shanxi Yungang shiku wenwu baoguansuo 1980, 7, 92. For more images of the bookcases, see Shen H. 2006, 82; Wang et al. 2015, 50–56; Liu X. 2015, esp. 70–71; Li R. 2015, 219–20. The hall with the bookcases was first built in 1038 as part of the monastery under Xingzong; the upper section was added under Daozong's patronage. The Liao Canon was stored in the bookcases after 1068.

FIGURE 4.30 Detail of the wall cabinets. 1038. Liao. Wood. Upper Avatamsaka Monastery, Datong, Shanxi

2.2.2 In Butterfly Binding (Small Characters)

The Liao Canon in butterfly binding and small characters as found in the Tiangong Pagoda reflects a newly developed book format popular in the Song.[107] Fang Guangchang authenticates three printed booklets of the *Mahayana Origin of the Mind Visualization Sutra* (*Dasheng bensheng xindi guanjing* 大乘本生心地觀經) (fig. 4.22) as rare specimens.[108] The framing design here differs from that used in the scroll format (figs. 4.21a–b), showing double contour lines, with outer ones thicker than inner. The title appears in a lined column; underneath is the character *bi* 壁, the 487th in the *Thousand Words*, suggesting that the text was originally from the 487th case. The textual layout is also different in that each page contains ten lines of twenty characters each.[109]

Several other Liao printed texts discovered in the Tiangong Pagoda and dated prior to the Liao Canon samples were also in butterfly binding, including the *Avatamsaka Sutra*, dated to 1042 and sponsored by the Princess of Yan (fig. 4.7), as well as assorted dharani booklets (fig. 4.17), each with a unique textual layout.

The Liao Canon in butterfly binding as well as its scroll-format counterpart may also have made its way to Korea, where it may have been connected to what the Korean monk Miran 宓庵 (1226–1292) described as the "Khitan edition of the Buddhist canon" (*Danben dazing* 丹本大藏) noted for its "refined paper and densely laid out characters" (*zhibo zimi* 紙薄字密).[110] Some discrepancies are notable. While Miran emphasizes that the Liao Canon he saw contained "less than two hundred cases" (*han weiying yu erbai* 函未盈于二百) and "fewer than a thousand album-books" (*ce buman yu yiqian* 冊不滿于一千),[111] the 487th *Thousand Words* numbering that marks the Tiangong Pagoda specimen suggests that the edition it belonged to contained many more than "two

107 Zhang and Han 2006, 154–55; 2009, 89.

108 For a meticulous study, see Fang 2015a, esp. 23–25. The Japanese monk Jōjin mentioned the *Xindi guanjing* 心地觀經 during his trip to Kaifeng in 1073; see Wang L. 2009, 552. For a Song printed version in concertina binding style from the National Palace Museum, see Song ed. 2014, 76–77.

109 Note that a colophon dated 1070 that was not original to the text was inserted to the first page and thus cited mistakenly in previous scholarship; see Fang 2015a, 23–24; Du and Li 2013, 25; Du C. 2016, 62. Cf. Hucker's translation of the "Classics Printing Bureau" which was "under the Court of State Ceremonial." See Hucker 1985, 581 (no. 7979).

110 Fang 2015a, 13; Du C. 2016, 64. Korean primary sources recorded multiple transmissions of the Liao Canon to Korea in 1063, 1072, 1099, 1107, and 1122; see Chen and Zhu 2009, 402–403; Xu 2010, 172, 190–91.

111 Chosŏn Kosŏ Kanhaenghoe 1914, 13: 96.

hundred cases." One way to explain the discrepancy is to consider the possibility that the Liao Canon transmitted to Korea was re-packaged.

2.3 *Four Editions of the Illustrated* Lotus Sutra

Although the Liao produced Buddhist printed texts in large quantities, very few printed frontispieces remain, suggesting that the majority originally did not have images. Among those extant, five frontispieces accompany the individually printed *Lotus Sutra* in scroll format, found in the Fogong Pagoda and classified by past scholarship as Editions Jia 甲, Yi 乙, Bing 丙, Ding 丁 (table 4.2; figs. 4.31a–b, 4.33a–b, 4.34a–d).[112] Embedded inscriptions suggest that they and their texts were printed in Yanjing around the year 1025.

The five extant frontispieces preserve three compositional templates unique to Liao designs (figs. 4.31a, 4.33a, 4.34a–b). Unlike the Northern Song *Lotus Sutra* produced in Hangzhou (see ch. 3), which consisted of seven chapters, the text here originally had eight. Also unlike the Song Hangzhou version, three of the five frontispieces here show elaborate landscape elements. Even

TABLE 4.2 The four printed editions of the incomplete *Lotus Sutra* in scroll format

Edition	*Juan* 3	*Juan* 4	*Juan* 8	Additional information of makers
Jia 甲		x		A cartouche in the upper right corner of the frontispiece identifies the cutters as Zhao Shoujun 趙守俊 and his two sons from Yanjing.
Yi 乙	x		x	
Bing 丙		x	x	A colophon at the end of the text of *juan* 4 identifies Pang Kesheng 龐可昇 as the copyist of the text; Sun Shouyi 孫壽益, Zhao Congye 趙從業 and his brother Zhao Congshan 趙從善 as cutters.
Ding 丁		x (fragment)		A cartouche at the lower left corner of the frontispiece identifies the cutter as Fan Shao 樊紹.

112 For selected pages of these printed texts, see Shanxi sheng wenwuju et al. 1991, 80–182. For past scholarship, see Drège 1999, 56–58; Huang 2014b, 421–23.

a

b

FIGURES 4.31A–B Frontispiece to the *Lotus Sutra*, juan 3 (edition Yi). ca. 1025. Liao. Woodblock print. Scroll. Discovered in the Fogong Pagoda, Yingxian, Shanxi
a. Complete view
b. Detail of the Parable of the Medicinal Herbs

when several illustrate the same parables, designs differ. For example, in the parable of the medicinal herbs (figs. 4.31a–b), the designer of the Liao frontispiece features rain-making troops in the sky, including a dragon, a thunder god striking a chained drum that is partially shown, and a wind god releasing a wind bag. The weather gods summon beneficent rain to nurture the plants and herbs depicted on the ground; the piece strongly focuses on rain-making. Its Hangzhou counterpart, produced by the Yan Family and dated just forty-four years later (figs. 0.4, 3.20), illustrates the same parable with a home-coming

FIGURE 4.32
Detail, the parable of the poor son. Late 8th or early 9th century. Mural. South wall of Mogao Cave 159, Dunhuang, Gansu

scene, showing a man riding an ox and two farmers dressed in raincoats on their way to a fenced dwelling.[113]

As regards the parable of the poor son, shown in the left corner of the picture plane (fig. 4.31a), the Liao scene highlights the kingly father in his palace, calling to mind the Tang-dynasty mural of Mogao Cave 159 in Dunhuang (fig. 4.32).[114] The Southern Song Hangzhou versions, on the other hand, highlight the poor son's hut (fig. 3.37b). In the parable of the illusionary city (figs. 4.0, 4.33a–c), matching the Southern Song design (figs. 3.38a–b), the Liao version places the city in the upper left corner of the picture plane, but unlike the Song depiction of two tigers in front of the city gate to refer to the danger of the journey, it highlights tall mountains and waterways surrounding the city (figs. 4.0, 4.33b). Slender trees dotting the mountain path and the rugged tops of the cliffs indicate danger along winding paths, but there are no tigers. On the other hand, the verticality of the mountains and their dense, parallel textural lines recall mountains in certain illustrations of the *Secret Treasures* woodcuts (fig. 2.29i) and the Liao landscape painting discovered in the tomb in Yemaotai (fig. 2.36).[115]

Further visual comparison indicates that even frontispieces bearing the same designs are based on different blocks. Those of the Jia (figs. 4.33a–b) and Ding (fig. 4.33c) editions, for example, are obviously cut by different artisans. As indicated by the cartouche in the upper right corner, the frontispiece of the Jia

113 Huang 2011b, 145–46 (figs. 14A, 16); Huang 2014b, 408–10 (fig. 18), 421–23 (fig. 32).
114 See also DHSKQJ 7: 99 (fig. 89).
115 Kobayashi 2017, 25–27.

a

b c

FIGURES 4.33A–C Two versions of the same frontispieces design, originally accompanying the *Lotus Sutra*, juan 4. 1025. Liao. Woodblock print. Scroll. Discovered in the Fogong Pagoda, Yingxian, Shanxi
a–b. Details of edition Jia
c. Detail of edition Ding

a

b

c

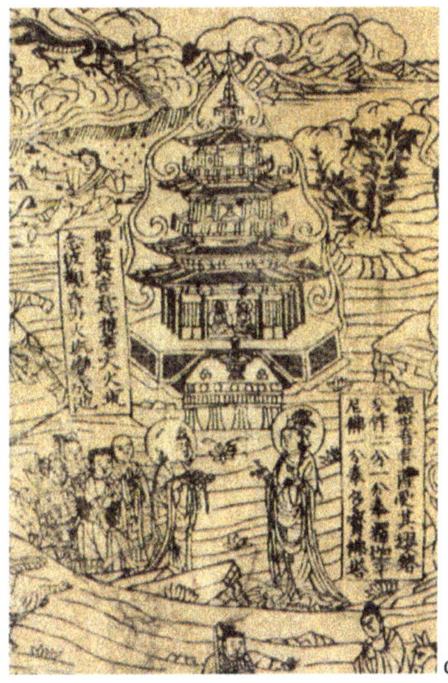
d

FIGURES 4.34A–D Details. Frontispieces to the *Lotus Sutra*, juan 8. ca. 1025. Liao. Woodblock print. Scroll. Discovered in the Fogong Pagoda, Yingxian, Shanxi
a and c. Details of edition Yi
b and d. Details of edition Bing

edition was cut by the Yanjing artisans Zhao Shoujun 趙守俊 and his two sons Zhao Congye 趙從業 and Zhao Congshan 趙從善. They also worked on other printed specimens discovered in the Fogong Pagoda and may be related to the cutter Zhao Jun 趙俊, who joined forty-four other artisans to cut the blocks of a text associated with the *Lotus Sutra* narrated by the monk Quanming 詮明 of the Minzhong Monastery in Yanjing (table 4.3). The incomplete frontispiece from the Ding edition, on the other hand, was cut by Fan Shao 樊紹, as indicated in a cartouche in the lower left corner (fig. 4.33c). They also reveal further minute stylistic differences, such as the cropping of architectural motifs in the background in their upper left corners (figs. 4.33a–b).

TABLE 4.3 Liao cutters recorded in printed Buddhist texts

Names of cutters	Date	Text	Discovery site
Fan Chengzun 樊承遵	1016	*Lotus Sutra* in small character in scroll format; based on the version collected in Shengshousi in Yanjing (De et al. 1994, 17 (fig. 38), 22–23)	White Pagoda, Qingzhou
Fan Shao 樊紹	1025 (?)	*Lotus Sutra* frontispiece, Edition Ding	Fogong Pagoda, Yingxian
Fan Zun 樊遵	1003	*Chengzan dasheng gongde jing*	Fogong Pagoda, Yingxian
	1007	*Fo xingxiang zhong anzhi fasheli ji* (De et al. 1994, 23) *The copy discovered in Qingzhou was dated 1021 and it was based on the Yanjing original cut by Fan Zun in 1007	A copy based on the original version was printed in 1021 and discovered in Qingzhou
Li Cunrang 李存讓	1003	*Chengzan dasheng gongde jing*	Fogong Pagoda, Yingxian
Mu Xianning 穆咸寧	1003	*Chengzan dasheng gongde jing*	Fogong Pagoda, Yingxian
Qu Shunqing 麴舜卿	Before 1049	*Dharani* scroll rolled up with the other printed text *Fo xingxiang zhong anzhi fasheli ji*; not with the metal sheet; placed at the bottom of a bodhisattva statue in the south chamber.	White Pagoda, Qingzhou

TABLE 4.3 Liao cutters recorded in printed Buddhist texts (*cont.*)

Names of cutters	Date	Text	Discovery site
Sun Shouyi 孫壽益	1025	*Lotus Sutra* in scroll format, *juan* 4, edition Bing	Fogong Pagoda, Yingxian
Zhao Congshan 趙從善	1025	*Lotus Sutra* frontispiece in scroll format, *juan* 4, edition Jia	Fogong Pagoda, Yingxian
		Lotus Sutra in scroll format, *juan* 4, edition Bing	
Zhao Congye 趙從業	1025	*Lotus Sutra* frontispiece in scroll format, *juan* 4, edition Jia	Fogong Pagoda, Yingxian
		Lotus Sutra in scroll format, *juan* 4, edition Bing	
Zhao Jun 趙俊 (and other 44 anonymous cutters)		*Fahua jing xuanzang huigu tongjin chao*, *juan* 6	Fogong Pagoda, Yingxian
Zhao Shoujun 趙守俊	1003 1025	*Chengzan dasheng gongde jing* *Lotus Sutra* frontispiece, *juan* 4, edition Jia	Fogong Pagoda, Yingxian

In a similar vein, the two frontispieces from the Yi (figs. 4.34a, c) and Bing (figs. 4.34b, d) editions, accompanying the eighth volume of the *Lotus Sutra*, are of the same design but printed from different blocks.[116] A comparison of individual motifs in their upper left parts (figs. 4.34c–d), including the shrubs, figures, raindrops, as well as the offerings placed on the table in front of the pagoda reveals minute differences. Curiously, the common motifs of a multi-storied pagoda recall the timber structure of the Fogong pagoda (fig. 4.6).[117] Shifting to the center of the foreground, the common figural design in the kneeling position (figs. 4.34a–b) is reminiscent of a similar figure with his back to the viewer in the two identical frontispieces decorating the Liao Canon (figs. 4.25a–b).

All except the Yi edition (fig. 4.31a) that have been mounted in scroll format bear textual information that links their production to Yanjing. The colophon

116 I disagree with Jean-Pierre Drège, who stated that these two frontispieces are identical; see Drège 1999, 56.

117 Yan et al. 1982, 18.

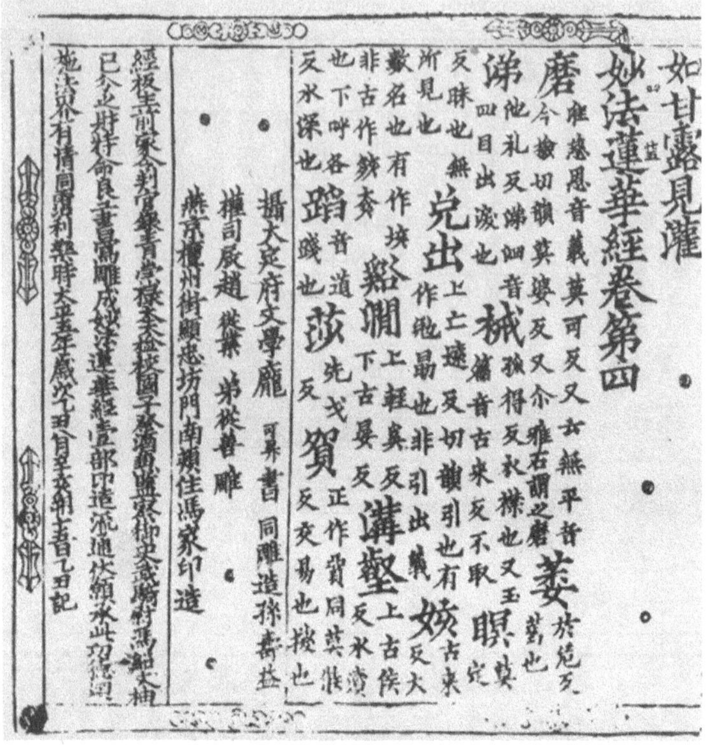
如甘露見灌
妙法蓮華經卷第四
攝大定府文學龐 可昇 書 同雕造孫壽益
權司辰趙 從業 弟從善 雕
燕京檀州街顯忠坊門南頰住馮家印造

FIGURE 4.35 Detail. *Lotus Sutra*, juan 4 (edition Bing). 1025. Liao. Woodblock print. Scroll. Discovered in the Fogong Pagoda, Yingxian, Shanxi

embedded at the end of the Bing edition provides its date, maker, and donor (fig. 4.35).[118] Dated 1025, it identifies the two Zhao brothers who worked with their father on cutting the frontispiece of the other edition (table 4.3), and the Feng family (Fengjia 馮家) located in the Xianzhong 顯忠 Ward, Tanzhou 檀州 Street in Yanjing (map 4.2) as the publisher. It is unclear whether the latter indicates a commercial printshop or a well-to-do household associated with the high-ranking military official Feng Shaowen 馮紹文.[119]

118 For a transliteration of the colophon, see Zhang and Han 2006, 164.

119 Feng Shaowen held multiple positions, including the ritual official in the Chancellor of the Directorate of Education (*Guozijian jijiu* 國子監祭酒), the Investigating Censor (*Jiancha yushi* 監察御史), and the Commandant of Military Calvary (*Wuqi wei* 武騎尉). For these posts in English, see Hucker 1985, 145 (no. 795), 299 (no. 3540), 568 (no. 7741). It requires more research to determine whether Feng Shaowen was the military leader with the same name who once served in the early Northern Song army in Sichuan and rebelled

FIGURE 4.36
Detail of a temple seal. Back of the *Lotus Sutra*, juan 4 (edition Ding). Discovered in the Fogong Pagoda, Yingxian, Shanxi

As shown in map 4.2, Tanzhou Street was located near the major market of Yanjing, where the Liao traded goods with north China.[120] The calligrapher Pang Kesheng, mentioned in a text deposited in the White Pagoda in Qingzhou (see above), was also listed as the sutra copyist. Given that all four printed editions of the *Lotus Sutra* share common visual and textual features, it is likely that they were all sponsored by the Feng Family in Yanjing and that some printed copies were collected by temples in the city. The latter is specifically suggested by a seal stamped at the back of the edition Ding. It reads, "Baoji Lecture Hall" (Baoji jiangyuan 寶集講院) (fig. 4.36), and may refer to the imperially sponsored Baojisi 寶集寺 (Monastery of the Treasured Assembly) in Yanjing (see chs. 5, 7).[121] It remained an important temple even under Mongol rule when it housed copies of the Buddhist canon reprinted in the mid-thirteenth century (figs. 5.18a–b).

3 Liao Yanjing as Printing Center

Evidence points strongly to Yanjing as the main printing center under Liao rule.[122] Major Buddhist temples and elite monks associated with them

---

in 965; see XZZTJCB 6: 162. Officials in Liao Yangjing and ordinary people also served as Buddhist sponsors; see Xu 2010, 150–54.

120 Researchers debated about its location and orientation in today's Beijing. The Tanzhou Street may have been located along the South Street of the Naoshikou 鬧市口 and the Changchun 長椿 Street, just north of the Inner Street of the Guang'an Gate (Guang'an men neijie 廣安門内大街). Cf. the maps of Liao Jin Yanjing published by various scholars, reproduced in Liu W. 2016, 88–90; Zhao 1982. For the location of the market in Liao Yanjing, see Zhuge 2016, 102. Researchers offered different reconstructions of the old Beijing streets; see Yu J. and Yu G. 1989; Hou and Yue 2008; Zhuge 2016.

121 The temple was established in the Tang, and was closely associated with the Yuan court; see YYTZ 1: 31; Chen G. 1992, 6; Chikusa 2000, 218–24; Yang W. 2017; Xu 2010, 167.

122 Zheng 1989; Chen J. 2000.

(table 4.4) joined selected family-based printshops to form a vibrant community in support of the growing Buddhist print culture. The Hongfa, Haotian, and Minzhong Monasteries were all involved in printing; others, such as the Tianwangsi 天王寺 (Monastery of Heavenly Kings), Shengshousi 聖壽寺 (Monastery of Sagely Longevity), Hongyesi 弘業寺 (Monastery of Vast Karma), and Xianlusi 仙露寺 (Nunnery of the Dew of Immortality), also housed elite monastics who composed, collated, or sponsored printed texts.[123] Dates on relevant documents suggest that the prime period lasted from 990 to 1071. Here are the details:

TABLE 4.4 Buddhist temples in Liao Yanjing mentioned in Buddhist printed texts

<table>
<tr><th>Temple</th><th>Location</th><th>Date</th><th>Text</th><th>People</th><th>Deposited pagoda</th></tr>
<tr><td rowspan="2">Haotiansi 昊天寺</td><td rowspan="2">棠陰坊 Tangyin Ward</td><td rowspan="2">After 1059</td><td rowspan="2">Foshuo bashi jing 佛說八師經 (butterfly binding)</td><td>Printed by the Fuhui Tower of the Haotian Monastery</td><td rowspan="2">Fogong Pagoda</td></tr>
<tr><td>Donor: Woman Li Han dedicated to her deceased husband</td></tr>
<tr><td rowspan="3">Hongfasi 弘法寺</td><td rowspan="3"></td><td rowspan="3">1069</td><td rowspan="3">Lotus Sutra (butterfly binding)</td><td>Printed by the Hongfa Monastery</td><td rowspan="3">Tiangong Pagoda, Fengrun</td></tr>
<tr><td>Supervisor: Monk Fangju of the Monastery</td></tr>
<tr><td>Collator: Monk Zhiyan of the Tianwangsi</td></tr>
</table>

123 YYTZ 1: 27, 29; Zheng 1989, 147–49; Li R. 2015, 72–75; Bi 1996, 62–76. The Shengshou Monastery was re-named the Kaitaisi 開泰寺 (Monastery of Opening Peace) in 1017.

TABLE 4.4 Buddhist temples in Liao Yanjing mentioned in Buddhist printed texts (*cont.*)

Temple	Location	Date	Text	People	Deposited pagoda
		1071	*Shi moke yanlun tongzan shuke, juan* xia 釋摩訶衍論通贊疏科卷下 (scroll)	Printed by the Hongfa Monastery Manager: Monk Xing'an of the Hongfa Monastery Collators: Monk Fangju of the Hongfa Monastery and Monk Zhiyan of the Tianwangsi Supervisor: Official Han Zimu of the Sutra-printing Bureau	Fogong Pagoda, Yingxian
		1071	*Shi moke yanlun tongzan shuke* 釋摩訶衍論通贊疏科, *juan* 10 (scroll)	Printed by the Hongfa Monastery Manager: Monk Xing'an of the Hongfa Monastery Collators: Monk Fangju of the Hongfa Monastery and Monk Zhiyan of the Tianwang Monastery Supervisor: Official Han Zimu of the Sutra-printing Bureau	
Hongyesi 弘業寺		1003	*Chengzan dasheng gongde jing* 稱贊大乘功德經（千字文號女）(scroll)	Sponsor: Monk Daozhuan of the Shengshou Monastery Copyist: Monk Zhiyun of the Hongye Monastery	Fogong Pagoda, Yingxian

TABLE 4.4 Buddhist temples in Liao Yanjing mentioned in Buddhist printed texts (*cont.*)

Temple	Location	Date	Text	People	Deposited pagoda
Minzhongsi 憫忠寺		990	*Shangsheng jing shu kewen* 上生經疏科文 (scroll)	Author: Monk Quanming 詮明 of the Minzhong Monastery	Fogong Pagoda, Yingxian
			Cheng weishi-lun shuji yingxin chao kewen 成唯識論述記應新抄科文, *juan* 3		
			Fahua jing xuanzan huigu tongjin xinchao 法華經玄贊會古通今新抄, *juan* 2, *juan* 6		
		1007	*Fo xingxiang zhong anzhi fa sheli ji* 佛形像中安置法舍利記 (scroll)	Compiler: Monk Zhiguang of the Minzhongsi Cutter: Fan Zun Copyist: Pang Kesheng	White Pagoda, Qingzhou
			Xindiao zhu zazan. 新雕諸雜讚 (butterfly binding)	Printed by the Minzhongsi	Fogong Pagoda, Yingxian
Shengshousi 聖壽寺 (a.k.a. Da Kaitaisi 大開泰寺)	Located to the northwest of the Haotiansi	1016	*Lotus Sutra* in small characters (scroll)		White Pagoda, Qingzhou

TABLE 4.4 Buddhist temples in Liao Yanjing mentioned in Buddhist printed texts (*cont.*)

Temple	Location	Date	Text	People	Deposited pagoda
Tianwangsi 天王寺	延慶坊 Yanqing Ward	1069	*Lotus Sutra* in small characters (butterfly binding)	Printed by the Hongfa Monastery Supervisor: Monk Fangju of Hongfa Monastery Collator: Monk Zhiyan of the Tianwang Monastery	Tiangong Pagoda, Fengrun
		1071	*Shi moke yanlun tongzan shuke, juan* xia 釋摩訶衍論通贊疏科卷下 (scroll)	Author: Monk of the Yongtasi 永泰寺 (Monastery of Eternal Peace) Manager: Monk Xing'an of the Hongfa Monastery Collators: Monk Fangju of the Hongfa Monastery, and Monk Zhiyan of the Tianwang Monastery Donor: Li Cunyin	Fogong Pagoda, Yingxian
		1071	*Shi moke yanlun tongzan shuke* 釋摩訶衍論通贊疏科, *juan* 10 (scroll)	Printed by the Hongfa Monastery Manager: Monk Xing'an Collator: Monk Fangju Supervisor: Official Han Zimu of the Sutra-printing Bureau	

TABLE 4.4 Buddhist temples in Liao Yanjing mentioned in Buddhist printed texts (*cont.*)

Temple	Location	Date	Text	People	Deposited pagoda
Xianlusi 仙露寺		1059	*Jin guangming jing* 金光明經十卷 (butterfly binding)	Donor: Nun Lingzhi 比丘尼靈志	Tiangong Pagoda, Fengrun
Yangshansi 仰山寺	Located behind the Yang Family printshop; to the west of the Zhulinsi	990	*Shangsheng jing shu kewen* 上生經疏科文 (scroll)	Printed by the Yang Family Printshop in front of the Yangshan Monastery	Fogong Pagoda, Yingxian
Yongji yuan 永濟院 (Cloister of Eternal Salvation)	Located in the Shou'an shan Mountain in the northwestern outskirt of Beijing		*Gaowang Guanshiyin jing* 高王觀世音經	Donor of 1000 copies: Woman Zhou, the wife of Ren Weisheng of the Yongji Cloister	Fogong Pagoda, Yingxian
Yuquansi 玉泉寺 (Monastery of Jade Springs)	Located on today's Mt. Shou'an in the suburb of Beijing	1101–1110	Temple ordinations	Issued by the Yuquansi in Yong'an shan Mountain, dated to the Qiandao reign.	Fogong Pagoda, Yingxian

3.1 *Mapping Temples and Monastics*

Of particular importance is the Hongfa Monastery, possibly the main printing center designated by the Liao government. As shown in map 4.2, it was close to today's West Second Ring Road (Xi erhuan lu 西二環路), that is, north of the Outer and Inner Streets of Guang'an Gate Street (Guang'an men wai/nei dajie 廣安門外/內大街). In Liao times, this neighborhood was noted for a north-south avenue stretching from the Tongtian 通天 Gate in the north to the east-west street near the Qingjin 清晉 Gate in the west. Liao imperial and aristocratic residences clustered here.[124] By 1071, the official Sutra Printing Bureau (Yinjing yuan 印經院) was established there and put in charge of

124 Zhuge 2006, 60; Yu J. and Yu G. 1989, 28.

FIGURE 4.37
Detail of a seal. Back of the *Shimoke yanlun tong zan shu ke*, juan 2. 1071. Liao. Discovered in the Fogong Pagoda, Yingxian, Shanxi

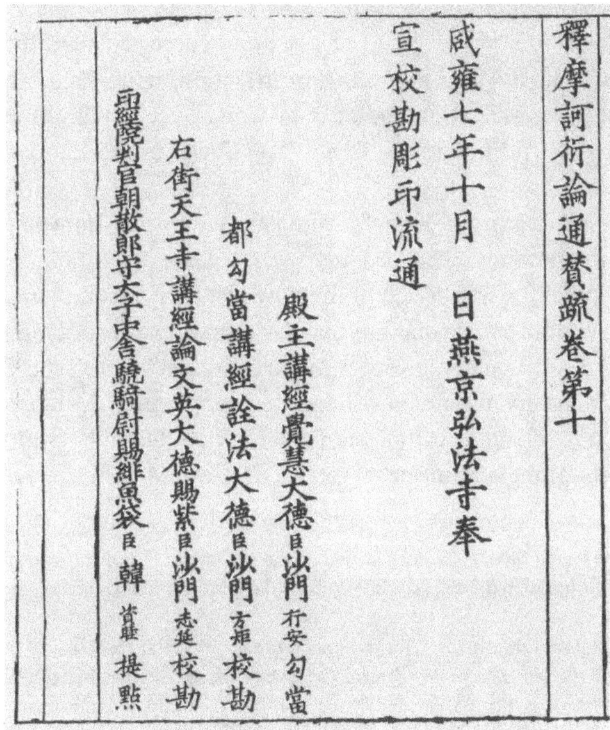

釋摩訶衍論通贊疏卷第十
咸雍七年十月　日燕京弘法寺奉
宣校勘彫印流通
殿主講經覺慧大德臣沙門行安勾當
都勾當講經詮法大德臣沙門方矩校勘
右街天王寺講經論文英大德賜紫臣沙門志延校勘
印經院判官朝散郎守太子中舍驍騎尉賜緋魚袋臣韓資睦提點

FIGURE 4.38
Detail. Colophon of the *Shimoke yanlun tongzan shu*, juan 10. 1071. Liao. Woodblock print. Discovered in the Fogong Pagoda, Yingxian, Shanxi

all government-sponsored Buddhist printing.[125] This is evident in at least two specimens in scroll format, dated 1071 and found in the Fogong Pagoda (figs. 0.9, 4.37–4.38).[126] According to them, Han Zimu 韓資睦 was appointed by the Bureau and served as the Temple's superintendent (*tidian* 提點), while elite monks from the Hongfa and Tianwang Monasteries were managers (*goudang*

125 Du C. 2016.
126 Shanxi sheng wenwuju et al. 1991, 289–312.

勾當) and collators (*jiaokan* 校勘) of printed texts.[127] At the back of one specimen is a rare official stamp that reads, "[imperial] order to bestow [the text] to Yanjing" (*xuanci Yanjing* 宣賜燕京) (fig. 4.37), referring to a governmental seal impressed to acknowledge the official gifting of the printed texts to a certain temple. This may or may not have been the Fogong Monastery, where the text was eventually deposited.[128]

Next to the Hongfa Monastery was the Haotian Monastery (map 4.2), built in 1059 on residential land in the Tangyin Ward donated by the Princess of Qin and Yue.[129] It may also have been involved in the printing of Buddhist texts, as documented in a rare fragment of the *Sutra of Eight Teachers Preached by the Buddha* (*Foshuo bashi jing* 佛說八師經) (fig. 4.39), a short text identifying killing, stealing, being lustful, bad mouthing, intoxication, aging, sickness, and death as the eight teachers.[130] Donated by a lay woman on behalf of her deceased husband, this was printed in the Fuhui 福慧 Tower of the Haotian Monastery.[131]

Next, across the street from the Hongfa Monastery, was the Tianwang Monastery, located in the Yanqing 延慶 Ward (map 4.2).[132] The extant Tianning 天寧 Pagoda in modern Beijing was added to the now-lost temple compound in 1119, sponsored by a Khitan prince and built by the prominent Kou 寇 family builders who were also in charge of other imperial monastic projects.[133] While the Tianwang Monastery may not have been a printing center, the monk Zhiyan who resided there served as sutra collator in multiple Buddhist printing projects based at the Hongfa Monastery (table 4.4). Given that both were

127 Monk Fangju of the Hongfa Monastery once served as the supervisor of the *Lotus Sutra* in butterfly binding format dated 1069; see Tangshan shi Fengrun qu wenwu guanli suo 2010, 10.

128 Cf. the extant stamped seal that reads "Yingzhou Secretariat" (Yingzhou wenshu 應州文書) at the back of the *Shimoke yanlun tongzan shu*, *juan* 10; see Shanxi sheng wenwuju et al. 1991, 306. A similar seal that reads "Huguo Monastery Imperially Bestowed Collection Record" (Xuanci Huguo si cang ji 宣賜護國寺藏記) is said to be stamped at the back of the Liao Buddhist scripture collected in the Huguo Monastery, located in today's Liaoning province in northeast China; see YJXBZ, 184–85.

129 YYTZ 1: 23; Zheng 1989, 140–41; Yu J. and Yu. G. 1989, 30–31; Xu 2010, 145–46. For an in-depth study of the construction history and the spatial layout of the Haotian Monastery in the Liao, see Li R. 2016.

130 Cf. the text of the same title in T.14.581.

131 Scholars suggested that the Fuhui Tower may be a building in the temple compound housing the Buddhist books; see Li R. 2015, 65; Li R. 2016, 289. Though no specific date, the Sutra of the Eight Teachers donated by the lay woman should be dated after 1059, when the temple was built; see Zheng 1989, 141–42.

132 YYTZ 1: 31; Yu J. and Yu G. 1989, 35.

133 Li R. 2015, 53–55.

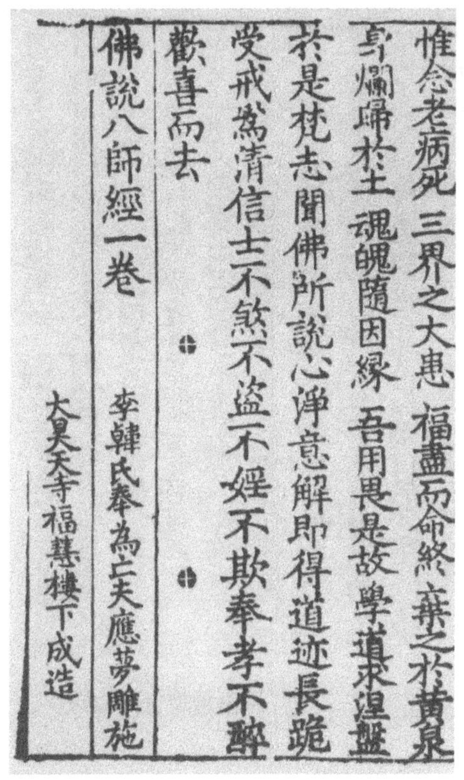
惟念老病死三界之大患福盡而命終棄之於黃泉
身爛歸於土魂魄隨因緣吾用畏是故學道求湼槃
於是梵志聞佛所說心淨意解即得道迹長跪
受戒為清信士不煞不盜不婬不欺奉孝不醉
歡喜而去
佛說八師經一卷
李韓氏奉為亡夫應夢雕施
大昊天寺福慧樓下成造

FIGURE 4.39
Detail. *Sutra of Eight Teachers Preached by the Buddha*. Liao. Woodblock print. Discovered in the Fogong Pagoda, Yingxian, Shanxi

located in the same neighborhood, it was convenient for the monks in the two temples to collaborate.

The imperially-sponsored Minzhong Monastery, today's Fayuansi 法源寺 (Monastery of the Source of the Dharma), was in a different neighborhood, located near what is today Ox Street (Niujie 牛街) (map 4.2). It is the only Liao temple discussed here that survives in modern Beijing.[134] A collection of eulogies used in multiple Buddhist gatherings in butterfly binding was printed there (fig. 4.40). Its elite monk Quanming was in charge of compiling the standard Buddhist bibliography and collating the Liao Canon. He also authored several works whose printed specimens were deposited in the Fogong Pagoda (table 4.4),[135] including the oldest Buddhist text printed in Yanjing (dated 990)

134 When the Northern Song Emperor Zhenzong passed away, the Minzhong Monastery held a memorial altar on behalf of the Liao court. See XZZTJCB 98: 2282.

135 Shanxi sheng wenwuju et al. 1991, 282, 288.

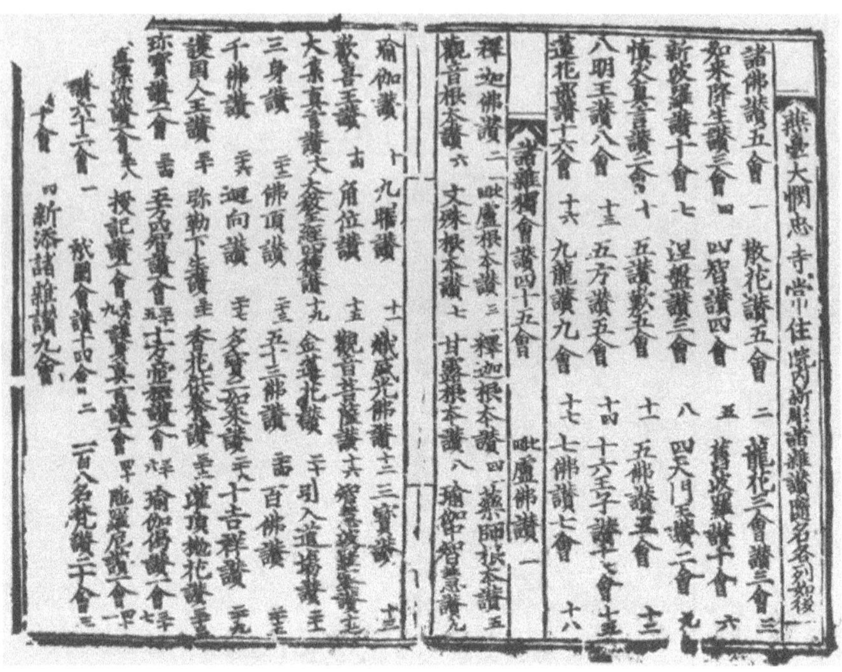

FIGURE 4.40 Detail. A collection of eulogies used in multiple Buddhist gatherings. Liao. Woodblock print. Butterfly binding. Discovered in the Fogong Pagoda, Yingxian, Shanxi

and the incomplete commentary of the *Lotus Sutra*, whose original blocks took a team of forty-five or so cutters to work on.[136]

While earlier scholars have acknowledged the contribution of Yanjing monks to Buddhist print culture, they have said little about the participation of nuns and their institutions.[137] In 1059, the nun Lingzhi 靈志 from the Xianlu

136 Cf. the numbers of cutters stated in the colophons attached to *juan* 2 and *juan* 6, reproduced in Shanxi sheng wenwuju et al. 1991, 354, 374.

137 As early as in the sixth century, nuns were actively involved in sponsoring Buddhist visual and material culture, including the image making in the Yungang grottoes. In Tang-dynasty Chang'an, furthermore, select temples housed elite nuns, some of whom came from imperial families whereas others developed strong ties to the court. For a stele dated 503 and discovered in 1956 that documents Nun Tanmei's 曇媚 sponsorship of the Buddhist image, see Xin 1986. For more nuns sponsoring icon-making in the sixth century, see Shao 2014. For the Fayunsi 法雲寺 (Monastery of the Dharma Cloud) in Tang Chang'an, see Zhang M. 2015, 36–40. For a classic study of Tang nuns, see Li Y. 1989.

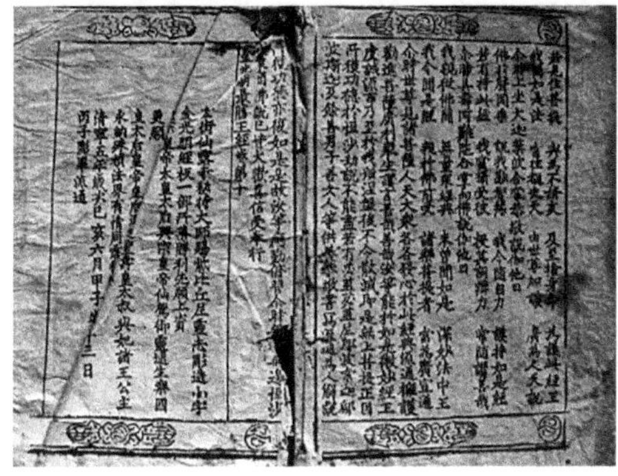

FIGURE 4.41
Detail. *Golden Light Sutra* in small characters. 1059. Liao. Butterfly binding. Discovered in the Tiangong Pagoda, Fengrun, Hebei

Monastery, located in the Xianlu Ward close to the marketplace (map 4.2),[138] sponsored the block cutting of the *Golden Light Sutra*, whose printed version in butterfly binding format was discovered in the Tiangong Pagoda in Fengrun (fig. 4.41). Judging from her title, "Grand Teacher Hongchi, the nun who received the purple robe from the court" (Hongchi dashi cizi biqiuni 弘持大師賜紫比丘尼), she was closely affiliated with the court. The Xianlu Monastery was founded in Tang times and served as a major center for female practitioners under the Liao and Jin.[139] In 949, the nun Dinghui 定徽 received an imperial order to manufacture a reliquary for the Buddha's tooth.[140] In the early twelfth century, under Jurchen rule, the nunnery accommodated over 1800 imperial women arrested in the Northern Song capital Kaifeng as part of the dynastic upheaval, suggesting that it was of an immense size.[141]

3.2 *Mapping Publishers*

Contrary to the abundant information available on Buddhist institutions involved in printing, little is known about publishers producing Buddhist printed texts and woodcuts. To date, we can identify two families, Feng and Yang, both in the Xianzhong Ward of Yanjing (map 4.2), as the publishers of

138 Yu J. and Yu G. 1989, 38–39. According to the Yuan source, the Xiashengsi 下生寺 (Monastery of Avatar Birth) located in the same Xianlu Ward may also be populated by nuns; it was founded by Nun Zhiguo 志果; see YYTZ 1: 32.

139 YYTZ 1: 32.

140 For additional financial support from the imperial members and high-ranking officials, see QLW, 70–71; Xiang 1995, 4–5; Li R. 2015, 72.

141 SCBMHB 98: 724. The Jin occupied most of the former Liao territory in 1122, and gave Beijing to Northern Song temporarily in 1123, and took it over after the Jin defeated the Northern Song in 1127; see Yu J. and Yu G. 1989, 4.

Buddhist texts. While tentatively identified as commercial printshops, they may also have been private households.[142] The Feng Family's shop, publisher of the illustrated *Lotus Sutra* (figs. 4.31a, 4.33a, 4.34a–b, 4.34d), was located near Tanzhou Street, possibly a north-south axis near the major trade market. This neighborhood is today's Naoshikou 鬧市口 and Changchun 長椿 Street, just north of the Inner Street of the Guang'an Gate (Guang'an men nei dajie 廣安門內大街).[143]

The other publisher, the Yang Family, printed the oldest extant Liao Buddhist text, the *Commentaries of the Sutra of Maitreya Bodhisattva's Ascent to the Tusita Heaven* (*Shangsheng jing shu ke wen* 上生經疏科文; fig. 4.42a), a set of commentaries to the *Maitreya Sutra*, collated by the monk Quanming (a.k.a. Quanxiao 詮曉) of the Minzhongsi (table 4.4). Dated 990, it was found in the Fogong Pagoda and bears unusual hand-written markings in red, which call to mind the red dots and handwritten notes in the other comparable commentary of the *Maitreya Sutra*, collated by the same monk and sold in auction in 1999 (fig. 4.42b).[144] Judging from the similarity of their calligraphy, authorship, and print style, it is possible that they were products of the same Yang Family printshop. The red hand markings and notes suggest that the texts were used for reciting or study purposes.

The Yang Family's shop was located "in front of the Yangshan Monastery in Yanjing" (Yangshan si qian 仰山寺前) (map 4.2). Indirect sources help us map its approximate location to the west of the Zhulinsi 竹林寺 (Monastery of the Bamboo Grove), converted in 1062 from the residence of the Princess of Song and Chu (Song Chu guo dazhang gongzhu 宋楚國大長公主).[145] It is also likely that it was close to the Feng Family printshop, not far from Tanzhou Street and the commercial district.

---

142 We can only approximate the location of the Yang Family Printshop based on the textual description that it was "in front of the Yangshansi," which was in turn located "to the west of the Zhulinsi," which was located in the Xianzhong Ward.

143 While most researchers agreed that Tanzhou Street must have been in the commercial district, some interpreted it as an east-west street in Liao Yanjing, overlapping today's Guang'anmen Inner Street; see Yu J. and Yu G. 1989, 27–28. Researchers offered different reconstructions of the old Beijing streets; see Zhao 1982; Hou and Yue 2008; Liu W. 2016, esp. 88–92 (the author opposed the hypothesis that the Tanzhou Street may be along the east and west axis, see 92 [footnote 4]); Zhuge 2016. For the location of the market in Liao Yanjing, see Zhuge 2016, 102.

144 Li 2002b, 101 (fig. 44); Zhang and Han 2006, 164 (fig. 31).

145 For the Yangshan Monastery, see XJZJY, 72. For the Zhulin Monastery, see YYTZ 1: 33; Xu 2010, 131. For researchers who mapped the Zhulin Monastery in the northwest section of the Liao Yanjing, see the maps by Hou Renzhi and Yue Shengyang reproduced in Liu W. 2016, 88, 90 (figs. 12, 15). The fifteenth-century Nun Huiying 惠顥 of the Zhulin Monastery commissioned a bronze bell in 1453; see Xu 1936.

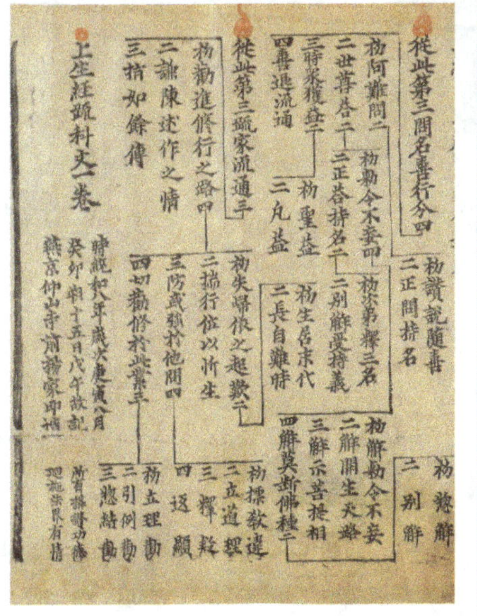

上生經疏科文一卷

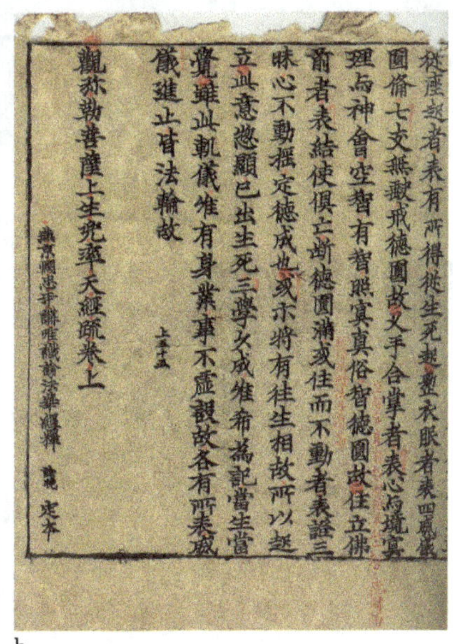

觀彌勒菩薩上生兜率天經疏卷上

a b

FIGURES 4.42A–B Details. Two versions of *Maitreya Sutra Commentaries* composed by Monk Quanming (or Quanxiao). Liao. Woodblock print
a. Detail. *Maitreya Sutra Commentaries*. Discovered in the Fogong Pagoda, Yingxian, Shanxi
b. Detail. *Maitreya Sutra Commentaries*, juan 1

•••

Buddhist printed texts and images excavated from various pagodas in north China shed light on the extensive circulation of Buddhist print culture under Khitan rule. Imperial patrons, Buddhist temples, elite monastics, professional cutters, and printshops in Yanjing formed a vibrant network that stimulated Buddhist print culture in eleventh-century north China. Part of yet wider imperial and Buddhist connections and nationwide transportation systems, Buddhist books and woodcuts produced in Yanjing circulated widely in other parts of the Khitan Liao empire and reached other areas, including the Western Capital in Shanxi and the Supreme Capital in Inner Mongolia. It is difficult to gauge with certainty the extent of the spread of Buddhist print culture in the Khitan Empire beyond the regions of Shanxi-Hebei and the Buddhist pagoda of the Upper Capital. That said, books printed under the Liao reached well beyond that kingdom, to the Xi Xia (ch. 6) in northwest China as well as to the Uighur homeland in Eastern Central Asia (fig. 10.1). In addition, Buddhist printing in Liao Yanjing paved the way for Beijing's Buddhist print culture during the Jin and Yuan periods (ch. 7).

地藏菩薩相

CHAPTER 5

Southern Shanxi as the New Printing Center under Jin Rule

After the Jurchen conquered the Liao in the early twelfth century, southern Shanxi replaced the Liao capital Yanjing as the most vibrant center of Buddhist books and print culture (map 0.4).[1] Ample natural resources of pear and jujube trees provided excellent raw materials for woodblocks, while white hemp paper made by local mills and ink produced in specialized workshops facilitated printing.[2] The growing elite population, including "elite celebrities" (*mingshi* 名士) coming from southern Shanxi, may also account for the prosperity of its print culture.[3] An anecdote of the Pingyang Examination Office, recorded by the leading Jin scholar and Taiyuan 太原 native Yuan Haowen 元好問 (1190–1257), notes that students excelling in the examination were all from "East of the [Yellow] River" (Hedong 河東), a historical term referring to what is today southwest Shanxi.[4] Some local elite members in turn became major players in vernacular and theatrical literature at the time.[5]

Jin print culture in southern Shanxi developed on both official and popular levels. Before 1130, when the Jin relocated their main capital to Beijing, then called Central Capital (Zhongdu 中都), the government established the Institute of Literature (Jingji suo 經籍所) in Pingyang 平陽 or Pingshui 平水 (today's Linfen 臨汾) to take charge of printing government-sponsored

FIGURE 5.0 ← Detail of fig. 5.25b. *Foshuo Shengtian jing*. 1155. Jin. Woodblock print. The New Orleans Museum of Art

1 Wu 1950, 454; Zhang and Han 2006, 174; Zhang and Han 2009, 102–103; Qi and Li 2004. Fan Zhang referred to this larger southern Shanxi area as "the He-Fen region between the Yellow and Fen Rivers"; see Zhang F. 2014, 345. For more studies of Jin history, see Franke 1994a; Bol 1987; Wang J. 2018; Iiyama 2021.

2 Zhang and Han 2006, 174; Zhang and Han 2009, 103; Zhang D. 2006, 34. For a study of the elite in north China under Jurchen and Mongol rules, see Iiyama 2021.

3 Zhang B. 2017, esp. the chart in 39–40; Guo and Li 2016, esp. 30–31.

4 See the anecdote entitled "Cranes in the Examination Office in Pingyang" (Pingyang gongyuan he) in XYJZ 4: 77. In the same text Yuan recorded a story of a blind old sculptor from Pingyang, who craved a magnificent wooden Buddha statue for a Buddhist temple in Jiaocheng; see "The Elder Jia Carving Wood" (Jiasou kemu 賈叟刻木) in XYJZ, 2: 37. For more studies of the Jin examination-based society, see Wang J. 2018, 28–62; Iiyama 2021.

5 Li W. 2014; Yao et al. 2012.

© SHIH-SHAN SUSAN HUANG, 2024 | DOI:10.1163/9789004700017_007

religious scriptures.[6] Even more pertinent, however, was the print culture on the popular level, carried by the efforts of commercial publishers and block cutters. Family-based printshops in Pingyang produced high-quality work. They included those of the Ji 姬 (fig. 5.1a) and Xu 徐 Families (fig. 5.1b), which made picture-based single-sheet prints; the Zhang 張 Family (fig. 5.1c), who reprinted books of the Northern Song; and the Wei 衛 Family, who printed Buddhist scriptures with frontispieces (fig. 5.1d). In Zhaocheng 趙城 county, also in the larger Pingyang area, there was the printshop of the Pang 龐 Family (fig. 5.1e), specializing in the reprint of Northern Song books.[7] Some shops, moreover, notably those of the Zhang and Pang Families, ran publishing businesses for generations even after the fall of the Jin, when southern Shanxi was taken over by the Mongols.[8] The printshop of the Pang Family, for example, was in charge of adding frontispieces (fig. 5.10d) to texts in the famous Jin Canon, when the region was already ruled by the Mongols before the Yuan dynasty was formally established.

This chapter explores the popular development of Jin print culture in southern Shanxi, highlighting documented cutters and family-based printshops as well as the intended audience and supporters. Because Buddhist printed specimens from the Jin are scarce, the study first takes a broader look at local publishing beyond Buddhist contents, including reprint editions of Northern Song illustrated books and ephemera of single-sheet prints.

It then examines two major cases of Buddhist printing. The first, a most ambitious undertaking, was the printing of the Jin Canon. A project lasting over thirty years and undertaken in the latter half of the twelfth century, it was organized mostly by villagers. After the blocks were completed, a local leader petitioned the government to take charge, and they were duly transported to the Central Capital and stored at an imperially sponsored temple, where they stayed throughout the Jin-Yuan transition. While the original blocks of the Jin Canon produced in southern Shanxi did not include any illustrations, several extant printed editions are adorned with frontispieces (figs. 5.10d, 5.22b, 5.25a). Since the editions are most likely associated with donors who acquired them in the capital, the images were probably added individually by artisans upon the owners' request. None of these frontispieces is dated to the Jin, although

6 Franke 1994a, 454; Zhang and Han 2006, 174; 2009, 103. For more on the printing in Pingyang, see Yu 1958.

7 For more on the printer's colophon, see Poon 1973; Tsien 1985, 376 (fig. 1233).

8 For the Pang Family printshop in the Northern Song and the Jin, see Yu 1958, 28; Zhou and He 2009, 49. In the latter half of the thirteenth century, it was in charge of adding the frontispieces to the Jin Canon, the texts of which were originally cut and printed in twelfth-century southern Shanxi; see Jiang 1977, 236–37.

a

b

c

d

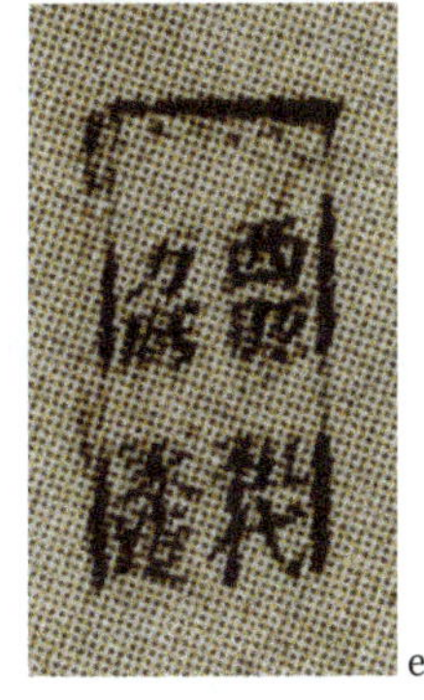

e

FIGURES 5.1A–E
Printers' colophons
a. Colophon of the Ji Family printshop. *Four Beauties*. Jin. Woodblock print. Single sheet. Discovered in Khara Khoto. The State Hermitage Museum, St. Petersburg
b. Colophon of the Xu Family printshop. *Guan Yu*. Jin. Woodblock print. Single sheet. Discovered in Khara Khoto. The State Hermitage Museum, St. Petersburg
c. Colophons of the Zhang Family printshop. *Revised Zhenghe Reign Classified and Consolidated Historical Materia Medica*. 1249. Woodblock print. National Library
d. Colophon of the Wei Family printshop. *Gaowang Guanshiyin jing*. 1173. Jin. The New Orleans Museum of Art
e. Colophon of the Pang Family printshop. *Jin guangming zuishengwang jing*, juan 1

one design (fig. 5.10d), found in numerous extant copies, was made locally in Shanxi. It was printed by the Pang Family, whose business continued into the latter half of the thirteenth century. The second case of Buddhist printing at the time concerns two rare illustrated books discovered inside a Buddhist statue in the New Orleans Museum of Art (figs. 5.25a–5.27). Both the image and the texts exhibit strong popular flavor, while colophons add unique information about local donors and publishers not documented in the official histories.

1 Reprinting Northern Song Illustrated Books

Extant illustrated books reprinted in Pingyang that closely match Northern Song originals attest to a direct link between the dynasties. First is the acupuncture manual *Newly Edited and Supplemented Illustrated Scripture of*

FIGURE 5.2 Detail. *Illustrated Scripture of Acupuncture and Moxibustion*. Reprinted in Pingyang by the Chen Family printshop in 1186

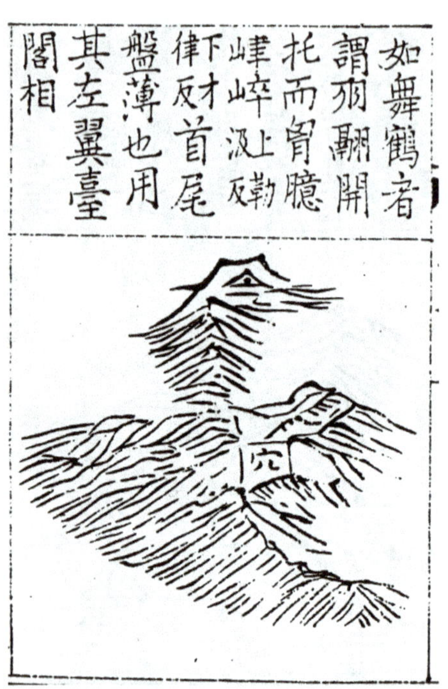

FIGURE 5.3 Detail. *New Book on Earth Lines*. Reprinted in Pingyang in 1192

Acupuncture and Moxibustion Based on Points Shown on a Copper Figurine (*Xinkan buzhu tongren shuxuan zhenjiu tujing* 新刊補注銅人腧穴針灸圖經). Printed by the Chen Family in 1186, the manual contains fifteen illustrations that detail acupuncture points corresponding to various inner organs. Each illustration features a male figure, either seated on a chair or standing on a mat (fig. 5.2).[9]

Next, in 1192, the geomancy manual, *New Book on Earth Lines* (*Dili xinshu* 地理新書), originally by the Northern Song Wang Zhu 王洙 (997–1057), was reprinted in Pingyang. It features seventy-seven Fengshui charts, showing mountains in various forms that mimic animals or man-made objects (fig. 5.3).[10] This edition is the only Jin reprint extant today but, given that the work was required reading for Jin official examinations, it was in high demand at the

9 Yu 1958, 30; Qi and Li 2004, 40.

10 DLXS; Yu 1958, 31; Huang 2012, 143–44; Huang 2014c, 143–44; Jin 2012.

time and multiple reprint editions were probably printed in Pingyang, Kaifeng, and other places under Jin rule.[11]

Then again, in 1249, when Pingyang had already fallen to the Mongols, Zhang Cunhui 張存惠 of the Zhang Family printshop published a fully illustrated reprint edition of the *Revised Zhenghe Reign Classified and Consolidated Historical Materia Medica* (*Chongxiu Zhenghe jingshi zhenglei beiyong bencao* 重修政和經史証類備用本草, hereafter referred to as the *Revised Materia Medica*) (figs. 5.4a–d).[12] Based on the Northern Song edition printed in the early twelfth century, the work, as stated in his preface, also relied on a now-lost Jin reprint edition of the same book by the Pang Family publisher in Xiezhou.[13] Zhang's preface is framed by an elaborate "tortoise-borne stele" design (fig. 5.4a).[14] He also included two stylish trademarks, one in bell shape and the other in the form of a Chinese zither positioned vertically (fig. 5.1c). The bell-shaped trademark reads, "Studio of Hidden Brightness" (Huiming xuan 晦明軒) (fig. 5.1c);[15] the zither design reads, "Printed by the Zhang Family of the Pingyang Prefecture" (Pingyang fu Zhang zhai yin 平陽府張宅印) (fig. 5.1c).

The *Revised Materia Medica* describes 1,748 medicines and has over 170 illustrations. The publisher claims that he replaced selected illustrations he deemed distorted and incorrect with new ones based on his personal observation of nature.[16] Most illustrations—featuring minerals, herbs, bodies of water, animals, fish, and insects—occupy an elongated space equivalent to a quarter of a page. Images of botanical plants form the majority of illustrations, mostly rendered in frontal view. Selected images, however, such as those depicting grapes,

---

11 The Northern Song illustrated manual *Sanli tu* 三禮圖 was also reprinted in southeast Shanxi in the thirteenth century. For more about the Northern Song-Jin print culture transmission, see Zhang 1935, 23–24; Zhang and Han 2006, 177.

12 CZJZBB. The dating is based on the commentary of the Qing writer Qian Qianyi, who once owned the book; the references of the reprint are based on the preface by Ma Gexin at the opening of the 1249 reprint. See Lin Z. 2014, 531–34; for a brief biography recorded in the Shanxi gazetteer (1475), see 541. For more studies, see Wu 1950, 454–55; Wu 1971, 187–88; Xue 2002, 121–22; Zhang F. 2014, 346–47.

13 See Zhang Cunhui's preface in CZJZBB, 2. Also see Zhou and He 2009, 49.

14 Zhang F. 2014, 346. For a comparable stele-shaped framing design for the dedicatory colophon illustrated in the *Lotus Sutra* frontispieces (dated 1330) by the Yuan painter Zhu Bao 朱珤(寶), see fig. 9.39b of this book; Ge 1995, 37 (fig. 13). This decorative convention may be traced back to the eight-century portable painting of the Buddha Preaching, originally discovered in the Dunhuang library cave and now in the British Museum (1919,0101,0.6); see Whitfield et al. 1990, pl. 1.

15 For comparable publisher's trademarks in bell shape, see Lin Shenqing 1999, 93, 109, 123.

16 Zhou and He 2009, 50. Among the illustrations updated or added by Zhang Cuihui are the "illustrations of three types of bamboo and two ways of making salt." See Zhang F. 2014, 346.

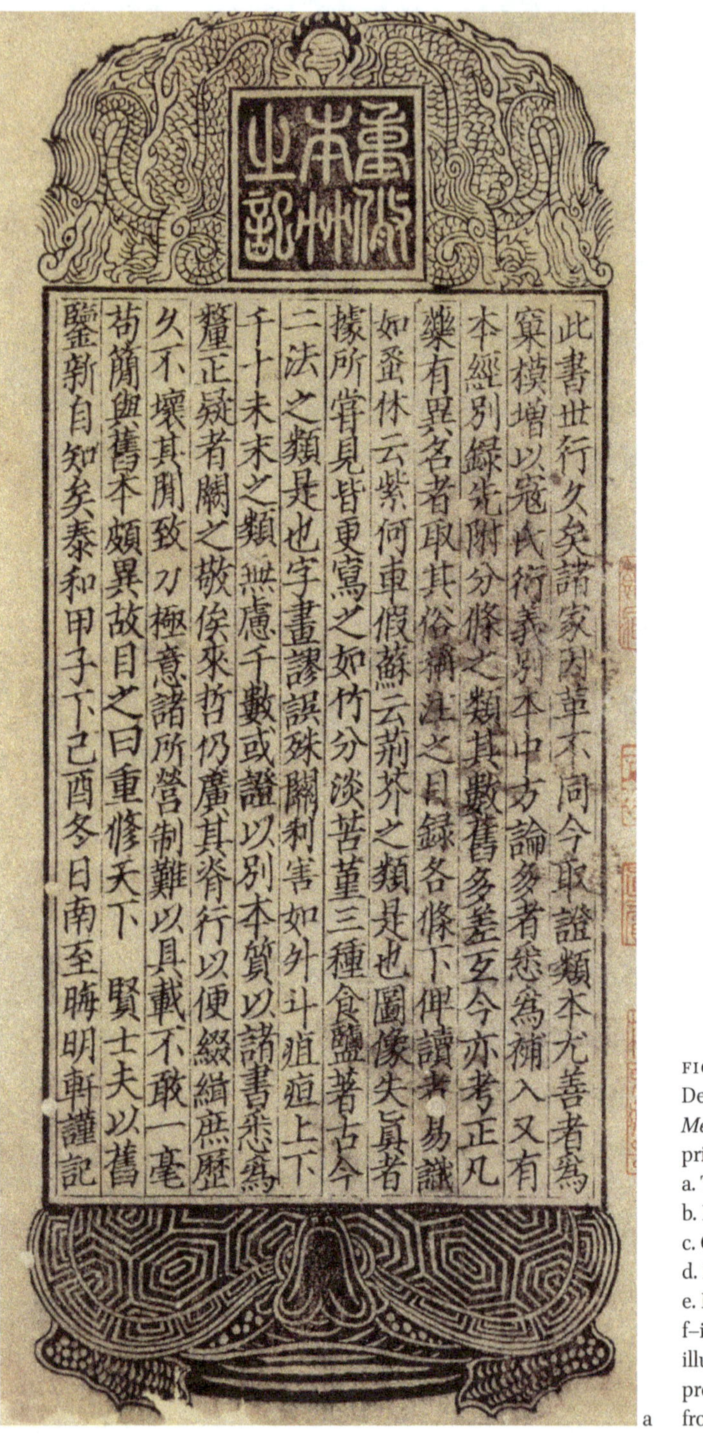

此書世行久矣諸家因革不同今取證類本尤善者為
窠模增以寇氏衍義別本中方論多者悉為補入又有
本經別錄先附分條之類其數舊多差互今亦考正凡
藥有異名者取其俗稱注之目錄各條下俾讀者易識
如蚤休云紫何車假蘇云荊芥之類是也圖像失真者
據所嘗見皆更寫之如竹分淡苦堇三種食鹽著古今
二法之類是也字畫謬誤殊關利害如升斗疽疸上下
千干未末之類無慮千數或證以別本質以諸書悉為
釐正疑者闕之敬俟來哲仍廣其脊行以便綴緝庶歷
久不壞其間致力極意諸所營制難以具載不敢一毫
苟簡與舊本頗異故目之曰重修天下　賢士夫以舊
鑒新自知矣泰和甲子下己酉冬日南至晦明軒謹記

a

FIGURES 5.4A–I
Details. *Revised Material Medica*. 1249. Woodblock print. National Library.
a. The publisher's colophon
b. Lychees
c. Grasshoppers from Shuzhou
d. Raw silver from Raozhou
e. Frogs
f–i. Details of continuous illustrations depicting the processes of extracting salt from water

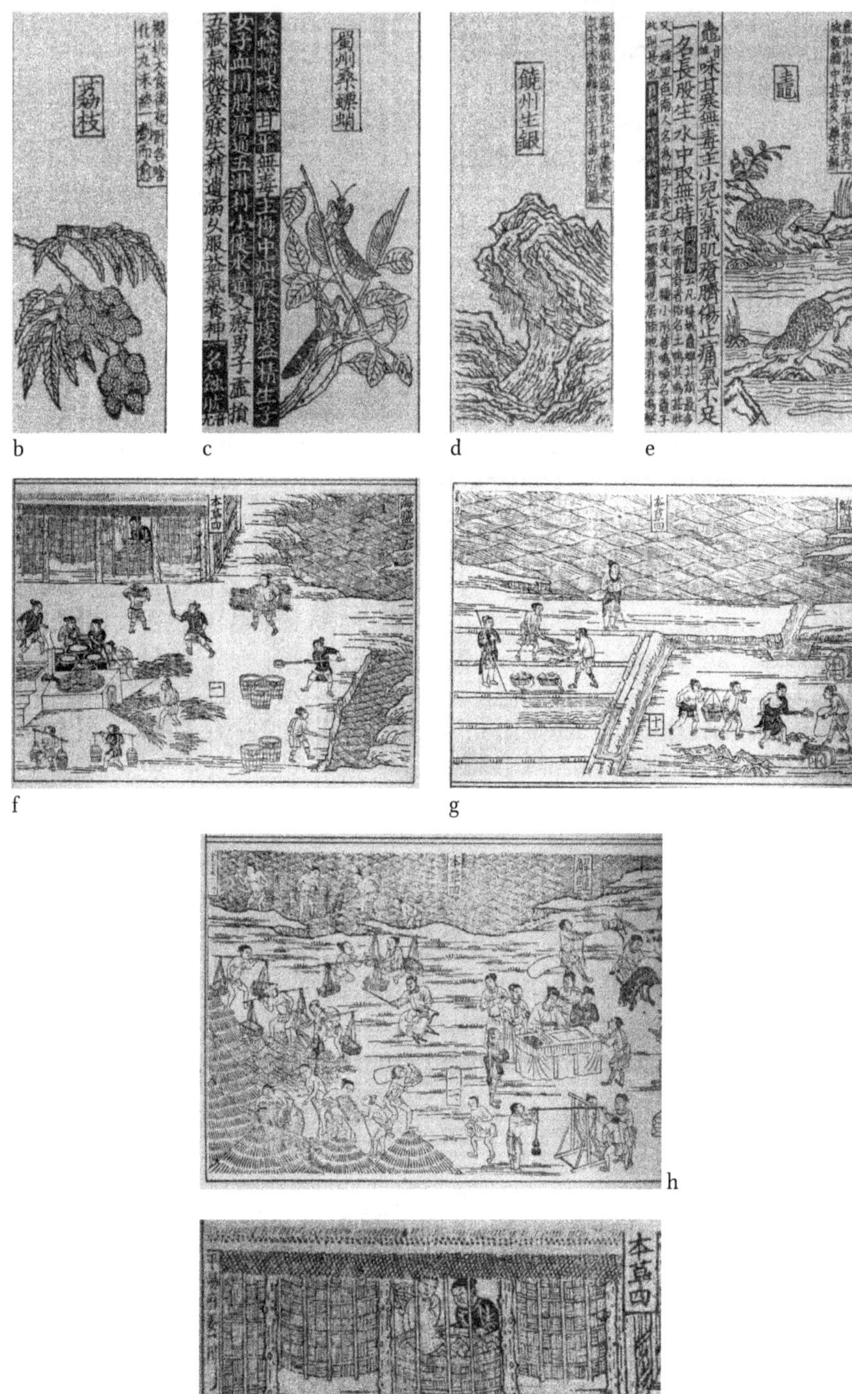
荔枝
蜀州桑螵蛸
饒州生銀
本草四
b
c
d
e
f
g
h
i

lychees (fig. 5.4b), and grasshoppers (fig. 5.4c), represent meticulously drawn items on cropped branches positioned diagonally. Quite possibly, such close-up and cropped views of plants and insects, originally available in Northern Song printed encyclopedias, inspired similar compositions in Southern Song painting that show birds, flowers, and insects in album leaves and fan paintings. While most illustrations do not show any background, some, notably those treating silver and frogs along river shores (figs. 5.4d–e), feature landscape settings with bodies of water, rocks, and mountains.[17] Viewed together, the *Revised Materia Medica* preserves not only the Song interest in natural science and medicine but also inherits its visual legacy in realistic representations of birds-and-flowers, fish, insects, and landscapes.

One of the illustrations constitutes a rather exceptional case. It consists of an expansive array of large-size, continuous narrative scenes that run through three full folded pages and represent panoramic views of labor-intensive activities concerning salt production (figs. 5.4f–h). A reader turning the pages of the book may view dynamic narrative scenes that show workers carrying buckets to transport water from the saline sea or lake surrounding the land, as well as other laborers working with pans and jars used for salt evaporation. The final page (fig. 5.4h) shows a government official seated at a desk, supervising what looks like a "harvest scene": workers weigh the salt with a mechanical device, while piles of salt lie on the ground alongside triangular straw mounds.[18] The meticulous renditions of man-made things demonstrate the Northern Song legacy not only in the artistic *jiehua* tradition but also in "know-how" books that use illustrations to explain complex procedures in science and technology.[19]

Another aspect of this work is the "local pride" the Shanxi publisher displays as he illustrates the salt-making process. These are the only illustrations that have a cutter's signature, notably "Jiang Yi from Pingyang" (Pingyang fu Jiang Yi 平陽府姜一) (figs. 5.4i), which appears on each of the three pages.[20] Jiang was among thirty or so cutters documented in the Zhang Family's reprint edition. Many cutters also worked on blocks for other books published in Pingyang at

17 For illustrations with landscape settings, see CZJZBB 3: 82; 4: 101–102, 109–10, 112; 5: 129, 133; 6: 168; 19: 404; 22: 448–49, 453–54.

18 For more discussions, see Miya 2018, 2: 835; Kobayashi 2017, 93–94 (fig. 13). For a comparable Ming imperial edition (dated 1587), whose printed illustration bear hand-painted colors, see Ma 2021, 50.

19 For a comparable *jiehua* painting, see the tenth-century *Water Mill* in Osaka Municipal Museum, well studied in Liu H. 2002.

20 Jiang's three signatures read, "Published by Jiang Yi of the Pingyang Prefecture" (Pingyang fu Jiang Yi kan 平陽府姜一刊), "Cut by Jiang Yi" (Jiang Yi diao 姜一刁), and "Cut by Jiang Yi of Pingshui" (Pingshui Jiang Yi diao 平水姜一刁). See also Lin Z. 2014, 538; Zhou and He 2009, 50.

the time.[21] The first illustration is labeled "Sea Salt" (*haiyan* 海鹽), referring to the general principle of salt production; quite possibly, it was based directly on a Northern Song original. The second and third pages bear the title "Xie [Area] Salt" (*Xieyan* 解鹽), referring to the government-controlled salt industry at the lakes in Xiezhou; they may be new additions celebrating southern Shanxi.[22] It is also possible that the Zhang Family was not the first publisher to insert the illustrations, especially since the preface mentions the consultation of an earlier edition by the Pang Family publisher in Xiezhou who may well have been the first to introduce these pictures.

2 Exhibiting Popular Culture in Pingyang Prints

While illustrated books reprinted in Pingyang best demonstrate the direct legacy of Northern Song arts and book culture, single-sheet prints in non-book form produced by local printshops showcase popular culture developing in southern Shanxi. The best examples are the *Four Beauties* by the printshop of the Ji Family in Pingyang (fig. 2.7) and the *Guan Yu* 關羽 (fig. 5.5) produced by the "Xu Family Printshop of the Pingyang Prefecture"; the latter features a popular martial god whose legendary birthplace was associated with Xiezhou. The two prints represent rare forerunners of the so-called "paper horse" (*zhima* 紙馬) or New Year's pictures (*nianhua* 年畫) (fig. 5.6),[23] printed ephemera displayed on walls either for festive celebrations or everyday decoration. Both prints were discovered in Khara Khoto, the ruins of the former Tangut Xi Xia kingdom (see ch. 6), suggesting the long-distance transmission of Jin prints.[24]

Even though the two prints were produced by different printshops, their common visual features reflect a local style. Both show a similar compositional template: the title is rendered horizontally in large calligraphy and placed on top of an elongated composition; in addition, there are intricate framing designs in meandering patterns on the borders.[25] Read from right to left,

21 For a chart detailing the cutters working on multiple books, see Lin Z. 2014, 536–37.

22 Salt was among the monopoly goods under government supervision. But the center of salt production in the Jin was Shandong, Manchuria and Mongolia, and not Shanxi; see Franke 1994a, 294–95.

23 ZGBHQJ 2; Wang S. 2008; Kobayashi 2017, 79.

24 The Pingyang prints were likely transmitted to Xi Xia via the Jin-Xi Xia interstate border markets and the Jin's courier network. See Franke 1994a, 297–98; Yang and Chen 2012, 62–97; Zhang and Han 2006, 178.

25 Past scholarship referred to such geometric patterns as the so-called "thunder patterns"; see Kobayashi 2017, 76.

FIGURE 5.5 *Guan Yu*. Jin. Woodblock print. Single sheet. Discovered in Khara Khoto. The State Hermitage Museum, St. Petersburg

FIGURE 5.6 Throne of the Stove God. Qing. Woodblock print. Ink and color on paper.

FIGURE 5.8 Detail of martial figures. Jin. Brick tomb, Pingyang, Shanxi

the title of the *Four Beauties* reads, "Elegant ladies of various dynasties, with beauty that could topple the kingdom" (*suichao yaotiao cheng qingguo zhi fangrong* 隨朝窈窕呈傾國之芳容) (fig. 2.7). Organized similarly, the title of the *Guan Yu* print reads, "Throne of the Loyal, Courageous, Martial, and Peaceful King" (*Yiyongwu'anwang wei* 義勇武安王位) (fig. 5.5). These titles recall horizontal banners displayed above theatrical stages, as shown in a wall painting of the Shuishen miao 水神廟 (Water God Temple) in Hongdong, southern Shanxi (fig. 5.7). This may well have served as a visual commemoration of a theatrical performance by an itinerant troupe, led by the lead actress Zhongduxiu 中都秀, who once performed in the temple to celebrate the completion of the renovation in 1324.[26]

A closer examination of the figural motifs in both prints suggests that the featured figures were all characters in popular drama and stories familiar to local viewers in southern Shanxi. They include the historical beauties Wang Zhaojun 王昭君 (ca. 54–19 BCE) and Banji 班姬 (ca. 45–117) (fig. 2.7), the martial hero Guan Yu (fig. 5.5), celebrated in the fictional history of the Three

26 Zhang F. 2014, 344. For more studies, see Jing 2001; Huang 2012, 206 (fig. 4.18); Qu 2018, 53–59.

FIGURE 5.7 Theatrical performance. 1324. Yuan. Mural. South wall of the Water God Temple, Hongdong, Shanxi

Kingdoms (Sanguo 三國) period (220–280) as well as a popular martial god.[27] The loud designs of the meticulous geometric and floral designs crowding the figures' garments, headdresses, and floral hats may reflect the gaudy garments of performing entertainers at the time. Some types, such as the martial figures holding flags and weapons in the *Guan Yu* print, match designs found in a brick tomb in Pingyang (fig. 5.8).[28] Selected "stage props" in the *Four Beauties*, such

27 For the most updated study of Guan Yu in religious culture, see Haar 2017 (Xiezhou was identified as the center of the cult in north China; see ch. 4). Multiple Ming-Qing printed versions of illustrative booklets on the cult of Guan Yu address him as the Loyal, Courageous, Martial, and Peaceful King, and trace his origin to Xiezhou, Shanxi; for a specimen printed in 1564, see ZGDJBHQJ 12: 109–14.

28 For more visual examples, see Shanxi sheng kaogu yanjiusuo 1999. The pine tree in the *Guan Yu* print recalls similar motifs in the other anonymous single-sheet print (X-2531) discovered in Khara Khoto and now in Hermitage Museum, likely also a product of Jin Pingyang; see Piotrovsky 1993, 242–43 (pl. 63).

FIGURE 5.9
Detail of General Mengtian. Yuan. Blue and white ceramic. Vase. Excavated in Changde, Hunan. Hunan Provincial Museum

as Banji's fan with an ink bamboo painting and Wang Zhaojun's scroll showing mock writing in cursive script, evoke a more elite taste introduced into folk art. The rolled-up hair style of Luzhu 綠珠, furthermore, is reminiscent of Northern Song court style, reflected in the female attendant in the Seiryōji *Maitreya* single-sheet print illustrated by Gao Wenjin (fig. 2.18e). Based on these stylistic connections, Kobayashi Hiromitsu suggested that both *Four Beauties* and *Guan Yu* may have been based on earlier single-sheet prints made in Northern Song Kaifeng.[29]

Some of the pictorial designs were transmitted and repurposed later in other media. A Yuan blue-and-white porcelain dish excavated in Hunan (fig. 5.9), for example, recycles the pictorial convention of a seated general and a soldier holding a flag as illustrated in the Xu Family print (fig. 5.5). The flag identifies the seated figure as "General Mengtian" (Mengtian jiangjun 蒙恬將軍),

29 Kobayashi 2017, 75–79.

possibly a character in the fourteenth-century popular novel about the Qin unifying the other six states.[30]

Intriguingly, these Pingyang prints were discovered among the Xi Xia ruins in Khara Khoto, over a thousand miles away from their original place of production. They were found alongside the Jin printed script of the earliest extant "all-keys-and-modes" (*zhugongdiao* 諸宮調), a popular colloquial literary form used in storytelling, probably also produced in southern Shanxi.[31] The script features a romantic story local to Shanxi: its protagonist was the tenth-century Liu Zhiyuan 劉知遠 (895–948), a native of Taiyuan and local official in southern Shanxi who ascended the throne of the Later Han 後漢 (947–950) as Gaozu 高祖 (r. 947–948). The author of the script used vernacular idioms native to the area, reflecting that he himself was from this region.[32] The "all-keys-and-modes" penetrated into funerary art as well. The tomb of a lay woman named Zhang, dated 1200 and located in Houma, about 48 miles south to Pingyang, bears three walls of citations identified as part of the *Three Kingdoms Records in All-Keys-and-Modes* (*Sanguozhi zhugongdiao* 三國志諸宮調), transcribed in modest ink calligraphy.[33] The content touches upon the heroes of the Three Kingdoms contemporaneous to Guan Yu, whose deified image as a martial god is represented in the Xu Family print (fig. 5.5).

The transmission of the "all-keys-and-modes" script as well as the two Pingyang single-sheet prints to the Xi Xia territory in northwest China suggest that there was widespread interstate circulation of Pingyang printing and theatrical culture. In fact, excavated documents from Khara Khoto record trading information associated with the Jin and Xi Xia border markets, located in northern Shanxi, Inner Mongolia, Shaanxi, and Gansu (map 0.2).[34] Other historical sources also note that the Xi Xia government sent envoys to acquire Confucian and Buddhist books from the Jin, including the Jin Canon whose original blocks were carved in Shanxi.[35]

30 Shanghai bowuguan 2012, pl. 68.

31 Idema 1978; Idema 2018, 1–38; Franke 1994a, 309; Long 2003; Li W. 2014, 76–93; Zhang F. 2014, 343–44, 350–51 (for the specimen in the National Library of China, see fig. 19).

32 Long 2003, 32, 78–79.

33 For the "all-keys-and-modes" copied in ink on the north and south walls of the Tomb M4 in Ershui, Houma, see Li W. 2014, 86–87. For a study, see Yan 2003.

34 Yang and Chen 2012, 63–99, especially 83, 86, 96.

35 JS 60: 1408; Yang and Chen 2012, 205.

3 The Jin Canon

The prospering print culture in southern Shanxi opens a window into the local and historical context of Buddhist printing. The most sensational story here is that of the Jin Canon (figs. 5.10a–b), parts of which were first discovered in the 1930s in the Guangshengsi 廣勝寺 (Monastery of Encompassing Victory), located in Hongdong, Zhaocheng (map 0.4).[36] Some texts were printed from original blocks, others from later ones added to the original. Soon after his visit to the temple in 1934, Jiang Weixin published an extensive report on the find.[37] He still saw the golden inscription, "Long Live the Emperor" (*huangdi wansui* 皇帝萬歲), on a pillar in the main hall, indicative of the temple's glory under the Yuan, when the court placed imperial portraits here.[38] Jiang further notes that the printed specimens of the Jin Canon were carefully stored in six large bookcases inside the Maitreya Hall of the upper monastery section (*shangsi* 上寺).[39] 4957 *juan* in total, these texts were mounted in scroll format; most were printed on white mulberry paper, but some also used yellow wax paper.[40] Jiang estimates that about a quarter of the extant specimens came from later blocks that were recut in Beijing in the thirteenth century.[41]

In order to protect the Canon during the Sino-Japanese war, it was relocated several times between 1938 and 1942. The monks first hid it in the pagoda near the main hall, then Communist troops moved it into a deserted coal mine. The relocation resulted in partial damage, dispersion, and loss. Some villagers picked up individual specimens and used them to wrap medicines or repair windows. Surviving sections became part of the collection of the National Library in 1949. After seventeen years of conservation, this incomplete set joined the Dunhuang manuscripts, the Ming *Yongle Encyclopedia* (*Yongle dadian* 永樂大典), and the Qing-dynasty *Complete Books of the Four*

---

36 They are duly reproduced in the *Zhonghua dazangjing* 中華大藏經; see ZHDZJ. For more about Guangsheng Monastery, see Steinhardt 2024, 127–32.

37 Jiang 1977; Li 2002b, 104–108; Li F. 1991; Li F. 2012; Wang Z. 2003; Xian 2010; Zhang D. 2006. For the architectural details, murals, and sculptures of the Guangsheng Monastery, see Chai and Ren 2006.

38 Jiang 1977, 217–18; Jing 1991; 1994, 53.

39 For the temple compound of the upper monastery, see Chai and Ren 2006, 17–46. For a recent study, see Qu 2018.

40 The original Jin Canon was estimated to have 7000 *juan*, filling 682 sutra cases; see Jiang 1977, 222; Li 2002b, 104. For the extant copies of the Jin Canon in the National Library in Beijing, see the reproductions in ZCJZ.

41 Jiang 1977, 226; Su 1964b, 15.

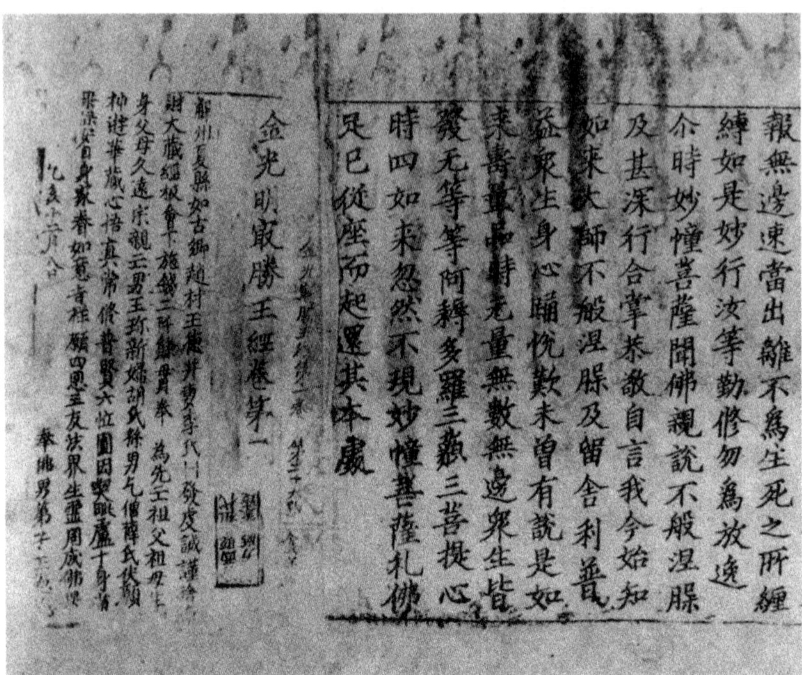

報無邊速當出離不為生死之所纏
縛如是妙行汝等勤修勿為放逸
尒時妙幢菩薩聞佛親說不般涅槃
及甚深行合掌恭敬自言我今始知
如來大師不般涅槃及留舍利普
益衆生身心踊悅歎未曾有說是如
來壽量品時无量無數無邊衆生皆
發无等等阿耨多羅三藐三菩提心
時四如來忽然不現妙幢菩薩礼佛
足已從座而起還其本處

金光明最勝王經卷第一

a

稱計也四者天地成已久住不壞不
可以日月歲數而稱計也是為四事
長久無量無限不可以日月歲數而
計量也

頌曰
百旬芥易盡 三災理自傾 石火無恒燄
電光非久停 飢寒自相啖 刀兵競相征
疫病無醫勠 空勞怨苦聲 覩感無相救
殘害有餘情 遺文虛滿目 徒欣冒貴纏
太息波川逝 悲斯苦業縈 生滅恒數遍
煎迫未安寧

法苑珠林卷第一

大宋咸平元年奉
勅印

b

FIGURES 5.10A–B Extant specimens of the Jin Canon. Jin. Woodblock print
a. Donor's colophon, *Golden Light Sutra*, juan 1
b. Colophon copied after the Northern Song Kaibao Canon. *Fayuan zhulin*, juan 1

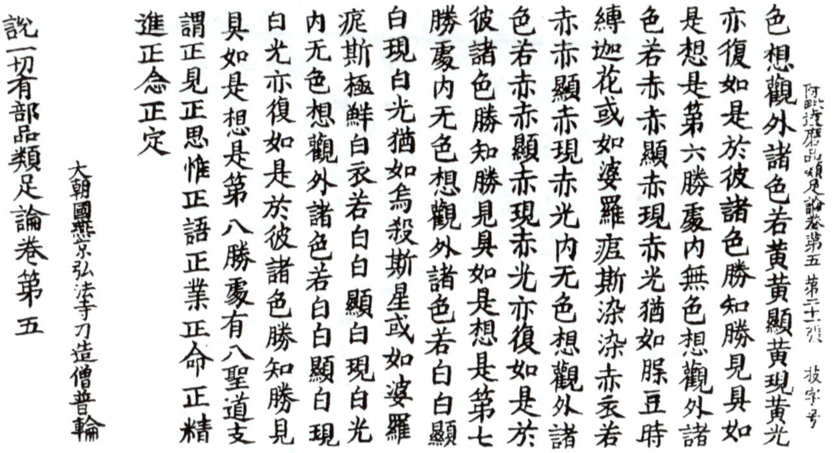

阿毗達磨品類足論卷第五 第二十一張 枝字号
色想觀外諸色若黃黃顯黃現黃光
亦復如是於彼諸色勝知勝見具如
是想是第六勝處內無色想觀外諸
色若赤赤顯赤現赤光猶如槃豆時
縛迦花或如婆羅痆斯染染赤衣若
赤赤顯赤現赤光內无色想觀外諸
色若赤赤顯赤現赤光亦復如是於
彼諸色勝知勝見具如是想是第七
勝處內无色想觀外諸色若白白顯
白現白光猶如烏殺斯星或如婆羅
痆斯極鮮白衣若白白顯白現白光
內无色想觀外諸色若白白顯白現
白光亦復如是於彼諸色勝知勝見
具如是想是第八勝處有八聖道支
謂正見正思惟正語正業正命正精
進正念正定
大朝國燕京弘法寺刁造僧普輪
說一切有部品類足論卷第五

FIGURE 5.11 Detail. *Shuo yiqie you bu pin lei zu lun*, juan 5. 13th century. Woodblock print

FIGURE 5.12 Frontispiece to the *Mahāprajñāpāramitā Sutra*, juan 103. 13th century. National Library of China

Repositories (*Siku quanshu* 四庫全書) as one of the Library's top treasures.[42] Because it was discovered in Zhaocheng, it came to be called the Jin Canon from Zhaocheng (*Zhaocheng Jinzang* 趙城金藏).[43]

42 For a discussion of the repair, see Du 2003. For more studies, see Li 2002b, 107–108; Chai and Ren 2006, 13.

43 For the true size reproductions of the extant specimens, see ZHDZJ.

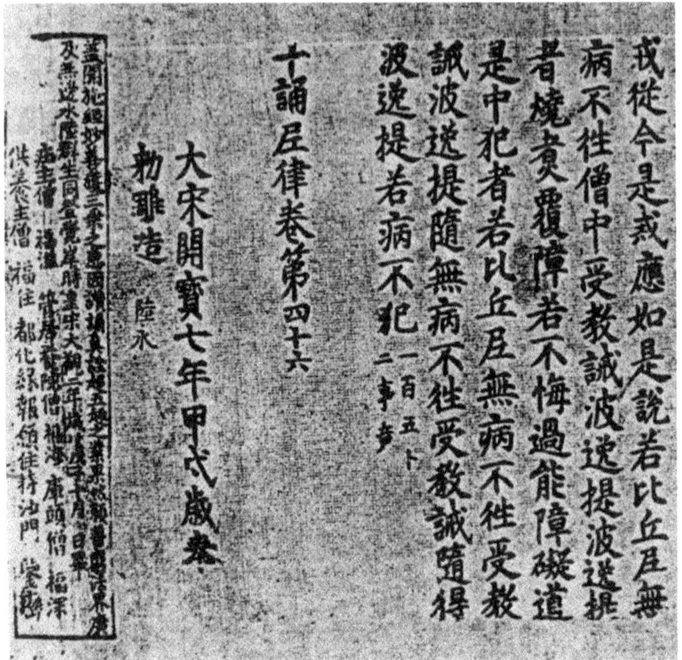
戒從今是戒應如是說若比丘尼無
病不往僧中受教誡波逸提波逸提
者燒煮覆障若不悔過能障礙道
是中犯者若比丘尼無病不往受教
誡波逸提隨無病不往受教誡隨得
波逸提若病不犯一百五十二事竟
十誦尼律卷第四十六
大宋開寶七年甲戌歲奉
勑雕造 陸永

FIGURE 5.13 Detail. *Shisong ni lü*, juan 46. Kaibao Canon. Calligraphy Museum, Taitō, Tokyo

The Jin Canon (fig. 5.10b) is a direct copy of the Northern Song Kaibao Canon (fig. 5.13).[44] Both versions share a similar textual layout, each line containing fourteen characters. The Jin Canon has a further single line as part of the framing design on the upper and lower borders, which the Kaibao Canon lacks. Selected Northern Song colophons found in the Kaibao Canon, such as the one dated 998 by the government-sponsored printing bureau, were directly copied in the Jin Canon (fig. 5.10b), further highlighting the Song-Jin connection. It is likely that samples of the Kaibao Canon were at the disposal of the producers of the Jin Canon. This is suggested by multiple specimens of the Kaibao Canon that bear a dedicatory colophon (dated 1108) by the monk Jianluan (figs. 2.29e, 5.13), abbot of the Qingliansi, located in southeast Shanxi (map 0.4).[45]

Unlike the Liao Canon (see ch. 4), which was commissioned by the Khitan ruling house and produced by elite monks living in imperially sponsored

44 Li 2002b, 108.

45 A temple stele dated 1105 documents Jianluan's endeavor to rebuild and expand the temple, including also the renovation of a building as a sutra library to house the newly acquired printed sutras; see Chen Yuquan 2009, 166–68.

temples in Yanjing, the Jin Canon was supported by a grass-roots network in rural northern China. The block cutting, supervised by a community organization based in the Tianning Monastery in Anyi, Xiezhou, took a little over thirty years to complete (map 0.4).[46] Fund-raising campaigns led by the Buddhist master Yin Shennai 尹矧迺 (?–1176) and his disciples, including a young woman called Cui Fazhen 崔法珍 (?–ca. 1183), solicited support from villagers to pay for the cutting. Sometime after 1178, thanks to her effort, the blocks were transported to the capital in Beijing and housed in a royally sponsored temple. Following this, the Jin Canon went through an "afterlife," as the temple reprinted its blocks to provide on-demand service to other temples and individuals nationwide.[47]

After the Mongol conquest of Beijing in the thirteenth century, new blocks (fig. 5.11) were cut in the same temple to replace worn out ones. Copies of the Jin Canon found in the Guangsheng Monastery in the 1930s may well have been printed in Beijing with blocks both original and recut. The monastery commissioned the printshop of the local Pang Family to furnish its printed Jin Canon; besides mounting the texts in scrolls, they also added a uniform frontispiece design to each text (fig. 5.12; hereafter the Guangsheng frontispiece).[48] A customized label that reads "Guangsheng Monastery in Zhaocheng County" (*Zhaocheng xian Guangsheng si* 趙城縣廣勝寺) is embedded in each frontispiece, highlighting local pride and the monastery's exclusive sponsorship. The height of the frontispiece is taller than that of the framed text it accompanies, an inconsistency that suggests that it was not part of the original Jin Canon but later added in the mid-thirteenth century.

3.1 *Mapping the Social Network: Villager-Donors, Fund-Raisers, and Temples*

Over forty dated donors' colophons preserved in the extant specimens shed light on the local network. The earliest colophon dates to 1149; the latest, to 1173. As marked in map 0.4, documented donors were mainly villagers living within 200 miles of the project's headquarters in the Tianning Monastery in Anyi. They bear witness to a concentric network, centered in southwest Shanxi

46 Chen Haodong questioned the received wisdom and argued that the Tianning Monastery in charge of the printing of the Jin Canon was not the one in Xiezhou, but the one in Jiangzhou 絳州. He also argued that the Guanghuasi 廣化寺 (Monastery of Wide Transformation) in Puzhou 蒲州 may have been the other hub in charge of the printing of the Jin Canon block. See Chen H. 2018.

47 For an example of such a request, see the Puzhaosi 普照寺 (Monastery of Universal Radiance) discussed in Jiang 1977, 233.

48 See ZGBHQJ 1: 65.

and expanding to the southeastern and central parts of Shanxi, as well as to Shaanxi in the west.[49]

A close reading of selected colophons reveals most donors' humble economic means. Ma Fuchang 馬福昌 and his younger brother from a village in Anyi (map 0.4), for example, "donated a home-raised living mule" (*she ziji jia shengluo yitou* 捨自己家生騾一頭), which caused them to be listed as the sponsors of seven *juan* of the canon. Other donations came in various forms, including fabric donated by a woman in Anyi, a knife from a woman named Dong, a Buddhist statue offered by a villager from Ronghe 榮河, and "fifty branches of a pear tree" (*lishu wushi gen* 梨樹五十根) donated by Yang Chang 楊昌 from Wanquan 萬泉 (map 0.4).[50] Yang's pear tree branches probably were useful raw materials for woodblocks.[51]

While it seems reasonable to assume that villagers who gave donations in kind constituted mainstream resources, the case of Wang De 王德 from Xiaxian 夏縣 is an exception. His grand donation of two thousand strings of cash caused his name to be listed repetitively in ten cases of texts throughout the Jin Canon, including the one shown here (fig. 5.10a).[52] As of the late twelfth century, one string could purchase about twenty-four liters of rice.[53] Compared to other households who contributed animals and trees they raised themselves, Wang De was far wealthier.

It is also likely that the donors of the Jin Canon included ethnic non-Han people. In this context, Zhang Xiumin calls attention to an unusual Jurchen donor, a woman called Tudan 徒單, maybe a servant working for the Wang Family in Taiyuan. Her humble contribution supported the cost of a woodblock.[54]

As noted earlier, Cui Fazhen and her Buddhist teacher Master Yin Shennai were two major agents soliciting funds for the cutting of the canon. Information about the Master Yin is sparse, but his leadership of the Jin Canon project is recorded on a stele in the Dayinsi 大陰寺 (Monastery of Great Seclusion) in Jiangxian 絳縣 (map 0.4), southern Shanxi, dated 1297.[55] A native of Huaizhou

49 Jiang 1977, 223–26; Li 2002b, 105. Li Fuhua estimated that there were about 140 colophons; see Li F. 1991, 3.

50 Jiang 1977, 225–26; Zhang and Han 2006, 183 (esp. footnote 1).

51 Cf. the Southern Song monk Liaoqin 了懃, whose donation in 1216 funded thirty pear woodblocks for the Qisha Canon; see Li 2002a, 132; Li 2002b, 120.

52 Jiang 1977, 225–26.

53 Von Glahn 2010, 470*n*13; Qi X. 1999, 2: 1241.

54 Zhang and Han 2006, 182.

55 The stele was engraved by Yang Yuan 楊瑗, and commissioned by the monk Liaowei 了威 of the Dayin Monastery. The text was composed by Monk Wenxiu 文秀; the title of the stele was inscribed by Monk Baoding 寶定. For a complete transliteration of the stele, see Wang Z. 2003, 16–17. For more studies, see Yang 2002; Wang Z. 2003; Xian 2010; Zhang D.

懷州 (in modern Henan), he visited many Buddhist pilgrimage sites. At the Guanyin pagoda in Sizhou 泗州, Anhui, he burnt his left arm to receive the bodhisattva's magical support. On his way to Mt. Wutai, he encountered Emperor Huizong of the Northern Song in Guide 歸德 prefecture (Henan). The emperor was moved by his devotion and bestowed an orchard upon him that was later turned into a monastery. On Mt. Wutai, Yin further witnessed the manifestation of Mañjuśrī and had a vision of the Buddha who advised him to cut blocks of the Buddhist canon in the Jin-Jiang 晉絳 area (southern Shanxi).[56]

In rural Shanxi, he recruited numerous lay disciples to help him with the printing of the Canon, including also his major successor, the woman Cui Fazhen, originally from Luzhou 潞州 (map 0.4). During the Song-Jin wars, Luzhou was the headquarters of the Jurchen troops; its relatively stable and prosperous social situation caused the town to become home to major donors of the Jin Canon.[57] To show her parents her determination to follow Master Yin, Cui severed her left arm. Altogether Master Yin attracted about 3000 disciples to the Tianning Monastery in Jintai 金台, matching the name of the institution in Xiezhou, where the Jin Canon block cutting took place.[58] The master and his disciples "traveled through He 河 (Hedong), Xie 解 (Xiezhou), Xi 隰 (Xixian), Ji 吉 (Jixian), Pingshui 平水, and Jiangyang 絳陽 (Jiangzhou)"—mostly rural places located between Pingyang and Jiangxian (map 0.4)—to "solicit funds for building more temples and cutting the blocks of the Buddhist canon."[59] Master Yin died in 1176, two years before the blocks of the canon were completed. The unfinished project passed down to Cui Fazhen, then also known as the "young maiden bodhisattva" (*tongnü pusa* 童女菩薩).[60] Among her many accomplishments was the Jin court's endorsement, making it possible for the blocks to be transported to the capital and stored in a temple for wider circulation.[61]

The story of Cui's submission of the Jin Canon to the Jin court in Beijing is well documented. Li Jining notes the importance of the lengthy record inserted in a text and added to the Qisha 磧砂 Canon in the Ming dynasty (fig. 5.14). Dated 1411 and entitled *Monastic Record of the Initiating [Story of]*

2006. For more on the irrigation projects organized by the monks of the Dayin Monastery to establish "systems of water use that gave priority to Buddhist communities" in the thirteenth century, see Wang J. 2018, 186–87.

56 Wang Z. 2003, 16.

57 About fifteen colophons in the Jin Canon acknowledge that donors were from Luzhou; see Li F. 1991, 5. For Luzhou's role in Song-Jin war, see Hsu Y. 2021, 116–17.

58 Wang Z. 2003, 18 (endnote 28).

59 Wang Z. 2003, 17; Zhang D. 2006, 33.

60 Wang Z. 2003, 17; Zhang D. 2006, 34.

61 Wang Z. 2003, 17.

the Woodblocks of the Buddhist Canon by the Imperially Awarded Great Master Hongjiao (*Zuichu chici Hongjiao dashi diaozangjingban yuan ji* 最初勑賜弘教大師雕藏經板院記; hereafter *Monastic Record*), this was narrated by the early Ming monk Bao Shanhui 鮑善恢 (ca. 1403–1424) from Hangzhou. Partially based on a now-lost Jin government-issued stele composed by the high-ranking official Zhao Feng 趙渢, it dates from 1193.[62] It says,

> Fazhen, the daughter of Cui Jin from Changzi county in the state of Lu, from early childhood was deeply interested in Buddhist teachings. At the age of thirteen, she severed her arm and became a nun. She once vowed to cut the woodblocks of the Buddhist canon. It took her over thirty years to achieve this goal. In 1178, she presented one set of the printed canon to the court. Upon imperial order, monks from the ten major monasteries in the Left and Right Streets of the capital welcomed her and the canon with fragrant flowers. She was then hosted at the Da Sheng'ansi 大聖安寺 (Great Monastery of Sagely Peace) …
>
> An imperial edit ordered the Sheng'an Monastery to set up an ordination platform for her, shave her hair, and receive her oaths as a nun. [The court] awarded [her] tens of thousands of cash, withdrawing 5,000,000 from the Prime Ministry to transport the blocks. By 1181, all blocks had made it to the capital. There were 168,113 blocks in total, with 6980 *juan* of texts. The court ordered five well-versed monks including Daozun to collate them properly. In 1183, the court bestowed an honorary purple robe upon Fachun and gave her the honorific title "Great Master Who Advocates the Teachings" …
>
> The blocks were stored in the Da Haotian Monastery in order to facilitate the canon's circulation … Liu Fashan and over fifty others [showed their devotion and) severed their arms, burned off their fingers, poked out their eyes, or cut open their livers. Some even gave up their family property and sold their sons and daughters in order to help to fund the block cutting of the canon, which took thirty years altogether …
>
> 潞州長子縣崔進之女，名法珍，自幼好道，年十三歲，斷臂出家。嘗發誓願，雕造藏經。垂三十年，方克有成。大定十有八年，始印經

62 Li Jining first discovered this record at the end of the *Dabao jijing* 大寶積經, *juan* 29, a text discovered inside the Buddhist statue of the Bolinsi 柏林寺 (Monastery of the Cypress Forest) in Beijing in 1966; see Li Jining 1998, 70–71. Because the text of the 1193 stele was composed of the Jin official Zhao Feng, he calls it the "Zhao Feng Stele." See Li 2002b, 109–13; ZWFJWX 3.32: 446–63; Zhang and Han 2006, 182–83. Inscriptions are preserved in JWZ 111: 1592–93.

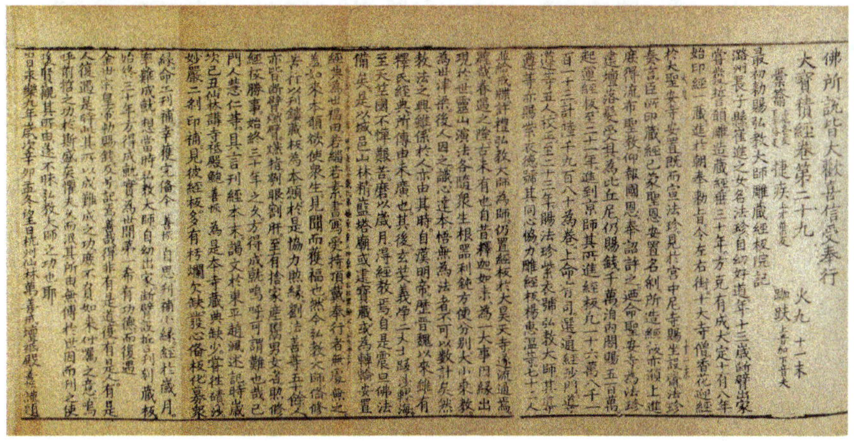

FIGURE 5.14 Detail of *Monastic Record by Bao Shanhui*. At the end of *Dabao jijing*, juan 29. Qisha Canon. 1411. Ming. Woodblock print

> 一藏進於朝。奉勑旨，令左右街十大寺僧，香花迎經，於大聖安寺安置……
>
> 奉詔許之，乃命聖安寺為法珍建壇，落髮受具，為比丘尼。乃賜錢千萬，洎内閣賜五百萬，起運經板。至二十一年，進到京師。其所進經板，几一十六萬八千一百一十三，及陸千九百八十為卷。上命有司選通經沙門導遵等五人校正。至二十三年，賜法珍紫衣，號弘教大師……
>
> 仍置經板於大昊天寺，遂流通焉……劉法善等五十餘人，亦皆斷臂、燃臂、燃指、剜眼、割肝，至有捨家產、鬻男女者，助修經板盛事，始終三十年之久……[63]

3.2 *The Jin Canon in Beijing*

After its blocks were transported to Beijing, the Jin Canon had an influential afterlife, mostly because temples and individuals nationwide could pay to request copies of selected texts. While the *Monastic Record* by the Hangzhou monk Bao Shanhui in 1411 identifies the Haotian Monastery as the temple storing the blocks,[64] other sources place it into the Hongfa Monastery in the Central Capital. The latter includes the local gazetteer on Yuan-dynasty Beijing (*Shuntian fuzhi* 順天府志), transcribed in the imperially sponsored *Yongle Encyclopedia* of the early Ming. It says:

---

63 For a punctuated transliteration of the record, see Li 2002b, 109–10. For more about Bao Shanhui, see Li 2002a, 127–28.

64 For the location of the temple in Liao-Jin Beijing, see Li R. 2016, 287; Yue 2005, 85.

> The Hongfa Monastery was located in the historical district [of Beijing]. Fazhen, the daughter of Cui Jin, submitted one set of the printed canon to the [Jin] court in 1178. [The court] ordered the Sheng'an Monastery to set up an ordination platform for Fazhen and sanction her as a nun. In 1181, the blocks were transported to the capital [Beijing]. In 1183, [Fazhen] was granted an imperial purple robe and [the honorable title of] "Great Master who Advocates the Teachings." The Hongfa Monastery stored the blocks in the area west of the temple. A stele was erected to commemorate the event in 1193. [It was] composed by Zhao Feng, the Assistant Director of the Palace Library and the Senior Compiler of the Hanlin Academy. Dang Huaiying, the Expositor-in-waiting at the Hanlin Academy, wrote the title of the stele in seal script.
>
> 弘法寺在舊城。金大定十八年潞州崔進女法珍印經一藏進于朝，命聖安寺設壇為法珍受戒為比丘尼。二十一年以經版達京師。二十三年賜紫衣弘教大師。以弘法寺收貯經版，及弘法寺西地與之。明昌四年立碑石，秘書丞兼翰林修撰趙渢記。翰林侍講學士黨懷英篆額。[65]

Intriguingly, the text credits Zhao Feng with the stele inscription, copied in full by Bao Shanhui in his *Monastic Record* and contained in the Qisha canon. It is likely that he provided misleading information, confusing the Haotian and Hongfa Monasteries.

Additional sources suggest that blocks of the Jin Canon were stored in the Hongfa Monastery. Both institutions were sponsored by the Khitan Liao imperial house (map 4.2) in the eleventh century (ch. 4), but only the Hongfa Monastery was engaged in printing, evident from extant scriptures printed by the temple as well as from records of its leading monks who managed, collated, and supervised the printing of various Buddhist books, including the Canon (table 4.4). A late twelfth-century epigraphic source further identifies it as the temple where the Jin Canon was printed. In 1187, the monk Zhizhao 智照 (d. 1195) from the Puzhaosi 普照寺 (Monastery of Universal Radiance) in Jizhou 濟州, Shandong, heard that the Hongfa Monastery kept the blocks of the Canon; he duly went there and requested two sets.[66] He paid for them with 2,000,000 strings of cash and stored them in two locations in his home temple. The first set he placed in

---

65 For a punctuated version of *Yongle Encyclopedia, juan* 4650, see Su 1964b, 14–15.

66 Cited from a stele composed by Zhao Feng, also author of the stele cited in the *Monastic Record*. See the "Stupa Memorial for Chan Master Zhaogong from the Puzhao chansi in Jizhou" (*Jizhou Puzhao chansi Zhaogong chanshi taming* 濟州普照禪寺照公禪師塔銘) in JWZ 111: 1592–94; Jiang 1977, 232–33.

a revolving sutra cabinet: it was printed in scroll format and mounted in yellow brocade and red rods. The second he stored in bookcases attached to the temple's interior walls: it was mounted in "Indian-style booklet format" (*fance* 梵冊) and packaged in lacquer boxes with gold inscriptions.[67]

After the Mongols took over Beijing in the latter half of the thirteenth century, the Hongfa Monastery recruited monk-cutters from the Imperial Secretariat District (Zhongshu sheng 中書省)—an area beyond Beijing that covers what are today Hebei, Shandong, and Shanxi—to cut new blocks and replace old ones.[68] Extant specimens previously owned by the Guangsheng Monastery preserve such added texts, each ending with a colophon that acknowledges the cutters, such as "monk cutter Pulun at the Hongfa Monastery in Yanjing, the Great Dynasty Country" (*Dachaoguo Yanjing Hongfasi diaozao seng Pulun* 大朝國燕京弘法寺雕造僧普輪) (fig. 5.11), and "Wang Puci of this temple" (*bensi Wang Puci* 本寺王普慈), probably a monk of the Hongfa Monastery.[69] Monk-cutters also came from other temples, located in the larger Imperial Secretariat District.[70] Because Yanjing was the official name of Beijing under the Mongols from 1215 to 1264, it is likely that Pulun and other monk-cutters added blocks to the Jin Canon at this time, that is, before the Yuan dynasty was officially established.[71] The other six colophons in the added blocks give the dates of 1238, 1242, and 1243, suggesting that the replacement blocks were added then.[72]

3.3 *Later Added Frontispieces*

There are four kinds of frontispiece designs attached to the texts of the Jin Canon, dating from the late twelfth to the early fourteenth centuries. The first three appear in extant printed specimens discovered in the Guangshang Monastery (fig. 5.12), at Dunhuang (fig. 5.15a), and in Turfan (figs. 5.16a–b). While the extant texts associated with them were probably printed at the Hongfa Monastery, they themselves were added later by individual owners in various locales.

The Guangsheng frontispiece design is best known among the three; it was replicated hundreds of times as illustrated at the openings of many texts in the

67 Cf. Hao Chunwen's discussion of the so-called "fan jiazhuang" 梵夾裝 format of Dunhuang manuscripts; Stephen F. Teiser translated the term as the "Brāhama (or Indian-style) board format," or "pothi format." See Teiser's translation of Hao 2020, 20.

68 Jiang 1977, 227–29.

69 Su 1964b, 15.

70 Jiang 1977, 228–29.

71 ZHDZJ 44: 39a; Jiang 1977, 229; Su 1964b, 15; Dang 1999, 117.

72 Called "budiao" 補雕, these added blocks were thus identified as the reprint version.

a

FIGURES 5.15A–B
Details. *Avatamsaka Sutra*. Jin Canon. Discovered in Mogao Cave B53, Dunhuang, Gansu

b

華嚴經第

十佛刹微塵數世界圍
佛号遍法界普照明
諸佛子如是十不可說佛刹
香水海中有十不可說佛刹微塵數
世界種皆依現一切菩薩形摩尼王
幢荘嚴蓮花住各各荘嚴際无有間
斷各各放寶色光明各各光明雲而
覆其上各各荘嚴具各各刧差別各
各佛出現各各演法海各各衆生遍
充滿各各十方普趣入各各一切佛
神力所加持此一一世界種中一切
世界依種種荘嚴住遞相接連成世
界網於花藏荘嚴世界海種種差別
周遍建立尒時普賢菩薩欲重宣其
義承佛威力而說頌言
花藏世界海 法界等无別 荘嚴極清淨
安住於虛空 此世界海中 刹種難思議
一一皆自在 各各無雜乱 花藏世界海

a

b

FIGURES 5.16A–B
Details. *Buddha Preaching* frontispiece (MIK III 23). Yuan. Woodblock print. Museum für Asiatische Kunst, Berlin
a. Complete View
b. Detail of the donor's family

FIGURE 5.17 Detail of fig. 6.55. Frontispiece to the "Vows of Samantabhadra" chapter from the *Avatamsaka Sutra* (TK 142). Xi Xia. Woodblock print. Concertina. Institute of Oriental Manuscripts, St. Petersburg

extant Jin Canon discovered at the monastery. Its template bears a title column in the upper right corner, which reads, "Guangsheng Monastery in Zhaocheng County" (*Zhaocheng xian Guangsheng si* 趙城縣廣勝寺) (fig. 5.12). It features the Buddhist pantheon with the seated Buddha in the center, flanked by ten monk-disciples and two guardians, all rendered smaller. Among the monk figures, one holds a long leaf, another carries a case of scriptures, and yet another holds a healing bowl.[73] Both the foreground and background are infused with floating clouds in circular floral shapes and horizontal strips. An image of a neatly cut-off tree adorns the upper right corner.[74] Most likely, this frontispiece

73 It is not clear if the leaf held by the monk here has any symbolic meaning. Cf. a similar leaf motif held by a "medicine god" (*yaoshen* 藥神) in the sixteenth-century *Peacock King Sutra* woodcuts, and by a Daoist "perfected being" (*zhenren* 真人) in the seventeenth century Daoist woodcuts depicting Lord Lao's eighty-one transformations; see ZGFJBHQJ 23: 171; ZGDJBHQJ 40: 101.

74 Curiously, multiple Hangzhou frontispieces of the *Avatamsaka Sutra* dated 1291 and associated with the Tangut monk Li Huiyue also depict tall trees at the border of a composition (see ch. 9, figs. 9.32a).

a

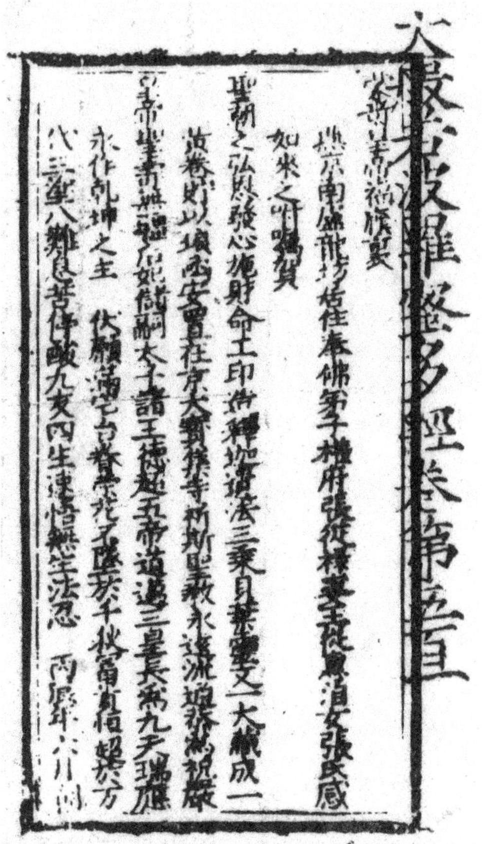

b

FIGURES 5.18A–B
Details of the reprint of the Jin Canon. 1256. Woodblock print
a. Frontispiece
b. Colophon

design was commissioned by the Guangsheng Monastery and executed by the local printshop of the Pang Family in southern Shanxi in the mid-thirteenth century, soon after the abbot received the Canon.

3.3.1 The Guangsheng Frontispiece

The publisher's seal (fig. 5.1e) stamped in selected texts traces its long reputation to "the ancestral generation" (*zudai* 祖代) in Fenxi 汾西 county,[75] literally "west of the Fen River," an area close to the temple. The publisher must have been the same "Pang Family printshop from Xiezhou," whose now-lost reprint of the Northern Song *Revised Materia Medica* was acknowledged by its fellow publisher, the Zhang Family from Pingyang, in its celebrated reprint version in 1249 (figs. 5.1c, 5.4a–i). A colophon (fig. 5.1e) stamped several times at the end of selected texts of the Jin Canon also acknowledges the leading cutter of the Pang Family. It reads, "Produced by Pang in-attendance (*daizhao* 待詔) of the printshop with business in Zhaocheng county since the ancestral generation. [He is] the leading senior [artisan] in-attendance in Fenxi county. Dated to the fifteenth day of the ninth month of 1262." The date uses the Mongol "Zhongtong" 中統 reign period, established prior to the official inauguration of the Yuan dynasty.[76] The title "in-attendance" literally refers to an official ranking in government. While it sometimes refers to a court painter, here it is simply a flattering honorific adopted by local professional craftsmen, including painters and sculptors.[77] A paper document (fig. 5.19a), discovered inside the cache of a Jin-to-Yuan wooden statue of a standing bodhisattva now in the Nelson-Atkins Museum (fig. 5.19b), records artisans with the same title as having repaired the statue in 1349 on behalf of a temple located in a village near the Guangsheng Monastery.[78] The title was actively used in this manner until the early Ming. Thus, an inscription on the interior surface of a removable panel (fig. 5.20a), attached to the back of a seated Guanyin now at the Metropolitan Museum (fig. 5.20b), states that the image was carved by "the woodcarver in-attendance Feng Xiaozhong and his son Feng Beigong of our village" (*bencun kanmu daizhao Feng Xiaozhong bing nan Feng Beigong* 本村刊木待詔馮孝中幷男馮備工) in 1385. Supported by villagers from Eastern Peace Village in Hongdong county, it was produced for a new temple that served as a guardian

75 This seal was retrieved from the *Daboruo jing*, juan 43; see Jiang 1977, 236–37.

76 The original inscription in Chinese reads, "趙城縣祖代經方（坊）龐待詔自造汾洒（西）縣主座老待詔，中統三年九月十五日記"; see Jiang 1977, 237.

77 Jiang 1977, 237.

78 For more discussion, see Qu 2017, 74–75 (fig. 4); Qu 2018, 170 (fig. 4.5). For the state, see the Nelson-Atkins Museum of Art, "Standing Bodhisattva," Works, Accessed December 24, 2023. https://art.nelson-atkins.org/objects/18434/standing-bodhisattva. Note that prior to 1349, when this statue was repaired, a major earthquake took place in 1303 and destroyed 70 percent of the buildings in the Pingyang area; see Wang J. 2018, 166.

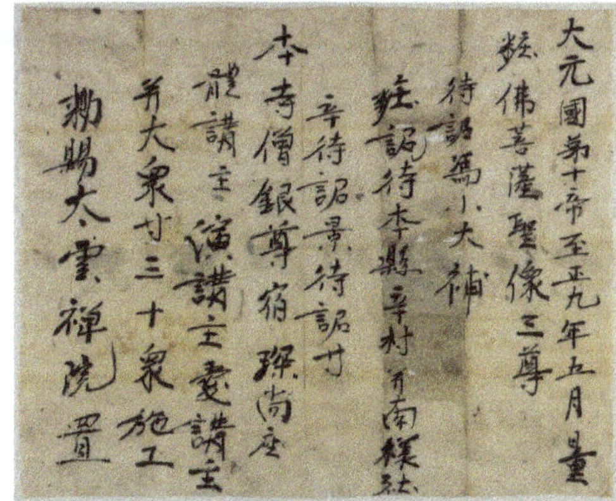

FIGURE 5.19A
A document listing the artisans who worked on the repair of the statue. 1349. Yuan. Ink on paper. Discovered inside the statue of Standing Bodhisattva. The Nelson-Atkins Museum of Art, Kansas City, Missouri

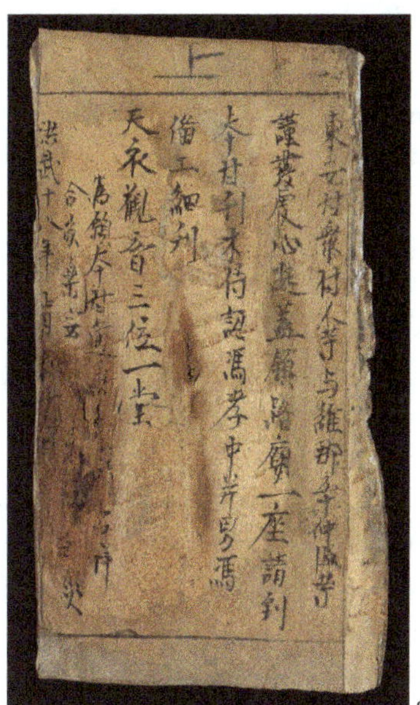

FIGURES 5.20A–B Bodhisattva Avalokiteshvara in Water Moon Form. 1385. Ming. Wood (willow) with gesso and traces of pigment; single woodblock construction. The Metropolitan Museum of Art
a. Inscription on the wooden panel attached to the back of the statue
b. Wooden statue

of the road (*zhenlu miao* 鎮路廟).[79] All this suggests that Pang in-attendance was the designer and block-cutter of the Guangsheng frontispiece.

79 Qu 2017, 75. For the statue and the inscribed wooden panel, see the Metropolitan Museum of Art, "Bodhisattva Avalokiteshvara in Water Moon Form (Shuiyue Guanyin)," Asian Art, Accessed December 24, 2023. https://www.metmuseum.org/art/collection/search/42727.

FIGURE 5.21
Seated bodhisattva. 12th or 13th century. Jin-Yuan. Polychrome wood. Upper Guangsheng Monastery

The Guangsheng frontispiece further shares stylistic features with local sculptures and murals originally housed in there. The masculine and round facial features as well as the robust torso of the Buddha (fig. 5.12) recall the wooden statue of the seated Mañjuśrī (fig. 5.21) still *in situ*.[80] Researchers have dated this statue to the Jin dynasty, relating it to a wooden statue made in the same region and dated 1195, which is now in the Royal Ontario Museum (fig. 5.22).[81] The same common style extends to wooden statues produced in southern Shanxi in the Jin, Yuan, and Ming periods, so that scholars call it summarily the "Fen River school wooden sculptural style" (*Fenhe mudiao liupai* 汾河木雕流派).[82]

Similar masculinity can be found in murals of regional temples that date from the thirteenth and fourteenth centuries. They include the mural of the Medicine Buddha, now at the Metropolitan Museum of Art (fig. 5.23) but originally from the Lower Guangsheng Monastery, as well as the Seven Buddhas mural, now in the Palace Museum in Beijing. Previous scholars have identified local itinerant muralists such as Zhu Haogu 朱好古 and his apprentices,

80 Chai and Ren 2006, 99, 267.

81 Qu 2017, 73; Sickman 1935, 14. Chai Zejun and Ren Yimin dated the statue to the Ming period, citing the date of 1452, when the temple hall was renovated; see Chai and Ren 2006, 98–99. Jiang Weixin thought the statue may have been dated to the Yuan period; see Jiang 1977, 218.

82 Sickman 1935, 14; Qu 2017.

FIGURE 5.19B Standing Bodhisattva. Jin. Wood with polychrome and gilding. The Nelson-Atkins Museum of Art, Kansas City, Missouri

FIGURE 5.22 Wood figure of Avalokiteśhvara (Guanyin). ca. 1195. Jin. Polychrome wood. Royal Ontario Museum, Toronto, Canada

who worked on the murals of the Daoist temple Yonglegong 永樂宮 (Palace of Eternal Joy) in southern Shanxi as the local painters who spread the style.[83]

83 Meng 2008, 2011; Steinhardt 1987b. For a recent study of the Yonglegong as the Quanzhen Daoist pilgrimage center with the help of local residents and villagers in the thirteenth century, see Wang J. 2018, 96–117. For more about its architecture, see Steinhardt 2024, 116–27.

FIGURE 5.23 *Buddha of Medicine Bhaishajyaguru*. ca. 1319. Yuan. Mural. Water-based pigment over foundation of clay mixed with straw. The Metropolitan Museum of Art

The cloud motifs in circular floral shapes and horizontal strips (fig. 5.12) in the Guangsheng frontispiece in addition carry local features that may have inspired later art. Similar motifs of round and multi-centric clouds appear strongly in the murals filling the east and west walls of the Water God Temple, dated around 1324 (figs. 5.24).[84] It was built after a major earthquake destroyed seventy percent of the buildings in this area in 1303.[85] The horizontal strips of clouds with an upward-turning, hook-like shape at the end are particularly noticeable in a rain-making scene in the upper right corner of the east wall.[86] Records mention twelve muralists as having painted the east and west walls,

84 Nancy Steinhardt links the pagoda depicted in this mural detail to the "thirteen-story glazed-tile pagoda" of the Upper Guangsheng Monastery; see Steinhardt 2024, 130–31 (fig. 4.16).

85 Chai and Ren 2006, 327–33. For a classic study of the temple, see Jing 2001. For a fresh perspective of the temple dedicated to a water-providing god promoted by the irrigation associations formed by local people to manage the Huo Spring irrigation system, see Wang J. 2018, 166–214.

86 Among celestial divinities in charge of the weather, three wind gods lead a procession in the sky, releasing two tiger-skinned bags and thereby sending wind diagonally across a temple complex, shown with a radiating pagoda. This may represent the upper monastery compound at the time when the mural was completed. See Qu 2018, 58–59; for a comparison of an on-site photo of the temple with the mural, see 146 (figs. 2.4–2.5). Cf. Chai and Ren 2006, 9–10, 118. For an alternative mural representation of the Guangsheng Monastery compound, see the mural (Yuan or Ming?) on the north wall of the western sub-hall of the upper monastery, reproduced in Chai and Ren 2006, 274 (fig. 129).

FIGURE 5.24 Motifs of round and multi-centric clouds. 1324. Yuan. East wall of the Water God Temple

noting many as related: fathers and sons, masters and apprentices, fellow villagers from Hongdong county.[87] Their work matching the printed frontispiece and the design of the wooden sculpture shows how the Guangsheng frontispiece fits within long-lasting local artistic practices shared across media.

3.3.2 The Dunhuang Fragments

Discontinuous fragments of the *Avatamsaka Sutra* printed from Jin Canon blocks were discovered in the deserted cave B53 in the northern district of the Mogao grottoes at Dunhuang (fig. 5.15b). They were accompanied by a frontispiece fragment (fig. 5.15a), now separate from the text but originally attached to it. Since most documents in the cave can be dated to the Yuan period, the fragments too are assumed to go back to this time.[88] Li Jining convincingly identifies the fragments as the tenth *juan* of the *Avatamsaka Sutra* in its 80-*juan* version, part of the original Jin Canon blocks.[89] Its textual layout and cut characters are identical with the printed specimen of the Jin Canon found in the

87 The muralists painting the east wall were Wang Yanda 王彥達 and his son, Hu Tianxiang 胡天祥, Gao Wenyuan 高文遠 and his apprentice Guan 關 in-attendance, Yuan Yancai 元彥材 and his son, Xi 席 in-attendance and his apprentice Hao Shan 郝善. The muralists in charge of the wets wall were Zhao Guoxiang 趙國祥 from the Dong'an 東安 Village, and Shang Junxi 商君錫 from Zhou 周 Village, and Jing Yanzheng 景彥政 from Nanyang community (Nanyang she 南樣社); see Qu 2018, 56–57.

88 For the survey of the documents found in Mogao Cave B53, see Peng and Wang 2000–2004, 1: 187–99 (for the *Avatamsaka Sutra* fragments, see 190–91). For a comparison of the Dunhuang finds with the Jin Canon specimen of the *Avatamsaka Sutra* in the National Library, see Li 2002b, 114–18.

89 It was juan 10, the third segment of the fifth part of the "Huazang shijie pin" (Huazang shijie pin di wu zhi san 華藏世界品第五之三); see Li 2002b, 115. See also Li J. 2007.

Guangsheng Monastery:[90] The textual layout in both has fourteen characters per line and the calligraphic style is the same. In addition, both versions bear block numbering information on the right border and list an abbreviated sutra title and chapter (*juan*) number in smaller characters. Li further notes that the Guanshengsi version, in the end of the chapter, preserves the dedicatory colophon of the donor Fan Xing 樊興 from Liangxu 梁許 village in Hejin 河津 county (map 0.4),[91] located in southwestern Shanxi along the Fen River.

Although there is not much evidence of the Dunhuang frontispiece, it is highly possible that, quite like its Guangsheng counterpart, it was added to the Jin Canon text by its later owner. Its overall design compares closely to a modular design shared by the Xi Xia frontispiece to the "Vows of Samantabhadra," extracted from the *Avatamsaka Sutra* (figs. 5.17, 6.55). Discovered in Khara Khoto, it probably dates to the late twelfth century (see ch. 6).

Both the Dunhuang fragment and the Xi Xia frontispiece show a seated icon with a jeweled crown and the *vajra* or "wisdom fist" mudra (*zhiquanyin* 智拳印). The accompanying cartouche on the top identifies this as the "Teaching master, the Great Universal (Vairocana) Buddha" (*jiaozhu da piluzhena fo* 教主大毗盧遮那佛). Kneeling in front of the Buddha is a back-facing bodhisattva atop a lotus seat. In both cases, the figure is labeled as the "Bodhisattva who Utters Victorious Sound between his Eyebrows" (Meijian shengyin pusa 眉間勝音菩薩), a prominent bodhisattva attending the assembly of Vairocana Buddha as discussed in several commentaries of the *Avatamsaka Sutra* traceable to the Tang dynasty.[92] A child commonly identified as Child Sudhana (Shancai tongzi 善財童子) in both cases appears kneeling on a piece of matting to the right of the bodhisattva. Next to him is a group of bodhisattvas in profile, all turning their heads upward and with their feet on lotus seats, reflecting a Himalayan style. Finally, both the Dunhuang frontispiece and the Xi Xia specimen share similar decorative patterns of lotus petals in the bottom border. All these minute similarities suggest that the Dunhuang frontispiece was originally a Xi Xia product. Given that Dunhuang was part of the Xi Xia territory in the twelfth century and that much Buddhist literature flowed back and forth between the Xi Xia and the Jin (see ch. 6), it is highly possible that the *Avatamsaka Sutra* fragment was originally printed in Beijing's Hongfa Monastery after 1181, once the blocks were stored there. After it reached Xi Xia territory, its new owner

90 See Li 2002b, 117 (fig. 50).

91 For the full citation of this colophon, see Li 2002b, 117.

92 See the commentary by the Tang monk Chengguan 澄觀 (737–838) in T.36.1736: 212.

had a frontispiece made to adorn the text, probably sometime close to the end of the twelfth century.[93]

3.3.3 The Turfan Frontispieces

A Prussian expedition at the turn of the twentieth century discovered five identical copies of the same—mostly damaged—frontispiece design in Turfan and took them back to Berlin (fig. 5.16a).[94] The design represents a buddha-preaching scene, with three lay devotees standing in the left corner of the picture plane. While their generic appearance makes it hard to argue visually who they represent (fig. 5.16b), the Uighur colophon in the upper left corner indicates that they may show a Uighur family: father (Toyincoy Tutung), mother (Oyul Yitmis Tngrim), and son (Buyanocóy).[95]

As Peter Zieme notes, the frontispieces may have accompanied the *Perfection of Wisdom Sutra* (*Daboruo boluomi duo jing* 大般若波羅蜜多經), one of six texts in the Jin Canon acquired by the Uighur merchant Buyanocóy Baxsi in Beijing's Hongfa Monastery.[96] The dedicatory colophon in the Uighur language is also recorded separately in another document, originally found in Turfan and now in Berlin. It sheds light on the printing location and the donor's intention. It says,

> The layman Buyanocóy Baxsi … the merit may reach both of my holy ones, my mother and my father … on the *posatha* fasting day, the eighth of the sixth month of the monkey-wu year of the ten-heavenly-stem series, has ventured to order to print these sutra jewels of the Tripitaka: the *Perfection of Wisdom Sutra*, *Avatamsaka Sutra*, *Lotus Sutra* …, *Merciful Repentance Ritual*, and the *Diamond Sutra* from the printing blocks of the Hongfa Monastery in the Central Capital.[97]

---

93 Li Jining also mentioned the possibility that the Dunhuang text may have been printed in the Jin time and transmitted to the Xi Xia territory, although he did not discuss the image at all; see Li 2002b, 118.

94 Zieme 1996; Dang 1999, 114–17; Zieme 2007, 86, 95–97.

95 Zieme 1996, 412–13.

96 The fragment labeled as MIK III 23 verso shows that the back of the frontispiece was superimposed onto the front side of *juan* 184 of the *Perfection of Wisdom Sutra*, which bears the character *shu* 戍 of the numbering system using the *Essay in a Thousand Words*; see Zieme 1996, 421 (pl. 4). The Turfan frontispiece specimens were mounted in butterfly binding format. Additional smaller fragments of printed texts were found in Turfan in 1927–1935; see Dang 1999, 104–106.

97 Cf. the English translation in Zieme 1996, 415. For a translation in Chinese, see Dang 1999, 110.

There are two major reasons to link the frontispiece to this colophon. First, the name of the lay donor here is close to that of the son in the frontispiece: Buyancóy and Buyanocóy Baxsi. Second, the back of the frontispiece was superimposed onto a fragment of the printed text of the *Perfection of Wisdom Sutra*, whose layout and numbering are in line with that preserved in the Jin Canon specimens. The "monkey-*wu*" year is hard to date, but previous scholars have suggested 1188, 1248, and 1308 as possibilities.[98] The Central Capital most likely indicates Beijing, matching its official name before 1272.

Peter Zieme dates the frontispiece to 1308, citing the unique Mongolian dress style of the donor figure who stands closest to the viewer and holds an incense burner (fig. 5.16b). The wide braided waist of the man's clothing matches numerous visual examples of male clothing dated to the Mongol era, making 1308 the most likely date.[99] The donor's dress is also similar to Mongolian-style garb featured in Turfan printed fragments of the so-called "family portrait" of Mengsusu (figs. 0.3), an elite Uighur with close ties to Qubilai Khan (see ch. 10). It is thus likely that the frontispiece showing the family of Buyanocóy was added to the Jin Canon the Uighur merchant acquired in Beijing around 1308 and was duly transported back to Turfan. Alternatively, Buyanocóy may have commissioned an artisan in Turfan to add a frontispiece to adorn the printed text after the text was transported to his homeland.

3.3.4 The Baojisi Edition of 1256

Yet another version of a frontispiece design is a Beijing product, dated to around 1256. The image is a "side product" of an effort of recutting blocks of select texts in the Jin Canon, a monumental effort funded by the layman Zhang Conglu 張從祿 who livedin Bejing under Mongol rule. Because Zhang donated the reprint edition to the Da Baojisi 大寶集寺 (Great Monastery of Gathered Treasures), scholars call this version the Baojisi edition (Baojisi ben 寶集寺本) (figs. 5.18a–b). The institution may well have had its own scribes cut the blocks. Numerous texts from the edition are extant, including specimens found in Khara Khoto and the Sakya Monastery in Tibet, plus various others reproduced in the modern compilation *Zhonghua dazang jing* 中華大藏經.[100]

98 Zieme first proposed 1248 and later revised this to 1308; see Zieme 1996, 413. Dang Baohai disagreed with Zieme and proposed the date of 1188; see Dang 1999, 116–17.

99 Zieme 1996, 416. Dang Baohai disagreed with the Yuan dating proposed by Zieme. He argued that the Mongolian dress already existed before the Yuan, and that the frontispiece may have been printed in Jin Zhongdu (today's Beijing) in 1188; see Dang 1999, esp. 113.

100 ZHDZJ; ECHSCWX 4: 365; Su 1964b, figs. 1–2; DYPGZGMT, 4 (no. 00898).

A dedicatory colophon dated 1256 (fig. 5.18b), stamped repetitively at the end of each *juan* of the extant texts, sheds light on the lay donor who funded the reprint. It begins with a note of thanks to Möngke 蒙哥 (1209–1259), the Mongol ruler at the time, and identifies layman Zhang Conglu, his wife Wang Conghui 王從惠, and their daughter living in the Lulong Ward 盧龍坊, as the main donors. Traceable to Tang times and one of twenty-six districts in Liao Yanjing, Lulong Ward was located near today's Liulichang 琉璃廠 in Beijing.[101] With the funds donated by the Zhang Family, artisans cut and printed a set of the Buddhist texts, which were in turn mounted in yellow scrolls, placed in containers decorated with precious stones, and stored at the Great Baoji Monastery. Back in the eleventh century, the temple collected the printed *Lotus Sutra* produced locally (fig. 4.36), as suggested by the temple's seal discussed above.[102]

It is reasonable to assume that a frontispiece (fig. 5.18a) was added to the selected texts of this reprint edition during the mounting process. The square-shaped frontispiece features a sword-holding guardian, seated at the center against a landscape background with distant mountains on top of wavy water. There is also a barefoot demonic attendant who stands in the right corner of the picture plane, wearing animal-skinned leg warmers and holding a long pole. A cartouche in the upper left corner reads, "Divine Guardian Protecting the Dharma" (Hufa shenwang 護法神王). The guardian image in these extant specimens reflects the Yanjing printing legacy transmitted from Liao times (figs. 4.26–4.28).

According to Su Bai, specimens of the same frontispiece and colophon were found among over five hundred *juan* of texts in the Baoji Monastery edition as discovered in the Sakya Monastery, Tibet.[103] Quite possibly, these printed texts were brought there by Qubilai Khan's first imperial preceptor, Phakpa (a.k.a. Basiba 八思巴, or 'Phags pa, 1235–1280), when he went back to Tibet in 1260 and 1270 (see ch. 7). They may also have been given to the temple as a sort of "payment" for rituals performed by the Tibetan monks.[104] In addition to

101 CYL, 48. The epitaph of the high-ranking Liao official Li Neizhen 李內貞 (898–978) living in the tenth-century Lulong Ward, was discovered in the eighteenth century in the neighborhood; see STJSWZXB 12: 1.

102 For a punctuated transliteration of the entire colophon, see Su 1964b, 17; Xiong 2003c, 204–205.

103 Su 1964b, 15–18; Xiong 2003c, 205–208; Xie ed. 2010, 371. According to Xiong Wenbin, the last Emperor of the Southern Song, Zhao Xian 趙顯 (1271–1323), was sent to Sakya Monastery to study Tibetan when he was just a child; he was later killed in 1323. See Xiong 2003c, 206–207.

104 Li F. 1991, 7; see also Li F. 2012, 317. For more of the material transfer between the Yuan court and the temples in Tibet, see Allsen 1997, 2002; Jing 2004.

the specimens found in Tibet, several other fragments of the same frontispiece design appear in the Russian collection.[105] Some are also found in the Bezeklik cave site near Turfan, the headquarters of the Uighurs (see ch. 10) and an area that gradually became part of the Mongol Empire, beginning in the thirteenth century.[106] One of the frontispiece fragments from the Russian collection, for example, is originally attached to the *Āgama Sutras* (*Ahan jing* 阿含經), discovered in Khara Khoto, the former territory of the Xi Xia kingdom (see ch. 6).[107] It shows the seated guardian with his chest and left arm missing. Detailed comparisons suggest that the Khara Khoto fragment and the specimen in Tibet were both based on different blocks sharing the same design. They reflect mass produced copies made in Beijing in the mid-thirteenth century, and were subsequently distributed to Tibet, the former Xi Xia territory, and the Uighur homeland (see ch. 10).

4 The New Orleans Finds

Village people from southern Shanxi not only formed the collective backbone of the Jin Canon's block cutting, they also sponsored individually circulated Chinese indigenous scriptures adorned with frontispieces. Two little-studied printed texts were discovered in the 1980s inside a wooden bodhisattva statue (fig. 5.27), held by the New Orleans Museum of Art: the *Sutra Narrated by the Buddha on Rebirth in Heaven* (*Fo shuo shengtian jing* 佛説生天經) (figs. 5.25a–c), dated 1155; and the *Guanyin Sutra Promoted by King Gao* (*Gaowang Guanshiyin jing* 高王觀世音經; hereafter the *King Gao Sutra*) (figs. 5.26a–b), dated 1173.[108] The statues exhibit the Fen River school wooden sculptural style shared by the statues in the Royal Ontario Museum (fig. 5.22) and the Nelson-Atkins Museum (fig. 5.19b). The two deposited printed specimens enrich our understanding of the Jin frontispiece art, popular Buddhism, and lay Buddhists in southern Shanxi. Comparable woodcuts made in Xi Xia and Northern Song further suggest the reach of inter-regional exchange at that time.

---

105 ECHSCWX 4: 365–66; ECDHWX 15: 248, 253.

106 ZGFJBHQJ 4: 263.

107 In earlier publications, I follow Chikusa Masaaki's lead to identify TK 274 as a Liao frontispiece printed in Yanjing; see Chikusa 2003, 22–23; Huang 2014d, 138*n*29, 149, 174 (fig. 20); 2017b, 293–94.

108 Wood 1986; Han 1993; Huang 2014d, 152–53; Huang 2017b, 296–97 (fig. 25).

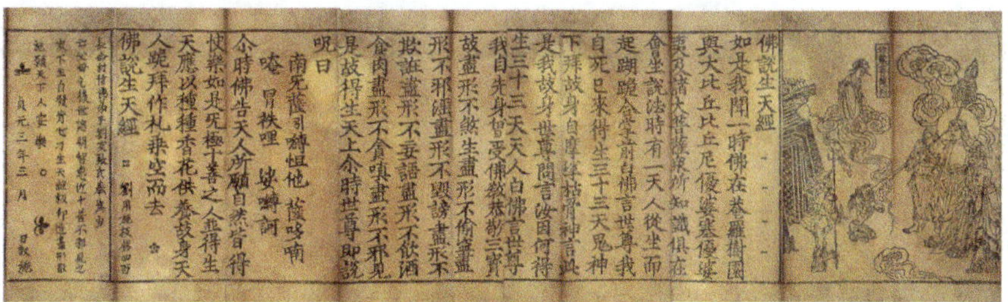

佛說生天經
如是我聞一時佛在菴羅樹園
與大比丘比丘尼優婆塞優婆
夷及諸大菩薩衆所知識俱在
會坐說法時有一天人從坐而
起踟蹰合掌前白佛言世尊我
自死已來得生三十三天鬼神
下拜故身自摩娑枯骨神言與
是我故身世尊問言汝因何得
生三十三天天人白佛言世尊
我自先身曾受佛教恭敬三寶
故盡形不殺生盡形不偷盜盡
形不邪婬盡形不毀謗盡形不
欺誑盡形不妄語盡形不飲酒
食肉盡形不貪嗔盡形不邪見
是故得生天上尒時世尊即說
呪曰
南无薩引嚩怛他 薩哆喃
唵 冒袟哩 娑嚩訶
尒時佛告天人所願自然皆得
快樂如是死極十善之人並得生
天應以種種香花供養故身天
人跪拜作礼乘空而去
佛說生天經 ⁘ 劉用施抜錢四百
長命封信佛弟子劉友張氏奉為少
亡父母乞後世聰明智恵近十善不邪見之
家下生自發肯心刁生天經板印造盡形散
施願天下人安樂 ○
貞元三年三月 日散施

a

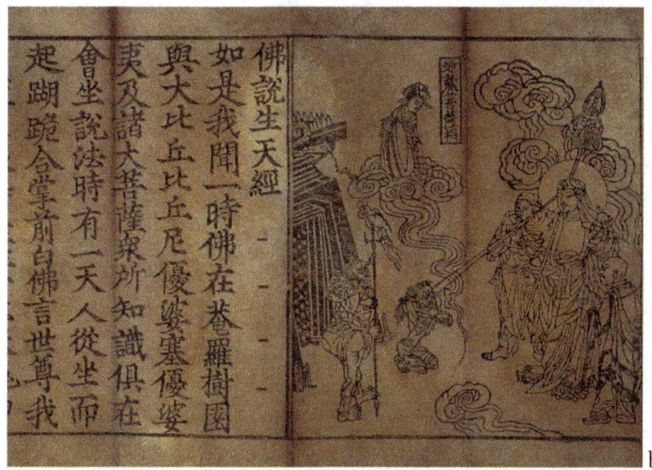

b

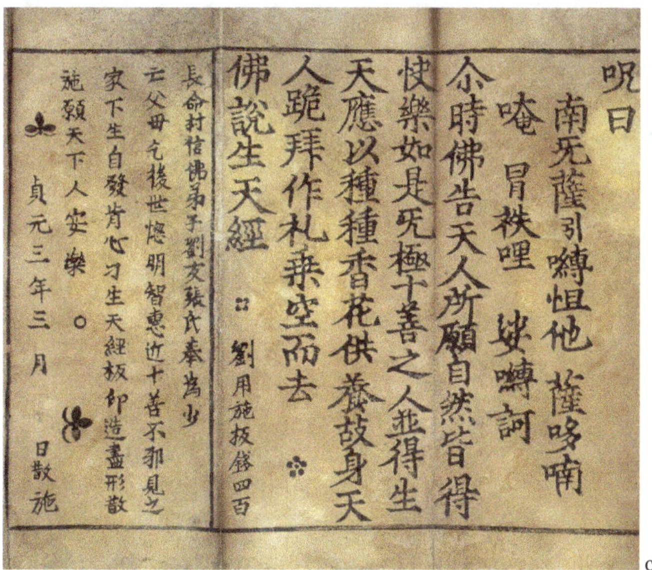

c

FIGURES 5.25A–C Details. *Foshuo Shengtian jing*. 1155. Jin. woodblock print. The New Orleans Museum of Art

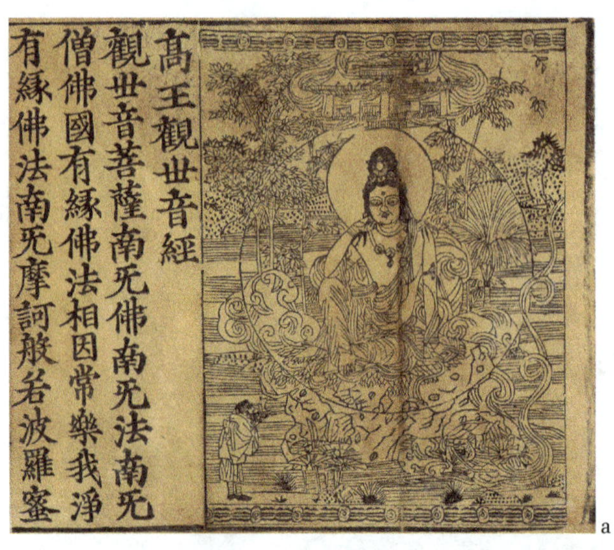

a

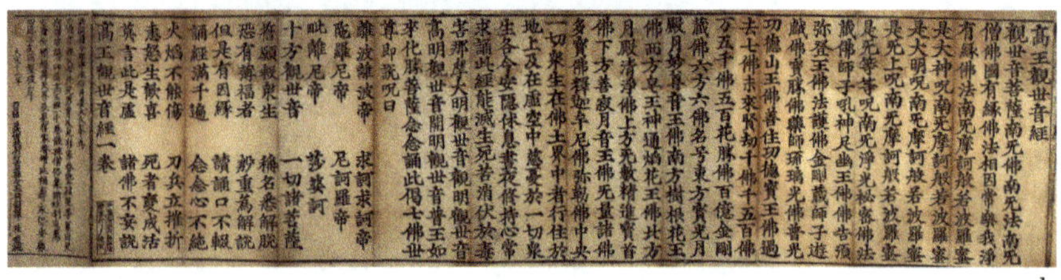

b

十方觀世音　一切諸菩薩
誓願救衆生　稱名悉解脱
恐有薄福者　殷重爲解説
但是有因緣　讀誦口不輟
誦經滿千遍　念念心不絶
火焰不能傷　刀兵立摧折
恚怒生歡喜　死者變成活
莫言此是虛　諸佛不妄説
高王觀世音經一卷

洪洞縣令鄭律承信并妻大氏奉為
亡過宗親父母并兒男等及見存家眷暨孩兒等累因災
病謹啓誠懇印造高王經一千卷散施僧俗集斯妙利追薦
亡靈伏願超昇天界及見存家眷增延福壽永保安康
四恩三友同登彼岸
大定十三年
日承信校尉行洪洞縣令飛騎尉鄭律 珪 散施

c

FIGURES 5.26A–C Details. *Gaowang Guanshiyin Jing*. 1173. Jin. woodblock print. The New Orleans Museum of Art

FIGURE 5.27
Guanyin. Jin. Wooden statue with pigments. The New Orleans Museum of Art

4.1 *Rebirth in Heaven*

The *Sutra on Rebirth in Heaven* is a short indigenous Buddhist text printed on paper (fig. 5.25a), quite possibly related to an earlier, now-lost text called *Sutra on [Attaining] Rebirth Heaven and Overcoming Destiny by [Being] a Monk Sitting in Meditation* (*Zuochan biqiu mingguo shengtian jing* 坐禪比丘命過生天經), recorded in multiple Tang and pre-Tang Buddhist bibliographies.[109] Framed as a conversation between the Buddha and a "heavenly being" (*tianren* 天人) reborn in the highest of the thirty-three heavens (*sanshisan tian* 三十三天), the text features nine specific "rebirth commandments." They include the classic ten precepts, close to similar rules advocated in other sutras at that time:[110] to abstain from killing, stealing, adultery, criticism, lying, arrogant talk, drinking, meat eating, gluttony, and seeing anything inappropriate.

The notion of being reborn in heaven also appears in Daoism. The Tang text, *Scripture on Rebirth in Heaven and Attaining Dao Spoken by the Heavenly Worthy of Primordial Beginning* (*Yuanshi tianzun shuo shengtian dedao jing* 元始天尊說生天得道經) notes that to become immortal, one should fast, cleanse the five organs and six viscera, and eliminate all blockages in the 360 joints of the body. In addition, one must avoid the ten evil deeds and 108 worries, which overlap with the Buddhist commandments.[111] According to multiple thirteenth-century liturgical manuals, moreover, priests performing rites for souls trapped in hell, here called underground prison, also recite a certain *Scripture of Rebirth in Heaven* (*Shengtian jing* 生天經) while circumambulating the altar.[112]

The two-fold frontispiece attached to the Jin printed text exhibits a popular flavor (figs. 5.0, 5.25a–b). Flanked by a monk and an attendant, the caped bodhisattva Dizang stands in front of the gate of the underground prison, which is guarded by demonic jailors, and sets free a female soul dressed in fine garments and seen ascending on clouds. In Chinese Buddhism, Dizang was widely known as a savior "helping the dead to evade the reach of the ten kings [of hell]" and delivering "all sentient beings from suffering, especially those trapped in the lower regions of rebirth."[113] The composition reveals two

---

109 T.55.2145, 23c; T.49.2034, 67c. This new discovery raises doubts about Han Qi's claim that *Sutra on Rebirth in Heaven* was never included in the Buddhist canon; see Han 1993, 212, 214.

110 See the "ten good deeds" (*shi shan* 十善) in the text collated by the Southern Song scholar Wang Rixiu 王日休 (?–1173) in T.12.364, 337b.

111 For the version preserved in the Ming Daoist Canon, see DZ 24, 1: 806. For dating and more study, see Lagerwey in Schipper and Verellen 2004, 555–56.

112 DZ 466, 7: 196c; DZ 407, 6: 556; Lagerwey in Schipper and Verellen 2004, 555.

113 Teiser 1994, 6.

pictorial memes combined into a memeplex: the gated underground prison and Dizang. A tenth-century prototype of this appears in a Dunhuang manuscript of the *Sutra of the Ten Kings of Hell Preached by the Buddha* (*Foshuo shiwang jing* 佛說十王經) (fig. 5.28). Here Dizang appears as an oversized monk standing in front of the flaming prison gate and greeting the sinners.[114] Both his staff with interlocking rings and the bladed underground prison, depicted in the Dunhuang manuscript, provide visual prototypes of similar motifs depicted in the Jin frontispiece (figs. 5.0, 5.25a). The longevity of the memeplex of Dizang standing in front of a gated prison is further supported by a seventeenth-century painting depicting a King of Hell (fig. 5.29).[115] It appears in the lower left of the overall composition, below the scene of the karmic scale discussed before (fig. 0.8).

With a slight alteration, the designer of the Xi Xia printed frontispiece to the "Vows of Samantabhadra" chapter from the *Avatamsaka Sutra* dated 1196 (figs. 5.30, 6.22) replaced Dizang with Child Sudhana while keeping the overall compositional scheme. Here Sudhana stands in front of a similar gated underground prison, which is positioned diagonally, and faces two jailors depicted as similar demonic types.[116] Mimicking the dogs clinging to the top of the prison fence in the Dunhuang prototype (fig. 5.28), here a dog climbs on the gate. Beyond China, the fourteenth-century Japanese printed version of a Chinese indigenous text, *Maudgalydyana Saves His Mother* (*Mulian jiumu* 目連救母), features an illustration with a similar meme of a monk standing in front of a gated prison, inside of which hungry ghosts are struggling in flaming waters.[117]

A dedicatory colophon (fig. 5.25c) at the end of the Jin *Sutra on Rebirth in Heaven* identifies its donors as the layman Liu You 劉友 and his wife Woman Zhang 張氏 from the Longevity Village (Changmingcun 長命村; see map 0.4). They donated 400 strings of cash to sponsor the blocks in 1155 on behalf of Liu's deceased parents. The village still appears on modern maps and is located in Hongtong county, about 23 miles from Linfen. In the Jin context, it was part of the Jin Canon network (map 0.4), which means that the cutter, illustrator,

114 While the picture scroll cited here bears no inscriptions, other comparable illustrations from Dunhuang manuscripts (such as P. 2870, P. 2003) are all accompanied with the citations from the *Scripture of the Ten Kings of Hell*. See also similar scenes in other Dunhuang *Ten Kings of Hell* scrolls, reproduced in Teiser 1994, 194–95 (figs. 14a–c). For alternative representations of Dizang, one with a cloth cap, see the Dunhuang manuscript (P. 4523) and the Dunhuang hanging scroll painting (MG 17793).

115 For the other three scrolls from the same incomplete set from the Musée Guimet collection, see Delacour 2010, 321.

116 Huang 2017b, 291 (fig. 16), 297.

117 For the image, see Teiser 2007, 241 (fig. 10.1).

FIGURE 5.28 Detail. *Ten Kings of Hell* (1919,0101,0.80). 10th century. Ink and color on paper. Manuscript. The British Museum

FIGURE 5.30 Detail. Frontispiece to the "Vows of Samantabhadra" chapter (TK 98). 1196. Xi Xia. Woodblock print. Institute of Oriental Manuscripts, St. Petersburg

FIGURE 5.29 *King of Hell* (EO 787). 17th century. Ming. Ink and color on paper. Hanging scroll. Musée des Arts Asiatiques-Guimet

and publisher of the sutra commissioned by Liu You and his wife may all have gained their experience by working in a Buddhist printing enterprise in the Pingyang region.

4.2 *The* King Gao Sutra

Also discovered inside the New Orleans statue is the illustrated *King Gao Sutra* (figs. 5.26a–c), whose end bears a stamp of the Wei Family printshop in Hongdong, Pingyang (fig. 5.1d), and a dedicatory colophon dated 1173 by the donor Yelü Gui 耶律珪, the magistrate (*xianling* 縣令) of Hongtong (fig. 5.26c). He and his wife Woman Tai (Taishi 大氏) sponsored one thousand copies to seek redemption on behalf of his deceased parents and to accumulate merit for their children and other family members.

Inspired by the "Universal Gateway" chapter of the *Lotus Sutra* (see ch. 3), the *King Gao Sutra* was one of the most widely printed indigenous scriptures promoting the cult of Guanyin.[118] It is also referred to as the *Sutra of Ten Phrases* (*Shiju jing* 十句經) or the *Sutra that Breaks the Sword* (*Zhedao jing* 折刀經).[119] Its earliest version, apparent in the sixth century, is said to have consisted of only ten sentences to promote the chanting of Guanyin's name day and night.[120] The notion of "breaking the sword" relates to a miracle often included in the expanded version of the text. It involves a criminal who lived during the time of Gao Huan 高歡 (496–547), the founder of the Northern Qi 北齊 dynasty (550–577), that is, the "King Gao" referred to in the title. Because the criminal chanted Guanyin's name one thousand times during his incarceration, when the executioner raised his sword to behead him, it broke into pieces. King Gao was so moved by this miracle that he pardoned the criminal.[121] Compared

118 Yü 2001, 110–15. Liu Shufen compares specific verses of the sutra with those in the *Lotus Sutra*; see Liu S. 2007, 149–50. For more studies, see Makita 1976, 284–85; Yü 2001, 23–24, 94, 98–99, 110–18, 123, 143, 148, 151, 168, 170, 176, 186, 242, 261, 300; Liu S. 2007, 147–53.

119 Shi et al. 1991, 39; Yü 2001,111, 115; Liu S. 2007, 148.

120 Yü 2001, 113–15. This is in line with the earliest extant stele of the *King Gao Sutra* in southern Shanxi. Dated 593, it was commissioned by thirty-one village people from what is today Huguan 壺關 county in southern Shanxi (map 0.4), about 131 miles east of Pingyang. See Liu S. 2007, 147–50. Cf. the other stele dated 548 commissioned by a group of villages organized by Monk Zhilang in Pingding 平定, Shanxi; see Liu S. 2007, 151. While Liu rightly pointed out that these six-century stele sources predated the Fangshan stone slabs dated 616 and several other seventh-century Buddhist catalogues, which Chün-fang Yü cited as the earliest textual sources listing the *Guanyin Sutra Promoted by King Gao* (Yü 1995, 106–107; Yü 2001, 23, 99), Chün-fang Yü also mentioned a sixth-century Northern Qi Buddhist stele in San Francisco Asian Art Museum bearing the carved text; see Yü 2001, 110–13 (fig. 3.4).

121 Saliceti-Collins 2007, 74. For the possible candidates of the criminal mentioned in the story, see Yü 2001, 111–14.

to the *Lotus Sutra* prototype, the story narrated here is much more personal, making it even more accessible to popular folk. Its essence is summed up in easy-to-memorize verses at the end of the Jin printed version (fig. 5.26c):

Chant the sutra a thousand times,	誦經滿千遍
Evoke [Guanyin] in your heart without stopping:	念念心不絕
Then fire cannot harm you,	火焰不能傷
Knives and weapons break immediately,	刀兵立摧折
Resentment and anger give rise to delights and joy,	恚怒生歡喜
And the dead turn back into the living.	死者變成活

The Jin printed version of the *King Gao Sutra* is decorated with a two-fold frontispiece. Enclosed in a large circle, Guanyin is seated in a casual posture on a rock amid water (fig. 5.26a). He is surrounded by various plants and covered by a canopy that imitates palatial architecture. The overall iconography is called the Water Moon Guanyin (Shuiyue Guanyin 水月觀音), and its setting refers his sacred domain known as Potalaka—a pictorial convention also preserved in the contemporary Buddhist mural in the Yanshan Monastery (fig. 5.31), about 261 miles north of Hongtong.[122] In the lower left corner, a figure with a non-human face offers a tray to Guanyin. His hat, garment, and shoes resemble those of a monk. The frontispiece is further decorated with geometric shapes such as circles and wavy horizontal lines at the top and bottom border.

The *King Gao Sutra* was known widely in the Liao, Song, and Xi Xia. The Liao printed version discovered in the Fogong Pagoda was one of the thousand copies donated by the lay woman Zhou 周, associated with the Yongji Cloister (see Table 4.4).[123] The text records the miracle of the criminal not included in the Jin version and ends with the verses found in its concluding section. A fragmented frontispiece attached to the Liao text shows some architectural and figural motifs, which differ greatly from the Jin frontispiece.

Select Northern Song designs may have provided a prototype for the Jin frontispiece design. This includes a tenth-century bronze mirror,[124] a single-sheet print of an Esoteric multi-armed Cintamani-cakra (Ruyilun Guanyin

---

122 For more study of the Water Moon Guanyin, see Yü 2001, 94, 184, 189, 224, 228, 232–47. For the murals at the Yanshan Monastery in Fanzhi, Shanxi, see Yang ed. 2018.

123 For the reproduction of the text, see Shanxi sheng wenwuju et al. 1991, 200 (fig. 32). It is not sure if this Yongji Cloister was the one identified in Zunhua, Hebei; see Shi et al. 1991, 39.

124 The mirror is in the Seiryōji collection; see Nara Kokuritsu Hakubutsukan ed. 1996, fig. 63.

FIGURE 5.31 Water Moon Guanyin. 1158–1167. Jin. Mural. West wall of the Wenshu Hall, Yanshan Monastery, Fanzhi, Shanxi

FIGURE 5.32 Cintamani-cakra. Northern Song. Woodblock print. Single sheet. Gankouji, Nara

FIGURE 5.33 Drawing copied after a Chinese painting. 12th century. Heian period, Japan. Ink on paper. Ninnaji Temple, Kyoto

如意輪觀音) (fig. 5.32),[125] and a twelfth-century Japanese ink drawing (fig. 5.33), copied from a Northern Song painting.[126] The frontal and casual seated position of the deity, the rocks surrounded by water, and various plants all resonate with the Jin frontispiece.

125 For additional copies of similar designs made in Northern Song China and Japan, see Uchida 2015. See also Huang 2017c, 9–10, 46 (fig. 10).

126 The now-lost Northern Song painting was donated by the layman Chen in Quanzhou on behalf of his son. The Japanese drawing is from the illustrated Esoteric Buddhist manual *Besson zakki* 别尊雜記; see Nara Kokuritsu Hakubutsukan 2009, 106 (pl. 94); Matsumoto 2019, 1: 207 (fig. 91).

The Jin frontispiece in turn became the predecessors of similar Xi Xia frontispieces (figs. 5.34–5.37, 6.62) that adorn various Guanyin-related texts in Chinese and Tangut. Produced in the late twelfth century, they include two frontispieces associated with the *King Gao Sutra* in Chinese (figs. 5.34, 5.35), and three that adorn the "Guanyin" chapter of the *Lotus Sutra* in Tangut (figs. 5.36, 5.37) and Chinese (fig. 6.62).[127] These Xi Xia examples represent two compositional modes. The first (figs. 5.34, 5.36, 5.37) stages Guanyin singularly in a frontal position, enclosed by a large circle.[128] In one case (fig. 5.34), he is seated atop the rocky platform supported by a pillar base amid water, similar to the rocky design in the Jin counterpart (fig. 5.26a). Alternatively, both frontispieces to the Tangut-script versions (figs. 5.36, 5.37), which follow a shared design template, omit the rocky support, and simply depict Guanyin in a circle, floating on water. A devotee dressed like an official is presenting offerings to the deity; this recalls a side figure depicted in the Jin frontispiece (fig. 5.26a), although the tight legging of the Jin figure suggests that he may represent a pilgrim monk.

The second compositional mode (figs. 5.35, 6.62) shifts the central Guanyin to the right of the picture plane, with a narrative scene that highlights the miracle of the prisoner's failed execution. In the foreground of the *King Gao Sutra* (fig. 5.35), the image of two donors dressed like noblemen suggests that the printed text may have been commissioned by Xi Xia royal or elite members (see ch. 6).[129] A print discovered in Turfan (fig. 5.38), likely a Xi Xia work transmitted to that region, represents Guanyin in a similar posture and setting.[130]

•••

During the twelfth century and under Jurchen rule, southern Shanxi became the new printing center in north China. Diverse local productions, including reprints of illustrated books and the Jin Canon, were all based on the Northern Song prototypes, attesting to the region's close connection to Song book and publishing culture. Going beyond simply copying Song models, however, single-sheet pictorial prints made by commercial publishers in the area

127 Saliceti-Collins 2007, 73–77, 218 (figs. 2.24, 2.25); Shi 2004, 159; Liu 1985.

128 Linrothe 1996a, 33.

129 For a similar rendition of noble male and female donors in a Xi Xia painting discovered in Khara Khoto, see Piotrovsky 1993, 180, 207, 239. A Tangut-script Xi Xia single-sheet print depicting ten realms of the world also depicts Guanyin in a similar style; for a study of this print, see Kitsudō and Arakawa 2018.

130 Chen A. 2020, 35, 37 (fig. 1–11), 39.

celebrate local popular culture. They were transmitted as far as the neighboring kingdom of the Xi Xia in northwest China, reflecting the cross-regional reputation of Shanxi print culture and its legacy beyond the Jin.

Unlike the Liao Canon, sponsored by the ruling class, the Jin Canon, especially at its initial block-cutting stage, exemplifies ambitious grass-roots effort, bringing together local monastics and villagers. Extant specimens were most likely printed in the Hongfa Monastery in Jin-to-Yuan Beijing, where the blocks were stored after 1181, and subsequently dispersed to the Guangsheng Monastery as well as to Dunhuang, Turfan, and Tibet. They testify to the presence of an active Buddhist network and dynamic Book Roads well beyond the dynastic framework. This is especially evident from the fact that owners of the sutra copies added customized frontispieces to the texts from the late twelfth to the early fourteenth centuries. The two illustrated indigenous scriptures found inside a Buddhist statue, originally made in southern Shanxi and now in the New Orleans Museum, further reveal lay support of Buddhist print culture "on the ground." Praying on behalf of family members, such lay donors may have donated the sutra copies to a local temple, which owned the New Orleans statue, and subsequently deposited them inside.

FIGURE 5.34 Frontispiece to the *King Gao Sutra* (K.K.II.0248a). Xi Xia. Woodblock print. Discovered in Khara Khoto

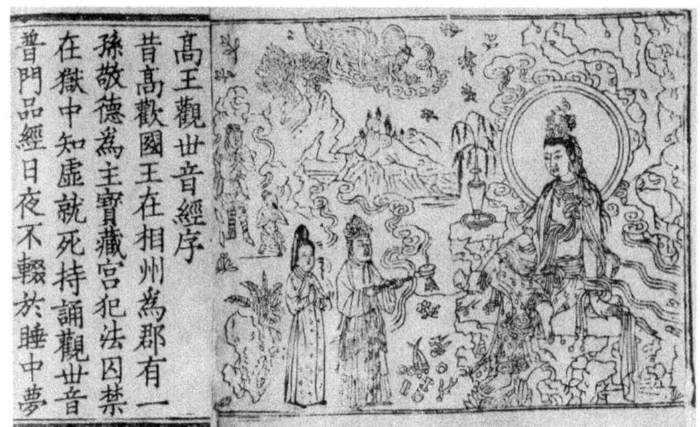

FIGURE 5.35 Frontispiece to the *King Gao Sutra* (TK 117). Xi Xia. Woodblock print. Discovered in Khara Khoto

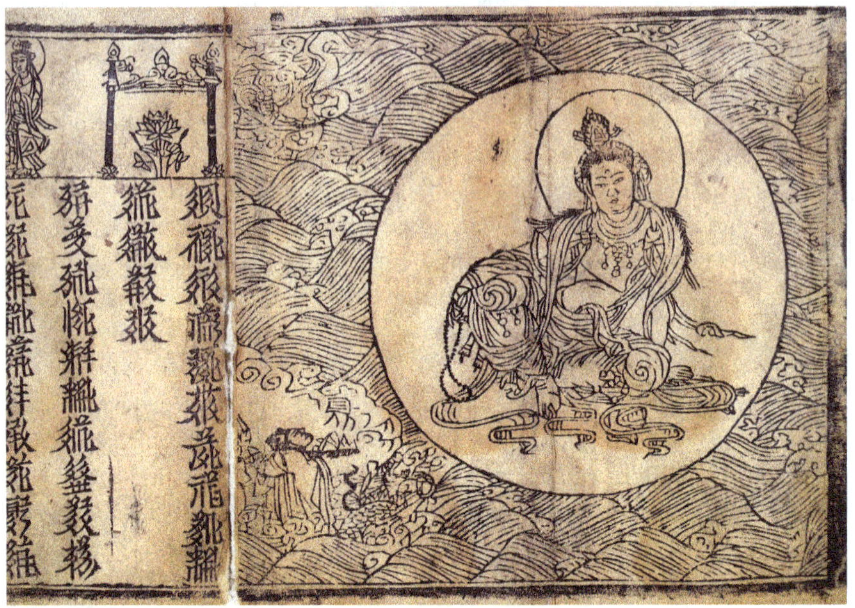

FIGURE 5.36 Frontispiece to the "Guanyin" chapter of the *Lotus Sutra* in Tangut. Xi Xia. Woodblock print. Discovered in Khara Khoto

FIGURE 5.37 Frontispieces to the "Guanyin" chapter of the *Lotus Sutra* in Tangut. Xi Xia. Woodblock print. Discovered in the Heli Stupa in Dunhuang, Gansu. Dunhuang Academy

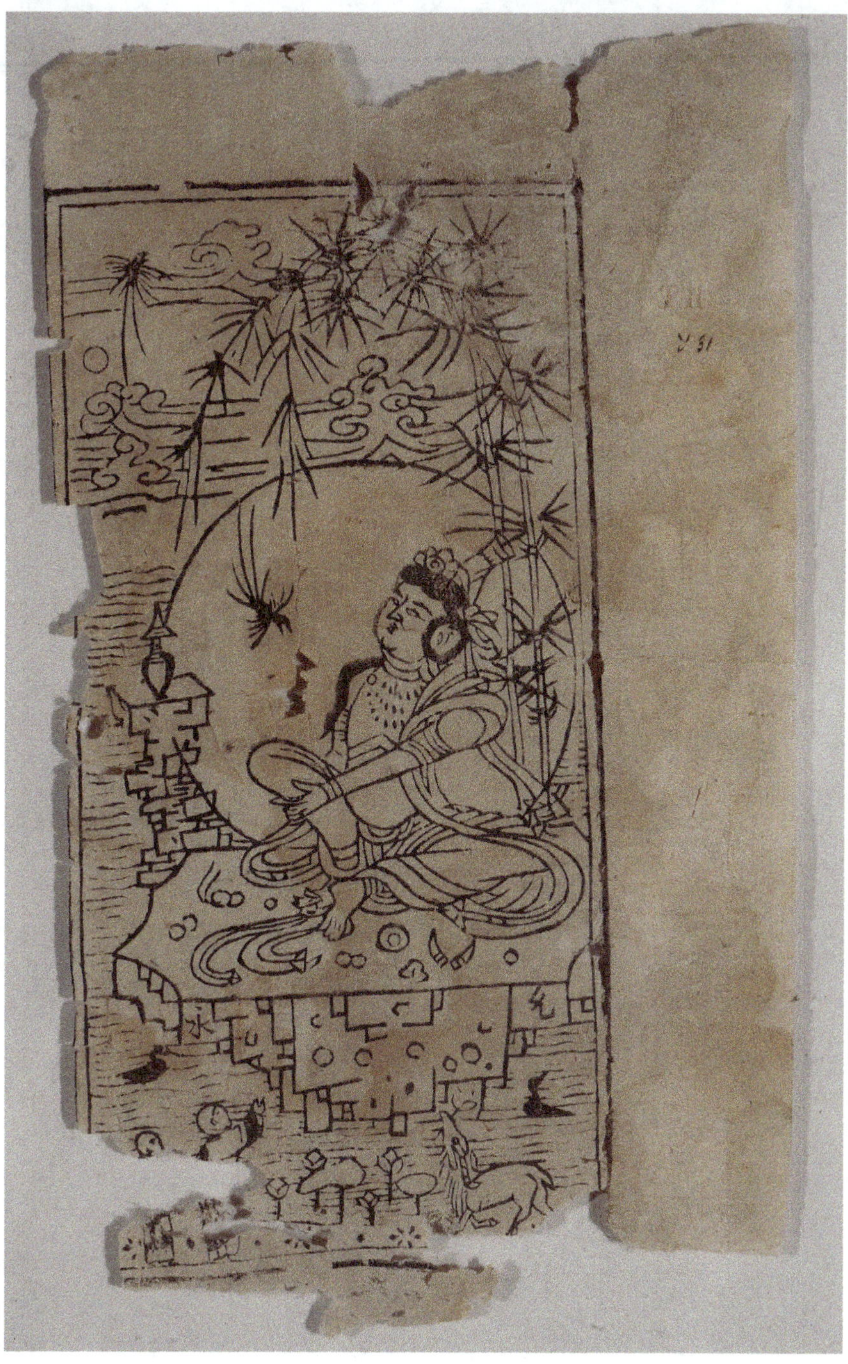

FIGURE 5.38 Guanyin print (III 6709). Xi Xia (?). Woodblock print. Discovered in Yarkhoto, Xinjiang. Staatliche Museen zu Berlin, Museum für Asiatische Kunst

CHAPTER 6

Tangut Royal Patronage and Xi Xia Buddhist Printing

On the fifteenth day of the ninth month of 1189, the Tangut Emperor Renzong of the Xi Xia kingdom celebrated the fiftieth anniversary of his ascendance to the throne in a grand Buddhist retreat in the Da Duminsi 大度民寺 (Great Monastery of Saving the People). No longer extant, the temple was once located in what is today Yinchuan 銀川, Ningxia, the Xi Xia capital in Xingqing prefecture (Xingqing fu 興慶府) (map 0.2).[1] Known as the Maitreya Retreat, the assembly was held in the hope of helping the emperor's deceased mother and all other participants to be reborn in the Tusita Heaven, the Buddhist paradise where Maitreya bodhisattva, the future Buddha, resides.[2] An international group of elite Buddhist monks were invited, some holding high-ranking positions granted by Renzong.[3] They chanted Esoteric and Mahayana texts in Tibetan, Tangut, and Chinese. A repentance rite was held on-site together with other activities for merit creation, such as feeding monastics and poor people, releasing animals and birds, and pardoning prisoners.

The highlight was Renzong's donation of great quantities of recently printed Buddhist scriptures and paintings. A virtuous ruler, he believed that his support of Buddhist activities would accumulate personal merit as well as

FIGURE 6.0 Detail of fig. 6.5. Frontispiece of the *Maitreya Sutra* in Tangut script (no. 78). ← 1189. Xi Xia. Woodblock print. Concertina. Institute of Oriental Manuscripts, St. Petersburg

1 Cf. the Map of Xi Xia (*Xi Xia dixing tu* 西夏地形圖) in the Qing-dynasty *Xi Xia jishi benmo* 西夏紀事本末; see XXJSBM: 22. For more on the Xi Xia capital, see Xu 1989, 52–93; Dunnell 1989. According to Ruth Dunnell, 1189 was "a year of change in East Asia." While the Xia Emperor Renzong was celebrating his steady long enthronement, the neighboring state, the Jurchen Jin, just lost its ruler Emperor Shizong (r. 1161–1189), whereas the Southern Song Emperor Xiaozong abdicated the throne; see Dunnell 1994, 205. For more on Renzong's sponsorship of Buddhism and Buddhist art, see Linrothe 1995, 1998; Dunnell 1996; Meinert 2020.

2 For an introduction to this deity, see Yü 2020, 79–80.

3 The complete name of the assembly is *Doushuai neigong Mile guangda fahui* 兜率內宮彌勒廣大法會. Shi Jinbo suspected that most of the monks invited to this assembly were Esoteric monks from Tibet; see Shi 1988, 165; Shi 2001, 72; Dunnell 2009, 48, 69–70.

© SHIH-SHAN SUSAN HUANG, 2024 | DOI:10.1163/9789004700017_008

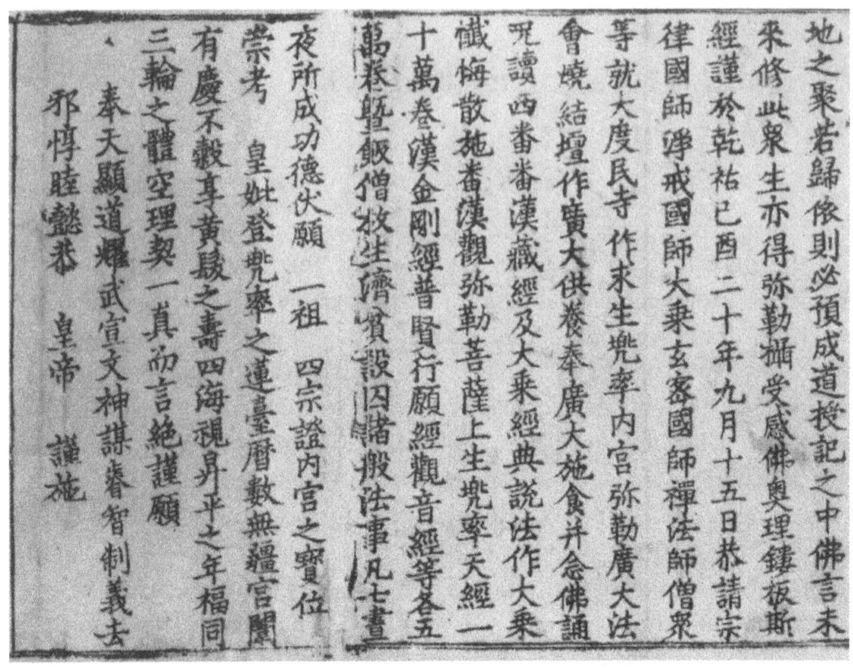
地之衆若歸依則必預成道授記之中佛言未
來修此衆生亦得弥勒攝受感佛奥理鏤板斯
經謹於乾祐己酉二十年九月十五日恭請宗
律國師淨戒國師大乘玄密國師禪法師僧衆
等就大度民寺作求生兜率内宫弥勒廣大法
會燒結壇作廣大供養奉廣大施食并念佛誦
呪讀西番番漢藏經及大乘經典説法作大乘
懺悔散施番漢觀弥勒菩薩上生兜率天經一
十萬卷漢金剛經普賢行願經觀音經等各五
萬卷暨飯僧放生濟貧設囚諸般法事凡七晝
夜所成功德伏願　一祖　四宗證内宫之寶位
崇考　皇妣登兜率之蓮臺曆數無疆宫闈
有慶不穀享黃髮之壽四海視昇平之年福同
三輪之體空理契一真而言絶謹願
奉天顯道耀武宣文神謀睿智制義去
邪惇睦懿恭　皇帝　謹施

FIGURE 6.1 Detail of the colophon. The *Maitreya Sutra* in Chinese (TK 58). 1189. Xi Xia. Woodblock print. Concertina. Institute of Oriental Manuscripts, St. Petersburg

enhance his moral and political authority.[4] Thus, he gave away one hundred thousand *juan* (scrolls) of copies of the *Maitreya Sutra* in Tibetan, Tangut, and Chinese, as well as fifty thousand scrolls of copies of the Chinese *Diamond Sutra*, the "Vows of Samantabhadra" chapter from the *Avatamsaka Sutra* (hereafter "Vows of Samantabhadra"), and the *Guanyin Sutra*.[5]

Details of the Retreat are documented in a dedicatory prayer (fig. 6.1), included at the end of several extant print versions of the *Visualization Sutra of Maitreya Bodhisattva's Rebirth in the Tusita Heaven Above* (*Guan Mile pusa*

4 Ruth Dunnell called Renzong "a semidivine Buddhist ruler," see Dunnell 1994, 203.

5 For the text, see ECHSCWX 2: 309–15; cf. T.14.452. Imre Galambos discusses select Dunhuang manuscripts that copied the sutra (such as S. 5555) or the mantra (such as P. 3932) at the end of the text; the mantra also appears in the Xi Xia printed versions (2020, 59–60n136–37). The "Vows of Samantabhadra" is extracted from the last chapter of the *Avatamsaka Sutra*; the *Guanyin Sutra* is based on the twenty-fifth episode of the *Lotus Sutra*. Cf. the *Daizōkyō* versions of the scriptures mentioned in the colophon in T.14.452; T.10.293: 844–48; T.9.262: 56–58.

shangsheng duoshuaitian jing 觀彌勒菩薩上生兜率天經; hereafter called the *Maitreya Sutra*) in Chinese, discovered in Khara Khoto, Inner Mongolia, together with several specimens of its Tangut counterpart. Each printed text was originally decorated with an elaborate frontispiece (hereafter the *Maitreya* frontispiece), available in at least five completely preserved versions (figs. 6.2–6.6), and had some cartouches in Chinese or Tangut.[6]

A Chinese among the five complete versions was mistakenly classified as a Dunhuang document in the Russian collection (figs. 6.4a–b).[7] It is quite similar to the TK 81 version (figs. 6.3a–b) in terms of its carving style; also, both prints bear the name of the cutter Zhang Zhiyi 張知一 (figs. 6.3b, 6.4b).[8]

Small fragments of the same design were also discovered in Khara Khoto and in the Baisigou Pagoda, another Xi Xia ruin in Yinchuan (fig. 6.7).[9] Viewed together, it becomes apparent that these illustrated texts and other extant specimens may have come from the hundreds of thousands of scriptures Renzong distributed to temples nationwide.[10]

The large-scale, multi-lingual, and illustrative Buddhist printing practices under Tangut rule have no precedent in history.[11] Extant printed materials associated with the Maitreya Retreat provide superb resources to probe into the social and visual dimensions of Xi Xia Buddhist printing. Geographically,

6 For the complete colophons of the Chinese versions (TK 58 and TK 81), see ECHSCWX 2: 47–48, 314–15. For a punctuated version, see Shi 1988, 267–68. Note that Shi mistranslates "seven days and nights" as "ten days and nights" in the colophon. Based on a comparison of the Chinese and Tangut colophons, some scholars think that the Tangut version was based on the Chinese (e.g., Nie 2009). For the fragments in the Stein collection (K.K. II. 0233. B, K.K. II. 0280. a, K.K. II. 0290. A, K.K. II. 0280. B), first discovered in Khara Khoto and now in the National Museum, New Delhi, see Toyo Bunko Digital Archive Viewer, "Innermost Asia: vol. 3, LXII," Digital Silk Road, Accessed December 24, 20230. http://dsr.nii.ac.jp/toyobunko/viewer/index.html?pages=T-VIII-5-A-a-3/V-3&pos=80&lang=en.

For more studies of the *Maitreya* frontispieces, see Drège 1999, 53–54; Linrothe 1996a, 33–36 (fig. 5); ZGBHQJ 1: 71, 82; Chen and Tang 2010, 152–57; Saliceti-Collins 2007, 142–48; Huang 2014d, 138–39; Huang S. 2021a, 560–61.

7 See no. 11580 in ECDHWX 15: 257–58.

8 For the signatures of the cutter, see ECDHWX 15: 258; ECHSCWX 2: 308.

9 Li Jinzeng 2016, 11: 4953–54.

10 When assessing the documents discovered in Khara Khoto, Imre Galambos points out that "twice as many dated Buddhist texts come from the time of [Renzong's] reign than from all other periods of the Tangut state together" (2015, 113). See also Meinert 2020, 248.

11 The sheer number surpasses the 84,000 copies of the *dharani* scrolls supposedly sponsored by Qian Shu, king of the Wu-Yue kingdom in the tenth century; see Huang 2011a, 137–42.

FIGURE 6.2 Detail. Frontispiece of the *Maitreya Sutra* in Chinese (TK 58). 1189. Xi Xia. Woodblock print. Concertina. Institute of Oriental Manuscripts, St. Petersburg

a

b

FIGURES 6.3A–B Details. Frontispiece of the *Maitreya Sutra* in Chinese (reconfigured from TK 81, TK 82, and TK 83). 1189. Xi Xia. Woodblock print. Concertina. Institute of Oriental Manuscripts, St. Petersburg

rather than in the Khitan or Jurchen territories in northern China, it centered in the northwest, from where the Tangut court, the Buddhist temples it patronized, as well as the multiethnic and multi-lingual host of monks actively created cross-regional connections—including those with the neighboring Song, Liao, and Jin. Located at a crossroad frequented by Silk Road travelers and sandwiched among many diverse cultures—Uighur, Tibetan, Khitan, Jurchen, and Chinese (map 0.2)—the Tangut kingdom was not simply "a transition zone" but a transregional hub accumulating, diffusing, producing, and re-interpreting "religious knowledge" from all around.[12] Just as social networks created a world of interconnected artisans, buyers, and patrons, so did workshops produce prints that both created and revealed the intersecting and often interrelated connections across prints, paintings, and other works of art. Borrowing Michael Pye's notion of syncretism in religious studies,[13]

12 See Meinert's discussion of Central Asia as the place where "all civilisations connected and interacted through the large network of trade routes," and her definition of the "primary node" as a major cultural center (2015, 1, 9).

13 Pye 1994.

a

b

FIGURES 6.4A–B Details. Frontispiece of the *Maitreya Sutra* in Chinese (no. 11580). 1189. Xi Xia. Woodblock print. Concertina. Institute of Oriental Manuscripts, St. Petersburg

I use the term "visual syncretism" to describe this interconnectivity. Examining frontispieces associated with the Maitreya Retreat, it becomes obvious that artisans often borrowed and built upon Chinese models, especially of the Southern Song and here particularly from Hangzhou. Although the Xi Xia and the Southern Song did not share a border, the kingdom's networking reached far, and its connections to Buddhist temples and trade centers all through the region brought Chinese and other models to the attention of local artisans looking for ways to effectively mass-produce enormous quantities of key texts.

FIGURE 6.5 Detail. Frontispiece of the *Maitreya Sutra* in Tangut script (no. 78). 1189. Xi Xia. Woodblock print. Concertina. Institute of Oriental Manuscripts, St. Petersburg

FIGURE 6.6 Detail. Frontispiece of the *Maitreya Sutra* in Tangut (no. 941). 1189. Xi Xia. Woodblock print. Institute of Oriental Manuscripts, St. Petersburg

FIGURE 6.7
Detail, fragments of the *Maitreya Sutra* frontispiece. Xi Xia. Woodblock print. Discovered in Baisigou, Ningxia

1 The Xi Xia Network

Buddhist temples, monks, and imperial donors and patrons formed the basic components of the Xi Xia network, centered on major temples—including archaeological sites of Buddhist grottoes and pagodas—transportation routes, and border markets (map 0.2).[14] Most important were Buddhist temples connected to the Tangut court and important for Buddhist printing.[15] They served in various functions: first, they probably were sites for the royal donation of

14 For more about the economy of Xi Xia, see Shi 2021.

15 Shi 1988, 117–34; Xu 1989, 79–93; Qin 2014 (for a chart of the temples, see 18).

printed books as part of ritual performances; second, they may have been the location of production, where Buddhist translating, block cutting, and printing took place; and third, they most likely were the recipients of printed books and thus sites that housed Buddhist collections.

A web of temples, including also caves, clustered in and around the Tangut capital of Xingqing and the nearby Mt. Helan 賀蘭山 (Mountain of Congratulatory Orchids), as well as around other sites of Buddhist communities in the west of the kingdom. These include Khara Khoto and other parts of the Hexi corridor (today Gansu), such as Liangzhou 涼州 (modern Wuwei 武威), Ganzhou 甘州 (today Zhangye 張掖), Guazhou 瓜州, and Shazhou 沙州 (modern Dunhuang) (see map 0.2). They were previously occupied by the Tibetans or Uighurs, before the Tangut conquered the area in the eleventh century.[16]

Major Buddhist temples near the capital were tied to royal power and intimately involved in printing. The Gaotaisi 高台寺 (Monastery of the High Platform) and Chengtiansi 承天寺 (Monastery of Supporting Heaven) were major temples built by the founding emperor Li Yuanhao 李元昊 (1003–1048) and his consort Lady Mozang 沒藏 (?–1056), in 1047 and 1055, respectively.[17] Prime sites of Buddhist book collections, they housed the Northern Song printed copies of the Kaibao Canon, multiple copies of which the Tangut court had requested from the Northern Song court on multiple occasions. The Da Dumin Monastery, site of the Maitreya Retreat, was also a large temple near the capital with, as archaeological remains suggest, a landmark ordination platform.[18] Furthermore, the Zhoujiasi 周家寺 (Zhou Family Temple) in the capital was associated with Buddhist printing,[19] among others employing the cutter Wang Huishan 王惠善, who participated in cutting the court-sponsored blocks for the illustrated *Lotus Sutra* in 1146 (figs. 0.1, 3.23). His work was rewarded by the royal family, who provided daily food for all artisans.[20] Excavations of the ruins

16 Mainstream scholarship uses the year of 1036 as the date when the Tangut conquered the Dunhuang area. For more, see Dunnell 1994, 179–80; Cui 2010a, 34, 52–54; Yang and Chen 2012, 333–73; Shi 1988, 110–34; Qin 2014; ZGDHBHQJ 10: 5, 39–44, 63–95; 11: 225–49; Zhu 2007; Yang 2011; Sha 2013.

17 XXSSJZ, 212; Shi 1988, 63, 112–13; Yang and Chen 2012, 290–91; Huang 2014d, 137; Huang 2017b, 282. For the possible location of the Gaotai Monastery in the eastern suburb of Xinchuan city, see Xu 1989, 83. The current Chengtian Pagoda reconstructed in the Qing dynasty, associated with part of the original Chengtian Monastery compound, still is a landmark of Yinchuan; see Lei et al. 1995, 17, fig. 3.

18 Nie 2003, esp. 95, 97.

19 Ruth Dunnell speculated that Monk Huihai active in the mid-twelfth century was a member of the Sino-Tangut Zhou clan who owned the Zhou Family Temple; see Dunnell 2009, 45.

20 Shi 1988, 95; Shi 2004, 134; Fan and Yang 2009, 128.

FIGURE 6.8 A block of Tangut text. Xi Xia. Woodblock. Discovered in Hongfo Pagoda, Ningxia

of the Hongfo 宏佛 Pagoda, discovered not far from the original Xi Xia capital, yielded more than two thousand blocks with neatly cut Tangut characters, suggesting that there may have been a printing center in a monastic setting nearby (fig. 6.8).[21]

The Tangut court's connection to temples went beyond the capital, as documented in a poem, entitled "Eulogy of the Imperial Tour Westwards to Offer Incense." Discovered in Khara Khoto, it recounts an imperial excursion to major temples in the west (map 0.2), referring to either the travels of Renzong in 1176 or those of his son, Huanzong 桓宗 (r. 1193–1206), in the early 1200s.[22] According to the poem, the emperor departed from the capital and journeyed west. His first major stop was Liangzhou, home of the imperially sponsored Shengrongsi 聖容寺 (Monastery of the Holy Countenance).[23] Archaeological finds in Haimudong 亥母洞 (Grotto of the Ultimate Mother), a Tibetan Buddhist cave temple in this area, yielded some of the earliest movable-type

21 Lei et al. 1995, 209; Shi 2004, 76.

22 For the original document (121V) in Tangut, see ECHSCWX 10: 286. The eulogy can be translated as "Yujia xixing shaoxiang ge" 御駕西行燒香歌 in Chinese. Yang Fuxue and Chen Aifeng translate the eulogy into Chinese and identify the tour with Emperor Renzong's trip taken in 1176 (2012, 252–67). Su Hang disputes the received interpretation and proposes that the emperor mentioned in the eulogy was Emperor Huanzong and the tour may take place in 1201–1204 (2014). See also Yang B. 2017, 156.

23 For a survey of the extant site, see E 2014, 2: 391–98.

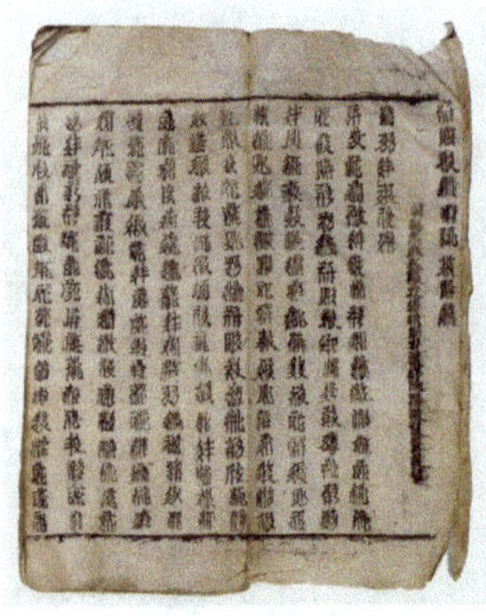
a

b

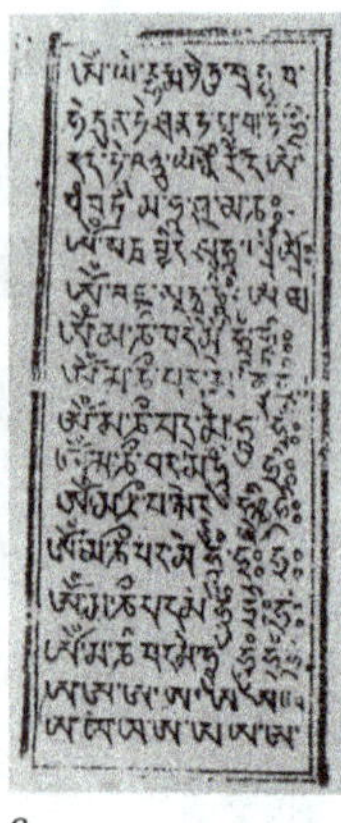
c

FIGURES 6.9A–C Buddhist artifacts. Xi Xia. Discovered in Haimudong, Wuwei, Gansu. Xi Xia
a. Detail, movable type *Vimalakirti Sutra* in Tangut, after 1140
b. Clay tablet of a multi-armed deity
c. Printed slip of Tibetan charms. Woodblock print

specimens of the *Vimalakirti Sutra* in Tangut sponsored by Emperor Renzong (fig. 6.9a).[24] There were also molded clay tablets of Esoteric Buddhist icons (fig. 6.9b), some bearing Sanskrit and Tibetan charms on the back, others containing paper slips of printed Tibetan charms deposited inside (fig. 6.9c).[25] All this further highlights the striving Tibetan Buddhist community well connected to the royal court and print culture at the time. At his next stop, Ganzhou, the emperor first visited the reclining Buddha (fig. 6.10) in the Dafosi 大佛寺 (Monastery of the Big Buddha).[26] Built under Xi Xia rule in the late eleventh century, this caught the attention of the Italian traveler Marco Polo in the thirteenth century and of the Persian envoys sent by the Timurid court in the

24 For more about the Tangut clay and wooden movable types, see Shi and Yasen 2000, 38–56 (for specimens of the *Vimalakirti Sutra* comparable to those in Wuwei, see 39); Shi 2020, 92–105. For an unusual "imagetext" in the form of a buddha, using movable types, discovered in the Baixiang 白象 pagoda in Wenzhou 溫州, Zhejiang, see Tsien 2002, 157 (fig. 2).

25 Shi 2004, 78–80; Niu 2013, 158–59; Chen and Tang 2010, 198 (fig. 3.20), 200 (fig. 3.23–1), 344 (fig. 6.17); Su 1996, 270–71; Zhang and Cai eds. 2020, 25. Cf. a dharani sheet printed in red and inserted into a miniature stupa-shaped clay *caca* discovered in Mogao Cave 464; see Peng and Wang 2000–2004, 3: 103, color pl. 12. For more visual examples of Xi Xia clay tablets produced discovered in Khara Khoto, Gansu, and Ningxia, see Zhang and Cai eds. 2020, 8–41.

26 Yang and Chen 2012, 260. For more representations of the death of the Buddha in Chinese visual culture, see Lee 2010. Qin Yu listed six temples in Ganzhou constructed under Xi Xia rule; see Qin 2014, 18.

FIGURE 6.10 Reclining buddha. Wofo Monastery, Zhangye, Gansu. Xi Xia. Renovated in the Qing

early fifteenth.[27] After this, the emperor stopped at the Matisi 馬蹄寺 (Monastery of Horses' Hoofs), a temple known for its Tibetan Buddhist heritage.[28] Extant printed documents suggest that multilingual monks once gathered at the Chandingsi 禪定寺 (Monastery of Absorption Samadhi) and Huguosi 護國寺 (Monastery of Protecting the State) in this region to translate Tibetan Buddhist texts into Tangut.[29] Further west, the court's temple network also covered the Yulin and Mogao caves in Guazhou and Shazhou, considered "sacred palaces of the world" (*shijie shenggong* 世界聖宮) at the time.[30]

1.1 *Monks of Many Sorts*

Thanks to the ruling classes' support of Buddhism, many monks of diverse ethnic and sectarian backgrounds were active in Tangut territory and contributed to its Buddhist print culture.[31] Elite monks were appointed by the court

27 Chen B. 1985, 63–65. According to the Ming imperial stele dated to the Xuande reign, the temple was first constructed in 1098; see Dong 2003, 31. For Marco Polo's comment on Ganzhou, see also Dang 2010, 20. For Timurid envoys' visit, see Maitra 1970, 38–39; He 1981, 113–15. I would like to thank Yusen Yu for sharing the Timurid documentation with me. For more studies of the Dafosi and its collection of Buddhist books, see Dong 2003; Kong 2010. For a survey of the extant site, see E 2014, 2: 367–84.

28 For a survey of the extant site, see E 2014, 2: 359–66. For the history of the Tibetan community in Ganzhou, see Su 1996, 255–63.

29 Shi 1988, 121, 123–24; Cui 2010a, 186–87. Shi Jinbo notes the illustrated single-sheet Tibetan prints produced in Xi Xia (2004, 70–72). Uighurs constituted a significant part of the local community in the western part of the Xia kingdom; see Dunnell 1994, 180; Yang and Chen 2012, 346–68. For more on Uighurs as northern neighbors of the Tangut, see Galambos 2011.

30 Yang and Chen 2012, 250–67; Cui 2010a, 67; Sha 2018, 11. The term "sacred palace" (*shenggong* 聖宮) also appears in a Uighur inscription of a pilgrim visiting Yulin Cave 3; see Matsui and Arakawa 2017, 291. Previous scholars have speculated that the inscription written on the north wall of the corridor of Yulin Cave 15 may refer to the visit of a Tangut emperor; see Yang and Chen 2012, 267. For a complete transliteration of the inscription, see Matsui and Arakawa 2017, 296–97.

31 Shi 1988, 135–54.

to translate and compile sutras; others were involved either as donors or block cutters. In the early days, multi-lingual Uighur monks well versed in both Tangut and Chinese held leading roles in Buddhist translation, supporting the Tangut rulers' efforts to create Buddhist sutras in their native tongue.[32] As the connection with Himalayan Buddhist circles intensified in the late twelfth and early thirteenth centuries, Tibetan monks grew in status.

There are ample visual representations of monks in Xi Xia woodcuts and paintings, revealing the extent of the international Buddhist community. In Tangut visual culture, monks are represented to showcase their diverse roles, ranging from religious leaders, deceased souls awaiting salvation, to donors of printed scriptures, and woodblock artisans.

The *Picture of Sutra Translating in Xi Xia* (fig. 6.11), an oft-cited two-fold frontispiece decorating an esoteric Buddhist scripture in Tangut, reprinted in the Yuan dynasty (early fourteenth century), provides a vivid picture of the multi-ethnic translation team working at the early Tangut court.[33] It may be based on a Xi Xia prototype, designed to commemorate the completion of translating the Buddhist canon into Tangut.[34] In the foreground are Empress Dowager Liang 母梁氏皇太后 (?–1099) and Emperor Huizong 夏惠宗 (1060–1086 r. 1068–1086),[35] who provided crucial support for Buddhist translations. The central figure seated frontally against a threefold landscape screen and depicted larger than the others is a Uighur monk. The Tangut colophon rendered in a horizontal line at the top identifies him as the state preceptor Bai Zhiguang 白智光, who translated numerous Buddhist texts from Chinese into Tangut, beginning in 1038.[36] More colophons rendered vertically on both his sides indicate that sixteen monks and laymen assisted with the translation.[37] Placed in groups of eight seated on either side of the central figure, they are shown in front of long tables displaying books, ink cakes, and brushes as they hold brushes and

32 For Uighur monks in the Gaotai and Chengtian Monasteries constructed by the founding emperor and empress, see Shi 1988, 31–32; Fan and Yang 2009, 123–24; Yang 1998; Yang 2003a.

33 Shi 1979; Shi 1988, 76–79; Shi 2020, 129–30; Cui 2010a. 191–93.

34 Peng 2011, 3.

35 Although he is depicted here as a mature, kingly figure with a mustache and a long beard, it is more likely that this is an imaginary image by the Yuan illustrator rather than his true appearance: the emperor died young, at the age of twenty-six. For more about Empress Dowager Liang and her clan in Tangut politics, see Dunnell 1994, 193–95; Galambos 2015, 110–11.

36 Different scholars proposed different translations of the colophon. For two versions of translation, see Shi 1979, 215; Peng 2011, 4. For more on Bai Zhiguang, see Shi 1988, 73–74; Huang 2014d, 140; 2017b, 284.

37 Shi 1979, 218.

FIGURE 6.11 *Picture of Sutra Translating in Xi Xia*. Frontispiece of the Tangut *Pratyuttpanna-bhadra-kalpa-sahasra-buddha-nama-sutra*. Yuan. Woodblock print. National Library of China

books in scroll or folded format. Name markers in Tangut script accompany each figure, indicating that there were three Tangut, two Tibetan, one Indian, and eleven Chinese monks;[38] however, they do not bear visual features that

38 In 1979, Shi Jinbo translated the names of the eight monks and proposed that four out of eight were Tangut; he assumed that the other four with Chinese last names were Chinese (1979, 218–19). More recently, the Russian scholar K. B. Leping re-identified the

can be directly linked to their ethnicities. Items on the tables suggest that the monks were engaged in multilingual translation. On the left side of the picture plane is a book with pseudo writings. On the right, a leaf-like artifact in front of the second monk may refer to a palm-leaf scripture—a popular material and format of Indian Buddhist scriptures.[39]

Tangut, Tibetan, and Indian monks appear frequently in other Xi Xia woodcuts and paintings. Their various garments and hats may reflect their different lineages and identities. A frontispiece published by Shi Jinbo shows the Tangut monk Baoyuan 寶源 from the Da Dumin Monastery, active in the second half of the twelfth century. A court appointed state preceptor (*guoshi* 國師), he appears as a monk with a pointed lotus-shaped cap who faces devotees kneeling in front of him in a garden (fig. 6.12).[40] His cap is similar to the lotus-shaped headgear of the Tangut state preceptor Zhihai 智海, depicted in the mural of the Yulin Cave 29, dated around 1193.[41]

Tibetan monks, of both the Karma Kagyu and Sakya sects, were active at the Tangut court, especially in the late twelfth and early thirteenth centuries.[42] The monk Fashizi 法獅子 (Tib.: Chos-kyi sen-ge), who was affiliated with the Da Dumin Monastery, was appointed state preceptor.[43] Indeed, all the three monks raised to this highest Buddhist rank in the Tangut state, were Tibetan. First established in the late twelfth century, the system of imperial preceptor was

Tangut cartouches and argued that one cannot readily assume that those with Chinese last names were in fact Chinese (Peng 2011, 4–6; Jia 2014a, 22). For a study of the Tangut and Chinese names, see Tong 2013; Tong 2015. For Chinese monks in Xi Xia, see Fan and Yang 2009, esp. 128–29. In general, Tibetan and Uighur monks in Xi Xia enjoyed a higher status than Chinese. See Fan and Yang 2009. Tong Jianrong has called attention to many names combing Chinese family with Tangut first names; see Tong 2015, 105–23.

39 Shi 1988, 78.

40 Shi 2015, 131–32; Sha ed. 2022, 199. Many monks were bestowed the title of a state preceptor; see Shi 1988, 143–47. For more on their caps, see Xie 2002, 1: 266–67. 2: 92–93 (pls. 90–91); Xie 2003, 74–78; Xie et al. 2010, 171, 214–15, 273–74; Gao 2009, 218; Liu Yuquan 1996, 132; Sha ed. 2022, 185–210.

41 The Yulin Cave 29 mural was painted by the Tangut artist Gao Chongde 高崇德 from Ganzhou and sponsored by members of the elite, including the Shazhou Military Commissioner Zhao Mayu 趙麻玉, his family members who held posts in the Tangut government, and a monk who was an imperial prince. See ZGDHBHQJ 10: 65 (fig. 82); Xie 2002, 1: 266–68; 2: 73 (pl. 71). For a complete transliteration of the Tangut inscriptions retrieved from this cave, see Matsui and Arakawa 2017, 311–18 (cf. the translation of the donor's name as Zhao Maji 趙麻吉 in 312). For more studies of the donors, see Liu Yuquan 1996; 2011, 362–64; Dunnell 2001, 121–22; Yang B. 2017, 156; Ning and He 2017; Sha ed. 2022, 241–57.

42 Sperling 1987; Chen Q. 2000; Shen 2018, 116–18.

43 Shi 2002, 41; Shi 2015, 132; Nie 2003, 95–98; Dunnell 2009, 51–54.

FIGURE 6.12
Depiction of the Tangut national preceptor Baoyuan. Xi Xia. Woodblock print

perpetuated in Yuan China under Mongol rule.[44] The Great Vehicle Mysterious National Preceptor (Dasheng xuanmi guoshi 大乘玄密國師; Tib.: Gtsang-po-pa Dkon-mchog seng-ge), whose name was mentioned on Renzong's guest list to the Maitreya Retreat (fig. 6.1), was granted this title later in his career.[45] He was the disciple of Dus-gsum mkhyenpa (1110–1193), the first head of the Karma Kagyu sect, recommended to Renzong after his teacher declined the ruler's invitation to serve as the court teacher in Buddhist matters.[46]

Scholars have proposed various hypotheses to identify certain monks' images in Xi Xia paintings as reputable Tibetan masters documented in textual sources, but there is no firm evidence.[47] Two monks (figs. 6.13b–c), with distinctive hats that can be traced back to Chinese official hat conventions, seen in the lower corners of the *Medicine Buddha* (fig. 6.13a), are tentatively identified as Tibetan monks of the Karma Kagyu sect.[48] The one with a black hat in the lower left corner (fig. 6.13b) may be Gtsang-po-pa Dkon-mchog seng-ge.[49] The monk in the lower right (fig. 6.13c) may be dGe shes gTsang pa dung khur ba, who arrived in Xi Xia at the same time. He is shown wearing a yellow hat

44 Shi 1988, 137–47; Shi 2001, 71–72; Shi 2002, 39–41; Shi 2004, 120; Dunnell 1992; 2001, 111–12; 2009, 64–78; Xie et al. 2010, 127; Chen Q. 1991; Yang and Chen 2012, 305–307.

45 Chen Q. 2000.

46 Stein 1966, 286; Sperling 1987; Dunnell 1992, 96–97; Shi 1988, 143–44.

47 For select studies, see Samosyuk 2001; Dunnell 2001; Stoddard 2008, 16–17; Xie and Cai 2020a; Meinert 2020, 260–69.

48 Xie and Cai 2020a–b. Cf. Samosyuk 1998, 99–101.

49 Xie and Cai 2020b, 60–61. This identification challenges the earlier identification proposed in Stoddard 2008, 16–17; Xie and Cai 2020a, 46–47, 54.

a

FIGURES 6.13A–C *Medicine Buddha* (X. 2332). Xi Xia. Colors on linen. Hanging scroll. The State Hermitage Museum, St. Petersburg
a. A complete view
b–c. Details of monks

b

c

with drapes on both sides, a style associated with the Tshalpa Kagyu, a lineage of Karma Kagyu.[50]

Indian monks, present in the Tangut Buddhist community,[51] most likely played a role in the translation of texts, drawing on Sanskrit versions.[52] As Ruth Dunnell suggests, the dark-skinned monk in thangka featuring the Tantric deity Vajravārāhī may be Indian (fig. 6.14).[53] In terms of dress, he differs from stereotypical monk images, being hatless and garbed in an orange-red-edged yellow cloak and a brown inner garment.[54] Images that seem to show Tibetan and Indian monks tend to appear in the lower borders of iconic paintings.[55] Depicted as deified figures with halos, they may have been Buddhist teachers of certain lineages.

Unlike the images of deified monks as subjects of veneration, selected woodcuts and paintings highlight monks as devotees awaiting salvation. A woodcut (fig. 0.13) and a thangka painting (fig. 6.15) representing the theme of

50 The style of the yellow hat is known as *dwags po sgom tshul zhwa*; see Xie and Cai 2020a, 51.

51 Yang and Chen 2012, 215–29.

52 For Sanskrit writings discovered on the wall of the western Baisikou Pagoda and a miniature stupa found in a tomb in Wuwei, dated around 1200, see Yang and Chen 2012, 221–24.

53 Dunnell 2001, 120. Dunnell also speculates that the Kashmiri monk Jayananda (fl. 12th century) "may very well be one of the Indian donor figures in the paintings" (2001, 110). See also Samosyuk in Piotrovsky 1993, 149. For a complete painting, see Piotrovsky 1993, 147–48.

54 Kira Samosyuk suggests that the monk depicted at the lower right corner of the *Medicine Buddha* (x. 2332) may also be an Indian; see Samosyuk 2001, 168; Piotrovsky 1993, 121.

55 For the complete view of the two paintings, see Piotrovsky 1993, 121 (fig. 7), 148 (fig. 22).

FIGURE 6.14
Detail of an Indian monk. *Vajravārāhī* (x. 2393). Colors on linen. Hanging scroll. The State Hermitage Museum, St. Petersburg

Amitabha Welcoming both show a dying monk in the lower left corner of the picture plane, waiting for the buddha's salvation.[56] In the woodcut version, the standing monk bears a cartouche that identifies him as "Disciple Gao Xuanwu" (Dizi Gao Xuanwu 弟子高玄悟).[57] Quite possibly, the image was commissioned by Gao's disciple or a temple affiliated with him to ensure his chances of rebirth in heaven. The brightly colored thangka shares a similar composition, depicting a monk dressed in brown seated under a tree. A new-born baby enclosed in a white cloud radiating from his head symbolizes his reborn form: he is about to be escorted to heaven by the rescuing bodhisattvas who offer him a large lotus seat.

In a woodcut fragment of the *Sutra of the Profound Kindness of Parents Preached by the Buddha* (*Foshuo fumu enzhong jing* 佛說父母恩重經) (figs. 6.16a–b) in codex format, two monks standing amid clouds with their hands in prayer position represent donors of the printed scripture. Because the overall pictorial convention recalls the monkish donors depicted in the Southern Song *Lotus Sutra* printed in Hangzhou (figs. 3.1a–b),[58] it is plausible to identify the two monks as donors of the text. The last paragraph (fig. 6.16b), apparently added to further endorse the choice of renunciation, states that the Buddha advised all men and women to leave the family (*chujia* 出家) in order

56 For more studies, see Piotrovsky 1993, 185 (fig. 40); Lee 1996; Wang M. 2022, esp. 211, 216 (fig. 6.6); Sha ed. 2022, esp. 100.

57 Also see ZGFJBHQJ 3: 237.

58 See also Huang 2020, 60 (fig. 9b).

FIGURE 6.15 *Greeting the Soul to the Pure Land of Amitabha* (X. 2410). Colors on linen. Hanging scroll. The State Hermitage Museum, St. Petersburg

a

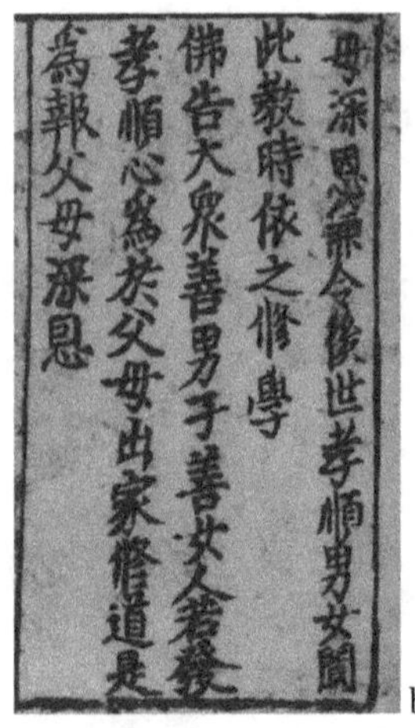
母深恩[illegible][illegible]令後世孝順男女聞
此教時依之修學
佛告大衆善男子善女人若發
孝順心爲於父母出家修道是
爲報父母深恩

b

FIGURES 6.16A–B
Details. *Sutra of the Profound Kindness of Parents* (TK 139). Xi Xia. Woodblock print. Concertina. Institute of Oriental Manuscripts, St. Petersburg
a. Woodcut fragment of the monk-donors
b. The last page of the text

to perform perfect filial piety and repay the profound kindness (*shen'en* 深恩) of the parents.

An intriguing case records an Indian monk as a block cutter: he signed his name as "Zhiyuan from the Western Realm [India]" (Xitian Zhiyuan 西天智圓) at the end of an illustrated *Dharani Sutra* in Chinese (fig. 6.17a).[59] While he may or may not have known the language, he skillfully transmitted the text in running script, based on the rendition by the scribe Suo Zhishen 索智深, quite possibly a Tangut craftsman related to Suo Zhizun 索智尊 and the elite Suo family of Dunhuang.[60] Both the monk Zhiyuan and Suo Zhishen, moreover, may have worked for a certain Puhuasi 普化寺 (Monastery of Universal Transformation), whose affiliate Li Zhibao 李智寶 appears as a donor of the printed text.[61] The large elongated seal stamped on the upper part is in Sanskrit *nāgāri* script; the content may refer to spells.[62] The Indian monk Zhiyuan may also have participated in cutting the block of the frontispiece, which represents a generic scene

59 The term "Western Realm" often refers to India; see Dunnell 2001, 110.

60 For the Tangut family name Suo, see Tong 2013, 184. Suo Zhizun appears as a monk holding a blue vase of lotus flowers in a group of donors-as-monks (*zhuyuan seng* 助緣僧) on the north wall of the corridor in Mogao Cave 61. For the transliteration of the names of the Tangut monk-donors, see Shi 1988, 289; Matsui and Arakawa 2017, 249–52 (esp. 251). For more about Suo Zhizun, see Sha 2018, 12.

61 Yang and Chen 2010, 108; Yang and Chen 2012, 214; Shi 1988, 47; Shi 2004, 135. Cf. the text with the same title in T.19.937. For more on the India-Xi Xia exchange, see Yang and Chen 2010; 2012: 211–29.

62 I am grateful for Yong Cho and Ellen Gough for their help with the Sanskrit seal. Cf. a round-shaped seal in non-Chinese script, stamped at the end of the same text but based on different blocks (TK 76), perhaps also cut by Zhiyuan; see ECHSCWX 1: color plate 32; ECHSCWX 2: 162.

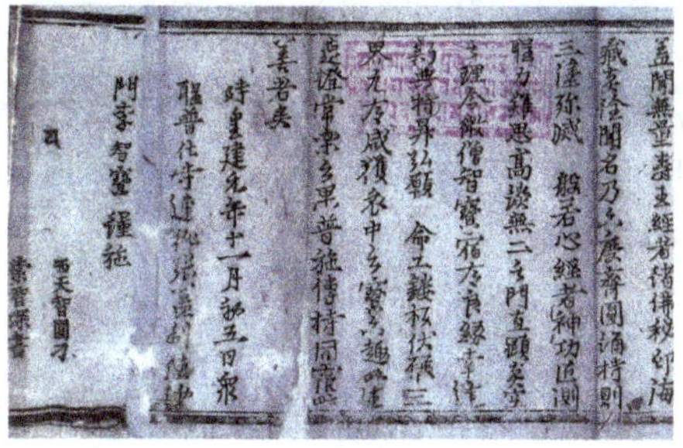
a

b

FIGURES 6.17A–B Details. *Dharani Sutra of the Infinite Life Buddha* (TK 21). 1210. Xi Xia. Woodblock print. Institute of Oriental Manuscripts, St. Petersburg
a. Detail of the colophon
b. Detail. Frontispiece to the text

of the Buddha preaching in a garden, complete with balustrades and a banana tree in the background (fig. 6.17b).

All this is indicative of a complex interactive network in Buddhist printing at the time. While much information is available on multiethnic Buddhists within Tangut society and their outreach, this was not a one-way street. Tangut monks also traveled to India and transmitted Buddhist teachings from there, while the Tangut court donated precious materials to decorate a new stupa in Tibet.[63]

1.2 *Empress Luo as Donor and Sponsor*

Emperor Renzong and his second consort Empress Luo, who was of Chinese descent, were most enthusiastic royal donors and patrons of Buddhist illustrated printing.[64] After Renzong died in 1193, their seventeen-year-old son ascended the throne as Emperor Huanzong, making Empress Dowager Luo the single most powerful female patron of Buddhist printing at court.[65] Based on her active involvement in politics, scholars have compared her support of Buddhism to that of Wu Zetian 武則天 (r. 690–705), "the sole female ruler in Chinese history."[66] Empress Luo may have also donated illustrated printed books sponsored at the Maitreya Retreat. Multiple extant copies of

63 Yang and Chen 2012, 212–13; Shi 2002, 36.

64 For more on Empress Luo's support of Buddhism, see Bai 2007; Yang B. 2017.

65 She was aggressively involved in a political rebellion in 1206. For her control of politics after Renzong died, see XXJSBM 22: 214–16. For more studies, see Dunnell 1994, 204; Shi 1988, 43–47.

66 Wong 2018, 17. Dorothy Wong highlights Wu Zetian's role in the shaping of an international Buddhist art style in Tang China and eighth-century Japan (2018, 57–94, 167–220).

the illustrated *Diamond Sutra* (figs. 6.18a–c) and the "Vows of Samantabhadra" (figs. 6.19a–b) bear her dedicatory colophons, dating their production to within a few months of the Retreat.[67] Since their titles match those of texts distributed by Renzong at the time, they may well have been printed for the occasion.[68] Selected copies of the *Diamond Sutra*, moreover, show a seal of the Wenjiasi daoyuan 溫家寺道院 (Cloister of the Wen Family Monastery) (figs. 6.18a–b), which may refer to an imperially sponsored temple in the capital to receive imperially-bestowed texts.[69] At the end of the "Vows of Samantabhadra," stories of seventh-century miraculous occurrences highlight the efficacy of the *Avatamsaka Sutra* (fig. 6.19a).[70] Their inclusion, possibly a byproduct of Wu Zetian's promotion of the sutra's teachings to legitimize her power, also reflects the political ambitions of Empress Luo.[71]

Empress Luo's ties to Buddhist temples are further documented in a large Tangut seal stamped in the opening of the hand-copied *Jeweled Rain Sutra* (*Baoyu jing* 寶雨經) in Tangut (fig. 6.20). This was translated under the auspices of Empress Dowager Liang, another major Buddhist donor.[72] Both empresses

For more about Empress Wu, see Rothschild 2008. For studies of the Xia Empress, see Bai 2007; Yang B. 2017, 157*n*4.

67 An additional specimen of the same frontispiece design attached to the *Diamond Sutra*, now in the Institute of Oriental Manuscripts, St. Petersburg, is mislabeled as a Dunhuang specimen (no. 11581); see ECDHWX 15: 258. Some fragments from the identical frontispiece design of the "Vows of Samantabhadra" are in the Stein collection in New Delhi (KK II 0227a, KK II 253c, KK II 0175.iv); see Stein 1928, 3: LXII; ZGBHQJ 1: 82 (fig. 12); Drège 1999, 49. For a study of Avatamsaka Buddhism and the text in Xi Xia, see Solonin 2013, 175–89.

68 Chen and Tang 2010, 133–34, 140–41. For the reception of the Avatamsaka teachings in Xi Xia, and its connection to Buddhism in the Liao, see Nishida 1975–1977; Solonin 2007, 2008, 2013; Shi 1988, 156–57; Cui 2010b. For a Xi Xia fragment of the printed frontispiece to the *Avatamsaka Sutra* (TK 114) based on the Southern Song frontispiece design associated with the *Brahma Net Sutra* (*Fanwang jing* 梵網經), see Huang 2014d, 146–48, 173–74 (figs. 18–19); Huang S. 2021a, 569–70.

69 Scholars tend to interpret the seal as the marking of the temple where the texts were printed (Shi 1988, 99, 121–25; Chen and Tang 2010, 132–33). I think it is more likely that the seal referred to the temple where the texts were collected. In the other extant copy (TK 18), an unidentifiable private seal was stamped at the end, complete with a hand-written signature that reads "Li Shanjin" 李善進, suggesting that the copy may have been bestowed to Li Shanjin; see ECHSCWX 1: 354; Bai 2007, 136.

70 Solonin 2013, 186.

71 Bai 2007, 136–37.

72 See also Shi 2004, 98; ECHSCWX 24: 68; Kira Samosyuk in EGABCHY, 1: 18 (fig. 14); ZGFJBHQJ 3: 192; Shi 2020, 88 (fig. 39). The same seal was also stamped on a hand-written copy of the twentieth chapter of the *Foshuo chang ahan jing* (no. 150), decorated with an identical printed frontispiece. See ECHSCWX 15, unnumbered page, color plate 3. Because both manuscripts bear the numbering system of the *Thousand Words*, scholars have speculated that they were originally part of the Buddhist canon in Tangut, sponsored by

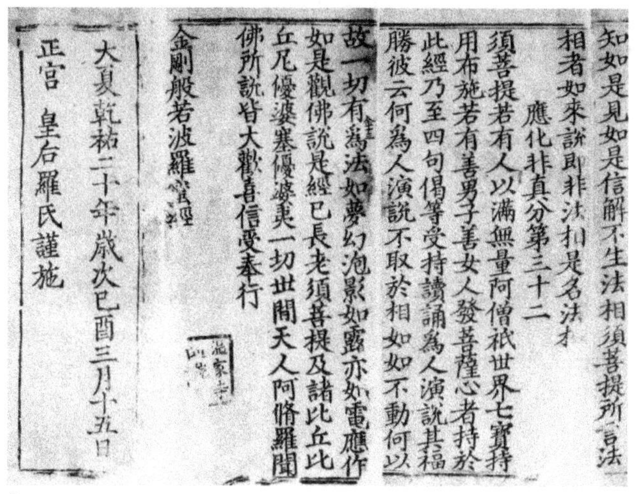

知如是見如是信解不生法相須菩提所言法
相者如來説即非法相是名法相
應化非真分第三十二
須菩提若有人以滿無量阿僧祇世界七寶持
用布施若有善男子善女人發菩薩心者持於
此經乃至四句偈等受持讀誦為人演説其福
勝彼云何為人演説不取於相如如不動何以
故一切有為法如夢幻泡影如露亦如電應作
如是觀佛説是經已長老須菩提及諸比丘比
丘尼優婆塞優婆夷一切世間天人阿脩羅聞
佛所説皆大歡喜信受奉行
金剛般若波羅蜜經
大夏乾祐二十年歲次己酉三月十五日
正宮皇后羅氏謹施

a

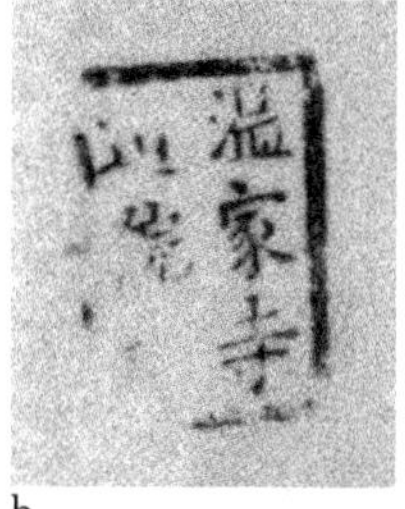

b

金剛經啓請
若有人受持金剛經者先須志心念淨口業真
言然後啓請八金剛四菩薩名号所在之處常
當擁護
淨口業真言
修唎修唎摩訶修唎修修唎薩婆訶

c

FIGURES 6.18A–C Details. Copies of the *Diamond Sutra* (TK 14). 1189. Xi Xia. Woodblock print. Concertina. Institute of Oriental Manuscripts, St. Petersburg
a. Detail of the dedicatory colophon by Empress Luo
b. Detail of a seal
c. Detail of the frontispiece

were well aware of the text's political implications, as Wu Zetian legitimized her own rule by promoting it: it mentions how the Buddha foretold that a bodhisattva manifesting in female form would be the future ruler.[73]

Empress Luo. See Shi 1988, 45; Shi 2004, 98–99. For the *Jeweled Rain Sutra* in Chinese, see T.16.660; for the Tang Dunhuang mural in Mogao 321 pertinent to this sutra, see DHSKQJ 9: 180–202.

73 Bai 2007, 140; Yang B. 2017, 155.

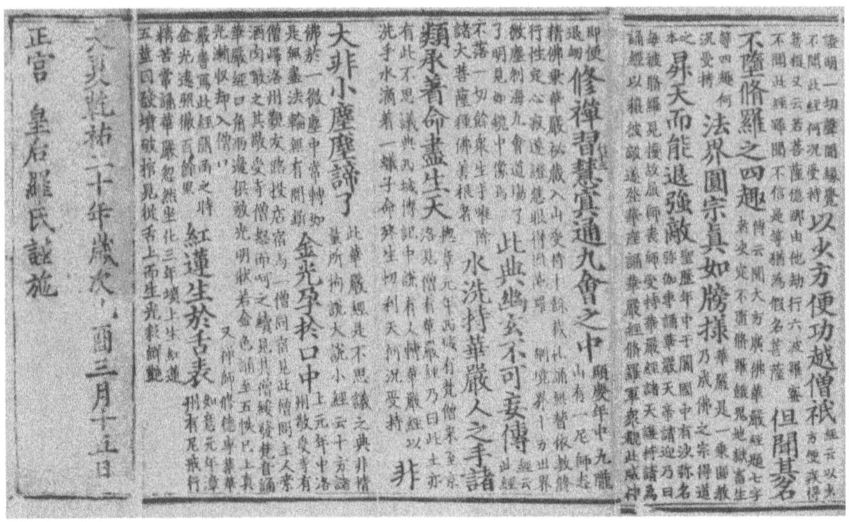

大夏乾祐二十年歲次己酉三月十五日

正宮皇后羅氏謹施

a

b

FIGURES 6.19A–B Details. "Vows of Samantabhadra" chapter from the *Avatamsaka Sutra* (TK 61). 1189. Xi Xia. Woodblock print. Concertina. Institute of Oriental Manuscripts, St. Petersburg
a. Dedicatory colophon by Empress Luo dated 1189
b. Frontispiece

A stamped five-line Tangut inscription acknowledges the formal donation. It says,

> Empress Dowager Luo, the pure and devout disciple of the Great White High Kingdom, recently had the complete Tangut Canon transcribed. All people under heaven [should] celebrate and praise [her]! [The copied

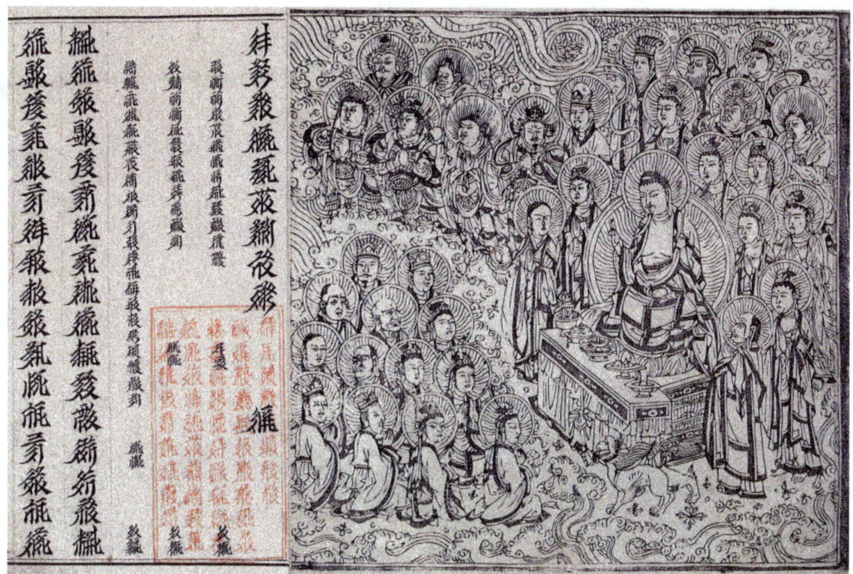

FIGURE 6.20 Detail of a printed frontispiece and a large seal in Tangut script. Part of the hand-copied *Jeweled Rain Sutra* (no. 87). Xi Xia. Woodblock print. Institute of Oriental Manuscripts, St. Petersburg

canon has] been deposited in a temple library. It shall be read and venerated forever.[74]

The Tangut seal inscription does not specify which temple received the bestowed text. It is, therefore, entirely plausible to assume that she distributed copies to several institutions.

Empress Dowager Luo continued her activities after Renzong passed away. In 1195, she presided over a Buddhist book-gifting ceremony dedicated to Renzong and donated thirty thousand newly printed Chinese and Tangut copies of the *Sutra of Transformation of the Female Body* (*Foshuo zhuan nüshen jing* 佛說轉女身經) (figs. 6.21a–d).[75] This is a Chinese Buddhist text about a young woman known as Wugou guang 無垢光 (Unsullied Pure Light) who turns out to be a bodhisattva.[76] Its key teaching is that, while ordinary women can only obtain salvation by abandoning their impure body, "some women are

74 My translation is based on the Chinese translation in Shi 1988, 45; Shi 2004, 98.

75 As a great patron of art, she also donated "more than 30,000 colored devotional paintings in hanging scroll format to officials and citizens." For a punctuated transliteration of the complete colophon, see Shi 1988, 275.

76 Cf. the *Foshuo zhuan nushen jing* in T.14.564. For more studies of the sutras on sexual transformation, see Balkwill 2016; Balkwill, 2021.

a

b

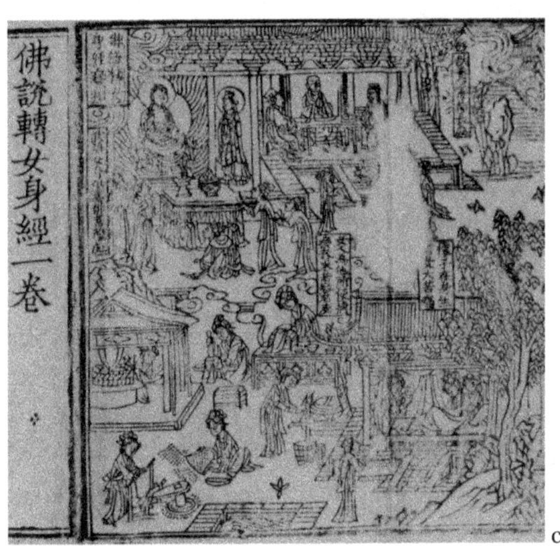

c

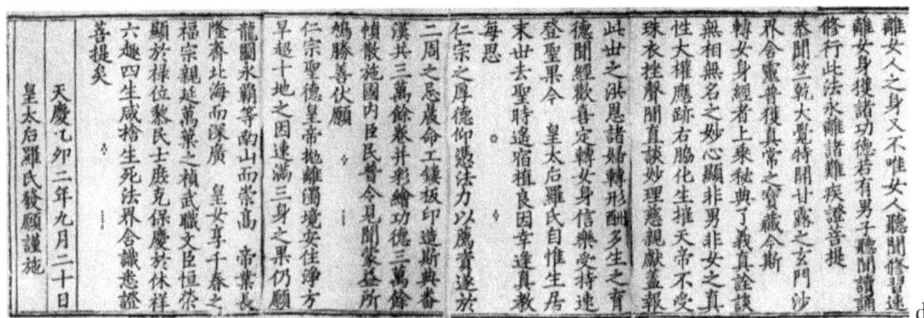

離女人之身又不唯女人聽聞修習速
離女身獲諸功德若有男子聽聞讀誦
修行此法永離諸難疾證菩提
恭聞竺乾大覺特開甘露之玄門沙
界含靈普獲真常之寶藏今斯
轉女身經者上乘秘典了義真詮該
無相無名之妙心顯非男非女之真
性大權應跡右脅化生推天帝不受
珠衣挫聲聞直談妙理慈親獻蓋報
此世之洪恩諸婦轉形酬多生之育
德聞經歡喜定轉女身信樂受持速
登聖果今 皇太后羅氏自惟生居
末世去聖時遥宿植良因幸逢真教
每思
仁宗之厚德仰憑法力以薦資遊於
二周之忌晨命工鏤板印造斯典番
漢共三萬餘卷并彩繪功德三萬餘
幀散施國內臣民普令見聞蒙益所
鳩勝善伏願
仁宗聖德皇帝抛離濁境安住淨方
早超十地之因速滿三身之果仍願
龍圖永霸等南山而崇高 帝業長
隆齊北海而深廣 皇女享千春之
福宗親延萬葉之禎武職文臣恒恭
顯於祿位黎民士庶克保慶於休祥
六趣四生咸捨生死法界含識悉證
菩提矣
天慶乙卯二年九月二十日
皇太后羅氏發願謹施

d

FIGURES 6.21A–D Details. *Sutra of Transformation of the Female Body* sponsored by Empress Dowager Luo. 1195. Xi Xia. Woodblock print. Concertina. Institute of Oriental Manuscripts, St. Petersburg
a–c. Details of the frontispiece (TK 8)
d. Detail of a colophon (TK 12)

in fact bodhisattvas in disguise"—a notion that may have had strong appeal for Empress Dowager Luo: by mass-producing this text, she in fact promoted "an image of herself as a bodhisattva."[77]

Its expansive sixfold frontispiece (fig. 6.21a) contains a unique array of narrative illustrations unlike anything else in East Asian art.[78] Unsullied Pure Light's magical birth appears in two continuous scenes near the center (fig. 6.21b). It shows first her conception as she enters her mother's womb, then her birth as a naked baby standing in a lotus flower. She is surrounded by a tapering cloud emanating from her mother's right armpit, a feature that closely echoes the story of the miraculous birth of the Buddha.[79] The lower left section further represents women engaging in daily activities (fig. 6.21c), ranging from giving birth through doing laundry in a bucket, pounding medicine in a tripod, and sifting grain, to turning a wheel-shaped machine and more.[80] The upper left section depicts what seems most crucial to make a woman's bodily transformation possible: venerating the Buddha and an accompanying bodhisattva.

In 1196, to commemorate the third anniversary of Renzong's death, Empress Dowager Luo made an unprecedented donation in a grand Buddhist ceremony, as documented in a colophon at the end of the "Vows of Samantabhadra"

77 Saliceti-Collins 2007, 103, 105.

78 The most thorough study of this frontispiece remains Saliceti-Collins 2007, 103–105. It depicts fifteen episodes. For the transliteration of the cartouches, see Chen and Tang 2010, 154.

79 This story is depicted in the Xi Xia mural on the east wall of Yulin Cave 3; see DHSKQJ 4: 212 (fig. 195); Jia 2020, 64–65 (fig. 2-1-3).

80 Saliceti-Collins 2007, 104.

(fig. 6.22a). The sheer numbers of Buddhist items she donated are stunning: ninety-three thousand copies of both Tangut and Chinese versions of the *Sutra of Transforming the Female Body*, the *Sutra of Benevolent Kings* (*Renwang jing* 仁王經),[81] and the "Vows of Samantabhadra"; 77,276 devotional paintings in hanging-scroll format, including representations of Buddha Shakyamuni's biographies framed in eight pagodas (*Bata chengdao xiang* 八塔成道像);[82] as well as 171 banners and 16,088 rosaries. She also sponsored the ordination of three thousand Tibetan, Tangut, and Chinese monks, released prisoners fifty-two times, fed the poor sixty-five times, released 70,779 sheep, and issued one Grand Pardon.[83]

The printed text is adorned by an elaborate sixfold frontispiece with minute narrative depictions of Child Sudhana's visits to the fifty-three sages (fig. 6.22b), a popular visual repertoire also shared in the *Illustrated Eulogies by Mañjuśrī*, printed in Southern Song Hangzhou and a possible source of inspiration for multiple Xi Xia woodcuts (figs. 6.67c, 6.69a–b).[84] As mentioned earlier (see ch. 5), the scene depicting Sudhana's visit to the prisons of hell (fig. 5.30), shown in the lower left corner, matches Dizang's visit to hell as featured in a twelfth-century frontispiece produced in Jin Pingyang (fig. 5.25b), that is, about twenty years before. A recent study of the Yulin Cave 2 constructed under Xi Xia rule further suggests that the printed frontispiece of the "Vows of Samantabhadra" sponsored by Empress Dowager Luo may have served as a direct model for the mural on that very theme.[85]

---

81 Cf. *Renwang huguo boruo boluo mi duo jing* 仁王護國般若波羅蜜多經 in T.8.246. For a study of this sutra, see Orzech 1998.

82 The title of the paintings recalls the eleventh-to-twelfth century murals known as the "Eight Pagodas Sutra Tableux" (*Bata bian* 八塔變), representing Buddha's biographical stories in eight scenes, their common compositional scheme framed by a pagoda. Prime examples include those depicted in the early eleventh-century Mogao Cave 76, and two Xi Xia caves—Yulin Cave 3 and Wugemiao 五個廟 Cave 1. For the plates, see DHMGK 4: 190–206 (figs. 177–93); 211–24 (figs. 194–213), 230–33 (figs. 220–23); 5, figs. 106–109; 21: 259 (fig. 261). For studies, see Xie and Yu 2011; Chen Q. 2017; Jia 2020, 61–108.

83 Shi 1988, 44–45. For a punctuated transliteration of the complete colophon, see Shi 1988, 273–74; note that Shi dated the colophon to 1195.

84 Drège 1999, 50–51 Huang 2014d, 145–46, 153, 173; Huang 2017b, 290–91, 297.

85 For a scene-by-scene comparison, see Sha ed. 2022, 331–35. Local Xi Xia military officials active in Guazhou may have joined the Tangut court to co-sponsor the construction of the cave, see Sha ed. 2022, 341–42.

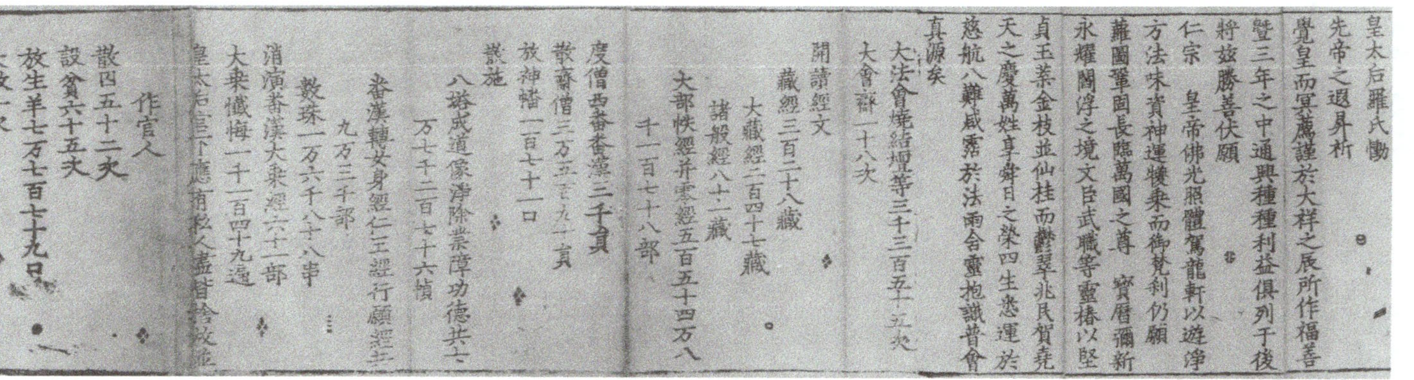
皇太后羅氏慟
先帝之遐昇祈
覺皇而冥薦謹於大祥之辰所作福善
暨三年之中通興種種利益俱列于後
將茲勝善伏願
仁宗 皇帝佛光照體駕龍軒以遊淨
方法味資神運犢乘而御梵剎仍願
藩圖鞏固長臨萬國之尊 寶曆彌新
永耀閻浮之境文臣武職等靈椿以堅
貞玉葉金枝並仙桂而欝翠兆民賀堯
天之慶萬姓享舜日之榮四生悉運於
慈航八難咸霑於法雨含靈抱識普會
真源矣
大法會燒結壇等三千三百五十五次
大會齋一十八次
開讀經文
藏經三百二十八藏
大藏經二百四十七藏
諸般經八十一藏
大部帙經并零經五百五十四万八
千一百七十八部
度僧西番番漢三千員
散齋僧三万五千五百九十員
放神幡一百七十一口
散施
八塔成道像淨除業障功德共七
万七千二百七十六幀
番漢轉女身經仁王經行願經共
九万三千部
數珠一万六千八十八串
消演番漢大乘經六十一部
大乘懺悔一千一百四十九遍
皇太后宮下應有私人盡皆捨放施
作官人
散四五十二夾
設貧六十五夾
放生羊七万七百七十九口
大赦一次

a

b

FIGURES 6.22A–B Details. "Vows of Samantabhadra" chapter from the *Avatamsaka Sutra* (TK 98). 1196.
Xi Xia. Woodblock print. Concertina. Institute of Oriental Manuscripts, St. Petersburg
a. Colophon
b. Frontispiece

1.3 *Interstate Connections*

Buddhist printing under Xi Xia rule also benefited from its extensive interstate network, especially connections to the Song and Jin.[86] A flourishing painting and print culture produced sophisticated visual materials, including murals, printed illustrations, and books that in turn provided references to Xi Xia woodcutters and other artists. As noted earlier, printed materials produced in Northern Song Hangzhou (figs. 0.2, 0.4) and Jin Pingyang (figs. 2.7, 5.5) were discovered in the Xi Xia ruins in Khara Khoto, suggesting that local artists had access to print cultures of other states via interstate connections.

1.3.1 To the Northern Song, Liao, and Jin

The interstate circulation of books in the tenth to thirteenth centuries were far more vibrant and complex than official regulations suggest. Books and other objects—including paintings and calligraphy—traveled across borders, transmitted both legally and illegally, directly and indirectly. Tributes, border markets, smuggling, and wars in this context constituted four major stimuli fostering an active culture of interstate circulation.[87]

Buddhism, as a key facet of the "interdependent cultural tradition of northern and northwestern China,"[88] played an important role in cross-regional exchange at the official level. Thus, from 1031 to 1073, the Xi Xia rulers lodged six requests with the Northern Song government to receive copies of the Kaibao Canon.[89] On the other hand, the Northern Song sent Buddhist monks as undercover agents to the Xi Xia court to scout out political information. Most likely, they also brought images or illustrated books along, which in turn became visual resources for Xi Xia artists and artisans.[90] While the Liao prohibited the export of books to the Northern Song, they supplied many Buddhist texts to the Tangut, exerting a significant impact on Xi Xia Buddhism. The Tangut court intended to duplicate the entire textual corpus of Liao Buddhism, internalizing teachings and practices associated with the Avatamsaka, Chan, and Esoteric schools.[91] It may have acquired the Liao Canon in 1062 as additional reference material for collating the compiled texts, in turn based on the Northern Song Kaibao Canon.

86 For a recent study of Jin-Xia relation, see Ma 2022.

87 Border markets and smuggling account for two major factors of interstate book circulation; see Liu P. 2006, esp. 153.

88 Solonin 2008, 70.

89 Shi 1988, 63; Huang 2014d, 137.

90 Yang and Chen 2012, 207–208, 311.

91 Solonin 2007; Solonin 2008; Solonin 2013.

Reciprocally, the Xi Xia also contributed to Buddhism in the Liao: in 1050, the Tangut embassy sent Uighur monks to the Liao as part of a tribute payment. In 1095, the Xi Xia dispatched Buddhist manuscripts copied on palm leaves to the Liao.[92] As regards the Xi Xia-Jin exchange, in 1154, the Tangut government sent envoys to purchase Buddhist and Confucian texts.[93] From 1162 to 1189, the Jin sent annual missions to the Tangut court to participate in Renzong's birthday celebrations.[94] While the Jin-Xi Xia Buddhist book exchange is poorly documented, it is possible that gifts exchanged by these envoys also included books with images that then provided pictorial samples for local woodcut designers or painters.[95]

Another major venue of exchange appears in interstate markets that dotted the eastern and southeastern borders of the Xi Xia territory (map 0.2). Song-Xi Xia border markets were held variously in today's Shaanxi and Ningxia provinces, while those on the Xi Xia-Liao border, established in the eleventh century, operated mainly in Datong, the Western Capital of the Liao in northern Shanxi and other places in Inner Mongolia.[96] The Jin became an immediate neighbor of the Xi Xia after conquering the Liao and the Northern Song in 1125. To facilitate the Xi Xia-Jin trade, some border markets originally set up for trade with the Song and the Liao in Shanxi and Inner Mongolia were reused.[97] The most popular goods traded here were precious stones and falcons from Xi Xia, and textiles and iron from Jin. Both states bought horses from each other and traded goods obtained elsewhere. Citing the Song scholar Hong Hao's 洪皓 (1088–1155) travelog to the Jin, Ruth Dunnell points out that Uighur merchants who passed through Xi Xia territory on their way to the Jin capital Beijing had to pay a ten percent tax on the value of all goods they transported.[98] Other

92 See Shi 1988, 397; Chen and Zhu, eds. 2009, 1001–1002; Yang and Chen 2012, 196–97; Huang 2014d, 140. For Tangut-Khitan intermarriages and Liao political support, see XXJSBM 28–29: 279–97. For more on Xi Xia manuscript culture beyond Buddhism, see Galambos 2015.

93 Yang and Chen 2012, 203.

94 Liu J. 2005, 79; Dunnell 1991, 161–62, 171–76.

95 Some scholars speculated that the Jin Canon might have been transported into Xi Xia from the Jin; see Chen and Yang 2006, 40, 42; Ma 2022, 87–88. For a recent study that acknowledges the stylistic connection between Jin landscape painting and the landscape mural from the Xi Xia Yulin Cave 3, see Sha ed. 2022, 295–325.

96 Chen and Zhu 2009, 1001–1002; Yang H. 2010, 152–53.

97 Yang and Chen 2012, 81–83; Huang 2014d, 150.

98 Dunnell 1994, 180. For more on Hong Hao's travelogue, see Lin H. 2013. For more Uighur-Tangut trade, see Yang and Chen 2012, 58–59, 102–103; Yang 2002.

exotic items, such as spices, gems, and jades which Xi Xia traders acquired along the Silk Road were also sold to the Jin. Likewise, the Jin traded tea, silk, rice, and perhaps books.[99]

Some books and artifacts produced near the border had a better chance of transmission to a neighboring state. This may have been the case with the refined Northern Song *Diamond Sutra Commentaries*, dated 1016 and found in the Khara Khoto ruins.[100] The book's donors were located in places near the Xi Xia border, exemplified by the official Liang 梁 who served at a post in Danzhou 丹州 (modern Shaanxi). This suggests that the book was a local product printed near Danzhou and later transported to Xi Xia lands.[101] Indeed, border inhabitants (*bianmin* 邊民) easily crossed state lines and were potential agents for transmitting books and images.[102] This may have been the case with the layman Zhao Zhong 趙仲, a native from the Jin border town of Zhenrong 鎮戎 (today Guyuan 固原, Ningxia; map 0.2), who visited a Xi Xia Buddhist site. A Buddhist banner, dated between 1190 and 1227 and bearing Zhao's dedicatory prayer written in ink, was discovered in the Hongfo Pagoda near the Xi Xia capital.

1.3.2 To the Southern Song

Even though the Southern Song was never an immediate neighbor of the Xi Xia, the Jin most likely served as intermediaries to get goods from one to the other—possibly also including illustrative books and paintings that then served as visual sources for Xi Xia artists. Jin-Song border markets are documented for many areas, including what is today Jiangsu, Anhui, Hubei, Henan, Gansu, and Shandong.[103]

Ancient paintings, rubbings, and other antiquities, originally collected at the Jin court and later transmitted to the Southern Song via such border markets, are among what Zhou Mi 周密 (1232–1298) has called "objects

99 Yang and Chen 2012, 94–98, 113–51; Huang 2014d, 151.

100 The printed specimen is the fifth chapter of the *Jingang boruo jingchao* 金剛般若經鈔 (TK 149); see ECHSCWX 3: 254–79.

101 Shi 2004, 69 (fig. 33). There are, however, additional donors (villagers and monks) acknowledged on the edges of selected pages. For a transliteration of the donors' information, see Tang 2010, 100.

102 For a case study of the "border residents" living in the Liao-Northern Song border in today's Hebei province, see Li Y. 2011.

103 Ma Xujun identified certain Southern Song artifacts as "exotic products" included in the Jin-Xia trade goods; see Ma 2022, 98. For a more comprehensive list of Southern Song-Jin border markets, see Wang K. 2006, 26.

acquired from the border markets" (*quechang wu* 榷場物).[104] In northern China, Yuan Haowen, a great scholar under Jin rule, once spotted a Southern Song landscape screen painting bearing the handwriting of the Southern Song scholar Zhu Xi 朱熹 (1130–1200) in a tavern in Taiyuan (Shanxi).[105] On the darker side, smugglers transported commodities, including books, either by land or on coastal sea routes.[106] Merchants from the Southern Song, for example, were caught smuggling cartloads of books across the Huai 淮 River border in order to sell them in Jin territory for greater profit.[107]

2 Transmediated Designs

Professional painters used a variety of visual tools to transfer designs across media.[108] An ink drawing of a seated buddha with dotted holes along the contour lines (fig. 6.23), discovered in Khara Khoto, is an example of a Xi Xia pounce. By pasting the pounce onto a wall and pounding powder over the dotted holes, an artist could efficiently transfer the design on a wall.[109] Pertinent to this is a rare image-to-be on the wall of the western of the Baisikou 拜寺口 Twin Pagodas (fig. 6.24). Its visible dotted contour suggests that it may have been an underdrawing transferred by a dotted pounce.[110]

Extant preparatory drawings are rare. In addition to the fragmented drawing described earlier (fig. 0.14), which reflects the popular design of the *Amitabha*

---

104 One example is the *Painting of the Divine Lady of the Wu Mountain* (*Wushan shennü tu* 巫山神女圖) by the Tang painter Li Sixun 李思訓 (fl. 651–716). It is said to have belonged to the Jin Emperor Zhangzong 章宗 (r. 1189–1208) and was later in the private collection of the Southern Song official Jia Sidao 賈似道 (1213–1275). See YYGYL, 147; Liu P. 2006, 156–57; Duan 2016, 107–108.

105 Yao ed. 1990, 391; Liu P. 2006, 156.

106 Wang K. 2006, 26–33 (for the sea route, see 30).

107 JYYLCYZJ, jia 6: 177; Liu P. 2006, 157.

108 For classic studies of *fenben* and finished murals, using Dunhuang drawings and murals as primary examples, see Fraser 1996, 2003; Sha 2007.

109 Saliceti-Collins 2007, 39 (fig. 1.6). For comparable Dunhuang pounces dated to the tenth century, see Drège 1999, 103; Fraser 2003, 103, pl. 14; Sha 2007, 215.

110 The image looks like the Esoteric Buddhist deity Mahākāla; cf. a comparable but not identical iconography in the single-sheet Xi Xia print discovered in Khara Khoto, reproduced in Piotrovsky 1993, 168–69. The underdrawing was found on the surface of an outside niche on the eighth story of the western pagoda of the twin Baisikou Pagodas located near today's Yinchuan, Ningxia. Previous scholars have suggested that the pagoda may go back to either the Xi Xia or the Yuan. See Lei et al. 1995, 244 (fig. 160). It is likely that the underdrawing refers to a painted image produced in the Xi Xia period, while the clay molded sculpture superimposed onto the painted image was added under the Yuan.

FIGURE 6.23 A hand-drawn pounce of a seated buddha (TK 157V). Xi Xia. Ink on paper. Institute of Oriental Manuscripts, St. Petersburg

FIGURE 6.24 The underdrawing of a martial god. Xi Xia. The eighth story of the western of the Baisikou Twin Pagodas, near Yinchuan, Ningxia

Welcoming commonly shared in portable paintings (fig. 0.12), and the printed frontispiece (fig. 0.13),[111] a little-studied ink drawing on paper (fig. 6.25), may have been a preparatory drawing of the workshop responsible for painting the bodhisattva on the south wall of the Yulin Cave 3 (fig. 6.26).[112] The close similarity of the drawing and the mural beyond iconographical concerns, evident

111 The Eastern Thousand Buddhas Cave (Dong qianfodong 東千佛洞) 7 provides a rare example of a Xi Xia mural that represents a comparable theme; for a plate, see Sha ed. 2022, 100 (fig. 3–19).

112 DHSKQJ 18: 228 (fig. 191). For the most updated study of this mural, focusing on the paired iconographies and representations of Mañjuśrī and Samantabadhra, see Jia 2020, 127–56. The dating of the Yulin Cave 3 is still controversial; see Wang 1980; Zhao 1999, 2004; Dunhuang yanjiu yuan 1997, 2011; Jia 2014a–b; 2020, 217. Rob Linrothe famously hypothesized that the kingly figure standing beneath the protective Esoteric Buddhist deity Ushnishavijaya featured in the mandala wall painting in Yulin Cave 3 may symbolize Renzong himself presiding over a Buddhist ritual; see Linrothe 1996b; Sha 2018, 11; Meinert 2020, 255–57 (fig. 10.2). Jia Weiwei, however, argues that the royal figure should be identified as the kingly deity Indra (Dishitian 帝釋天), based on a Tibetan ritual manual translated into Chinese and introduced to Xi Xia; see Jia 2020, 51, 208, 217. Zhang Shubin has identified the narrative pictures at the bottom of the south wall as the representations of Monk Tanyi's visualization of Puxian bodhisattva in the form of a woman; he suggested that Yulin Cave 3 may have been associated with a female patron; see Zhang S. 2019. For a study of the *jiehua* representations in Xi Xia murals, see Wang 2007; Wang 2019, 158–71.

FIGURE 6.25 *Mañjuśrī Bodhisattva* (x. 2442). Xi Xia. Ink on paper. Drawing. The State Hermitage Museum, St. Petersburg

FIGURE 6.26 Detail of the bodhisattva Mañjuśrī crossing the sea. Xi Xia. North side of the west wall. Yulin Cave 3, Guazhou, Gansu

FIGURE 6.27 Drawing of a reclining bodhisattva (K. K. II. 0313. d) discovered by Stein in Khara Khoto. Xi Xia. Ink on paper

in the shared hook-like, angular markings at the end of selected lines, suggests that they may have been associated with the same workshop. Similarly, a drawing of what looks like a seated bodhisattva (fig. 6.27),[113] discovered in Khara Khoto by Sir Aurel Stein, may have been used as a preparatory sketch or design sample to be transferred onto murals in larger size.[114]

3 Visual Syncretism of the *Maitreya* Frontispieces

The *Maitreya* frontispieces (figs. 6.2–6.7) commissioned by Renzong provide the best visual examples for probing into the visual syncretism in Xi Xia Buddhist woodcuts. Like most cases in the history of Chinese print culture, the illustrators or image designers of the Xi Xia Buddhist frontispiece woodcuts often went unrecorded. Nevertheless, it is most likely that these exquisite frontispieces were designed by artist(s) working for the Tangut court. The block cutting and printing may have taken place in imperially sponsored temples, as suggested above. It may also have been carried out in various governmental offices, such as the Character-cutting Office (Kezi si 刻字司), devoted mostly to the printing of texts in Tangut script, and the Craft and Technology Bureau (Gong yuan 工院), which was known for movable-type printing as well.[115]

While there are different versions of the *Maitreya* frontispieces, they all have a common design. Each frontispiece is an eight-fold accordion book, with densely packed pictorial motifs pertinent to the content explained by the accompanying scripture.[116] Viewed from right to left, the composition is divided into three parts, demarcated by two vertical bands of vajra motifs framing the middle part.[117]

The first part, which spreads over the first two folds, shows the Buddha preaching, seated frontally on a highly adorned throne and flanked by his entourage (figs. 6.2–6.5). A generic scene, it yet echoes the content of the *Maitreya Sutra*, in which Buddha Shakyamuni explains to his kneeling disciple Upali the way to enlightenment by citing the example of the bodhisattva

113 Stein 1928, LXI. See also Toyo Bunko Digital Archive Viewer, "Innermost Asia: vol. 3, XLI," Digital Silk Road, Accessed December 24, 2023. http://dsr.nii.ac.jp/toyobunko/viewer/index.html?pages=T-VIII-5-A-a-3/V-3&pos=79&lang=en.

114 Comparable but not identical likenesses of the bodhisattva Guanyin reclining on a rock can be found in two mirror images on the corresponding walls of the Yulin Cave 29.

115 Shi 2004, 102–109, esp. 104–106; Cui 2010a, 221–23. For more on paper making in Xi Xia, see Shi 2004, 169; Shi 2007a, 525; Cui 2009; Niu 2013, 279–304.

116 Cf. the Chinese translation by Ququ Jingsheng, see T. 14.452.

117 Drège 1999, 53; Saliceti-Collins 2007, 143–44.

Maitreya, "who presently resides in a palace in Tusita Heaven and will descend to Earth in the future to become a fully enlightened Buddha."[118] The second part, which occupies the middle five folds, is the most elaborate depiction of Maitreya's palace in the Tusita Heaven. In the foreground is a horizontally extended wall, adorned with pendant jewelry, demarcated by a gate in the center and two gates at both ends that are revealed partially. Two groups of heavenly guardians are riding patrol on mushroom-shaped clouds outside the gates. Inside the wall is the magnificent palace. The bodhisattva Maitreya is seated inside the main hall, populated by celestial maidens and officials. In front of the hall, numerous musicians and monkish figures are seated in the courtyard, paying tribute to Maitreya. Next to the palace is the third part. It is composed of six vignettes of narrative scenes laid out in a three-by-two grid. Each vignette highlights a devotional act that can lead to rebirth in Maitreya's paradise: a lay couple makes offerings to the Buddha, a practitioner meditates in a hut, a sculptor creates a Buddhist statue, a scholarly devotee reads Buddhist texts by a desk, two lay people bow to a buddha, and two laymen clean a Buddhist pagoda.

The complex design of the *Maitreya* frontispieces reflects two major artistic conventions, the Indo-Himalayan and the Chinese, both current in eleventh-to-twelfth century China and Tibet.[119] The Indo-Himalayan style is most prominent in the first section, whereas the rest of the frontispiece is dominated by the Chinese style. Together, the two styles form the core visual vocabulary of Xi Xia Buddhist art. They show the unique "Tangut way" of assembling different styles. Instead of blending styles, the makers of the frontispieces juxtaposed them in a compartmental fashion.

The notion of stylistic juxtaposition is akin to what the religious studies scholar Michael Pye describes as "syncretism," as opposed to "synthesis." According to Pye, syncretism refers to a situation when "the potential claims of the constitutive elements are still alive" and "dynamically open," whereas synthesis entails "a new conclusion."[120] If we extend Pye's notion of religious syncretism to the visual dimension, two layers of cultural implications are worth noting, especially in the case of the *Maitreya* frontispieces. First, the aesthetic logic of juxtaposing two styles in one single composition may reflect the designer's ambition of catering to multicultural viewers living in Xi Xia society. Second, the segmentation of disparate styles may also reflect the labor division

118 Saliceti-Collins 2007, 143.

119 For selected studies of the Himalayan, Indian, and Chinese inspirations in Xi Xia art, see Linrothe 1996a; Xie 2002; Xie et al. 2010, 119–261; Huang 2014d.

120 Pye 1994, 220.

of woodcut artisans. The artisans went through a patchwork or collage-like process when it came to the complex task of designing a frontispiece such as the *Maitreya* frontispieces. They first selected stock motifs from a repository of images at their disposal, then assembled them into a whole composition. It is also likely that the hybrid display of styles reflects multiple artisans who specialized in different styles or iconographies having been assigned to cut or design different segments of the frontispiece. A deeper visual examination of the two juxtaposed styles in the next section further connects the *Maitreya* frontispieces to multiple media of Xi Xia visual productions and their possible artistic sources in Himalayan and Chinese traditions.

3.1 *The Buddha's Entourage in Indo-Himalayan Style*

The opening scene of the Buddha preaching to his disciples (figs. 6.2–6.6, 6.28) blends eastern Indian Pala and Tibetan artistic styles.[121] This is prominent in the seated Buddha's top knot, S-shaped torso, and thin garment. Comparable designs are widely shared in other Xi Xia woodcuts (fig. 6.29–6.31), portable paintings (fig. 6.32), and murals (figs. 6.33–6.34).[122] Their prototypes can be found in early twelfth-century Tibetan painting (fig. 6.35), which itself integrated Pala elements.[123] Shifting to the standing bodhisattvas in the *Maitreya* frontispieces, their slender, S-shaped bodies, thin clothing, raindrop-shaped

121 For the transnational legacy of the Pala style, see Huntington et al. 1990. For more studies of the Pala-Tibetan style of Xi Xia Buddhist art, see Jia 2014b, 66; Piotrovsky 1993, 116–17; Xie 2002, 1: 44–45; ECHSCWX 3: 73; Saliceti-Collins 2007, 129–31, 257–59 (figs. 3.6, 3.8, 3.9); Stoddard 2008, 34–35 (fig. 18); Xie et al. 2010, 123–24 (fig. 2). Xie Jisheng claimed that because the Tibetan style was featured in the opening section of the *Maitreya* frontispiece, it was considered the superior style; see Xie 2002, 1: 197. This is problematic, as there are multiple Xi Xia frontispieces in which the opening sections are in Chinese style whereas the rest of the frontispieces are in Tibetan style. Note that even within this section dominated by the Pala-Tibetan style, selected figural motifs showing officials with caps are depicted in Chinese style and can be compared to the Xi Xia mural in the Eastern Thousand Buddhas Cave 2; see ZGDHBHQJ 10: 92 (fig. 118). For more on the strong reception of the Pala style in Xi Xia Buddhist art, see Xie and Chang 2011; Jia 2020, 32–33.

122 See ZGDHBHQJ 10: 110 (fig. 142); ZGDHBHQJ 10: 129 (fig. 167). For more iconographic studies of the woodcuts TK 164, see Jia 2020, 209–10, 273–74; for the plates, see ECHSCWX 4: color pl. 3. Cf. the Eastern Thousand Buddhas Caves 2, which was most likely constructed under Renzong's patronage; see Gao ed. 2009, 52; Zhang B. 2012, 104; Xie 2003; Meinert 2020, 270–71; Kogou et al. 2020. Xie Jisheng has raised the possibility of so-called counter-influence from Xi Xia to Tibet, citing the mural style of the Dratang Monastery; see Xie et al. 2010, 120–21.

123 The pointed draperies draped over the Buddha's left shoulder in the Tibetan painting cited here form a direct prototype for the Xi Xia woodcuts. Pala style of eastern India played a dominant mode in Tibetan Buddhist art in the eleventh to thirteenth centuries; see Kossak 2010, 39–63.

FIGURE 6.28 Detail. Frontispiece to the *Maitreya Sutra* in Tangut (no. 941). Xi Xia. Woodblock print. Concertina. Institute of Oriental Manuscripts, St. Petersburg

FIGURE 6.29 Detail. Frontispiece to the Tangut printed text *Xianzai xianjie qianfo ming jing*, juan 1 (no. 7188). Xi Xia. Woodblock print. Concertina. Institute of Oriental Manuscripts, St. Petersburg

FIGURE 6.30
Detail of a printed frontispiece to the written manuscript of the *Dashasahasrika Prajñāpāramitā* in Tangut dated 1182 (no. 206; TANG 164). Xi Xia. Woodblock print

FIGURE 6.31 One of the three frontispieces to *Jingli sheng dabeixin guanzizai* (TK 164). Xi Xia. Woodblock print. Concertina. Institute of Oriental Manuscripts, St. Petersburg

FIGURE 6.32
A Buddha, Two Bodhisattvas and Two Buddhist Disciples (x. 2342). 12th–13th centuries. Xi Xia. Ink and color on cotton or silk. Hanging scroll. The State Hermitage Museum, St. Petersburg

FIGURE 6.35
Detail. *Buddha with Attendants*. Central Tibet. Early 12th century. Distemper on cloth. Private collection

FIGURE 6.33
Detail of two seated buddhas. Xi Xia-Yuan. Mural. North wall, Yulin Cave 4, Guazhou, Gansu

FIGURE 6.34
Detail of a bodhisattva. Xi Xia-Yuan. Mural. South slop of the main chamber, Mogao Cave 465, Dunhuang, Gansu

FIGURE 6.36
Detail of a bodhisattva. Late 11th century. Mural. Dratang Monastery, Central Tibet

FIGURE 6.37
Detail. *Portrait of a Monk* (X. 2400). Xi Xia. Colors on linen. Hanging scroll. The State Hermitage Museum, St. Petersburg

FIGURE 6.38
Portrait of a Lama, Possibly Dromton. Tibet. Last quarter of the 11th century. Distemper on cloth. Thangka. The Metropolitan Museum of Art

FIGURE 6.39 *Buddha adorned.* 11th–12th centuries. Sandstone. Musée des Arts Asiatiques-Guimet

FIGURE 6.40 Detail. Eight Pagodas. South side of the east wall, Mogao Cave 76. Early 11th century. Northern Song

FIGURE 6.41
A backrest decorated with the paired makaras, goats, and elephants. Possibly 11th century. Clay with colored pigments. Discovered in Mogao Cave B77, Dunhuang

headdresses, large round earrings, tube-shaped hairstyles, and arch-shaped haloes rendered with double contour lines also demonstrate a Pala-Tibetan melange. The late eleventh-century Tibetan prototype, a mural in the Dratang Monastery in Central Tibet (fig. 6.36), serves as an oft-cited prototype.[124]

The highly ornamental backrests in the opening scene of the *Maitreya* frontispieces reflect a shared visual idiom also frequently used in other Xi Xia woodcuts and paintings (figs. 6.29, 6.30, 6.32, 6.37).[125] Such backrests often included paired geese on both sides at the top, sometimes radiating strings of gems from their mouths. On occasion the paired geese are replaced with water creatures (known as Makara), shown with their mouths wide open. On the right and left of the backrest, next, is a pair of vertically positioned goat-like animals, either turning toward the throne or facing away. At times they stand on top of a pair of other animals, such as elephants. An eleventh-century Tibetan painting of a lama contains all the animal symbols in one single backrest design (fig. 6.38). A simpler pattern is preserved in a Pala sculpture dated

124 Zhang Yasha argues convincingly for the fusion of Tibetan, Pala, and Central Asian styles of the murals in Dratang Monastery; see Zhang Y. 2008.

125 For more examples of comparable backrests, see Xie 2002, 2: 74 (pl. 72); Xie et al. 2010, 129 (color plate 2–4–1), 202 (color plates 3m–3–8, 3m–3–9). For the earlier style of the Himalayan style backrest in Sui and Tang art, see Li 2006. According to Xie Jisheng, the Khara Khoto portrait of a monk (x 2400) may represent a Tangut monk, and the lay figures standing in the lower corners of the picture plan refer to the noble donors of the painting; see Xie 2002, 1: 169–70; 2: 46 (pl. 43).

to the eleventh or twelfth century (fig. 6.39).[126] Such Pala-inspired decorative conventions already existed in Buddhist art in northwest China prior to the Xi Xia period: examples include the eleventh-century mural in Mogao Cave 76 (fig. 6.40)[127] and the clay backrest originally found in Cave B77 in the northern district of the Mogao site (fig. 6.41).[128]

3.2 *Constructing the Tusita Heaven from Mural Conventions*

The second part of the *Maitreya* frontispiece demonstrates a strong Chinese style. The overall composition offers a panoramic view of celestial figures in the walled palace (figs. 6.0, 6.42, 6.44, 6.49). The exhaustive array of paradisiacal buildings is rare in printed frontispieces. The designer may have had access to stock motifs shared by Xi Xia painters working on murals and paintings, following prototypes such as the large-scale murals in Xi Xia Buddhist grottoes (figs. 6.43a–b). They borrow pictorial conventions from other earlier or contemporary Buddhist murals produced in the neighboring kingdom of Qocho along the Silk Road, as well as in the Northern Song and Jin territories in today's Shanxi.

The Xi Xia mural *Maitreya's Paradise* (figs. 6.43a–b) on the east wall of the Wanfodong 萬佛洞 (Cave of the Ten Thousand Buddhas) on Mt. Wenshu 文殊山 Grottoes (map 0.2) provides the closest comparison.[129] The mural depicts the Tusita Heaven as a multilayered building compound.[130] From a cross-regional perspective, it reveals pictorial designs that recall the tenth-to-twelfth century mural associated with the royal patronage of the Qocho kingdom discovered near the Uighur capital Beiting 北庭 (near today's Jimsar) (fig. 6.45),[131] as well as the Northern Song and Jin murals in Shanxi

126 This author would like to thank Eric Huntington for his input.

127 DHMGK 5, fig. 109.

128 The Pala style of the mural of Mogao Cave 76 may reflect the Song-Indian exchange at that time. For more studies, see Xie et al. 2010, 186–98; Xie and Yu 2011; Toyka-Fuong 1998.

129 This is a Buddhist site southwest of today's Jiuquan 酒泉, Gansu, where Emperor Renzong may well have stopped by during his journey to the west in 1176.

130 Yao ed. 2019, 64–82; Wang 2019, 14–15, 164–65; ZGDHBHQJ 11: 165–85; Zhang 1985.

131 According to Tian Chen, "The likeness between these images suggest a shared pictorial template used by mural artists working along the Silk Road and documents religious exchange of elite monks and artisans." See Chen T. 2020. Liu Yongzeng noted the similarity between the Mt. Wenshu and Gaochang murals, adding that the female figural motif in the Gaochang mural reflects a stylistic influence from the "central kingdom" (zhongyuan); see Liu Y. 2020, 11. For more studies, see Zhang 1985, 260–62, 264, 271 (endnote 2); Zhongguo shehui kexue yuan kaogu yanjiusuo ed. 1990, 27–37; Meng 1990. Kitsudō Kōichi and Arakawa Shinaro's recent study of the illustration of the *Ten Realms of Mind Contemplation* provides another Buddhist iconography attesting to the Uighur

FIGURE 6.42 Detail of fig. 6.5. Frontispiece of the *Maitreya Sutra* in Tangut (no. 78). Xi Xia. Woodblock print. Concertina. Institute of Oriental Manuscripts, St. Petersburg

(figs. 6.46a, 6.46c, 6.47).[132] To contextualize the rich Xi Xia murals from Mt. Wenshu more locally, the images reflect a thriving multicultural Buddhist community in the locale under Tangut rule.[133] The intended audience most likely was a multicultural Buddhist community, as is evident from inscriptions about donors in Uighur, Tangut, and Chinese. An inscription accompanying a monkish donor image identifies the figure as a donor monk from the Haizangsi 海藏寺 (Monastery of Oceanic Repositories) in Wuwei; the other monkish image shows that he was of elite status.[134]

Compositionally, the Mt. Wenshu mural and the Maitreya frontispiece both represent the paradise as an architectural compound framed by a wall with multiple gates stretching in the foreground and inner palatial buildings piled up in multiple horizontal rows above the wall. Maitreya appears seated in the upper row of the central hall of the main palace. To cater to the horizontal composition, the overall architectural construct in the mural version is consolidated, keeping a tight space between each layer.

---

and Xi Xia connection; see Kitsudō and Arakawa 2018. For more on Xi Xia-Uighur artistic connection, see Yang and Chen 2012, 176–94.

132 Chai and He 2006; Gu D. 2015; Li L. 2015; Li L. 2016.

133 Zhang 1985, 256; Yao ed. 2019, 5–6; ZGDHBHQJ 11: 184 (fig. 182); Wang Yanyun 2003; Wang 2007.

134 Zhang 1985; Shi 1988, 133–34. The Mt. Wenshu mural shares pictorial conventions with other Xi Xia Buddhist cave murals associated with the Tangut elite class or court in the late twelfth century. See ZGDHBHQJ 10: 78 (fig. 100); DHSKQJ 21: 247–51; Gao ed. 2009, 46 (fig. 1–55). Cf. a similar composition in Eastern One Thousand Buddhas Grottoes (Dong qianfo dong 東千佛洞), Cave 7; see Wang 2019, 163 (fig. 8–1–7).

FIGURE 6.43A Detail. *Maitreya Paradise*. Xi Xia. Mural. East wall, Cave of the Ten Thousand Buddhas, Mt. Wenshu Grottoes, Zhangye, Gansu

The mural is comparable to the *Maitreya* frontispiece design not only in its overall composition but also in its minute individual motifs, including the group of kneeling figures, each holding a tray of a crown, which is in turn transformed into a miniature celestial palace in a white band (fig. 6.43b).[135]

135 Similar scenes are depicted in Buddhist murals in Gaochang (E204 cave mural) and Northern Song Kaihua Monastery in Shanxi; see Chen T. 2020.

FIGURE 6.44
Detail. Frontispiece of the *Maitreya Sutra* (TK 81). Xi Xia. Woodblock print. Concertina. Institute of Oriental Manuscripts

FIGURE 6.43B Detail. *Maitreya Paradise*. Xi Xia. Mural. East wall, Cave of the Ten Thousand Buddhas, Mt. Wenshu Grottoes, Zhangye, Gansu

FIGURE 6.45 Detail. *Maitreya Paradise*. 10th–12th centuries. Mural. Cave E204, ruins of the Gaochang Kingdom, near today's Jimsar city, Xinjiang

As identified by the cartouch of the Xi Xia Maitreya frontispieces in Chinese (fig. 6.44), these kingly figures represent the "five hundred billion of kings offering jeweled crowns" (*wubaiyi tianzi fengshi baoguan* 五百億天子奉施寶冠).[136] According to the *Matireya Sutra* following the frontispiece, the five hundred billion of celestial kings kneel down to dedicate their crowns as offerings (*gongju* 供具). As they swear a sincere vow, the jeweled crowns are transformed into jeweled palaces (*bagoong* 寶宮), but their number is 10,000 times of that of the jeweled crowns.[137]

The woodcut representing the Tusita Heaven highlights Xi Xia's transregional artistic connections with the mural practices in Shanxi, located not far away. The murals in the Northern Song Kaihua Monastery located in Gaoping, and in the Jin Yanshan Monastery in Fanshi 繁峙 (map 0.2) are but two examples. The Kaihua Monastery houses the largest collection of Northern Song murals available for comparison.[138] The much-damaged mural (fig. 6.46a) on the north wall in the main hall, here juxtaposed with a reconfigured modern drawing (fig. 6.46b),[139] represents Maitreya's palatial paradise in a multi-layered fashion similar to the Xi Xia murals and woodcuts.[140]

The architectural compound depicted in the Shanxi mural is bordered by a gated wall in the foreground. Heavenly beings are depicted gathering in a courtyard in the middle layer. In the top layer, Maitreya is seated in an open-door hall, overlooking the assembly. Details such as the kneeling kings offering crowns (fig. 6.46c), the gate tower with an open door, and the mushroom-shaped clouds, are motifs that recur in the second section of the Xi Xia *Maitreya* frontispiece.

136 Yao ed. 2019, 69, 71–73. Other minute details, such as the radiating strips filled with miniature palaces, ponds, and banners, which may refer to the visualized imagery, and the enclosed baby reborn from a lotus in the almost invisible lotus pond cutting through the edges of the raised palatial ground, are also comparable to the motifs in the *Maitreya* woodcuts.

137 ECHSCWX 2: 309–10.

138 For an introduction, see Jin Weinuo in ZGMSQJ, huihua bian 13, 44–45; Chai and He 2006, 16–22; ZGSGBHQJ 1: 62–64. For the murals, see Yan and Cheng 2016, 32; Chai and He 2006, 114–24.

139 See Chai and He 2006, 124 (fig. 57). Gu Dongfang challenged the earlier identification of this mural as the Guanyin's assembly, and re-identified it as the sutra tableaux expounding the *Mile shangsheng jing*; see Gu 2015, 14–21. For more studies of the Kaihua murals, see Zhao 2016, 43–59; Gu 2009; Zhang and Liu eds. 2015, 54–59.

140 I agree with Izumi Takeo's latest claim, which challenges the conventional view identifying the mural as a representation of the Guanyin assembly; see Izumi 2019, 45.

Depictions of lay men and women (fig. 6.46d), segregated by gender, on the lower right and left corners of the same wall are labeled as "*yi*-society men" (*yiren* 邑人) and "*yi*-society women" (*yipo* 邑婆) respectively. They may have been donors from a Buddhist society who contributed funds for the temple construction.[141]

Inscriptions by Guo Fa 郭發, an otherwise undocumented local professional painter, on the pillars inside the main hall record the date and working procedure of the Kaihua Monastery murals.[142] In 1096, he prepared the surface of the west wall in the sixth month, started drafting the Guanyin image in the tenth month, and completed it in the eleventh month. His plan was to add colors to the Guanyin image in the spring of 1097. While this image is no longer extant, the majority of the extant murals on the west wall are considered to be a tour de force.[143]

Mural practices in Shanxi temples continued to flourish even after the area was taken over by the Jurchen in the twelfth century. This is evident in a mural that survived in the Wenshudian 文殊殿 (Mañjuśrī Hall) of the Yanshan Monastery (fig. 6.47).[144] As documented in an inscription on its west wall, the mural, completed in 1167, was executed by a group of painters led by Wang Kui 王逵 (active 1158–1167), a professional artist from the area who lived through the fall of the Northern Song and once worked as a contracted painter for the Jin court.[145] The minute details of the architecture demonstrate their visual

141 Gu Dongfang counts approximately twenty-one men on the right and seventeen women on the left; for a transliteration of the accompanying cartouches, see Gu 2015, 20.

142 For the inscriptions, see Chai and He 2006, 17.

143 For a complete view of the extant murals on the west wall, see Yan and Cheng 2016, 36–38. For more details, see ZGSGBHQJ 1: 140–75; Chai and He 2006, 114–20 (figs. 41–49).

144 Cf. the faded color of the mural reproduced in Chai and Zhang 1990, 112 (fig. 49). For more studies, see Karetzky 1980; Chang ed. 2013; Li L. 2015, 2016.

145 Other muralists mentioned in the inscription include Wang Hui 王輝, Wang Qiong 王瓊, Fuxi 福喜, and Ruixi 瑞喜, all of whom may be Wang's disciples or assistant painters. See Chai and Zhang 1990, 25. According to the stele found in situ, in 1158 Wang Kui and the other painter Wang Dao painted the now-lost mural in the Water Land Hall of the same temple; he was referred to as a contracted artisan working for the Jin court (*Yuqian chengying huajiang* 御前承應畫匠) at that time; see Chai and Zhang 1990, 2 (for dating, see 3). For more about Wang Kui's career, see Chang ed. 2013, 3–6; Li L. 2015, 73 (esp. footnote 2); Li L. 2016, 52–54. For more on the Yanshan murals, see Meng 2005; Zhang and Liu eds. 2015, 7–8, 27, 31–32, 75–87; Zhao 2016, 61–79; Zhang and Liu eds. 2015, 80–87.

a

b

FIGURES 6.46A–D Details. *Assembly of Maitreya's Tusita Heaven*. 1096–1097. Northern Song. Mural. East side of the north wall, Kaihua Monastery, Gaoping, Shanxi
a. A complete view
b. Line drawing of fig. 6.46a
c–d. Details of fig. 6.46a

knowledge, inherited from the Northern Song tradition.[146] Most comparable to the *Maitreya* frontispieces (fig. 6.48) are the figures placed neatly within the complex pictorial space created by the stairs, balustrades, doors, windows, and

146 Among the motifs that reflect a direct reference to the Northern Song *jiehua* repertoire are the water mill and the city gate; see the plates in Chai and Zhang 1990, 124, 159. For more discussion, see Li L. 2016, 52–53.

FIGURE 6.47 Detail of the architectural and figural motifs. 1158–1167. Jin. Mural. West wall of the Wenshu Hall, Yanshan Monastery, Fanzhi, Shanxi

FIGURE 6.48 Detail. Frontispiece of the *Maitreya Sutra* in Chinese (TK 58). 1189. Xi Xia. Woodblock print. Institute of Oriental Manuscripts, St. Petersburg

pillars (fig. 6.47).[147] The stylistic features shared across the *Maitreya* frontispiece and the Northern Song and Jin murals in Shanxi suggest a large image-sharing network across media and regions.[148]

The arch-shaped chains of pendant jewelry or garlands decorating the paradisiacal walls (fig. 6.49) exhibit recurring ornamental designs widely seen in Xi Xia art and architecture. Comparable examples include the beaded curtains repainted on the upper walls of the passageway of the Mogao Cave 61 (fig. 6.50)[149] and the molded and painted garlands suspended from the fron-

147 The motif of a city wall depicted on the west wall of the Wenshu Hall in Yanshan mural (see Chang ed. 2013, 66–67) compares closely to the similar motif depicted on the narrative vignette at the bottom of the south wall of Yulin Cave 3. This further suggests that artists working for the Xi Xia elite and royal court were accessible to the pictorial conventions reflected in the Yanshan murals.

148 Jia Weiwei noted that the multi-armed, multi-headed Guanyin mural in Xi Xia Yulin Cave 3 compares closely to that depicted in the Jin-dynasty Chongfusi 崇福寺 (Monastery of Venerating Happiness) in Shuozhou, Shanxi, offering further visual evidence of the Xi Xia and Shanxi connection; see Jia 2020, 183–84.

149 Mogao Cave 61 went through partial renovation in the Xi Xia period, the result of a group effort of both the Xi Xia royal family and the Chinese elite families in Dunhuang. See

FIGURE 6.49 Detail of fig. 6.5. Frontispiece of the *Maitreya Sutra* in Tangut script (no. 78). 1189. Xi Xia. Woodblock print. Concertina. Institute of Oriental Manuscripts, St. Petersburg

FIGURE 6.50 Detail of decorative motifs. Xi Xia. Mural. Southern slope adjacent to the ceiling of the passage way. Mogao Cave 61

tally positioned monstrous faces covering the surfaces of the Baisikou Twin Pagodas (fig. 6.51; map 0.2), which may be in the vicinity of a now-lost summer palace of the Tangut court.[150] Similar garland designs also existed in both China and India. They are reminiscent of the terracotta tiles of pendant

---

Sha 2018, 12. Yang Binghua further argues that a donor image depicted on the north wall of the corridor may be Empress Dowager Luo; see Yang B. 2017. For more studies of Dunuhang cave temple constructions and inscriptions dated to the Xi Xia period, see Chen B. 1985, 1–55; Liu Yuquan 1996, 2011.

150 Niu 2013, 101–12. For the Tangut royal summer palace in Baisikou, cited from the Ming Ningxia gazetteer, see 106. The renovated western pagoda decorative motifs of painted pendant jewelry in red, which look different from the molded motifs in the case of the eastern pagoda; see Lei et al. 1995, 94, 257. For the eastern pagoda, see Lei 1996, 59 (fig. 7); Chen and Tang 2010, 201 (fig. 3.25). I am grateful for Yong Cho who shared with me the photographs of the pagodas he took in situ in 2016.

The original exterior of the Baisigou Pagoda (map 0.2 of this book) located near Yinchuan also preserves a rougher version of painted ornamental motifs of pendant jewelry in ink similar to those in both the frontispiece woodcuts. For the painted motifs, see Lei et al. 1995, 163 (fig. 4); Zhao 2015, 184 (fig. 4–3–1).

FIGURE 6.51 Detail of decorative patterns. Xi Xia. Relief carvings. The Eastern Baisikou Pagoda, Ningxia

FIGURE 6.52 Detail of the pendant garlands. 7th century. Tang. Terracotta tiles. The pagoda of the Xiuding Monastery, Luoyang, Henan

garlands with frontal monstrous faces decorating the seventh-century pagoda of the Xiudingsi 修定寺 (Monastery of the Cultivation of Samadhi) in Luoyang, Henan (fig. 6.52).[151] Turning to the Himalayan tradition, they also resemble the garland relief carvings adorning the pillars of the eleventh-to-twelfth century Pala-style statue introduced earlier (fig. 6.39).[152]

3.3 *Multiple Blocks*

Emperor Renzong donated 100,000 copies of the *Maitreya Sutra* at the Maitreya Retreat in 1189—a production that would have required at least five sets of blocks, since one block is good for about 20,000 copies. Its frontispieces survive in various versions (figs. 6.2–6.6), which suggests that the images were produced by numerous different artisans.[153]

For example, the first vignette of the third section in four different versions reveals a surprising discrepancy (figs. 6.53a–d). A cartouche on the upper left of the picture plane in the two Chinese versions reads, "venerating [the Buddha] with flowers and incense" (*huaxiang gongyang* 花香供養) (figs. 6.53a, 6.53c); it was translated into Tangut in the two versions accompanying Tangut texts (figs. 6.53b, 6.53d). The scene depicts a couple standing in the lower left corner, making offerings to a statue of a seated buddha inside a hall. The most telling discrepancy lies in the varying styles of the Buddhist statues depicted in the four versions. In two that are closely comparable (figs. 6.53a–b), the artists depict a statue with a slender S-shaped torso and clothed in a thin robe, reminiscent of the Indo-Himalayan buddha represented in the first section of all the versions (figs. 6.2–6.6). Nevertheless, minute differences are apparent in the triangular markings on the left edges of the steps in front of the hall (figs. 6.53a–b). The other two versions (figs. 6.53c–d), on the other hand, differ greatly from the previous two. Here the statues are in Chinese style, evident in loose robes that fully cover the body, rendering the contours less visible. The stylistic discrepancy also reflects the varied qualities of the cutters. Among the four versions, the last in Tangut (fig. 6.53d) is the roughest.

---

151 Jia Weiwei identifies the images in the relief vignettes as the so-called seven Buddhist treasures (*qi zheng bao* 七政寶); see Jia 2020, 283–84 (fig. 4–2–22).

152 For comparable visual examples of the architectural garlands, in murals from Lhasa and India, and a miniature model of the copper mountain in India, see Huntington 2019, 176.

153 This is evident in the comparison of the multiple versions of the heavenly kings; see Huang 2014d, 138, 169 (figs. 1–3); Huang S. 2021a, 560–61.

a

b

c

d

FIGURES 6.53A–D Multiple versions depicting offering flowers and incense to the Buddhist icon. The *Maitreya Sutra*. 1189. Xi Xia. Woodblock print. Institute of Oriental Manuscripts, St. Petersburg

a. Detail (TK81)
b. Detail (no. 78)
c. Detail (TK 58)
d. Detail (no. 941)

4 Workshop Practice and Modular Designs

An effective way to speed up mass production is to reuse existing motifs and compositional templates—a standard approach widely deployed in arts-and-crafts workshops. Four groups of frontispieces bear witness to this, each potentially modified to fit different themes or iconographies. As they are associated with Tangut royal patronage, they also reveal details of how exactly Buddhist woodcuts were produced under Xi Xia rule.

4.1 *The First Group*

Frontispieces in the first group all share the modular design of a kneeling figure with his back to the viewer featured in the central foreground of a more or less centralized composition (figs. 5.15a, 5.17, 6.54–6.58). He appears either as a bodhisattva with a raised topknot decorated in jewelry or sashes (figs. 5.17, 6.54–6.56) or as a monk with his head shaved (figs. 6.57–6.58).[154] In addition to the Russian collection, fragments collected elsewhere include the incomplete frontispiece described earlier (fig. 5.15a). This was originally attached to a printed text of the Jin Canon, discovered in Mogao Cave B53; it appears in a fragment now in the Gansu Provincial Museum as well as in one discovered by Stein in Khara Khoto (fig. 6.56). The legacy of the figural design of the kneeling figure lasted through Yuan and Ming times (see pt. 3 below) and appears even in *Chosŏn* Korea.[155]

The first two frontispieces (figs. 6.54, 6.55) accompanying different versions of the "Vows of Samantabhadra" chapter of the *Avatamsaka Sutra* may have been produced by the same group of artisans.[156] Both show a bodhisattva kneeling in front of the main icon, identified as "Lord of the Teaching, Great Universal Buddha," that is, Vairocana, a buddha central to Avatamsaka teachings.[157]

154 Huang 2014d, 153–56.

155 Jahyun Kim identifies similar kneeling figural motifs (called the "listener" motifs) in Chosŏn Buddhist paintings representing the buddha-preaching scene; she traces the visual convention to Ming Buddhist woodcuts. See Kim 2021.

156 This is based on an incomplete colophon at the end of the first version (TK 72); see ECHSCWX 2: 106 (no. 26–24). For more study, see Shi 2004, 134; Dunnell 2009, 45; Drège 1999, 48–49 (fig. 5).

157 For more on the cartouches identifying individual figures represented, see Huang 2014d, 153–54; Chen and Tang 2010, 140 (note that Chen and Tang misidentified a kingly figure labeled as Prince Wuguang, depicted to the left of the kneeling figure in TK 72, as the donor of the print). Comparable Xi Xia woodcuts represent Vairocana either with or without a crown; cf. two versions of frontispieces to the *Avatamsaka Sutra* (TK 243 and TK 246) reproduced in Chen and Tang 2010, 166.

FIGURE 6.54 Frontispiece to the "Vows of Samantabhadra" chapter from the *Avatamsaka Sutra* (TK 72). 1161. Xi Xia. Woodblock print. Concertina. Institute of Oriental Manuscripts, St. Petersburg

FIGURE 6.55 Frontispiece to the "Vows of Samantabhadra" chapter from the *Avatamsaka Sutra* (TK 142). Xi Xia. Woodblock print. Concertina. Institute of Oriental Manuscripts, St. Petersburg

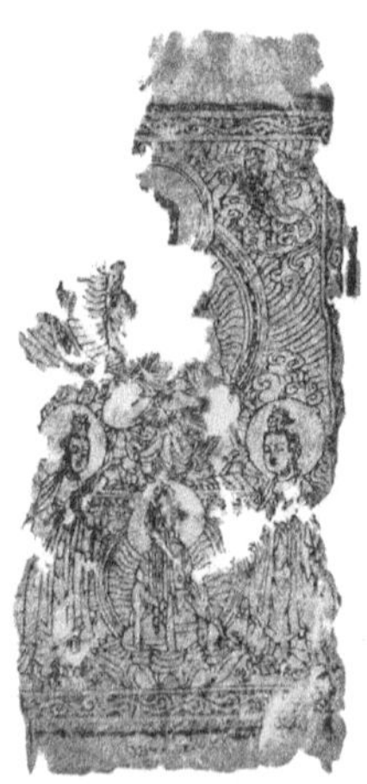

FIGURE 6.56
Fragment woodcut discovered by Stein in Khara Khoto (K. K. II. 0285. b. viii). After Stein 1928, 3: LXIV

FIGURE 6.57 Frontispiece to *Āryamañjuśrīnāmasaṃgīti* (no. 707; TANG63). Xi Xia. Woodblock print. Concertina. Institute of Oriental Manuscripts, St. Petersburg

FIGURE 6.58 Detail. Frontispiece to the *Diamond Sutra* (G11). Xi Xia. Woodblock print. Gansu Provincial Museum

As both have similar lotus petals decorating the bottom edges,[158] it is likely that they were associated with the Tangut royal family.[159]

The common template shared by the woodcuts in this group went beyond the frontispieces to the *Avatamsaka Sutra*. The modular figure, originally a bodhisattva, was altered to show a monk in the same posture. A fragmented frontispiece in Indo-Himalayan style, accompanying an Esoteric Buddhist text in Tangut (fig. 6.57), and a frontispiece to the *Diamond Sutra* (fig. 6.58) are good examples of the flexible use of this motif.[160] While the kneeling monk in the

158 The lotus petals may reflect the designer's novel comparison of the Avatamsaka cosmology to the Lotus Repository World. Cf. a different visual approach expounding the similar concept in a Southern Song-inspired Xi Xia frontispiece fragment, representing miniature buddhas, "each enclosed in a lotus petal floating in the ocean." See Huang 2014d, 146–47, 173 (fig. 18).

159 The first version illustrated here (fig. 6.54 of this book) ends with additional miracle tales associated with the *Avatamsaka Sutra*, printed in small characters whose style is similar to the miracle tales printed at the end of the "Vows of Samantabhadra" dated 1189 and sponsored by Empress Luo (fig. 6.19a of this book). The second version (fig. 6.55 of this book) was donated by An Liang in commemoration of the 100th day after his mother's death. An Liang also donated seventy-two paintings and forty-nine lamps; he commissioned Tibetan monks to recite charms and other monks to recite the *Lotus Sutra*. It is highly possible An Liang was from the royal family.

160 The kneeling monkish motifs in these two cases are comparable to a similar motif in the other frontispiece decorating the *Amitabha Sutra* in Tangut (no. 7564); see ECHSCWX 22, 1 (color plate 3).

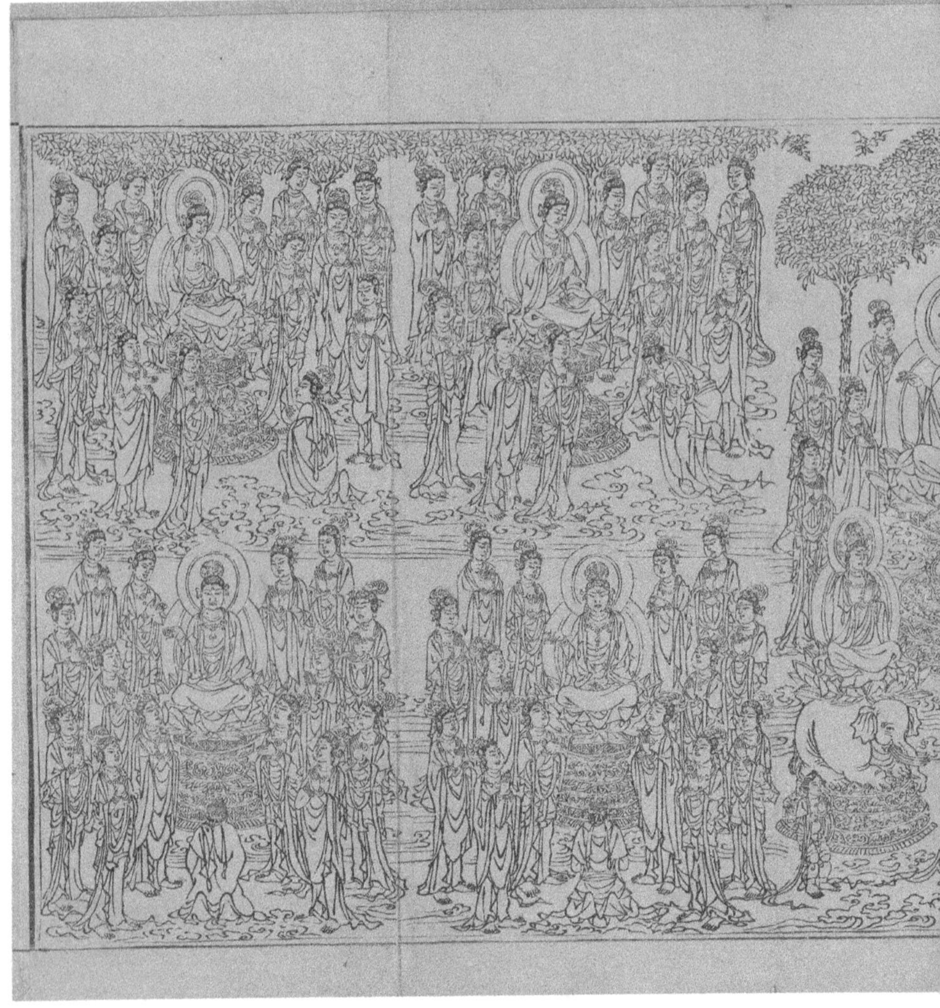

FIGURE 6.59 Frontispiece to the *Avatamsaka Sutra*. Northern Song. Woodblock print. Concertina. National Palace Museum

Esoteric text wears a robe of a different style, having one shoulder exposed, his counterpart in the Chinese version is fully covered.

The motif of a kneeling figure with his back to the viewer may have been derived from prototypes of the Northern Song, whose frontispiece to the *Avatamsaka Sutra*, printed in the Longxingsi 龍興寺 (Monastery of Dragonlike Prosperity) in Hangzhou during the Chunhua reign (990–994), is the earliest extant version (fig. 6.59).[161] Among nine scenes of the Buddha's various assem-

161 Huang 2014d, 155; ZGFJBHQJ 2: 18–19.

blies, five utilize the same design with a kneeling bodhisattva, comparable to the Xi Xia examples.[162] A rare printed frontispiece fragment, first discovered in a pagoda in Yunnan and originally from the kingdom of Dali (937–1253) in southwest China, shows a similar template depicting nine assemblies,

162 In the four side scenes in the lower register of the composition, furthermore, selected side figures show their raised heads slantly, not unlike the side figures depicted in the Xi Xia frontispiece (TK 142). Cf. Xie Jisheng's linking of the side figures in TK 142 to the figural motifs in the mural of the Dratang Monastery in Central Tibet; see Xie 2002, 1: 246–47.

a

b

FIGURES 6.60A–B Details. Left side of the west wall, Kaihua Monastery, Gaoping, Shanxi. 1096. Northern Song

suggesting a Song-Dali connection.[163] The Kaihua Monastery in Shanxi, introduced before (figs. 6.46a–d), houses a Northern Song mural on its east wall that represents the *Avatamsaka Sutra* (figs. 6.60a–b).[164] It features a comparable figure, a kneeling monk turned "inward" to face the Buddha, and also a monumental mountain above. Interestingly, he has taken off his shoes and, before kneeling down, carefully placed them in front of his mat, facing away from it (fig. 6.60b). Other comparable motifs appear in various Song-to-Qing visual sources, ranging from a Daoist stele to temple murals and printed frontispieces.[165]

4.2 *The Second Group*

The second group (figs. 6.18c, 6.19b, 6.61a–6.63), probably produced in a Tangut royal workshop, contains frontispieces with shared landscape and figural motifs. Those to the *Diamond Sutra* and the "Vows of Samantabhadra"

163 The specimen was found inside a Dali pagoda in Yunnan. For a new study, see Chen J. 2023.

164 For the mural, see ZGSGBHQJ 1: 179 (fig. 110); Huang 2014d, 156.

165 Phillip Bloom has suggested that the motif may show an avatar for the viewer, stimulating his engagement with the frontispieces he gazed at; see Bloom 2013, 249; Bloom 2018; Huang 2014d, 156; Huang S. 2021a, 578. Other researchers cite Liao frontispieces dated around 1003 as alternative visual prototypes; see Saliceti-Collins 2007, 119–20, 246 (fig. 2.63); Huang 2014d, 155, 175 (fig. 23).

(figs. 6.18c, 6.19b), donated by Empress Luo, share landscape and figural motifs in their first folds (figs. 6.61a–b) that appear based on a common template. Other features indicate that Xi Xia woodcut designers revamped a sectional design of a block to create different frontispieces.[166]

The landscape setting, noted for its overhanging rocks topped with shrubs, that extends diagonally toward the picture plane (figs. 6.61a–b), is inspired by Southern Song models.[167] In the *Diamond Sutra* (fig. 6.61a), the rocks and trees in the first fold correspond to similar motifs in its fourth fold (fig. 6.18c); together, they create an enclosed frame for the scene of the Buddha preaching as shown in the second and third folds. This is not the case in the "Vows of Samantabhadra" (fig. 6.19b), which has no corresponding rocks and trees in its fourth fold. It is thus possible that the landscape motifs were first created for the frontispiece to the *Diamond Sutra* and later copied onto the "Vows of Samantabhadra" in a cut-and-paste fashion.[168] To make the ready-made design of the first fold fit in the overall composition, the woodcut designer used additional flowing clouds and overlapping figures across the first and second folds, thus creating a continuous effect.[169]

The rocks, shrubs, and clouds can be further linked to a frontispiece to the "Guanyin" chapter of the *Lotus Sutra* (fig. 6.62), where similar motifs appear but are positioned differently.[170] It shows three rocks placed in interlocking angles in the middle of the composition. They function effectively as a divider that separates the main icon of Guanyin on the right from other narrative scenes. The similarities between the two go beyond the frontispieces: the calligraphy also matches. It is possible that the frontispiece to the "Guanyin" chapter goes back to a royal workshop and formed part of the fifty thousand *juan* of copies distributed at the Maitreya Retreat. A similar if more modest rendition of a

166 For two frontispiece specimens based on the left part, see ZGBHQJ 1: 82–83.

167 Cf. comparable motifs of overhanging rocks and shrubs in the Southern Song court painting staging the Daoist Official of Earth; reproduced in Huang 2012, 283 (fig. 6.2).

168 That the frontispiece to the "Vows of Samantabhadra" is copied partially after the frontispiece to the *Diamond Sutra* can be further supported by a comparison of the cartouches in both frontispieces. Unlike the multiple cartouches accompanying most figures depicted in the frontispiece to the *Diamond Sutra*, only two cartouches copied after the first fold of the *Diamond Sutra* are present in the frontispiece to the "Vows of Samantabhadra." Jean-Pierre Drège notices that it has only two cartouches, but does not offer an explanation (Drège 1999, 49).

169 Li Zhitan did not think that the first fold belongs to the original frontispiece; he only reproduced the second, third, and fourth folds of the frontispiece as a complete design. See ZGBHQJ 1: 72 (fig. 108).

170 For more about this frontispiece's stylistic connection to the Southern Song conventions, see Saliceti-Collins 2007, 59–60; Huang 2014b, 415–16.

FIGURES 6.61A–B Comparison of the landscape motifs in three frontispieces associated with the Tangut royal patronage in 1189. Xi Xia. Woodblock print. Institute of Oriental Manuscripts, St. Petersburg
a. Detail of the frontispiece to the *Diamond Sutra* (TK 17)
b. Detail of the first and second folds of the frontispiece to the "Vows of Samantabhadra" (TK 61)

FIGURE 6.62 Frontispiece to the "Guanyin" chapter of the *Lotus Sutra* (TK 90). 1189. Xi Xia. Woodblock print. Concertina. Institute of Oriental Manuscripts, St. Petersburg

diagonally positioned rock with shrubs appears in the Xi Xia frontispiece to the *King Gao Sutra* (fig. 5.35).[171]

The two frontispieces sponsored by Empress Luo (figs. 6.18c, 6.19b, 6.61a–b) similarly show discrepancies in the grouping and labeling of figural motifs

171 Saliceti-Collins 2007, 73–77.

FIGURE 6.63 Frontispiece to the *Diamond Sutra* (TK 179). 1189. Xi Xia. Woodblock print. Institute of Oriental Manuscripts, St. Petersburg

that expose their "add-on" quality. They also bear a close relationship with other Xi Xia woodcuts. The two cartouches of the eight vajrapāṇis (*ba jingang* 八金剛) and ten disciples (*shi dizi* 十弟子) in the first fold of each frontispiece are not consistent with the guardians and monks spread across the first three folds of the picture plane. Neither frontispiece depicts sufficient numbers of figures to match those claimed in the cartouches. For example, the *Diamond* Sutra depicts five vajrapāṇis instead of eight (fig. 6.18c). In the "Vows of Samantabhadra," most figures depicted in the other folds of the frontispiece are not accompanied by cartouches (fig.6.19b), highlighting the incoherence of the two cartouches in the overall design. The first fold here is clearly cut and pasted from the first fold of the *Diamond Sutra* frontispiece and not entirely connected to the second fold, although the common cloud motifs in both provide the deceptive effect of continuous composition.

The reference to the eight vajrapāṇis and ten disciples may have been taken out of context from an earlier Xi Xia *Diamond Sutra* frontispiece (fig. 6.63), likely copied after a Southern Song prototype (fig. 6.64).[172] In the first fold of this Xi Xia frontispiece (fig. 6.63), ten monkish disciples and eight guardians

172 The ornamental motifs of waves and Buddhist treasures framing the Southern Song frontispiece cited here recall similar decorative framing of the *Golden Light Sutra* frontispieces dated 988 and discovered in the tomb of the lay woman Su Siniang in Jiangsu province (see fig. 2.37b of this book). See also Huang 2017c, 49 (fig. 16); ZGBHQJ 1: 36 (fig. 47); ZGFJBHQJ 2: 17.

FIGURE 6.64 Frontispiece to the *Diamond Sutra*. Southern Song

match the accompanying labels. A multi-armed figure with his arms raised and holding two swords appears in the third fold. It is cloned in the third fold of Empress Luo's frontispiece to the *Diamond Sutra* (fig. 6.18c). Both the fluid linear style of the images and the elegantly rendered calligraphy of the printed text further suggest that this work, too, may have been produced by the Tangut royal workshop.[173]

4.3 *The Third Group*

The third group, evident in three frontispieces (figs. 6.65a–c) associated with three Esoteric Buddhist texts in Tangut translated from Sanskrit or Tibetan sources, features a common composition that shows a buddha and a multi-armed bodhisattva seated on raised podiums on the right and left, surrounded by monks and guardians.[174] The pairing of a buddha on the right and a bodhisattva on the left calls to mind the frontispiece to the Tangut-script *Mahasitavani Sutra* (fig. 6.66), which pairs an oft-recycled Chinese-style buddha with a Pala-style multi-armed deity.[175] This may reflect the woodcut designers' syncretic approach, which compartmentally juxtaposes Indo-Tibetan and Chinese styles in one single frontispiece instead of blending them into one.

173 Both the fluid linear style of the frontispiece and the elegantly rendered calligraphy in the accompanying printed text prompted past scholarship to speculate that this work, too, may be made by the Tangut royal workshop; see Chen and Tang 2010, 134.

174 Chen and Tang 2010, 137, 139 (figs. 2.92–2, 2.92–4); Piotrovsky 1993, 269.

175 Shi 2004, 103, 112. Cf. ZGBHQJ 1: 82–83; Linrothe 1996a, 32 (fig. 3); Xie 2002, 1: 92 (fig. 34); Xie et al. 2010, 100 (fig. 1).

a

b

c

FIGURES 6.65A–C Three frontispieces with a modular design. Xi Xia. Woodblock print. Institute of Oriental Manuscripts, St. Petersburg
a. Frontispiece to the *Sutra of the Buddha Mother*, juan 9 (no. 6236)
b. Frontispiece to the *Mahamayurividyarjni Sutra* in Tangut (TANG 61, no. 1)
c. Frontispiece to the *Sutra of the Great Thousand Kingdoms*, juan 2 (no. 32)

FIGURE 6.66 Frontispiece to the *Mahasitavani Sutra* in Tangut (no. 43). Xi Xia. Woodblock print. Institute of Oriental Manuscripts, St. Petersburg

FIGURES 6.67A–C
Botanical motifs
a. Detail of 6.65a. Frontispiece to the *Sutra of the Buddha Mother*, juan 9 (No. 6236). Xi Xia. Woodblock Print. Institute of Oriental Manuscripts, St. Petersburg
b. Detail of fig. 6.65c. Frontispiece to the *Sutra of the Great Thousand Kingdoms*, juan 2 (no. 32). Xi Xia. Woodblock print. Institute of Oriental Manuscripts, St. Petersburg
c. Detail. *Illustrated Eulogies by Mañjuśrī*. Southern Song. Woodblock Print. Concertina. Otani University Library

The pairing of the two divine figures also sets the compositional paradigm for later frontispieces that adorn the Qisha Canon produced in Yuan Hangzhou (fig. 8.14).

A close comparison of the three frontispieces of this group (figs. 6.65a–c) reveals that the cutters or block designers modified minute details while following a common compositional template. The first (fig. 6.65a) and second (fig. 6.65b) resemble each other most closely, although minor differences occur, such as the monks in the first folds and the parallel lines at the edge of the fourth folds. A major difference between the first two versions from the third (fig. 6.65c) lies in the minute details and changing positions of selected figural motifs. While the multi-armed seated figure in the first two has eight arms, in the third he has only six. A recurring guardian with flaring hair in the fourth fold of the first two versions appears also in the third fold of the third—plus, his face and flaring hair are directionally reversed. Similarly, one figure with an animal-faced hat and another with a bird's beak appear in the third fold of the first two versions and in the fourth fold of the third. A lesser notable difference lies in the rendering of a cluster of leaves sprouting behind the halo of the multi-armed deity. In the first two versions (figs. 6.65a, 6.67a), the leaves recall similar motifs decorating the halo of the Buddha in the Northern Song *Lotus Sutra* frontispieces, produced by the Qian and the Yan Families (figs. 0.4, 3.14b, 3.18). The banana leaves in the third version (figs. 6.65c, 6.67b), on the other hand, are reminiscent of botanical motifs widely used in garden scenes in Southern Song paintings and woodcuts, such as the Southern Song *Illustrated Eulogies by Mañjuśrī* (fig. 6.67c), printed by the workshop of the Official Jia in Hangzhou (see ch. 3).[176] The motif remains a popular stage prop of garden settings in many Xi Xia frontispieces, especially the fourth group.

4.4 *The Fourth Group*

The fourth group (figs. 6.68a–f), mostly associated with Tangut royal patronage, also attests to the popularity of Southern Song Hangzhou woodcut designs in the modular repertoire of Xi Xia artisans. Most impressive in the context are garden settings, complete with rocks, banana leaves, and balustrades.

The two frontispieces sponsored by Empress Dowager Luo, the "Vows of Samantabhadra" (figs. 6.22b, 6.68a) and the *Transformation of the Female Body* (figs. 6.21a, 6.68b–c), are most refined and sophisticated. The designer of the former illustrated multiple episodes of Child Sudhana's visits to sages in a continuous garden setting that spreads over the upper portion of the

176 Multiple scenes in the *Illustrated Eulogies by Mañjuśrī* represent similar garden settings; for the scenes with comparable banana leaves, see ZGFJBHQJ 2: 72–73, 81.

a

b

c

FIGURES 6.68A–C Details of Southern Song-inspired garden motifs from two frontispieces sponsored by Empress Dowager Luo. Xi Xia. Woodblock print. Institute of Oriental Manuscripts, St. Petersburg
a. Detail, frontispiece to the "Vows of Samantabhadra" chapter from the *Avatamsaka Sutra* (TK 98). 1196
b–c. Details, frontispiece to the *Transformation of the Female Body* (TK 8). 1195

six-fold frontispiece. Similar images also appear in the latter (fig. 6.68b). The rocks, plants, and balustrades in both resemble the pictorial conventions in the Southern Song *Illustrated Eulogies by Mañjuśrī* (figs. 6.69a–b, 9.36). Screens decorated with painting or mock calligraphy and placed outdoors stand out as much as Southern Song-inspired "garden furniture."[177] Three screens in variant scenes of the "Vows of Samantabhadra" feature landscape, plants, and

177 Huang 2014d, 145–46, 172–73 (figs. 13–17). For more studies of the painted or calligraphic screens in paintings, see Wu ed. 2021.

FIGURES 6.69A–B Details of Child Sudhana's visits to sages. *Illustrated Eulogies by Mañjuśrī*. Southern Song. Woodblock print. Concertina. Otani University Library
a. The twenty-fifth visit
b. The twenty-sixth visit

calligraphy (fig. 6.68a). Similarly, a painted screen in the *Transformation of the Female Body* features reeds along the shore (fig. 6.68c), which recalls the painted screen in the *Illustrated Eulogies of Mañjuśrī* (fig. 6.69b).[178]

Several two-fold frontispieces feature garden motifs. The frontispiece to the *Amitabha Sutra*, sponsored by Emperor Renzong (fig. 6.68d), bears lush plants and impressive rocks outside the balustrade.[179] The balustrades with honeycomb patterns compare closely to the garden imagery depicted in contemporaneous Xi Xia murals, found in Yulin Cave 3 (fig. 6.70) and on Mt. Wenshu

178 For more discussion of the comparable scenes in *Illustrated Eulogies by Mañjuśrī*, see Huang 2017c, 22, 62 (fig. 37); Chen Y. 2023, 200, 202–203, 244 (fig. 23), 248 (fig. 33).

179 This is mainly based on the Tangut colophon printed to the right of the frontispiece. Jia Weiwei discusses Empress Dowager Cao's 曹 (Renzong's mother) sponsorship of 3000 copies of the *Amitabha Sutra* and the construction of the Amitabha Hall in 1156; see Jia 2020, 125 (for more scholarship on the Amitabha cult and art in Xi Xia, see her footnote 1).

d

e

FIGURES 6.68D–F Modular designs of frontispieces with a garden setting. Xi Xia. Woodblock print. Institute of Oriental Manuscripts, St. Petersburg
d. Frontispiece to the *Amitabha Sutra* in Tangut sponsored by Emperor Renzong (no. 763). Concertina
e. Frontispiece to the *Sutra of Impermanence* (TK 137)
f. Frontispiece to the *Diamond Sutra* commissioned by Ren Dejing (TK 124). 1167

(fig. 6.71).[180] It is likely that the twofold frontispiece to the *Sutra of Impermanence Preached by the Buddha* (*Foshuo wuchang jing* 佛説無常經) (fig. 6.68e), which includes comparable balustrades with honeycomb openwork designs and tiled floors, is also a workshop product associated with royal patronage.[181]

---

180 Jia Weiwei cites the Tangut inscription on the north wall of the corridor of the Yulin Cave 3 and argues that the aristocratic Tanguts may be the donors of the cave; she dated the cave to 1086–1139 (2020, 51–52, 217). The mural representation with the balustrade motif cited here is from one of the multi-vignettes crowding the lower parts of the south, north, and west walls of the Yulin Cave 3. For a discussion of the vignettes associated with the *Visualization Sutra* on the south wall, see Jia 2020, 112–15. The narrative mural associated with a miracle story of the *Lotus Sutra* and the Samantabhadra bodhisattva, depicted on the west wall of the Yulin Cave 3, includes a hut motif comparable to the Song-inspired pictorial convention often seen in such woodcuts as the *Mizangquan* and the *Lotus Sutra* frontispiece. See Zhang S. 2019, 24 (fig. 3).

181 The *Sutra of Impermanence* was popularly copied in northwest China at the time, as reflected in multiple manuscripts in Dunhuang library cave and Xi Xia printed texts in Chinese and Tangut discovered in Khara Khoto; see Cui 2013. Cf. the version in T.17.801. The compositional scheme featuring the zig-zag balustrade with floor tiles in a garden,

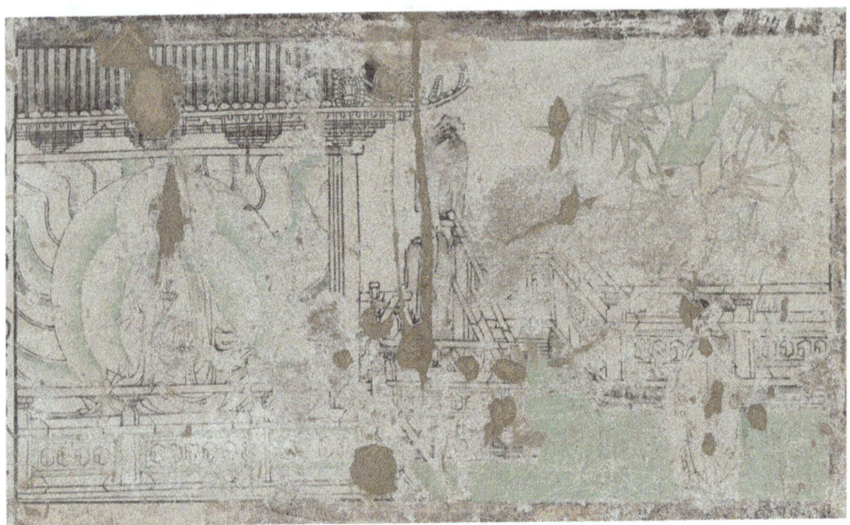

FIGURE 6.70 Detail of the balustrades with honeycomb patterns. Xi Xia. Mural. South wall, Yulin Cave 3, Guazhou, Gansu

FIGURE 6.71 Detail of the balustrades with honeycomb patterns. Xi Xia. Mural. Cave of the Ten Thousand Buddhas, Mt. Wenshu Grottoes, Gansu

Also of royal workshop style is a frontispiece to the *Diamond Sutra* dated 1167 (fig. 6.68f). Both the banana tree behind the balustrade and the floor tiles reflect recurring stage props of frontispiece designs of the period. This extant specimen, however, looks incomplete, as it only shows part of the Buddhist pantheon led by a kneeling monk and aristocratic lay devotees; it misses the presence of the Buddha, who may have been depicted in the right part of the overall composition. It may have been sponsored by Ren Dejing 任得敬, who refers to himself in the dedicatory colophon as King of Qin and Jin (Qinjin guowang 秦晉國王).[182] Ren was a controversial politician active during Renzong's reign.[183] Previously having served the Northern Song dynasty as a controller-general near the Tangut border, he surrendered to the Xia and eventually rose to high rank by marrying his daughter to Emperor Chongzong (r. 1086–1139), Renzong's predecessor, as well as through bribes and conspiracies.[184] In 1165, he controlled the Tangut army, insisting that Emperor Renzong treat him as an equal in charge of Lingzhou 靈州 and Xiazhou 夏州. In 1167, he fell severely ill. Having "found no cure in medicine," he turned to sponsoring the printing of the *Diamond Sutra* in the hope of religious salvation.[185]

• • •

Buddhist print culture under Tangut rule in many regards was unprecedented. Printed frontispieces retrieved from archaeological finds in Khara Khoto and other sites in Ningxia and Gansu form the largest and most diverse repository of Buddhist woodcuts from the multi-centered Song-to-Yuan period, attesting to a thriving print culture in northwest China. Compared to their counterparts produced in Song Hangzhou, most Xi Xia frontispieces were commissioned and donated in massive numbers by Tangut royalty, especially

---

such as that shown in fig. 6.68e of this book, recalls the fifteenth-century illustrated book, *Orthodox Essentials of Eating and Drinking* (*Yinshan zhengyao* 飲膳正要), originally compiled in 1330 and sponsored by the Mongol Yuan court. For more discussions of this work, see Kobayashi 2017, 97 (figs. 17–18); Clunas 2007, 199–200 (fig. 170).

182 Its current composition appears incomplete, mostly because the subject to whom the group of figures led by a monk are paying tribute, likely a buddha, is missing in the overall composition.

183 Shi 1988, 261; Shi 2004, 109.

184 Ren's daughter was the Empress Dowager Ren, who died in 1169–1170. For more discussion of Ren Dejing in political history, see Dunnell 1994, 198–204. For more about Han Chinese surrendering the Tangut regime, see Yang and Chen 2012, 309–10.

185 This is stated in his colophon; see Shi 1988, 39–40, 261. Ren was accused of treachery and executed in 1170; see Dunnell 1994, 202–203.

Emperor Renzong and Empress Luo. This is quite different from the situation under the Song, where Buddhist prints were mainly produced and sold by commercial printshops. Contrary to Chinese-based Buddhist print culture supported by non-Han regimes under the Khitan and Jurchen, bilingual (Chinese and Tangut) Buddhist printing supported by the Tangut royal house may reflect a more aggressive state policy using Buddhist print culture as a means to advocate the Tangut language; it may also reflect the active participation of Tangut-speaking members from its Buddhist community.

The extraordinary print runs ranging from fifty thousand to one hundred thousand or more claimed in the royal donors' dedicatory colophons required a massive division of labor across large teams of artisans in workshop fashion. I contend that most workers producing Buddhist woodcuts were based in the Tangut capital near today's Yinchuan in Ningxia, either affiliated with imperially sponsored temples or working in governmental institutions. The multiethnic, multicultural, and international Buddhist community in the Xi Xia kingdom, combined with the interstate connections forged by diplomatic exchange and the widespread trade of books and art through border markets turned the Tangut realm into a cultural crossroads, making Indo-Tibetan, Chinese, and other styles accessible to local woodcut artisans.

Renzong's grand book-gifting ceremony at the Maitreya Retreat in 1189 was the source of multiple related works of printing and art. The *Maitreya* frontispieces he sponsored (figs. 6.2–6.7), the two frontispieces donated by Empress Luo dated 1189 (figs. 6.18c, 6.19b), the frontispiece to the "Guanyin" chapter of the *Lotus Sutra* (fig. 6.62), and the Southern Song-inspired frontispiece to the *Diamond Sutra* (fig. 6.63) all bear similar features. They may accordingly be extant specimens of the tens of thousands of printed Buddhist scriptures donated by the Tangut court at the Maitreya Retreat and later distributed throughout the network of Buddhist temples.

The visual interconnectivity of royally sponsored woodcuts reveals specific practices applied under Tangut royal patronage. Block cutters prepared multiple sets of blocks to meet the demands of extraordinarily large print runs. While they followed shared templates to create basically the same composition, there are nuanced discrepancies in minute details, revealing that different hands were responsible for cutting different versions. The notion of workshop practices offers an additional aspect to unpack the juxtaposition of multiple styles or "visual syncretism" in Xi Xia woodcuts. Artisans worked together on any complex frontispiece. One person may have used a Himalayan model to compose one section, while his co-worker applied a more Chinese model in another section. Beyond iconographical concerns, Xi Xia woodcut artisans recycled, reassembled, and appropriated certain modular designs to create seemingly different frontispieces suitable for different Buddhist texts.

Chinese prototypes loom large in all four groups of design motifs. The modular design of a kneeling figure with his back to the viewer may go back to Northern Song prototypes found in murals and woodblock prints. The modular designs underlining the other three groups reference landscape and garden motifs, which in turn highlight visual connections to Song-era Hangzhou in general and Southern Song Hangzhou in particular. This is somewhat surprising, given that the Southern Song was not an immediate neighbor of the Xi Xia kingdom. Quite possibly, the Southern Song illustrated books or other image-bearing objects made their ways to Xi Xia lands not so much through direct exchange but through third parties, most likely the border markets of the Jin.

The relationship between Xi Xia print culture and its Hangzhou counterpart, however, is clearly reciprocal and not unidirectional. This is evident in the Tangut legacy as manifest in the art of Hangzhou frontispieces under the Mongol-Yuan. Here feedback loops as outlined in the introduction above expand to transcend the geographical framework, working also temporally. The Xi Xia, it becomes clear, not only serve as recipients, getting input from neighboring cultures, but also as transmitters who—after digesting and transforming art and techniques—spread them into the Mongol Yuan (see pt. 3 below) and the Ming (figs. 11.15i, 11.34).

www.ingramcontent.com/pod-product-compliance
Lightning Source LLC
LaVergne TN
LVHW010851110826
845149LV00005B/1381

* 9 7 8 9 0 0 4 7 4 5 8 1 0 *